S0-FJM-537

READINGS IN PRICE theory

RICHARD E. NEEL
Associate Dean, School of Business Administration, and Professor of Economics
Georgia State University
Atlanta, Georgia

H01 

Published by

SOUTH-WESTERN PUBLISHING CO.

CINCINNATI WEST CHICAGO, ILL. DALLAS PELHAM MANOR, N.Y.
BURLINGAME, CALIF. BRIGHTON, ENGLAND

ISBN: 0-538-08010-8

Library of Congress Catalog Card Number: 72-86896

2 3 4 5 K 7 6 5 4 3

Printed in the United States of America

TABLE OF CONTENTS

PREFACE

To find enough excellent articles to develop a book of readings in price theory is a relatively easy task. In this respect, the editor expresses his regret that space limitations make it impossible to include all of the outstanding articles in price theory.

From the many articles available, the editor has assembled a collection which will hopefully be of optimum usefulness and readability to the student and the instructor of price theory. The goal is a broader and deeper understanding of price theory than can be obtained solely from the use of a textbook, however well prepared it may be. The articles in this book have been selected for their effectiveness in supplementing the leading texts in the field, and most of the articles are to be found on the suggested reading lists of the leading textbooks in price theory.

The articles range from one or two which might be termed "classics" to several which contain some of the most recent developments in price theory. The editor has made a special effort to include a number of articles which, in addition to effectively covering important segments of price theory, discuss critically the contributions made by some of the leading writers to the subject. This is one of the distinguishing features of this collection and makes it possible not only for the student to obtain a better understanding of the theory itself but also to gain an awareness of some of the major contributors to this body of theory.

To increase further the usefulness of this collection, each of the eight sections is prefaced by an introduction which contains a short synopsis of each article. These introductions are designed to facilitate the student's understanding as he reads each article in its entirety. In addition, the introductions are designed to interrelate the various sections so that the book represents a meaningful and integrated whole.

This reader is basically intended for the undergraduate course in intermediate price theory, but it may be used effectively in graduate price theory courses also. It assumes that the student has completed a rigorous course in principles of economics. A sophisticated understanding of mathematics is not a prerequisite for the use of this book, but a working knowledge of elementary calculus will be helpful in a few articles.

These articles have been selected for their readability, yet care has been taken not to sacrifice rigor and quality. All of the articles have been reproduced in their entirety, including very valuable appendices, footnotes, and references. The final section contains some applications of price theory for the purpose of indicating some of its possible uses in the business setting.

The editor is very grateful to the authors and the publishers of the articles included in this book. Formal source acknowledgements and author identifications appear at the bottom of the first page of each article.

Richard E. Neel

SECTION I. SCOPE AND METHOD OF ECONOMICS

What is the subject matter of economics and what is the methodology employed by economists? Section I is devoted to a consideration of these very important questions.

The classic article by Lange is concerned with the nature, scope, and method of economics. Garb and Melitz analyze some of the major methodological issues in economics. Specifically, Garb examines the use and the role of the principle of causality in economics, and Melitz looks at the importance of realism in economic assumptions and the significance of testing economic assumptions. In the process, they discuss some of the positions taken on methodological points by several distinguished economists and review their contributions to the literature in this area.

Economics is defined by Lange as the social science which studies the ways in which scarce resources are administered to satisfy human wants. The "administration," or allocation, problem arises because certain wants are not satisfied due to the scarcity of some resources.

Professor Lange delineates theoretical economics and applied economics as the main branches of economic inquiry, and he outlines the methodology employed in each branch. He also differentiates welfare economics (normative or social economics) as the branch of economics which is concerned with evaluating the actual administration of scarce resources in terms of specified social objectives.

Lange identifies the three basic "units of economic decision" as households, firms, and public services (which are usually operated by some branch of government). The totality of the units of economic decision is an economy or an economic system. The administration of scarce resources may be organized in different ways. *Private capitalism* exists when all or most of the production is done by privately owned firms whose objective is profit maximization. Although planning may serve a coordinating function in a capitalistic economy, the market is the principal method of coordinating the economic units under capitalism. Under *socialism*, in contrast, production is performed by public services, and planning has a much larger coordinating role than it does under capitalism. In a *mixed economy*, production activities are engaged in by both private firms and public services.

Garb points out that for many years the principle of causality has been used as a major means of explaining economic phenomena. That is, economists often assume that if cause-and-effect relationships are known, then prediction is possible; yet, according to Garb, "economists have a poor record of prediction." In this article, Garb analyzes the possibility that the poor record of prediction is attributable to the failure of the strict causal approach in economics.

In considering the place of the principle of causation in economics, Garb reiterates that our record of discovery of causal relationships has been disappointing and has been in part responsible for the greater emphasis being placed on the use of more sophisticated mathematical and statistical tools and the social and behavioral sciences by contemporary economists.

In view of the problems associated with the employment of the causal principle, what is the answer? Garb indicates that a probabilistic approach to causality based on statistical regression analysis constitutes an improvement, particularly for certain purposes.

He points out that the problems associated with the probabilistic approach are being dealt with and that the success of these attempts will help "to determine whether economists will be able to rely to a greater degree on the more formal methods of science or whether Professor Knight is indeed correct in his position that economic prediction and control must largely depend upon trained judgment, insight, and common sense."

Melitz states that the rapid advance of modern science is generally attributed in large part to the development of deductively related bodies of general statements called theories. Among the "social theories," economic theory has been the "most viable one"; but in spite of the venerability of economic theory at the present time, Melitz maintains that it does not command as much respect as do some of the theories developed in the physical sciences. In fact, for well over a century, economic theory and its assumptions have been subject to frequent attacks. Melitz examines some of the replies which have been made by the proponents of economic theory to those who have made these attacks.

The major portion of Melitz' article is devoted to an analysis of Friedman's article, entitled "The Methodology of Positive Economics," and to Machlup's article, entitled "The Problem of Verification in Economics." Melitz seeks to show that Friedman and Machlup give an "exaggerated defense" of economic theory. His discussion centers on the positions taken by Friedman and Machlup on the use of realistic assumptions in economics and the significance of testing economic assumptions. His general thesis is that "unrealism of assumptions is a serious drawback, granted that inaccurate assumptions may be sufferable and, indeed, wise." He tries to show, further, that tests of all economic assumptions are valuable.

In his conclusion, Melitz states that, although he has "argued extensively the significance of tests of economic assumptions," it should be reiterated that he has made no effort to promote the idea that it is absolutely essential to have true assumptions in scientific work. His central argument has been that every inaccuracy in assumptions is disadvantageous, since it either impedes testing or may give rise to false hypotheses and predictions. Melitz further points out that he does not intend to imply that grave damage is suffered by economic theory each time a negative result of a test of an economic assumption takes place. Instead, the actual "disconfirmatory significance of any negative test finding" largely depends on the individual circumstances involved.

1. THE SCOPE AND METHOD OF ECONOMICS*

Oscar Lange†

The Subject Matter of Economics

Economics is the science of administration of scarce resources in human society. Human beings, living within the framework of a given historical civilization, experience various wants, such as of food, shelter, clothing, education, social prestige, entertainment, expression of religious, national, or political attitudes, and others. Some of the wants result from biological needs which must be satisfied for the very preservation of life. Most of them, however, are products of life in civilized society, frequently of the very existence of the means to satisfy them, and even the wants which result from biological needs assume forms determined by the standards of the particular civilization under which the human beings live. The wants can be satisfied by means of appropriate objects called *goods*, e.g., land, coal, cattle, buildings, ships, railroads, machinery, stocks of raw materials and the uses of such objects or of persons called *services*, like of transportation, of housing, of workingmen, of teachers, of managers, and of artists, etc. The goods and services are the *resources* which serve to satisfy human wants. Some of the resources, air, for instance, are so plentiful that all wants dependent upon them can be fully satisfied. Others, however, e.g., oil or the services of human beings, exist only in quantities which are not sufficient to satisfy all wants dependent upon these resources. In this case, we say that the resources are *scarce*. When resources are scarce, certain wants must go unsatisfied. Men make decisions which, given the organization and institutions of society, determine the distribution of the scarce resources among the different persons as well as the uses to which the scarce resources are put. In other words, the resources are administered. The study of the ways in which scarce resources are administered is the task of the science of economics.

The administration of scarce resources is influenced by the standards of civilization and by the organization and institutions of the society in which men live. The influence is a two-fold one. The wants which the resources serve to satisfy are products of standards of civilization historically developed in society. The ways in which scarce resources are procured, adapted to various purposes, distributed among different persons are all results of social

*From *Review of Economic Studies*, Vol. XIII, No. 19 (1945–1946), pp. 19–32. Reprinted by permission of the publisher and the author's wife.

†Oscar Lange, deceased, formerly of the University of Warsaw.

organization and social institutions. Forms of ownership, institutions like corporations and banks, technical knowledge acquired in institutes of research and transmitted by schools, regulation by government agencies, habits and moral standards all influence the ways of administering scarce resources. Economics is thus a *social science*, i.e., it deals with a subject which depends on the standards and forms of life in human society. It differs from sociology, the science of social actions and relations (patterns of repeated social actions) between men, by being interested in the actions of men toward the scarce resources which serve to satisfy their wants. These actions are dependent upon social actions but are distinct from them. We shall call them *economic actions*. While dependent on social actions, economic actions, in turn, influence and even create social actions and relations. The last mentioned influence provides subject-matter for a special field of study. We might name it *economic sociology*, the science of the effect of economic actions upon social actions and relations. Subjects, such as the sociology of industrial relations, bureaucracy in corporations, trade-unionism, belong to this field. The present essay is limited to economics, i.e., the study of economic actions. This includes a study of the influence of social organization and institutions upon the ways and methods of administration of scarce resources.

Like any other science, economics is not content with merely descriptive knowledge. It tries to discern general patterns of uniformity in the administration of scarce resources. The possibility of establishing such patterns of uniformity is based on two observed facts. Human actions with regard to scarce resources are subject to uniform patterns of repetition. For instance, most people react to an increase in their income by spending more money on goods and services. Within the framework of given social organization and institutions, the uniformities in economic action of individuals or groups of individuals produce certain uniformities in the distribution and use of scarce resources. Thus, an increase in the quantity of bank loans to businessmen or corporations makes them increase their demand for resources with a consequent rise in employment and/or prices. The branch of economics which deals with such patterns of uniformity and combines them in a coherent system is called *theoretical economics* or *economic theory* (also economic analysis). Statements enunciating the patterns of uniformity are referred to as *economic laws*. Economic laws are, like all other scientific laws, conditional statements. They assert that such and such happens regularly whenever such and such conditions are satisfied (i.e., whenever such and such other observations take place). No scientific law applies when its prerequisite conditions do not occur. Since the administration of scarce resources is influenced by social organization and institutions, such organization and institutions are among the conditions implied in economic laws. Consequently, economic laws which hold under one type of social organization may fail to do so under another type. Most economic laws are thus "limited historically" to certain given types of social organization and institutions. This, however, does not imply any basic difference between the laws of economics (or of other social sciences) and the laws of the natural sciences. The latter, too, are contingent upon conditions which are subject to change. Different laws of the natural sciences have different degrees of historic permanence, usually a much higher one than the laws of economics, though even this is not always the case (some laws of meteorology are less permanent than some laws of economics). The difference is but one of degree. Like all scientific laws, economic laws are established in order to make successful prediction of the outcome of human actions. In economics the laws serve to predict the result of policies, i.e., of actions of public or private agencies with regard to the administration of scarce resources. Such predictions, however, are difficult. This is due to the fact that the number of conditions circumscribing the validity of economic laws is very great, and it is difficult to ascertain whether they are all satisfied in any one situation. Still, some successful predictions are being made with the aid of economic science.

Theoretical economics does not exhaust the field of economic inquiry. Economics also studies and describes the particular ways and methods of administering scarce resources as they occur in the history of human society, past and present. Observations are made and classified and interpreted with the aid of the uniformities established by economic theory. This pursuit provides the subject-matter of *applied economics.* Applied economics is subdivided into several parts. The most important are economic history — the study of administration of scarce resources in the human societies of the past — and institutional economics, the study of the influence of particular social institutions upon the administration of scarce resources. The effect of trade-associations upon prices, quality and output of goods, or the effect of collective farming in agriculture on the efficiency of production are examples of problems which fall in the last-mentioned field.

Theoretical economics puts the patterns of uniformity in a coherent system. This is done by presenting the laws of economics as a deductive set of propositions derived by the rules of logic (and of mathematics) from a few basic propositions. The basic propositions are called assumptions or postulates, the derived propositions are called theorems. Theoretical economics thus appears (like all other theoretical sciences) as a deductive science. This, however, does not make it a branch of pure mathematics or logic. Like the rest of economics, economic theory is an empirical science. Its assumptions or postulates are approximative generalizations of empirical observations; e.g., the assumption that business enterprises act so as to maximize their money profit. Some inaccuracy of approximation (e.g., some considerations, like safety, may keep enterprises from maximizing money profit) is accepted for the sake of greater simplicity. The theorems, in turn, are subjected to test by empirical observation. A deductive set of theorems to be subjected to empirical test is also called a *theory*, *hypothesis*, or a *model.* We can thus say that theoretical economics provides hypotheses or models based on generalization of observations and subject to empirical test.

Since the assumptions (postulates) underlying a model are only approximative, the theorems do not correspond directly to results of empirical observations. In order to establish such a correspondence, special procedures must be provided. First, the concepts used in theoretical models are not adequate representations of empirical observation. For instance, a theoretical model speaks of "the price" of a specified good, but experience fails to produce anything like the specified "good" and its "price." There are hundreds of quality-grades and thousands of sellers each charging a different price. Experience is much richer than the language of science can make allowance for. In order to bridge the gap between theoretical concepts and empirical observations, it is necessary to have a procedure of *identification*, which contains rules establishing a correspondence between the two. Such procedures have to be provided by the different branches of applied economics. Furthermore, the theorems of theoretical economics are never borne out exactly by empirical observation. At best, they do so only "approximately." This raises the question as to what is to be considered as an acceptable degree of approximation inducing us to accept a hypothesis as "true" and what degree of approximation is to be judged as insufficient, making us reject the hypothesis as "incompatible with the facts." The question can be answered only in terms of a procedure of *verification* (testing) which establishes rules according to which hypotheses are accepted as "empirically verified" or rejected as "empirically unverified" or "empirically refuted." A recently developed special branch of economics deals with such procedures of verification. It is called *econometrics* and is based on the principles of mathematical statistics.

The administration of scarce resources empirically observed can be evaluated in terms of certain social objectives. Such objectives may consist in the best satisfaction of the wants of private persons according to their own preferences or in marshalling scarce resources for certain collective enterprises—e.g., industrialization of a country according to time-table, as in the Soviet Union, or successful prosecution of war, or enactment of certain ideas of social justice—or, finally, of a combination of all. The social objectives being given, rules of use of scarce resources can be found which are most conducive to the attainment of these objectives. The use of resources which follows these rules is referred to as the "ideal" use. The rules of "ideal" use of resources provide a standard by which the actual use can be evaluated as to its social desirability. The use of resources empirically observed may be compared with the "ideal" use and measures may be recommended to bring the actual use into closer correspondence with the "ideal" one. This provides subject-matter for another branch of economic science, usually called *welfare economics* (also normative economics or social economics). The rules of "ideal" use of resources are general statements; they express uniform patterns of economic action which, if adopted, are most conducive to the social objectives aimed at. They are conditional statements because they are valid only under given social objectives and empirical conditions; they require empirical verification.

(A rule of the "ideal" use of resources may prove in practice not to be conducive to the social aims desired.) The rules of "ideal" use of resources can thus be considered as a special kind of economic laws. This makes it convenient to include welfare economics in theoretical economics as a supplementary branch of the latter.

The Objectivity of Economic Science

The statements of economic science have objective validity. This means that two or more persons who agree to abide by the rules of scientific procedure are bound to reach the same conclusions. If they start with the same assumptions, they are bound, by the rules of logic, to derive the same theorems. If they apply the same rules of identification and verification, they are bound to reach agreement as to whether the theorems should be accepted as "true" or rejected as "unverified" or "false." The test of verification decides whether the assumptions are adequate or not. In the latter case, they have to be replaced by new ones which lead to theorems able to stand the test of verification. The final verdict with regard to any statement of economic science is thus based upon an appeal to facts, i.e., to empirical observations. "The proof of the pudding is in the eating." This verdict has interpersonal validity because facts are interpersonal, i.e., can be observed by everyone.

The interpersonal validity of statements holds also for welfare economics. There is no necessary interpersonal agreement about the social objectives which provide the standard of evaluation for welfare economics. Different persons, social groups and classes may, and frequently do desire different social objectives. Once, however, the objectives are stated and certain assumptions are made about empirical conditions, the rules of "ideal" use of resources are derived by the rules of logic and verified by the rules of verification. This procedure is interpersonally objective, i.e., everyone who applies it is bound to reach the same conclusions. The situation may be compared with that of two physicians treating a patient. There is no necessity of interpersonal agreement about the objective of the treatment. One physician may want to heal the patient, the other may want to kill him (e.g., the patient may be a Jew in a Nazi concentration camp; one physician may be a fellow prisoner who wants to help him, the other physician may be a Nazi acting under orders to exterminate Jews). But once the objective is set for the purpose under discussion (either of the two physicians may, of course, refuse to act upon it), their statements as to whether a given treatment is conducive to the end under consideration have interpersonal validity. Any disagreement between them can be settled by appeal to fact and to the rules of scientific procedure.

Our conclusion about the objectivity of economic science may seem startling. Economists are rather notorious for being unable to reach agreement and for being divided into opposing "schools of thought," "orthodox" and "unorthodox," "bourgeois" and "socialist," and many others. The existence of profound disagreement among economists, however, does not refute our thesis about the objectivity of economics as a science. The disagreements can all be traced to one or more of the following sources:

(1) Disagreement about social objectives. This is the most frequent source of disagreement, but acts as such only as long as it is implicit and unrecognized. If the social objectives are stated explicitly, the disagreement disappears. For any given set of social objectives and with given assumptions as to empirical conditions, conclusions are drawn with interpersonal validity by the rules of logic and of verification.

(2) Disagreement about facts. Such disagreement can always be resolved by further observation and study of the empirical material. Frequently, however, the empirical data necessary to resolve the disagreement are unavailable. In such cases, the issue remains unsettled. The conclusion that the issue cannot be settled with the data available has interpersonal validity. Agreement is reached to withhold judgment.

(3) Failure to abide by the rules of logic, of identification and of verification. The disagreement can be removed by correct application of these rules.

The disagreements are thus all due to failure to abide by the rules of scientific procedure and can be resolved by strict application of these rules. Economists, as well as other scientists, however, are not automatons acting on the basis of the rules of scientific procedure. As human beings they are subject to a great multiplicity of influences, some conscious, most of them subconscious, which determine their conclusions as laid down in the literature of economics. There are influences, sociological and psychological, which sometimes are unfavorable and sometimes favorable to the application of scientific procedure. The persistence of disagreements indicates that the harmful influences are very strong. It is desirable to have a picture of these influences, harmful as well as helpful.

Economists, like other human beings, live under the institutions of a historic society and under the standards of its civilization. They share in its beliefs and values, prejudices and interests, horizons and limitations. They depend for their living, advancement, and recognition on the institutions of the society in which they live, e.g., on universities, research institutes, publishers, press, government, and business establishments. Most of these institutions have other, more important, objectives than the "untrammelled pursuit of truth," and even those which have this objective are dependent on the rest of society and must make their adjustments and compromises. Furthermore, economists are brought up as members of a particular nation, social class, religious or philosophical group, and political tradition, etc. All this exposes economists, and also other scientists, to a multiplicity of influences other than the rules of scientific procedure. Those influences which are conscious are easily recognized and overcome if they interfere with honest application of scientific procedure. Though even in this case, many may choose to limit their scientific inquiry to "safe" fields where there is little danger of conflict with powerful and dominant interests and prejudices. The really important influences, however, are those which are subconscious. The economist subject to them is unaware of their existence; the influences operate through processes of rationalization of subconscious motivations. The result is the production of *ideologies*, i.e., systems of beliefs which are held not on grounds of their conformity to scientific procedure but as rationalizations of subconscious, non-logical, motives. Ideologies have no interpersonal validity. They convince only those who share the same subconscious motivations and undergo the same processes of rationalization.

The study of ideologies, of the conditions of their origins and influences, has become the subject-matter of a special discipline, the *sociology of knowledge*. This discipline has established valuable insights into the sociological and psychological conditions of scientific inquiry. Its most important contribution is the recognition of the fact that all scientific production contains an ideological element. This holds for the natural sciences as well as for the social sciences. The history of the Copernican theory in astronomy and of the theory of evolution in biology provides an example. For a long time the attitude of astronomers and of biologists to these theories was influenced by their general attitude, friendly or hostile, to dominant ecclesiastic doctrines and by their personal dependence or lack of dependence on ecclesiastic institutions. The history of economics is full of instances of the ideological element in economic science. The most important stepping-stones in the development of economics were not merely scientific but also ideological with far-reaching social consequences.

The existence of an ideological element in each science has caused some representatives of the sociology of knowledge to deny the objective validity of scientific statements, particularly in the domain of the social sciences. Such a conclusion is unwarranted. The validity of scientific statements can be ascertained with impersonal objectivity through an appeal to facts. Predictions derived from scientific statements are or are not borne out under the test of verification. The outcome is entirely independent of human motivations, conscious or subconscious; it depends entirely on the correctness of the scientific procedure applied in establishing the statements. Eclipses predicted do or do not occur, bridges stand the stress of traffic or break down, patients get healed or die, whatever the personal motivations of the astronomer, the engineering scientist or the medical man. Certain economic situations lead to unemployment or to inflation, whatever the economist's personal liking or disliking of the capitalist system. The validity of scientific statements does not depend on human motivations; it depends entirely on the observations of the rule of scientific procedure and is, therefore, interpersonal.

The ideological element in scientific inquiry need not always be a handicap in reaching interpersonally valid results. If this was not the case, little scientific progress would have been made. Ideological motivation may also stimulate the development of science. Discoveries have been made in physics and chemistry as a consequence of the desire to make profits or to promote national defense (indeed, the very development of these sciences is closely related to modern industry and warfare). Biological science has been stimulated by motivations of human sympathy for the sick and the suffering. Most important contributions of the social sciences are due to passion for social justice and betterment. The discoveries of classical economics were thus ideologically motivated by passion for freedom and justice as well as by the interests of the industrial middle class. The progress of institutional economics was substantially motivated ideologically by the desire for justice and for the improvement of the lot of the industrial working class. Some relation seems to exist between the nature of the motivations and their favorable or unfavorable influence upon the development of economics and other social sciences. "Conservative" motivations, i.e., motivations resulting from the desire to maintain established social institutions and standards of civilization tend to disfavor, while "progressive" motivations which result from the desire to change and improve social institutions and standards of civilization tend to favor the attainment of scientifically valid results in the domain of the social sciences. For it is the desire for change and betterment, whether conscious or subconscious which creates the inquisitiveness of mind resulting in scientific investigation of human society.

The Units of Economic Decision and Their Co-ordination

Administration of scarce resources, or economic activity, is carried on by various units such as individual persons, families, business corporations, or agencies of the government. Each of these units has disposal over certain resources and makes decisions as to their use. We shall call them *units of economic decision* (or of economic activity). Three kinds of use of resources are ordinarily distinguished: (1) *consumption* or the use of resources for direct satisfaction of wants; (2) *production* or the preparation and adaption of resources for the satisfaction of wants through actions such as changing physical, chemical, and biological qualities, changing location in space, and storing for future use; (3) *exchange* or the use of resources for procurement of resources from other units of economic decision. Accordingly, the units of economic decision are frequently classified as consumers and producers, respectively. These classes, however, are not mutually exclusive. For the same unit is frequently a consumer and producer at the same time (a farm, for instance); almost all units in modern society engage in exchange. There are practically no units engaging in exchange alone; e.g., commerce involves always some change in location or some storage of resources.

A more important classification is one according to the objectives which guide the decisions of the units. On this basis three types of units can be distinguished:

(1) *Households.* The objective of the decisions of these units is consumption, i.e., satisfaction of wants. Households may engage in exchange and in production, but these activities are undertaken with the purpose of providing for the satisfaction of

wants of members of the unit. Households appear in different forms, namely, as individual persons, families, corporations, and even public agencies (e.g., a municipal orphanage). In our society, the family is the dominant form of a household.

(2) *Firms or Business Enterprises.* These are units which engage in exchange with the purpose of making a money profit, i.e., a difference between the money value of the resources sold and the money value of the resources bought. Firms are practically always producers; they are distinguished from other producers by the objective of their activity, namely the acquisition of money profit. Firms assume diverse forms: individual enterprises, business corporations, and also government agencies. In our present society, the corporate form is dominant.

(3) *Public Services.* These are agencies operated with the purpose of contributing to the attainment of certain social objectives (usually called public welfare). Instances of public services are schools, hospitals, research institutes, publicly owned and operated utilities, the post-office, the army and navy, etc. In most cases, public services are operated by some branch of government, national, state or local. But this is not always the case, e.g., privately endowed universities or hospitals. Certain public services are also operated jointly by two or several governments or by governments and private institutions.

The three objectives which serve as a basis for this classification can always be conceptually distinguished. Accordingly, each unit of economic decision will be considered as being either a household, a firm, or a public service. Under certain circumstances, the pursuit of one of these objectives may imply exactly the same actions as the pursuit of another one. Thus, a public service may, according to the social objective chosen, act exactly like a business enterprise. In such cases, it is necessary to ascertain the real objective of the decisions (e.g., attainment of a social objective or pursuit of money profit). This can be done by varying the circumstances hypothetically in such a way that the different objectives imply different actions and by inquiring into the actions which will be followed. It should also be noticed that individual persons may be members of several units of economic decision. For instance, a person can be a member of a household and, at the same time, a member of several business firms.

The decisions of a unit may be independent of the decisions of other units and exert no influence on them. The unit is then said to be an isolated unit. Isolated units of economic decision are by necessity, households. In modern society, however, decisions of the various units influence each other; they are interdependent. The totality of interdependent units of economic decision is called an *economy* or an *economic system.* If the decisions of the different units in an economy are to be carried out, they must be consistent with each other. Thus, the quantity of resources which units wish to consume must be equal to the quantity which the same or other units wish to produce; the quantity of resources which units wish to acquire by exchange must be equal to the quantity which other units wish to give up in the exchange; the total quantity of a resource desired by the units must be equal to the quantity available in the economy. When the decisions of the various units in the economy are consistent with each other, the economy is said to be in *equilibrium.* Unless the economy is in equilibrium, the decisions of the units cannot all be translated into actions. In order for action to become possible, the decisions must be co-ordinated, i.e., brought into consistency with each other.

There are two principal methods by which decisions of the various units are co-ordinated. One is *planning*, i.e., co-ordination by a central authority with power to influence the decisions of the units. The means used by the planning authority to influence the decisions of the units are many. The planning authority can prescribe quotas, i.e., quantities of resources to be produced or consumed, bought or sold by each unit. It can also use more indirect means as, for instance, subsidies and taxes to encourage or discourage certain decisions. Another means of planning is regulation, the setting of rules which the units must observe in their decisions and actions. The planning authority may extend over the whole economy or over a part of it. It may be public, e.g., an agency of government, or private, as, for instance, a trade association or a cartel. We may, accordingly, distinguish between private and public planning.

The other method of co-ordination is the *market*. A market is a pattern of regular, recurrent exchange relations between units of economic decision. Regular exchange between a large number of units presupposes the use of a generally accepted medium of exchange, namely of money. The units thus transact their exchange in two stages, sale and purchase; they sell their resources for money and buy with the money the resources desired. The ratio at which money and resources are exchanged in the market is called the price. Meeting in the market, the various units match their offers and bids, their supplies and demands, against each other. They adjust and readjust their quantities offered and demanded and their prices, until co-ordination of their decisions is reached. Thus, through an interplay of the units in the market, equilibrium of the economy is attained. This happens quite unintentionally, as a by-product of the pursuit by each unit of its own individual goals (consumption, money profit, or public service). The market thus automatically produces a result equivalent to that of planning. Its operation has, therefore, been compared (by Adam Smith and others) to that of an invisible hand which produces co-ordination out of the autonomous decisions of many separate units. Not all markets, however, are able to produce such co-ordination, nor is the co-ordination obtained always consistent with accepted social objectives. In such cases, planning is used either to reach the co-ordination otherwise unobtainable or to correct the co-ordination produced by the "invisible hand" of the market.

Planning and the market do not exclude each other. Planning may utilize the uniformity of behavior patterns of units operating in the market as one of the means of influencing their decisions. This happens, for instance, when the planning authority imposes tariffs or pays subsidies in order to influence the quantities bought or sold. Sometimes regulation — a special method of planning — is necessary in order to enable the market to achieve co-ordination of the units' decisions. The two methods of co-ordination co-exist with each other. However, in different historic societies, one or the other of these methods plays the preponderant role and appears as the chief means of co-ordinating all the units in the economy. The development of economics as a science is closely connected with the growing preponderance of the market in modern times. The co-ordinating operation of the market and, at times, the failure of the market to achieve co-ordination of decisions have posed the intellectual problems which have led to the emergence and growth of economic science.

Capitalism and Other Forms of Economic Organization

The history of human society confronts us with different ways in which administration of scarce resources is organized. Of all types of economic activity, production is the one to which men devote their major time and attention. We, therefore, classify the forms of economic organization according to the units of economic decision which are dominant in the performance of production. In older times, almost all producers were households; administration of resources was carried on in isolated units. Such a form of economic organization is usually called a domestic economy. The growing interdependence of households through exchange of goods and services had led to the emergence of the firm or business enterprise as the dominant producing unit in the economy. At present, in most of the advanced countries, production is done by firms.

Firms or business enterprises have as their objective one single magnitude, namely, money profit. In this they differ from households and public services. A household, for instance, desires to satisfy several wants, not to pursue merely one magnitude as an objective. Similar considerations hold for public services. Having one single magnitude for an objective, the firm attains the objective the better the greater the value of the magnitude attained. In other words, pursuing money profit for its objective, a firm wants to *maximize* it. It uses the resources at its disposal — its capital — in such a way as to obtain the greatest possible money profit. An economy in which all or most of production is done by firms is called a *capitalist economy*; the economic organization which leaves production to firms is called *capitalism.* In our present economy, most of the firms or business enterprises are privately owned (most frequently they are private corporations). It is, however, possible to envisage an economic organization in which production is assigned to publicly owned profit-maximizing enterprises. We shall use the term *state capitalism* to denote such an economic organization. For the sake of distinction, we may describe our present economic organization as *private capitalism.* Since a publicly owned profit-maximizing enterprise operates exactly like a private firm, this distinction is of no importance for economic theory, however significant it may be from the point of view of sociology or political science.

Pursuit of money profit implies participation in exchange. Firms regularly buy and sell resources. The market is, therefore, an integral part of the capitalist economy. It is, indeed, the chief method by which various units of decision in the capitalist economy are co-ordinated. Planning, however, is not excluded as a method of co-ordination under capitalism. It played an important part in early capitalism (mercantilist policy, e.g.) and increases steadily in importance in the present capitalist economy. The existence of the market is not sufficient for the economy to be capitalist; a market, for instance, exists in an economic organization in which production is done by households which regularly exchange part of their products. For the economy to be capitalist, according to our definition, money profit must be the sole objective of the units engaged in production. This excludes an economy in which the satisfaction of wants competes with the profit-making objective. A craftsman may refuse to use an opportunity of making an additional money profit because it is not worth the effort involved or because he prefers to devote his time to the satisfaction of specific wants, such as company, entertainment, etc. A farmer may fail to maximize money profit because he prefers to consume some of his products instead of selling them. In order that the producing unit pursue money profit as its sole objective, it must be entirely separated from the owner's (or owners') household and, in addition, all services of persons employed by the unit must be purchased in the market.

The condition that all services of persons employed by the producing unit be purchased in the market implies that these persons do not own the enterprise. They must be either pure laborers paid wages or salaries or slaves purchased by the enterprise. In antiquity business enterprises operated with slave labor played a considerable role. Some authors, therefore, speak of capitalism in ancient Greece and Rome. In modern times, however, business enterprises employ the services of free wage and salary earners. The existence of a class of laborers working for wages and salaries endows capitalism with specific sociological features. Capitalism as a form of economic organization is, therefore, a subject of study of economic sociology as well as of economics.

Firms, as defined by us, are but approximative representations of certain units of economic decision found in experience. Although in the present economy, money profit is the chief objective of most units engaged in production, some other objectives are always co-existent. Among these other objectives are, for instance, prestige, social standing, desire for a "quiet life," social responsibilities, and, most important of all, desire for safety, i.e., dislike of decisions involving risk. Strictly speaking, the empirical units called "firms" or "business enterprises" are households which desire to satisfy these specific wants alongside with making money profit; they are ready to sacrifice some money profit to attain the other objectives. The pursuit of money profit, however, dominates the other objectives to such an extent that the units mentioned conform approximately to our theoretical concept of a firm. The extent of approximation between the theoretical concept and its empirical counterpart justifies the assumption that the units engaged in production pursue the single objective of money profit as a useful simplification of analysis. The consequences of the other objectives being present can be introduced at a later stage, whenever necessary. However, the desire for safety may be of such prominence that it sometimes becomes necessary to introduce it from the very beginning in the analysis of the firm. This can be done by redefining the firm as pursuing profit "discounted for risk" as a single objective. The presence of a desire for safety among firms will be considered as compatible with the capitalist character of the economy.

Another form of economic organization to consider is *socialism.* This is an economic organization where production is done by public services operated for the satisfaction of the wants of the community. Socialism is the objective of important social and political movements in many countries, e.g., the Labor Party in Great Britain, and in some of the Dominions, the Co-operative Commonwealth Federation in Canada, the socialist and communist movements in the various countries of Europe. One country, the Union of Soviet Socialist Republics, has established a socialist economy. In a socialist economy production is a public, not private, responsibility. All the units of economic decision charged with production need not be owned and operated by the central government. They may be owned and operated by branches of provincial and local government, by citizens' associations like co-operatives, unions, or collective farms, by special public service corporations, or foundations. There may be substantial decentralization of units of decision in a socialist economy. All these units, however, must be public services, i.e., they must be operated for the satisfaction of the wants of the whole community and not merely of members of the unit. In principle, the co-ordination of the decisions of the various units may be effected by either planning or the market. In practice, both methods prove necessary, as is similar under capitalism. Most socialists, however, assign planning a much greater role under socialism than it has under capitalism. In the U.S.S.R. planning serves as the basic method of co-ordination between producing units, the market playing an important subsidiary role in co-ordinating the decisions of households with the decisions of the producing units. If socialism is adopted by more countries, the socialist economies in different countries will probably differ substantially as to types of producing units, their degree of centralization, and as to the relative importance of planning and the market as methods of co-ordination, just as the capitalist economy differs from one country to another and in different historical periods.

History seldom confronts us with an economic organization corresponding exactly to our theoretical classifications. In most cases, production is carried on by all three types of units of economic decision, by households, by firms, and by public services. Thus, in the United States at present, households like small farms or craftsmen and public services like publicly owned power plants or transportation services engage in production alongside with business enterprises. Elements of a domestic economy and of a socialist economy co-exist with those of a capitalist economy. But one of the three types (for instance, business enterprises in the United States) may be so dominant (in terms of the amount of resources at the disposal of units of this type) that the economy may be described as approximately domestic, capitalist, or socialist. For purposes of theoretical analysis, we then disregard the other elements and introduce them, if necessary, at a later stage. Such a procedure is sometimes called construction of "ideal types" of economic organization. Economic theories can then be developed which describe the operation of such "typical" economies, e.g., the economics of capitalism or the economics of socialism. In some cases, however, this proves impossible because several types of units of economic decision are equally important in production, or although one type is dominant, some other type is too important to be disregarded even in a first approximation. For instance, in many countries of Europe big industry and finance are operated as public services, while medium-sized and small industry are operated by business enterprises; in addition, farming is frequently operated by households exchanging but a small part of their products in the market. In such case we speak of a *mixed economy.*

An instance of mixed economy occurs when the government chooses to leave production to private firms (or sometimes to households) or to conduct it through public services, depending upon, in each case, which course promises to contribute more to the satisfaction of the wants of the community. This may be called a *service economy* because production is assigned to the unit which best serves the social purpose. But it can be considered as a special kind of socialist economy. The purpose of production here is always satisfaction of the wants of the community; the operation of production is merely delegated to private firms if they do it better than, or at least just as well as, public agencies. In such an economy private firms can be considered as a special kind of public service in which the managers are remunerated by being allowed to make whatever money profit they can. Furthermore, in a service economy the government must have the power to decide in each case whether a private firm or a public agency is to be charged with production. This presupposes an alignment of political power similar to that in a socialist society. The service economy type of socialism, rather than the "ideal type" excluding all forms of private business enterprise, is the objective of contemporary socialist movements; the political programmes of the socialist and communist parties are explicit in stating that private enterprise shall continue to operate under socialism in small farming, small trade, and small industry. It is, therefore, an important subject of study for economic science.

The Postulate of Rationality

We have seen that the pursuit by firms of a single magnitude for an objective implies the desire to maximize it. A unit in pursuit of money profit but not desirous of maximizing it obviously must be striving for additional objectives. It is ready to sacrifice some money profit for the attainment of some other objective or objectives. Thus, there appears to be an essential difference between firms and households. Firms pursue a single objective, a magnitude which they want to maximize; households, instead, are concerned with the satisfaction of many different wants, theirs being a multiplicity of objectives. However, since resources are scarce, wants must be weighed against each other and decisions must be made as to which wants to satisfy and to what extent; resources must be allocated accordingly. This implies the existence of given preferences which guide the household in choosing one allocation rather than another. We may now ask whether these preferences can be ordered along a scale. When this is possible, the household can be interpreted as pursuing a single objective, namely, the most preferred allocation of the resources among its different wants. The household appears then as maximizing a magnitude. We call this magnitude *utility*. The decisions of the household are interpreted, in this case, in a way similar to those of firms, i.e., as resulting from the pursuit of a single objective.

The possibility of interpreting decisions of households in a way similar to decisions of firms suggests the adoption of a general postulate covering both cases. We call it the *postulate of rationality*. A unit of economic decision is said to act rationally when its objective is the maximization of a magnitude. Firms thus act rationally, by definition, while households do so only when their preferred allocations of resources among different wants can be ordered along a scale. The postulate of rationality is the assumption that all units of economic decision act rationally. This assumption provides us with a most powerful tool for simplification of theoretical analysis. For, if a unit of decision acts rationally, its decisions in any given situation can be predicted by mere application of the rules of logic (and of mathematics). In absence of rational action such prediction could be made only after painstaking empirical study of the uniformities in the decision patterns of the unit. For a unit which acts rationally, these uniformities or laws can be deduced immediately by logic and the decisions predicted, accordingly. Thus, the postulate of rationality is a short-cut to the discovery of laws governing the decisions of units and to the prediction of their actions under given circumstances.

Though a short-cut designed to save elaborate empirical investigation, the postulate of rationality is, nevertheless, but an empirical assumption. It is a hypothesis which, in each case, must be verified by confronting the logical deductions obtained from the postulate with the observations of experience. The use of the postulate is justified only when the logical deductions agree with the results of empirical observation with an acceptable degree of approximation. Otherwise, the postulate would lead us to make predictions which fail to be borne out by observed facts. This needs to be stressed because some economists believe that the postulate of rationality can be used as an *a priori* principle, not subject to empirical verification. In such case, however, the conclusions derived from the postulate of rationality could not have any empirical relevance, either. Theoretical economics would become a branch of pure logic or mathematics without empirical implications, whatsoever. If the laws deduced from the postulate of rationality are to serve as a basis of making predictions about the decisions of units encountered in experience, this postulate must be treated as an empirical hypothesis.

The hypothesis that producing units act rationally, i.e., with the objective of maximizing money profit, is verified with satisfactory approximation in the capitalist economy. It serves, therefore, as a useful tool of simplification in the study of that economy. The situation is more doubtful with regard to households. Here the verification of the hypothesis is much more precarious, and we must expect much larger discrepancies between results of empirical observation and conclusions derived from the postulate of rationality. There seems, however, to be some difference between households operating in the capitalist economy and households of the domestic economy of pre-capitalist societies. The dominance of business enterprises with a tangible and quantified magnitude (money profit) as their objective has created a mental habit of considering all kinds of decisions as a pursuit of a single objective, expressed as a magnitude. Some authors call this mental habit the "capitalist spirit." It spreads beyond the specific decisions of business enterprises and affects the mode of operation of other units, including households. Under the influence of the mental habit mentioned, households are encouraged to order their preferences along a scale, i.e., to maximize utility. In capitalist society, therefore, the decisions of households are more likely to conform to the deductions derived from the postulate of rationality than in societies which preceded the rise of modern capitalism.

Public services act rationally when the social objective they aim at can be expressed as a single magnitude to be maximized. The magnitude is then called *public welfare*. Public welfare exists as a magnitude when the community, or more exactly the agencies of the community responsible for the judgment, have preferences as to the distribution of resources among members of the community as well as to the allocation of resources among the various wants of each member, and when, furthermore, these preferences can be ordered along a scale. In this case, the decisions of public services in any given situation can be derived by the rules of logic from the postulate of rationality. But the community seldom has such definite and ordered preferences. Because of this, the study of the operation of public services has to be based on the observations of institutional economics and economic history rather than on logical deductions from the postulate of rationality. However, there is a different way in which the postulate of rationality is useful in the study of public services. Instead of accepting it as an empirical hypothesis, we can consider conformity of public services with the postulate of rationality as a social objective. In other words: we can set up a chosen set of ordered preferences, i.e., some concept of public welfare, as our own (i.e., the student's) social objective and require that all public services be guided by this objective as a norm. This leads to rules of "ideal" use of resources and provides a basis for critical evaluation of the actual administration of resources by public services as well as by firms and households. The postulate of rationality becomes then the basis of a theory of welfare economics.

There is a difference between the rationality of households and firms and the rationality, whether (approximately) actual or normative (as in welfare economics), of public services. The first involves the pursuit of a private objective—utility or profit, respectively; the latter involves pursuit of a social objective, namely, public welfare. We can speak of *private* and *social rationality*, accordingly. Private rationality need not necessarily exclude social rationality. If the community's preferences as to allocation of resources among the various wants of each member coincide with the individual preferences of the members, then each member, by maximizing his private utility, contributes to the attainment of maximum public welfare. Under certain conditions the maximization of money profit by firms implies maximization of public welfare too. In such cases, their own private rationality makes the members of the community act as if they were public services; private rationality then implies social rationality. The existence of such situations underlies the idea of the service economy. If all firms were always subject to these conditions, the capitalist economy could be considered as a special case of a service economy in which it is found expedient to delegate all production to private firms. This, indeed, is the famous doctrine of *laissez-faire* which maintains that the capitalist economy, provided it is not hampered by government planning, spontaneously operates in such a way that it secures the maximum of public welfare. Accordingly, non-interference in the spontaneous operation of the capitalist economy is considered to be the best way of assuring the "ideal" use of resources. Most contemporary students of welfare economics consider this claim to be false and point out many conflicts between the private rationality of business enterprises and social rationality as postulated by welfare economics. The private rationality of business enterprises is also in conflict with the social objectives accepted by most citizens of modern democratic society. This accounts for the increasing tendency toward planning under contemporary capitalism and also for the socialist movements present in most capitalist countries.

A final observation has to be made about the procedure of verification of the postulate of rationality. There is some difference in procedure between firms, on the one hand, and households and public services on the other. Money profit is a quantity which can be observed empirically (like, for instance, velocity in physics). The theoretical concept of money profit, therefore, can be easily identified with corresponding empirical observations (the procedure of identification involves an interpretation of bookkeeping categories). Direct observation tells, then, whether firms do or do not maximize money profit. Utility and public welfare, instead, are purely theoretical constructs; there are no empirical observations which would serve as their counterparts (just like in the case of the concept of potential in physics). But this does not preclude verification by indirect devices. The uniformities of decision patterns are different when utility or public welfare, respectively, are maximized than when they are not. This difference in the uniformities mentioned makes it possible to verify empirically the hypothesis of rationality of acts of households and of public services.

2. THE PROBLEM OF CAUSALITY IN ECONOMICS*

Gerald Garb†

Introduction

At least since Adam Smith's *An Inquiry into the Nature and Causes of the Wealth of Nations*,[1] causality[2] has been a major form of explanation in economics. The applicability of strict causal concepts to economic phenomena has always been accepted almost without question, this, even though physicists have challenged the concept of causality, and even though many philosophers (and some economists) have gone over to probabilistic modes of expression. Let us put the problem another way. We often assume that if cause-effect relationships are known, prediction is possible. Economists have a poor record of prediction. Is this because, even after two centuries, most relevant causal relationships have eluded economists? Is it because of lack of data, errors in data, or nonquantitative knowledge? Or is it because the strict causal approach has failed in economics? Much has been written on the first two questions, but has not the time come to analyze the last one?

*From *Kyklos*, Vol. XVII, Fasc. 4 (1964), pp. 594–609. Reprinted by permission of the publisher and the author.

†Gerald Garb, Professor of Economics, Lehigh University. The author wishes to thank Professors B. M. Olsen and C. W. Harrell for comments on a draft of this paper.

[1]As this title suggests, Smith sought to discover the causes of economic phenomena. Even though Smith has a general causal approach which is evidenced throughout the work by many causal statements, he never explains what he means by causation, nor does Ricardo. Yet, in the *Principles*, Ricardo employs the word "cause" at least 26 times in the first chapter alone, and many more times in succeeding chapters. J. S. Mill expressly states that the aim of political economy is the search for the causes that govern the production and distribution of wealth. See his *Principles of Political Economy*, Ashley ed., p. 1. Marshall repeatedly stresses that the economist must discover the causes of economic phenomena, and even the causes of the causes. For examples, see his *Principles of Economics* (8th ed.; London: 1936), pp. 3, 4, 29, 30, 31, 34, 36, 40, 43, 44, 773, 776, 778, and 779. Keynes, like Marshall and others, did not ignore processes of interaction in economics. However, anyone who believes that Keynes did not conduct much of his analysis in causal terms should see *The General Theory of Employment, Interest and Money* (New York: Macmillan Co., 1936), esp. pp. 57, 78, 79, 93, 95, 116, 123–124, 136, 165, 171–173, 198, 200, 201, 250, 254, 269, 297–298, 300, 301, 318, 322, 329, 331, 340, and 381. But for lack of space, these examples could easily be increased by such venerable names as Malthus, Menger, Veblen, and many others. Examples could also be easily produced from contemporary writings. To take one, Gottfried Haberler introduces his study of the business cycle with the following: "The present study confines itself to the task of analysing existing theories of the business cycle and deriving therefrom a synthetic account of the nature and possible causes of economic fluctuations." *Prosperity and Depression* (new revised and enlarged edition; London: W. H. Allen & Co. Ltd., 1958), p. 1.

[2]In this paper, I shall use the following terms as synonyms: causal principle, causality, principle of causality, and causation.

Traditionally, the nature and precise meaning of the causal principle have been regarded as lying beyond the pale of economic discussion. In recent years, the idea of causality has received some explicit recognition in the areas of mathematical economics and econometrics; efforts have been made in these areas to define the concept, as well as to incorporate it into mathematical systems. However, these efforts have been limited and are as yet incomplete. These investigations into the causal mode of explanation have generally been restricted to mathematical and logical systems analysis. They have not penetrated the body of general economic thought. In the latter there exists a vague and disturbing uneasiness concerning the nature and scope of the causal principle, and this often leads to a predilection to substitute the word 'association' for the word 'causation.' Nevertheless, we refuse to abandon the search for causes. We are determined to discover *the* causes of economic growth, of inflation, of the business cycle.

Vagueness can only lead to confusion and misunderstanding in any science. Therefore, this paper undertakes to clarify the idea of causality and to determine the place, if any, of causality in economic thought. To the obvious charge that the analysis of causality has taxed the greatest philosophical minds since antiquity and that it is thus presumptuous for economists to attempt a resolution of the problems involved, we can only answer that progress in economics is being impeded by these problems and hence they must at least be made explicit and considered by economists.

The Principle of Causality

The main purpose of this section is to consider the meaning of the causal principle. Even a cursory review of the historical development of ideas about causality would go beyond the limits of this paper. A voluminous literature exists on this subject, ranging from Aristotle's great codification to the thoughts of such men as Galileo, Hobbes, Locke, Hume, and in our own day, Carnap, Nagel, Reichenbach and Russell. We are primarily concerned with how this concept may be employed in economics. For this purpose, we shall dip into the literature when necessary.

Before proceeding to meanings, something must be said about the widespread idea that developments in physics have shown that the principle of causality is not applicable in scientific thought. This does not appear to be wholly true. We must distinguish between microphenomena and macrophenomena. Causality was challenged in microphysics, and even here it received support in the writings of Bohm and de Broglie. By physical standards, economists deal with macrophenomena only, and here certain forms of causality have been strongly defended.[3]

[3]See Ernest Nagel, "The Causal Character of Modern Physical Theory," *Readings in the Philosophy of Science*, edited by Herbert Feigl and May Brodbeck (New York: Appleton, 1953), pp. 436–7; and Bertrand Russell, *Human Knowledge: Its Scope and Limits* (New York: Simon and Schuster, 1948), pp. 201–2, 460.

Some discussion of the relationship between the traditional deductive method in economics and causality is necessary in order to provide additional background and perspective for our treatment of the causal principle. J. N. Keynes advises us: "The economist cannot help endeavouring to trace effects to their causes, and to assign to causes their effects. But the deduction of causal connexion needs the assistance of some apparatus of reasoning, inductive or deductive or a combination of these."[4] In recent times one economist who has done much to explore these relationships is Frank H. Knight. Knight's thought on these matters may be characterized as follows.

First, Knight considers the causal principle to consist of a functional relationship, the cause being the independent variable and the effect the dependent variable.[5] *Second*, Knight distinguishes between economic theory and applied economics; the latter is a statistical and inductive study, whereas the former is deductive and is concerned with the discovery of more general laws largely causal in character.[6] *Third*, economic theory is difficult and vague because of the problems involved in separating constants, independent variables, and dependent variables; and because of disturbing lags from cause to effect.[7] *Finally*, as a result of the foregoing, prediction and control in economics must depend more on trained judgment, insight into human nature and social values, and common sense than on the formal methods of science.[8]

Actually J. N. Keynes and Knight are representative of two widely held viewpoints in economics. Keynes represents the view that explanation in economics depends upon the discovery of cause-effect relationships. The latter are uncovered by means of deductive and/or inductive reasoning. Knight would agree with this approach up to a point, but would add that the subject matter or data of economics is so complex that neat theories must perforce give way in application to the trained judgment of the expert.

How are we to interpret the position of those other groups of economists who avoid or ignore causal relationships? For example, Lionel Robbins tells us that ". . . we no longer enquire concerning the causes determining variations of production and distribution. We enquire rather concerning the conditions of equilibrium of various economic 'quantities'. . . ."[9] As another example, we can cite Milton Friedman's well-known essay, *The Methodology*

---

[4]J. N. Keynes, *The Scope and Method of Political Economy* (4th ed.; London: Macmillan Co., 1917), p. 176.

[5]See Frank H. Knight, *On the History and Method of Economics* (Chicago: University of Chicago Press, 1956), pp. 40, 94–5 and 138–9; and *The Ethics of Competition* (New York and London: Harper and Bros., 1935), p. 128.

[6]Knight, *The Ethics of Competition, ibid.*, p. 143.

[7]*Ibid.*, pp. 139–41, and Knight, *On the History and Method of Economics, op. cit.*, p. 203.

[8]In particular, see Knight, *The Ethics of Competition, op. cit.*, p. 132 and p. 146, and *On the History and Method of Economics, op. cit.*, p. 177.

[9]Lionel Robbins, *An Essay on the Nature and Significance of Economic Science* (2d ed., revised and extended, London: Macmillan Co., 1935), p. 67.

of Positive Economics.[10] In this essay, Friedman does not discuss, or even mention, causal relationships. One explanation of why some economists emphasize cause and effect while others avoid it can be offered in terms of the difference between general theories and the specific applications of these theories. It is mainly in the specific applications that we look for causes. For example, we may wish to determine the cause of a particular inflationary situation, or we may attempt to discover causal factors common to all inflations. However, in order to find causes in this sort of diagnostic situation, we generally think in terms of a more general theoretical framework. We may say, for example, that a certain inflation was caused by an increase in the money supply, but this diagnosis rests on our general theoretical ideas concerning individual behavior, supply and demand, equilibrium, and so forth. This distinction between general and applied theories can be compared to the difference between maps and itineraries.[11] Mapmakers are not concerned with particular starting points or destinations, only with the general representation of a region. Once the map is completed, showing the configuration of landmarks, it may be used for many different purposes, including the determination of numerous specific itineraries. In general, most mapmakers in economics create their maps for the purpose of plotting definite itineraries; hence, the usual mixture of causal analysis and general economic theory.

Let us review briefly some of the recent attempts by economists to clarify the causal principle. Samples of the kind of analysis occurring in economics appear in the work of Herman Wold, Herbert Simon, and Guy Orcutt. Wold has written extensively on the place of the causal principle in econometrics.[12] He (with Strotz) defines causality as follows:

> For us, however, the word in common scientific and statistical-inference usage has the following general meaning. *z* is the cause of *y* if, by hypothesis, it "would be" possible by *controlling z* indirectly to control *y*, at least stochastically. But it may or may not be possible by controlling *y* indirectly to control *z*. A causal relation is therefore in essence asymmetric, in that in any instance of its realization it is asymmetric.[13]

Wold (with Jureen) believes that causal relationships can be expressed by means of statistical regression analysis in which there is a dependent (effect) variable and an independent (cause) variable or variables.[14] Finally, the

[10]Milton Friedman, "The Methodology of Positive Economics," *Essays in Positive Economics* (Chicago: University of Chicago Press, 1953), pp. 3–43.

[11]See Stephen Toulmin, *The Philosophy of Science* (Torchbook edition; New York: Harper and Bros., 1960), pp. 119–22.

[12]See especially, H. Wold and L. Jureen, *Demand Analysis* (New York: Wiley, 1953); H. Wold, "Causality and Econometrics," *Econometrica* (1954), pp. 162–177; and Robert H. Strotz and H. O. A. Wold, "A Triptych on Causal Systems," *Econometrica* (1960), pp. 417–63.

[13]Strotz and Wold, *ibid.*, p. 418; see also Wold, "Causality and Econometrics," *op. cit.*, p. 165.

[14]See Wold and Jureen, *Demand Analysis*, *op. cit.*, pp. 31–33, *et passim.*

idea is advanced that it is the theorist who must invest each relationship with a causal interpretation.[15] In both controlled experiments and the analysis of nonexperimental data, the causal relationship (that is, the choice of the dependent and independent variables) must be justified by theoretical inference or by experience and then confirmed by the results.

Herbert Simon has been concerned with devising ways in which causal concepts can be introduced into symbolic logic and econometric models.[16] We shall not focus here on Simon's methods, but rather on his approach to the idea of causation. Simon builds his theory on three basic premises: (1) the causal relation is asymmetrical, (2) the "undertaking is logical rather than ontological," and (3) no time sequences are involved.[17] Even though his approach is based on static models, Simon maintains that empirical testing of his causal relationships would validate his approach for scientific purposes.

Whereas Simon's approach is mainly theoretical, Orcutt is interested in harnessing causal relationships for the use of the policymaker.[18] Orcutt feels that basically a causal relation should be asymmetrical, but he also says:

> Causal relations may sometimes be set up as unidirectional relations which are complete and exact within well-defined limits, but they need not be set up in this way. Thus, when we say that *A* is a cause of *B*, we often mean that if *A* varies, then *B* will be different in a specified way from what it *would have been* if *A* had not varied. We do not, however, exclude the possibility that *B* would have changed by a unknown amount even in the absence of any variation of *A*.[19]

Furthermore, to apply controls with some degree of confidence, the policymaker must know the effects of these controls; that is, he must know which actions (causes) will produce what consequences (effects). But as the above definition reveals, Orcutt's approach to causality is inexact and indefinite.

Although Wold, Simon, and Orcutt are not the only economists who have concerned themselves with the principle of causality itself,[20] they have in fact devoted considerable attention to this problem. However, their work has

[15]*Ibid.*

[16]Simon's work on causality has been conveniently collected in *Models of Man* (New York: Wiley, 1957), Chaps. 1–3.

[17]See *Ibid.*, pp. 12, 50–51.

[18]See Guy H. Orcutt, "Toward Partial Redirection of Econometrics," *The Review of Economics and Statistics* (1952), pp. 195–213; and "Actions, Consequences, and Causal Relations," *The Review of Economics and Statistics* (1952), pp. 305–13.

[19]Orcutt, "Actions, Consequences, and Causal Relations," *ibid.*, pp. 305–6.

[20]For example, see Trygve Haavelmo, "The Probability Approach in Econometrics," *Econometrica* (1944), *Supplement*, pp. 22; also, T. W. Hutchison, *The Significance and Basic Postulates of Economic Theory* (London: Macmillan Co., 1938), pp. 70–2. Hutchison states: "The possibility of prognosis in economics is based on or intimately connected with the problem of causality in economic events," p. 70. But he concludes: "We certainly do not volunteer here to give any other meaning to concepts like 'the causes of a trade depression' than, simply, 'certain events immediately preceding or accompanying a trade depression,'" p. 72.

appeared in the context of econometrics and hence has not been adequately comprehended or even noticed by the general body of economists. In addition they have not gone far enough in their attempts to explain and solve the problems of causality.

The foregoing remarks, as well as the deficiencies in the approaches of Wold, Simon, and Orcutt, will become clearer after we define the causal concept with greater precision. There is really no consensus to be found, even among philosophers, on the precise meaning and application of the causal principle, but those economists who have considered the problem seem to lean toward a simple functional approach. It may be enlightening to consider some of the various possible definitions, rather than to lay down immediately a definition, however precise.[21]

First of all, we can discard all definitions of the type

(1) *A therefore B (or B because of A).*[22]

This expression is a factual statement explaining a relationship of actual events *A* and *B*. For scientific purposes, it is necessary to employ a conditional statement of the form

(2) *If A then B.*

This is a fairly general formulation of the causal principle. To make it more precise, certain, and definite, we may state it as

(3) *If A then B always.*

What does this formulation mean? *First*, there are no exceptions; it is the statement of an invariable law. *Second*, it is conditional in that we are stating what must happen to *A* in order to have *B* occur. *Third*, the relationship is asymmetrical, since the existence of *A* is necessary for the occurrence of *B*. Note that *A* does not necessarily have to precede *B* in time; all that is required is that *A* does not come into existence *after B*.

The major problem with definition (3) is that it can be interpreted as meaning that *A* is only the *sufficient* cause of *B*. In other words, we do not know from this formulation whether or not there may be a *D* such that "if *D* then *B* always." To express *A* as both the necessary and sufficient condition for *B* to occur, the relationship must be expressed as

(4) *If A then (and only then) B always.*

This eliminates disjunctive multiple causation in which any one of a number of causes may produce the same effect; it does not eliminate conjunctive

[21]Our approach to a definition of causality leans on the excellent study by Bunge. See Mario Bunge, *Causality* (Cambridge, Mass.: Harvard University Press, 1959), Chapter 2.

[22]Let *A* and *B* symbolize phenomena, situations, or events.

multiple causation in which B results from an event which is composed of distinguishable components; i.e., $A = A_1 \cdot A_2 \cdots A_n$. The latter is really just a more complicated *single* cause.

If we are to accept (4) as a precise formulation of the causal relationship, there remains another immediate problem to be resolved. Do we mean by (4) simply an invariable, repetitious, one-to-one relationship, or do we mean that A in some sense *produces* B? A distinguished philosopher posed and answered this question succinctly as follows:

> Since repetition is all that distinguishes the causal law from a mere coincidence, the meaning of causal relation consists in the statement of an exceptionless repetition — it is unnecessary to assume that it means more. The idea that a cause is connected with its effect by a sort of hidden string . . . is anthropomorphic in its origin and is dispensable; *if— then always* is all that is meant by a causal relation.[23]

Since the eighteenth century when David Hume "popularized" this view of causality (called the constant-conjunction view), it has been widely held and defended by both scientists and philosophers.[24] The chief difficulty with this view is that a correlation between A and B can be called a causal relationship and the definition will still be satisfied. Economists seem to be well aware that some kind of distinction exists between mere correlation and causality. They recognize, for example, that two variables (A and B) may always vary together (high correlation) and yet their joint variation may be the result of the influence of a third variable (C).[25] In terms of events this can mean that whenever event A occurs, event B will occur; yet both events will occur only whenever event C occurs. The approach that holds that in this case there is a causal relationship between A and B may be satisfactory for some purposes. However, it appears that economists would do well to distinguish between correlation and causation. That is, A and B are correlated (not causally related), while C is regarded as the cause of A and B. The objection may be raised that this is no improvement, since now we can regard A, B, and C as being correlated. Once granted that A and B have always been observed together, what difference can it make whether or not we think in terms of correlation or causation? For the economist, this distinction becomes critical once he enters the realm of policy-making and control. For example, if A and B are unrelated and their joint occurrence is dependent upon that of C, it would not be possible to alter B by changing A, or vice versa; it would be necessary to change C in order to change both A and B. That is, assuming a change in B to be desirable, a controlled change

[23]Hans Reichenbach, *The Rise of Scientific Philosophy* (Berkeley and Los Angeles: University of California Press, 1951), p. 158.

[24]For a recent defense see R. B. Braithwaite, *Scientific Explanation* (New York: Harper and Bros., 1960), esp. Chapter 9.

[25]See Mordecai Ezekiel and Karl A. Fox, *Methods of Correlation and Regression Analysis* (3d ed.; New York: Wiley, 1959), esp. pp. 475–7.

in *A* will not produce a change in *B*, but a controlled change in *C* will. This sort of consideration is vital to the economic policy-maker. Therefore, let us define the causal relationship as follows:

(5) *If A, then (and only then) B is always produced by A.*

This definition contains the idea that *B* is engendered or generated by *A*, which implies something more than a mere constant conjunction.

The "constant conjunction" approach to causality can be based entirely on observation; i.e., we need merely observe the joint occurrence of *A* and *B*. The "production" approach requires in addition that we ask *why* the relationship exists in order to determine whether *A* actually produces *B* in the sense discussed above. In this case, it is necessary to understand the relationship. In economics, and in other sciences, this understanding results from the construction of theories which serve to explain why *A* should indeed produce *B*. These are causal type theories. There are, of course, types of scientific explanation other than causal; and hence, there may be economic theories that are not causal. However, if they are causal, they must involve observation in order to establish the relationship as well as the construction of theories in order to determine "production." The theory may precede the observation, or *vice versa*, but both are necessary. In the case of the construction of models based on empirical relationships, causality cannot enter the model in a meaningful way without the prior development of theory.[26] In general, the necessity of theory construction in order to establish causal relationships has been largely responsible for pushing economists beyond the traditional borders of economics and into other social sciences.

To revert to our analogy of maps (theories) and itineraries (cause to effect), we find that we need maps covering more territory in order to find the starting points of certain itineraries. This development is particularly evident in the theory of economic growth and in the theory of the firm.

Causality and Economics

Our definition of causality (5) appears to be inclusive and precise. It seems to represent the kind of relationship for which economists have been searching since the time of Adam Smith. And no wonder, for in terms of both explanation and prediction, the rewards of discovery would seem to be high. But our record of discovery of such causal relationships is disappointing. We still search for the fundamental cause or causes of economic growth, the business cycle, inflation, and the behavior of the consumer and the firm. We attribute our failures to insufficient and inadequate observation or data, and to a certain amount of insularity and naivete in our development of theories.

---

[26]For a general discussion of the difference between models and theories in economics, see A. G. Papandreou, *Economics As a Science* (New York: Lippincott Co., 1958), Chapter 6.

These views have been at least partly responsible for the emergence of two pronounced trends in contemporary economics. One is the application of more sophisticated mathematical and statistical tools, as represented by mathematical economics and econometrics; the other is evidenced by the growing interest of economists in other social and behavioral sciences.

Many of these activities revolve around causality. Indeed, Wold states that ". . . causal relations are of central importance in economic analysis, in theory as well as in the applications."[27] Moreover, he believes that ". . . econometric analysis should be laid out along causal lines. . . ."[28] A leading growth theorist informs us that ". . . the inquiry into human actions has to be conducted at different levels, because there are proximate causes of growth, as well as causes of these causes."[29] Given these developments, we must now question the suitability of applying to economic problems a precise definition of causality as represented by (5).

The first problem concerns the interpretation of A and B as events. Is A to be considered as belonging to a class of identical events or of similar events? Even in the physical sciences it is held that no two events can be identical in every detail. Therefore, if A is to be considered as belonging to a certain class of similar events, which seems more appropriate in economics, how much alike must these events be in order to belong to the class?

It would appear that the more detailed and rigid we make the requirements for membership in a class, the fewer will be the number of members in the class. That is, by adding more and more details we finally describe a particular event. In terms of our definition of causality, if we have fewer A's we shall have fewer corresponding B's (and *vice versa*); and hence, with less experience our causal relationship will be more tenuous. On the other hand, if the class is broadly defined to include events that are just roughly similar, there will be more members in the class, more cases of a causal relationship; but our experiences will cover relationships which show a correspondingly wider range of variation.

If we reject vague, all-inclusive classes and search for causal regularities among well-defined concepts, we must face another difficulty—the continual emergence of new and novel events and situations. We all say that "the world of Alfred Marshall is not the world of today," and "the U.S. economy has changed since the thirties." It is true that new configurations are always evolving, which means that in economics established causal relationships may change with time and also new relationships may emerge.

Compared with the physical sciences, causal relationships in economics are often not very enduring. Moreover, we cannot adjust our causal theories to the impact of a change in the environment on a causal relationship if this

---

[27]Wold, *Demand Analysis, op. cit.*, p. 74.

[28]*Ibid.*, p. 128.

[29]W. Arthur Lewis, *The Theory of Economic Growth* (Homewood, Ill.: R. D. Irwin, Inc., 1955), p. 11.

change is unique and if we are consequently unable to assess the significance of the change. Indeed, we may simply be unaware of the change for some period of time during which one or more causal relationships are altered. Included in this set of problems is the emergence of new events that do not fit into any established class.

The economist must also recognize that even at best the causal explanation may be, and usually is, found in conjunction with some other form of explanation. It would be outside the scope of this paper to consider in detail these other possible modes of economic explanation, but we can at least point out some of them.

(1) *Interaction (or reciprocal causation)*: the relationships are no longer asymmetrical. There may be strong causal lines with varying degrees of feed-back.

(2) *Statistical*: the event is an element in a population so defined that the occurrence of the event can be explained in terms of probability.

(3) *Teleological*: behavior is explained in terms of goals, i.e., goal-directed activity.

(4) *Dialectical*: a synthesis of two opposing forces or tendencies.

(5) *Taxonomic*: the classification of events and their consequent explanation in terms of class membership.

(6) *Structural or organismic*: the behavior of a part is explained by its relationship to the whole.

(7) *Reduction*: the whole is explained after it is reduced to smaller parts, the behavior of the part being understood.

One or more of these modes of explanation may occur together or may occur in connection with a causal explanation; in the latter case, causality must be only a partial explanation.

In view of the usual joint occurrence of causality with other forms of explanation (rarely does any form of explanation occur in all its pristine purity), as well as the other difficulties involved in defining and applying a precise causal concept in economics, how can the economist employ the causal principle other than in the traditional loose and unsatisfactory way? One answer to this question is that of Wold and others, who employ statistical methods to handle the causal relationship. For example, Wold uses theory and experience to set up the following model.[30]

$$d_t = 2 - p_t + z_t$$

$$s_t = p_{t-1} + z_t$$

$$p_t = p_{t-1} + r(d_{t-1} - s_{t-1}) + z_t.$$

The model relates demand, d, supply, s, and price, p; t serves as a time index referring to periods; and z indicates disturbances. The model incorporates the causal hypotheses that consumers react to a change in price in the same

[30]Wold, *Demand Analysis, op. cit.*, pp. 12–15.

period and producers react to a price change of the preceding period. The z variables ". . . sum up the effect of causal factors that have not explicitly been taken into account in the model."[31] Wold feels that causality is ". . . brought out by the use of statistical regression analysis."[32]

Regression analysis cannot be employed for causal purposes without interpretation based on economic theory. Although Wold is cognizant of this, he does not seem to be adequately aware of the many exceptions in economics to his approach to causality or indeed, of the importance of other forms of explanation. Still, Wold's method has the virtue of being based on the application of probability ideas to causal relationships.

Causality and Probability

We have already considered some of the difficulties involved in a certainty approach to causality. Can there be a probabilistic approach which will eliminate these difficulties? A prior and more fundamental question is whether or not the principle of causality can be expressed in terms of probability. Traditionally, and even today, the probabilistic expression of causality has been rejected by proponents of the various forms of rationalism and idealism. On the other hand, empiricists often strongly defend the consistency and even advocate the necessity of a probability approach to causality. The latter position is often held to be applicable to all forms of knowledge. As Russell puts it: "Knowledge, I maintain, is a matter of degree. We may not know 'Certainly *A* is always followed by *B*,' but we may know 'Probably *A* is usually followed by *B*' . . . ."[33] Thus, all forms of causal certainty are rejected in favor of varying degrees of probability. If this approach is felt by many philosophers and physical scientists to be appropriate and necessary in the physical sciences, how much more applicable is it in the seemingly more complex and ever-changing world with which economists deal? In view of the difficulties confronting a certainty approach to causality, let us rephrase our definition of causality (5) to include probability.

(6) *If A, then (and only then) there is some degree of probability that B will be produced by A.*

These considerations seem to put us into Wold's camp. Unfortunately most of the objections that we raised against Wold's use of regression analysis as a general approach still hold. There is still the problem of dealing with nonquantitative data. There may not be enough observations to warrant regression analysis; indeed, there may be only one unique observation on the basis of which we wish to make a prediction; i.e., we want to know the effect

[31]*Ibid.*, p. 15.
[32]Wold, "Causality and Econometrics," *op. cit.*, p. 165.
[33]Russell, *Human Knowledge, op. cit.*, p. 427.

of a non-recurring event. Moreover, if a regression line is used for predictive purposes, a change in the environment may invalidate the regression line as a predictive device. Finally, the use of regression analysis for purposes of prediction has been challenged on other purely statistical grounds.[34] It should be pointed out and emphasized that Wold's inclusion of residual variables (z's) in his equations does not eliminate all of these objections. Therefore, Wold's approach to probabilistic causality, and all other similar approaches, must be termed incomplete.

To complete the probabilistic approach to causality, two additional categories of economic events must be developed. One of these categories would include events that may be only roughly similar, that may recur relatively infrequently, and that may be non-quantitative in certain or all respects. The other category would encompass non-recurring events. Indeed, most of the causal relationships with which economists struggle fall into these two categories, rather than into Wold's well-developed framework. Unfortunately these two proposed categories are not very well developed, and many difficult problems must be solved before a workable approach to probabilistic causality is evolved. For example, how much alike must events be in order to be regarded as similar? This question is partly dependent upon the problem of quantifying qualitative knowledge. How do we handle causal relationships which occur infrequently and with varying amounts of lag between cause and effect? Most difficult of all, how do we evaluate non-recurring events? Obviously this question is also related to the problem of similarity, since beyond some point we may feel that an event is no longer similar to other events, and hence is unique or non-recurring.

These perplexing questions lie beyond the scope of this paper. However, there is a growing body of thought dealing with such problems, as represented in the work of Reichenbach,[35] Rescher,[36] Keynes,[37] and Churchman,[38] to name but a few of those who have concerned themselves with these problems. These are hopeful developments, for in the end their success will help to determine whether economists will be able to rely to a greater degree on the more formal methods of science or whether Professor Knight is indeed correct in his position that economic prediction and control must largely depend upon trained judgment, insight, and common sense.

---

[34]For example, see A. M. Mood, *Introduction to the Theory of Statistics* (New York: McGraw-Hill Book Co., 1950), pp. 297–9; see also discussion of this range of problems in *Demand Analysis*, *op. cit.*, Chapter 2.

[35]Hans Reichenbach, *The Theory of Probability*, translated by E. H. Hutten and Maria Reichenbach (2d ed.; Berkeley and Los Angeles: University of California Press, 1949).

[36]Nicholas Rescher, "On the Probability of Nonrecurring Events," *Current Issues in the Philosophy of Science*, edited by Herbert Feigl and Grover Maxwell (New York: Prentice-Hall, 1961), pp. 228–37.

[37]J. M. Keynes, *A Treatise on Probability* (London: Macmillan Co., 1929).

[38]C. West Churchman, *Prediction and Optimal Decision* (Englewood Cliffs, N. J.: Prentice-Hall, 1961).

3. FRIEDMAN AND MACHLUP ON THE SIGNIFICANCE OF TESTING ECONOMIC ASSUMPTIONS*

Jacques Melitz†

INTRODUCTION

The spectacular advance of modern science is usually attributed very largely to the development of deductively related bodies of general statements known as theories. The construction of theories in science has not only brought improvements in order and clarity and broadened the scope of empirical generalization but has also scored extraordinary predictive successes, some of which were never even envisaged when the theories began. No wonder that, as awareness of the possibility of "social sciences" grew in the nineteenth century, there emerged an enormous zeal for the erection of social theories. Of the social theories that thrived during the nineteenth century, the most viable one has proven to be an offspring of the preceding century, when this general zeal had not yet begun, that is, economic theory. Despite the venerability of economic theory at present, it still does not command nearly as much respect as some of the theories in the physical sciences. This is, of course, a rank understatement: for well over a century, economic theory has been subject to frequent attacks, including completely subversive attempts. The theory and its assumptions have been the victims not only of constant opposition but of abuse.[1] In the face of such extreme antagonism, partisans have traditionally armed themselves with some sort of a reasoned reply.

During the period 1880–1920 the friends and advocates of economic theory adopted on the whole a moderate, conciliatory stance. They agreed that economic theory made false assumptions, and admitted that the value of the

*From *Journal of Political Economy*, Vol. LXXIII, No. 1 (February, 1965), pp. 37–60. Reprinted by permission of the University of Chicago Press and the author.

†Jacques Melitz, Economist, Ministry of Finance, France. The author owes an inestimable debt to Carl G. Hempel and Paul Benacerraf for guidance and criticism in the early stages of preparation of this paper some six or seven years ago. He has also benefited from comments by Gaston V. Rimlinger.

[1]To illustrate, without attempting to be compendious: Thorstein Veblen, "Why Economics Is Not an Evolutionary Science," *Quarterly Journal of Economics*, Vol. XII (1898), reprinted in *The Place of Science in Modern Civilization and Other Essays* (New York: Viking Press, 1912), pp. 56–81; Barbara Wootton, *Lament for Economics* (London: W. H. Allen and Co., 1938); and Sidney Schoeffler, *The Failures of Economics: A Diagnostic Study* (Cambridge, Mass.: Harvard University Press, 1955).

theory depended greatly on the degree of accord between the assumptions and the facts. Yet they insisted, first, that the assumptions did correspond broadly with events, and second, that the sacrifice of some accuracy for simplicity was justified in view of the complexities of facts. Further, they emphasized the importance of combining the use of simplifying assumptions with several protective measures: (1) the pursuit of intensive inductive study in all areas of economics, whether closely related to economic theory or not; (2) the determination of reasonable proximity between major assumptions and facts prior to any application of economic theory to practice; and (3) the alteration of theoretical assumptions, to whatever degree possible, in keeping with the particular case involved.[2]

With the notable advance of the purely logical branch of economic theory in the 1920's and 1930's, this conciliatory support of economic theory lost enormous appeal among theorists. A tendency arose, partly unconscious, to avoid the impression that economic theorists bore the responsibility to make their assumptions as realistic as they could, given practical limitations in knowledge, returns to additional theoretical invention, and time. Increasingly, economic theory was described in a manner suggesting no positive declarations about facts. Concomitantly, some narrow characterizations of economic theory took hold, such as "box of analytical tools," "filing cabinet," "conceptual framework," and "procedural device." A growing number of people also hinted broadly, both inside and outside the classroom, that theory is its own reward.

In 1948 Milton Friedman tried to supply a logical foundation for the developing attitude that the realism of assumptions is not a genuine, or is only a secondary concern. While granting that the assumptions of economic theory are false, he denied any significant resulting handicap. In his view, assumptions must simply work, that is, yield reliable results. Whether or not assumptions correspond with the facts is—with a few reservations—without interest. Since, according to Friedman, all previous attacks on economic theory had been founded principally on observed discrepancies between economic assumptions and facts, these attacks were mostly beside the point.[3] In 1955 Fritz Machlup joined forces with Friedman, claiming

[2]See John Neville Keynes, "On the Deductive Method in Political Economy," *The Scope and Method of Political Economy* (London: Macmillan Co., 1891), Chap. vii, pp. 204–35; Alfred Marshall, *Principles of Economics* (London: Macmillan Co., 1961), *passim*, esp. pp. 24–31, 636–46 (1st ed.; 1890); Henry Sidgwick, *The Principles of Political Economy* (3d ed.; London: Macmillan Co., 1901), pp. 35–52 (1st ed.; 1883); and his "Political Economy: Method," in R. H. I. Palgrave (ed.), *Dictionary of Political Economy*, Vol. III (2d ed.; London: Macmillan Co., 1913), pp. 133–37 (1st ed.; 1899). For highly similar views, see Vilfredo Pareto, *Cours d'economie politique*, Vol. I (Lausanne, 1896–97), pp. 304–5, Vol. II, pp. 1–8; his *Manuel d'économie politique*, trans. Alfred Bonnet (2d ed.; Paris, 1927), pp. 1–39 (1st ed. [Italian]; 1906); and Knut Wicksell, *Lectures on Political Economy*, Vol. I, trans. E. Classen, (ed.) with Introduction by Lionel Robbins (London: Kelley, 1934), pp. 9–11 (1st ed. of Vol. I [Swedish]; 1901).

[3]Milton Friedman, "The Methodology of Positive Economics," *Essays in Positive Economics* (Chicago: University of Chicago, 1948), p. 3–43.

to bring with him the support of the experts in the philosophy of science and logic and of a whole tradition in economics (or "political economy"). Machlup, in fact, sides with Friedman only with regard to so-called "fundamental assumptions" but still, on this count alone, must be viewed as an ally.[4]

This paper attempts to show that Friedman and Machlup offer an exaggerated defense of economic theory. Previous attempts to show this in connection with Friedman are all, in my opinion, somewhat unsatisfactory, by virtue of incompleteness if nothing else.[5] The argument presented here is that the most judicious defense of economic theory is the one that was prevalent in the 1880–1920 period. Thus, my general thesis is that unrealism of assumptions is a serious drawback, granted that inaccurate assumptions may be sufferable and, indeed, wise. I will try to show, further, that tests of economic assumptions — all economic assumptions, regardless of categorization — are valuable and bear implications for economics, apart from psychology, sociology, history, or any other bordering discipline. The discussion focuses first on Friedman's position, then on Machlup's, and the article concludes with a few summary remarks.

THE FRIEDMAN THESIS

Thesis and Qualifications

Friedman maintains that the accuracy of assumptions is not pertinent to the test of a hypothesis. In his view, the validity of any statement can be determined only by checking the truth of its implications. To contemplate the realism of assumptions in testing a hypothesis is wrong. His section on "The Significance and Role of the 'Assumptions' of a Theory" qualifies this argument in several ways, and it may be best to observe these qualifications at once.

First, Friedman recognizes a difficulty in his position if a statement (A) is used to derive a hypothesis (B) while in a different context, B serves to derive A. A simple example, slightly adapted from the illustration in Friedman's essay, may be presented. Imperfect competition, together with several

[4]Fritz Machlup, "The Problem of Verification in Economics," *Southern Economic Journal*, Vol. XXII (July, 1955), pp. 1–21.

[5]See Tjalling C. Koopmans, *Three Essays on the State of Economic Science* (New York: McGraw-Hill Co., 1957), pp. 135–42; Eugene Rotwein, "On 'The Methodology of Positive Economics,'" *Quarterly Journal of Economics*, Vol. LXXIII (November, 1959), pp. 554–75; Ernest Nagel, "Assumptions in Economic Theory," *American Economic Review, Papers and Proceedings*, Vol. LIII (May, 1963), pp. 211–19; and Paul Samuelson, "Discussion," *ibid.*, pp. 231–36. While broadly in agreement with all of these writings, I am particularly in close accord with Koopmans and the philosopher Nagel. For some generally favorable appraisals of Friedman's position, mixed, except in the first case, with light criticisms, see Campbell R. McConnell, "Advocacy versus Analysis in Economics," *Southern Economic Journal*, Vol. XXII (October, 1955), pp. 155–56; K. Klappholz and J. Agassi, "Methodological Prescriptions in Economics," *Economica*, Vol. XXVI (February, 1959), pp. 60–74; and G. C. Archibald, "The State of Economic Science," *British Journal for the Philosophy of Science*, Vol. X (May, 1959), pp. 58–69.

other assumptions, implies price stability, but under a different set of conditions, price stability implies imperfect competition. Thus, imperfect competition may be an assumption of a hypothesis of price stability and vice versa. In cases of this sort, Friedman admits, evidence bearing on either statement would be relevant in determining the validity of the other. To quote:

> What are called the assumptions of a hypothesis can be used to get some indirect evidence on the acceptability of the hypothesis in so far as the assumptions can themselves be regarded as implications of the hypothesis. . . .[6]

However, he softens the impact of this concession by maintaining that "in so far as the assumptions can themselves be regarded as implications of the hypothesis," the realism of the assumptions "generally refer[s] to a class of phenomena different from the class which the hypothesis is designed to explain." In his view, "the weight attached to this indirect evidence depends on how closely related we judge the two classes of phenomena to be."[7]

Further, Friedman acknowledges that the confirmation of an assumption is partial support for a hypothesis:

> Suppose it can be shown it [the hypothesis] is equivalent to a set of assumptions including the assumption that man seeks his own interest. The hypothesis then gains indirect plausibility from the success for other classes of phenomena of hypotheses that can also be said to make this assumption; at least, what is being done here is not completely unprecedented or unsuccessful in all other uses.[8]

Finally, as I understand him, Friedman concedes that, whenever a satisfactory test is absent, the realism of assumptions may contribute toward the evaluation of a hypothesis. In his words:

> The decisive test is whether the hypothesis works for the phenomena it purports to explain. But a judgment may be required before any satisfactory test of this kind has been made, and, perhaps, when it cannot be made in the near future, in which case, the judgment will have to be based on the inadequate evidence available.[9]

In the light of these qualifications, the opening description of Friedman's thesis may seem to exaggerate his position. Indeed, he is careful never to say that the realism of assumptions is "irrelevant" without adding the adverb "largely."[10] Nevertheless, the qualifications play a minor, rather inconspicuous role in his essay as a whole. They appear after the close of the main arguments, which are stated quite categorically. Moreover, Friedman's attitude

---

[6]Friedman, *op. cit.*, p. 28.

[7]*Ibid.*

[8]*Ibid.*, p. 29.

[9]*Ibid.*, p. 30.

[10]Cf. Rotwein, *op cit.*, p. 555, footnote 6, and pp. 567–68. See also Koopmans, *op. cit.*, pp. 137–39.

toward past and prospective tests of economic assumptions reveals an extremely low degree of concern over his qualifications. In disputing previous tests of profit maximization, Friedman not only questions the workmanship of the experiments, but denies the logical basis for them. The unqualified version of Friedman's thesis, therefore, presents a reasonably accurate image of his position; and, at the very least, this version of his thesis requires concentrated attention.

Argument 1: The Inverse Relation of Realism and Abstraction

In arguing his position, Friedman opens with an avowedly paradoxical view. "To be important," he maintains, "a hypothesis must be descriptively false in its assumptions." The main relevant paragraph may be quoted in full:

> In so far as a theory can be said to have "assumptions" at all, and in so far as their "realism" can be judged independently of the validity of predictions, the relation between the significance of a theory and the "realism" of its "assumptions" is almost the opposite of that suggested by the view under criticism. Truly important and significant hypotheses will be found to have "assumptions" that are wildly inaccurate descriptive representations of reality, and, in general, the more significant the theory, the more unrealistic the assumptions (in this sense). The reason is simple. A hypothesis is important if it "explains" much by little, that is, if it abstracts the common and crucial elements from the mass of complex and detailed circumstances surrounding the phenomena to be explained and permits valid predictions on the basis of them alone. To be important, therefore, a hypothesis must be descriptively false in its assumptions; it takes account of, and accounts for, none of the many other attendant circumstances, since its very success shows them to be irrelevant for the phenomena to be explained.[11]

Clearly Friedman is correct in asserting that the provision of simple and reliable hypotheses with wide application requires considerable abstraction. On what grounds, however, does he claim that abstraction involves the use of false assumptions? Evidently Friedman considers abstraction as implying the assumption that some aspects of reality are absent. It is admittedly true that, in ordinary English usage, "assume that *x* is absent" may be substituted for "abstract from *x*" in many contexts. There is no meaningful sense, however, in which a hypothesis may be said to require the assumption that what it abstracts from is absent. No hypothesis hinges on such an assumption in any way. For instance, the statement that the marginal productivity of factors is inversely related to quantity involves abstraction from the sequence in which goods are produced. But the statement does not rest upon the assumption that goods are produced without any time relation to one another. In abstracting, we leave some facts out of consideration. This commits us to the view that these facts do not matter, not to the assumption that the facts do not exist.

[11]Friedman, *op. cit.*, pp. 14–15.

Further problems arise due to Friedman's failure expressly to limit his use of the term "assumption" in the previous quotation to allegations of the absence of perceptible facts. In saying that "important assumptions" "must be descriptively false," Friedman seems to argue that abstraction involves false allegation beyond the mere assertion that certain observable aspects are gone. This suggestion cannot be seriously contemplated. Abstraction is clearly consistent with the exclusion of false classes of implications from statements, and cannot require the admission of false information. In fact, as Friedman would probably agree despite his opposite suggestion, abstraction is the major instrument for achieving scope without sacrificing accuracy.

To elaborate, the exercise of everyday concepts and terms almost invariably leads to error in attempts to develop broad generalizations. Abstraction, and the subsequent introduction of technical terms, allows the elimination of ambiguities and exceptions from statements. As long as difficulties arising in the use of everyday terms can be traced to some specific classes of implications in a statement, increased abstraction enables superior formulation. Countless examples are available in economics. Thus, to present a simple case, reliance on ordinary concepts and terms poses serious obstacles in defining the general relation of buyers' behavior to prices. Yet the use of highly abstract concepts and terms makes possible the compact and trustworthy statement that "the demand for all non-inferior goods is negatively sloping."[12]

In conclusion, the relationship between abstraction and truth is not as recondite as Friedman would have everyone believe. Quite conformably with prevalent suppositions, abstraction facilitates the attainment of truth, and does not necessitate the acceptance of false assumptions, or immersion in "unrealism" of any sort.[13]

Argument 2: The Uninformativeness of Knowledge of Discrepancies Between Assumptions and Facts

Next, Friedman sets forth a more substantial argument, evolved with the aid of an intriguing illustration. Though Friedman's presentation is intricately bound up with his illustration, a general formulation of the argument is possible. The starting-point, which remains somewhat implicit in his text, is that assumptions need only be approximated. That is, some finite departure from an assumption can be admitted in all or nearly all cases. The tolerable degree of discrepancy, theoretically speaking, can exceed any perceived deviation. Thus, while the acceptable deviation is sometimes discernible only with the

[12]For a highly illuminating and developed example see Carl G. Hempel, "The Theoretician's Dilemma: A Study in the Logic of Theory Construction," in Herbert Feigl, Michael Scriven, and Grover Maxwell (eds.), *Minnesota Studies in the Philosophy of Science: Concepts, Theories, and the Mind-Body Problem*, Vol. II (Minneapolis: University of Minnesota Press, 1958), pp. 41–46.

[13]Cf. Nagel, *op. cit.*, pp. 214–16.

use of refined instruments, at other times it may be evident to the unassisted senses. Since the acceptable deviation between assumptions and facts can be either "large" or "small," knowledge of the actual magnitude of a discrepancy, by itself, yields meager, nearly useless information. The proper way to resolve whether an assumption is adequately fulfilled is to check the observable implications of the hypothesis in question. If the implications are true, the assumption is warranted. Otherwise the assumption must be rejected. It follows (barring the aforementioned special circumstances which Friedman discusses later) that the actual correspondence between assumptions and reality is irrelevant. To quote the central passage:

> We may start with a simple physical example, the law of falling bodies. It is an accepted hypothesis that . . . the distance travelled by a falling body in any specified time is given by the formula $s = \frac{1}{2} gt^2$, where s is the distance travelled in feet and t is time in seconds. The application of this formula to a compact ball dropped from the roof of a building is equivalent to saying that a ball so dropped behaves *as if* it were falling in a vacuum. Testing this hypothesis by its assumptions presumably means measuring the actual air pressure and deciding whether it is close enough to zero. At sea level the air pressure is about 15 pounds per square inch. Is 15 sufficiently close to zero for the difference to be judged insignificant? Apparently it is, since the actual time taken by a compact ball to fall from the roof of a building to the ground is very close to the time given by the formula. Suppose, however, that a feather is dropped instead of a compact ball. The formula then gives wildly inaccurate results. Apparently, 15 pounds per square inch is significantly different from zero for a feather but not for a ball.[14]

Some aspects of Friedman's position can hardly be disputed. There is no question, for instance, that many discrepancies between assumptions and reality are quite acceptable. He is also correct in holding that mere size cannot determine whether a discrepancy is large or small. Whether 15 pounds air pressure, or any other positive amount less than infinity, is significantly greater than zero, to echo Friedman, clearly depends on the experiment at hand. One degree of seller influence over price will invalidate the assumption of perfect competition in some instances, but not others. Does this mean that the disparity between an assumption and reality has no bearing on the testing of a hypothesis?

To cope with this question, a distinction must first be introduced between two types of assumptions: (1) statements which are used in conjunction with the hypothesis in order to deduce predictions, and (2) statements which serve in deriving the hypothesis itself. For want of better names, the two types may be referred to, respectively, as "auxiliary" and "generative" assumptions. Some frequently employed assumptions usually function in one role rather than the other. In economics, for instance, "*ceteris paribus*" is typically an "auxiliary" assumption and "profit maximization" a "generative"

[14]Friedman, *op. cit.*, pp. 16–17.

assumption. But logically speaking, every assumption may serve in either capacity, depending on the particular test involved. To illustrate, the assumption of perfect competition may be used in deriving the hypothesis, say, that all firms in industry *Y* produce where marginal cost equals price, and may therefore function as a "generative" assumption. However, in relation to the hypothesis, say, that every perfectly competitive firm in industry *Y* produces where marginal cost equals marginal revenue, perfect competition is an "auxiliary" assumption. This hypothesis does not presuppose perfect competition, but will only yield implications about the behavior of particular firms under the assumption that those firms are perfectly competitive.[15] In Friedman's example, the assumption of a vacuum is clearly an "auxiliary" one.[16] His argument, however, is intended to apply to "generative" as well as "auxiliary" assumptions, and thus, must be examined with regard to both.[17]

In respect to "auxiliary" assumptions, consider a hypothesis, *H*, which, like any ordinary hypothesis, is expressible as saying that if certain types of conditions, $c_1, c_2, \ldots, c_n$, are realized, a certain type of event, *E*, occurs. *H* does not yield any predictions alone, but only in conjunction with a set of statements A_x, affirming that the conditions, $c_1, c_2, \ldots, c_n$, are true.[18] The members of A_x are "auxiliary" assumptions. Suppose, in accord with a fundamental implicit understanding in Friedman's argument, that the maximum tolerable discrepancy between $c_1, c_2, \ldots, c_n$ and the facts is not known. Now

[15] I do not mean to exclude the possibility of a particular statement serving both as an "auxiliary" and "generative" assumption at once in an experiment. A simple illustration of this possibility can easily be constructed. Suppose that increasing marginal cost is among the assumptions employed in deriving the hypothesis that a fall in the output of butter will result in a rise in the price of margarine. In testing this hypothesis, we may determine that the output of butter has fallen without immediate evidence of the fall, relying mainly on the probable impact of medical reports about the cholesterol content of butter, and the blanket assumption of increasing marginal cost. Should this be done, increasing marginal cost would function both as an "auxiliary" and a "generative" assumption of the hypothesis.

[16] Cf. Nagel, *op. cit.*, p. 212.

[17] In developing the distinction between "generative" and "auxiliary" assumptions, I have chosen to avoid the conventional distinction between (1) "fundamental assumptions" and theorems and (2) assumptions "which refer to the antecedent clause of a conditional theoretical statement" (see Nagel, *op. cit.*). The latter two-part distinction divides statements on the basis of an accepted definition of a theory, and results in a fairly defined list of "fundamental assumptions" and theorems and an automatic exclusion of most assumptions from this "theoretical" group. On the other hand, my distinction is purely functional and permits any statement to belong to either the "generative" or the "auxiliary" classification, to shift from one to the other group, and even to belong to both groups on occasion. Since some economic assumptions sometimes function as "generative" and at other times as "auxiliary" assumptions, this classification has clear expository value.

[18] For further exposition, see the classic paper by Hempel and Paul Oppenheim, "Studies in the Logic of Explanation," *Philosophy of Science* (1948), Vol. XV, pp. 135–75; reprinted and abridged under the brief title of "Logic of Explanation," in Herbert Feigl and May Brodbeck (eds.), *Readings in the Philosophy of Science* (New York: Appleton, 1953), pp. 319–52.

imagine that by using H and A_x together a statement about a specific spatio-temporal location, namely, an observation statement, O, is derived.

If O is found to be true, then by inductive logic, both H and A_x acquire a degree of confirmation. That is, the outcome increases the probability that both H and A_x are true. However, it may be shown that any evidence contrary to A_x will also play a role in the interpretation of the test result. Given any deviation between A_x and reality, then along with the chance that the experimental conditions conform adequately to the requirements, it is also possible that the facts fall outside the boundary conditions for testing H. If this possibility should hold, H would be consistent with false results. Thus, as long as the facts do not correspond fully with A_x, the truth of O is not necessarily favorable to H. Consequently, the greater the evidence opposed to A_x, the lower the degree of confirmation which the truth of O confers upon H. This reasoning applies without modification to Friedman's experiment with the compact ball. In this example, the accuracy of the predicted time of fall increases the probability of truth of the law of falling bodies and the assumption of a vacuum. However, the presence of 15 pounds of air pressure per square inch admits the possibility that the test is faulty, and thereby diminishes the significance of the result. In arriving at a different conclusion, Friedman simply ignores the chance of an invalid experiment.

Suppose, next, that O is tried and found false. As long as the experiment deserves attention, or in other words, is not manifestly a fraud, the result increases the probability that H is false. But the more the discrepancy between assumed conditions and reality, the greater the chance that the requisite test conditions are unfulfilled. Consequently, the greater is this discrepancy, the less reason there is to expect H to yield true implications, and the less disconfirmatory is the falsehood of O. In Friedman's example of the feather, therefore, the false prediction weakens the probability that the law of falling bodies is true, but the actual degree of environmental air pressure reduces the weight of the result. Friedman manages somehow to reach a strikingly different conclusion. He interprets the false predicted time of fall to mean that the assumption of a vacuum is false while the law of falling bodies is true. It may be readily seen that, if this interpretation could be logically sustained, all contradictory results would be attributable to the experimental environment, and no hypothesis could ever be disconfirmed. When a prediction is false, we must allow for the possibility that the hypothesis — in this case, the law of falling bodies — is wrong. The logician Carl G. Hempel advances this point in a somewhat different context, while, by sheer coincidence, employing the same example:

> Let us imagine, by way of analogy, a physicist propounding the hypothesis that under ideal conditions, namely in a vacuum near the surface of the Earth, a body falling freely for t seconds will cover a distance of exactly 16 t^2 feet. Suppose now that careful experiment yields results differing from those required by the hypothesis. Then clearly the physicist

> cannot be content simply to infer that the requisite ideal conditions were not realized: in addition to this possibility, he has to allow for the alternative that the hypothesis under test is not correct.[19]

The unusual persuasiveness of Friedman's conflicting conclusions in his illustration can be explained. In his example, there are covering general laws enabling fairly accurate predictions of the magnitude of the errors which the law of falling bodies will yield both in the instance of the feather and the compact ball. In addition, the reader knows beforehand, on the basis of general experience and education, that the law of falling bodies is liable to give a fairly accurate forecast of the time of fall of the compact ball, but will necessarily yield miserable results in the experiment of the feather. It is this prior knowledge, rather than the test results, which accounts for the reasonable appearance of Friedman's inferences. Supposing that all grounds for anticipating the outcome of his experiments were removed, say, by the substitution of x and y for the terms "feather" and "compact ball," then the lack of justification for his conclusions would become patent.[20]

To summarize the main conclusions attained thus far in this section, given ignorance of the extent to which deviations between "auxiliary" assumptions and the facts can be tolerated, all evidence opposed to these assumptions increases the ambiguity of test results. Regardless of the test outcome, any discrepancy between "auxiliary" assumptions and reality raises some likelihood that the experiment is invalid. As a consequence, the lower the evidential support for A_x, the smaller the significance of both positive and negative results. The realism of "auxiliary" assumptions, therefore, is plainly relevant.[21]

---

[19]Hempel, "Typological Methods in the Social and Natural Sciences," *American Philosophical Association, Eastern Division*, Vol. I, *Science, Language, and Human Rights* (Philadelphia: 1952), p. 78 (the title of the paper is not present in the book, but appears on the reprints). Cf. Andreas G. Papandreou, "Theory Construction and Empirical Meaning in Economics," *American Economic Review, Papers and Proceedings*, Vol. LIII (May, 1963), pp. 205–10; Archibald, "Discussion," *ibid.*, pp. 227–29, and his "The State of Economic Science," *op. cit.*, pp. 61–62.

[20]Cf. Koopmans, *op. cit.*, p. 139.

[21]In his article, Rotwein (*op. cit.*, pp. 556–64) argues to the same effect, maintaining that under positive air pressure, a true test outcome does not necessarily support the law, and that "the probable inaccuracy of the prediction grows as the values of the variables of the given case depart from those under which we have been led to expect the prediction" (*ibid.*, p. 563). But unfortunately, he rests his argument on some obscure considerations, including the nature of causality and human predispositions toward chance, and does not adequately emphasize the logical issues raised by Friedman's position.

The argument in the text regarding "auxiliary assumptions" also emerges quite clearly in Papandreou's *Economics as a Science* (Chicago: Lippincott Co., 1958) and in his aforementioned article in the section on methodology of the *American Economic Review, Papers and Proceedings* of 1963. I am, however, quite skeptical regarding Papandreou's general emphasis. He seems to be largely preoccupied with the fact that, unless the truth of "auxiliary" assumptions can be ascertained, hypotheses cannot be—and the term here is quite crucial—*refuted.* He builds his distinction between "theories" and "models" on the issue of possible refutation, and devotes much attention to the types of logical structures which hypotheses may assume in order to be refutable if they derive from a "model" (consisting of irrefutable statements) rather than a "theory" (refutable) (see Papandreou, *Economics as a Science*, *op. cit.*, pp. 8–9, 101–20 [esp.

Friedman's argument may now be examined with regard to "generative" assumptions. Suppose *H* is derived from a set of statements or "generative" assumptions, A_g; and presume, for the sake of simplicity, that no member of A_g belongs to A_x. Now consider the significance of evidence opposed to A_g with regard to *H*.

Unlike testimony conflicting with A_x, such evidence would not interfere with the interpretation of outcomes of any tests of *H*. "Generative" assumptions are not logically required in deducing observation statements. Consequently, whatever the facts with respect to A_g, the results of checking observation statements derived from *H* and A_x can be unambiguously interpreted as either for or against *H*. Together with this point, it may be noted that the falsehood of A_g would not preclude the truth of *H*. False assumptions, like all other false statements, may bear true and non-trivial implications. The statement that all animals can fly, for instance, correctly implies that under a wide variety of circumstances, all winged animals can fly. As long as any false matter included in A_g is not also contained in *H*, the falsehood of A_g is perfectly compatible with the truth of *H*. In principle, therefore, no mere volume of evidence contradicting A_g need cause *H* to be abandoned. Furthermore, concurrent with a large amount of such contradictory evidence, *H* may enjoy great predictive success, and possess high confirmation.[22]

---

pp. 116–17], and p. 141; and "Theory Construction and Empirical Meaning in Economics," *op. cit.*). The trouble with this perspective, in my opinion, is that although general scientific statements may be capable of refutation in principle, as a rule scientific hypotheses are rejected because of disconfirmation, or in other words, on grounds of high probability of error. The main reason for this fact is that even in the most advanced sciences, as Friedman suggests, there is usually room for doubting whether the appropriate conditions for an experiment were adequately fulfilled. Consequently, as long as statements can be disconfirmed, which is true of those in Papandreou's "models," I do not see why the issue of refutability, as such, should be of particular concern. This criticism applies, a fortiori, to Geoffrey P. E. Clarkson's recent methodological work by the somewhat misleading title of *The Theory of Consumer Demand: A Critical Appraisal* (Englewood Cliffs, N.J.: Prentice-Hall, 1963). Clarkson utterly confuses the issues of refutation and disconfirmation (see, for example, his pp. 21–22, 82–83, 142). He maintains, contrary to the foregoing text, that if "auxiliary assumptions" are not known to be "true," in the strict sense, the results of experiments are neither *confirmatory* nor *disconfirmatory* (see his pp. 95–96 in particular). He also bases a whole program of reform of existing consumer theory essentially on the absence of *refutability* of this theory, which he interprets as implying lack of "empirical meaning."

[22]In his attempt to refute Friedman, Clarkson (*ibid.*) argues in sharp opposition to these views that "the prediction of an event can only be employed as a means of testing a theory when some parts of the theory have already been well confirmed" (p. 90), and moreover, contrary to his own position at some points (for example, p. 80), that "the derived laws [of the theories of utility and demand] could be empirically confirmed if and only if the basic postulates were empirically confirmed" (p. 103). This view rests on a confusion between "auxiliary" and "generative" assumptions, or perhaps more appropriately in this context, between "antecedent conditions" and "general theoretical statements." Proceeding on the basis of an example where the major hypothesis has the form "if *R*, then *S*," Clarkson concludes correctly that unless *R* is true, the truth of *S* does not necessarily support the hypothesis. However, he treats *R* as a general theoretical statement, whereas, of course, *R* is an "antecedent condition" (or an "auxiliary"

(Contd.)

Yet these factors do not establish Friedman's case. While the falsehood of A_g does not thwart the testing of H or refute the hypothesis out of hand, it may nevertheless reduce the probability that H is true. If Friedman's thesis is to be meaningful, he must be maintaining, in effect, that evidence opposed to A_g would not raise the odds against H. Framed in this manner, his position is extremely weak.

In case A_g is true, then all of its implications, including H, must be true. However, if A_g is false, then some of its implications must be false, and these implications may affect the substance of H. Whatever the past success of H may be, should the hypothesis bear false contents, it may yield false predictions in the future. Thus, broadly speaking, the more the evidence conforms to A_g, the greater the rational basis for confidence in H; and vice versa, the less this evidence agrees with A_g, the less this basis for confidence.[23] Furthermore, it may also be observed that H may derive an important measure of its existing support from the testimony favorable to A_g. If A_g did not possess sufficient factual corroboration to warrant some faith in its conclusions, this assumption would most likely not be used to develop hypotheses or hunches. There is every reason to think, therefore, that a marked reduction in the evidential basis for A_g would notably undermine H. In fact, in cases where hypotheses derive from a well-established general theory, the bulk of their support often stems from the theory. There are surely many instances in the physical sciences where hypotheses have been dismissed only because some covering laws or theories had come under serious question.

Argument 3: The Presence of "Undesigned" Classes of Implications

Friedman, however, is not satisfied to maintain, as the preceding arguments would imply, that if assumptions work they should be used, regardless of the extent of their unrealism. In addition, he holds that false information contained in assumptions may not concern classes of implications which the hypothesis is "designed to explain." Every hypothesis, he believes, harbors some implications which are completely without interest, and only findings concerning the other implications are pertinent. This argument, it may be

---

assumption) in the example and, even if occasionally employed elsewhere in a "generative" role, can hardly be taken to be a "general theoretical statement." (In order to crosscheck this point, consider first that R cannot logically imply S or the hypothesis would simply be R, and next, that the economic postulates and theorems do not appear as subordinate clauses of more general economic statements.) Clarkson's error underlines the importance of the related distinctions between "antecedent conditions" and "general theoretical statements," and "auxiliary" and "generative" assumptions (see *ibid.*, pp. 88–92, and compare with pp. 19–20 where the same reasoning is correctly presented in relation to "antecedents").

[23]Cf. Nagel, *op. cit.*, p. 215; Rotwein, *op. cit.*, pp. 568–69; and also William J. Baumol, *Business Behavior, Value and Growth* (New York: Macmillan Co., 1959), p. 6.

noted, is not entirely consistent with his previous stand. If false information can be countenanced with complete equanimity, there is no need to plead that some of the implications of assumptions are "undesigned." Evidently, Friedman recognizes that false assumptions pose the danger of false predictions, and thus, that false assumptions have a certain likelihood not to "work."[24]

The notion that hypotheses contain "undesigned" classes of implications has serious merit. Every hypothesis (*H*) is limited to some specific classes of events by conditional clauses and other verbal restrictions. Each condition for the application of *H*, for instance, eliminates a whole class of implications which, in the absence of the condition, would follow from *H* together with its "auxiliary" assumptions (A_x). There is always a chance that these conditions are insufficiently restrictive in various ways, or that the sentence component of *H* asserting what happens under these conditions is too comprehensive. As presently stated, *H* and A_x may admit various classes of implications that concern types of events which the investigators are not interested in explaining or classes of implications which they have overlooked and would not accept upon notice. There are, in fact, some general reasons to think that most scientific statements are never perfectly consistent with the researchers' proper empirical interests and intentions. First of all, the assertion of all necessary qualifications and limitations of scope would often require intense consideration of outside problems, perhaps in different fields. In addition, this assertion would frequently cost an inordinate amount of time and resources from the perspective of current concerns.

However, the likelihood that negligible kinds of discrepancies exist between economic assumptions and facts is not a warrant for discarding any contradictory test evidence. Before any negative results can be safely dismissed, it is necessary to be able to discern the "undesigned" classes of implications. Friedman views this ability as present to an important degree in economics. According to him, every hypothesis in economic theory is attended by a set of rules defining the class of phenomena which the hypothesis is supposed to explain.[25] While these rules are inexact, and Friedman deplores the failure to devote greater attention to their elaboration, he believes that "to a considerable extent the rules can be formulated explicitly."[26]

The issue of the existence of these rules can be examined, first, from a highly common-sense point of view. If economic rules of application of the sort which Friedman describes can be formulated to any significant degree, then what are some examples? What, for instance, is a rule determining any one class of "undesigned" implications of the postulate of profit maximization? Are there any kinds of producers who are not supposed to try to maximize their profits, or kinds of conditions under which no producer is expected to do so? Admittedly, it may not matter for most purposes whether producers

[24]Cf. Rotwein, *op. cit.*, p. 560, footnote 5, the paragraph extending on pp. 560 and 561, and pp. 565–67.

[25]Friedman, *op. cit.*, p. 24

[26]*Ibid.*, p. 25.

try to maximize their profits to the very last cent, but given the wide range of functions which the profit-maximization postulate serves in economics can any practical deviation from the assumption be confidently termed completely inconsequential? Likewise, what are the rules for finding the "undesigned" classes of implications of the theorem of negatively sloping demand for non-inferior goods? Friedman supplies no answer to these questions. The only support for his view that can be inferred from his essay is the indication that the same firm or industry may be regarded as perfectly competitive for some purposes, but not for others. However, economic theory, in its most unlimited form, does not clearly assert the omnipresence of perfect competition. Hence, the specification of rules concerning the proper application of this assumption, or the supply of guidelines determining when perfect competition can and cannot be assumed, does not plainly entail any "undesigned" classes of implications. Moreover, Friedman's one or two examples of legitimate and illegitimate applications of the assumption of perfect competition to a single industry do not provide a single tenable rule of application regarding perfect competition, let alone with respect to any other economic assertions. While these examples may be fairly convincing, it would be very difficult to infer a general rule of application from them.[27]

Aside from the practical problem of identifying rules of application in economics, it may be observed, more generally, that if any "undesigned" classes

[27] *Ibid.*, pp. 36–37. Archibald has made a highly related point with regard to Friedman's major example, involving the cigarette industry, and in return has received a sharp rebuke from Friedman (Archibald, "Chamberlin versus Chicago," *Review of Economic Studies*, Vol. XXIX [October, 1961], pp. 2–28, esp. pp. 3–4; Friedman, "More on Archibald versus Chicago," *ibid.*, Vol. XXX [February, 1963], pp. 65–67; and Archibald, "Reply to Chicago," *ibid.*, pp. 68–71). In his answer, Freidman maintains that his example is intended to show the importance of specifying the rules of application, rather than existing knowledge of those rules. But I must confess that, whatever Friedman may say elsewhere in his paper regarding the need for developing and elaborating the economic rules, like Archibald, I cannot help but read the cigarette example and the entire surrounding context as an attempt to show the current availability of such rules and the neglect of the critics of economic theory of their existence. The following three opening statements of paragraphs shortly prior to the cigarette example set the tone for the illustration:

"The confusion between descriptive accuracy and analytical relevance has led not only to criticisms of economic theory on largely irrelevant grounds but also to misunderstanding of economic theory and misdirection of efforts to repair supposed defects" (Friedman, "The Methodology of Positive Economics," *op. cit.,* p. 34).

"This tendency is perhaps most clearly illustrated by the interpretation given to the concepts of 'perfect competition' and 'monopoly' and the development of the theory of 'monopolistic' or 'imperfect competition' " (*ibid.*).

"As always the hypothesis as a whole ["that, for many problems, firms could be grouped into 'industries' such that the similarities among the firms in each group were more important than the differences among them"] consists not only of this abstract model but also of a set of rules, mostly implicit and suggested by example, for identifying actual firms with one or the other ideal type and for classifying firms into industries" (*ibid.,* pp. 35–36).

As may be gleaned from these quotations, the general trend of Friedman's argument is that, in refusing ever to apply various assumptions to particular economic units, the critics of economic theory, Marshallian and otherwise, are blind to the existence of certain "rules."

of implications could be properly identified, they could then be eliminated. In other words, if we could pinpoint precisely something that we do not wish to say, we could cease to say it. Thus, in order to substantiate his contention that certain adverse test results can be completely disregarded, Friedman should be able to show that, by introducing appropriate qualifications and conditions, he could narrow the empirical scope of economic theory without impairing the explanatory and predictive value of the theory. Until he can meet this test, there is every reason to think that all negative findings must be accepted as disconfirmatory.[28]

To elaborate on this view beyond the point reached in the preceding section, assume that there is reason to suspect, along with Friedman, that some of the testimony advanced, say, against the profit-maximization postulate does not impair the theoretical statement. Granted, however, the inability to reconcile the postulate satisfactorily with the contrary evidence, how can we be sure? Even though the negative results, as such, appear trivial, the part of the theory to which the results pertain may carry latent significance. In any general theory including many theorems, the interrelations among statements and definitions may be extremely complex, and any particular aspect of a statement which appears negligible in itself may nevertheless play an important part in the theory as a whole. Thus, the falseness of any portion of the theory may be an unsuspected cause of many false predictions. Furthermore, even if certain practical errors in the theory have not borne any adverse effects in the past, they could become catastrophic in the future. Theories are supposed to provide new and untried hypotheses, and whatever may be the past record, later hypotheses may be highly influenced by on-going theoretical mistakes. Thus, any errors uncovered in assumptions may also be considered as clues regarding the possible improvement of the theory.

---

[28]Cf. the following statement by Koopmans: "To state a set of postulates, and then to exempt a subclass of their implications from verification is a curiously roundabout way of specifying the content of a theory that is regarded as open to empirical refutation" (Koopmans, *op. cit.*, p. 139). See also Nagel, *op. cit.*, pp. 217–18.

There is a great deal of reciprocity between the argument at this point and Samuelson's criticism of Friedman in his "Discussion" (Samuelson, *op. cit.*). Samuelson stresses that whatever is known to be false in an argument should simply be purged. While this view is correct, I think it bears emphasis that to remove false information from a statement requires knowledge of the false *classes* of implications rather than merely the false *instances* themselves. In other words though a statement may be known to be imperfect, there may be no clear avenue of improvement. Samuelson's failure to give adequate consideration to this point has led him, in my view, to an important error in criticizing Friedman. Samuelson supposes that a favorable outcome of a check of an implication of a general statement only supports the whole statement if no parts of the statement are known to be false. However, since there may be no obvious way to remedy the defects of the statement, the only suitable interpretation of a favorable test result may be as adding a degree of confirmation to the statement as a whole. The basis for this interpretation is that every favorable result enhances the chances that the statement, as constituted, will yield true predictions in the future. However, Samuelson's error in refusing to accept some positive results as confirmatory is far less serious than that of Friedman in supposing that some negative outcomes are non-disconfirmatory.

There is also a noteworthy and curious inconsistency in Friedman's position. While minimizing the importance of contradictory findings, he sometimes displays a lively appreciation of the impact of evidence supporting any fragment of a theory on the entire theoretical edifice.[29] It is quite rational to believe that every favorable result confers some degree of confirmation on every part of a theory and all logically affiliated hypotheses. But granted this view, it is difficult to see how the converse effect of negative results can be denied.

Economic Theory as a Set of "As If" Statements

In connection with the problem of "undesigned" implications, a particular semantic proposal by Friedman that is enjoying some following should be discussed; namely, the idea of regarding assumptions as "*as if*" statements. Specifically, the proposal is that assumptions be construed to mean that certain events take place *as if* the assumptions were true, instead of being understood as outright assertions. The basis for the appeal of this construal is obvious; it would mean that assumptions, as conventionally stated, are never even supposed to be true. Thus, the construal is in keeping with Friedman's view that certain fallacies in assumptions have no bearing. In addition, the construal answers the conspicuous demand of many economists for some sort of logical protection against unfriendly criticism of economic theory. A quotation will make Friedman's proposal clearer:

> Consider the problem of predicting the shots made by an expert billiard player. It seems not at all unreasonable that excellent predictions would be yielded by the hypothesis that the billiard player made his shots *as if* he knew the complicated mathematical formulas that would give the optimum directions of travel, could estimate accurately by eye the angles, etc., describing the location of the balls, could make lightning calculations from the formulas, and could then make the balls travel in the direction indicated by the formulas. . . .
>
> It is only a short step from these examples to the economic hypothesis that under a wide range of circumstances individual firms behave *as if* they were seeking rationally to maximize their expected returns . . . and had full knowledge of the data needed to succeed in this attempt.[30]

The "*as if*" construal of economic assumptions, whatever its appeal, has some important drawbacks. In particular, the construal is inconsistent with the explanatory and predictive function of economic theory and scientific statements in general. With regard to the explanatory function, suppose the question arises why a given individual shoots expert pool. The answer that he shoots expert pool because he is a competent mathematician, and can make the balls travel in accord with complicated calculations, etc., can at least be accepted. But the reply that he shoots pool *as if* he were a competent

[29]See, for example, footnote 8, and the associated quotation in the text.

[30]Friedman, "The Methodology of Positive Economics," *op. cit.*, p. 21.

mathematician, and so forth, is beside the point. This answer concerns the question "how possibly" rather than the question "why." The correct answer to "how possibly," of course, is completely independent of the actual state of affairs and the genuine reasons why. Thus, Friedman might as well have said that the billiard player shoots the balls into the pockets *as if* the balls were magnetized and the pockets were magnets; or *as if* there were invisible ridges in the table shifting in accord with the player's will and leading the balls into the pockets. The question "why" calls for an assertion of fact, suitable for an introduction with the term "because." Statements of possibilities and suggested analogies do not constitute explanations. In sum, the economic postulates cannot appear in an "*as if*" form when they are used in explanation. Since the postulates frequently serve in order to explain, the "*as if*" construal would seriously misrepresent these statements.

The "*as if*" formulation is also impossible to reconcile with the predictive function of general scientific statements. Departing from the rather trivial example of the expert pool player, consider the assertion that businessmen behave *as if* they were trying to maximize their profits, or (if such an alternative be possible) that under certain conditions businessmen behave *as if* they were attempting to maximize profits. Given the requisite circumstances, if any, what can we predict, or in other words, what observable implications can we derive from this "*as if*" statement? Unfortunately no observable implications seem to follow. If businessmen act only *as if* trying to maximize profits, then evidently they do not exactly try to maximize profits, at least not all of the time, and perhaps sometimes they do not even try to maximize profits at all. As a result, no specific conclusion about businessmen's actions, however vague and tentative, can be strictly derived from the statement. In basing any prediction on the assumption of profit maximization, it may safely be concluded that there is implicit reliance on the declaration that, maybe only under some *specified* conditions, and maybe only with regard to some *defined* subgroup, businessmen really and truly try to maximize their profits.

Since "*as if*" statements can serve neither to explain nor to predict, Friedman's proposal to interpret the economic postulates as "*as if*" statements should be rejected.[31] Broadly speaking, in using the economic postulates

[31]A similar objection can be raised against all of the weak characterizations of economic theory mentioned in the introduction, such as "box of analytical tools," "filing cabinet," "conceptual framework," etc. Admittedly, these characterizations are true as far as they go, but they fail to acknowledge the explanatory and predictive functions of the theory. To elaborate, the characterizations are correct in stressing that economic theory provides a compact, efficient way of structuring and storing masses of information, which is useful, for instance, in writing textbooks and cataloguing data; and they are also correct in stressing that the theory helps in raising questions and suggesting possible replies. But since the theory is continually employed in the further effort to explain and predict the future, it does not seem accurate to depict economic theory as a mere analytical device (for viewing things, asking questions, compiling knowledge, etc.). In employing these weak characterizations, therefore, it may be said that economists have unduly modest pretensions. The most acceptable characterization, I submit, is that economic theory is a set of general statements about the world.

to explain and predict, we commit ourselves to what they say about the world; and thus, it would seem almost mandatory to interpret them accordingly as straightforward declarations of fact.

Conclusion

In conclusion, lest the point be lost amid the criticisms, I would like to emphasize the presence of an important measure of agreement with Friedman in these pages. Most notably, I concur fully with his view that the disconfirmation of an assumption, as such, does not disqualify any hypothesis. First, false "auxiliary" assumptions impede testing but do not carry the least suggestion that the hypothesis is false.[32] Second, false "generative" assumptions may bear true and non-trivial implications. A hypothesis about price behavior founded partly on the profit-maximization postulate could be true, granted that the postulate is false. There is no doubt that, in arguing this general point of view, Friedman faces strong opposition from many quarters. Many writers, mostly in the social sciences and humanities, evidently regard assumptions as the pillars on which whole theories and even entire disciplines stand. Judging from some accounts, science is a pyramid with assumptions on the bottom and empirical knowledge sitting precariously on top. Friedman's strenuous objection to this extreme position is amply justified. Allowing that assumptions are often an important source of support for hypotheses, that they affect what is looked for and the interpretation of what is found, surely it is fundamentally the facts that support theories, rather than the other way around. If all corroborating evidence for empirical theories were lost, it would seem that theories and their assumptions would soon collapse. On the other hand, the destruction of all assumptions could not negate all the previous testimony of our senses. As Friedman ably points out, although this is by no means the only relevant consideration, the facts apprehended at any moment in time are always compatible with infinitely many assumptions.

Unfortunately, however, Friedman does not confine his remarks to the previous points. (To some extent, however, he fosters the quite contrary impression that everything that he says is logically attendant; witness the disarming title of his main section, concerning the irrelevance of the truth of assumptions: "Can a Hypothesis Be Tested by the Realism of Its Assumptions?") Friedman also states that a test of assumptions is completely pointless, unless, as he mentions only after concluding his main arguments, a few special kinds of circumstances hold. This position must be unreservedly rejected. As noted, the greater the deviations between test conditions and "auxiliary" assumptions, the lower the ability to perform tests; and the greater the extent to which "generative" assumptions are inaccurate, the lower is the probability that the derived hypotheses are true. More generally, with regard to "generative" assumptions, the more unrealistic these assumptions, the weaker

[32]Cf. Nagel, *op. cit.*, p. 215.

the basis for relying on them in order to develop hypotheses or hunches. Hence, contrary to Friedman, tests of economic assumptions are generally useful in testing and appraising hypotheses, and in indicating possible avenues of improvement in theory and hypotheses.[33]

THE MACHLUP VIEW

Introduction

In his article on "The Problem of Verification in Economics" in the *Southern Economic Journal* in 1955,[34] Machlup adopts Friedman's view of the irrelevancy of tests of assumptions, but only with respect to one particular type of assumptions, namely, "fundamental assumptions." Other assumptions, Machlup believes, require some degree of corroboration in an experiment.[35] In support of his position regarding "fundamental assumptions," Machlup follows a special line of reasoning. To begin with, he holds that "fundamental assumptions" *cannot* be tested "directly" or "independently." To quote him: "There is no way of subjecting fundamental assumptions to independent verification";[36] and "Fundamental assumptions are not directly testable and cannot be refuted by empirical investigation."[37] In addition, Machlup also argues, particularly with respect to economics, that "fundamental assumptions" are not *supposed* to be tested "independently" since they can be properly *understood* as making no factual declarations. These two arguments are not fully consistent: If "direct" tests of "fundamental

[33]Nagel (*ibid.*) fully corroborates these conclusions. He reasons that if "unrealistic" is understood in the sense of false, rather than abstract, Friedman's arguments are wrong. Nagel's article suffers, however, from a failure (or at least the strong symptoms thereof) correctly to assess Friedman's main objectives. Perhaps intending to give the benefit of a doubt, Nagel interprets Friedman's support of unrealistic assumptions strictly as an effort to defend the use of abstract theory. That is, Nagel does not acknowledge Friedman's interest in undercutting the rational basis for testing assumptions and in denying the relevance of the results of tests of assumptions. Concomitantly, Nagel focuses largely on what seems to me to be a subsidiary aspect of Friedman's position, namely, the view that abstract theoretical terms could, if so desired, be completely eliminated from statements. Nagel regards this view as an essential link in Friedman's effort to establish the acceptability of abstract theory whereas, if my reading is correct, the view is a secondary accompaniment of Friedman's attempt to show that certain aspects of assumptions are "undesigned" and that the facts relating to them are negligible. Whatever the true significance of this view, Nagel's refutation is conclusive. I may also note that Nagel does not mention Friedman's argument for "undesigned" classes of implications. Yet on all issues where this paper and Nagel's meet, there is, I believe, total agreement.

[34]Machlup, *op. cit.*

[35]See *ibid.*, pp. 8–16, and the interesting paragraph on pp. 18–19. Machlup fails to recognize his disagreement with Friedman regarding "non-fundamental" assumptions. According to Machlup, the "only serious flaw in the otherwise excellent essay" by Friedman is the failure to consider the requirement of "understandability" (*ibid.*, p. 17, footnote 42).

[36]*Ibid.*, p. 9.

[37]*Ibid.*, p. 11.

assumptions" are entirely precluded, as the first argument says, then the argument that these assumptions may be properly interpreted in a way rendering "direct" tests inappropriate is completely superfluous. Nevertheless, Machlup develops both arguments together and does not separate the two.[38]

Machlup's stand is of interest largely as an example of a certain kind of opposition to direct testing of theoretical postulates. Concern with his stand is also dictated by his taunting suggestion that his conclusions are commonly accepted in the field of the philosophy of science. "Logicians and philosophers of science," he asserts, "have long tried to make this perfectly clear."[39] No attempt will be made to deal with Machlup's position as a whole; the aim will be only to treat a few important selected topics in connection with his stand, namely: (1) the distinction between "direct" and "indirect" tests; (2) the argument that "fundamental assumptions" are inherently impossible to test directly; and (3) the argument that it is illegitimate to test "fundamental assumptions" because they can be appropriately understood as rules, or more generally, as making no declarations about facts.

The Distinction Between Direct and Indirect Tests

The distinction between direct and indirect tests plays a central part in the writing of Friedman and Machlup, since both authors contend that, for one reason or another, postulates can be properly tested only in a roundabout or indirect way. The reason for discussing the distinction with regard to Machlup is that he deals with this distinction more explicitly and more satisfactorily than Friedman.

Friedman presents the distinction by contrasting testing by mere "perception" of "descriptive accuracy" with testing by checking the validity of

---

[38]Machlup's confusion of the two arguments is particularly evident on p. 11 of the article. Later on, in his rejoinder to a reply by Terence W. Hutchison, Machlup admits the error, saying: "Perhaps it was confusing when in addition to stating that these fundamental assumptions *need not* be independently verified, I also indicated that they *cannot* be so verified" ("Rejoinder to a Reluctant Ultra-empiricist," *Southern Economic Journal*, Vol. XXII [April, 1956], p. 487). Also in the same general passage (*ibid.*, p. 488), Machlup abandons the argument that "fundamental assumptions" are inherently impossible to test directly. In his subsequent writing, however, including one lengthy methodological article, Machlup makes a number of cross-references to his 1955 essay, without indicating the least change in his position (see Machlup, "Operational Concepts and Mental Constructs in Model and Theory Formation," *Giornale degli Economisti e Annali di Economia*, Vol. XIX [September–October, 1960], pp. 553–82; and *Essays on Economic Semantics* [Englewood Cliffs, N.J.: Prentice-Hall, 1963], pp. 48, 79). It may also be noted that his reply to Hutchison is a spirited defense on the whole (see Hutchison, "Professor Machlup on Verification in Economics," *Southern Economic Journal*, Vol. XXII [April, 1956], pp. 476–83; and Machlup, "Rejoinder to a Reluctant Ultra-empiricist," *op. cit.*, pp. 483–93). The original article by Machlup and the subsequent exchange with Hutchison have been translated into Italian in a book under the authorship of Machlup, Hutchison, and Emile Grunberg titled *IL Problema della Verifica in Economia* (Milan: 1959). Hereafter, Machlup's original article will be referred to briefly as "Verification" and his reply to Hutchison as "Rejoinder."

[39]Machlup, "Verification," *op. cit.*, p. 10.

derived implications; and Machlup does essentially the same at one point.[40] The distinction between comparing a statement against the facts and checking its implications, however, is highly superficial. Every test involves a checking of something which follows from a statement or set of statements by implication. Thus, while Friedman may wish to regard an investigation of the propensities of individual businessmen *a, b, c, . . . , n,* to maximize profits as a mere test of the descriptive accuracy of the profit-maximization postulate, the fact remains that this test constitutes a check of bona fide implications. At best, the distinction between checking a statement, as such, and checking its implications can be understood as one between a check of a whole as opposed to a check of only a part of a statement. The latter distinction, however, makes sense only with regard to statements whose entire empirical content is amenable to checking with a finite set of observations (for example, "this tree is an elm"). In the instance of statements yielding an infinite set of implications requiring separate observations, which comprises the whole class of general theoretical statements, checking the entire empirical content of the statements is not feasible.

In an effort to advance beyond the crude distinction between comparing statements against the facts and checking their implications, Machlup asserts that a direct test entails the derivation of implications from a statement alone whereas an indirect test involves the derivation of implications from a statement in conjunction with other statements. This proposed definition, while a step in the right direction, is also inadequate. The definition provides no basis for a distinction between direct and indirect tests of conditional statements, which constitute, of course, the dominant portion of the entire output of scientific hypotheses. A conditional statement, by itself, yields no *observable* implications whatever, and can never be tested in complete isolation from other statements.[41] The statement "if *x*, then *y*" does not imply anything about the world at any particular spatio-temporal location unless it is brought together with an affirmation that *x* is true. The combined assertion of "if *x*, then *y*" and "*x* is true" implies *y* and whatever observable implications *y* may bear. Thus, according to the proposed definition of a direct test, no direct test of the main assertion "if *x*, then *y*" is possible, and all tests of conditional statements are indirect.[42]

[40]To quote the relevant passage in Machlup: "The point to emphasize is that Mill does not propose to put the *assumptions* of economic theory to empirical tests, but only the *predicted results that are deduced from them*" ("Verification," *op. cit.*, p. 7).

[41]Though, of course, the statement "if *x*, then *y*," by itself, does bear infinitely many conditional implications. For one thing, the statement implies itself. More significantly, the statement yields implications of the form "if *z* implies *x*, then *z* implies *y*."

[42]To offer an economic example, consider the conditional assertion: "If wages are inflexible, then a fall in the aggregate demand for goods will cause unemployment." This assertion, alone, says nothing whatever about observable conditions at any specific point in space and time. But a conjunction of this assertion and the statements that "wages are inflexible" and "government spending on goods and services has declined" implies a present rise in unemployment. Thus, on the basis of the present definition, the only possible test of the hypothesis is indirect.

The only tenable distinction between a direct and an indirect test, agreeing with the general intentions of Machlup and Friedman, is one between a test that employs only statements that are logically essential for the derivation of observable implications and a test that uses additional statements. In other words, an indirect test involves the checking of implications derived from a statement together with one or more others that are not required in order to draw some observable implications by means of the first. Machlup's reply in his exchange with T. W. Hutchison[43] indicates an attempt, although not an altogether successful one, to formulate the distinction in this way.[44]

The Impossibility of Testing "Fundamental Assumptions"

Machlup's argument that "fundamental assumptions" are impossible to test directly rests essentially on the experience in physics.[45] As frequently noted, the physical postulates cannot be directly tested. Like many other observers, Machlup is extremely impressed with this point and prone to generalize on its basis. However, the difficulty of testing the physical postulates in any relatively straightforward manner is easy to diagnose; it arises from the fact that these postulates contain various highly abstract terms, such as atom and molecule, whose counterparts in nature are not subject to immediate sensory observation. It does not follow that there are significant barriers to direct testing of postulates in other disciplines, particularly in a field as distantly related to physics as economics.[46] The experience of physics

[43]See Hutchison, "Professor Machlup on Verification in Economics," *op. cit.*; and Machlup, "Rejoinder," *op. cit.*

[44]Machlup, *ibid.*, pp. 484–85.

[45]See Machlup, "Verification," *op. cit.*, pp. 9–10.

[46]Cf. Koopmans, *op. cit.*, p. 135. In his article on "Operational Concepts and Mental Constructs in Model and Theory Formation," (*op. cit.*), Machlup maintains that the theoretical concepts of economics are highly abstract, and thus, by intimation, supports his earlier thesis that the economic postulates require indirect testing. However, Machlup's argument rests entirely on the supposed classification of all scientific concepts into two groups: "operational concepts" and "pure constructs." "Operational concepts" are those which can be defined as a set of operations. "Pure constructs," on the other hand, are either mathematical, or else bear only "some indirect reference to facts of experience" and are "derived through idealization, heroic abstraction, or inventions" (*ibid.*, p. 577). In order to show that the economic concepts of "price" and "quantity" are "theoretical" or "pure constructs," Machlup is satisfied to point out the inadequacy of any purported operational definition of either term. Given, however, Machlup's own demonstration of the extreme weaknesses of "operationalism," or the thesis that all scientific concepts should be "operational," his bipartite division of concepts is untenable. For example, as Machlup indicates quite clearly (*ibid.*, p. 558), all objects of sensory perception such as ants or lilacs cannot be operationally defined, lest the concepts be made synonymous with the operations of the observer in identifying these objects. Yet the concepts of an "ant" and a "lilac" can hardly be regarded as "pure constructs." The need for some intermediary classification (or classifications) is clear, and the possibility that many economic concepts belong to this (these) intermediary grouping(s) is equally plain. Thus, Machlup's argument for the high abstractness of the economic concepts does not stand.

does not signify that "fundamental assumptions," in general, are impossible to test directly.[47]

To elucidate the falsehood of the thesis that empirical postulates cannot be tested directly, first, the status of a statement as a postulate in a theoretical system implies nothing about the testability of that statement. Any general statement can serve as a postulate in a deductive system. Furthermore, a "lower-level" hypothesis in one deductive system can be a "fundamental assumption" in another. To carry the argument further, there is no reason, in principle, why in a certain system the theoretical postulates might not be more readily testable than the theorems and many of the "lower-level" hypotheses. In one of his writings, the noted philosopher Rudolf Carnap emphasizes this practical possibility,[48] which derives mainly from the feasibility of introducing new terms at any step in a deductive sequence. Since the terms which are imported after a deductive process has begun can be highly technical, the derived statements of a theory may be more abstract and less susceptible to direct testing than the underived ones. A single economic example, intended to be correct, but not to supply the ground for any generalization about abstract relations in economics,[49] will do. The assertion that indifference

[47] Machlup provides very little evidence of philosophical support for his view. His two lengthy quotations from prominent philosophers ("Verification," *op. cit.*, p. 10) do not say, as he supposes, that scientific postulates are impossible to test directly, but rather that postulates which are only indirectly testable have proven to be extremely valuable in science. His most impressive citation of philosophical support is the statement by Richard B. Braithwaite: "The empirical testing of the deductive system is effected by testing the lowest-level hypotheses in the system." This assertion, though in seeming agreement with Machlup, actually offers him no assistance. Braithwaite uses the term "lowest-level" hypothesis to mean any general statement which is last in a deductive order, regardless of the simplicity of the derivation. Moreover, in the relevant context, the statement refers unambiguously to the possibility of a direct test (see Braithwaite, *Scientific Explanation: A Study of the Function of Theory, Probability and Law in Science* [London: Cambridge, 1953], pp. 12–13). Machlup also claims that Nassau W. Senior, John Elliot Cairnes, and John Stuart Mill denied "the independent objective verifiability of the fundamental assumptions" of economic theory ("Verification," *op. cit.*, p. 6). There is no doubt, however, that all three of these writers held that at least some of the "fundamental" economic assumptions could be independently (and "objectively") verified, for example, the "law of diminishing productiveness of the soil" and the "law of population." For explicit indications see Senior, *An Outline of the Science of Political Economy* (London: 1836), pp. 26, 30–50, and 81–86; Cairnes, *The Character and Logical Method of Political Economy* (London: 1875), pp. 77, 88–89 (1st ed., 1857); and Mill, "On the Definition of Political Economy; and the Method of Investigation Proper to It," *Essays on Some Unsettled Questions of Political Economy* (London: 1844), pp. 145–46 (essay written in 1829–30, and appearing first in the *London and Westminster Review*, October, 1836). Moreover, Mill's essay "On the Definition of Political Economy" clearly opposes the notion that the economic postulates require no direct testing. In this essay, Mill vigorously argues that the main economic assumptions should never be put to work without priorly ascertaining their general applicability to the particular case involved (see *ibid.*, pp. 139–41, and 149–50).

[48] Rudolf Carnap, "Foundations of Logic and Mathematics," *International Encyclopedia of Unified Science*, Vol. I, No. 3 (1939), pp. 61–67, esp. 64.

[49] In this connection see the interesting though rather unusual comment by Herbert Simon, in his "Discussion," *American Economic Review, Papers and Proceedings*, Vol. LIII (May, 1963), pp. 229–31.

curves are convex, everyone will probably admit, is much more abstract than the statement that consumers always prefer variety to uniformity of goods. Yet as is generally well known, the latter assertion can serve as a partial basis for deriving the convexity of indifference curves. The main reason for this condition, evidently, is that the special terms "indifference curve" and "convex" are injected at a late point in the argument.[50]

The Illegitimacy of Direct Tests of Empirical "Rules"

Perhaps the most challenging part of Machlup's stand, requiring some detailed attention, is his view that the economic postulates *ought not*, or cannot *legitimately* be tested directly because they can be understood not to be assertions of fact. His main support for the belief, as the reply to Hutchison explicitly shows, is the following:

> Logicians have long debated the possibility of propositions being synthetic and yet *a priori*, and physicists are still not quite agreed whether the "laws" of mechanics are analytical definitions or empirical facts. The late philosopher Felix Kaufmann introduced as a middle category the so-called "rules of procedure," which are neither synthetic in the sense that they are falsifiable by contravening observations nor *a priori* in the sense that they are independent of experience; they are and remain accepted as long as they have heuristic value, but will be rejected in favor of other rules (assumptions) which seem to serve their explanatory functions more successfully.[51]

To quote a closely related passage in the "Rejoinder":

> In his comments on the nature and significance of the maximization postulate Professor Hutchison conveys the impression that he recognizes as scientifically legitimate only two kinds of statements: Propositions which by empirical tests can, at least conceivably, be proved to be false, and definitions without empirical content. If so, he rejects a third category of propositions used in most theoretical systems: the heuristic postulates and idealized assumptions in abstract models of interdependent constructs useful in the explanation and predictions of observable phenomena. . . .
>
> Logicians have long recognized this intermediate category of propositions, which are neither *a priori* nor *a posteriori* in the strict sense of these terms.[52]

On the basis of the general content of Machlup's essay, his argument can be interpreted substantially as follows:

Step I. Logicians "have long recognized" the presence of statements which are neither "*synthetic*" nor "*a priori*";

[50]Cf. Hutchison, *op. cit.*, pp. 481–82.
[51]Machlup, "Verification," *op. cit.*, p. 16.
[52]Machlup, "Rejoinder," *op. cit.*, p. 486.

Step II. Some special terms have been addressed to such statements;

Step III. These terms are applicable to the postulates of economic theory; and therefore

Step IV. Like all other statements which are suited to bear those labels, the economic postulates ought not to be tested independently.

In order to avoid prolonged discussion, I will confine myself to the principal issues related to economics. It is convenient to begin with Step III. With close bearing to this step, one can question Machlup's assertion (which does not emerge fully above) of the equivalence or at least equal admissibility of a variety of different portrayals of the economic postulates. Machlup is explicitly indifferent as to whether the postulates are understood as "rules of procedure," "heuristic postulates," "idealized assumptions," "useful fictions," "resolutions," or "definitional assumptions," to list only his most prominent appelations.[53] Yet some of these terms differ greatly, and the application of all of the appelations to the economic postulates does not seem appropriate.

The conception of the economic postulates as "definitional assumptions," if not illogical, is certainly misleading. The adjective "definitional" is usually understood to pertain either to sentences defining a concept or term, or to a particular concept or term. Given this construal of the term, the economic postulates are clearly not "definitional." Whatever other meaning may be assigned to "definitional," the term retains the connotation "necessarily true." Yet we know that the assertion of non-optimizing behavior, for example, involves no inherent contradiction. More generally, it would spell a great misfortune for economics if the economic postulates were necessarily true, since then all of their implications would be empirically irrefutable and no hypotheses or predictions could be derived from them.[54]

---

[53]See Machlup, "Verification," *op. cit.*, pp. 9, 16; and "Rejoinder," *op. cit.*, pp. 486, 487, including footnote 5.

[54]Hutchison is responsible for considerable confusion, I believe, on the question of the logical truth-status of the economic theoretical statements. In his *The Significance and Basic Postulates of Economic Theory* (London: Macmillan Co., 1938), he argues that the postulates and theorems of economic theory are tautological and hence necessarily true. Though by this time Hutchison may have altered his opinion, his early view continues to exert influence among economists, and therefore deserves attention. His sole supporting arguments for his 1938 position are: first, that "in formulating a system of definitions one is in one and the same process formulating a series of analytical-tautological propositions of pure theory" (*ibid.*, p. 30); and second, that every proposition which follows by implication within a deductive system is a tautology. With regard to the first argument, the construction of a theoretical vocabulary does not necessitate any statements at all, and granted that tautologies can usually be manufactured easily, any set of technical terms can be used to formulate non-tautological statements, given a sufficient vocabulary and adequate syntactical rules. Otherwise, of course, no technical terms could ever serve in order to obtain empirical statements. As for the view that all theoretical implications are tautological, which applies to theorems and not postulates, here again a logical mistake is involved. If statement X is derived from Y, then X is necessarily true if Y is true, but not if Y is false. Hutchison's view easily leads to a *reductio ad absurdum* since every statement is theoretically derivable from infinitely many others. Incidentally, among those who have indorsed Hutchison's argument are some eminent economists.

Nor is it clear that all economic postulates can be interpreted as "idealized assumptions." On the basis of current philosophical usage, an "idealized" assumption is one which holds true only under certain limiting conditions which can never be even closely approximated in practice outside of the laboratory. Accordingly, the "assumption" of a "pure gas," for instance, is "idealized." If this special philosophical meaning is accepted, then objective factors largely determine whether a given statement is "idealized" or not, and it cannot simply be postulated at will that the "fundamental" economic assumptions are "idealized." In particular, "optimizing behavior" is not a very convincing example of an "idealized assumption."

Avowedly, though, the postulates of economic theory can be interpreted as "procedural rules," "heuristic postulates," "useful fictions," or "resolutions." Consequently, the subsequent treatment of Machlup's position will be restricted to these possible appelations. Despite some difference in meaning between the four terms, the notion of a "rule" seems to approximate all four; and therefore I will focus on the interpretation of the economic postulates as rules.

Machlup strongly suggests that there are some logically unimpeachable grounds, established by philosophers, for viewing the economic postulates as rules. Judging from his account, it has been conclusively shown that certain scientific propositions, particularly theoretical postulates, are not statements about the world, but rules or something similar. Yet his only attempt to corroborate this impression is the consideration, implicit in his reference to Felix Kaufmann, that some propositions that relate to experience (and thus are not "a priori") are retained in science despite contradictions by the facts (and therefore are not "synthetic"). According to Kaufmann, Machlup's principal authority, any proposition which is known to contain a single false implication, and is nevertheless retained, must be understood as a rule of procedure.[55] Kaufmann's position, however, is highly debatable. At most, Kaufmann is able to show that, if false propositions are interpreted as statements instead of rules, there is some difficulty in reconciling the use of these propositions with prediction. In support of the view that false scientific propositions can be rationally understood as statements rather than rules, though, it can be argued (1) that in predicting, one questions whether any of the operating premises are really false; and (2) that predictions can always be based on false statements if sufficient allowance is made for the probability that the predictions are false. In fact, the general trend in philosophy seems opposed to the interpretation of any empirical propositions as rules.[56] On

[55]See Felix Kaufmann, *Methodology of the Social Sciences* (London: Oxford, 1944), pp. 83–89.

[56]See Nagel, "Review" of Stephen Toulmin, *The Philosophy of Science*, in *Mind*, Vol. LXIII (July, 1954), pp. 403–12, reprinted in Nagel, *Logic without Metaphysics* (Glencoe, Ill.: Free Press, 1956), pp. 303–15; Hempel, "Deductive-Nomological vs. Statistical Explanation," in Feigl and Grover Maxwell (eds.), *Minnesota Studies in the Philosophy of Science*, Vol. III, *Scientific Explanation, Space, and Time*, pp. 110–13; and also H. Gavin Alexander, "General Statements as Rules of Inference?" *Minnesota Studies in the Philosophy of Science*, Vol. II, *op. cit.*, pp. 309–29.

the basis of widespread philosophical opinion, every empirical proposition in science can be formulated and understood simply as a factual statement. Thus, as might have been supposed apart from any philosophical considerations, there is no logical necessity to view the economic postulates as rules.

Suppose, however, that the economic postulates are nevertheless construed as rules. Then there arises the central problem connected with Machlup's argument, involving Step IV: How would the "rules" interpretation of the economic postulates affect the possibility and legitimacy of independent tests? Machlup seems to suppose an enormous adverse effect. But in order to explain, he always falls back upon the idea of a contradiction in the very notion of a direct test of a rule. This contradiction, it may be shown, is illusory.

To begin with, a proposition cannot be blindly accepted in science because of its construal as a rule. Science is not an art or game of skill, where the object is to accomplish a certain end within defined constraints. The object of science is to explain and predict events, and the adequacy of any rules employed in science must be judged in the light of their contribution to this objective. Thus, even supposing that the construal of empirical postulates as rules disposes of the question of their "truth," "falsehood," "confirmation," or "disconfirmation," the issue of the "usefulness," "adequacy," "reliability," or "correctness" of the postulates will still remain.[57] This issue must be resolved on the basis of empirical findings.

Machlup, in fact, recognizes that indirect tests affect the usefulness of empirical rules. But if the construal of postulates as rules does not remove the need for testing, the construal, as such, does not justify any opposition to direct testing. Consequently, Machlup's objection to the direct testing of postulates is not implicit in the construal of postulates as rules. So far as I can see, none of the proponents of the construal of theoretical postulates as rules, including Kaufmann,[58] have ever advocated self-imposed limitations

[57]At one point in his "Rejoinder" to Hutchison (*op. cit.*, p. 486), Machlup does not rely on the interpretation of "fundamental assumptions" in some non-declarative form, such as "rules" or "resolutions," etc., in defending the view that "fundamental assumptions" are neither true or false and cannot be disconfirmed. Instead, he implicitly consents to regard the postulates as assertions, but argues (1) that they predicate only "about ideal constructs"; and (2) that "they cannot be 'falsified' by observed facts . . . because auxiliary assumptions can be brought in to establish correspondence with almost any kind of facts." These remarks lack cogency. First, according to general understanding in logic, assertions are either "true" or "false" whether they predicate about ideal constructs or anything else (cf. Kaufmann, *op. cit.*, p. 87). Second, to import new "auxiliary assumptions" in the face of contradictory evidence does not avert the possibility of disconfirmation, but merely revises the original assertion. Upon complete formulation, the "auxiliary assumptions" of every statement are implicit. The only reasonable ground for arguing that "fundamental assumptions" cannot be disconfirmed and are neither true nor false, in my opinion, is that they possess some non-declarative form. This is the sole inferable ground for the argument in Machlup's original article.

[58]Kaufmann bases his designation of certain empirical propositions as rules exclusively on their actual treatment in the relevant disciplines. While raising the question of the best method of determining the reliability of these particular "rules," he offers no answer (see Kaufmann, *op. cit.*, pp. 85–87, 233). It is also noteworthy that much of Kaufmann's emphasis is on different kinds of "rules."

on direct testing. Moreover, Machlup's view cannot be justified. To cite the main criticism, inherent in the discussion of Friedman's thesis, the results of direct tests bear on the usefulness of empirical "rules." The most pertinent previous argument is that the correspondence between "generative" assumptions and facts alters the probability of true predictions, and thus modifies the "reliability," "usefulness," etc., of those assumptions, or in terms of the present convention, "rules."

CONCLUSION

Having argued extensively the significance of tests of economic assumptions, it should be emphasized one last time in closing that there has been no effort in this paper to promote the idea that true assumptions are absolutely essential in scientific work. Indeed, since a single false implication suffices to render an entire statement false, it would be genuinely astounding if any moderately important true scientific hypothesis were in stock. The central argument in these pages has been that every inaccuracy in assumptions is disadvantageous. The essential basis for this conclusion is that every falsehood in assumptions either hinders testing or potentially gives rise to false hypotheses and predictions. This conclusion, which is not new in economics, as noted in the introduction, currently requires stress due to the serious challenge of Friedman and Machlup.

The argument in this paper does not imply, it is important to add, that economic theory suffers grave damage each time a negative result of a test of an economic assumption takes place. The actual disconfirmatory significance of any negative test finding always depends largely on the individual circumstances involved; in particular, the character of the experiment, the quality of the execution, and the nature of the results. Thus, the outcome of former tests of the economic postulates may be barely detrimental. But even if this were so, future tests of these assumptions might prove very upsetting. In general, the potential impact of a disconfirmatory test result corresponds closely to the intensity of current reliance on the statement in question. On this basis, and in order to highlight the significance of the preceding argument, I may venture the opinion with regard to economics that there are certain *conceivable* outcomes of tests of profit maximization which, *if they actually took place*, would prove devastating.

SECTION II. DEMAND THEORY

This section deals with the theory of consumer demand. Many of the major contributions to this literature are reviewed and several of the important methodological and definitional issues are discussed. Coverage is given to both the utility and the indifference curve approaches to consumption theory and demand curves. Also, some of the more recent developments in consumer theory are considered.

In distinguishing between the classic and the current approaches to cardinal utility, Ellsberg provides a basis for gaining a better understanding of some of the measurement problems encountered in the theory of demand. Yeager compares the Hicksian demand curve with the Marshallian demand curve and counters the arguments of some of the proponents of the latter conception of the demand curve. Houthakker reviews the major developments in and contributions to consumption theory between the time of Hicks' *Value and Capital* and the writing of his survey article. Lancaster develops a new approach to consumer theory built around the concept of the technology of consumption. Phlips discusses a theory which explains consumer choice when there are differentiated "products," and he considers the implications of this approach for aggregate demand curves and the demand curves of a firm. Suggesting that demand curves should be thought of as a class of functions with each demand curve being derived from indifference curves in a unique way, Usher illustrates the derivation of the conventional demand curve and then examines six different types of demand curves.

The publication of *The Theory of Games* by von Neumann and Morgenstern rekindled interest in the concept of "measurable utility." Their concept of measurable utility was viewed with skepticism by those economists who espoused the classical conception, as implied in the writings of Marshall and Jevons, for example. Ellsberg maintains that von Neumann and Morgenstern, by concentrating on the general concept of "measurability," obscured the unique features of their approach. According to Ellsberg, the major source of misunderstanding is "ambiguity concerning the differences in derivation and application" between the "new" concept of measurable utility and the classic one. Ellsberg attempts to distinguish clearly between these two concepts, chiefly "by examining the different operations by which they are defined and tested."

Initially, Ellsberg points out the similarities between the old and the new approaches to a "cardinal utility" and draws some conclusions on their points of contrast. He then examines in considerable detail the operational bases of the classic and the current approaches; he concludes with a detailed analysis of the peculiarities of the von Neumann-Morgenstern theory.

Yeager indicates that he is trying to clarify some points raised in the literature relating to Milton Freidman's Marshallian demand curve. Yeager first summarizes the innovations in demand theory proposed by Friedman, indicating that Friedman objects to the "Hicksian" concept of the demand curve and, instead, prefers to use a "Marshallian" demand curve.

Yeager examines the "implied claim" that Friedman's concept has an "advantageous rough-and-ready simplicity." He points out that objections to the Hicksian demand curve are essentially objections to the use of partial-equilibrium analysis as an approach to the complexities of reality and, as such, "lose their force." Yeager discusses the Chicago school's insistence that demand curves represent only "genuinely attainable alternatives" or "conceptually attainable alternatives." Yeager maintains that this insistence, as well as their predilection for comparative-static predictions, suggests a reluctance to consider questions of disequilibrium, of equilibriating processes, and of the stability or instability of equilibrium. Further, this insistence seems to overlook Patinkin's "illuminating distinction" between individual-experiments and market-experiments; rather, it has the effect of attempting to build market-experiment considerations directly into the individual-experiments.

Yeager objects to the claim that the Friedman approach is more "useful" than the Hicksian approach in working with practical problems. He stresses that the real world "never contains an actual entity corresponding to *the* demand curve for a commodity."

In his survey article, Houthakker covers the major contributions which were made to the theory of consumer's choice during the time period bounded by Hicks' *Value and Capital* (1939) and the writing of this survey article. In the first section, Houthakker considers the logical foundations of the theory of consumer's choice. Beginning with the early history of this theory, he covers such important concepts as cardinal utility, ordinal utility, and Samuelson's revealed preference.

The second section is devoted to developments within the classical theory. In this section, some of the contributions considered are those concerned with the theory of rationing, duality, substitution, and complementarity.

Pointing out that several of the assumptions underlying classical consumption theory are "for the most part unrealistic," Houthakker proceeds in section three to a consideration of developments which go beyond, or are outside, the classical framework. He discusses attempts to extend the classical theory to such important subjects as indivisible commodities, uncertainty, and short- and long-term dynamics.

The final section deals with "problems of aggregation, including the possible interactions between consumers' preferences." Here Houthakker is concerned with aggregation at the household level, random variations of preferences, and the effect of social interaction on the transmission of preferences.

Indicating that technology is generally thought of as applying to production and not to consumption, Lancaster is now concerned with developing a concept of the technology of consumption. Central to this concept is the idea that goods, as such, are not the immediate objects of preference or utility or welfare, but that they have associated with them "characteristics" which are important to the consumer; the consumer's aim is to attain his most desired "bundle of characteristics."

Lancaster regards the typical consumption activity as having a single input (a good) and joint outputs (a bundle of characteristics). He points out that the jointness of the characteristics is "really the core of the whole approach." Traditional consumer theory has viewed the relationship between goods and characteristics as merely one-to-one in both directions. In Lancaster's construction, there may be several combinations of goods which give rise to the same bundle of characteristics and this is an important distinction between his approach and the traditional approaches to consumer theory.

In Lancaster's model, the consumer must make two types of decisions. Initially he makes an efficiency choice in rejecting combinations of goods which do not enable him to reach the efficiency frontier, and then he makes a private choice in finding his preferred point on the frontier. The existence of the efficiency considerations constitutes a "radical departure" from the traditional theory.

Lancaster then considers whether it is possible to have change, innovation, and technical progress in consumption technology, just as there is in production technology. He concludes that the technology of consumption is the subject of "continual change and innovation" and that this change does lead to increased welfare.

Phlips reconsiders "certain interpretations and criticisms" of demand curves based on the theory of monopolistic competition. Definitionally, Phlips defines the term "commodity" to represent a group of "products." A "differentiated commodity" represents a group of differentiated products produced by one "industry." Thus, using his example, cigarettes in general are considered to be a differentiated commodity, but individual cigarette brands are each defined as products.

Phlips suggests that only choices between commodities ("an" automobile versus "cigarettes") are explained by utility theory. He argues that the choice of a particular brand is to be explained by "another theory," the elements of which he discusses. If this latter type of choice is not explained by utility theory, then "traditional consumer demand curves refer to commodities (i.e., *groups* of products) and not the particular products which belong to these groups."

Phlips then considers the implications of these ideas for the aggregate demand curve for the market of an industry, for the aggregation of demand curves for products, and for the construction of demand curves of a firm.

Usher maintains that the inconsistency in the treatment of income in the derivation of the conventional demand curve "leads to the notion of demand curves as a class of functions, each derived from indifference curves in a unique way." He points out that an economic problem which calls for the use of a demand curve "will in general contain the information necessary for deciding which species of demand curve is relevant to it."

After illustrating the derivation of the conventional demand curve, Usher follows with a "digression" on the derivation of the supply curve from the production possibility curve. He then examines six different types of demand curves: (1) the production demand curve, which is the curve facing an industry in perfect competition; (2) the average revenue curve of the monopolist; (3) the compensated demand curve; (4) the short-run agricultural demand curve; (5) the demand curve facing a trader; and (6) the conventional money-income demand curve.

Usher concludes by considering several topics which are common to many types of demand curves. These include the slopes of demand curves, income and substitution effects, and community indifference curves.

4. CLASSIC AND CURRENT NOTIONS OF "MEASURABLE UTILITY"*

Daniel Ellsberg†

I

It is ten years since von Neumann and Morgenstern, in their famous aside to the economic profession, announced they had succeeded in synthesizing "measurable utility." That feat split their audience along old party lines. It appeared that a mathematician had performed some elegant sleight-of-hand and produced, instead of a rabbit, a dead horse.

The most common reaction was dismay. To "literary" economists who had freshly amputated their intuitive feelings of cardinal utility at the bidding of some *other* mathematicians, it seemed wanton of von Neumann and Morgenstern so soon to sprinkle salt in their wounds with the statement: "It can be shown that under the conditions on which the indifference curve analysis is based very little extra effort is needed to reach a numerical utility."[1] To others, who had said all along that surgery was unnecessary, the verdict was no surprise but still welcome, coming as it did from an unexpected (non-Cambridge) source. But before long both these groups had joined in expressing doubts that von Neumann and Morgenstern had succeeded in doing what (these readers believed) they had set out to do. The spokesman for the "cardinalists," interpreting their cause as his own, was forced to conclude that they "seem to me to have done as much harm as good to the cause to which they have lent their distinguished aid."[2]

However, it is now clear that the impression that von Neumann and Morgenstern were leading a reactionary movement was erroneous. Their cause, if it can be so dignified, is a new one, not that to which Professor Robertson alluded. The operations that define their concepts are essentially new, and their results are neither intended nor suited to fill the main functions of the older, more familiar brands of "cardinal utility." It is unfortunate that old terms have been retained, for their associations arouse both hopes and antagonisms that have no real roots in the new context.

---

*From the *Economic Journal*, Vol. LXIV, No. 255 (September, 1954), pp. 528–556. Reprinted by permission of the publisher and the author.

†Daniel Ellsberg, Senior Research Associate, Center for International Studies, Massachusetts Institute of Technology.

[1]Von Neumann and Morgenstern, *The Theory of Games* (Princeton: Oxford, 1944), p. 17.

[2]Professor D. H. Robertson, *Utility and all That* (London: Macmillan Co., 1952), p. 28.

In the latest writings the theory has been formulated unambiguously, so that the subject presents little difficulty to one approaching it now for the first time. This article is directed, instead, at readers who came early to the controversy, and who followed the theory in its various stages closely enough to become thoroughly confused.

By concentrating their discussion on the general concept of "measurability," von Neumann and Morgenstern unfortunately obscured the unique features of their particular construction. Later expositions have tended to follow them in this,[3] or to stress the empirical content of the von Neumann-Morgenstern results.[4] Very little attention has been given to the major source of misunderstandings: ambiguity concerning the differences in derivation and application between the new notion of "measurable utility" and the concept of the same name implied in the writings, say, of Marshall and Jevons. This article will attempt to distinguish clearly between the two concepts, chiefly by examining the different operations by which they are defined and tested.[5]

This procedure may provide some valuable exercise in the use of the operational approach, which in economic literature has been honored chiefly in footnotes. This approach regards the basic definition of a technical concept in scientific usage as: "What is measured by" a particular set of operations. Two different sets of operations are presumed to measure two different "things," although under certain conditions (discussed later) it is justifiable to treat the two concepts as identical. A scientific proposition is operationally meaningful if definite conceivable results of given operations are defined which would *refute* the statement; if it does not *restrict* the class of results which are to be expected, it cannot be useful for scientific purposes. The meaningfulness of concepts and propositions is a necessary, though not a sufficient, condition for their scientific usefulness.[6] This point of view will prove useful in the concluding section in clarifying the *difference* in meaning of two concepts bearing the same name.

---

[3]This is the only shortcoming of the otherwise excellent article by Alchian, "The Meaning of Utility Measurement," *American Economic Review* (March, 1953), p. 26. The present paper may serve as a complement to Alchian's.

[4]Friedman and Savage, "The Utility Analysis of Choices Involving Risk," *Journal of Political Economy* (August, 1948), p. 279. Mosteller and Nogee, "An Experimental Measurement of Utility," *Journal of Political Economy* (October, 1951), p. 371. I have also benefited from reading as yet unpublished papers by Professors Bishop, Marschak and Allais.

[5]This paper was originally written as the first chapter in a thesis, entitled "Theories of Rational Choice Under Uncertainty: The Contributions of von Neumann and Morgenstern," submitted for undergraduate honors at Harvard University, April, 1952. The thesis was written under the valuable guidance of Professor John Chipman. I am also greatly indebted to Professors Paul Samuelson, Robert Bishop, Oskar Morgenstern and Frederick Mosteller for the opportunity to discuss problems and to read unpublished writings on the subject, and to Mr. Nicholas Kaldor for his comments.

[6]These concepts and the general point of view were first formulated explicitly by Percy W. Bridgman, in *The Logic of Modern Physics* (New York: Macmillian Co., 1927), who declared them to be implicit in the thinking of modern physicists. The

The next section will describe the similarities between the old and new approaches to a "cardinal utility" and will present, in advance, some of the conclusions to be drawn as to their points of contrast. The next two parts examine the operational bases of the two theories, and the final section will analyse the peculiarities of the von Neumann-Morgenstern construction.

II

Suppose that a man who prefers *A* to *B*, *B* to *C*, and *A* to *C* must choose between having *B* for certain or having a "lottery ticket" offering *A* with probability *p* or *C* with probability $1 - p$.[7] Without asking him outright, is it possible to predict his choice? If so, what sort of data are necessary?

Economists of the school of Jevons, Menger, Walras and Marshall, on the one hand, and on the other those following von Neumann and Morgenstern would answer "Yes" to the first question. But their predictions would be based on quite different types of data.

For von Neumann and Morgenstern, it would be necessary to observe the man's behavior in other risk situations, involving different outcomes or the same outcomes with different probabilities. The older economists, of whom we will take Marshall as typical, would ask no knowledge of his other risk behavior. They assumed it possible, by observation or interrogation, to discover a man's intensities of liking for sure outcomes; on the basis of this knowledge alone, they were ready either to predict or to prescribe his choice between prospects.

This divergence is concealed by the fact that both schools would summarize the results of their investigations in the same symbolic shorthand, arriving at expressions that are formally identical. Under both procedures the results of experiment would be expressed by assigning a triplet of numbers, U_a, U_b, and U_c, to the three outcomes, with the property: $U_a > U_b > U_c$. This triplet is a utility index for the three outcomes, since their order of magnitude reflects the order of preference. Next, both Marshall and von Neumann-Morgenstern would form the expression:

$$(1) \qquad 1 \cdot U_b \gtreqless p \cdot U_a + (1-p)U_c$$

where p and $1 - p$ are the respective probabilities of *A* and *C*. Each side of this relationship is a sum of the utility numbers corresponding to the outcomes of a given prospect multiplied by their respective probability numbers. Since the probabilities sum to unity, the result is a weighted arithmetic mean of the

terms, and the emphasis on restrictiveness and refutability of propositions, have become familiar to economists largely through Samuelson's *Foundations of Economic Analysis* (Cambridge: Harvard University Press, 1948), but the other main propositions are less well known.

[7] A "lottery ticket" of this sort, offering a set of alternative outcomes with stated probabilities summing to unity, will hereafter be known as a *prospect*. If one outcome is offered with unit probability, *i.e.*, with no uncertainty, it will be known as a *sure outcome.*

utilities, variously known as the mathematical expectation of utility, the expected utility, the moral expectation, moral expectancy, actuarial value of utility and the first moment of the utility-probability distribution.[8]

In each case the prediction (or advice) would have the man choose the prospect with the highest mathematical expectation of utility. Or if the two sides of the relationship (1) were equal, he should be indifferent between the two prospects. A man whose behavior conformed to this rule could be said to be "maximising [*sic*] the mathematical expectation of utility."

With this much similarity between the two approaches, it is natural that they should commonly be confused. Yet the most misleading point of similarity remains: the fact that in both cases "utility" is said to be "measurable." The necessity of this assumption is seen more clearly if the left-hand side of expression (1) is rewritten $p \cdot U_b + (1-p)U_b$ and terms collected to form the relationship:

$$p(U_a - U_b) - (1-p)(U_b - U_c) \gtreqless 0 \tag{2}$$

This is merely relationship (1) in a different form. The rule would now have the man accept the prospective offering *A* or *C* if the left-hand side of (2) were positive, reject it if the left-hand side were negative, or be indifferent between it and the sure outcome *B* if the left-hand side were equal to zero. The important point here is that relationship (2) shows clearly that the rules rely on comparing *differences* in utility.

If only preferences were known, the triplet of utility numbers could be replaced by another with the same ordinal relationships. In general, such a monotonic transformation would not preserve equality, or given inequalities, among differences between utility numbers. The rule of maximizing expected utility would lead to prediction or advice which would depend on the particular index used, and if preferences were the only guide, the choice of index would be arbitrary. The rule would be meaningless, therefore useless.

In order for the rule to give definite results, it would be necessary to find some "natural"[9] operation that would give meaning to differences in utility numbers, hence to the numerical operations implied by the rule. The new index, summarizing the results of the additional operation as well as preferences, would belong to a more restricted set of indices than the set of all ordinal utility indices. Any two indices in which corresponding differences as well as absolute utilities satisfied the same inequalities would be related by a

[8]Of these, "mathematical expectation of utility" and its shorter form, "moral expectation," will be used below. Both must be carefully distinguished from the "mathematical expectation of *money*," which is a weighted sum of the money outcomes, rather than of their utility numbers.

[9]Von Neumann and Morgenstern use this term to signify an operation other than numerical or logical manipulation of a mathematical model. A mathematical model is useful if the results of a "natural" operation can be correlated with numbers in such a way that numerical operations can symbolize and substitute for the "natural" operation.

linear, and not merely any monotonic, transformation.[10] It is, then, necessary to find some aspect of behavior that can be described only by a set of numbers determined up to a linear transformation: a set, moreover, which is one of those expressing preferences. So much is necessary in order for the rule of maximizing expected utility to be meaningful. Its usefulness, if any, must depend on the particular aspect of behavior which serves this purpose, if one can be found.

To say that both the Marshallian and the von Neumann-Morgenstern theories require a "measurable utility" is precisely to say that they require a utility index determined up to a linear transformation. At this point the similarity ends. In general, the order of magnitude of the differences between corresponding numbers would be different for the two indices; therefore, predictions based on the rule of maximizing moral expectation would differ for the two approaches. Moreover, it might be possible to find a measurable index by one method and not the other. Even if both should "exist," they would be in general monotonic, and not linear, transformations of each other.

III

Such theorists as Jevons, Menger, Walras, and Marshall conceived of the crucial natural operation in the measurement of utility as taking place within the mind of a subject; it was a process of weighing introspectively the amounts of "satisfaction" associated with different outcomes.

Such an operation appeared more of an objective basis for theory to them than it would to modern economists. In their view, in the realm of reasonable men one man's introspection was as good as another's, and the theorist's own internal calculations were likely to correspond roughly to those of his subject; to this extent the results of the subject's operation were "observable." However, if challenged to produce less-subjective evidence, it would undoubtedly have occurred to Jevons that the most natural way to obtain the results of the man's introspective measurements would be to ask for them.

The first rough outline of the subject's pattern of "satisfaction" would emerge from an "indifference-map" experiment, in which he is asked to rank the events, A, B, and C in order of preference. If he can compare the events and if his preferences are transitive ("consistent"), *e.g.*, if he prefers A to B, B to C, and A to C, the results of this experiment are summarized by any triplet of numbers satisfying: $U_a > U_b > U_c$. This triplet is a "non-measurable" utility index, determined up to a monotonic transformation.

[10]For an excellent exposition of the concepts of linear and monotonic transformations, the reader is referred to the article by Alchian, *op. cit.* Briefly, two indices are related by a linear transformation if for every point x on one index, the corresponding point y on the other index satisfies a relationship of the form: $y = ax + b$, where a and b are constants. The two indices differ only with respect to scale and origin.

If the difference between two numbers in one index is greater than, less than, or equal to the difference between two other numbers, the corresponding differences in the other index will have the same ordinal relationship.

In what we will call a "Jevonsian"[11] experiment the man would next be asked to rank his preferences of A to B and his preference of B to C. If he finds that he can state, for example, that his preference of A to B exceeds his preference of B to C, we could summarize this information by any triplet of numbers satisfying the two inequalities: (a) $U_a > U_b > U_c$, and (b) $U_a - U_b > U_b - U_c$.

Finally, if A and B were sums of money, we could ask the man to vary the sum of money represented by B until he could tell us that he found his preference of A to B' equal to his preference of B' to C. If he finds such a B', then the results of this last operation would be expressed by any triplet of numbers satisfying the relationships: (a) $U_a > U_b > U_c$, and (b) $U_a - U_b = U_b - U_c$. Any two triplets obeying these relationships must be related by a linear transformation; they represent utility indices differing only by scale and origin.

The Jevonsian index for the individual, if one can be found, is thus "measurable"; which in this case means nothing more or less than that the subject was able to give consistent answers to these particular questions. It might be objected that, in fact, subjects will be unable to answer the questions, or will answer them inconsistently. This is an empirical matter. If the events were the possession of (a) one million dollars, (b) two dollars, and (c) one dollar, it seems likely that most people would answer the question (and moreover, would state specifically that their preference of A to B exceeded their preference of B to C)[12] For such people, the notion of a cardinal utility index would not be "meaningless"; if it had no other meaning, it might at least imply that their answers to this sort of question could be predicted. Inconsistency is to be expected, particularly with respect to utility differences that are almost equal. But inconsistency also appears (in lesser degree) in the "indifference-map" experiment; in each case the most important information gained concerns choices which the subject finds easy to make.[13]

The more damaging attack has been on the usefulness of the method, though here again the case is not conclusive. If the only "consistency" discovered were consistency of answers with other answers, the results would be trivial. But Marshall and his predecessors regarded such answers as revealing the subject's internal measurements of satisfaction.[14] Since they believed the man based his decisions to act on the results of this introspective operation, they hoped to use the results of a Jevonsian experiment to predict his decisions.

---

[11]This name is suggested by J. C. Weldon, who points out that it implies no more than that Jevons assumed that preferences could be directly compared. "A Note on Measures of Utility," *Canadian Journal of Economics and Political Science* (May, 1950), p. 230.

[12]At least, they would probably do so if asked point-blank and not given time for doubts as to whether the question "meant" anything (induced, perhaps, by the writings of Samuelson). This could be made part of the conditions of the experiment.

[13]The above discussion follows Weldon, *op. cit.*

[14]Such information might itself be of interest in welfare economics; it might, though it need not, influence the evaluations on which a social-welfare function must be based.

As the ordinalists have demonstrated, decisions in the marketplace under conditions of certainty can be predicted on the basis of the "indifference-map" experiment alone. But this is not true of behavior under uncertainty or risk. With a Jevonsian utility index it is possible to frame meaningful hypotheses placing definite restrictions on observable behavior in risk situations.

The particular rule which Marshall and Jevons proposed (rather more for normative purposes than descriptive) was that the "rational" man would maximize the mathematical expectation of utility. In terms of the expression (1) cited earlier:

$$(1) \qquad U_b \gtreqless p \cdot U_a + (1-p)U_c$$

the rational man should (would) choose the prospect if the right-hand side were greater, the sure outcome *B* if the left-hand side were greater. If U_b, the utility that can be had for certain if the prospect is rejected, is regarded as the opportunity cost of the prospect, then the expression (2):

$$(2) \qquad p(U_a - U_b) - (1-p)(U_b - U_c) \gtreqless 0$$

represents the mathematical expectation of *gain* (measured in utility) associated with the prospect. The first term is the amount of utility that the man stands to win by accepting the gamble (in excess of the utility cost of the gamble) multiplied by the probability of winning, and the second term is the amount of utility he stands to lose multiplied by the probability of losing. The man should take any gambles whose expectation of gain is positive, reject all whose expectation of gain is negative, be indifferent to those whose expectation of gain is zero.

One point about this procedure must be emphasized, for it is in sharp contrast to that of von Neumann and Morgenstern. The utility index, and its measurability, on which the Marshallian predictions were based was not derived from any risk behavior, and did not depend on any sort of consistency in that behavior. The rule of maximizing expected utility on the basis of a Jevonsian index led to prediction, or prescription, of a man's choices among prospects without any previous observation of his behavior in the face of risk.

Actually in the main field of consumer behavior characterized by risk—gambling—Marshall was not sanguine about the usefulness of the rule as a descriptive hypothesis. He took it as a universal empirical law that answers in the Jevonsian experiment would reveal diminishing marginal utility. In other words, if *A*, *B*, and *C* are three sums of money such that $A > B > C$, and if $A - B = B - C$, then he assumed that corresponding utility numbers would satisfy the inequality: $U_a - U_b < U_b - U_c$. A "fair" gamble is defined as one in which the mathematical expectation of *money* gain is zero, expressed by:

$$(3) \qquad p(A - B) - (1-p)(B - C) = 0$$

where p is the probability of winning A, $1\text{-}p$ the probability of winning C, and B is the cost of the gamble (in the above case, p must equal ½). But, granted decreasing marginal utility, the corresponding expectation of *utility* gain is negative, so the rational man would never accept a fair gamble, or, *a fortiori*, an unfair gamble.

As Marshall was well aware, people did accept fair and even unfair gambles; but this behavior disputed their rationality, not (the curvature of) their utility index. The latter was established once and for all by tests that did not involve risk. Because of the existence of "pleasures of gambling"[15] (which Marshall measured by the acceptance of unfair bets), Marshall would have rejected the observation of risk behavior as an alternative operation for measuring people's intensities of liking for outcomes.

The particular Marshallian rule governing risk behavior is not implied by his concept of utility or by the methods of measuring it. An early form of the rule is stated by Jevons:[16]

> If the probability is only one in ten that I shall have a certain day of pleasure, I ought to anticipate the pleasure with one-tenth of the force which would belong to it if certain. In selecting a course of action which depends on uncertain events, as, in fact, does everything in life, I should multiply the quantity of feeling attaching to every future event by the fraction denoting its probability.

The reliance of this approach on measurability (of "quantity of feeling") is obvious; but it is equally obvious that the measurability of "pleasure," and even the general principle that likings for prospects should be based on likings for outcomes and their probabilities, does not imply this particular rule of decision-making. On the basis of a given Jevonsian index, Marshall or Jevons could just have easily proposed that the rational man base his preference on the mode, the median, the range, variance or other properties of the distribution of utilities. These rules would have been just as meaningful, and possibly more useful (especially if they took into account measures of "risk" as well as "central tendency"). In fact, it was the feeling that the emphasis on mathematical expectation was arbitrary and unrealistic which led to the decline of the concept even before doubts arose that a measurable utility could be discovered to make it meaningful.

---

[15]Unfair gambling could be "rationalized" if introspective tests revealed that the happiness derived from gambling outweighed the "expected loss of satisfaction" implied by the odds. However, Marshall wished to retain the normative connotation of "rationality" at the expense of predictive value. In his view, the pleasures of gambling "are likely to engender a restless, feverish character, unsuited for steady work. . . ." (*Principles of Economics*,[London: 1925], Mathematical Appendix, Note IX, p. 843.) Granted that marginal utility was decreasing, and that pleasures of gambling could be ignored because "impure," then unfair gambling was unequivocally irrational, an "economic blunder."

[16]W. Stanley Jevons, *The Theory of Political Economy* (London: Macmillan Co., 1911), p. 36.

IV

What von Neumann and Morgenstern asserted, in their famous digression,[17] was the possibility that the notion of maximizing the mathematical expectation of utility might (*a*) be made meaningful, and (*b*) describe a wider range of risk behavior than in its old usage, *if "utility" were measured (defined) in a special way.* Since they were concerned only with risk behavior, the operation they proposed was the observation of choices in risk situations. If a person's preferences among *prospects* — described merely in ordinal terms — should satisfy certain, apparently weak, axiomatic restrictions, then von Neumann has proved that it would be possible to find a set of numbers which could express these preferences in a particularly convenient way.

This set of numbers would be *a* utility index, because it would be one among all the sets of numbers (related by monotonic transformations) expressing the person's preferences (*not* "intensities of preference" or "quantities of feeling") among sure outcomes. The novelty would be that this same set of numbers, applying explicitly only to sure outcomes, could also summarize the person's preferences among prospects. In a complete description of the individual's entire preference-structure, it would be unnecessary to list prospects separately or to record explicitly his preferences among prospects; these preferences would be known, through observation, but they could be expressed implicitly by the numbers attached to sure outcomes.

Clearly the class of indices which could express with such economy preferences both among sure outcomes and among prospects must be smaller than the class of all ordinal utility indices (in most of which it would be necessary to list prospects individually). In fact, it turns out that all indices with this property, if any exist, will be related by linear transformations. Yet the index is not "measurable" in the sense that it is correlated with any significant economic quantity, such as quantity of feeling or satisfaction, or intensity, such as intensity of liking or preference. It is derived from *choices,* and describes only *preferences.* It would be "cardinal" ("measurable") only to the extent that the numerical operation of forming mathematical expectations on the basis of these numbers would be related to observable behavior, so as to be empirically meaningful.

Von Neumann and Morgenstern might simply have proposed the empirical hypothesis that an index of the desired sort could be found for certain individuals. However, this proposition, which we will call the Hypothesis on Moral Expectations, has little inherent plausibility. The major feat of von Neumann and Morgenstern is to show that the Hypothesis on Moral Expectations is *logically equivalent* to the hypothesis that the behavior of given

[17]The theory which follows occupies only a few pages in the introduction to their book, and plays no role in the theory of games. The latter theory requires a commodity which is not only measurable but intercomparable and freely transferable, so pay-offs are expressed in money, not in von Neumann-Morgenstern "utility."

individuals satisfies certain axiomatic restrictions. Since these axioms appear, at first glance, highly "reasonable," the second hypothesis seems far more intuitively appealing than the equivalent Hypothesis on Moral Expectations. It is thus more likely to be accepted on the basis of casual observation and introspection, although the two hypotheses would both be contradicted by exactly the same observations.

Most expositions follow von Neumann and Morgenstern in focusing all attention on the second hypothesis, *i.e.*, on the empirical relevance of the axioms. Once this is accepted, the Hypothesis on Moral Expectations "goes along free" in the form of the Theorem on Moral Expectations, which states conditionally that *if* an individual's behavior conforms to the axioms, a von Neumann-Morgenstern index can be computed for him (this proposition rests on logic rather than observation, and it has been established by several different proofs). Empirical test of the proposition is thus displaced to the axioms which imply it. The logical relationship of the axioms to the Hypothesis is usually left obscure, for the demonstration is too difficult for most readers.[18] Therefore, the reader must generally take it on faith that behavior violating a particular axiom conflicts with the possibility of finding a von Neumann-Morgenstern index. Instead, we will follow the straighter, though less persuasive, route of describing how the Hypothesis on Moral Expectations would be tested directly.

We can state the Hypothesis in the following form. For a given individual (it is asserted that) a set of numbers *exists* (*i.e.*, can be found) with the two properties: (1) it is one of the sets expressing the individual's actual preferences among sure outcomes (*i.e.*, it is one of his ordinal utility indices); (2) numbers are assigned to sure outcomes in such a way that, if "moral expectations" of *prospects* were computed on the basis of these numbers, one prospect would have a higher moral expectation than another if, and only if, the person actually preferred the former to the latter, and two prospects would have the same moral expectation if, and only if, the person were indifferent between them.

If from the set of all utility indices (related by monotonic transformations), one index can be found such that "moral expectations" computed on the basis of this particular set of "utilities" arrange prospects according to an individual's actual preferences among them, then any other index related to the first by a linear (not merely by any monotonic) transformation will also have this property. Thus, if one such index exists, an infinite set will exist: though

[18] Von Neumann and Morgenstern did not present a proof deriving the Theorem from the axioms until the second edition of *The Theory of Games* (Princeton: Oxford, 1947); they describe it, with terrific understatement, as "rather lengthy and may be somewhat tiring for the mathematically untrained reader" (p. 617). A different, slightly easier proof, is given by Marschak in "Rational Behaviour, Uncertain Prospects, and Measurable Utility." *Econometrica* (April, 1950). A genuinely simple proof has finally been presented by Samuelson, in "Utility, Preference, and Probability," abstract of paper given before the conference on *Les Fondements et Applications de la Theorie du Risque en Econometrie,* 1952.

still a tiny subset of all indices expressing ordinal preferences among outcomes. The Theorem on Moral Expectations states that such a set does exist, if and when the axioms apply. The Hypothesis states that the index actually does exist for given persons.

Having found such an index, we could submit it to a monotonic increasing transformation—*e.g.*, we could take the square or the log of each number—and the resulting set of numbers would be a perfectly valid utility index of outcomes. But it would not serve any more as a utility index of prospects as well; it would no longer be true that moral expectancies would correspond to the individual's actual preferences among prospects.

Our approach will consist of trying to find an index (hypothetically) with the two properties specified, noting in the process the type of behavior which would make this impossible. The "operational content" of the theory should be most obvious from this point of view, since it is intimately related to the body of behavior "ruled out" by the Hypothesis. The greater the amount and importance of this behavior, the more powerful does the Hypothesis appear, though the less immediately plausible.

The basic operation in deriving a von Neumann-Morgenstern utility index is the observation of an individual's behavior in the very simplest situation involving risk: a choice between a sure outcome and a prospect involving two possible outcomes with given probabilities. The essential restriction the Hypothesis puts on behavior is that, by observing a person's choice in situations of this simple type, it must be possible to predict his choices among sets of prospects each offering a multitude of prizes with complex odds (some of the prizes possibly being other prospects). In the discussion below, the notation, $(A, p; B)$, signifies a prospect offering outcome A with probability p or B with probability $1 - p$.

To fix the origin and unit of the utility index we seek, we assign arbitrary numbers to two outcomes (order of magnitude in order of preference); this guarantees that the index, if we can find one, will be unique. For example, let us assign to the money-sums \$1,000 and \$0 the utility numbers 10 and 0: *i.e.*, $U_{1000} = 10$, $U_0 = 0$. Now we consider a third sum, say, \$500, which the individual ranks between the first two; the problem is to find a utility number U_{500} that satisfies the Hypothesis on Moral Expectations, consistent with his preferences and with the two numbers already assigned arbitrarily. The crucial datum in the procedure is the probability $\dot{p}$ at which the person is indifferent between having \$500 with certainty or a prospect (\$1,000, $\dot{p}$; \$0).[19] Suppose that this $\dot{p}$ is $\frac{8}{10}$; *i.e.*, he tells us, or we observe, that he is indifferent between \$500 and (\$1,000, $\frac{8}{10}$; \$0). The Hypothesis on Moral Expectations then implies that it is possible to find a number U_{500} with the two properties:

[19]The axioms require that he be indifferent at one and only one p. Tests have already shown that this perfect consistency is never encountered, but "indifference" might be defined stochastically (*e.g.*, if an individual rejected a prospect with given odds as often as he accepted it, he might be said to be "indifferent" to it).

(4) $0 < U_{500} < 10$ (since he prefers \$1,000 to \$500 and \$500 to \$0), and

(5) $$1 \cdot U_{500} = \tfrac{8}{10} \cdot 10 + \tfrac{2}{10} \cdot 0$$

Obviously such a number *can* be found: $U_{500} = 8$. So the Hypothesis has passed the first test.

Even in this first application, the Hypothesis was not tautologous. It was conceivable that the individual would prefer the certainty of \$500 to any prospect (\$1,000, p; \$0) for *any p* whatever: perhaps from extreme conservative principles or moral scruples against gambling. The Hypothesis would then imply that it was possible to find a number U_{500} satisfying both the following two relationships:

(6) $$0 < U_{500} < 10$$

and

(7) $$U_{500} > p \cdot 10 + (1 - p) \cdot 0, \text{ for } all\ p,\ 0 < p < 1.$$

But no such number exists; for any given U_{500} satisfying (6), there would exist a p, such that (7) would not hold. Therefore, the Hypothesis would be contradicted.

Similarly, the Hypothesis would be contradicted if the individual should prefer any prospect (\$1,000, p; \$0) to the certainty of \$500; say, from an obsession with gambling.

It might seem that such behavior might well occur, thus rejecting the Hypothesis on the basis of one observation. But proponents of the Hypothesis could point out that it is unusual to have such "absolute" likes or dislikes: to feel so strongly either for or against gambling as to ignore entirely the relative stakes and odds.[20] They might suggest that such behavior, though it may exist, is statistically unimportant, so that it is reasonable to hypothesize that there will be *some* $\dot{p}$ at which the subject will be indifferent. A man with a marked taste for security might pick $\dot{p} = 9{,}999/10{,}000$; a born gambler might indicate $\dot{p} = 1/1{,}000$. In either case it would be possible to find a number U_{500} consistent with these preferences.

Thus, the Hypothesis puts very weak limitations in this initial application to the man's preferences among risky alternatives. The drastic test is to investigate whether or not his *other* choices will be "consistent" with this first choice. Let us return to our original result, $U_{500} = 8$. On the basis of our single observation (fixing $\dot{p}$ at $\frac{8}{10}$) we must be able to predict the individual's choice among any set of prospects involving the three outcomes, \$1,000, \$500 or \$0, with any probabilities. Given any set of prospects, we compute the moral expectations

[20]As John Chipman has put it, this is the "every man has his price" axiom.

of each prospect on the basis of the utility number (two of which, in this case, were fixed arbitrarily and the third derived from a single observed choice), and pick the prospect with the highest moral expectancy. No rationale for this procedure has been given here. It is not suggested that the individual makes his choice by a similar calculation. We are merely examining the implications of the hypothesis that it is possible to describe his behavior "as though" he did.

Thus, we compute the moral expectation of the prospect ($1,000, $\frac{1}{2}$; $0) as: $\frac{1}{2} . 10 + \frac{1}{2} . 0 = 5$. If, when confronted with the choice between this prospect and the certainty of $500 ($U_{500} = 8$), our subject does not definitely prefer the latter, then it is not true that moral expectations computed on the basis of our utility numbers arrange prospects according to the individual's actual preference; our triplet does not have properties of a von Neumann-Morgenstern index. More than that, if this triplet is not one of those whose existence is implied by the Moral Expectations Hypothesis, *then no such triplet can be found,* and the hypothesis is thereby invalidated. For, once two numbers had been arbitrarily chosen, the third one was uniquely determined by our initial observation;[21] any other value for U_{500} would be inconsistent (in terms of our hypothesis) with that particular choice.

If on the contrary, no serious[22] inconsistency appears, we can proceed to find utility numbers for other sums of money. If we observed that the subject was indifferent between $200 and ($500, $\frac{1}{4}$; $0), we would define $U_{200} = 2$. Our set of utility numbers corresponding to $0, $200, $500 and $1,000 is now 0, 2, 8, 10. If these are the unique set implied by the Hypothesis, then the individual should be indifferent between a 50-50 chance of $0 or $1,000, and a 50-50 chance of $200 or $500, since: $\frac{1}{2} . 0 + \frac{1}{2} . 10 = \frac{1}{2} . 2 + \frac{1}{2} . 8$. If, in fact, he prefers one to another, then the existence theorem is contradicted; the axioms on which it may be based do not apply to this individual.

More complicated tests can be devised. One of the "prizes" in a prospect might be another prospect, say, a "lottery ticket" offering a $\frac{4}{5}$ chance of $1,000 and a $\frac{1}{5}$ chance of $0; if the other prize is $200, the two prizes being offered at equal odds, this would appear in our notation: ($200, $\frac{1}{2}$; ($1,000, $\frac{4}{5}$; $0)). This "complex" prospect might be compared to the "simple" prospect: ($500, $\frac{5}{8}$; $0). The person "should" be indifferent between them, since:

$$\frac{1}{2} . 2 + \frac{1}{2}(\frac{4}{5} . 10 + \frac{1}{5} . 0) = \frac{5}{8} . 8 + \frac{3}{8} . 0$$

A new test would be to confront the subject with a choice between the above complex prospect and the simple prospect with three prizes: ($1,000, $\frac{2}{5}$; $200, $\frac{1}{2}$; $0, $\frac{1}{10}$). Suppose that U_{200} is yet to be computed, and that the individual is found to prefer the complex "lottery ticket" to the above simple one. Then the Hypothesis would imply that a number U_{200} can be found satisfying both:

[21]Since indices satisfying the Hypothesis are determined "up to two arbitrary constants," the specification of two values determines the index uniquely.

[22]In a real experiment we would have to decide in statistical terms what to regard as a "reasonable" approximation to consistency with the Theorem.

$$(8) \qquad 0 < U_{200} < 10, \text{ and}$$
$$(9) \qquad \tfrac{2}{5}.10 + \tfrac{1}{10}.0 + \tfrac{1}{2}.U_{200} < \tfrac{1}{2}(\tfrac{4}{5}.10 + \tfrac{1}{5}.0) + \tfrac{1}{2}.U_{200}$$

Since (9) implies $U_{200} < U_{200}$, it is clearly impossible to find a number with the desired properties.

Von Neumann and Morgenstern's controversial Axiom 3 : $C:b$[23] rules out this type of behavior by assuming that a person will be indifferent between two prospects which are derivable from each other according to the rules of probabilities. By application of these rules, any complex prospect offering other prospects as prizes may be reduced to a simple prospect, and the axioms require the individual to be indifferent between this derived prospect and the original one. This implies that the individual is indifferent to the number of steps taken to determine the outcome. On the contrary, a sensible person might easily prefer a lottery which held several intermediate drawings to determine who was still "in" for the final drawing; in other words, he might be willing to pay for the possibility of winning intermediate drawings and "staying in," even though the chances of winning the pot were not improved thereby. A longer time-period of suspense would usually also be involved, but it need not be. The crucial factor is "pleasure of winning," which may be aroused by intermediate wins even if one subsequently fails to receive the prize. Many, perhaps most, slot-machine players know the odds are very unfavorable, and are not really motivated by hopes of winning the jackpot. They feel that they have had their money's worth if it takes them a long while to lose a modest sum, meanwhile enjoying a number of intermediate wins — which go back into the machine to pay for the pleasure of the next win. Von Neumann and Morgenstern single out axiom 3 : $C : b$, which excludes this type of behavior, as the "really critical" axiom[24] — "that one which gets closest to excluding a 'utility of gambling.' "[25]

The final major test of the Hypothesis would be to give the subject a choice between two such prospects as (\$500, p; \$1,000) and (\$200, p; \$1,000), where p is the same in each and where \$500 is preferred to \$200. For any p he must prefer the first to the second. If, for example, he was indifferent between them at some $p = P$, the Hypothesis would imply that there was a U_{500} such that:

$$(10) \qquad 2 < U_{500} < 10, \text{ and}$$
$$(11) \qquad P.U_{500} + (1 - P)10 = P.2 + (1 - P)10.$$

Together these imply that $U_{500} > 2$ and $U_{500} = 2$, which can be true of no number (we are assuming in this example that U_{500} has not already been determined by some other experiment).

---

[23]Von Neumann and Morgenstern, *op. cit.*, p. 26.

[24]*Ibid.*, p. 632.

[25]*Ibid.*, p. 28.

It is the "Strong Independence Axiom" ruling out this sort of preference which Samuelson has emphasized, presenting it as the "crucial" axiom.[26] It seems rather hard to justify this emphasis, since the axiom seems indubitably the most plausible of the lot. After all, all of the axioms are necessary to the final result, and this particular one is almost impregnable (even people who did not follow it in practice would probably admit, on reflection, that they should) whereas others (such as 3 : *C* : *b*) are contradicted by much everyday experience. One might almost suspect Samuelson, who counts himself a "fellow traveller"[27] of the von Neumann-Morgenstern theory, of using the axiom (his invention) as a mantrap, luring critics past the really vulnerable points to waste their strength on the "Independence Assumption."[28]

In all this it has been emphasized that the Hypothesis on Moral Expectations sets a double condition for an acceptable index, the first part being that it must be one of the individual's ordinal utility index. Some critics seem to have overlooked this; for example, I. M. D. Little:[29]

> Suppose that . . . we had given *C, A, B,* the utility numbers $10\frac{4}{5}$,10, 9, because the consumer was 'indifferent' between (*A* certain) and (*C* with probability $\frac{5}{9}$ or *B* with probability $\frac{4}{9}$). It follows that . . . if the consumer is given the choice between *B* and *A, A* must be taken. In fact *B* might well be taken.

If, as the last sentence suggests, the consumer preferred *B* to *A* (and *C* to both), we would start the experiment with this information. If we should then observe that he was indifferent between *A* and (*C*, $\frac{5}{9}$; *B*), then we would not be able to assign any utility number at all to *A*, for it would be impossible to find one satisfying the two conditions: $U_a < U_b < U_b$ and $U_c = \frac{4}{9} . B + \frac{5}{9} . C.$ This behavior contradicts the Hypothesis, but the conflict would show up in the impossibility of finding a von Neumann-Morgenstern index, not in the index, once having been "certified," turning out to be inconsistent with ordinal preferences. This is a small point, but criticism which may be quite pertinent loses force if framed in a way that suggests the critic has not understood the conditions of the experiment.

Another type of criticism that goes wide of the mark uses examples involving only "utils," with no mention of the sums they represent or the particular observations on which they were based. Baumol, for example, cites two

---

[26]Samuelson, "Utility, Preference, and Probability," *op. cit.* Also, "Probability, Utility, and the Independence Axiom," *Econometrica* (October, 1952), p. 672.

[27]Samuelson, "Probability, Utility, and the Independence Axiom," *op. cit.,* p. 677.

[28]Dr. Alan S. Manne's article, "The Strong Independence Assumption—Gasoline Blends and Probability Mixtures," *Econometrica* (October, 1952), p. 665, gives an interesting example of a physical situation in which superposition does not apply, which may be more relevant to linear programming than to the present subject. Although it raises a doubt, I do not think his criticism is really damaging in this context. The argument in the same issue by H. Wold, "Ordinal Preferences or Cardinal Utility?" is definitely invalid.

[29]I. M. D. Little, *A Critique of Welfare Economics* (Oxford: Toronto, 1950), p. 30.

lottery tickets with prizes expressed in utils (*i.e.,* utility units, rather than money).[30] He computes their moral expectations, but asks, "Yet who is to say" that it is "pathological" for the subject to prefer the one with the lower expectation. To this a defender can retort: (*a*) Baumol gives no indication that the utility numbers were correctly derived; (*b*) it would not, of course, be "pathological" in any case; but (*c*) if it happened that the utility numbers were actually derived, for example, from the person's previous choice between the very two prospects cited, then it would be "inconsistency" of a sort usually defined as nonrational for him to switch his choice on this occasion. The crux of the matter is that it is impossible to decide on intuitive grounds whether it is "plausible" to choose the prospect with the higher moral expectation if only utils are cited and if the person's past choices are not known, since an appraisal of "plausibility" must be based on the money sums involved and on the person's pattern of behavior in risk situations.

We have described above the main types of behavior that conflict with the Hypothesis on Moral Expectations. It is possible to give long lists of factors in risk situations which would lead to these types of behavior.[31] Among those which have not been mentioned earlier are: feelings of skill, or, in general, the feeling that the "real" odds are more favorable than the stated odds (*e.g.,* belief in personal luck, or in "winning streaks"); inability to compute compound probabilities, and thus to derive simple prospects from complex ones; influence of the other elements in the risk situation besides the money prizes and the probabilities — *e.g.,* the atmosphere of the gaming-room. The Theorem could possibly be framed so as to allow for these considerations, but in any practical application they would undoubtedly have some effect.

Whether or not these factors would lead to *serious* inconsistency is open to question; it seems very likely that they would in the field of gambling, but Samuelson suggests that they may be less important in business and statistical problems.[32]

The only laboratory test of the Hypothesis has been performed by Professor Frederick Mosteller, who derived utility curves for a group of subjects on the basis of their choice among simple gambles, and used these data to predict their choices among other and more complicated gambles.[33] The experiment sidestepped pitfalls which could not be avoided in practical application by abstracting from the major sources of inconsistent behavior: (*a*) all probabilities were

---

[30]William Baumol, "The Neumann-Morgenstern Utility Index — An Ordinalist View," *Journal of Political Economy* (February, 1951), p. 65.

[31]Maurice Allais, in "Notes théoriques sur l'Incertitude de l'Avenir et la Risque" (as yet unpublished), and Professor Robert Bishop, in a paper that has not been published as yet, outline these considerations in detail.

[32]Samuelson, "Probability, Utility, and the Independence Axiom," *op. cit.,* p. 677.

[33]Frederick Mosteller and Philip Nogee, "An Experimental Measurement of Utility," *Journal of Political Economy* (October, 1951), p. 399.

known; (*b*) all calculations were performed for the subjects and their misconceptions eliminated;[34] (*c*) only small sums were used; (*d*) no social influences or any "other factors" were present; (*e*) behavior was observed only in one special risk context (and that an artificial one). The fact that Mosteller found only mild consistency despite these "ideal" conditions might be interpreted as distinctly unfavorable to the hypothesis (though, considered in themselves, the results were inconclusive).

V

In deriving a "Jevonsian" utility index, we would begin as in the preceding section by assigning two arbitrary values; since, like the von Neumann-Morgenstern index, it is determined up to a linear transformation (if it can be found at all). As before, we might assign the utility numbers 10 and 0 to the outcomes \$1,000 and \$0. To find U_{500}, instead of confronting the individual with a choice between prospects, we would ask him to rank his preference of \$1,000 to \$500 and his preference of \$500 to \$0. Suppose he should tell us that the two preferences were equal; we would then assign the utility number $U_{500} = 5$. But on the basis of the von Neumann-Morgenstern experiment (let us assume that the same individual was the subject) we assigned the number $U_{500} = 8$. Is there not a conflict here?

To anyone who has skimmed the literature in this field it will not be obvious that the two sets of results are independent, hence do not conflict, for certain passages, particularly in *The Theory of Games*, gives quite the opposite impression. A close examination of the texts can, in fact, settle the question definitely. Instead of referring immediately to the literature, however, it is rewarding to examine a more general type of analysis, which might have made the issues intelligible to economists from the beginning.

Bridgman states the central proposition of the operational approach thus:[35]

---

[34]In the first two sessions subjects were not instructed on computing odds, and calculations were not performed for them. Behavior in these sessions was quite different from behavior in the rest of the experiment. Although these interesting results were not discussed in the article cited, Mosteller informed me that a definite finding of the experiment was that all the subjects behaved very differently before and after they had received lectures on dealing with probabilities. Moreover, their behavior showed a trend factor throughout the experiments as they grew increasingly familiar with the various gambles.

Even if the final conclusions had been much more favorable than they were, these observations would have dictated great caution in extrapolating them to situations outside the laboratory.

[35]Percy W. Bridgman, *The Logic of Modern Physics* (New York: Macmillan Co., 1927). The first sentence is on p. 6, the second on p. 10 (my italics).

Although such notions as the meaningfulness and restrictiveness of hypotheses have been made familiar to many economists by followers of Bridgman, the above proposition and the following ones, which are the very heart of the operational approach, are not widely known among economists.

> We must demand that the set of operations equivalent to any concept be a unique set, for otherwise there are possibilities of ambiguity in practical applications which we cannot admit. . . .
>
> *If we have more than one set of operations we have more than one concept*, and strictly there should be a separate name to correspond to each different set of operations.

The word "should" above should be interpreted as meaning that it is *useful,* in terms of certain specific purposes, to adopt the proposed point of view (this applies as well to the word "should" in this sentence). Because of incautious phrasing in his early writing, it has often been thought that Bridgman regarded his own definitions and classifications as logical imperatives. Actually (as he has since made explicit), it is not necessary to insist on his approach dogmatically or exclusively; without making any unique claims, it is easy to show the value of his point of view (which admittedly is not the most natural) in helping to avoid certain types of confusion.

Of course, in everyday usage we very commonly use the same term to cover different operations, on the grounds that they measure the "same thing." If we take the strict operational point of view that a "thing" is "what is measured by a particular operation," we need not ban the practice of treating two different operations as measuring the "same thing," but we must insist that it be justified by a direct argument. In an important passage, Bridgman indicates the nature of an adequate justification:[36]

> If we deal with phenomena outside the domain in which we originally defined our concepts, we may find physical hindrances to performing the operations of the original definition, so that the original operations have to be replaced by others. These new operations are, of course, to be chosen so that they give, within experimental error, the same numerical results in the domain in which the two sets of operations may be both applied; but we must recognize in principle that in changing the operations we have really changed the concept. . . . The practical justification for retaining the same name is that within our present experimental limits a numerical difference between the results of the two sorts of operations has not been detected.

It would hardly be possible to find a passage more pertinent to a comparison of the economic theories discussed here. It may be helpful to give some economic illustrations; several examples of pairs of operations which differ but are usually treated as equivalent exist within the boundaries of our discussion.

(1) In the indifference map experiment the operations (*a*) of interrogating the individual as to his preferences, or (*b*) observing his actual choices (Samuelson's "revealed preference"), are usually regarded as alternative.

(2) In the "Jevonsian" experiment two operations are usually thought to be involved: (*a*) inquiring of the subject how he ranks his preferences; (*b*) the subject's own

[36]Percy W. Bridgman, *The Logic of Modern Physics* (New York: Macmillan Co., 1927); the first two sentences are on p. 23; the third, on p. 16 (in the latter sentence, Bridgman refers to the measurement of length by ordinary and by Einstein's operations).

subjective process of "weighing" satisfactions. The first is said to measure differences in satisfaction on the assumption that it approximates the results of the second. The basis of this assumption is that in the area where they can both be applied — the area of our own introspection — they give identical results (to the extent that we *can* balance satisfactions and that we tell the truth).

(3) In the von Neumann-Morgenstern experiment we used the operation (*a*) of asking the subject to name a $\dot{p}$ at which he would be indifferent; but we also suggested the possibility (*b*) of observing his choices when confronted with various pairs of prospects many times. Mosteller used the latter operation in his empirical tests.

In each case, the alternative operations are regarded as roughly identical. Actually, most economists who have had practical experience in applied theory are well aware that the results of interrogation and of observing actual behavior are almost never identical. Moreover, minor differences in the operations (such as the wording of questions) do "make a difference."[37] When a pair of operations is accepted as measuring the "same thing" it is because the divergence between the results is not regarded as significant. But as the range of application of each operation is widened over time, divergences appear in the area of overlap, and as precision increases, small differences become significant. Too often, theorists are unprepared for these phenomena and are thrown into confusion at the emergence of ambiguity and paradox.[38] One who accepts the propositions of the operational approach, on the other hand, not only expects these problems to arise but also knows where to watch for them. This (and nothing more pretentious) is the chief virtue which is claimed for the approach.

The relevance of the above discussion to the present problem can now be stated. Probably many readers of *The Theory of Games* and some later articles have received the impression that the third pair of operations above was being proposed as "measuring the same thing" as the second pair. In other words, many have interpreted the von Neumann-Morgenstern experiment as a more precise or practical, though indirect, approach to the results of the Jevonsian experiment: *i.e.,* basically, to the results of the subjective calculation of satisfactions. But if the operational point of view were more common as a habit of thought, readers would have placed the burden of proof on the (supposed) exponents of such an equivalence, challenging them to exhibit evidence. In fact, as they would have discovered, there are no such exponents. And the evidence does not exist, for in general the two operations do not produce even approximately the same results.

Let us recall the results of our hypothetical von Neumann-Morgenstern experiment: $U_0 = 0$, $U_{200} = 2$, $U_{500} = 8$, $U_{1,000} = 10$. If the von Neumann-Morgenstern index for this individual were plotted as a function of money

[37]The operational approach may be useful in reminding us that differently worded questionnaires measure, in general, "different things."

[38]Such confusion was prevalent in physics prior to the revolutionary theories of Einstein and Planck. The operational approach was proposed as a means of avoiding such a state of mind in the future.

incomes, interpolating a smooth curve, the graph would be concave upward between $0 and $500; in this range it would show "increasing marginal utility." This shape would reflect merely the fact that in this range of money outcomes the individual accepted "unfair" bets and that his choices among prospects showed consistency of a certain type.

In contrast to this, Marshall and Jevons predicted almost unconditionally one general feature of a "utility" curve derived from an experiment of the Jevonsian type; it would be concave downwards throughout its whole length, exhibiting non-increasing marginal utility at all points. Among those economists who believe that a Jevonsian experiment can have consistent results at all, few have ever disputed this opinion.

If Marshall's prediction does hold, then the numbers inferred from the two experiments will certainly conflict for any person who is observed to accept a gamble at odds which are not distinctly favorable, let alone odds that are actually unfair. If such a person has a von Neumann-Morgenstern index it will have a range of increasing marginal utility, which is assumed to be contradictory to the Jevonsian index. Marshall himself pointed out that there were such people, even among those otherwise "rational."

Thus we can state: the von Neumann-Morgenstern and Jevons-Marshall operations do *not* measure the "same thing." The former do not simply tend to measure the Marshallian "utilities" with greater precision, *i.e.,* to a higher number of significant figures. In general, the ranking of first differences in "utility" as a function of money will be different, depending on which "utility" is being measured; if the functions are continuous, the second derivatives will not in general have the same sign.

To those who accepted the apparent inference that the gambling operation allowed an "estimate" of the results of a Jevonsian experiment, a moment's thought should have suggested the question: Why is an estimate necessary? If risk behavior reveals something about differences in satisfaction, presumably it is because those differences in satisfaction are the decisive factor in decision-making. But in that case we might as well ask about satisfactions directly.[39]

This discussion has not established yet that von Neumann and Morgenstern do not themselves regard their operation, mistakenly, as measuring differences in satisfaction. The evidence for this is their repeated rejection of the notion that an individual reaches decisions in risk situations by calculating

---

[39]It is perhaps conceivable, though unlikely, that his feelings of satisfaction might be difficult for an individual directly, being only semi-conscious, though influencing his behavior. But if it were true that his risk behavior was a reliable and convenient guide to his feelings of differences in satisfaction, this would ensure that the Jevonsian experiment *could* always be performed. For even if the subject were an economist, say, who detested introspection, he could note tacitly his reactions to hypothetical lottery tickets (or even, if conscientious, plot his behavior at bingo games and horse races) before replying to questions about differences in satisfaction.

On the other hand, to say that the Jevonsian experiment cannot lead to consistent results is to say that any consistency revealed by the von Neumann-Morgenstern experiment is not closely related to satisfaction.

differences in utilities, their brand or any other (such as Jevonsian utilities). But much confusion probably stems from the fact that they are prone to write in large, clear type about comparing differences in preferences and to discard such notions in fine print at the bottom of the page. Thus, they formulate their "continuity" axiom (which rules out the "absolute" rejection of lottery tickets or the "absolute" love of gambling discussed earlier) as follows:[40]

> No matter how much the utility of *v* exceeds . . . the utility of *u*, and no matter how little the utility of *w* exceeds . . . the utility of *u*, if *v* is admixed to *u* with a sufficiently small numerical probability, the difference that this admixture makes from *u* will be less than the difference of *w* from *u*.

This leaves a strong impression, to put it mildly, that the notions of quantity of utility and differences in quantities are an integral part of the argument . . . unless the reader follows a footnote on to the next page:[41]

> The reader will also note that we are talking of entities like 'the excess of *v* over *u*,' or 'the excess of *u* over *v*' or (to combine the two former) the 'discrepancy of *u* and *v*' (*u, v,* being utilities) merely to facilitate the verbal discussion—they are not part of our rigorous, axiomatic system.

One other passage in the "literary" discussion is probably the greatest single source of misunderstanding; it concerns a situation in which an individual is offered a choice between a sure outcome, *A*, and a 50-50 chance of *B* or *C*, where *C* is preferred to *A* and *A* to *B*:[42]

> . . . any assertion about his preference of *A* against the combination contains fundamentally new information. Specifically: If he now prefers *A* to the 50-50 combination of *B* and *C*, this provides a plausible base for the numerical estimate that his preference of *A* over *B* is in excess of his preference of *C* over *A*.

This passage seems clearly to imply that the von Neumann-Morgenstern operation aims at the same "entities" (*i.e.*, utility differences) as the Jevonsian experiment, being merely more indirect. But again, the crucial withdrawal is in the footnote:[43]

---

[40]Von Neumann and Morgenstern, *op. cit.*, p. 630. Since the content of this passage is not under discussion, the reader is advised to pass his eyes over it rather swiftly.

[41]*Ibid.*, p. 631 n. This is not the only time in their book that the authors introduce notions in a "literary" discussion of their theorems that they simultaneously disown, informing the reader that it all comes out in the axioms. Of course, the very inclusion of a verbal discussion is a concession to non-mathematicians; but one can do only so much in the name of "heuristic devices." It is not a recommendation of the empirical relevance of axioms to say that they can be made plausible in literary translation only by identifying them with notions (such as subjective utility differences) which are actually irrelevant.

[42]Von Neumann and Morgenstern, *op. cit.*, p. 18.

[43]*Ibid.*, p. 18 n.

> Observe that we have only postulated an individual intuition which permits decision as to which of the two 'events' is preferable. But we have not directly postulated any intuitive estimate of the relative sizes of two preferences — *i.e.,* in the subsequent terminology, of two differences of utilities.

The equivocal word here is "estimate." This implies that the procedure tries to approximate the results of an introspective operation. Actually in the von Neumann-Morgenstern experiment described above utility differences were not "estimated" but computed exactly. They were related precisely to certain risk choices; no other evidence, intuitive or otherwise, was allowed to influence the results.

The authors themselves point out the ambiguity:

> Are we not postulating here — or taking it for granted — that one preference may exceed another, *i.e.,* that such statements convey a meaning? Such a view would be a complete misunderstanding of our procedure.[44]

Their procedure is actually to use the risk choices to *define* the utility differences — to make this notion meaningful in a new way — not to "estimate them." Very likely it was the above passage which led Professor D. H. Robertson to imagine that von Neumann and Morgenstern had proposed a method for estimating relative differences in desirability. It is easy to spot this inference in his critical account of their theory:[45]

> Thus in the case of a man who does not know how to choose — *i.e.,* who chooses by the toss of a mental coin — between the certainty of *B* and an even chance of *A* or *C,* these authors offer 1 as a measure of the ratio of *AB* to *BC*. . . . But it is clear that this would only be *true* for a particular type of man, namely, one who is content to be governed entirely by mathematical expectations. . . . (My italics.)

In the case of the behavior described, von Neumann and Morgenstern would *define* the ratio of utility differences as 1; and in a matter of definition there can be no question of truth and falsity. Those standards could be applied only to a *hypothesis* that the scale defined by von Neumann and Morgenstern bore some empirical relation to some other data, not involving risk: for example, the hypothesis that it approximated the results of a Jevonsian measurement. It is clear from the context of Robertson's remarks that he believed, like most readers, such a hypothesis was implied. It has been the argument of this paper that this belief is mistaken.

In the same passage Robertson adopts essentially the Marshallian position:[46] ". . . we can make no sense of his actions in the face of uncertainty without supposing that he can form some estimate of the relative difference in desirability between pairs of situations." Whatever the plausibility of this

[44]*Ibid.*, p. 20.
[45]D. H. Robertson, *Utility and all That* (London: Macmillan Co., 1952), p. 28.
[46]*Ibid.*, p. 28.

argument, it has no relevance to the von Neumann-Morgenstern theory. Where Marshall postulated a type of "consistency" between men's risk choices and their feelings of relative differences in desirability of the outcomes, von Neumann and Morgenstern hypothesize simply a consistency between risk choices and other risk choices. By coincidence, it happens that the particular form of "consistency" prescribed by Marshall (he might well have chosen some other rule than the maximization of "expected utility") would imply von Neumann-Morgenstern "consistency"; though not vice versa. A man who had a Jevonsian index *and* who obeyed Marshall's dictum would have a von Neumann-Morgenstern index; but the existence of the latter index implies neither of the first two conditions (and the existence of the former index implies neither of the last two conditions). Thus, the von Neumann-Morgenstern axioms cover all those who are "rational" in the Marshallian sense; in addition, they may apply to others who would be "irrational" in Marshall's terms, *e.g.,* bettors who accepted unfair bets[47]: and still others for whom no Jevonsian index can be defined.

Von Neumann and Morgenstern describe their procedure thus: "We have practically defined numerical utility as being that thing for which a calculus of mathematical expectations legitimate."[48] The word "practically" is unnecessary; from an operational point of view, they *have* so defined it. Does such a "thing" exist? Friedman and Savage have emphasized the use of the axioms, which put definite restrictions on behavior, as a basis for testable and fairly powerful predictions concerning risk choices.[49] *Should* it exist? Marschak has proposed that the axioms be regarded as defining "rational" behavior in risk situations; according to this view, which no other writer has supported, the axioms are of interest for normative purposes, even if no one actually does conform to them.[50]

Von Neumann and Morgenstern cited only the descriptive aspect of the theory. They were not particularly interested in predicting or prescribing people's preferences among prospects, but merely in describing them in terms of mathematical expectation: a necessity in their own theory of games, a convenience in any context. This original view of the subject, by far the least pretentious, is probably the most appropriate. The emphasis by Friedman and Savage on the meaningfulness of the hypothesis obscures the fact that many other hypotheses are just as meaningful, perhaps more useful, and even more convenient for predictive purposes (though not for description). For example,

---

[47]The theory, since it allows for this sort of behavior, cannot be said to rule out all forms of "pleasure in gambling." But proponents have rather overplayed this point. Although acceptance of unfair bets does not contradict the theory, there is ample behavior which does, including some other forms of "pleasure in gambling."

[48]Von Neumann and Morgenstern, *op. cit.,* p. 28.

[49]Friedman and Savage, *op. cit.*

[50]Marschak, *op. cit.*, p. 139; also, "Why 'Should' Statisticians and Businessmen Maximise 'Moral Expectation'?" *Proceedings of the Second Berkeley Symposium on Mathematical Statistics and Probability* (Los Angeles: 1951), p. 493.

hypotheses in terms of parameters of the *money* distribution, such as mathematical expectation and variance, might produce fully as good predictions as those based on a derived von Neumann-Morgenstern index, and they would certainly be easier to test. As for the normative aspect, there seems very little reason to advise a man who is extremely reckless (or excessively conservative) in some of his risk choices that he should be consistently reckless (or conservative) in his remaining risk choices. Nor does it seem that a person who behaves approximately in accordance with a von Neumann-Morgenstern index would be in any sense better off if he behaved *more* in accordance with it. If these conclusions are accepted (and von Neumann and Morgenstern would probably accept them), then one must answer the question, "What does it matter whether such a 'thing' exists?" very conservatively.

At any rate, it should be clear that Baumol's impression that "Neumann and Morgenstern consider the utility index obtained by them as the *only* true one"[51] is quite mistaken. So far as behavior under certainty is concerned, only the ordinal features of the index are relevant. The only numerical operation permitted is that of forming mathematical expectations, which is related to risk behavior; it makes no sense, for example, to *add* von Neumann-Morgenstern utilities. The cardinal features of the index—the relative differences between utility numbers—are used only to predict or describe risk behavior, and, moreover, are derived solely from risk behavior. Therefore, the results of a von Neumann-Morgenstern experiment cannot be "checked" against the results of any experiment not involving risk choices. This applies to simple introspection, to the Jevonsian experiment, and also to other attempts to base a cardinal utility on consumer behavior.[52] These latter have been rather thoroughly discredited by Samuelson and others because of their use of special unrealistic assumptions. But the existence or non-existence of a von Neumann-Morgenstern index and the existence of "measurable" indices based on these other operations are entirely independent matters. Each method might, out of the whole set of ordinal utility indices, select a different subset of indices reflecting some type of data in addition to preferences; if the indices inside each subset were related by linear transformations, each method would result in *a* "measurable" utility index. These indices might have entirely different shapes, but so long as they did not entirely overlap in application, there would be no need to single out any one of them as being the "true" utility index. Certainly von Neumann and Morgenstern make no such claims for their construction; they cite only its convenience in formalizing risk behavior. There is no reason to believe that a "measurable utility" derived by some other

---

[51]Baumol, "The Neumann-Morgenstern Utility Index—an Ordinalist View," *Journal of Political Economy* (February, 1951), p. 61.

[52]See Robert Bishop, "Consumer's Surplus and Cardinal Utility," *Quarterly Journal of Economics* (May, 1943). For criticism of these approaches see Samuelson, *Foundations of Economic Analysis*, pp. 174–9.

method could do this;[53] on the other hand, the von Neumann-Morgenstern index could not do the main jobs for which other constructions are intended. It would be of no aid whatsoever in formalizing consumer behavior under certainty (the goal of the Fisher-Frisch constructions: see Bishop, *op. cit.*), nor would it seem to be of any relevance in welfare evaluations (whereas a Jevonsian index might be).[54] If it is true, as Professor Robertson has complained, that von Neumann and Morgenstern have actually done harm to "the cause" of creating acceptance for a measurable utility with these last two objectives,[55] this is but a measure of the general misinterpretation of their results: a confusion for which they cannot evade all responsibility.

---

[53]Thus, Alchian is mistaken in asserting that "measurability 'up to a linear transform' both *implies* and is implied by the possibility of predicting choices among uncertain prospects, the universal situation" ["The Meaning of Utility Measurement," p. 49 (my italics)]. Actually, it is easy to conceive a "measurable" utility index which is neither derived from nor used to predict risk behavior.

[54]After I had reached these conclusions, I had the great benefit of conversation with Professor Oskar Morgenstern, who was kind enough to read and discuss with me an earlier version of this paper. Professor Morgenstern confirmed what were then speculations on the implications of the theory; he particularly confirmed that he and von Neumann had envisioned only limited application, to risk behavior alone.

[55]Robertson, *op. cit.*, p. 28.

5. METHODENSTREIT OVER DEMAND CURVES*

Leland B. Yeager†

Rival Demand Curves

This paper seeks to clarify some points raised in the literature that has grown up around Milton Friedman's Marshallian demand curve.[1] It examines some methodological precepts set forth in this literature: its insistence on a particular conception of empirical falsifiability and concrete applicability of theories and its insistence that theories deal only with actually or conceptually attainable positions of equilibrium. Published appraisal of this point of view has so far been remarkably scant.

First, it is necessary to summarize the proposed innovations in demand theory. Friedman objects to the currently prevalent conception of the demand curve (the "Hicksian" or, as Knight says, the "Slutzky-school" conception). For a particular commodity, this curve shows the alternative quantities per time period that the buyers would want to buy at various alternative prices, assuming no change in their tastes and so forth, in their *money* incomes, and in the prices of goods and services other than the particular one in question. A change in the commodity's own price will affect quantity demanded through the familiar "income effect" and "substitution effect." Friedman wants to work, instead, with what he calls a "Marshallian"[2] demand curve. Such a curve

*From *Journal of Political Economy*, Vol. LXVIII, No. 1 (February, 1960), pp. 53–64. Reprinted by permission of the University of Chicago Press and the author.

†Leland B. Yeager, Professor of Economics and Chairman of the James Wilson Department of Economics, University of Virginia. The author is indebted to Professor James M. Buchanan for the title of this article and for lengthy, patient, and exceedingly helpful, though not necessarily concurring, written comments on earlier drafts.

[1]Milton Friedman, "The Marshallian Demand Curve," *Journal of Political Economy*, Vol. LVII (December, 1949), pp. 463–95, reprinted in *Essays in Positive Economics* (Chicago: University of Chicago Press, 1953), pp. 47–99; as Friedman points out, his argument is an extension of that presented by Frank H. Knight in "Realism and Relevance in the Theory of Demand," *Journal of Political Economy*, Vol. LII (December, 1944), pp. 289–318. Further writings in the same tradition include Martin J. Bailey, "The Marshallian Demand Curve," *Journal of Political Economy*, Vol. LXII (June, 1954), pp. 255–61; Milton Friedman, "A Reply," *Journal of Political Economy*, Vol. LXII (June, 1954), pp. 261–66; Martin J. Bailey, "Saving and the Rate of Interest," *Journal of Political Economy*, Vol. LXV (August, 1957), pp. 279–305; James M. Buchanan, "Saving and the Rate of Interest: A Comment," *Journal of Political Economy*, Vol LXVII (February, 1959), pp. 79–82; James M. Buchanan, "*Ceteris Paribus:* Some Notes on Methodology," *Southern Economic Journal*, Vol. XXIV, (January, 1958), pp. 259–70.

[2]The present paper ignores the question of "what Marshall really meant." The merits of Friedman's approach and methodological precepts can be examined separately from matters of textual interpretation.

would show the alternative quantities of a particular commodity demanded at alternative prices on the condition of constancy in the buyers' tastes and so forth, in their *real* incomes, and in the prices of all close substitutes for and complements of the commodity considered. A change in the one particular price would be accompanied by a change in the average level of prices of substantially unrelated goods in such a way as to freeze the general purchasing power of money and thus the real income corresponding to the given money income. In principle, the offsetting changes in the other prices would be such as to keep buyers at the same utility levels as before.[3] These price changes cannot be exactly specified in practice because the necessary detailed knowledge of utility functions cannot be obtained and because of other complications. As an approximation, Friedman proposes adjustments to make the unchanged money income just barely adequate to buy the same assortment of goods in the new price situation as in the old situation.[4] Bailey proposes an alternative constant-real-income demand curve corresponding to the fixity of the community's production-possibility frontier; his approximation would keep constant a quantity index weighted by base prices.[5]

There is no need here to explore the relative merits of the Friedman and Bailey constructions; they both exemplify the same methodological approach.[6] Whatever the details may be, this approach is supposed to have advantages in comparison with the conventional Hicksian demand curve. It isolates the substitution effect of a price change for study, with the income effect being "eliminated," or removed from consideration.[7] A Friedman-Marshall demand curve *must* slope negatively: under the conditions presupposed in its very construction, a cut in the price of the commodity will without exception increase quantity demanded (or, in the limit, leave it unchanged). The theorist need not hedge his predictions to allow for the possibility of a strong inferior-good income effect outweighing a normal substitution effect. Friedman-Marshall predictions are meaningful because refutable if wrong.[8] The Hicksian demand curve, by contrast, "contains no empirical generalization that is capable of being contradicted. . . ."

---

[3]Friedman, *Essays, op. cit.,* esp. pp. 51–54.

[4]Cf. Friedman's summary statement in *Journal of Political Economy* (June, 1954), *op. cit.*, p. 263.

[5]Martin J. Bailey, *Journal of Political Economy* (June, 1954), *op. cit.*, esp. pp. 259–60.

[6]Constant real income in the utility sense and constant real income in the sense of outputs obtainable from a fixed total of resources converge in the neighborhood of equilibrium. Friedman, *Essays, op. cit.,* p. 63.

[7]Friedman, *Essays, op. cit.,* pp. 64–65.

[8]This claim is admittedly not made perfectly explicit — in print. It may be inferred from statements such as the one quoted in the next sentence of the text (from Friedman, *Essays, op. cit.*, p. 91). Furthermore, Knight (*Journal of Political Economy*, [December, 1944], *op. cit.*, p. 300) recommends drawing the demand curve with "utility and the objective purchasing-power of money . . . held constant," since "This procedure has the further great advantage of eliminating the spurious 'Giffen paradox'. . . ." Bailey's attempt in his 1957 article (already cited) to settle the question whether a rise in the rate of interest can be expected to increase or decrease saving bears an obvious though loose analogy to attempts to exclude the possibility of the Giffen paradox in the demand for an ordinary commodity.

In general, the Friedman approach is said to be more "useful" than its rival for dealing with practical problems.[9] This apparently means that the Hicksian approach, in regarding all prices as kept constant except the price of the particular commodity to which the demand curve refers, reflects the Walrasian notion that the quantity demanded of any particular commodity depends on *all* prices in the economic system. Such a striving for generality, elegance, and photographic accuracy in assumptions sabotages the treatment of practical problems and the search for the "concrete truth" stressed by Marshall. The more modest Friedman-Marshall approach does not try to take account of all prices in the system, not even by keeping them constant. Instead, it fixes the prices only of obvious substitutes and complements and concerns itself further only with the behavior of an average of all other prices rather than with those other prices individually. Because it has more modest aims than rival approaches, the rough-and-ready Friedman demand curve is a more practical and usable tool.

Setting aside until later the question of just what might be meant by the practical "usefulness" of a demand curve, we may now consider the implied claim that Friedman's concept has an advantageous rough-and-ready simplicity. Actually if we are going to find fault with the Hicksian demand curve for the complexity of in principle taking account of all prices in the system in order to keep all but one of them constant, we are even more entitled to question Friedman's concept on similar grounds. (Friedman and Bailey themselves have already noted most of what follows here, though apparently without taking it enough to heart. The only reason for repeating it is to lay the basis for considering their methodological precepts.) First of all, a great ambiguity surrounds the "Chicago"[10] demand curves as to just *which* other prices in the system are conceived to vary, and by how much, to offset the income effect of the change in the price of the particular commodity considered. Any specified set of price changes must be arbitrary, since the changes are not necessarily those that would occur in the real world in response to the change in underlying conditions that also caused the change in the price of the particular commodity. The Hicksian approach is also arbitrary in specifying no change in the other prices, but at least it is not ambiguous.[11] A related ambiguity in the Chicago approach concerns the starting price considered for the commodity, since the level of buyers' real income to be kept constant by offsetting price variations is different for different starting prices.

The Friedman method of offsetting price changes is not only an approximation to what would leave each individual on the same utility level as before; it is also a mere approximation to what would leave each individual just able to

[9]For remarks about usefulness, see Friedman, *Essays, op. cit.*, pp. 48, 56–57, 89, 93; Friedman, *Journal of Political Economy* (June, 1954), *op. cit.*, p. 263.

[10]Labels such as this are merely a convenient shorthand. As is clear from the context, they have a restricted meaning and imply no monolithic unity among all "Chicagoans."

[11]Bailey, *Journal of Political Economy* (June, 1954), *op. cit.*, pp. 260–261.

afford his original assortment of goods. For the individuals will in fact have been buying different original assortments, and any actually specified set of price changes will affect different individuals in different ways and will somewhat redistribute effective purchasing power. Friedman's construction is a mere approximation to an approximation to keeping each individual on the same utility level as before.[12] Bailey's construction, on the other hand, is incapable of being defined logically for each individual in the community; it can aim to keep approximately constant only the production possibilities available to the community as a whole.[13]

We see that neither Friedman's nor Bailey's construction can analyze how a particular price change affects quantity demanded under the assumptions both of an unchanged distribution of real income and of a constant level of real income or of production opportunities. Any price change or set of price changes is bound to benefit some and harm other members of the community; a rise or fall in some particular price is almost certain to reduce or increase the real opportunities available to those who happen to be actual or potential buyers of the commodity in question. In reality, then, the income effect is as inherent a part of the influences determining consumer behavior as is the substitution effect. Yet Friedman wishes to "eliminate" the income effect and consider only the substitution effect; he wishes to keep real income unchanged not merely for the community as a whole but even for the group of purchasers of the particular commodity in question.[14] This seems illegitimate: to abstract from the way a price change in the real world *does* affect the real income of a particular group of buyers and potential buyers is to abstract from a possibly important part of the reason why the price change will affect quantity demanded. These are perhaps the considerations that James Buchanan (a champion of the Friedman methodology) had in mind when he recognized that there is some justification for the widespread acceptance and use of the uncompensated or Hicksian demand curve in analyzing the behavior of one individual or some one group of individuals smaller than the whole community.[15] What does remain to be emphasized is that, in contemplating a

[12]Cf. *ibid.*, pp. 257–59. Friedman himself (*Journal of Political Economy* [June, 1954], *op. cit.*, p. 264) acknowledges his own earlier failure to deal explicitly with the problem of transition from the demand curve of the individual to the demand curve of the community.

[13]Bailey, *Journal of Political Economy* (June, 1954), *op. cit.*, pp. 258–59, crediting Friedman for the point.

[14]He makes this explicit on pp. 50–51 of his *Essays, op. cit.* Furthermore, in considering a price change due to subsidizing a particular commodity, Friedman postulates that the revenue to pay for the subsidy is raised from broadly the same group of individuals as those who benefit from it, "so that complications arising from changes in the distribution of income can be neglected . . ." (pp. 59–60). On p. 84, however, where he is seeking to reconcile the Giffen paradox with his interpretation of Marshall, Friedman envisages constancy in the real income of the community at large but not of the particular consumer group. In *Journal of Political Economy* (June, 1954), *op. cit.*, pp. 262–63, in connection with an international trade example suggested by Lloyd Metzler, Friedman does recognize that there are special problems for which the Hicksian demand analysis is appropriate.

[15]Buchanan, *Southern Economic Journal* (January, 1958), *op. cit.*, p. 262.

demand curve, we *always are* analyzing the behavior of a group smaller than the whole community; not everyone is a buyer of a particular commodity. (Or to be precise, even if every member of the community does buy at least some small amount of the commodity in question, not all members are buyers to the same extent; some members count importantly and others only trivially as buyers of the commodity.)

In developing his objection that a reduction in price along a Hicksian demand curve illegitimately implies a change in the productive capacity of the community, Friedman considers an excise subsidy that lowers the effective supply curve of commodity *X*. The new intersection with the Hicksian demand curve is *MN* units to the right of the old intersection. "But then," asks Friedman, "where do the resources come from to produce the extra *MN* units of *X?* Obviously our assumptions are not internally consistent. The additional units of *X* can be produced only by bidding resources away from the production of other commodities, in the process raising their prices and reducing the amount of them produced." A Hicksian demand curve "fails to give the correct solution even when all disturbing influences can be neglected" because "each point on it implicitly refers to a different productive capacity of the community."[16] It is noteworthy that Friedman refers to the community rather than to buyers and potential buyers of the particular commodity. Even supposing the productive opportunities open to the community to remain unchanged, it is perfectly easy to conceive of an improvement of the supply opportunities open to particular buyer groups. Perhaps, for instance, the ingredients used in making a product have become cheaper because of a shift in tastes away from other products made from these same ingredients.

On a more general plane, what is the objection, after all, to considering changes in the supply opportunities open not merely to particular groups but even to the community as a whole? Perhaps the product has been cheapened by advances in technology. What is illegitimate about asking how this price reduction will affect quantity demanded? And why must we somehow compensate out of the analysis the increase in people's real incomes that this cheapening does imply?[17]

Part of the explanation is that the Chicagoans are not typically concerned with examples involving changes in resources or technology; they deal with

---

[16]Friedman, *Essays, op. cit.,* pp. 61–62.

[17]Friedman, *Essays, op. cit.*, p. 63, does take note of this question; and he suggests redrawing a demand curve of his type to correspond to the appropriately higher but again constant level of real income. Bailey, *Journal of Political Economy* (June, 1954), *op. cit.*, p. 261, also recognizes that a change in actual supply conditions would cause a compensated demand curve of his type to shift; from this he concludes that the choice of a demand curve should depend on the problem in hand. We should bear these remarks in mind when we later turn to consider the claim that the Chicago approach best fits in with the ideal of keeping demand factors and supply factors as separate and independent as possible. It appears that the Chicagoans mingle supply and demand factors together despite their own precepts. Furthermore, if the proper conception of the demand curve does admittedly depend, after all, on each particular problem in hand, one wonders just what is left of the general methodological insights ostensibly connected with the Chicago curve.

price changes brought about by excise taxes and subsidies.[18] They are quite right in insisting that, with unchanged resources and technology, the tax or subsidy is necessarily accompanied by a revenue-disposal or revenue-raising aspect whose neglect may involve serious analytical error. If this other aspect impinges to any important extent on the same persons directly affected by the tax or subsidy, it may be necessary to take account of this effect on their real income by redrawing their demand curve accordingly. Perhaps this is a clumsy expedient, but no more so than to shift the demand curve when supply shifts because of changed resources or technology (see footnote 17.) In cases like this, shifting the curves seems a more straightforward and more generally applicable approach than trying to rig given demand curves in advance to take account of possible supply changes affecting real income. Even if a tax or subsidy is the cause of the supply and price change, there still is not much justification for trying to draw a given demand curve that gets rid of income effects, for the demanders of the particular taxed or subsidized commodity may very well have their real incomes changed. If the Chicagoans object that others in the community will necessarily have their real incomes changed in the opposite direction and that repercussions even onto the first market will occur, they are just pointing out the fact of general interdependence and the fact that partial analysis is only an approximation.

Ways of Allowing for General Economic Interdependence

Any demand curve drawn on a two-dimensional diagram is a piece of partial-equilibrium analysis and is incapable of reflecting, in itself, the full interdependence of all aspects of the economic system. Any demand curve is a way of contemplating how buyers would react to a change in supply price; but, in general, the particular price in question cannot change apart from other changes in the economic system. Sometimes, as Buchanan has persuasively shown,[19] theorists fail to take this incomplete character of partial-equilibrium analysis adequately into account and arrive at seriously wrong conclusions about the general-equilibrium aspects of the economy. But a warning against illegitimate use of *ceteris paribus* and against illegitimate neglect of general-equilibrium considerations, however necessary and persuasive, makes no conclusive case against the Hicksian demand curve. Objections to the Hicksian curve are essentially objections to any attempt to use partial-equilibrium tools, however supplemented, in an approach to the complexities of reality; as such, these objections lose their force.

Two expressions recur in the Chicago discussions of methodology: first, the question of "How can *one* price change?" and second, the insistence on

[18] For example, see Friedman, *Essays, op. cit.*, pp. 59–62; Bailey, *Journal of Political Economy* (June, 1954), *op. cit.*, pp. 255, 261; Bailey, *Journal of Political Economy* (August, 1957), *op. cit.*, pp. 283–84, 288; Friedman, "Leon Walras and His Economic System," *American Economic Review*, Vol. XLV (December, 1955), middle of p. 904.

[19] Buchanan, *Southern Economic Journal* (January, 1958), *op. cit.*

"genuinely attainable alternatives."[20] The question refers to the interdependence of all aspects of the economy: one item cannot change all by itself, devoid of all repercussions. This is of course true. Yet there is no harm in contemplating, for example, what would happen if government price-controllers tried to decree a change in one single price. There is no harm in considering how demanders would want to respond to various prices *if* they somehow could prevail. Part of the purpose of such an analysis might be to show the inconsistency among the plans of various members of the community at disequilibrium prices and to analyze the processes of groping toward equilibrium.

Relating to the same set of problems is the insistence that demand curves represent only "genuinely attainable alternatives" or "conceptually attainable alternatives"; "each point on a demand curve must represent an attainable equilibrium between demand and supply."[21] What this apparently means is that it is legitimate to ask ourselves what quantities of some product would be demanded only at prices which in fact can represent points of intersection between the demand curve and various supply curves under the supply possibilities open to the economy. (We can conceive of the effective supply curve being shifted about by one of the tax or subsidy schemes of which the Chicago theorists are so fond.) The insistence on attainable alternatives apparently forbids us to consider what quantities of the product people would want to buy at prices which cannot in fact prevail (at least not as equilibrium prices) under given supply conditions. This insistence on attainable price-quantity situations right along the demand curve itself is an example of the half-recognized inclination, mentioned previously, to build general-equilibrium considerations, and in particular supply considerations, right into the demand curve itself.[22]

Buchanan remarks that "in general, demand curves are useful only because they allow some predictions to be made regarding the effects of changes in supply."[23] In short, demand curves are useful only for the purpose of comparative statics, only to enable us to specify the new price-quantity equilibrium corresponding to changed supply conditions. Actually there are several uses of supply-and-demand analysis other than to make comparative-static predictions. There can be good reason for studying disequilibrium situations—for studying what demanders and suppliers would be wanting to do at a price at which their plans cannot in fact mesh. Precisely one of the characteristics of a disequilibrium situation, and one of the reasons why it cannot endure, is

[20]The question is attributed to Frank Knight, *op. cit.*, p. 261, where the other expression also occurs on, e.g., p. 264. A less epigrammatic version of the "one-price" remark appears in Knight's 1944 article, *op. cit.*, p. 299.

[21]Buchanan, *Southern Economic Journal* (January, 1958), *op. cit.*, p. 264. Compare Friedman's worry (*Essays, op. cit.*, p. 63) that the conditions for which the Hicksian demand curve is drawn are inconsistent with the conditions postulated on the side of supply.

[22]It is interesting that Friedman (*Journal of Political Economy* [June, 1954], *op. cit.*, p. 265) should have criticized Bailey's construction as seeming "to import supply considerations too directly into the demand function."

[23]Buchanan, *Southern Economic Journal* (January, 1958), *op. cit.*, p. 264.

that real incomes appear different to people from what they can actually be. We conceive of disequilibrium situations precisely in order to show that they are *not* genuinely attainable in the sense that the plans of various persons can be carried out and can mesh. We can study how the failure of plans to mesh would unleash competitive processes tending to establish a price or a set of prices at which plans finally would mesh. (In teaching the Law of Supply and Demand to beginning students, for instance, it is not enough to draw two curves on the blackboard and point to their intersection. It is necessary to show the competitive pressures that *would be* at work at prices "too low" or "too high" to be "genuinely attainable.") Consideration of disequilibrium and of equilibrating processes is further useful in helping us understand the consequences of interferences with these processes, such as price ceilings and wage floors.

The Chicagoans' insistence on attainable alternatives and comparative-static predictions suggests a reluctance to consider questions of disequilibrium, of equilibrating processes, and of the stability or instability of equilibrium. Perhaps this attitude stems from a feeling that such questions lead into talk about obscure "forces" and about things not observable in the marketplace. Yet in order to qualify as meaningful rather than metaphysical, propositions need not be falsifiable by direct observation, understood in the narrow behaviorist sense. Introspection and what people say may be counted among the numerous legitimate sources of empirical fact.[24]

Individual-Experiments and Market-Experiments

The Chicago insistence on genuinely attainable alternatives seems, further, to overlook Patinkin's illuminating distinction between individual-experiments and market-experiments.[25] An individual-experiment involves discovering, at least conceptually, the desired behavior of an individual person, of a small or large group of individuals, or even of all individuals in the community, acting

[24]Unfortunately, the arguments supporting this remark would strike some readers as long-exploded fallacies, while others would find them correct but too banal to bear repetition. These, like certain other propositions in economics, have met the paradoxical fate of becoming too hackneyed for continued attention even before a reasoned consensus on their truth or falsity has been reached. I can only urge readers to take the existing literature seriously. I especially commend to the Chicagoans some perceptive remarks by their own mentor: Frank Knight in *Journal of Political Economy* (December, 1944), *op. cit.*, p. 307. For an introduction to the literature on the use in economics of information on anticipations and plans, such as is obtainable from surveys, and for an explanation of the "realization-function" approach to using such information in combination with facts of a more obviously "objective" nature, see Franco Modigliani and Kalman J. Cohen, "The Significance and Uses of Ex Ante Data," in Mary Jean Bowman (ed.), *Expectations, Uncertainty, and Business Behavior* (New York: Social Science Research Council, 1958), pp. 151–64.

[25]Don Patinkin, *Money, Interest, and Prices* (Evanston, Ill.: Row, Peterson & Co., 1956), pp. 15, 275–81. Patinkin, though a Chicago Ph.D., is not included among the "Chicagoans" as I am using the term here.

in certain capacities, under certain specified circumstances. Whether these circumstances are compatible with other economic conditions and whether they can in fact prevail (whether they are genuinely or even conceptually attainable, to use the Chicago terminology) is beside the point: it is not the purpose of an individual-experiment, by itself, to describe the economic equilibrium that will tend to emerge. A demand curve is the standard example of the result of a set of (conceptual) individual-experiments; it shows the desired purchases of the buyers and potential buyers of a particular commodity under various specified circumstances, which include, notably, various alternative prices of the commodity. It is true that facts about the economic system other than those (the circumstances and attitudes of the demanders) reflected in the demand curve rule out many and perhaps all but one of these prices as genuine possibilities. But this does not invalidate drawing the demand curve in the way described. For the demand curve, by itself, is not meant to describe the prices that can in fact prevail. This description is possible only by an analysis that takes all of the relevant circumstances into account, including the results of other conceptual individual-experiments reflecting the circumstances and attitudes of groups other than the buyers and potential buyers of the commodity in question. This other type of analysis, which pulls together the results of various individual-experiments, examines the conditions under which the plans of various persons would and would not mesh, describes the processes at work when plans fail to mesh, and describes the equilibrium position, is what Patinkin means by market-experiments.

The anxiety to have even each demand curve by itself reflect attainable alternative positions for the whole economy is an attempt to build market-experiment considerations right into the conduct of individual-experiments. While this procedure strikes me as a source of confusion, it might perhaps be defended as a way of guarding against the worse confusion caused by misapplication of partial analysis to a description of aspects of the general equilibrium of the whole system; that this latter kind of confusion is widespread and serious can hardly be doubted by anyone who has studied Buchanan's lucid article on *ceteris paribus*. The errors so deftly examined by Buchanan may be interpreted as a confusion between individual-experiments and market-experiments in one particular direction: individual-experiment or partial notions have carelessly been carried over into analysis of market or general equilibrium. The Friedman-Buchanan school wants to move in the other direction, carrying market-experiment considerations directly into individual-experiments. It sees people so badly confusing individual- and market-experiments as to neglect relevant market considerations and reach wrong market conclusions on the basis of individual-experiment considerations inadequately supplemented. To prevent this error, the school insists (if I correctly interpret it) on building market-experiment considerations directly into the individual-experiments. I, on the other hand, do not believe that mistakes can so easily be prevented. Neither with the Chicago conception of demand curves nor with any other ready-made approaches can ingenious theorists mechanically guard their less perceptive or methodologically less alert colleagues against error. There is no easy way out: each theorist must himself grasp certain distinctions and must himself remain clearly aware of what he is doing. And the Chicago approach, blurring the distinctions between desired behavior and realizable behavior and between individual-experiments and market-experiments, seems not to contribute to the necessary clarity. Confusion in one direction can hardly be remedied by insisting on its counterpart in the opposite direction. Of course, this judgment may be a matter of personal opinion or taste: what seems simple to one person may be confusing to another, and vice versa. But if the issue does boil down to matters of personal opinion and preference and convenience, then the methodological precepts connected with the Friedman demand curve lose their force — which is precisely my argument.

The Example of The Demand for Money

The demand-curve issue may be sharpened up and summarized by considering both Patinkin's demand curve for cash balances and a powerful objection recently made to it. Patinkin re-examined the question whether the demand for money is of unitary elasticity with respect to the purchasing-power of the money unit, as traditionally supposed.[26] Is it true, in other words, that a postulated doubling or halving of the general price level would make people want to hold precisely twice or half as many dollars as before (in order to keep the real value of their cash balances unchanged)? Patinkin says no. A doubling of the price level would mean a halving of the real purchasing power of existing cash balances and a corresponding real impoverishment of their holders. Being poorer than before, people would have to economize on various uses of their incomes or wealth; in particular, they would somewhat cut down on their planned holdings of real cash balances. The total of nominal cash balances demanded would thus rise somewhat *less* than in full proportion to the assumed rise in the price level; the elasticity of demand for cash balances would prove to be less than unity.[27]

---

[26]Patinkin, *op. cit.,* pp. 28–30, 103–4, 388–389, 408–9. Buchanan's critique of Patinkin's position appears in the article already cited, *Southern Economic Journal* (January, 1958), *op. cit.*, pp. 262–64, 266–67.

[27]Patinkin's less-than-unitary elasticity depends on the fact that a change in the price level, postulated in an individual-experiment, implies a one-shot change in the real wealth of persons already holding cash balances. This one-shot change becomes negligible, however, in comparison with total real income considered over the fulness of time. The long-run-full-equilibrium amount of real balances demanded thus depends entirely on tastes and on the flow of real income (and on the costs of holding cash) and to only a vanishingly small extent on the one-shot change in wealth associated with the price-level change. With reference to long-run full equilibrium and to a population of immortal beings, then, the demand for cash balances does, after all,

(Contd.)

Speaking from the methodological standpoint of the Friedman-Marshall demand curve, Buchanan takes issue with Patinkin. For one thing, he says, the purchasing power of money cannot in fact be supposed to double or halve in the context of an unchanged money supply; the corresponding points on the Patinkin demand curve are not genuinely or conceptually attainable alternatives. Admittedly they are not; and precisely one of the reasons for contemplating them, anyway, is to show that they are not attainable because of the incompatibilities among the plans of various persons that they would imply and thus to show both the equilibrating process that would be touched off and the necessity and stability of the equilibrium price level. Incidentally, one of the further uses of contemplating the aggregate demand for cash balances at a disequilibrium price level is to understand the consequences of a government attempt to decree a disequilibrium price level, such as an attempt to decree a "roll-back" of an accomplished price inflation.

Another objection raised by Buchanan is that Patinkin's demand curve for money presupposes some definite existing supply of money. Supply influences demand. This fact not only is apparent from Patinkin's explanation of the less-than-unitary elasticity but also is explicitly stated by Patinkin. A doubling of the money supply would imply that the holders of the increased cash balances would feel richer than before at a not-yet-changed price level, and their demand curves not only for ordinary commodities but also for cash balances would shift to the right. The equilibrium supply-and-demand intersection would lie not only on a new money-supply curve but also on a new money-demand curve, indicating that the original demand curve was not a set of possible intersections with alternative supply curves. Patinkin gets into this alleged trouble because he draws an uncompensated demand curve, along which changes in the purchasing power of the money unit have wealth effects analogous to the income effects of price changes along an ordinary uncompensated Hicksian commodity demand curve. What Patinkin supposedly should have done instead is to devise some sort of compensated money demand curve, analogous to the Friedman-Marshall commodity demand curve, such that all points on it corresponded to a constant level of real wealth. This curve would consist of a set of conceivable intersections with various money supply curves and would, under traditional assumptions, have unit elasticity. Patinkin is of course aware of the uncompensated nature of his demand curve and is

---

have the traditional unit elasticity. Patinkin's inelasticity relates only to mortals operating in less-than-infinite time periods. Substantially this point is made in G. C. Archibald and R. G. Lipsey, "Monetary and Value Theory: A Critique of Lange and Patinkin," *Review of Economic Studies*, Vol. XXVI (1), No. 69 (October, 1958), pp. 1–22, esp. p. 9. This point seems to me to be less a refutation of Patinkin's argument than a spelling-out of something already implicit in it. Patinkin's emphasis is not on the degree of departure from unit elasticity (which may quickly become very slight) but on the distinction between an individual-experiment (portrayed in the demand curve for cash balances) and a market-experiment (portrayed in what he calls the "market-equilibrium curve"). Patinkin's discussion also helps show that the assumptions necessary to the quantity theory are less rigorous than traditionally supposed.

also aware of another type of curve that, under assumptions spelled out in admirable detail, would have the traditional unit elasticity. This other curve, which he calls the "market-equilibrium curve," expresses the comparative-static proposition that the equilibrium value of the purchasing power of the money unit is inversely proportional to the total money supply.

Patinkin makes perfectly clear what he is doing and, as Buchanan recognizes, cannot justly be accused of actual error. At worst he can be accused of an inexpedient approach conducive to error in the hands of persons less careful than himself. But this is a fuzzy charge — that a certain approach is not really erroneous, but conducive to error. Furthermore, an uncompensated money demand curve *is* useful; it is useful, for instance, in understanding the consequences of an attempt to "roll back" prices by decree. Precisely one of the difficulties is the fact that at a rolled-back price level, total real wealth (including the purchasing power of cash balances) would appear to the members of the community to be larger than it in fact could be under the objectively existing supply conditions. In understanding why disequilibrium price levels are untenable, we also understand the necessity of the equilibrium price level. There is more to economics than comparative statics; there is also the matter of equilibrating processes.

The question of expediency must be considered with special reference to Patinkin's listing of the supply of money among the factors affecting the demand for money. As the Chicagoans insist, it is admittedly desirable to apportion demand factors and supply factors into categories as separate and distinct as possible.[28] But what is to be done when the nature of the real world makes complete separation impossible? The only demand curve that never shifts is a curve — or hypersurface, rather — taking account of everything imaginable among the determinants of quantity demanded. A standard two-dimensional price-quantity demand curve is conceptually obtained by taking a cross-section or slice through a multidimensional hyperspace. To seek a curve that stays put on a two-dimensional price-quantity slice despite shifts in supply is to chase a will o' the wisp; the reason is the hard fact of reality that everything does depend on everything else. Shifts in price-quantity curves are an expedient necessary for dealing on flat sheets of paper with matters involving general interdependence. Of course, when this interdependence is negligible, as when we are dealing with a commodity without significant substitutes or complements and on which buyers spend only a small fraction of their incomes, then the shifts of the demand curve on a two-dimensional diagram are too small to worry about; and for practical purposes we can regard the demand curve as

[28]"We want demand functions precisely in order to analyze the effect of changes in supply; and they can be useful for this purpose only if the factors affecting demand can be regarded as largely independent of the factors affecting supply. We want demand analysis to be so constructed as to fit together and be consistent with supply analysis; yet we also want the two to be largely independent." Friedman, *Journal of Political Economy* (June, 1954), *op. cit.*, p. 265.

staying fixed in the face of supply changes. When interdependence is important, however, and when demand factors and supply factors cannot be kept substantially separate, the most straightforward way of dealing with this fact of reality is to follow Patinkin in recognizing that supply itself influences the position of the demand curve. The rival Chicago approach seems at least as awkward and at least as bedeviled with concepts of questionable operational meaning.

It is ironic, incidentally, that the criticism of Patinkin for allowing supply to affect demand should come from the very methodological camp which itself insists on building supply considerations directly into the demand curve. For this is what the Chicagoans are doing when they insist on constant-real-income or constant-production-possibility demand curves and criticize a Hicksian demand curve on the grounds that a fall in price along it implies an increase in real income which is incompatible with supply conditions.[29]

Usefulness and Operationality — Conclusion

One further aspect of the Chicago methodology remains to be considered. The Chicagoans repeatedly purport to compare the practical "usefulness" of different varieties of demand curve.[30] Though the present paper has so far uncritically adopted such references to "usefulness," I must now confess that, except perhaps in special contexts, I honestly do not know what it means to make practical "use" of one demand curve rather than of another. Sometimes Friedman seems to be claiming practical usefulness for his demand concept only in comparison with a Walrasian function into which, in principle, all prices individually enter. For the analysis of concrete real-world situations, it is of course impossible to draw up actual Walrasian demand functions; any demand curve for practical employment must be a partial curve. But as far as the choice between a Friedman demand curve and an ordinary Hicksian demand curve is concerned, it is hard to see what is meant by employing one rather than the other. Suppose a railroad hires a consulting economist to predict how the volume of railroad travel would respond to a cut in fares. Just what would it mean to tell this economist that the Friedman-Marshall demand curve is more "useful" and that he should work with it rather than with a

---

[29]So convinced is Friedman of the necessity for keeping real income constant along the demand curve that in one passage he interprets even the Hicksian construction as attempting to do this, though unsuccessfully. The real issue between rival concepts of the demand curve centers, he says, on the definition of the real income to be kept constant. The Hicksian construction goes astray by inappropriately defining real income as purchasing power over all goods except the particular one for which the demand curve is drawn. *Journal of Political Economy* (June, 1954), *op. cit.*, p. 262. This is certainly a strained reinterpretation of the forthright Hicksian specification that *money* income and all prices but one, and *not* real income, are to be supposed constant (in the individual-experiment sense, of course).

[30]Friedman concedes, for example, that the Hicksian approach is not actually "wrong." Though "formally valid," it is open to the objection of not being the most "useful" approach. Friedman, *Journal of Political Economy* (June, 1954), *op. cit.*, p. 262.

Hicksian curve? Can the economist really bother with deciding whether or not to suppose that the fare cut is accompanied by rises in other prices so as to keep constant the real incomes of passengers and potential passengers?

Similarly, what would it mean to claim greater operationality for the Friedman-Marshall demand curve on the grounds that it unequivocally predicts an inverse price-quantity relation, whereas the Hicksian demand theorists hedge this prediction with reference to the Giffen paradox?[31] The Chicagoans, correspondingly, could always explain away the failure of one of their own predictions on the grounds that real income had not been kept constant as it should have been. And, of course, anyone venturing a prediction could always take refuge in postulated changes in tastes, expectations, and so forth.

If a demand curve is to be conceived of as a set of predictions of the various price-quantity equilibria that would actually be established and observed under various supply situations, then it is appropriate to doubt whether opportunities to keep real incomes constant by compensating price variations can be created and whether the techniques of econometrics will ever develop to the point where it makes sense to draw a distinction between actual predictions by means of a Hicksian demand curve and actual predictions by means of a Friedman-Marshall demand curve. The overwhelming econometric difficulties in the way of actually drawing up one or both curves are not the main issue. More fundamentally, there is no such things as *the* Hicksian or *the* Friedman-Marshall relation between price and quantity demanded of a given commodity. The amount per time period that buyers would demand at any given price depends on how long a time period buyers are conceived of as having to adjust to a newly established price, on the price history of the commodity, and on innumerable other circumstances.

So far, this paper has uncritically tolerated the notion of the demand curve. Usually there is no reason to stress something that most economists are no doubt aware of anyway: that the real world never contains an actual entity corresponding to *the* demand curve for a commodity. Here, however, the point is relevant. Rather than as a set of numerical predictions, a demand curve might better be regarded as a pedagogical device for helping students grasp the inverse price-quantity relation asserted by the Law of Demand. A demand curve is an aid to straight thinking (helping avoid confusion, for example, between changes in demand and in quantity demanded). The demand curve—or rather the Law of Demand which it portrays, together with the Law of Supply—helps us understand why a free market tends to clear itself

[31]Actually, I do not regard mention of the Giffen paradox as a mere empty hedge. While I never expect to hear of an adequately documented real-world instance of it, the phenomenon could conceivably occur; and in being able to explain a range of potential phenomena to this extent broader than the range explainable by the Chicago demand theory, the Hicksian construction is superior. The assertion that an observed positive association between price and quantity demanded is an instance of the Giffen paradox need not be a metaphysical proposition. It can be meaningful: evidence can be obtained by questioning the persons involved. The legitimacy of this kind of evidence has already been alluded to.

(and seeing this depends on seeing what forces would be at work in a disequilibrium situation in which buyers' and sellers' plans did *not* mesh). The generalizations portrayed by demand and supply curves enter into explanations of the rationing and production-motivating functions of price. They help us understand how prices act as signals transmitting relevant information to decision-makers and how an economy without central planning can nevertheless be a co-ordinated economy. They help us understand, qualitatively and without numerical precision, what would happen to price and quantity when tastes or technology or taxes underwent specified changes. They help us understand the consequences of price ceilings and floors. We can go a long way in economic theory with a mere knowledge of the signs of partial derivatives. Of course, it is all the better, in definite historical situations, to have a pretty good idea of the magnitudes as well; the consulting economist for the railroad would certainly think so. But even this last consideration does not justify regarding demand curves as objectively existing things.

The Chicagoans sometimes appear to fall into just the non-operational metaphysics against which they warn other economists. In particular, their worries about which is the correct or most useful conception of the demand curve seem to imply that a substantive issue is involved and that a demand curve is something which objectively exists and whose properties should be rightly rather than wrongly perceived. To suppose so is to verge on the fallacy of "conceptual realism," the "reification" of concepts. Of course, Friedman implicitly disavows reification and implicitly recognizes that theoretical concepts, far from corresponding to actual things are but tools employed in the gathering and systematization of data.[32] In practice, however, the Chicagoans sometimes seem to forget this.

The foregoing survey of Chicago demand methodology provides new support for a familiar proposition that K. Klappholz and J. Agassi have recently restated with eloquence. They deplore "the illusion that there can exist in any science methodological rules the mere adoption of which will hasten its progress" and warn against the impatient "belief that, if only economists adopted this or that methodological rule, the road ahead would at least be cleared (and possibly the traffic would move briskly along it)." They recognize that methodological dogmas can even retard progress. This is particularly true, I might add, of methodological taboos. As the Chicagoans themselves have impressively illustrated in their work apart from propounding methodological advice, it is far more constructive to show the actual application of particular methods to particular problems: success speaks for itself. On the other hand, there is no warrant for *exclusive* insistence on particular methods, successful though they may have been in answering particular questions. Klappholz and Agassi will heed only the general "exhortation to be critical and always ready to subject one's hypotheses to critical scrutiny." Additional rules to reinforce this general maxim are "likely to be futile and possibly harmful."[33]

---

[32]Cf., e.g., Friedman, *Essays, op. cit.*, p. 57.

[33]K. Klappholz and J. Agassi, "Methodological Prescriptions in Economics," *Economica*, Vol. XXVI, N. S. (February, 1959), pp. 60, 74.

6. THE PRESENT STATE OF CONSUMPTION THEORY A SURVEY ARTICLE*

H. S. Houthakker†

INTRODUCTION

In the following survey I shall be mostly concerned with developments in the theory of consumer's choice during the last 25 years or so. My starting point, with which the reader is assumed to be reasonably familiar, is Hicks' classical exposition in the first three chapters and the mathematical appendix of *Value and Capital* [48]. Empirical research as such is outside the scope of this article, but the emphasis will be on those theoretical developments that are of importance for empirical research, rather than those connected with welfare economics. I have not, however, taken a narrow view of what may be important for empirical research, and have for instance devoted more space to the foundations of the theory than might otherwise be warranted.

The survey is divided into four sections. The first is devoted to the logical foundations of consumer's choice. It represents an effort to explain in nontechnical language what is inevitably a somewhat esoteric subject. The second section deals with the classical theory of consumer's choice, that is, the theory that operates with the aid of the infinitesimal calculus of constrained maxima and expresses its conclusions in terms of derivatives and elasticities. Under this heading come such subjects as substitution and complementarity, rationing, taste and quality variations, special preference structures, and duality. The third section, like the first and second, remains within the realm of the single individual, and discusses attempts to go beyond the classical framework by considering nonnegativity, dynamic phenomena, indivisibilities and uncertainty. The fourth and final section is concerned with problems of aggregation, including the possible interactions between consumers' preferences.

The usual disclaimers are in order here. While I have tried to cover all important developments in the last quarter century, much relevant material may have escaped my attention and, in any case, a judgment of what is important has a subjective element. I have not referred to contributions that

*From *Econometrica*, Vol. XXIX, No. 4 (October, 1961), pp. 704–740. Reprinted by permission of the publisher and the author.

†H. S. Houthakker, Professor of Economics, Harvard University. This is one in a series of survey articles which *Econometrica* has published with the support of the Rockefeller Foundation. The author gratefully acknowledges Paul Samuelson's helpful comments.

were not available in printed form at the time of writing, but occasionally the published material has been supplemented by my own speculations on possible future developments. Since the present survey is systematic rather than historical I have not hesitated to benefit from hindsight wherever this appeared to improve the exposition.

THE FOUNDATIONS

In many disciplines, be they mathematics or law, biology or literary criticism, the so-called foundations are the subject of more disagreement than are the substantive contributions. The view that foundations are fundamental, in fact, has been aptly dismissed by Savage [101] as "naive first-things-firstism." We need not go all the way with Friedman [33] in holding that a theory should be judged entirely by its conclusions, but few of us would still want to judge it entirely by its assumptions. If I start with the foundations, therefore, this is merely for convenience in exposition. The reader who dislikes hair-splitting is advised to skip section 1, *The Foundations*.

The principal qualification to Friedman's methodological position that needs to be made is that in a well-developed theory the distinction between assumptions and conclusions disappears. If a theory reaches logical (as opposed to empirical) perfection, the assumptions under which any conclusion is derived are just strong enough for that purpose; in other words the assumptions are necessary and sufficient for the conclusions, and each may be judged by the other. The theory then becomes a list of equivalent relations between two sets of concepts, neither one of which is more fundamental than the other. An example is the equivalence between points and lines in analytical geometry, or the duality between activity levels and shadow prices in linear programming.

The theory of consumer's choice has not quite reached this level of development, though it is close to it. In fact, the remarks just made about assumptions and conclusions may serve as a clue to the understanding of the historical development of consumption theory from its beginning to our day.

Early History

This history of the theory of consumer's choice is marked by a succession of generalizations. Gossen [42], who made the first systematic contribution to the subject, assumed that consumer's preferences could be represented by a sum of quadratic expressions in the quantities consumed, all cross-product terms being zero. Jevons [61] independently introduced a more general assumption, namely that the utility function is a sum of arbitrary functions with diminishing second derivatives, still not involving cross-product terms. Edgeworth [26] and Auspitz and Lieben [11] went further and regarded utility as a function of all the quantities, without restrictions on cross-derivatives. All these authors viewed utility as cardinal, but Fisher [29] and Pareto [86] realized that if a utility function reaches a maximum at a certain point then any order-preserving transform of that function also reaches a maximum there; hence, such maximization involves only ordinal properties. Neither, however, was able to draw the full conclusions from this realization. It remained for Slutsky [102] to do so. His principal conclusions were the Slutsky inequality, which declares the compensated own-price derivatives to be negative, and the Slutsky equation, according to which the compensated cross-price derivatives are pairwise equal to each other. The distinction between income effects and substitution effects, fruitful in many areas of economics, also goes back to him.

In the eyes of some economists the generalizations mentioned had so undermined the reality of the utility concept that Cassel [16] proposed to do away with it altogether and start economics from demand functions rather than from preferences, which he declared to belong to psychology. Nevertheless, Cassel found it necessary to attribute to the demand functions properties (such as homogeneity of degree zero) that are completely arbitrary unless demand functions are held to reflect underlying preferences. A somewhat less extreme position was adopted by Allen ([3], [4]; see also Allen and Bowley, [6]) who based consumption theory not on the utility function, but on the marginal rates of substitution between commodities, thus admitting only comparisons between commodity bundles that are infinitesimally close to each other. Neither Cassel's nor Allen's views, however, found general acceptance; in the authoritative work of Hicks [47, 48] and Wold [123] the fundamental notions are those of indifference and of ordinal utility, as they were in Slutsky.

Nevertheless, the gradual erosion of the concept of utility, which to Edgeworth was "as real as his morning jam" [97] into something as shadowy as a set of indifference curves or even less, inevitably raised the question where this erosion should stop.

The Introduction of Revealed Preference

In an epoch-making paper Samuelson [96] proposed to "purge demand theory of vestigial traces of the utility concept" and to base the theory on those properties of demand functions whose retention is necessary for the application of the theory. Moreover, he proposed to consider only conditions that can be expressed in terms of individual price-quantity situations rather than in terms of derivatives of demand functions. By the latter restriction he hoped to make the theory more immediately verifiable.

To achieve this program Samuelson looked at price-quantity relations not in terms of demand functions for single commodities, as Marshall and most of his followers had done, but in terms of value sums. Value sums, which are nothing but sums of quantities each multiplied by its relevant price, had long been familiar from the theory of index numbers, but Samuelson gave them a more central position. In particular he emphasized certain inequalities among the value sums obtained by combining two sets of quantities with two sets of prices in all four possible ways.

Consider an individual who buys the quantities $\overset{1}{q}_1, \overset{1}{q}_2, \ldots, \overset{1}{q}_n$ when the prevailing prices are $\overset{1}{p}_1, \overset{1}{p}_2, \ldots, \overset{1}{p}_n$. His total expenditure is consequently $\Sigma_i \overset{1}{p}_i \overset{1}{q}_i$. Consider a second bundle of commodities $\overset{2}{q}_1, \overset{2}{q}_2, \ldots, \overset{2}{q}_n$ whose cost $\Sigma_i \overset{1}{p}_i \overset{2}{q}_i$ is no more at the prevailing prices than the cost of the bundle which he actually bought, that is to say

$$\sum_i \overset{1}{p}_i \overset{2}{q}_i \leqslant \sum_i \overset{1}{p}_i \overset{1}{q}_i.$$

Consequently the consumer could have bought the second bundle when he actually bought the first. By choosing the first bundle rather than the second he revealed a preference for the first. Therefore, we can say that the first bundle is revealed to be preferred to the second, or in symbols

$$\overset{1}{q} R \overset{2}{q}.$$

Now consider the set of prices $\overset{2}{p}_1, \overset{2}{p}_2, \ldots, \overset{2}{p}_n$ at which the second bundle $\overset{2}{q}$ is actually bought. What can we say about the cost of the first bundle at the second set of prices? We know that the first bundle is revealed to be preferred to the second, and if this relation is to mean anything, the second bundle should not be revealed to be preferred to the first. According to the definition of the relation R, the second bundle would be revealed to be preferred to the first if $\Sigma \overset{2}{p} \overset{1}{q} \leqslant \Sigma_i \overset{2}{p} \overset{2}{q}$. The latter inequality must be false, hence $\Sigma_i \overset{2}{p} \overset{1}{q} > \Sigma_i \overset{2}{p} \overset{2}{q}$.

Consistency of preferences therefore requires that if the second bundle can be bought at the first set of prices, then the first bundle cannot be bought at the second set of prices. It may be noted that this implication goes only one way; if the second bundle is too expensive at the first set of prices, nothing follows about the cost of the first bundle at the second set of prices. In the terminology of symbolic logic, a discipline which has found fruitful applications in the foundations of consumer's choice, the implication just stated means that the relation R is antisymmetric.

What has been achieved so far is nothing but a generalization of the law of demand to arbitrary price changes. To see how it relates to the ordinary law of demand we need only put $\Sigma_i \overset{1}{p} \overset{2}{q}$ equal to $\Sigma_i \overset{1}{p} \overset{1}{q}$ and assume that the vectors p^1 and p^2 are identical except for one (say the first) price. After some subtractions we then get that

$$\text{if } \Sigma \overset{1}{p} \overset{2}{q} = \Sigma \overset{1}{p} \overset{1}{q} \text{ then } \Sigma(\overset{1}{p}_1 - \overset{2}{p}_1)(\overset{1}{q}_1 - \overset{2}{q}_1) < 0,$$

or in words: if a price changes in such a way that in the new situation the consumer can buy what he bought in the old, then the price change and the quantity change are necessarily of opposite signs. If p^1 and p^2 differ in more than one component the implication becomes

$$\text{if } \Sigma p^1 q^2 = \Sigma p^1 q^1 \text{ then } \Sigma(p^1 - p^2)(q^1 - q^2) < 0,$$

illustrating the fact (Hicks [48]) that complementarity is on balance weaker than substitution, so that on the whole the relation between price changes and quantity changes is still negative.

Considered as a deduction from the assumption of consistent preferences the above is interesting but hardly revolutionary. Its importance derives from Samuelson's suggestion that the generalized law of demand includes all or most of the observable implications of the theory of consumer's choice. This law might therefore provide the touchstone by which the adequacy of a system of axioms of utility could be judged: if the system implied less than the generalized law of demand, it would be too weak; if it implied more, it would be too strong. To put it in another way, suppose we regard the generalized law of demand as our basic postulate, what does it imply about consumer's preferences?

As a basic postulate on demand functions the generalized law of demand has later become known as "the weak axiom of revealed preference." In an appendix to his original paper Samuelson [96] used this axiom to show that demand functions are single-valued and homogeneous of degree zero. He was unable, however, to establish the symmetry of the substitution term in the Slutsky equation.

Axiomatic Analysis

At this point it remained an open question, therefore, whether the new approach had really exhausted the implications of the old one. In his later work, and especially in *Foundations of Economic Analysis* [97] Samuelson started a more systematic investigation of the equivalence of the two sets of axioms, one of which refers to a consumer's preferences and the other to his demand functions. Since the derivation of the weak axiom of revealed preference from utility theory is fairly obvious, the main question is how to derive the structure of preferences from a knowledge of value-sums only.

For this purpose it is convenient to extend the revealed preference relation R into a new relation S by allowing evidence from intermediate bundles. Suppose, for instance, that the bundle q^0 is revealed to be preferred to q^1, and that q^1 is revealed to be preferred to q^2. In that case we may say that q^0 is indirectly revealed to be preferred to q^2, or in formula q^0Sq^2. More generally we may consider a sequence of bundles q^0, q^1, . . ., q^{n-1}, q^n such that each bundle is directly revealed to be better than its successor in the sequence (q^0Rq^1, q^1Rq^2, . . ., $q^{n-1}Rq^n$); we then say again that q^0Sq^n. The effect of introducing the more comprehensive relation S is to increase the amount of information by which the preference relation between two bundles can be determined. Little [69] showed that, in the case of two commodities, it is possible to classify nearly all bundles into two classes: those to which q^0 is (directly or indirectly) revealed to be preferred and those which are revealed to be preferred to q^0, where q^0 is any fixed bundle. The expression "nearly all" refers to the fact that the bundles which cannot be thus classified form a one-dimensional set in two-dimensional space, or, in other words, a curve. This curve is deceptively similar to the well-known indifference curve, but Little preferred to call it a "behavior line"; the reasons that led him to this distinction will be discussed in the next subsection.

Little's proof was based on the weak axiom of revealed preference, on the differentiability of the demand functions, and on the so-called Lipschitz condition, which insures the boundedness of changes in demand and is fairly trivial in the case of consumption. These assumptions are not sufficient to prove a similar result for three or more commodities. We saw above that consistency of preferences implies that the relation R is antisymmetric. This consistency also implies that the relation S is antisymmetric, in other words, that it is not possible to get a contradiction by considering a chain of bundles, each of which is preferred to the preceding one, while the final one is revealed to be preferred to the initial one. Since R is merely a special case of S (a chain with one link), the antisymmetry of S implies the antisymmetry of R; the converse is not true, however. One counter-example may be found in (Hicks [51], p. 111).

To cover the case of three or more commodities it is necessary to introduce the antisymmetry of S as a separate axiom, which has become known as the strong axiom of revealed preference. It was shown by Houthakker [54] that the strong axiom, the Lipschitz condition and certain continuity conditions imply the existence of a consistent system of preferences from which the demand functions could have been derived. Part of this proof was corrected later by Corlett and Newman [18]. The strong axiom is very similar to a condition known as acyclicity introduced by von Neumann and Morgenstern [120] and also to a condition on demand functions proposed by Ville [119] in a somewhat different context.

With these developments the aim of the revealed preference approach, namely to formulate equivalent systems of axioms on preferences and on demand functions, had nearly been reached, although a number of subtle points remained to be cleared up. Before proceeding I have to deal with a number of misunderstandings which came to a head in the subsequent literature. Wold [125] declared the revealed preference approach to be nothing but a variant of Cassel's demand function approach, whereas in fact it avoids the basic weakness of Cassel's approach by specifying conditions on the demand functions. Allen [5], misinterpreting Corlett and Newman's paper mentioned above, denied that the strong axiom did what it was intended to do. Newman's endeavors to axiomatize revealed preference ([84] and elsewhere) were unfortunately vitiated by logical errors, but they did much to stimulate interest in the subject. The critical remarks of Green [44] and especially of Mishan [78], on the other hand, followed from nothing more illuminating than a failure to distinguish between properties of preferences and properties of demand functions.

Of greater interest was a point raised by Arrow [9], who argued that the strong axiom is redundant because in the case of direct comparisons between two commodity bundles there is only need for the weak axiom. Such direct comparisons, exemplified by the statement "I like bundle 1 better than bundle 2," are foreign to the revealed preference approach, which concerns itself with demand functions and not with choices outside a market context. Nevertheless, a question remained as to the influence of the continuity conditons present in Houthakker's proof; it was conceivable that demand functions which satisfy sufficiently strong continuity assumptions as well as the weak axiom would implicitly also satisfy the strong axiom. This question was settled by Gale [37], who gave an example of a set of demand functions that are continuous and satisfy the weak but not the strong axiom. He concluded that the introduction of the strong axiom was indeed necessary.

Lexicographic Preferences

We must now temporarily return to a matter raised in connection with Little's article of 1949 [69], namely his reasons for speaking of "behavior lines" rather than indifference curves. To explain Little's remarks on indifference curves, it is sufficient to refer to the case of two commodities discussed in every elementary textbook. According to the usual treatment, indifference curves are nonintersecting and concave to the origin; no point on any indifference curve is supposed to be preferred or dispreferred to any other point on that same curve.[1] To see which point is optimal in a given price-income situation, however, it is sufficient to find a point at which the budget line touches an indifference curve. All other points on or under the budget line are necessarily inferior to the tangency point; because of the strict concavity of the indifference curve, there is only one optimal point.

In this argument, it should be noted, nothing is said about the other points on the indifference curve which touches the budget line. Any point on an indifference curve, in fact, is chosen in some price-income situation in which it is compared not with points on the same indifference curve, but with points on or below a certain budget line. As long as budget lines are straight, therefore, it is never necessary to compare points on the same "indifference curve" with each other. In the study of market behavior the concept of indifference is never used at all, and this is why Little preferred the term "behavior line." Even if one point on an alleged indifference curve were

[1]Moreover, I have assumed throughout—though this is not always necessary—that the indifference curves have no kinks or flat sections.

preferred to another point on the same curve this would never show up in any actual market choice.

There is consequently no need for the traditional assumption that the points on behavior lines are neither dispreferred nor preferred to each other. All that matters is that the points on any behavior curve are preferred to any points on behavior curves closer to the origin, and dispreferred to any points on behavior curves farther away from the origin. Among the commodity bundles in two-dimensional space, therefore, there may be a hierarchy of preference orderings: the primary ordering is that between points on different behavior lines; in addition, there may be a secondary ordering of points on the same behavior line. An ordering of this hierarchical kind, which can easily be extended to three or more dimensions, is known as "lexicographical." Little's discussion (see also [70]) of these points was somewhat unconvincing; for clearer treatments see Georgescu-Roegen [39] and Chipman [17]. Debreu [23] established sufficient conditions for an ordering not to be lexicographical.

By undermining the concept of indifference, Little also forced a reconsideration of the utility function. Ordinal utility, as is well known, may be defined as a numbering of indifference classes, preferred classes getting higher numbers. The classical utility function is, therefore, a one-dimensional number or scalar. If the ordering is lexicographical, we can still define a utility function for each of the hierarchical orderings separately. Thus, there will be one utility function for the primary ordering, that holding between bundles on different behavior lines; a second utility function will permit a description of the preference relations between bundles on the same behavior line, and so on for three or more dimensions.

The utility of a given bundle is now no longer a scalar, but a vector, whose components correspond to the different levels of the hierarchy. To compare two bundles, we look first at the first component of the utility vector; if these are the same we look at the second component, and so on. To determine which bundle is optimal in a given price-income situation, however, we need never look beyond the first component of the utility vector, and the classical (ordinal) utility function is therefore adequate, though unnecessarily restrictive in the sense that not all of its properties are used in deriving demand functions. This, of course, was precisely the reason why the cardinal utility function was discarded at the end of the 19th century. A derivation of the classical demand conditions without the use of a scalar utility function was undertaken by McKenzie [75]. The second and further components of the utility vector only become relevant in such purely theoretical cases as that of a perfectly discriminating monopolist, who would vary prices as a function of quantities in such a way as to follow each individual's behavior line.

Although the conception of utility as a vector is only of theoretical importance when we study market choices, it is more relevant to other applications of consumption theory not covered in this survey. Thus, the notions of equivalent and compensating variations (Hicks, [49]) and of constant-utility index numbers need some redefinition. This can no doubt be done without giving up the purposes for which these notions have been introduced.

Axiomatic Analysis (Resumed)

We are now prepared for the culmination of the above discussion, which is the formulation of two sets of axioms, one referring to preferences and the other to demand functions, which are logically equivalent to each other. Probably the earliest rigorous formulation of a system of axioms of preferences was undertaken by Wold [123]. Wold's system was not influenced by the revealed preference approach and it is not surprising, therefore, that his axioms are somewhat too strong, in the sense that some of the properties of preferences he postulates are not revealed in demand functions. Thus, the notion of indifference plays a prominent part in Wold's axioms.[2] In this respect the system of Uzawa [118] is more satisfactory. His axioms on demand functions may be informally rendered as follows:

(a) The quantities demanded are single-valued functions of prices and income.

(b) These functions are continuous in prices and income.

(c) They satisfy the strong axiom of revealed preference; that is, $q^1 Sq^2$ and q^2Sq^1 cannot both be true (see sub-section entitled *Axiomatic Analysis*, page 109).

(d) The quantities demanded are nonnegative; since they also satisfy a budget constraint, this, together with the other axioms, implies that they are of bounded variation and satisfy the so-called Lipschitz condition.

(e) All income is spent (possibly some of it on the commodity "savings"); this means there is no saturation.

The axioms on the preference relation are as follows:

A. The relation is transitive, that is if q^1Pq^2 and q^2Pq^3, then q^1Pq^3.

B. The relation is "almost" connected; except for a set of lower dimensionality than the commodity space (corresponding to Little's behavior line), it is always true that q^1Pq^2 or q^2Pq^1.

C. The relation is antisymmetric: if q^1 is preferred to q^2, then q^2 is not preferred to q^1.

D. The strict concavity of indifference surfaces is replaced by the following argument. Suppose that the bundle q^2 lies on the straight line between the bundles q^1 and q^3, and that q^1 is not preferred to q^3; then q^2 is preferred to q^1. The main purpose of this axiom, which applies equally well to conventional indifference curves as to a lexicographical ordering, is to insure that on any budget surface there is only one preferred bundle; this is achieved by applying the axiom to successively shorter intervals (q^1, q^3), each obtained from its predecessor by leaving out dispreferred points.

---

[2]Another aspect of Wold's synthesis is in need of clarification. One of his theorems asserts that demand functions derived from consistent preferences are not merely unique but reversible as well (implying a one-to-one correspondence between prices and quantities). This theorem was questioned by Samuelson [98], but no consensus has been reached. Recent work by Afriat [1] would seem to be relevant here.

E. If a bundle q^1 contains at least as much of every commodity as another bundle q^2, then q^1 is preferred to q^2. This axiom restricts the validity of the theory of consumer's choice to a region of the commodity space where there is no saturation.[3]

Apart from certain minor technical complications, Uzawa has shown that these two axiom systems are equivalent to each other. He has also shown that the strong axiom of revealed preference (axiom (c)) may be replaced by the weak axiom provided the demand functions satisfy a certain regularity condition; unfortunately the economic meaning of this latter condition has not been spelled out.

Evaluation

Since Uzawa's contribution appears to settle the remaining problems concerning the relation between the classical approach to consumer's choice and the revealed preference approach (at least if everything is convex, continuous, and non-saturated), this is a suitable point for stock-taking. To what extent has the revealed preference approach satisfied the expectations which it raised? If we regard it primarily as an attempt at theoretical clarification, it has certainly been successful. As Samuelson [98] pointed out, the longstanding question of integrability has at least been brought to a conclusion. As far as the foundations of the static theory of choice for a single consumer are concerned, we now know where we stand.

The revealed preference approach also reinforced the emphasis on observable implications that is gradually transforming consumption theory from a mere philosophizing about utility to an essential component of empirical research. The approach has, perhaps, not yet opened as many new avenues of research as had at one time been hoped, and it has been of rather limited assistance in coping with the well-known difficulties of aggregation and interpersonal comparison (see section entitled *Aggregation and Interaction*, page 131), but future work may yet modify this slight disappointment.

This may be a suitable place to mention one possible application of the axioms of revealed preference, namely in the analysis of differences in tastes. The axioms refer to a single individual at one instant of time, hence a violation of the axioms could always be ascribed to a change in tastes. Conversely, we can regard the axioms, whether applied to different individuals or to different instants of time, as a test of equality of tastes, if consistency is taken for granted. The attractions of this test are its simplicity and generality. It would be of great interest for the empirical study of consumption to know how much variation in tastes (among individuals, among countries, or over time) there actually is.

---

[3]This exclusion of saturation is one of the main weaknesses of existing axiomatic formulations. The phenomenon was to some extent covered by Wagner [121].

DEVELOPMENTS WITHIN THE CLASSICAL FRAMEWORK

In this section I shall discuss some developments in what might be termed the superstructure of the theory of consumer's choice, that is to say, some theorems that follow from this theory if certain more special assumptions are added to the basic axioms discussed in the previous section. From the point of view of empirical research such special theorems are often of greater importance than the general axioms. In this section I confine myself to developments within the classical theory, that is, the static theory valid for a single consumer in which only small changes around an equilibrium point are studied. Generalizations outside this framework will be taken up in the succeeding two sections.

Rationing and the Le Chatelier Principle

It will be convenient to start with the theory of rationing. This subject was surveyed some years ago in *Econometrica* by Tobin [115], and a few remarks in the present context should therefore be enough. It may be recalled that Rothbart [93] and Graaff [43] developed the notion of a "virtual price system," which, if it prevailed in a free market, would lead a consumer to buy the same quantities as he does under rationing. For the rationed commodities the virtual price system consequently gives the shadow prices, to use the term that has since become familiar from linear programming.

A somewhat different line of inquiry was taken up by Tobin and Houthakker [116] who analyzed the influence of changes in the rations of the rationed commodities on the demand for the unrationed commodities.[4] If coffee is rationed and milk is not, then the derivative of milk consumption with respect to income when coffee is rationed turns out to differ from the same derivative when coffee is not rationed by an amount proportional to the free-market derivative of coffee consumption with respect to income and to the derivative of milk consumption with respect to the coffee ration. Similar relations hold for the derivative of milk consumption with respect to any price change (whether compensated or not). The effect of a change in the coffee ration on the demand for milk, moreover, turns out to be proportional to the substitution effect of a change in the price of milk on the demand for coffee in a free market. Thus, if the substitution effect shows coffee and milk to be complements in a free market, then an increase in the coffee ration will cause the demand for unrationed milk to increase, but if tea is a substitute for coffee, the demand for tea will go down. Clearly there is a close connection between the comparative statics of a free market and the comparative statics of partial rationing. In this and the following arguments it is always assumed

[4] A similar analysis for the case of so-called points rationing was undertaken by McManus [76].

that the ration is "effective," that is, that the consumer always buys as much as he is allowed to do. The opposite case will be briefly discussed in the sub-section entitled *Random Variations of Preferences*, page 133.

Of particular interest is the influence of a change in the number of rationed commodities on the own-price substitution effect, that is on the effect of a compensated change in the own-price of an unrationed commodity. Samuelson [97] showed in another context that the own-price substitution effect must become smaller in absolute value as the number of rationed commodities increases. Because of an analogy with thermodynamics he called this the Le Chatelier principle, and he pointed out that this provides an exact basis for Marshall's distinction of the long and the short run, the difference between the two lying in the number of commodities that are held constant ("rationed").

An intuitive argument in support of the Le Chatelier principle runs as follows: Suppose we consider the own-price substitution effect on sugar with and without coffee rationing. Consider a compensated decrease in the sugar price. If sugar and coffee are complements, then such a fall will cause the consumption of both sugar and coffee to decline. If coffee consumption is held constant by rationing, however, the fall in sugar consumption will be less because some additional sugar is needed to complement the fixed amount of coffee. On the other hand, if sugar and coffee are substitutes, the own-price substitution effect on sugar under coffee rationing will also be smaller, because there is now less possibility of substituting coffee for sugar. In the limiting case where coffee and sugar are neither substitutes nor complements, that is to say if they are "independent," the own-price substitution effect will be the same with and without rationing.

It is seen from this intuitive argument that the Le Chatelier principle depends on the possibility of classifying pairs of commodities into substitutes and complements. This classification is unique if we confine ourselves to infinitesimal price changes, but it is entirely possible that two commodities act as complements under small price changes but as substitutes under large price changes, and conversely. It follows — and this can also be shown graphically — that the Le Chatelier principle holds only in the small and not necessarily in the large.

Changes in Tastes

In the conventional theory of consumer's choice tastes are normally assumed to be constant, but for some empirical and theoretical purposes it is also useful to be able to talk about changes in tastes. Thus, Allen and Bowley [6] discussed the effects of variations in preferences among households on the observed relation between total expenditure and the expenditure on particular items (see also the sub-section entitled *Random Variations of Preferences*, page 133). Another example of the possible importance of changes in tastes is provided by advertising which is partly directed to bringing such changes about.

Ichimura [60] defined an "isolated change in wants" as a change in preferences by which the marginal rate of substitution of a given commodity for all other commodities is multiplied by some fixed factor; the marginal rates of substitution among the "other" commodities are left unchanged. He showed (see also Hicks, [50]) that the effect of such an isolated change on the demand for any other commodity is proportional to the cross-substitution effect in the Slutsky equation. Thus, the effect of an isolated change in taste for coffee on the demand for tea is inversely proportional to the effect on tea of a compensated change in the price of coffee. A more elaborate analysis of changes in tastes was given by Basmann [12].

Duality

A third development with some bearing on the question of complementarity, though even more important in its own right, is connected with the notion of duality. This notion has recently become widely familiar as a result of linear programming and related developments, but its use in the theory of consumer's choice is actually older. According to consumption theory the demand for each commodity is a function of all prices and of income. These quantities, in turn, are the arguments of the utility function (or, if we prefer to follow Little as in the earlier sub-section, *Lexicographic Preferences*, page 111, the first component of the utility vector). Hence, as Hotelling [53] pointed out, utility is indirectly a function of prices and income.[5] The function that depends on prices and income may be called the "indirect" utility function, to distinguish it from the conventional "direct" function. Its indifference curves were drawn by Hicks [52]; there is a related discussion of "price functions" in Wold [123].

Roy [94, 95] made effective use of the indirect utility function to derive many of the classical properties of demand functions. The analytical usefulness of the indirect utility function turns especially on Roy's equation, $q_i = -\Psi'_i / \Psi'_\mu$, where Ψ'_i and Ψ'_μ are the partial derivatives of the indirect utility function with respect to the ith price and income, respectively. The indirect utility function, therefore, leads to an explicit expression for the demand

[5]Prices and income together represent $n + 1$ variables if there are n commodities; hence some additional restriction must be imposed. One possibility is to treat one of the commodities as a numéraire (with a price of one), but it is usually more convenient to introduce n new variables $z_i = p_i / \mu\ (i = 1, \ldots, n)$ where μ is income.

If the latter procedure is adopted it appears that the weak axiom of revealed preference (see the earlier sub-section entitled *The Introduction of Revealed Preference*, p. 107), is symmetric in the vectors q and z; it reads now

$$\text{if } \Sigma\, z^1 q^2 \leqslant 1 \text{ then } \Sigma\, z^2 q^1 > 1.$$

Contrary to a suggestion by Wold [125], the dual of the weak axiom is not different from the weak axiom itself. Similar remarks apply to the strong axiom.

functions, which is not, in general, the case with the direct utility function. Court [19] and Houthakker [55] showed that maximizing the direct utility function subject to a budget constraint is equivalent to minimizing the indirect utility function subject to the same constraint, in which, however, the quantities are regarded as given and the maximization refers to prices and income. Samuelson [100] generalized this approach by introducing a function of all n quantities and n prices in which any m quantities and $n-m$ prices ($0 \leqslant m \leqslant n$) may be regarded as given and the remaining quantities and prices derived by optimization. He especially studied the second order conditions for a saddle point in such a "minimum equilibrium system."

Duality was also stressed by Hicks [51], who pointed out that the "indirect" approach is actually closer to the work of the founders of utility theory than the "direct" approach, as may be seen from an interpretation of the "indirect" approach in terms of marginal valuation, that is, of the money value put by an individual on an additional unit of a commodity. The many conclusions which Hicks derives from the "indirect" approach, or "p-theory," as he calls it, can unfortunately not be discussed here. In a sense, however, Hicks overstates the advantages of the "indirect" approach. Following Mosak [82] he uses the two approaches to define two kinds of complementarity (or substitution), which he calls "p-complementarity" and "q-complementarity." The former is defined by the effect on the marginal valuation of a commodity of a change in the quantity of another commodity, while the latter is defined, as customary, by the substitution effect in the Slutsky equation. In the normal case when there are no additional restrictions on prices or quantities these two concepts are equivalent, but Hicks considers also the case where the price (and hence the marginal valuation) of a third commodity is held constant. He correctly concludes that holding a third price constant may change a pair of p-complements into p-substitutes, and considers this proof that, if such restrictions are admitted, p-complementarity is no longer equivalent to q-complementarity. In fact, however, the complementarity with a third price held constant is perfectly dual to q-complementarity when the quantity of a third commodity is held constant by rationing. Thus, if eggs and butter are q-substitutes in a free market, they may become q-complements when bacon is rationed, and they will then also be p-complements if the price of bacon is held constant.

The Structure of Preferences

We have seen how in the early stages of consumption theory the concept of utility was gradually generalized so as to admit any shape of marginal utility and any relation between pairs of commodities. More recently this process has to some extent been reversed. It has been increasingly realized that utility theory should make some allowance for the fact that some commodities appear to be more closely related than others, and that specific items can often be meaningfully grouped into larger categories. Thus, it seems intuitively clear that there is a closer connection between oranges and bananas than between oranges and overcoats, and that this idea may be given more precision by saying that oranges belong under the heading "food" and overcoats under the heading "clothing." The notion of commodity groups had already been recognized by Leontief [65] and by Hicks [48]; the latter proved that for theoretical purposes a number of commodities may be considered as one group if their relative prices remain unchanged.[6] Although this grouping theorem has many useful applications, it does not come fully to grips with the problem just mentioned.

An important step in that direction was made by Leontief [66] with his discussion of the "internal structure" of functional relationships. In this theory, utility does not necessarily depend on the quantities consumed themselves; it may also depend on certain intermediate entities which themselves are functions of the quantities consumed, or of still further entities of the same kind. The utility function is then called "separable." Leontief's theory was not particularly directed to consumption, but Strotz [107] developed it in that direction by elaborating the concept of a "utility tree." Thus, utility may be a function of two quantities called "nutrition" and "amusement," while "nutrition" in turn depends on the quantities of "starches," "protein foods," etc., and "starches" in its turn depends on the quantities consumed of bread, rice, etc. Strotz also derived some of the observable implications of a utility tree in terms of demand functions; unfortunately they cannot be easily summarized. His analysis was corrected and expanded by Gorman [41].

An important special case of a utility tree is the case where the utility function is a sum of separate functions, each of which depends on only one quantity; this is essentially the case discussed by Jevons, often described as "independent utilities." Its special features had been investigated by a series of authors, among others Friedman [32], Bergson [13], and Samuelson [97]. Houthakker [58] showed that the case of independent utilities, or "direct additivity" as he called it, implies that the cross-derivatives of demand are proportional to the derivatives with respect to income, while a certain expression involving the own-price derivatives is the same for all commodities; these conditions are necessary and sufficient. Similarly he showed that the indirect utility function can be written as a sum of one-variable functions if and only if the cross-price derivatives are proportional to the quantities consumed. In general, a preference ordering cannot be both directly and indirectly additive; if it is, all income elasticities must be equal

[6]Leontief considered the case where a number of commodities are consumed in fixed proportions. According to a theorem of Houthakker [55], however, there are certain composite price changes which will change the ratios between any two quantities consumed. Hence, if two or more commodities are always consumed in fixed proportions they *must* be considered as one commodity for theoretical purposes.

to one. Some of the limitations of direct additivity were brought out by Green [45].

A somewhat different problem, also important for empirical research, was investigated by Fourgeaud and Nataf [31]. They found the class of preference orderings for which it is strictly legitimate to represent "real income" by an index number and to express prices in real terms. Roy's method of analysis (see the sub-section entitled *Duality*, page 117) proved to be especially useful here. Similar questions were also taken up independently by Rajaoja [91].

Cardinal Utility Reconsidered

Frisch [36] related the case of direct additivity to the concept of the flexibility of the marginal utility of income with respect to income, and showed how this flexibility can be derived from the demand functions. The importance of this result is that the flexibility is a cardinal rather than an ordinal concept, so that the old quest for measurable utility had suddenly acquired new respectability. It is indeed clear that direct and indirect additivity are not compatible with a merely ordinal interpretation of utility, for the equation $u(x_1,x_2) = u_1(x_1) + u_2(x_2)$ is not invariant under monotonic transformations of the utility function. Frisch [35] had previously made a well-known attempt at measuring utility, but this was based on the assumption that the marginal utility of income was independent of prices; Samuelson [97] showed that this implied that all Engel curves are straight lines through the origin, which is hardly a plausible assumption. The assumption of direct additivity is more plausible, at least if the "commodities" observed are relatively broadly defined (for instance, food, clothing), as Konus [64] had pointed out for the case of indirect additivity.

It is widely believed that the development of the theory of choice from Fisher and Pareto through Hicks and Allen has somehow eliminated the notion of cardinal utility altogether, and the study of additive utility functions may therefore seem to be a step backward. Actually what this development showed was not that utility cannot be cardinal, but merely that appeal to its cardinal properties is not necessary for deriving a number of fundamental conclusions on demand functions in general. This does not rule out the possibility of additional features, displayed by more special classes of demand functions, which restrict the transformations under which utility functions are invariant. Such additional features, for instance, are displayed by the classes of demand functions corresponding to directly or indirectly additive utility functions. While cardinality is not revealed by the most general demand function, it is revealed by these special classes. Cardinalists, such as Robertson [92], who view utility as necessarily cardinal under all circumstances, can clearly derive absolutely no comfort from the remarks of this section.

Complements and Substitutes

With this somewhat backhanded resurrection of cardinal utility the problem of defining complementarity and substitution has also been placed in a different light. Direct additivity means that there is no complementarity or substitution in the sense of Pareto and Edgeworth, whose definition was subsequently rejected because it involved cardinal utility. If we assume direct additivity, however, we can at least say what the observable implications of the absence of Pareto-Edgeworth complementarity or substitution are, and this may be of interest to those who feel that independence in this sense has some intuitive plausibility.

On the other hand, the results discussed in the sub-sections entitled *Rationing and the Le Chatelier Principle* and *Changes in Tastes*, pages 115 and 116, confirm the importance of the Hicks-Allen definition based on compensated price changes. We have seen that the relationship between two commodities according to this definition is also decisive for their relationship under partial rationing or under isolated changes in tastes.

Not to be confused with Pareto-Edgeworth substitutability is another notion which has played a role in discussions of the stability of general equilibrium; it is the notion of "gross substitutability" (Metzler, [77]). Two commodities are gross substitutes if the uncompensated cross-price-derivatives involving them are both positive. The assumption that has turned out to be particularly fruitful in stability discussions is that all commodities are gross substitutes for each other. As can easily be shown by summation over all commodities, this implies that all uncompensated own-price elasticities are less than -1: if raising one price increases the quantity bought of, and hence the expenditure on, all other commodities, then the expenditure on the commodity itself must go down (total expenditure being constant), and hence, the elasticity must be less than -1. The assumption of universal gross substitutability is therefore not as innocuous as it appears at first sight. Similarly, universal gross complementarity implies that all own-price elasticities are greater than -1.

Particular Utility Functions

The study of particular utility functions (or preference orderings) is of special interest to empirical demand analysis and to index number theory, neither of which subjects can be covered in this survey. Some functions that have found empirical application are the following. The quadratic (direct) utility function

$$\Psi^{\circ}(q_1, \ldots, q_n) = \sum_{i=1}^{n} a_i q_i + \tfrac{1}{2} \sum_{j=1}^{n} \sum_{k=1}^{n} A_{jk} q_j q_k$$

goes back to Gossen but was investigated in more detail by Bowley ([14] and elsewhere) and Wald ([122] and elsewhere). It gives rise to linear Engel curves (see, however, the *Nonnegativity* sub-section), which are on the whole unrealistic; moreover, the quantity-price relations corresponding to it are of a fairly intractable form. The "linear" utility function (Klein and Rubin, [63]; Samuelson, [97]; Stone, [105]) also gives linear Engel curves, which all go through the same point and hence are even more restrictive; its attraction is that the demand functions are linear in prices. The double-logarithmic demand functions that are so useful empirically unfortunately do not agree with theory because the sum of the expenditures on particular items is not identically equal to total expenditure, but it is possible to overcome this difficulty by slight modifications. Thus, Konus [64] and Leser [67] introduced what Houthakker [58] called the "indirect addilog" utility function

$$\Psi^*\left(\frac{p_1}{\mu}, \ldots, \frac{p_n}{\mu}\right) = \sum_{i=1}^{n} a_i\left(\frac{p_i}{\mu}\right)^{b_i}$$

where u is total expenditure. This function is additive in the sense of the previous sub-section, *The Structure of Preferences*, page 118; it implies, among other things, that the ratios of the expenditures on any two commodities are double-logarithmic functions of total expenditure and hence that the differences between income elasticities are constant. Leser used it for a partial solution of the problem first raised by Pigou [88] of deriving price elasticities from cross-section data. Another modification is "direct addilog" (Houthakker, [58]) for which

$$\Psi(q_1, \ldots, q_n) = \sum_{i=1}^{n} \alpha_i q_i^{\beta_i}$$

and for which the ratios between income elasticities are constant. As Arrow and Hurwicz [10] pointed out, however, a "direct addilog" utility function implies universal gross substitutability (see sub-section entitled *Complements and Substitutes*, page 121), which has empirically undesirable consequences for the own-price elasticities; "indirect addilog" similarly entails universal gross complementarity.[7]

It must therefore be concluded that no completely satisfactory utility function (or system of demand functions) has yet been found. Perhaps there is none, but the search has hardly started and should be pursued. The discovery of such a function might put empirical demand analysis on a much

---

[7]The preference orderings represented by direct and indirect addilog may be termed each other's "counterpart," since they have the same mathematical form but with the variables replaced by their duals. The counterpart of the (direct) quadratic utility function discussed above is the "indirect quadratic." The Engel curves corresponding to it are closely related to those proposed by Törnqvist [117], where the expenditure on any particular item is a ratio of linear functions of total expenditure. Törnqvist's curves do not add up to total expenditure and therefore cannot be exactly derived from utility analysis. Rajaoja [91] claimed to have done so, but her derivation involves approximations. The Engel curves for the "indirect" quadratic differ from Törnqvist's principally in that the *proportion* of total expenditure spent on an item (rather than the expenditure itself) is a ratio of linear functions of total expenditure.

firmer theoretical footing and contribute also to its statistical aspects. Of course, dynamic and aggregative considerations, taken up below, will also have a bearing on the further integration of theory and empirical research.

DEVELOPMENT OUTSIDE THE CLASSICAL FRAMEWORK

Limitations of the Standard Case

Classical consumption theory, to which I have confined myself so far, deals with a highly idealized standard case. It assumes that the consumer has definite preferences for varying quantities of a well-defined finite number of commodities, and that he chooses the best combination available to him subject to a given total expenditure. There is no explicit reference to time, and the theory, therefore, applies equally well to stocks as to flows. Moreover, since the analysis proceeds largely by means of classical calculus methods there is in general no way of knowing whether the maximizing quantities are negative or positive; furthermore, most of the theorems discussed so far (with the exception of those derived by revealed preference) describe the effects of small changes in the parameters, rather than large finite changes. The quantities themselves are assumed to be infinitely divisible.

It need hardly be said that these assumptions are for the most part unrealistic. The future usefulness of consumption theory will depend largely on the extent to which it will be possible to derive meaningful conclusions from more widely applicable assumptions. In reviewing what has been done so far I shall start with developments that stay most closely to the classical framework, and then proceed to dynamic and other generalizations.

Nonnegativity

Under the influence of linear programming it is by now generally recognized that meaningful maximization requires attention to the sign of the resulting magnitudes. Although changes in stocks, or some financial variables, can either be negative, zero, or positive, stocks themselves or quantities consumed can only be nonnegative. Nothing in ordinary calculus maximization guarantees a meaningful sign; to achieve this, additional constraints in the form of inequalities have to be imposed. Unless this is done, consumption theory can only make statements about small changes around a point which on other grounds is known to have only nonnegative components. An algorithm for maximizing a quadratic utility function with nonnegative variables was outlined by Houthakker [56, 57] who showed that in this case the Engel curves are no longer straight lines (as they are if no attention is paid to sign) but become continuous broken curves with linear segments. A comprehensive treatment of the effect of prices and income changes when nonnegativity is required has not been undertaken so far. There is a connection between nonnegativity and rationing, in which there are also additional constraints, though not in the form of inequalities.

An Infinite Number of Commodities

The question of nonnegativity has a bearing on a seemingly quite different approach, which is also a relatively mild generalization of classical consumption theory. I am referring to the extension to an infinite number of quantities, and indeed to a continuum of commodities, attempted by Court [19]. By introducing what he called "commodity spectra" Court was able to generalize the classical theorems of consumer's choice. Unfortunately it seems that in the case of infinitely many commodities the difficulty of obtaining meaningful signs is even more severe than in the case of a finite number. In the latter case we can at least assume that somehow we are at a point where all quantities are nonnegative, but this cannot be done when we have infinitely many and assume also, as seems reasonable (though Court apparently did not do so) that commodities that are close to each other on the spectrum are also close substitutes. To take an example, if part of our spectrum consists of shoes of different sizes and if size is regarded as a continuous variable, then shoes of almost the same size are evidently very close substitutes. It is also clear that if two commodities are close substitutes, then maximization without regard to sign will produce a negative quantity for one and a positive quantity for the other. (Consider, for instance, the extreme case where the quantities are X and Y and the utility function is $U = - XY$.) It appears, therefore, that if we maximize utility over a continuum of commodities, then "adjacent" commodities must have opposite signs, and the optimal spectrum is highly discontinuous if it exists at all. From an economic point of view nothing is gained by restricting maximization to continuous functionals, as is usually done in the conventional calculus of variations. The correct approach evidently is to maximize with nonnegativity constraints. In that case it appears that the maximizing spectrum must again be discontinuous, but not so irregular as in the previous instance. For any finite income the maximizing spectrum just consists of positive quantities for a finite number of commodities and zero for all others. It would seem that for the quadratic case at least one method of quadratic programming (see the subsection entitled *Nonnegativity*, page 123) can be extended to an infinite number of commodities without any great changes. The above remarks, however, are only intuitive conjectures, and the difficulties that arise seem to be worthy of the attention of professional mathematicians.

Despite these difficulties the extension of the classical theory of consumer's choice to a potentially infinite number of commodities, abstract though it may seem at first, promises useful results because it leads to statements not only on *how much* consumers buy, but also on *what* they buy. The latter problem was also attacked, along rather more pedestrian lines, by Theil [110] and Houthakker [55]. They assumed that each "commodity" or group of commodities is available in a continuous range of "qualities," of which each consumer buys exactly one. These approaches were suggested by the study of household budgets, where it has been found that the average price per unit of a "commodity" is invariably an increasing or constant function of total expenditure. It appears that this empirical regularity is not theoretically necessary, but there are a number of other statements that can be made about the influence of price changes of various kinds on quantities and qualities consumed. The price changes considered are not only those known from the classical theory, but also changes in the price differentials between different qualities.

Indivisibility

A more drastic departure from the framework of classical consumption theory is required by the study of indivisible commodities. Calculus or programming methods based on continuity cease to apply, though it seems likely that the recent development of integer programming may have some application in this area. Despite the practical importance of the problem of indivisible commodities, there is as yet nothing that can be described as a theory. That such a theory would have interesting features of its own is apparent from the suggestion of Morris [81] concerning what she called "complementary substitutes." She uses this somewhat paradoxical term to describe a phenomenon of which the following is an example. If a woman's income is so low that she can afford only one pair of shoes, she will buy a pair that can be worn on a great variety of different occasions. If she can afford two pairs, she will not buy two of the same kind as before, but two pairs that complement each other by being useful on different occasions. Phenomena of this kind will presumably be of importance in a general theory of indivisible commodities. One attempt at such a theory, by Theil [109], had some obvious flaws and seems unfortunately to have been abandoned by its author. Wagner [121] proposed an extension of the revealed preference approach to permit indivisible commodities.

Uncertainty

Still within the static framework, though again deviating in varying degrees from its basic assumptions, are theories involving uncertainty. Stimulated mostly by von Neumann and Morgenstern [120], a great deal of work has recently been done in this area, much of it by mathematicians and psychologists and mostly without specific reference to consumption. The survey of this field by Arrow [8] is still valuable. Among the approaches developed in this field, only two can be mentioned here. In the first, which is most closely associated with von Neumann and Morgenstern's conceptions (see for instance Luce [71]), the emphasis is on choice among objects which themselves have consequences with subjectively or objectively known probabilities; these objects may be visualized as generalized lottery tickets. The principal result in this approach, first obtained by Marschak [73] and definitively established by Herstein and Milnor [46], is that consistent choice among such tickets implies the existence of a cardinal utility function. The importance of this result for the study of consumption, however, would seem to be rather limited; even though the objects of consumer's choice are often affected by uncertainty, it is not yet clear that better explanations of consumer behavior can be obtained by emphasizing this particular aspect.

In this connection it may be useful to point out that the traditional theory of consumer's choice is not, as is often believed, a theory based on the assumption of certainty. What is assumed is that an individual can rank all objects available to him in order of desirability. Whether the results of obtaining these objects are certain or not is irrelevant, and in principle the classical theory applies just as well to lottery tickets as to any other object. What the new approach just referred to does contribute is a systematic analysis of probabilistic aspects on the *formation* of preferences. Such an analysis may no doubt be useful in contexts other than that of consumption.

Another approach involving uncertainty is more promising for consumption research. According to this line of thinking, which goes back at least to Georgescu-Roegen [38] and Armstrong [7] and was more recently developed by Davidson and Marschak [22], the fact that an individual *prefers* bundle *A* over bundle *B* does not mean that he will always *choose* bundle *A* rather than bundle *B* if both are available to him. It is assumed, on the contrary, that the individual will select bundle *A* over bundle *B* with a probability that depends on the strength of his preference of *A* over *B*. Thus, if the individual is indifferent between *A* and *B*, he will be equally likely to choose either. In this manner it is evidently possible to avoid the extreme deliberateness that classical theory attributes to the consumer. Another advantage, which it shares with the approach previously discussed, is the possibility of verification by means of psychological experiments. On the other hand this stochastic interpretation of the choice process seems to present formidable logical difficulties, and its implications for market behavior have not yet been worked out.

The Technology of Consumption

Diametrically opposed to the introduction of uncertainty into the theory of choice is another development which aims to render preferences less arbitrary by emphasizing the "technological" considerations underlying a large part of consumer's behavior. The conventional theory is not interested in the origin of preferences, but only in their consistency. The explanation of such empirical phenomena as Engel's law is outside its scope. We need not fall into deterministic materialism, however, to recognize that to some extent consumption is subject to laws similar to those of production. Thus, useful insights can be gained by looking at food expenditure from the point of view of nutrition, or at the purchase of appliances from the point of view of the allocation of time. It may be argued, for instance, that preferences really do not refer to specific commodities as such, but rather to the purposes which these commodities may serve. The relations between commodities serving the same purpose, or cooperating in the attainment of such purpose, could then sometimes be deduced from their objective properties rather than from subjective preferences, while the purposes themselves could still be subject to a preference ordering. There is an obvious connection here with the "utility trees" discussed in the sub-section entitled *The Structure of Preferences*, page 118. A technique such as linear programming may then help to explain choice at the "technological" level.

One of the earliest applications of what later became known as linear programming was made by Stigler [104] who determined a diet that would satisfy nutritional requirements at minimum cost. This early result was not such as to promise valuable insight into consumer behavior from this approach, for he found that the minimum cost diet would consist of a very small number of somewhat unpalatable commodities (such as navy beans, flour, and dried milk) and would be very cheap compared to actual expenditure on food. Clearly some essential factor determining actual food expenditures had been left out of account.

More recently, Smith [103] obtained a more realistic diet by imposing certain additional restrictions, mostly in order to avoid too much monotony. This, in fact, seems to be the road along which useful results can be derived. In another context, Wold [124] emphasized the role of day-to-day variety in food consumption habits. The effect of such variety is no doubt to make the food budget more expensive. It is conceivable that by taking into account the desirability of variety, and of more palatable foodstuffs, the pattern of food expenditures for different price-income constellations could be explained along these more or less "technological" lines. Similarly, the use of domestic appliances, of pre-cooked foods and of various transportation services could perhaps be explained by an explicit minimization of the time budget.

Supply Decisions

The mention of time serves to recall that in the classical theory of consumer's choice income is regarded as given. This implies that decisions concerning factor supply are independent of decisions concerning the use of income. Since supply of factors, especially of labor, no doubt enters into the consumer's preference ordering, an independence assumption is implied, similar to the one we encountered in the sub-section entitled *The Structure of Preferences* in connection with "additive" utility functions. Such independence, we know now, implies cardinal utility, and it appears, therefore, that the dichotomy between earning and spending decisions may have unsuspected implications for ordinal utility. On the other hand, it should also be pointed out, that this dichotomy may not always be realistic. While it is true that, for most people, the work they do does not affect the prices they pay (farmers are a notable exception) there may well be a connection through the influence of working time on leisure. Leisure is a complement of many recreational activities; it is also an important determinant of housekeeping habits. Yet leisure is not ordinarily regarded as a commodity which is bought by individuals, though in a realistic and comprehensive approach it properly should be so regarded.

Short-Term Dynamics

The complications just discussed all arise already in a purely static theory. We now come to dynamic complications, which are probably more important and which have received considerable attention in recent years. For expository purposes it is perhaps useful to make a distinction between short-term and long-term dynamics.

In short-term dynamics it is first of all necessary to distinguish between stocks and flows. Such a distinction hardly arises in static theory, where it makes little difference whether we interpret the analysis to refer to stocks or to flows, although for practical purposes the flow interpretation is usually the more intuitively appealing. Closely related to the stock-flow distinction is a phenomenon that Morgenstern [80] has described as the "reconstitution" of the demand curve. What he had in mind was the fact that yesterday's purchases have an influence on preferences for today's purchases; we may also express this by saying that yesterday's purchases have changed today's stocks, and that today's stocks influence preferences for today's flows. This is most obvious in the case of durable commodities, where the flows may often be usefully regarded as attempts to bring the stocks closer to some desired level. Stocks are not the only cause of reconstitution of the demand curve; habit formation is perhaps equally important.

From the point of view of short-term dynamics, stocks and habits are each other's negatives. The effect of a stock is to lower the marginal utility of the flows concerned (that is to say, the larger the stock, the lower the marginal utility of these flows) while the effect of a habit is to raise it. We can therefore define habits as negative stocks, as liabilities, if one likes.

The relation between stocks (or habits) on the marginal utility of flows is one of the three relations that are important in short-term dynamics. The other two are the effect of flows on stocks (the effect of a purchase is, generally speaking, positive for stocks, and negative for habits) and the relation of stocks or habits to the mere passage of time. The effect of time is negative for wasting assets, zero for perennial assets, and positive for growing assets; a similar classification can be made for habits. The number of stocks need not be the same as the number of flows; each stock may affect several flows, and conversely.

Although the concepts just described are implicit in some recent empirical work (for instance in Stone and Croft-Murray, [106]), there is as yet no well-developed theory of short-term dynamics. Such a theory would probably concern itself mostly with two problems: the relation between short-term elasticities with respect to prices and income (where stocks are regarded as fixed) to long-term elasticities (where again stocks are regarded as optimal) and the relation between short-term equilibrium and long-term equilibrium, including the question of when a stock-flow model will produce cyclical fluctuations. Some elements of the necessary theory are to be found in the work of Bushaw and Clower [15] on stock-flow relations; since these authors work with separate stock demand functions and flow demand functions, however, they do not yet seem to have done justice to the full interrelations of the problem. Cramer [20] made an interesting attempt to develop a pure stock theory of demand, but was unable to fit in the effects of price changes. In short-term dynamics indivisibilities are of special importance because durable commodities are often indivisible and a continuous adjustment of actual to desired stocks is impeded by transaction costs. The spasmodic adjustment that results has been described by Houthakker and Haldi [59], though not in the framework of a theory of choice. By taking those factors into account the theory becomes akin to inventory theory as recently developed in another context.

Long-Term Dynamics

Rather more attention than has been devoted to short-term dynamics has recently been given to long-term dynamics, especially to the theory of allocation over time. The problems raised here go beyond the framework of consumption, and I shall therefore not attempt a comprehensive discussion; the survey by Farrell [28] will be found useful for more details. The most important question that arises is the theory of saving. In a static theory nothing very interesting can be said about saving; it is just like any item of expenditure, and in relation to income, for instance, it may be inferior, a necessity, or a luxury. It is, incidentally, not correct to say that in a static theory there can be no saving at all; this misconception appears to be based on the naive view that saving is identical with not spending, while in fact it is more usefully regarded as the planned acquisition of certain (usually financial) assets or the reduction of liabilities.

The maximization of utility over time has been studied by a number of authors, including Tintner [113] and Klein [62]. These are for the most part fairly straightforward extensions of static maximization in which time is merely another dimension. In other words, no particular use is made of the fact that time is irreversible; since it may well be argued that attention to dating by itself does not make a theory dynamic, it would seem that these theories do not come to grips with the basic issues, although they are of undoubted usefulness as a first orientation. Among other relevant aspects these theories generally fail to pay attention to the finite length of human life. Even the assumption of immortality, however, does not seem to be a sufficient condition for the assertion (Friedman, [34]) that savings must be a constant proportion of permanent income.[8]

Of greater interest are theories in which the finiteness of human life is taken into account explicitly, and which in particular pay attention to the so-called life cycle. The most notable example of this kind of theory is by Modigliani and Brumberg [79].

Strotz [107] investigated the inconsistencies arising from the maximization of an instantaneous utility function, in which the needs of future periods are somehow discounted. Even under perfect foresight the consumption path followed during a period will in general not coincide with the path chosen as optimal at the outset.[9] The two paths coincide only if all future dates are discounted from the moving present at a constant rate of interest, but there is no reason why time preference should always be of this special form. Strotz analyzed two types of strategies by which inconsistency may be avoided and pointed out the practical difficulties preventing the adoption of either. This paper goes to the root of the problems of choice over time, but so far it has not led to further discussion.

The problem of uncertainty, already mentioned in connection with static theory, is of special importance in the dynamic theory of choice. Indeed it may well be argued that without uncertainty there would be no liquidity preference and that time preference would be merely technological.

The mention of liquidity preference recalls the connection between the theory of consumer's choice and monetary theory. While a discussion of the latter subject would transcend the scope of this survey, it may be noted that the controversy raised by Patinkin [87] has focused attention on the role of absolute (as distinct from relative) prices when financial assets and liabilities are brought into the picture. The upshot of recent discussions (mostly in the *Review of Economic Studies* of October, 1960) seems to be that the presence of financial items does not violate the basic irrelevance of absolute prices postulated by the theory of consumer's choice; this had already been argued by Leser [68].

---

[8]I do not discuss Friedman's book in the present survey because the problems with which it deals belong primarily to statistics rather than to economic theory. The "permanent income hypothesis," which has done so much to clarify recent empirical research, is essentially a theory about errors of measurement; it is logically independent of the proportionality of consumption to permanent income.

[9]This had already been pointed out in a different context by Smithies (1939).

AGGREGATION AND INTERACTION

Unlike the historian or the physician, the economist is not much interested in the behavior of single individuals. The elaborate analysis of individual behavior, with which we have been concerned in the three preceding sections, is no more than the basis for the theory of aggregate demand. Is such a basis really necessary? The question has occasionally been answered in the negative (for instance by Cassel; see the sub-section entitled *Early History*, page 106), though by and large the desirability of a microeconomic foundation for aggregate economics is not seriously doubted. The contribution of microeconomics to economic theory in general lies in the powerful assumption of rationality, that is, behavior according to a consistent pattern of preferences. It is true that this assumption has never been thoroughly verified, though the tests made by May [74] and by Papandreou and others [85] are encouraging. If economics were in a more advanced stage, the assumption would no doubt be made less freely, if only because we could then presumably say more about irrational behavior, a subject on which there is as yet little or no theory.[10]

The Household

The problem of aggregation over individuals is found in its purest form in the household, where some compromise between the preferences of the various members has to be found. Samuelson [99] analyzed the allocations that are necessary if a household is to have a consistent preference pattern. He pointed out that it is in general not rational for each member to get a constant fraction of income irrespective of price changes. Thus, if in a family the husband spends 10 percent of the family income on his own needs, and the price of haircuts goes up, a rational pattern can only be maintained if the percentage spent by the husband is slightly raised. There has to be a redistribution of income in such a way that the "ethical worth" of the marginal dollar spent on each member remains the same. While the term "ethical worth" seems unfortunate, the important point is that rationality requires a social welfare function which describes the relation of the utility levels of the individual members to the utility level of the household as a whole. Apart from certain obvious general characteristics, it does not matter how this social welfare function is constituted; consistency for the household as a whole only requires that income is redistributed in accordance with one

[10]The concepts of direct and indirect utility (see the sub-section entitled *Duality*, page 117) may be helpful here. These two functions have the same value if and only if the individual is consistent; otherwise direct utility is what he actually attains, indirect utility what he might attain if consistent. Hence a measure of inconsistency can perhaps be defined with the aid of these two functions (cf. also the final paragraph of the sub-section entitled *Uncertainty*, page 125).

such function.[11] In empirical research on household budgets much attention has been paid to the influence of household composition; Samuelson's theory may lead to a reconsideration of this subject.

This theory of the rational household (or, as Samuelson has called it in a wider context, the "good society") also has a bearing on the question of irrationality discussed in the preceding paragraph. One source of irrationality evidently is that the amount spent by the various individuals cannot be described by some social welfare function. For the individual with inconsistent behavior this might mean that he would act as if he were several persons instead of only one. Such behavior might, therefore, be described as "revealed schizophrenia" and it would be interesting to know if all inconsistent behavior is of this type.[12]

Special Functions

While the result of Samuelson just mentioned is evidently basic for any general theory of aggregation over individuals, there is also scope for more special results. Thus, it is often of interest to analyze the relation between aggregate consumption and aggregate income and prices when the relation between individual consumption, individual income, and prices has a specified form. DeWolff [24] showed that under certain conditions concerning the distribution of income, linear Engel curves for individuals imply a linear relation between aggregate consumption and aggregate income. This result was independently generalized by Gorman [40], but neither author took into account the difficulty of nonnegativity recalled in the sub-section entitled *Cardinal Utility Reconsidered*, page 120, according to which linear Engel curves are something of an exception. The linear case is also discussed at length by Theil [111]. Similar results for the double logarithmic Engel curve were derived by Tobin [114] and for the lognormal by Aitchison and Brown [2], though it should be pointed out that since neither of these curves satisfies the additivity criterion they are inconsistent with theoretical notions of consumer's behavior. In the latter two cases it is also necessary to make fairly restrictive assumptions about the size distribution of income among consumers.

The above mentioned results have a relation to the notion of the "representative consumer" well-known from the work of Marshall and Pigou. By means of this device, for instance, a selected group of individuals with different incomes can be represented as a collection of identical individuals, all having some average income and some average consumption. If $f(y)$ is

---

[11]The weak and strong axioms will then also hold for the household, although in general they do not hold for groups of individuals whose tastes are different.

[12]Sociologists and psychologists have recently become interested in the decision-making process within the household, which evidently has a bearing on the rationality of its aggregate preference pattern. See some of the papers in Foote [30], especially the paper by Kenkel. There is also a connection with the work on preference structures discussed in the sub-section entitled *The Structure of Preferences*, page 118.

the consumption-income relation for the individual, and if Y is some appropriate average of income, and if the size distribution of income is represented by $K(y, Y)$, then the representative consumer can be validly employed if the following equation holds:

$$f(Y) = \int_0^\infty K(y, Y) f(y) dy.$$

This is an integral equation of the second kind, which in general has a unique solution $f(y)$ for each given $K(y, Y)$. If $K(y, Y)$ and $f(y)$ are not related by such an equation, the distribution of income will have an independent influence on aggregate demand.

The above comments apply to the influence of income; much less can be said about the influence of prices (except on the basis of Samuelson's approach discussed in the preceding section). The discussion of market demand in Hicks ([48], esp. para. 12 of the Mathematical Appendix) may suggest to the unwary that microeconomic theorems can be immediately generalized to aggregates but, in fact, this is possible only for severely circumscribed distributions of income; indeed the distributions for which aggregation is exactly valid will be different for every commodity. (This is clear from some basic theorems on aggregation stated by Wold [123].) On the other hand the influence of the income distribution may well be small in reality, especially since this distribution seems to be governed by well-defined if little-understood empirical laws. Numerical examples purporting to show a large effect of redistribution are rarely convincing for this reason. If the distributional effects are normally small this will greatly enhance the usefulness of microeconomic theory.

Random Variations of Preferences

Although it was assumed so far that individuals all had the same demand functions (or more generally, preference patterns), this assumption can be relaxed to some extent by allowing random variations in preferences. Allen and Bowley [6] achieved this important generalization for the case of a linear preference scale (which is a slight extension of the quadratic utility function) by assuming that certain of the parameters occurring in these preference scales are normally and independently distributed; it appeared then that the aggregate Engel curves depend only on the average values of these parameters. It has not yet been possible to extend these results to the kinky Engel curves that result from nonnegativity; such an extension would be especially desirable because aggregation over individuals with varying preferences would presumably change those kinky curves into smooth curves.

Among the many interesting complications raised by random variations in preferences two deserve special mention. In the first place it may seem that observations on households with varying preferences may give information on substitution and complementarity. To take an example, if a household spends more on margarine than the average at its income level, then it may be expected to spend less on butter, and it may then seem plausible to derive an estimate of the substitutability of butter for margarine from observations on different households. It appears from the work of Prais [89] and of Theil and Neudecker [112] that this is not possible. In the second place, there is much empirical evidence that households with higher incomes show greater variation in their expenditures than households with lower incomes, presumably because the former have more latitude to follow their idiosyncracies. It would be interesting to incorporate this important fact into the theory of consumer's choice; it may also be explicable by the approach discussed at the end of the sub-section entitled *Uncertainty*.

Some attempts have also been made to relate random variations in preferences to the aggregate demand for indivisible commodities. The emphasis here is on the probability of a consumer's owning a certain durable (for instance a car) as a function of his income and possibly of prices. Farrell [27] and Cramer [21] have used normal and lognormal distributions for this purpose, though both seem to consider it a virtue of this approach that it does not follow from any theory of consistent or random choice. Somewhat similar results had been reached by Malmquist [72] who studied the aggregate demand for rationed commodities if rationing is not effective for all individuals.

Social Interaction and the Content of Preferences

Powerful though the assumption of random variation in preferences is, it also contradicts many intuitive notions on the social nature of human behavior. The formation of preferences is to some extent a social process, in which imitation and differentiation are important elements. The formation of preferences itself is usually held to be outside the realm of economic theory, but some of the consequences of social interaction are nevertheless of economic interest. These consequences have been explored by Duesenberry [25], primarily in an attempt to resolve a well-known contradiction between estimates of savings functions from cross-section and time-series data; since then other explanations have become available. While the "demonstration effect" agrees with casual observation, it has not yet been subjected to much theoretical analysis. Preliminary investigation (Prais and Houthakker, [90]) has suggested that when the budget constraint is properly taken into account the consequences of social interaction are not so straightforward as they seem at first sight. Perhaps the most that can be said at the present is that social interaction may produce patterns of correlation in the variation of preferences among individuals.

There is much to be said for regarding the explanation of the content of preferences (that is, of the question why an individual prefers one bundle of goods to another) as outside the economist's competence. Nevertheless, there is also a danger in such delimitations of responsibility, namely, that the problems thus excluded may not be studied at all. It is easy to say they belong to psychology, but this does not mean that psychologists will find them sufficiently interesting to look into them. Indeed, the whole concept of preference as used by economists may be hard to fit into the psychologist's framework.

Social interaction by itself can at best explain the transmission of preferences, but not their origin. And here are some questions of importance to many areas of economics. Engel's law, for instance, is fundamental not only in consumption research but also in the empirical study of economic development and international trade. It is undoubtedly a property of preferences, and probably hardly influenced by social interaction. The naive explanation in terms of stomach capacity does not get us very far, for the income elasticity of food expenditure reflects an increase of average price per unit of weight (that is, of "quality") rather than of physical quantity, except at very low income levels. There are similar empirical regularities for other items of expenditure, but again no explanation seems to have been attempted.

Although these empirical phenomena are little understood, their persistence and universality suggest that they are not readily amenable to change. This may seem surprising to those who, taking the claims of the more irresponsible advertisers or the best-sellers of popular sociologists at face value, believe that the preferences of modern man are largely shaped by Madison Avenue and its equivalents in other countries. In fact a large part of advertising does no more than inform the public of changes in prices and products. Most of the remainder is merely an attempt to sway consumers from one brand to another, a matter important to the firms concerned and to the student of marketing, but hardly to those interested in the basic patterns of consumption, which is the proper concern of the economics of consumption. Examples of advertising that changed the demand for a substantial commodity are hard to find. The prudent marketer tries to exploit consumer's preferences, not to alter them.

CONCLUDING REMARKS

It so happens that the four main sections of this survey appear in approximate order of decreasing development. The level of sophistication reached in the study of the foundations (at least in the standard case) is rarely found in economics. Compared to the achievement recorded in the other three sections, this sophistication may even seem disproportionate. In the second section a number of solid contributions were noted, and while much remains to be done, the directions of future research are fairly clear. On leaving the classical framework in the section entitled *Development Outside the Classical Framework*, page 123, we are in less completely charted territory where the greatest discoveries await the imaginative. In such vitally important subjects as dynamics, only a beginning has so far been made. The state of knowledge described in the section entitled *Aggregation and Interaction*, page 131, is not much better, but here it is not so clear that a great deal can be done pending more empirical research. It is also not certain that the error involved in applying microeconomic conclusions to aggregates is large enough to warrant a more concentrated effort in the analysis of aggregation than has so far been undertaken.

It is not within the scope of this survey to assess the general usefulness of consumption theory. Such a task cannot be taken up within the theory itself, but requires systematic reference to observations. It is nevertheless pertinent to point out — without further elaboration — that the theory of consumer's choice may historically have had more influence as a prototype to other branches of economics than as a guide to consumption research. While the relative importance of the two types of influence may change, I do not doubt that the theory will continue to be valuable in both these directions.

REFERENCES*

[1] Afriat, S. N. "The Axiomatic Concept of a Scale and the Logic of Preferences in the Theory of Consumers' Expenditures." (abstract) *Econometrica*, Vol. XXVIII (1960), pp. 693–5.

[2] Aitchison, J., and J.A.C. Brown. *The Lognormal Distribution with Special Reference to its Uses in Economics.* New York: Cambridge University Press, 1957.

[3] Allen, R. G. D. "Reconsideration of the Theory of Value, II." *Economica*, N.S., Vol. I (1934), pp. 196–219.

[4] ———. *Mathematical Analysis for Economists.* London: Macmillan, 1938.

[5] ———. *Mathematical Economics.* London: Macmillan, 1956.

[6] ———, and A. L. Bowley. *Family Expenditure: A Study of Its Variation.* London: Staples Press, 1935.

[7] Armstrong, W. E. "Determinateness of the Utility Function." *Economic Journal*, Vol XLIX (1939), pp. 453–67.

[8] Arrow, K. J. "Alternative Approaches to the Theory of Choice in Risk-taking Situations." *Econometrica*, Vol. XIX (1951), pp. 404–37.

[9] ———. "Rational Choice Functions and Orderings." *Economica*, N.S., Vol. XXVI (1959), pp. 121–7.

[10] ———, and L. Hurwicz. "On the Stability of the Competitive Equilibrium." *Econometrica*, Vol. XXVI (1958), pp. 522–52.

[11] Auspitz, R., and R. Lieben. *Untersuchungen über die Theorie des Preises.* Leipzig: Duncker and Humbolt, 1889.

[12] Basmann, R. L. "A Theory of Demand with Consumer's Preferences Variable." *Econometrica*, Vol XXIV (1956), pp. 47–58.

[13] Bergson (Burk) A. "Real Income, Expenditure Proportionality and Frisch's New Methods of Measuring Marginal Utility." *Review of Economic Studies*, Vol. IV (1936), pp. 33–52.

[14] Bowley, A. L. "Earnings and Prices, 1904, 1914, 1937–8." *Review of Economic Studies*, Vol VIII (1941), pp. 129–42.

[15] Bushaw, D. W., and R. W. Clower. "Price Determination in a Stock-Flow Economy." *Econometrica*, Vol. XVIII (1954), pp. 236–41.

[16] Cassel, G. *Theoretische Sozialökonomie.* Leipzig: Scholl, 1918.

[17] Chipman, J. S. "The Foundations of Utility." *Econometrica*, Vol. XXVIII (1960), pp. 193–224.

[18] Corlett, W.J., and P.K. Newman. "A Note on Revealed Preference and the Transitivity Condition." *Review of Economic Studies*, Vol. XX (1952), pp. 156–8.

[19] Court, L. M. "Entrepreneurial and Consumer Demand Theories for Commodity Spectra." *Econometrica*, Vol. IX (1941), pp. 135–62.

*Only publications mentioned in the text are listed; this is not a bibliography of the subject.

[20] Cramer, J. S. "A Dynamic Approach to the Theory of Consumer Demand." *Review of Economic Studies*, Vol. XXIV (1957), pp. 73–86.

[21] ———. *A Statistical Model of the Ownership of Major Consumer Durables.* New York: Cambridge University Press, 1961.

[22] Davidson, D., and J. Marschak. "Experimental Tests of a Stochastic Decision Theory," in Churchman, C. W., and P. Ratoosh (eds.). *Measurement: Definitions and Theories.* New York: Wiley, 1959.

[23] Debreu, G. "Representation of a Preference Ordering by a Numerical Function," in Thrall, R. M. (ed.). *Decision Processes.* New York: Wiley, 1954, pp. 159–65.

[24] DeWolff, P. "Income Elasticity of Demand: A Microeconomic and a Macroeconomic Interpretation." *Economic Journal*, Vol. LI (1941), pp. 140–5.

[25] Duesenberry, J. S. *Income, Saving and the Theory of Consumer Behavior.* Cambridge: Harvard University Press, 1949.

[26] Edgeworth, F. Y. *Mathematical Psychics.* London: Kegan Paul, 1881.

[27] Farrell, M. J. "Some Aggregation Problems in Demand Analysis." *Review of Economic Studies*, Vol. XXI (1954), pp. 193–203.

[28] ———. "The New Theories of the Consumption Function." *Economic Journal*, Vol. LXIX (1959), pp. 678–95.

[29] Fisher, I. "Mathematical Investigations in the Theory of Value and Prices." *Transactions of Connecticut Academy of Arts and Sciences*, Vol. I, No. 9 (1892), pp. 1–124.

[30] Foote, N. N. (ed.) *Household Decision-Making.* New York: New York University Press, 1961.

[31] Fourgeaud, C., and A. Nataf. "Consommation en Prix et Revenu Réels et Théorie des Choix." *Econometrica*, Vol XXVII (1959), pp. 329–54.

[32] Friedman, M. "Professor Pigou's Method for Measuring Elasticities of Demand from Budgetary Data." *Quarterly Journal of Economics*, Vol. LI (1935), pp. 151–63.

[33] ———. *Essays in Positive Economics.* Chicago: University of Chicago Press, 1953.

[34] ———. *A Theory of the Consumption Function.* Princeton: Princeton University Press, 1957.

[35] Frisch, R. *New Methods of Measuring Marginal Utility.* Tübingen: Mohr, 1932.

[36] ———. "A Complete Schema for Computing all Direct and Cross Demand Elasticities in a Model with Many Sectors." *Econometrica*, Vol. XXVII (1959), pp. 177–96.

[37] Gale, D. "A Note on Revealed Preference." *Economica*, N.S., Vol. XXVI (1960), pp. 121–7.

[38] Georgescu-Roegen, N. "The Pure Theory of Consumer's Behavior." *Quarterly Journal of Economics*, Vol. L (1936), pp. 545–593.

[39] Georgescu-Roegen, N. "Choice, Expectations and Measurability." *Quarterly Journal of Economics*, Vol. LVIII (1954), pp. 503–34.

[40] Gorman, W. M. "Community Preference Fields." *Econometrica*, Vol. XXI (1953), pp. 63–80.

[41] ———. "Separable Utility and Aggregation." *Econometrica*. Vol. XXVII (1959), pp. 469–81.

[42] Gossen, H. H. *Entwicklung der Gesetze des menschlichen Verkehrs, und der daraus fliessenden Regeln für menschliches Handeln.* Berlin: Prager, 1854.

[43] Graaff, J. de V. "Rothbart's 'Virtual Price System' and the Slutsky Equation." *Review of Economic Studies*, Vol. XV (1948), pp. 91–5.

[44] Green, H. A. J. "Some Logical Relations in Revealed Preference Theory." *Economica*, Vol. XXIV (1957), pp. 315–23.

[45] ———. "Direct Additivity and Consumers' Behaviour." *Oxford Economic Papers*, Vol. XIII (1961), pp. 132–6.

[46] Herstein, I. N., and J. Milnor. "An Axiomatic Approach to Measurable Utility." *Econometrica*, Vol. XXI (1953), pp. 291–7.

[47] Hicks, J.R. "A Reconsideration of the Theory of Value, I." *Economica*, N.S., Vol. I (1934), pp. 52–75.

[48] ———. *Value and Capital.* Oxford: Clarendon Press, 1939.

[49] ———. "The Four Consumer's Surpluses." *Review of Economic Studies*, Vol. XI (1943), pp. 31–41.

[50] ———. "A Comment on Mr. Ichimura's Definition." *Review of Economic Studies*, Vol. XVIII (1915), pp. 184–87.

[51] ———. *A Revision of Demand Theory*. Oxford: Clarendon Press, 1956.

[52] ———. "The Measurement of Real Income." *Oxford Economic Papers*, Vol. X (1958), pp. 125–62.

[53] Hotelling, H. "Edgeworth's Taxation Paradox and the Nature of Demand and Supply Functions." *Journal of Political Economy*, Vol. XL (1932), pp. 577–616.

[54] Houthakker, H. S. "Revealed Preference and the Utility Function." *Economica*, N.S., Vol. XVII (1950), pp. 159–74.

[55] ———. "Compensated Changes in Quantities and Qualities Consumed." *Review of Economic Studies*, Vol. XIX (1952), pp. 154–64.

[56] ———. "La Forme des Courbes d'Engel." *Cahiers du Seminaire d'Econométrie*, Vol. II (1953), pp. 59–66.

[57] ———. "The Capacity Method of Quadratic Programming." *Econometrica*, Vol. XXVII (1960), pp. 62–87.

[58] ———. "Additive Preferences." *Econometrica*, Vol. XXVII (1960), pp. 244–57.

[59] Houthakker, H. S., and J. Haldi. "Household Investment in Automobiles," in Friend and Jones (eds.). *Consumption and Savings.* Philadelphia: University of Pennsylvania Press, Vol. I (1960), pp. 175–224.

[60] Ichimura, S. "A Critical Note on the Definition of Related Goods." *Review of Economic Studies*, Vol. XVIII (1951), pp. 179–83.

[61] Jevons, W. S. *The Theory of Political Economy*. London and New York: Macmillan and Co., 1871.

[62] Klein, L. R. *The Keynesian Revolution*. New York: Macmillan, 1947.

[63] Klein, L. R., and H. Rubin. "A Constant-Utility Index of the Cost of Living." *Review of Economic Studies*, Vol. XV (1947), pp. 84–7.

[64] Konus, A. A. "On the Theory of Means." *Acta Universitatis Asiae Mediae*, Series Va, No. 24 (1939).

[65] Leontief, W. W. "Composite Commodities and the Problem of Index Numbers." *Econometrica*, Vol. IV (1936), pp. 39–59.

[66] ———. "Introduction to a Theory of the Internal Structure of Functional Relationships." *Econometrica*, Vol. XV (1947), pp. 361–73.

[67] Leser, C. E. V. "Family Budget Data and Price Elasticities of Demand." *Review of Economic Studies*, Vol. IX (1941), pp. 40–57.

[68] ———. "The Consumer's Demand for Money." *Econometrica*, Vol. XI (1943), pp. 123–40.

[69] Little, I. M. D. "A Reformulation of the Theory of Consumer's Behaviour." *Oxford Economic Papers*, Vol. I (1949), pp. 90–9.

[70] ———. *A Critique of Welfare Economics*. New York: Oxford University Press, 1950.

[71] Luce, R. D. *Individual Choice Behavior*. New York: Wiley, 1959.

[72] Malmquist, S. *A Statistical Analysis of the Demand for Liquor in Sweden*. Uppsala: Almquist and Wiksells, 1948.

[73] Marschak, J. "Rational Behavior, Uncertain Prospects, and Measurable Utility." *Econometrica*, Vol. XVIII (1950), pp. 111–141.

[74] May, K. J. "Transitivity, Utility and Aggregation in Preference Patterns." *Econometrica*, Vol XXII (1954), pp. 1–13.

[75] McKenzie, L. "Demand Theory Without a Utility Index." *Review of Economic Studies*, Vol. XXIV (1957), pp. 185–9.

[76] McManus, M. "Points Rationing and the Consumer." *Metroeconomica*, Vol. VIII (1956), pp. 118–34.

[77] Metzler, L. W. "Stability of Multiple Markets: The Hicks Conditions." *Econometrica*, Vol. XIII (1945), pp. 277–92.

[78] Mishan, E. J. "Theories of Consumer's Behavior: A Cynical View." *Economica*, N.S., Vol. XXVIII, No. 109 (1961), pp. 1–11.

[79] Modigliani, F., and R. Brumberg. "Utility Analysis and the Consumption Function: An Interpretation of Cross-Section Date," in Kurihara, K. (ed.). *Post-Keynesian Economics*. New Brunswick, N.J.: Rutgers University Press, 1954.

[80] Morgenstern, O. "Demand Theory Reconsidered." *Quarterly Journal of Economics*, Vol. LXII (1948), pp. 165–201.

[81] Morris, R. T. (Norris). *The Theory of Consumer Demand.* New Haven: Yale University Press, 1947.

[82] Mosak, J. L. *General Equilibrium Theory in International Trade.* Bloomington, Indiana: Principia Press, 1944.

[83] Newman, P. K. "The Foundations of Revealed Preference Theory." *Oxford Economic Papers*, Vol. VII (1955), pp. 151–69.

[84] ———. "The Foundations of Revealed Preference Theory." *Oxford Economic Papers*, N.S., Vol. VII, No. 2 (1966), pp. 149–69.

[85] Papandreou, A. G., *et al.* "A Test of a Stochastic Theory of Choice." *University of California Publications in Economics*, Vol. XVI, No. 1 (1957).

[86] Pareto, V. *Cours de'ēconomie politique.* Lausanne: F. Rouge, 1896–97.

[87] Patinkin, D. *Money, Interest and Prices.* Evanston, Ill.: Row, Peterson, 1956.

[88] Pigou, A. C. "A Method of Determining Numerical Values of Elasticities of Demand." *Economic Journal*, Vol. XX (1910), pp. 636–40.

[89] Prais, S. J. "Non-Linear Estimates of the Engel Curve." *Review of Economic Studies*, Vol. XX (1953), pp. 87–104.

[90] ———, and H. S. Houthakker. *The Analysis of Family Budgets.* New York: Cambridge University Press, 1955.

[91] Rajaoja, V. *A Study in the Theory of Demand Functions and Price Indexes.* Helsinki: Academic Bookstore, 1958.

[92] Robertson, D. H. *Utility and All That.* London: Macmillan, 1952.

[93] Rothbart, E. "The Measurement of Changes in Real Income Under Conditions of Rationing." *Review of Economic Studies*, Vol. VIII (1941), pp. 100–7.

[94] Roy, R. *De l'Utilitē, Contribution ā la Thēorie des Choix.* Paris: Hermann, 1943.

[95] ———. "La Distribution du Revenue entre les Divers Biens." *Econometrica*, Vol. XV (1947), pp. 181–204.

[96] Samuelson, P. A. "A Note on the Pure Theory of Consumer's Behaviour." *Economica*, Vol. V (1938), pp. 61–71, 353–4.

[97] ———. *Foundations of Economic Analysis.* Cambridge, Mass.: Harvard University Press, 1947.

[98] ———. "The Problem of Integrability in Utility Theory." *Economica*, Vol. XVII (1950), pp. 355–85.

[99] ———. "Social Indifference Curves." *Quarterly Journal of Economics*, Vol. LXX (1956), pp. 1–22.

[100] ———. "Structure of a Minimum Equilibrium System," in Pfouts, R. W. (ed.). *Essays in Economics and Econometrics.* Chapel Hill, N.C.: University of North Carolina Press, 1960.

[101] Savage, L. J. *The Foundations of Statistics.* New York: Wiley, 1953.

[102] Slutsky, E. "Sulla Teoria del Bilancio del Consomatore." *Giornale degli Economisti*, Vol. LI (1915), pp. 1–26.

[103] Smith, V. E. "Linear Programming Models for the Determination of Palatable Human Diets." *Journal of Farm Economics*, Vol. XLI (1959), pp. 272–83.

[104] Stigler, G. J. "The Cost of Subsistence." *Journal of Farm Economics*, Vol. XXVII (1945), pp. 303–14.

[105] Stone, R. *The Measurement of Consumers' Expenditure and Behaviour in the United Kingdom, 1920–38*, Vol. I. New York: Cambridge University Press, 1954.

[106] ———, and G. Croft-Murray. *Social Accounting and Economic Models.* London: Bowes and Bowes, 1959.

[107] Strotz, R. H. "Myopia and Inconsistency in Dynamic Utility Maximization." *Review of Economic Studies*, Vol. XXIII (1956), pp. 165–80.

[108] ———. "The Empirical Implications of a Utility Tree." *Econometrica*, Vol. XXV (1957), pp. 269–80.

[109] Theil, H. *De Invloed van de Voorraden op het Consumentengedrag.* Amsterdam: Poortpers, 1951.

[110] ———. "Qualities, Prices and Budget Enquiries." *Review of Economic Studies*, Vol. XIX (1952), pp. 129–47.

[111] ———. *Linear Aggregation of Economic Relations.* Amsterdam: North-Holland Publishing Co., 1954.

[112] ———, and H. Neudecker. "Substitution, Complementarity and Its Residual Variation Around Engel Curves." *Review of Economic Studies*, Vol. XXV (1958), pp. 114–23.

[113] Tintner, G. "The Maximization of Utility over Time." *Econometrica*, Vol. VI (1938), pp. 154–8.

[114] Tobin, J. "A Statistical Demand Function for Good in the U.S.A." *Journal of the Royal Statistical Society, Series A*, Vol. CXIII (1950), pp. 113–41.

[115] ———. "A Survey of the Theory of Rationing." *Econometrica*, Vol. XX (1952), pp. 521–53.

[116] ———, and H. S. Houthakker. "The Effects of Rationing on Demand Elasticities." *Review of Economic Studies*, Vol. XVIII (1951), pp. 140–53.

[117] Törnqvist, L. "Review of Work by H. Wold," *Ekonomisk Tidskrift*, Vol. XLIII (1941), pp. 216–25.

[118] Uzawa, H. "Preference and Rational Choice in the Theory of Consumption." *Proceedings of a Symposium on Mathematical Methods in the Social Sciences.* Stanford: Stanford University Press, 1960.

[119] Ville, J. "Sur les Conditions d'Existence d'une Ophélimité Totale et d'un Indice du Niveau des Prix." *Annales de l'Université de Lyon.* Vol. IX (1946), pp. 32–29.

[120] Von Neumann, J., and O. Morgenstern. *Theory of Games and Economic Behavior.* Princeton: Princeton University Press, 1944.

[121] Wagner, H. M. "An Eclectic Approach to the Pure Theory of Consumer Behavior." *Econometrica*, Vol. XXIV (1956), pp. 451–66.
[122] Wald, A. "A New Formula for the Index of the Cost of Living." *Econometrica*, Vol. VII (1939), pp. 319–31.
[123] Wold, H. "A Synthesis of Pure Demand Analysis." *Skandinavisk Aktuarietidskrift*, Vol. XXVI (1934–4), pp. 85–118, 220–63 and Vol. XXVII, pp. 69–120.
[124] ———. "Ordinal Preferences or Cardinal Utility?" *Econometrica*, Vol. XX (1952), pp. 661–4.
[125] ———. *Demand Analysis*. New York: Wiley, 1953.

7. CHANGE AND INNOVATION IN THE TECHNOLOGY OF CONSUMPTION*

Kelvin Lancaster†

We typically think of technology as applying to production rather than consumption, and my first task is to establish just what I mean by the technology of consumption.

I am drawing on ideas which have been set out in some detail in another paper of mine which is to be, but unfortunately has not yet been, published elsewhere.[1] This paper, "A New Approach to Consumer Theory," sets out a model of consumption and the consumer with certain features which provide the basis for the present explorations. I must necessarily start with a brief description of those features.

"A New Approach . . ." presents the following view of consumption. Goods, as such, are not the immediate objects of preference or utility or welfare, but have associated with them characteristics which are directly relevant to the consumer. The term "characteristics" was chosen for its normative neutrality; in my earliest draft of this idea I called them "satisfactions," but that has too many connotations. The consumer is assumed to have a preference ordering over the set of all possible characteristics vectors, and his aim is to attain his most desired bundle of characteristics subject to the constraints of the situation. The consumer's demand for goods arises from the fact that goods are required to obtain characteristics and is a derived demand.

An analogy to production theory is starting to appear. We are viewing goods as inputs into a process in which these characteristics are the outputs. The structure of consumption activities is, however, typically different from the structure of production activities. In the typical production activity we have joint inputs and a single output, while we shall regard the typical consumption activity as having a single input (a good) and joint outputs (a bundle of characteristics). Some consumption activities may require several goods, or even other inputs. For example, the activity, driving a car, requires the use of a consumer capital good, the using up of other goods (gas

*From the *American Economic Review*, Vol. LVI, No. 2 (May, 1966), pp. 14–23. This article may also be found in the author's new book, *Consumer Demand: A New Approach* (New York: Columbia University Press, 1971). Reprinted by permission of the publisher and the author.

†Kelvin Lancaster, Professor of Economics, Columbia University.

[1]In the *Journal of Political Economy*, (April, 1966).

and oil), and the labor of the consumer to give the bundle of characteristics associated with the activity. If we were discussing the theory of consumer durables, we would pursue this example further, but, in the present context, we shall think of the typical consumption activity as using up a unit of some good and deriving the bundle of joint characteristics from it.

The jointness of the characteristics is really the core of the whole approach. If we eat an apple, we are enjoying a bundle of characteristics— flavor, texture, juiciness. Another apple may have the same flavor but associated with a different texture, or be more or less juicy. A single good may have more than one characteristic, and a single characteristic may be obtainable from more than one good. Goods which share a common characteristic may have their other characteristics qualitatively different, or they may give the same characteristics but in a quantitatively different combination. If the relationship between goods and characteristics was merely one-to-one in both directions, so that the only characteristic of an apple was appleness and the only source of appleness was an apple, then there would be no operational difference between the traditional approach to consumer theory and that being portrayed here.

It will be assumed that characteristics are, in principle, intrinsic and objective properties of consumption activities. Given arbitrary units, each consumption activity is defined by its inputs (most often assumed to be a unit of a single good) and by the vector of characteristics which forms its output. It will further be assumed that the activities are linearly homogeneous, so that doubling the goods input give double the characteristics. Essentially psychological effects, such as the consumer's relative interest in different characteristics or effects similar to diminishing marginal utility, are assumed to make their appearance in the preference ordering of the characteristics vectors, not in the relationship between goods and characteristics.

The set of all possible consumption activities forms the consumption technology. In a highly developed economy, with many different goods and product variants, the technology will be complex; in a less developed economy, the technology will be simpler. In a country like the U.S.S.R. we may have a complex production technology combined with a relatively simpler consumption technology.

The consumption technology will relate goods on the one hand with characteristics on the other. In general, there is no reason why the number of characteristics and the number of goods should be related to each other (any more than the number of goods and the number of factors should be related in the production technology), and I shall make the working hypothesis that the number of goods in a complex consumption technology like that of the U.S. will probably exceed the number of operationally distinguishable characteristics. There may well be several combinations of goods which give rise to the same bundle of characteristics, and this gives rise to a very important distinction between the present and traditional approaches to consumer theory.

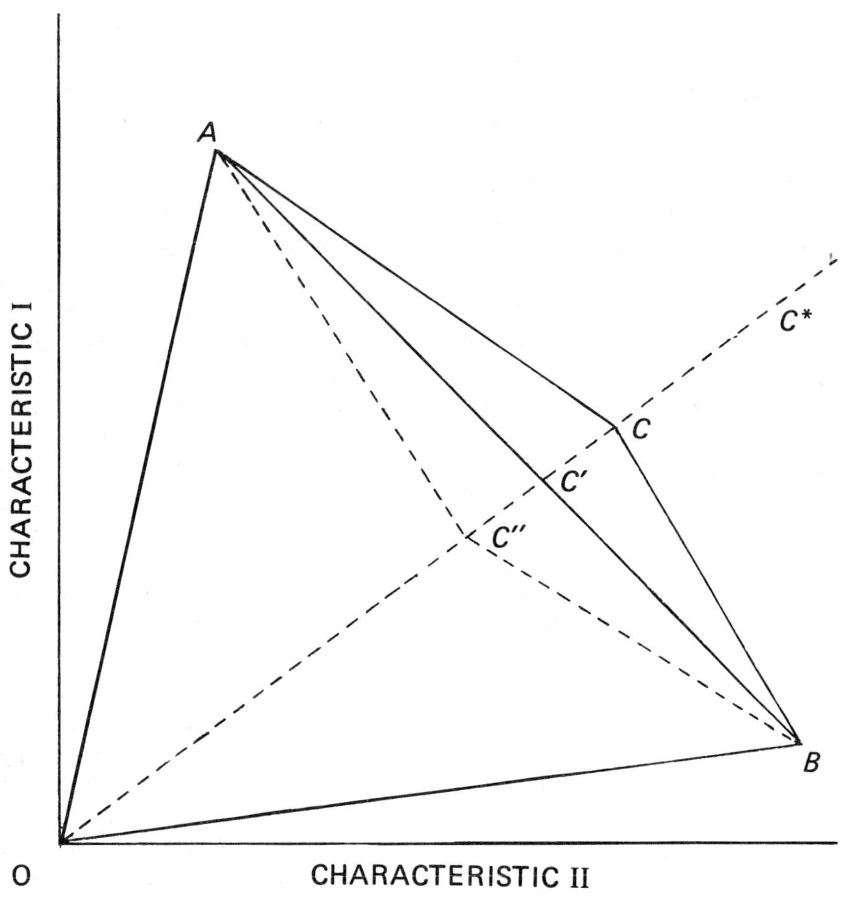

Figure 7-1

Consider a simple example of a consumer in a world of two characteristics and three goods. Each good gives rise to a vector of the two characteristics, and the consumption technology consists of the activities, consuming each of the goods separately, and consuming them in linear combination. If we impose a budget constraint on the goods, we can explore the characteristics vectors attainable by the consumer. The above illustration shows the two-dimensional characteristics space and the points *A*, *B* represent the characteristics attainable if the whole budget is spent on goods *A*, *B*, respectively. By spending the whole budget on combinations of *A* and *B*, characteristics vectors represented by points along the line *AB* can be attained. Now consider the third good, *C*, which gives rise to the characteristics in proportions represented by the line *OC**. The price of *C* will determine how far out along *OC** the consumer can get by spending all his income on *C*. If this price is low enough, this point might be represented by *C*. All the attainable bundles of characteristics for the given price-income situation are given by the points *A, B, C,* and their linear combinations, which are the points in and on the triangle *ABC*.

The consumer chooses his preferred characteristics bundle from the attainable set. Note that efficiency considerations arise—a radical departure from traditional theory—since, for any bundle of characteristics attainable by combinations of *A* and *B*, a larger bundle with the same proportions can be attained by *C* or by combinations of *A* and *C* or *B* and *C*. An efficient consumer will choose combinations on *ACB*, the efficiency frontier for characteristics. Just which point he chooses will depend entirely on his preferences. If consumers have well-distributed preferences and are efficient, we can expect to find that all three goods are sold, but that no single consumer consumes both *A* and *B*.

In this model, the consumer faces a double choice. He makes an efficiency choice in rejecting goods combinations which do not enable him to reach the efficiency frontier and a private choice in finding his preferred point on the frontier. If the markets are competitive so that all consumers face the same prices, and given the linearity of the consumption activities, the shape of the efficiency frontier is the same for all individuals. Income differences appear only as scalar enlargements or reductions of the typical frontier. Thus, efficient choice is objective and common to all individuals in a given price situation.

The efficiency frontier changes with relative prices, however. In the example given, if the price of *C* should rise so that the characteristics vector attainable by spending the whole income on that good moved to *C″*, *AB* would now be the efficiency frontier. No combination using *C* would be efficient and *C* would no longer have any buyers at that price. Price changes may give rise to a substitution effect between goods rising wholly from efficiency effects and unrelated to any convexity of the preference structure. This efficiency substitution effect has been discussed in detail in "A New Approach. . . ."

The general nature of the consumption technology has now been established, and the remainder of the paper will be devoted to answering the question: can we have change, innovation, and technical progress in consumption technology, just as we have in production?

In the case of production technology, considered in activity analysis form, changes in that technology can be regarded in one or more of the following ways:

(1) "Magic wand" effects, in which a particular input combination that gave a certain output in 1965 gives a greater output in 1966.

(2) Shifts from actual capabilities, or the upgrading in efficiency of those firms whose productivity is below the known technological potential. Strictly speaking, this is not a change in technology but it will manifest itself in aggregate data in a similar way.

(3) An identified technical change arising from the introduction of specified new activities.

(4) A change in the nature of inputs such as the introduction of new capital goods, new labor or management skills.

In analyzing production technology, output can be measured with relative ease, as can the input of broadly defined factors. This places much emphasis on magic wand effects, such as unexplained residuals. On the other hand, information concerning the detailed nature of inputs is more difficult to discover, so that the effects of changes in the nature of inputs are less emphasized. In consumption technology the situation is reversed; we have information concerning the changes in the goods which form the inputs, but little information concerning the outputs. We have no interest, therefore, in magic wand effects, but the other three effects can be important.

Since our model of consumer behavior provides scope for efficient choice and hence for the possibility that not all consumers are efficient, there is scope for technical progress in the special sense of increased consumption efficiency, even with no change in the nature of goods or consumption activities.

In consumption, as in production, the prime reasons for inefficient use of the existing technology are ignorance and lack of managerial skill. The consumer may not be aware that a certain good possesses certain characteristics or that certain goods may be used in a particular combination to give a specified bundle of characteristics. Producers or sellers may use advertising to ensure that no characteristics of their product regarded as particularly desirable should go unnoticed by consumers. They will go to less pains to ensure that consumers are aware of some other characteristics of their product.

Organizations such as the Consumers Union exist to provide more objective information on the characteristics of goods than is easily available elsewhere. Some consumers are willing to pay for information which assists in attaining efficient points on their characteristics possibility sets and, on the model presented here, are rational to do so. However, since efficient choices are the same for all consumers, there is a clear argument in favor of public information on these matters and in favor of legal requirements, such as composition and contents labeling, designed to increase knowledge of the available consumption technology.

We can use our model to demolish the old argument, favored by sellers of established products, that since consumers "reveal" their preference for the product already, labeling laws are unnecessary. Traditional theory may seem to lend some weight to this argument, but the present theory does not, since actual choice by consumers can no longer be regarded as revealing their preferences for characteristics — they may merely be making an inefficient choice.

The consumption technology, in a society like that of the United States, is very complex. Efficient consumption, even in the presence of adequate information concerning the technology, involves some managerial skill. As any social worker will testify, many households are noticeably deficient in this skill. Conventional consumer theory leads to a presumption that the family which spends its income on an eccentric collection of goods is simply revealing its preferences for that collection. Of course, this might be true, but it may also be that the family is consuming inefficiently. If the consumer's desired characteristics collection could be ascertained even in a very general way, some type of advising might lead to more efficient consumption.

A crucial difference between the production and consumption sectors is that the market mechanism does not tend to guarantee efficiency in consumption in the same way it does in production. In a society at subsistence level, the inefficient consumer may not survive. In a more affluent society he will survive, but will remain at a lower welfare level than that potentially available to him. Again, this leads to the presumption that public consumer education would be socially valuable.

A relatively static technology, in consumption as in production, will, if coupled with stable relative prices, probably lead to a situation in which the efficient activities become generally known and traditional. Traditional consumption patterns will be efficient only within a relatively unchanging choice situation and only optimal for consumers whose preferences on characteristics approximate the society mode. Tradition will be less useful when the technology is changing rapidly, when relative prices are changing considerably, or when the consumer's preferences diverge from the mode. Furthermore, the typical consumer will inherit his traditions from his social background, and they may not serve him at a radically different income level. We are all aware that the *nouveau riche* may consume differently from persons already established in the higher income group. This analysis suggests that it is at least possible that the desired characteristics of the new and old rich need not be different; the newcomers may be less efficient in achieving their aims. The same considerations may work in reverse, so that a consumer suddenly thrust from a wage income to welfare payments may take some time to discover efficient methods at the new income level, although at this level efficiency may be crucial.

One suspects that there may be great scope for increasing consumption efficiency in the kind of changing situations outlined above. These include the transition from peasant to market economies and from rural to urban societies in developing countries and, within countries, among social groups migrating from one region to another or from one income level to another.

Because the market system does not place pressure on consumers to be efficient, this aspect of technical progress has been stressed more than it might be in discussing production. But innovation in the true sense occurs in the consumption technology, and this takes place primarily through the introduction of new goods or new variants and product differentiation.

Traditional consumer theory is at its most unenlightening when confronted by the problem of new goods. Introduction of a new goods requires either that the preference function defined on n goods is thrown away, and with it all the knowledge of behavior based on it, and replaced by a brand new function defined on $n + 1$ goods, or the fiction that the consumer has a potential preference function for all goods present and future and that a new good can be treated as the fall in that good's price from infinity to its market level. Neither approach gets us very far.

In the present model, it may be that the good is so revolutionary that its characteristics are not possessed by any existing goods. We are no better off, in this case, than in the traditional one. But most new goods can be regarded as simply giving rise to existing characteristics in new proportions, and we have available an operationally meaningful way of approaching the problem. A new good of this kind—and this probably covers nearly all new goods and certainly all product variants—adds a new activity to the technology and is, in the proper sense of the word, an innovation in that technology. Whether the innovation is efficient depends entirely on the price of the new product. If the price is too high, its characteristics correspond to a point within the efficiency frontier and it will not be purchased by efficient consumers, except perhaps initial experimentation to discover whether it is efficient or not. If the price is sufficiently low, however, the new good will push part of the efficiency frontier forward and will enter the efficient technology. Unless that particular part of the frontier happens to contain no consumer's preferred characteristic collection, the new good will sell. Furthermore, the introduction of a successful new good will result in an increase in welfare, if other prices are unchanged.

It may not always be clear whether we should classify a new good as an innovation on the production or the consumption side, but it certainly seems most useful to regard a variant of an exist-product, involving no fundamental change in the technical nature of the production process, as an innovation in consumption technology. In terms of our model of consumption, the difference between a new product and a product variant is only the degree to which the characteristics mix of the new product differs from that of existing products. We have, in this model, a satisfactory technique for analyzing product differentiation.

Consider a simple model with two characteristics, derivable in different proportions from two goods. We can use the same diagram as before and suppose *A, B* to represent the two goods. If the goods are divisible and can be used in combination, the attainable characteristics collections for a consumer, given the budget constraint, correspond to the line *AB*. The introduction of a third good, *C*, whose characteristics vector lies between those of *A* and *B* can be regarded as a product variant, and this good will sell if its price is low enough to bring the characteristics vector to point *C′* or beyond in the diagram. Given this product variant, further variants lying between *A* and *C*, and *C* and *B* would, if suitably priced, expand the efficiency frontier and therefore be sold. If the relationships between the technical properties of the product variants and their relative prices is such as to give a convex frontier with every variant represented by a corner of the frontier, then all variants will be in demand, provided consumers preferences are well distributed.

If we consider the situation from the production end and look through the consumption technology, we see that a producer is ultimately selling characteristics collections rather than goods. The degree of product differentiation will depend on the possibilities, at the production end, of producing variants with characteristics, and at prices, that gives a convex frontier.

A producer with some monopoly power (and we might note that the theory of product differentiation presented here does not require imperfect competition as a prerequisite) will seek the profit maximizing price and differentiation policy. A theory of imperfectly competitive behavior can be built up by pursuing the above analysis, but it is not proposed to do this here.

If products cannot be utilized in combination, the analysis of product differentiation is somewhat different. Consider a highly simplified model of automobiles as consumption activities, expressed in terms of two characteristics, transportation per dollar of gas and comfort. Let two variants, Cadillacs and Volkswagens, be represented by *A* and *B* in the diagram. Now one cannot obtain a combination of these characteristics by taking half a Cadillac and half a Volkswagen, so that, although the points *A* and *B* are on the frontier, points on *AB* are not. Then a variant priced to give point *C″* might be preferred by some consumers to either *A* or *B*, and the convexity of the price-characteristics relationship is not a necessary condition for marketability in this case.

New goods and differentiated products may not simply add to the spectrum of consumption activities; they may replace previous goods. This replacement will occur when the characteristics and price properties of the new product push the frontier forward in such a way that some existing good is no longer part of the efficient set. This will, of course, happen if the new good, for the same outlay, gives more of all characteristics in approximately the same proportions as the old. Such a change seems to correspond to what is often meant by an "overall improvement in quality." In other cases a quality improvement may correspond rather to an increase in some characteristics, with the others unchanged.

Although the introduction of a new product or a new variant can be expected to increase welfare in the simple Paretian sense if the new product is actually purchased and if the existing product is still available at the old price, this may not be the case if the seller takes the old product off the market as he puts the new one on. If the new product, however much of some characteristics it may offer per dollar of outlay, offers less of some other characteristic than the old, then some consumer may be deprived of part of the efficient technology relevant to his particular tastes.

The distinction between the technology of production and that of consumption is a great convenience in analysis but is not based on an absolute criterion of any kind. The ultimate constraints on the system are resources; the ultimate products are characteristics. Some resources may be used to first produce goods which are all intermediate goods in the final analysis, and these goods may then be used in the consumption technology to produce characteristics. But some resources may directly enter the consumption technology without the production of goods as intermediates. As the technologies of both production and consumption change, activities may move back and forth between the consumption and production sectors. This is particularly true of the service and distribution phases of production.

Ultimately the supply of resources, particularly labor, is determined by characteristics. A particular job will have associated with it several characteristics: some will be, in relation to characteristics derived from goods, of a negative kind, but some may well be of a positive kind. The traditional idea of "nonmonetary advantages" has been an attempt to face this obvious fact. We can expand the idea of the consumption technology to include the activities associated with the consumer's sale of labor or other resources. Since labor as an activity may have some characteristics associated with it that are shared by goods, the particular work a consumer performs may partly determine his choice of goods. A taxi driver may spend less of his budget on taking weekend drives than the social norm; yet traditional theory would find no connection between his consumption and his occupation.

New occupations and even new work conditions can be considered as changes in consumption technology. They may also lead to changes in production technology, but this is not necessarily the case.

It would be possible to follow through the kind of analysis we have been making here at very much greater length than is available, but I think the point has been made. There is a technology of consumption. It is the subject of continual change and innovation, just as is the production technology. This change does lead to increased welfare, but the direction from which change comes, the incentives for change, and the analysis and measurement of change differ considerably between production and consumption.

8. DEMAND CURVES AND PRODUCT DIFFERENTIATION*

Louis Phlips†

Introduction

The purpose of this article is to reconsider certain interpretations and criticisms of demand curves, based on the theory of monopolistic competition.

At the outset I shall define some of the terms that will be used. In the following text the term "commodity" is to represent a group of "products." More precisely, a "differentiated commodity" is to represent a group of differentiated products produced by one "industry."[1] For example, according to my definition, cigarettes (in general) are a differentiated commodity; whereas individual cigarette brands are called here each as "products." The term "product" is used in its most restrictive sense; the slightest difference in quality (even if imaginary) between two goods is sufficient for these goods to be considered as two different "products."

My starting point is somewhat peculiar. I suppose that a consumer decided to buy a car and determined the maximum amount of money he would be ready to spend for it. This consumer next has to make a choice between the different brands whose prices do not exceed this sum. The determination of the maximum amount of money to be spent for this purchase is explained by utility theory. My question then is—does utility theory also explain his choice of a particular brand? Or more generally, does utility theory explain choices between differentiated products (belonging to the same commodity)? The second section is devoted to this question. It is suggested that this theory explains only choices between commodities (i.e., how much to spend for "a" car and how much for, say, "cigarettes"). It is also suggested that the choice between the products produced by one industry (i.e., which particular brand to buy) is to be explained by another theory. If this is true, traditional consumer demand curves refer to commodities (i.e., *groups* of products) and not the particular products of these groups.

*From *Kyklos*, Vol. XVII, Fasc. 3 (1964), pp. 404–417. Reprinted by permission of the publisher and the author.

†Louis Phlips, Professor of Economics, Universite Catholique De Louvain. The author gratefully acknowledges the advice and criticism of Dr. A. Heertje. He is also indebted to M. Dasgupta, who read the manuscript and corrected the English.

[1]An "industry" is defined as a group of firms producing "technically" or "physically" similar products satisfying a same want. On the usefulness of this definition for an "objective" delimitation of the concept of industry, see my note: "La théorie de la demande et le concept d'industrie," *Revue suisse d'économie politique et de statistique* (March, 1963), pp. 60–69 (English summary in *The Journal of Economic Abstracts*, Vol. I, No. 3 [1963], p. 362).

If this is accepted, then there is no need to reject the concept of an aggregate demand curve for a differentiated commodity: this idea is developed in The Aggregate Demand Curve section. The section after that is devoted to the demand curve of the firm. It will be suggested that the impact on a firm of (a) consumers' choice between differentiated products (within the same group) and (b) consumers' choice between differentiated commodities, could be illustrated by different curves.

The Individual Demand Curve

In current discussions of the theory of consumer behavior, the nature of the goods between which a consumer has to choose is not precisely defined. For ordinal utility theory, a circular and implicit definition is considered as satisfactory: diminishing marginal rate of substitution between two goods is considered as sufficient, for definitional purpose.[2] As the convexity of indifference curves is an essential postulate, the preceding definition gives the logical consistency of the theory. This procedure clearly does not answer the question which goods satisfy the convexity criterion: this question is simply begged.

However, when from utility theory one proceeds to the theory of the firm, and discusses the demand curve of a firm with a differentiated product, it is admitted without much discussion that this curve represents the impact of consumers' decisions taken according to utility criteria. This amounts to saying that utility theory explains the choice between two products within the same commodity, e.g., between two cigarette brands: the goods on which utility theory applies could thus be specific products, supplied by particular firms.[3]

Actually this is an unjustified extension of the scope of utility theory. Let us consider first, in order to sharpen our ideas, two homogeneous products; if we draw an indifference curve, it has, of course, a unitary slope. The marginal rate of substitution is constant and unitary. In this case, one would say these two products are to be considered as one single good. It should be noted that this is because the marginal rate of substitution is *constant* and not because the rate is unitary. It follows that any pair of products whose marginal rate of substitution is constant is to be considered as one good, from the point of view of utility theory, whether this rate is unitary or not. In order to show that utility theory cannot explain the choice between two given products, it is thus sufficient to prove that their marginal rate of substitution is constant.

---

[2]Cf. G. W. Nutter, "The Plateau Demand Curve and Utility Theory," *Journal of Political Economy,* Vol. LXIII, No. 6 (1955), p. 526.

[3]This thesis has been defended most explicitly by the Dutch economist A. Heertje in his book *De prijsvorming van consumptiegoederen op oligopolistische markten* (Leiden: 1960), p. 10 and pp. 25–27.

I suggest that the marginal rate of substitution of a particular brand (product) for another brand (product) belonging to the same industry (commodity) is indeed constant. It is difficult to prove this, especially as appropriate statistical information is not available to me. My suggestion is not new, however. And some statistical work has been done.

To my knowledge, G. W. Nutter[4] was the first to have noted that the marginal rate of substitution between products may be constant. The same idea has been taken up by L. E. Fouraker.[5] Strangely enough, these proposals were not given much attention. This may be due to the fact that E. H. Chamberlin rejected their arguments with force.[6] Yet, these seem to be valuable. Starting from homogeneous products, Nutter points out that between these products and "varieties" of a differentiated commodity, there is only a difference of degree: "The varieties are 'pure' substitutes for each other even though they may not be 'perfect' substitutes."[7] With the help of this terminology (certainly not very fortunate), Nutter wants to show that the degree of preference between two cigarette brands, for example, does not vary as the relative quantity of the products is altered. The idea is not, as Professor Chamberlin is asserting, that the consumer in question does "not distinguish between them, either at a one-to-one or at some other ratio."[8] On the contrary, consumers' preferences for a specific product are emphasized by the fact that the marginal rate of substitution is not unitary, while the constancy of this ratio illustrates the circumstance that these preferences are not related to quantities consumed and should accordingly sharply be distinguished from the "preferences" (or marginal utilities) of utility theory.[9]

Nutter's ideas did not score a great success, perhaps because they imply that consumers' decisions cannot be explained by a unique theory, whereas they seem to be unique. When a consumer buys something, he always buys a well specified product. (How could it be otherwise?) But this does not mean that this purchase is the result of one unique decision; on the contrary, it is normally the result of a series of decisions. In my view, a consumer is making two distinct steps: first, he has to decide how to allocate his budget

---

[4]G. W. Nutter, *op. cit.*, pp. 527, 528.

[5]L. E. Fouraker, "A Note on the Definition of a Commodity," *Southern Economic Journal*, Vol. XXIII, No. 1 (July, 1956), pp. 80–82; "Product Differentiation and Straight-line Indifference Curves," *American Economic Review, Papers and Proceedings*, Vol. XLVIII, No. 2 (1958), pp. 568–577.

[6]E. H. Chamberlin, "Discussion," *American Economic Review, Papers and Proceedings*, Vol. XLVIII, No. 2 (1958), pp. 598–599.

[7]G. W. Nutter, *op. cit.*, p. 527.

[8]E. H. Chamberlin, *op. cit.*, p. 598.

[9]If the constancy of the marginal rate of substitution characterizes the relations between products within an industry, the concept of industry may be defined with precision. This constancy would make it possible to identify the products to be taken together. One better understands Chamberlin's rejection of Fouraker's ideas if one remembers that Chamberlin considers the concept of industry as a "snare and a delusion."

between all "commodities"; secondly, the amount to be spent on one commodity being given, he has to choose a "product" (i.e., a particular supplier or a particular brand). The decision to travel by train rather than by plane is not to be confused with the decision to take the "Trans European Express" rather than an ordinary train—even if the individual decides both at the same time. As Nutter rightly emphasizes, a consumer thinks first[10] of buying "aspirins" before thinking of choosing "Bayer" aspirins.

This view of consumer behavior leads to the idea that traditional utility theory should be amplified by a theory of choice between products in all cases where the good considered by the former appears to be a differentiated commodity.

The essential elements of a theory of choice between two products (1 and 2) forming part of a differentiated commodity have been very well defined by L. E. Fouraker.[11] The data are: (a) a certain amount of money (determined by utility theory) to be spent for the given differentiated commodity; (b) the prices p_1 and p_2; (c) the preferences (resulting from objective or subjective product differentiation) of the consumer. The data can be represented graphically by a budget line and a field of linear indifference curves (the constant marginal rate of substitution measuring the degree of differentiation).

The optimal allocation of the given amount of money is clearly determined as follows: the consumer buys product 1 exclusively, when his marginal rate of substitution of 1 for 2 has an absolute value less than p_2/p_1; he buys product 2 exclusively, in the opposite case. If the two ratios are equal, he may buy product 1 exclusviely, or product 2 exclusively, or some combination of the two products; the allocation is indetermined.

Let us take an initial situation in which the marginal rate of substitution of 1 for 2 is higher than p_2/p_1. When p_1 is lowered, p_2 remaining constant, product 2 will be replaced by product 1 as soon as p_2/p_1 has an absolute value in excess of the rate of substitution. *Replacement* appears to be the typical reaction to a change in the ratio of the prices. There is no substitution effect between two products.[12] There is no income effect either between two products. A fall in the price of a cigarette brand does not incite to buying a greater quantity of another cigarette brand. An income effect could appear only if the representative price of the commodity (cigarettes as a whole) is lowered in the mind of the consumer, which would then lead to a greater

[10]In a logical order, of course.

[11]Product Differentiation and Straight-line Indifference Curves, *loc. cit.*, pp. 569–70. I do not agree, however, with the way Fouraker conducted his inductive tests. By taking butter and margarine together, he compared two groups of "technically" different products, i.e., two differentiated commodities. His test should have been limited to the choice between different margarine brands, *or* between different butter brands.

[12]Cf. G. W. Nutter, *op. cit.*, p. 528: "Mixing the grades together is not usually thought of as producing a superior service: more pleasure in smoking does not typically come from using several brands of cigarettes."

consumption of *another commodity* (beer, for instance). But there we are again in the field of utility theory.

It is now easy to define the main features of a demand curve derived from straight-line indifference curves. On the one axis one could measure well specified prices (prices fixed by a firm for a particular product), on the other, well specified units of the product under consideration. The "ceteris paribus" hypothesis refers to (1) the prices of the other products within a same differentiated commodity, and (2) the representative price of the differentiated commodity and all other commodities. There is a curve for product 1 only for the price range within which p_2/p_1 has an absolute value in excess of the marginal rate of substitution of 1 for 2; within this range, the curve has the form of a rectangular hyperbole, as the constant amount of money is spent entirely on product 1.

Let us now return to traditional utility theory. It has been admitted for a long time that, drawing an indifference field, the vertical axis measuring quantities of a good *A*, and the horizontal measuring quantities of a good *B*, *B* can represent any group of goods, on the condition that relative prices within the group are supposed to be constant.[13] M. Friedman,[14] referring to A. Marshall, has shown that group *B* may be divided into subgroups. More recently, several writers[15] extended Friedman's idea, showing that *A* may also represent a commodity group.[16]

My point is that, because of the convexity postulate (necessary in order to obtain a stable solution) *A* and *B cannot* stand for particular products or sub-groups of products, when these products form part of a differentiated commodity.[17] In that case, *A* and *B* cannot stand but for *groups*: these groups can identify themselves with differentiated commodities. They may

---

[13]Cf. J. R. Hicks, *Value and Capital* (2d ed.; New York: Oxford University Press, 1946), Chapter II, No. 4. See also W. Leontief, "Composite Commodities and the Problem of Index Numbers," *Econometrica*, Vol. IV, No. 1 (1936), pp. 55–57, and R. L. Basmann, "A Theory of Demand with Variable Consumer Preferences," *Econometrica*, Vol. XXIV, No. 1 (1956), p. 55.

[14]"The Marshallian Demand Curve," *Journal of Political Economy*, Vol. LVII, No. 6 (1949), p. 465 sqq.

[15]See I. F. Pearce, "A Method of Consumer Demand Analysis Illustrated," *Economica*, Vol. XXIII, N.S. (1961), pp. 371–394, and the references given at p. 371 of that article. See especially R. H. Strotz, "The Empirical Implications of a Utility Tree," *Econometrica*, Vol. XXV, No. 2 (1957), pp. 269–280.

[16]In a Marshallian perspective one does not see why good *A* should correspond to a well determined physical object. Cf. M. Friedman, *op. cit.*, p. 469: "Demand and supply are to him (Marshall) concepts for organizing materials, labels in an 'analytical filing box.' The 'commodity' for which a demand curve is drawn is another label, not a word for a physical or technical entity to be defined once and for all, independently of the problem at hand." See the famous note on p. 100 of the original eighth edition of the *Principles*.

[17]Here I am not following A. Marshall, who suggests, in footnote 16, that utility theory could be applied to sub-groups within a differentiated commodity.

be larger; but they cannot be smaller. There is, thus, a minimum limit to commodity grouping.[18]

As a direct consequence, the individual demand curve, derived from utility theory, refers normally[19] to a group of products, i.e., a commodity. The axes measure alternative average prices (or rather prices considered as representative for the group) and the amounts spent at the corresponding prices.[20] Specific quantities can be measured only for homogeneous commodities.

The Aggregate Demand Curve

Suppose the ideas laid down in the previous section are acceptable: what would be the implications as for the construction of an aggregate demand curve (for the market of an industry)? Probably, the reader already has realized that those ideas could allow us to tranquillize the conscience of the writers on monopolistic competition who had the courage to draw an aggregate demand curve for a differentiated commodity.

Let us briefly recall the main aspects of the controversy. It is well known that E. H. Chamberlin thought of an aggregate demand curve for a differentiated commodity.[21] However, he could not conceal his embarrassment, as the following quotation shows:

> . . . . In fact, the very concept of a demand curve for the general market of a differentiated product is open to the objection that people do not demand the product "in general," but particular varieties of it, so that the amount which any buyer will take depends not only upon the price but upon the variety which is offered to him.[22]

J. Robinson uses a "total demand curve," emphasizing, however, that the number of products under consideration is always a matter of convention.[23]

---

[18]This seems to support the following idea of A. Smithies: "Suppose it can be established empirically that the markets for different brands of coffee are definitely more closely interdependent than any one of them is dependent on the market for tea or any other competing product. In these circumstances, while it may be quite uninstructive to treat the markets for particular brands of coffee in isolation, we may be able to obtain useful results by considering the market for coffee as a whole, assuming everything outside it to remain unchanged. Considerations such as these determine the minimum extent of an imperfect market; . . ." Cf. A. Smithies, "Equilibrium in Monopolistic Competition," *Quarterly Journal of Economics*, Vol. LV, No. 1 (November, 1940), pp. 95–96.

[19]I.e., in all cases where a commodity is composed of several products.

[20]This conclusion is very similar to an idea advanced by J. M. Clark. Cf. J. M. Clark, "Realism and Relevance in the Theory of Demand," *Journal of Political Economy*, Vol. LIV, No. 4 (1946), p. 351.

[21]E. H. Chamberlin, *The Theory of Monopolistic Competition* (3d ed.; Cambridge, Mass.: Harvard University Press, 1939), pp. 82–83.

[22]*Ibid.*, p. 91, footnote 1.

[23]J. Robinson, "What is Perfect Competition?" *Quarterly Journal of Economics*, Vol. XLIX, No. 1 (November, 1934), p. 116 and pp. 113–114.

On the other hand, F. Zeuthen[24] suggests that an aggregate demand concept could be useful in an intermediary range between homogeneous and differentiated markets; accordingly, he gives himself much trouble to find particular features characterizing "temporarily" non-homogeneous and "approximately" homogeneous markets. Of course, this attempt was condemned to come at a dead end, for as long as a market is "temporarily" non-homogeneous, it is to be considered, in theory, as differentiated.[25] As to the "truly" or "definitely" non-homogeneous market, Zeuthen makes a categorical statement:

> .... Aggregate supply and demand functions for all sellers and buyers must here be replaced by an analysis of the interplay between the individual buyers and sellers. No aggregate demand function for the total market with one price and one quantity will be able to indicate the effect of the total demand, neither will a function between the price in any representative or arbitrary point of the (geographical) market and total quantity, nor a function between average price and total quantity. The total quantity is a function, not of one price, but of all the different prices in the individual parts of the market, and the price differences between them are not fixed because different combinations of actual transports will be realized in different price situations.[26]

In spite of these series of objections, G. J. Stigler has made use of a "total market demand,"[27] although stressing, in another context, that one is not allowed to add up individual demand curves of differentiated products: "The quantity axes of the various product diagrams are simply not the same; one measures three-room apartments, another four-room houses, and perhaps still another, restaurant meals (an excellent substitute for a kitchen)."[28] In general, however, writers dare not, at this moment, conceive of an aggregate demand curve for a differentiated commodity; especially as they think that the term "differentiated commodity" cannot have a precise meaning.[29]

If the conclusions of the second section are acceptable, these objections loose much of their strength. Indeed, these rest on the idea that utility theory applies to purchases of specific products, and that individual demand curves refer accordingly to particular products; under these conditions, aggregation has little meaning, and an average price is a poor expedient. As soon as the individual demand curve derived from utility theory is seen as referring to

[24]F. Zeuthen, "Monopolistic Competition and the Homogeneity of the Market," *Econometrica*, Vol. IV, No. 3 (1936), pp. 193–209.

[25]In fact, Zeuthen's reasoning is circular, as he is saying that the "approximately" non-homogeneous market is to be distinguished from the homogeneous market according to the possibility of utilizing an aggregate demand curve. Cf. F. Zeuthen, *op. cit.*, p. 196.

[26]F. Zeuthen, *op. cit.*, p. 197.

[27]G. J. Stigler, *The Theory of Price* (New York: Macmillan, 1947), p. 230 and pp. 235–36.

[28]G. J. Stigler, *Five Lectures on Economic Problems* (London: Macmillan Co., 1949), p. 16.

[29]See, for example, F. Ritzmann, *Der Monopolgewinn* (Zurich: 1962), p. 52.

a (differentiated) *commodity, product* differentiation ceases to be an obstacle to aggregation.[30] For the market demand curve is obtained by aggregating individual demand curves referring to commodities, *not* by aggregating curves referring to products. This market demand curve is neither better nor worse than its components. To have recourse to an average or representative price does not seem to be objectionable any longer, even though it lacks precision.

What about aggregation of demand curves for products, derived from straight-line indifference curves? This aggregate curve cannot but coincide with the demand curve of the firm selling the product under consideration, as each firm has "the monopoly of its product" by definition. The form of this curve depends on the structure of preferences within the market, i.e., on the dispersion of the (constant) marginal rates of substitution within the group of customers. This point will be taken up again in the final section of this paper.

The Demand Curve of the Firm

In this section, I shall try to elucidate some implications of the ideas developed in the second section as to the construction of demand curves of a firm. My essential point was that, in the mind of a consumer, budget allocation problems on the one hand, and problems of choice between particular suppliers or brands on the other, are stated in completely different terms. In short, the choice of a "product" was opposed to the choice of a "commodity." I have now to draw similar distinctions from the point of view of a firm.

(a) There is the problem to know how many customers a firm could take away from the other firms of its industry, aggregate demand being constant.

(b) There is also the problem to know which part of aggregate demand a firm is able to attract, without taking customers away from competitors, when aggregate demand increases as the average price of the industry falls.

(c) These two questions are different from a third one, which is to determine how many new customers the industry as a whole may gain by a fall in the average price of the differentiated commodity.

It would be interesting to have curves giving a separate answer to these questions, as they seem to be of vital importance for the firm. Traditional (i.e., Chamberlinian) demand curves do not seem to be satisfactory in this respect. On the one hand, aggregate demand curves for differentiated commodities are either rejected, or used with great suspicion: this means that

[30]This supposes that the differentiated commodity is the same for all individuals. In other words, the commodity must be delimitated by an "objective" criterion, different from the "market gap in the chain of substitutes." I suggested a criterion I believe to be "objective," in my note in *Revue suisse d'économie politique et de statistique* (March, 1963).

there is no clear answer to our third question. As to the questions (a) and (b), they are considered *en bloc*, with the aid of Chamberlin's famous *dd'* and *DD'* curves.

The *dd'* curve, considered as "the" demand curve of the firm, is based on the hypothesis that competitors' prices remain constant at a given level. Actually it represents the arrival of customers, taken away from the competitors, *and the arrival of new consumers*, who were not able to buy the products of the industry at higher prices. Indeed, Chamberlin is saying that *dd'* has evidently a greater elasticity than *DD'*; this is to say that, in order to draw the former, one has to add the customers taken away from competitors and the new customers entering the market.[31] This is also the point of J. Robinson[32] and of H. von Stackelberg.[33] As long as no distinction is made between product differentiation *within* a differentiated commodity and the (decreasing) marginal rate of substitution *between* differentiated commodities, this position is of course unattackable. As soon as such a distinction is made, one must regret that the *dd'* curve is defined as showing the aggregate effect of taking customers away from competitors *and* attracting new customers (who could not previously buy the commodity).

The *DD'* curve is based on the assumption that the prices of all products within the industry are always equal. At first sight, it seems to show how sales are increasing when new consumers enter into the market at lower average prices (no customers being taken away from competitors, for prices are supposed to remain equal). In fact, this is not the case, as Chamberlin stresses that "such a curve will, in fact, be a fractional part of the demand curve for the general class of product, and will be of the same elasticity."[34] The distribution of the market is thus supposed to remain unchanged, which comes to the same thing as eliminating our question (b), as referred above.

These characteristics of Chamberlin's curves support the view that there seems to be room for three other curves, corresponding to each of our three questions. First, one could think of an aggregate demand curve (*DA*) applying to the industry as a whole (question [c]). *DA* could be defined as representing the sales a producer could make if he succeeded in eliminating all his competitors (within the industry). This curve would be the same for all firms (within the industry under consideration) whatever the degree of differentiation of their products, as it refers to the heterogeneous *commodity* and not to a particular product.

---

[31]E. H. Chamberlin, *The Theory of Monopolistic Competition, op. cit.*, p. 90. See also M. Bouchard, "De la concurrence," *Economie Appliquée,* Vol. XIV, No. 1 (1961), p. 22.

[32]J. Robinson, "What is Perfect Competition?" *loc. cit.*, p. 116: "The stronger the competition from substitutes for this commodity the smaller the degree of competition within the industry necessary to secure any given elasticity of demand for each separate producer."

[33]H. von Stackelberg, "Probleme der unvollkommenen Konkurrenz," *Weltwirtschaftliches Archiv*, Vol. II, Bd. 48 (1938), p. 99.

[34]E. H. Chamberlin, *The Theory of Monopolistic Competition, op. cit.*, p. 90.

Secondly, one could draw a curve NN' on the assumption that the competitors immediately readjust their prices (i.e., make their prices equal) with the price of the firm under consideration. But NN' would not be a fraction of curve DA; it would measure the quantities of the firm's product bought by the consumers whose (constant) marginal rates of substitution of this product for any other product within the industry have absolute values less than 1.[35] The slope of the curve would measure what Zeuthen[36] calls "the power of expansion of the firm towards unsatisfied demand" and would give an answer to question (b). There seems to be no reason why this curve should be of the same elasticity as DA.

Finally, a curve nn' could answer question (a), if drawn on the assumptions that (1) all other prices remain unchanged and (2) that aggregate demand remains constant. This curve would illustrate exclusively the reactions of the *existent* customers of the industry, i.e., of the customers whose aggregate demand is measured by the point on DA to which nn' refers.

Figure 8-1 gives the DA curve, the NN' curve, and a few nn' curves corresponding to different points on DA. If we consider an industry composed of two firms selling each a differentiated product (the two products forming together a differentiated commodity), DA measures the approximate quantities q^* of the differentiated commodity, which this industry can sell at different alternative average prices p^*, or the quantities which one of these firms, e.g. firm 1, can sell at alternative prices p_1, on the assumption that it has the monopoly of this industry (and that accordingly $p_1 = p^*$). DA is obtained by summing up the individual demand curves *for the differentiated commodity*. The NN' curve is based on the assumption that $p_1 = p_2$, and may be more or less elastic than DA and nn'. The nn' curve is drawn on the assumption (1) that aggregate demand BP is constant, and (2) that p_2 is constant and equal to OB. For each $\overline{p}^*$ $(= \overline{p}_2)$ we have another nn' curve. Two of these other curves have been drawn, corresponding to OC, CQ and to OE, ER respectively. The distances BP, CQ, and ER are respective limits of these curves.

The link between the theory of the second section and the construction of NN' and nn' could be stressed. NN' rests on the assumption that the consumers, who just decided to spend a certain part of their budget for the differentiated commodity under consideration, are then confronted with a budget line (relative to products 1 and 2) whose slope is unitary $(p_2 = p_1)$. Under these conditions the slope of their straight-line indifference curves

---

[35]As the assumption $p_2 = p_1$ implies that the slope of the budget line is unitary, all consumers whose marginal rate of substitution is less than 1 (in absolute value) buy product 1 exclusively.

[36]F. Zeuthen, "Monopolistic Competition and the Homogeneity of the Market," *loc. cit.*, p. 200, and *Economic Theory and Method* (London: 1957), pp. 261–263. In his presentation, Zeuthen follows the traditional interpretation of utility theory.

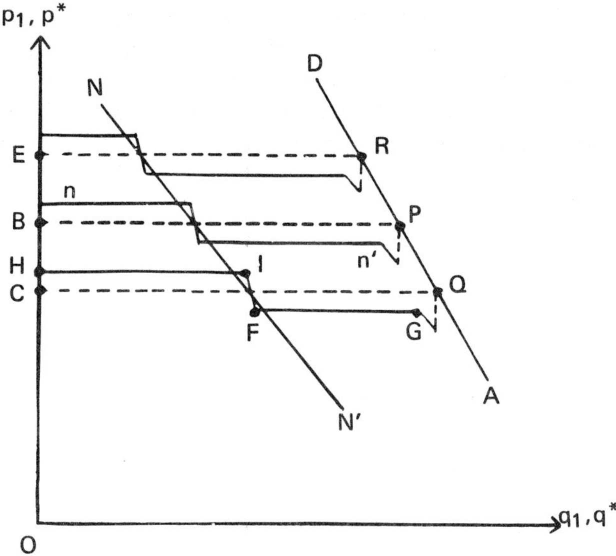

Figure 8-1

determines exclusively their choice among products. The different aggregate quantities of product 1, which would be bought at the corresponding alternative prices p_1 (= p_2 = p^*) give curve *NN'*.

The *nn'* curve is the sum of the individual demand curves *for product* 1 of the consumers whose aggregate demand is *PB*. Each individual curve starts at the price p_1 for which p_2/p_1 is just superior to the marginal rate of substitution of the consumer under consideration. If, at a certain price p_1, p_2/p_1 is equal to the marginal rate of substitution for a certain number of consumers, *nn'* takes the form of a "plateau-curve" similar to the one A. J. Nichol has described.[37] These consumers are "marginal."

Hence, the plateau *FG*, for example. As for the plateau *HI*, it measures the purchases (of product 1) of the consumer(s) with the highest marginal rate of substitution.

All this supports the view that the old "plateau demand curve" should be exhumed again. It is well known that Professor Chamberlin rejected Nichol's idea, among other things, because "nowhere is any reason given why these marginal buyers should be more numerous at one price than at another, which is the real meaning of the curve upon which Professor Nichol

[37] A. J. Nichol, "The Influence of Marginal Buyers on Monopolistic Competition," *Quarterly Journal of Economics*, Vol. XLIX, No. 1 (November, 1934), pp. 121–124.

bases his conclusions."[38] If, however, one allows for the fact that consumers are rather well informed about the qualities of competing products, one has to concede that there are quite good chances for a number of them to have the same marginal rates of substitution. As soon as the ratio of the prices attains this value, all these consumers become truly "marginal."

[38] E. H. Chamberlin, "Comments," *Quarterly Journal of Economics*, Vol. XLIX, No. 1 (November, 1934), p. 136.

9. THE DERIVATION OF DEMAND CURVES FROM INDIFFERENCE CURVES*

Dan Usher†

Judging from accounts in textbooks of economic theory, one would suppose that the theory of demand is a complete and consistent doctrine, at least in its elementary form in the two-commodity world without money where it is usually defined. There is, however, a small but significant inconsistency that enters demand theory between chapter 1 on the theory of consumer behaviour where the demand curve is defined, and later chapters where the demand curve is employed. The elimination of this inconsistency gives rise to a broader concept of the demand curve that covers the conventional textbook demand curve as a special case.

The inconsistency in the conventional demand curve arises over the notion of income. In the conventional derivation, it is supposed that income remains constant over movements along the demand curve, while in many uses of the demand curve, changes in income are co-ordinated with movements along the demand curve in some determinate way. To make allowance for income changes is to alter the way in which the demand curve is derived from indifference curves. If the view here is correct, it is not open to the economist to choose how he derives a demand curve from indifference curves for this is already implicitly defined each time a demand curve is used, and a rigorous restriction of the term 'demand curve' to the conventional textbook derivation would divorce the term from most of the contexts in which it now appears.

The paper begins by showing how the inconsistency in the conventional theory of demand leads to the notion of demand curves as class of functions, each derived from indifference curves in a unique way. An economic problem that calls for the use of a demand curve will in general contain the information necessary for deciding which species of demand curve is relevant to it. After a digression on the supply curve, six species of demand curves are examined one by one. The paper concludes with the examination of several topics common to more than one demand curve; these are community indifference curves, slopes of demand curves, and income and substitution effects. The n-commodity world and the transition from relative to money prices are taken up in

*From *Oxford Economic Papers*, N.S., Vol. XVII, No. 1 (March, 1965), pp. 24–46. Reprinted by permission of the Clarendon Press, Oxford, and the author.

†Dan Usher, Professor of Economics, University of British Columbia. This paper has benefited from comments by Francis Seton and Professor Sir John Hicks. In the latter case especially, this acknowledgement must not be taken to imply agreement with all the views expressed.

Appendix 1, and the application of ideas of this paper to the income vs. excise tax problem will be taken up in Appendix 2.

THE DERIVATION OF THE GENERIC DEMAND CURVE

The standard textbook definition of a demand curve supposes a two-commodity world in which one commodity is the numeraire and the other is by convention the commodity demanded. The subject of the demand curve, who is at first thought of as a single individual, is given an income in units of the numeraire commodity and allowed to exchange any part of this income for some of the other commodity at a given price. The functional relation between the given price and the quantity bought is the conventional demand curve.

The standard diagram[1] showing the derivation of the demand curve is presented as Figure 9-1. The vertical axis of the figure represents the numeraire commodity Q_1 and the horizontal axis represents the quantity demanded Q_2. (Amounts of Q_1 and Q_2 are indicated by q_1 and q_2). The initial income is Y. Prices, p, are slopes of lines radiating out of Y, and the amount demanded of Q_2 at any price is indicated by the tangency of the appropriate price line to an indifference curve. The locus of these points of tangency (subject to variation in the price P) is the price-consumption curve, from which the demand curve is derived. Demand curves of individuals are aggregated to yield a market-demand curve. The income applicable to a market-demand curve (where the relevant market is the nation as a whole) is the national income.[2]

Adherence to this notion of the demand curve is not as widespread among economists as textbooks would suggest. Walras and Wicksell had a notion of a demand curve applicable to a person who (in a two-commodity world) goes to market with given stocks of both goods and may purchase more of either depending on the going market relative price between them.[3] Pigou followed by Joan Robinson used a definition assuming not income but conditions of supply of all other commodities to be fixed during movements along

---

[1]See J. R. Hicks, *Value and Capital* (New York: Oxford University Press, 1953), Figure 7, p. 30.

[2]This version of the demand curve is generally attributed to Marshall. There is no hint of any other candidate for the demand curve in J. R. Hicks, *Value and Capital*, *ibid.*, or in Paul Samuelson, *The Foundations of Economic Analysis* (Cambridge, Mass.: Harvard University Press, 1947), or in H. Wold and L. Jureen, *Demand Analysis*, or in any current textbook (Friedman's excepted) that has come to my attention.

[3]See Leon Walras, *Elements of Pure Economics*, translated by William Jaffe (New York: Kelley Publishers, 1954), p. 93, and Knut Wicksell, *Lectures On Political Economy* (New York: Kelley Publishers, 1934), Vol. I, Part i. The exact derivation of this curve from indifference curves has been worked out in a manner similar to Figure 9-10 by K. Boulding, "The Concept of Economic Surplus," *American Economic Review*, Vol. XXXV (December, 1945), pp. 851–869. The currently accepted constant money-income demand curve is a special case of this curve in a two-commodity world.

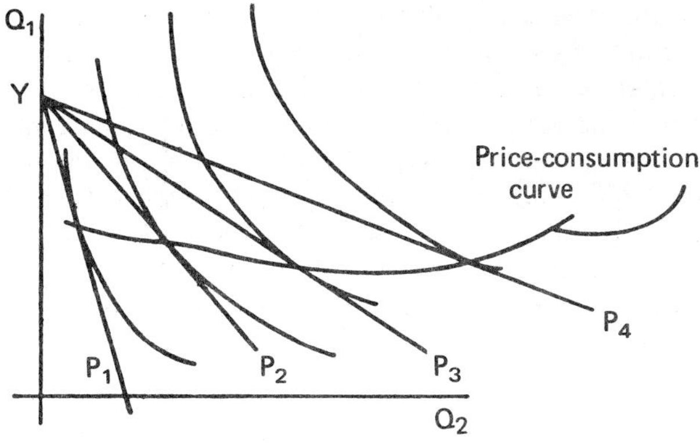

Figure 9-1

the demand curve.[4] Recently Friedman has made a strong case for a demand curve on which all points represent conditions of equal utility,[5] and in response to Friedman's paper Martin Bailey[6] revived Pigou's definition in a thorough and rigorous way.

The difficulty with the constant money-income demand curve arises not in its derivation but when the curve is used. To keep the demand curve consistent with its derivation, it is necessary to hold national income constant. But most of the applications of the demand curve are to situations in which whatever is causing a joint movement of quantity and price along the demand curve is affecting national income as well. Suppose the price of grain (in terms of manufactures) depends on its abundance or scarcity and that this in turn is caused by the weather. One would normally describe the set of alternative prices and quantities applicable to this situation as a demand curve, even

[4]In Joan Robinson, *The Economics of Imperfect Competition* (New York: St. Martin's Press, 1934), p. 20, she writes: "Marshall instructs us to draw up a demand schedule on the assumption that prices of all other things are fixed. This not only cuts off all hope of drawing realistic demand curves but it is somewhat illogical in itself. . . . The proper course is that suggested by Professor Pigou to assume not prices but the conditions of supply of all other commodities to be fixed. This still leaves of course many difficulties . . ." Joan Robinson's reference in Pigou contains no more on this point than the bald statement that the demand curve "may also be a function of conditions of supply of several other things." A. C. Pigou, "The Statistical Derivation of Demand Curves," *Economic Journal* (1930), reprinted in *Economic Essays and Addresses*, p. 64.

[5]See "The Marshallian Demand Curve," and "The 'Welfare' Effects of an Income Tax and an Excise Tax," both reprinted in Milton Friedman, *Essays in Positive Economics* (Chicago: University of Chicago Press, 1953), and Milton Friedman, *Notes on Lectures In Price Theory*, an abridged version of which has recently been published. [Ed. note: Milton Friedman, *Price Theory, A Provisional Text* (Chicago: Aldine Publishing Co., 1962).] Friedman recognizes several types of demand curves.

[6]Martin Bailey, "The Marshallian Demand Curve," *Journal of Political Economy*, Vol. LXII (June, 1954), pp. 255–266 (including Friedman's rejoinder). The demand curve of Figure 9-6 is the same as a construction in Bailey's paper.

though the income associated with points on this curve is not invariant.[7] Even the more conventional uses of the demand curve, as the average revenue curve of a monopolist, or as a description of the demand side of perfect competition, might involve income variation with movements along the demand curve.

If we knew the connection between changes in price and changes in income, this knowledge could easily be incorporated in the demand curve as illustrated in Figure 9-2. Each price line P_1 to P_4 cuts the vertical axis at the corresponding income Y_1 to Y_4 and the price-consumption curve is determined in the same way as before, though of course, the new price-consumption curve is different from the old one of Figure 9-1.

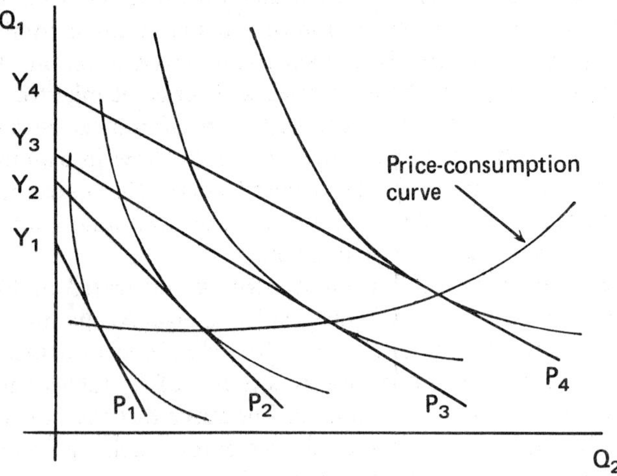

Figure 9-2

To each relation between income and price there corresponds a unique price-consumption curve from which a demand curve can be derived. Conversely any line passing through the field of indifference curves (q_1, q_2) defines a relation between income and price. This follows from the fact that any point in the field of indifference corresponds at once to a unique pair (q_1, q_2) and to a pair (P_1, Y), the latter being the combination of the slope of the indifference curve at (q_1, q_2) and the projection of this slope on the vertical axis.

This suggests a different way of deriving a demand curve. Suppose instead of using income and prices to derive a price-consumption curve, we take the price-consumption curve as given and derive the demand curve directly from it. A movement along a demand curve doesn't simply happen. It is caused by something, and this cause necessarily alters the amounts of Q_1 and Q_2 con-

[7]In this case income could be positively or negatively correlated with changes in the quantity of grain available depending on the elasticity of demand, or to be more precise, on slopes of indifference curves.

sumed, which in turn indicates the price P as the slope of an indifference curve at (q_1, q_2).

Define a demand curve as a function connecting quantity demanded, q_2, and its demand price, P, where the demand price is the marginal rate of substitution in use between the good demanded Q_2 and the numeraire Q_1 and where this price is measured by the slope of an indifference curve.

This definition does not specify a unique curve, for above each point q_2 on the horizontal axis lies a family of indifference curves each corresponding to a unique value of q_1 and each having its own slope. To pass from this general definition to a specific curve, it is necessary to specify which value of q_1 corresponds to each value of q_2, i.e., to set down the price-consumption curve.

We are proposing a generic[8] definition of a demand curve combined with a rule for specifying which curve is relevant to any given situation. In view of the difficulty of knowing how income varies with price, it might be supposed that this general definition is empty because the specifics it refers to cannot be discovered. Fortunately this is not true. We shall show in examples below that for a large variety of uses of the demand curve, the appropriate price-consumption curve is easily discovered from the economic context of the problem in which the demand curve appears.

The complete derivation of a demand curve is illustrated in Figure 9-3. The top half of the figure is like Figures 9-1 and 9-2 except that the price-consumption curve is given directly, and without reference to income. The price P corresponding to each quantity q_2 is indicated by the slope of the indifference curve cutting the price-consumption curve directly above q_2. The vertical axis in the bottom half of the figure measures price P instead of Q_1, but the horizontal axis is the same in the two figures. The sets of corresponding prices and quantities derived in the top half of the figure are illustrated as a demand curve in the bottom half.

A DIGRESSION ON THE DERIVATION OF THE SUPPLY CURVE FROM THE PRODUCTION POSSIBILITY CURVE

The supply curve is the function connecting the quantity produced and the supply price, the latter being defined as the marginal rate of substitution in production between Q_1 and Q_2. As long as resources are not being wasted, the supply price corresponding to any given output of Q_2 is the slope of the production possibility curve directly above it. The method of constructing

---

[8]The generic concept of the demand curve proposed here has much in common with the total demand curve advocated by I. F. Pearce, "Total Demand Curves and General Equilibrium," *Review of Economic Studies*, Vol. XX (1952–53), pp. 216–27. The main point of this article is anticipated in the final paragraph of Bailey's paper (*op. cit.*), when he states that "the choice of a demand curve for purposes of analysis should depend on the problem in hand" (p. 261). Friedman agrees and states: "There is no need to decide in advance what interpretation to use and no need to use only one" (p. 266).

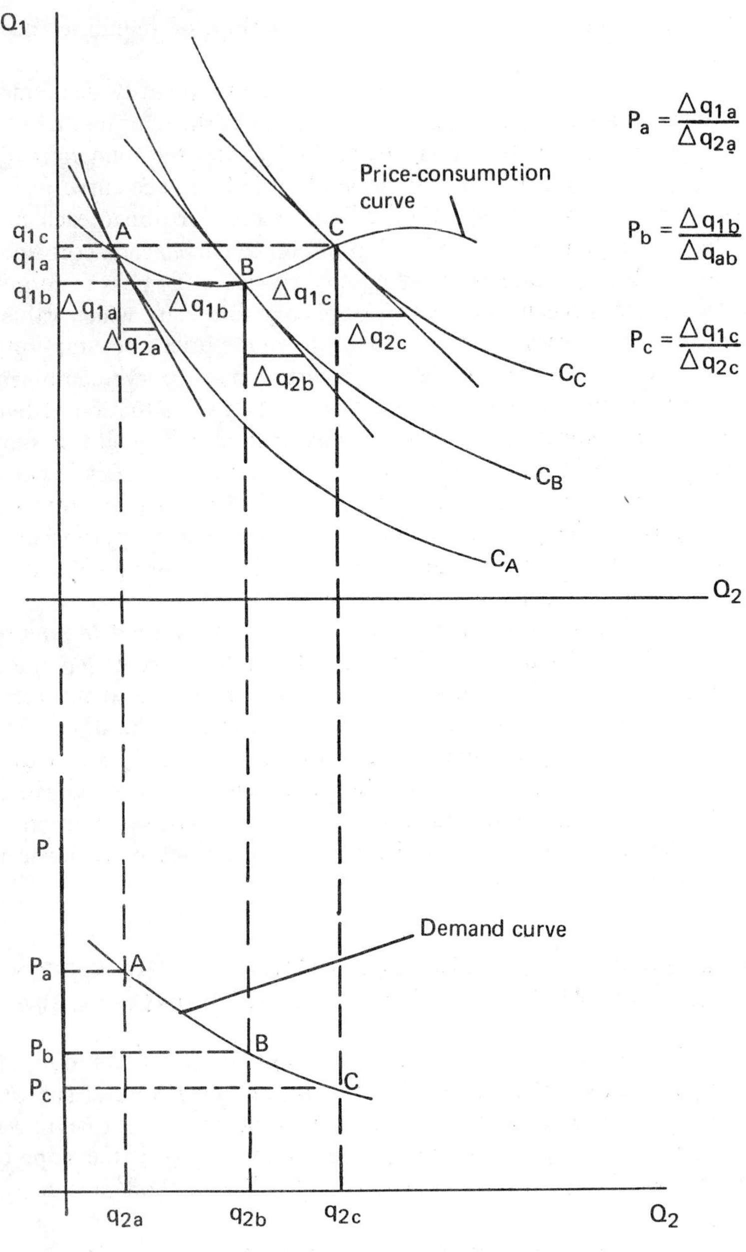

Figure 9-3

the supply curve is illustrated in Figure 9-4. The concavity of the production possibility curve ensures that the supply curve is upward sloping.

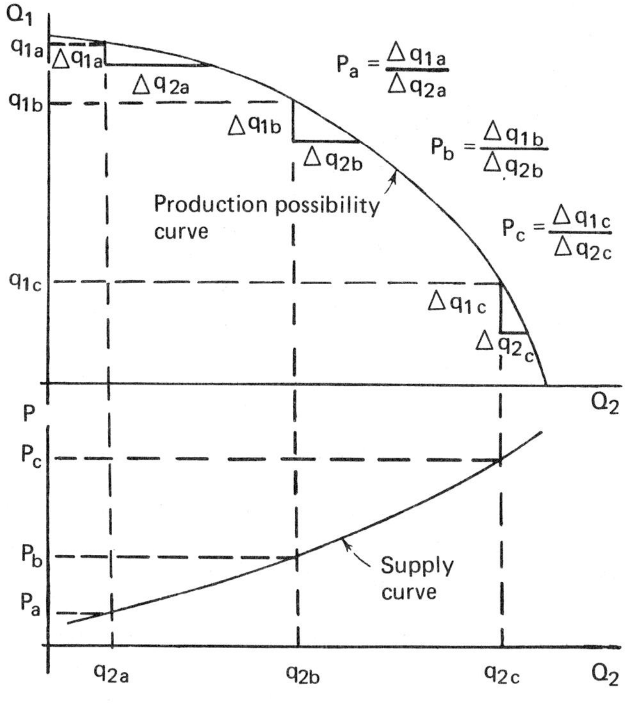

Figure 9-4

Long- and short-run supply curves can be distinguished by the proportion between fixed and variable factors of production. The shortest conceivable run is that in which no factors are allowed to vary so that no substitution between the goods is possible. The longest conceivable run is that for which the production possibility curve is a straight line. Production possibility curves corresponding to four runs are illustrated in Figure 9-5. The supply curve can be derived from each of them in the manner described in Figure 9-4.

A production possibility curve and its corresponding supply curve might be constructed subject to constraints. Unchanging prices of certain factors of production might be postulated in a supply curve constructed by adding up supply curves of firms in an industry.[9]

The variety of possible supply curves has an origin different from the variety of possible demand curves. In the former case, the conditions of the problem specify a single production possibility curve which in turn specifies a unique supply curve. In the latter there is always a set of indifference curves, and the conditions of the problem determine a price-consumption curve indicating the indifference curve relevant to any given quantity demanded.

---

[9]See J. R. Hicks, "A Note on the Elasticity of Supply," *Review of Economic Studies*, Vol. II (1934–5), pp. 31–37.

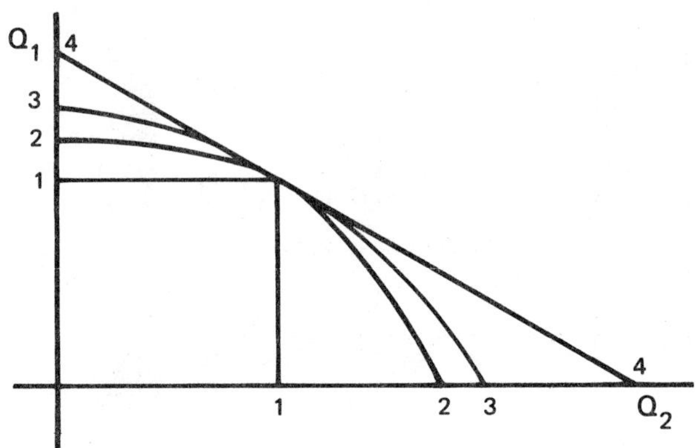

Figure 9-5

In a sense the production possibility curve acts as its own price-consumption curve. If Figures 9-3 and 9-4 were superimposed, the production possibility curve might equally well specify a demand curve, or appear as part of a construction out of which the demand curve is specified. When conditions of production and taste are joined in this way, the indifference curves must be those of the recipient of outputs indicated by the production possibility curve, i.e., they must describe tastes of a market or a community as a whole.

SIX TYPES OF DEMAND CURVES

The Production Demand Curve

This is the demand curve hinted at above for which the production possibility curve acts as a price-consumption curve in a diagram combining a community's tastes and opportunities.

The supply side of Figure 9-6 is reproduced unchanged from Figure 9-4, and the demand side is essentially Figure 9-3, where the production possibility curve acts as the price-consumption curve. The supply price associated with any output of Q_2 is the slope of the production possibility curve above it. The corresponding demand price is the slope of the indifference curve touching the appropriate point on the production possibility curve. Above the point q_{2a}, the slope of the production possibility curve is $\Delta q_1^S/\Delta q_2 (\equiv P_a^S)$ and the slope of the indifference curve cutting the production possibility curve is $\Delta q_1^D/\Delta q_2 (\equiv P_b^D)$. These slopes are the prices associated with q_{2a} on the supply and demand curves respectively. The market equilibrium is denoted

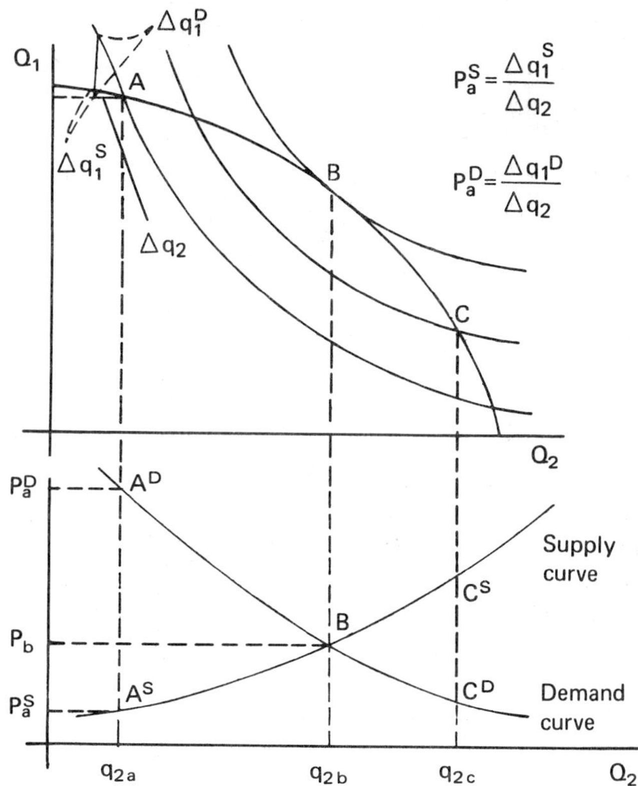

Figure 9-6

as *B*. At *B* the production possibility curve is tangent to an indifference curve, indicating an equality between demand and supply prices and a crossing of the demand and supply curves.

The production demand curve defined in this way is the curve facing an industry in perfect competition, on the understanding that other industries and factor markets are in competition as well. This curve specifies the price of Q_2 that the firms making it can expect to receive if through error or perversity the economy as a whole, the sum total of firms, chooses to produce a mix of Q_1 and Q_2 different from that required by the market equilibrium *B*.

If for instance, the output of Q_2 were q_{2a} instead of q_{2b} (which is what output of Q_2 ought to be) the corresponding output of Q_1 would have to be q_{1a} and the price the market would set on Q_2 would be P_a^D, the appropriate point on the production demand curve.

The AR Curve Facing a Monopolist

No distinction is made in the usual analysis of monopoly between the demand curve facing an industry in competition and the average revenue curve of a monopolist. Though the difference between them is never likely to be very large or very significant, the two curves are identical only when the monopolists' consumption is too small a part of total consumption to affect price formation on the demand side. The method used here enables us to consider the case where the monopolists' consumption is large enough to affect the demand price.

It is essential in deriving this curve to distinguish between the tastes of the community exclusive of the monopolist and the tastes of the monopolist himself. The community indifference curves in Figure 9-7 are those of the community exclusive of the monopolist. The monopolist is assumed to consume only the good Q_1 and to maximize his revenue (from the exclusive right to sell Q_2) in terms of the good Q_1. It is assumed that except for this monopoly grant the whole economy, product and factor markets, is in competition.

The monopoly grant is the right to choose the output of Q_2 — to buy this output from the factors of production and to sell it back to final consumers, so as to earn the difference between demand and supply price. Suppose the monopolist chooses the output q_{2a}. In conjunction with this output of Q_2, the rest of the economy produces an amount q_{1a} of Q_1 as indicated by the production possibility curve. The price the monopolist has to pay for this quantity of Q_2 is indicated by the slope of the production possibility curve. The monopolist buys an amount q_{2a} of Q_2 from the factors of production for an amount $q^*_{1a} - q_{1a}$ of Q_1, the ratio between the two amounts being the supply price. The monopolist acquires the quantity $q^*_{1a} - q_{1a}$ of Q_1, and more besides by selling the amount q_{2a} of Q_2 back to the community. The highest price the monopolist can set (if he wishes to sell the whole of his acquired stock of Q_2) is that corresponding to a slope of a line through q^*_{1a} cutting the vertical line below A at a point P where this price line is tangent to a community indifference curve. The monopoly profit corresponding to the output q_{2a} is an amount of q_1 indicated by the distance PA. The rational monopolist maximizes revenue by choosing an output of q_2 for which PA is the greatest; let it be supposed that this output is q_{2a}.

The average revenue curve tells the monopolist what price he can set at each possible output of q_2. This set of feasible price and output combinations is indicated by the locus of P over changes in q_2; this locus is indicated on Figure 9-7. As a rule it begins, from left to right, at the intersection of the production possibility curve and the vertical axis. It thereafter remains below the production possibility curve, rejoining it at the point B, the competitive equilibrium at which the monopoly profit disappears.

The supply curve in the bottom part of Figure 9-7 is constructed as in Figure 9-4. Here it serves as the monopolist's average cost curve. The demand curve is fixed by the locus of the point P. Marginal revenue and marginal cost curves are derived from demand and supply curves in the usual way.

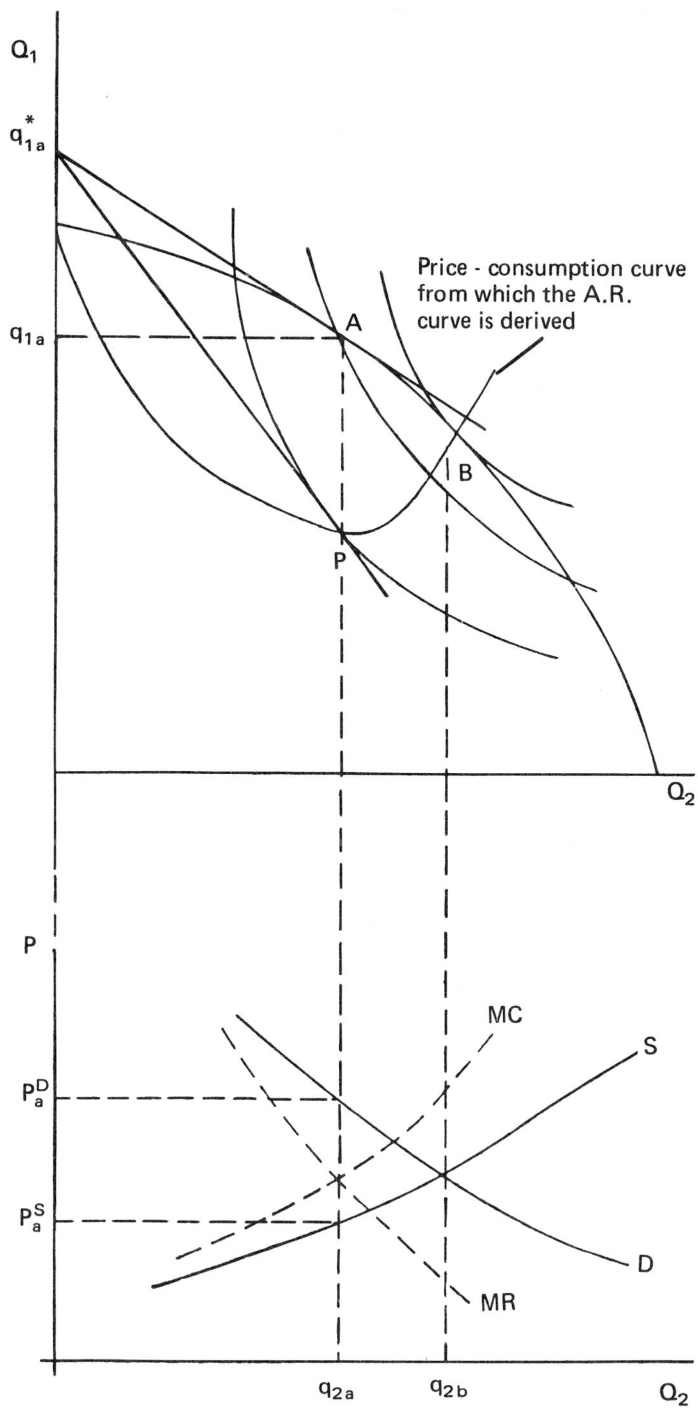

Q_1
q^*_{1a}
q_{1a}
A
Price - consumption curve from which the A.R. curve is derived
B
P
Q_2
P
MC
S
P^D_a
P^S_a
D
MR
q_{2a}
q_{2b}
Q_2

Figure 9-7

The Compensated Demand Curve[10]

The compensated demand curve is not employed in any practical situation. It is instead the curve that measures off areas of consumers' surplus. Figure 9-8 demonstrates a symmetry in the origins of consumers' and producers' surplus. The total surplus to a community in being able to produce Q_2 at all (measured

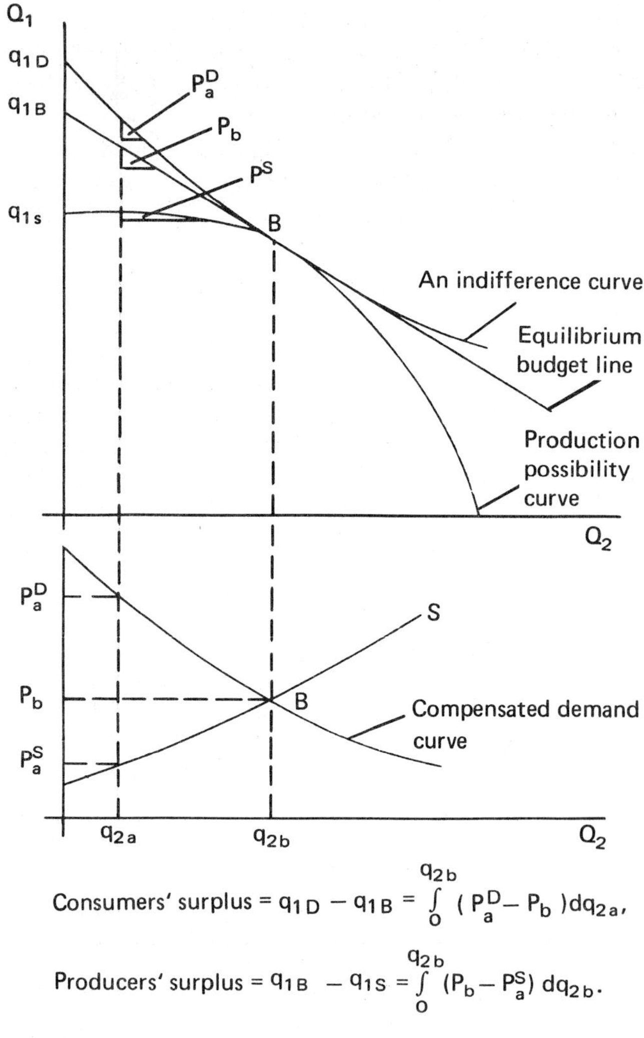

Figure 9-8

[10]For the *raison d'être* of this term see J. R. Hicks, *A Revision of Demand Theory* (New York: Oxford University Press, 1956).

in units of Q_1) is here defined to be the difference between the maximum amount of Q_1 that could be produced (the point q_{1S}) and the amount of Q_1 alone (the point q_{1D}) that would make the community as well off as it is at the equilibrium B attained when both goods can be produced in combinations consistent with the production possibility curve.[11] This total surplus divides naturally into consumers' and producers' surplus. The consumers' surplus is $q_{1D} - q_{1B}$, the difference between the amount of Q_1 that the community would be willing to exchange for the bundle of Q_1 and Q_2 consumed at equilibrium and the market value (in units of Q_1) of that bundle. The producers' surplus is $q_{1B} - q_{1S}$, the difference between the value of the bundle of goods consumed and the maximum quantity of Q_1 alone that could be produced.

The proof that consumers' and producers' surplus defined in this way correspond to areas under the demand curve and above the supply curve follows directly from the definition of an integral as the area under the integrated curve.

The Short-Run Agricultural Demand Curve

Imagine that a crop has already been planted and that this year's food output (Q_2) now depends on nothing but the weather. The demand curve associating possible outputs and resulting prices represents a situation in which only Q_2 is variable because the output of non-agricultural products (Q_1) is independent of climatic conditions. This demand curve is therefore specified by a horizontal line (Figure 9-9) the height of which is the given output of Q_1.

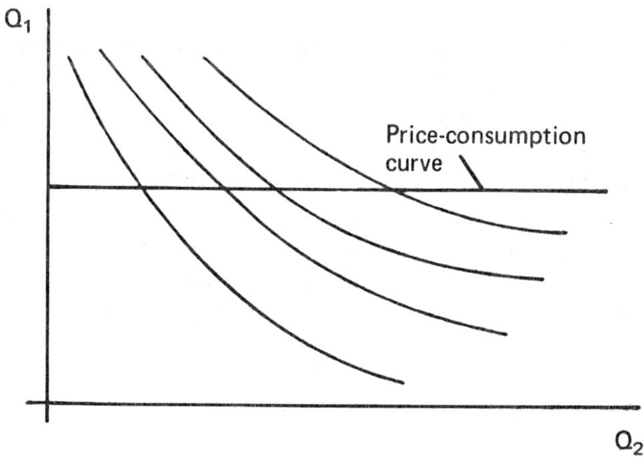

Figure 9-9

[11]There are, of course, many other definitions of surplus. See Don Patinkin, "Demand Curves and Consumer's Surplus," in *Measurement in Economics, Studies in Mathematical Economics and Econometrics in Memory of Yehuda Grunfeld*, edited by Carl Christ (Stanford: Stanford University Press, 1963).

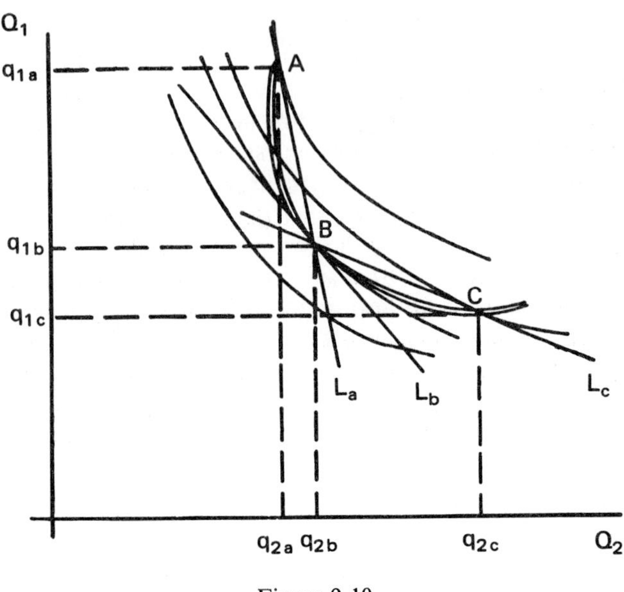

Figure 9-10

The Traders' Demand Curve[12]

Imagine a trader coming to a market with a stock of goods, and prepared to trade either of them if the price is right. His initial stock is *B*, q_{1b}, and q_{2b}. He will not trade unless the price ratio differs from L_b, tangent to his indifference curve at *B*, and representing his marginal rate of substitution in use of Q_1 and Q_2. He will buy whichever good is cheap relative to L_b. If the price ratio is L_c he will exchange $q_{1c} - q_{1b}$ for $q_{2c} - q_{2b}$. If the price ratio is L_a he will exchange $q_{2b} - q_{2a}$ for $q_{1b} - q_{1a}$. The locus of the points like *A*, *B*, *C* representing the bundles of goods he acquires at all possible price ratios is the price-consumption curve of the trader's gross demand for Q_2. As seen from a vertical axis through *B* (his initial stock of goods), the gross demand curve for Q_2 becomes a net demand curve to the right and a net offer, or supply curve of a sort, to the left.

The Constant Money-Income Demand Curve

This is the conventional demand curve of Figure 9-1. Analytically, this curve is a sub-species of the trader's demand curve, but it is open to much wider application. The only formal difference between the two curves is that the subject of this curve begins with a stock *Y* of one good (Q_1 by convention)

[12]The term was used by Leon Walras. See his *Elements of Pure Economics*, *op. cit.*, p. 93.

only. The economic difference between this demand curve and the trader's demand curve is that the good Q_1 can, to a degree of approximation, be thought of as general purchasing power allowing this curve to serve as a model of a consumer choosing how to spend his income.

The constant money-income demand curve has two valuable properties that might account for its historical precedence. The first is that it is naturally suitable to represent consumer behavior in a general equilibrium system.[13] Most of the demand curves examined so far indicate the price and quantity combinations that would be observed if certain changes took place in the economy, if a monopolist changed his output, or if there were a poor harvest of grain. The constant money-income demand curve describes the behavior of a consumer subject to a parameter, income that appears to the consumer as fixed but is in fact determined jointly by the demand and supply sides of the economic system.[14] This is precisely the role required of a demand equation in a general equilibrium system in which, given the demand equations, income is finally determined in equations pertaining to the behavior of productive agents.

The properties of the constant money-income demand curve that make it appropriate as one equation in a general equilibrium system, render it inappropriate as the demand curve in a simple demand and supply diagram such as the bottom half of Figure 9-6. One requires of this diagram an independence of the supply and demand curves so that one curve may shift while the other holds steady; the usefulness of the supply and demand concepts lies in that the forces acting on the market can be classified under one of these two headings exclusively. Unlike the production demand curve of Figure 9-6, the constant money-income demand curve is not invariant over changes on the supply side, because these changes generally cause a change in income. The constant money-income demand curve is not appropriate to the simple demand and supply diagram unless one is prepared to allow the whole demand curve to shift in conjunction with changes in price or quantity demanded.

The other valuable attribute of the constant money-income demand curve is its close connection with the statistical demand curve of the form

$$\text{quantity demanded} = f(\text{price, national income})$$

where the variables are measured by time series data. For reasons given in the last paragraph but one, the constant money-income demand curve is the appropriate basis for the statistical demand curve above if this equation is intended as one equation in a general equilibrium system in which other equations depict the supply side.

---

[13]See for instance, the treatment of demand in G. Debreu, *Theory of Value* (Cowles Foundation Monograph No. 17), especially criterion of section 5.5.

[14]In Patinkin's terminology, the constant money-income demand curve refers to an "individual experiment" while the production demand curve refers to a "market experiment." See Don Patinkin, *Money, Interest and Prices* (New York: Harper and Row, 1964), p. 15. See also Section III of Leland B. Yeager, "Methodenstreit Over Demand Curves," *Journal of Political Economy*, Vol. LXVIII (February, 1960), pp. 53–64. (Editor's note—In this volume see article 5, pp. 90–104.)

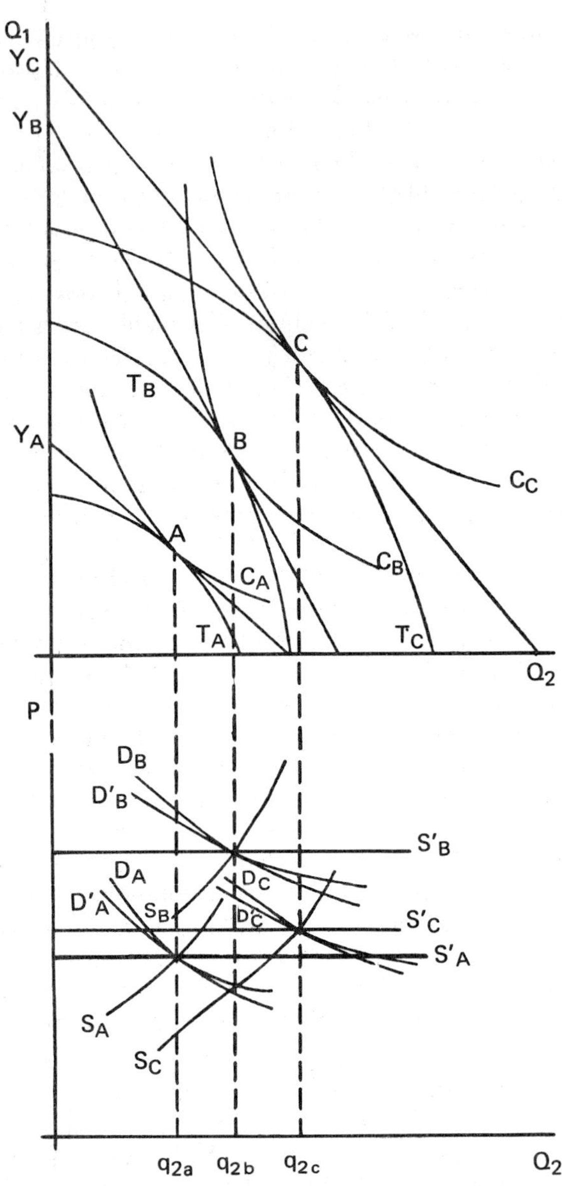

Figure 9-11[15]

[15]C_A, C_B, and C_C are indifference curves; Y_A, Y_B, and Y_C are incomes measured in units of Q_1; T_A, T_B, and T_C are production possibility curves. D_A, D_B, and D_C are production demand curves; S_A, S_B, and S_C are supply curves derived from T_A, T_B, and T_C; D'_A, D'_B, and D'_C are constant money-income demand curves associated with Y_A, Y_B, and Y_C; S'_A, S'_B, and S'_C are supply curves derived from the price lines $Y_A A$, $Y_B B$, and $Y_C C$ as if these were production possibility curves.

There is another possible interpretation of the statistical demand curve that would associate the equation with a modified production demand curve. One might require of a statistical demand curve that at any given time it show the actual variation of quantity with price indicated by the production possibility curve. As time passes, technology changes and the production possibility curve shifts. A demand curve that is to be accurate at more than one moment of time must shift along with the production possibility curve. Figure 9-11 illustrates the effect of shifts in production possibility curve and the demand curve. At times *A*, *B* and *C*, the production possibility curve takes up positions T_A, T_B, and T_C, specifying demand and supply curves D_A and S_A, D_B and S_B, and D_C and S_C respectively.

In practice too little is known about the shape of the production possibility curves or about demand prices off the point of equilibrium to permit shifts in the demand curve to be estimated in this way; most of the relevant information available can be summed up in the statistics of national income and of prices. At best, the production possibility curve can be approached by letting income and prices stand for its overall height and angle of inclination.

The advantage of the constant money-income demand curve as a rationale for statistical demand curves is that it is specified not by the information desired but by precisely the information available. Income and prices specify a production possibility curve exactly only if it is linear, in which case the production possibility curve is everywhere identical to its own budget surface. To make this assumption is to imagine a horizontal supply curve that shifts between points of equilibrium taking up positions S'_A, S'_B, S'_C in Figure 9-11 as income shifts from Y_A to Y_B to Y_C. The equilibria *A*, *B*, *C* are obviously points on the constant money-income demand curves D'_A, D'_B, D'_C corresponding to incomes Y_A, Y_B, and Y_C.

There is another discrepancy between the assumptions governing our theoretical demand curves and the facts described by a statistical demand curve. The relation between price and quantity in the theoretical demand curves described here is one of comparative statics. Points on a demand curve represent mutually exclusive alternatives each assumed to persist in perpetuity, and the quantity axis indicates amount per unit of time. On the other hand the values connected in statistical demand curves refer to quantities or averages associated with specific limited periods of time. The use of comparative static demand theory to explain market statistics rests on the assumption that the relation between variables at a point of time is not too different from what it would be if the variables were to maintain their current values indefinitely. Or at least it is assumed that deviations from comparative static relationships are more or less the same in all of the data to be explained. The comparative static demand theory fits an empirical study only in so far as the relationship between price and quantity demanded today is independent of what happened yesterday and what will happen tomorrow. Of course, this discrepancy applies to all of the demand curves discussed here.

ASPECTS OF DEMAND CURVES IN GENERAL

The Slope of the Demand Curve

Of the six demand curves described, only the compensated demand curve is necessarily downward sloping.[16] The negative slope of the compensated demand curve is imparted by the necessary concavity of any indifference curve from which it might be derived. The production demand curve is always downward sloping only in the neighborhood of equilibrium where the production possibility curve is tangent to an indifference curve. The rest of the demand curves may on occasion be upward sloping. This occurs when the price-consumption curve deviates markedly from the course of a single indifference curve and when this deviation has a considerable effect on the demand price.

Income Effects and Substitution Effects

Because of its association with the constant money-income demand curve, the familiar derivations of income and substitution effects are based on a model of adjustments of quantities resulting from given changes in price. Definitions of these effects could equally well be based on adjustments in prices due to given changes in quantities. This is illustrated in Figure 9-12.

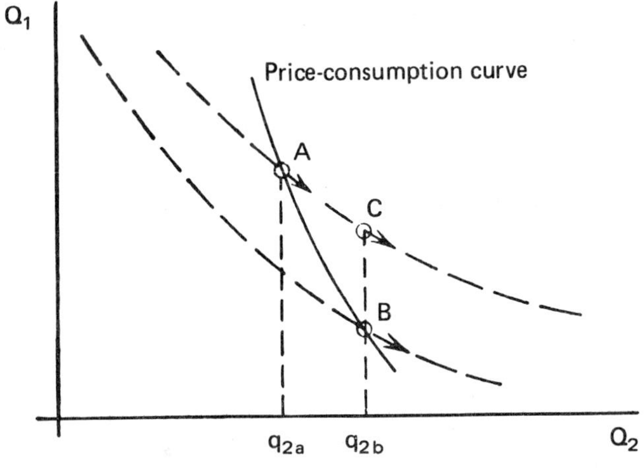

Figure 9-12

Imagine a movement along a demand curve from q_{2a} to q_{2b}. Suppose also that the price-consumption curve passes through the points A and B above q_{2a} and q_{2b} in the (q_1, q_2) plane. The substitution effect of this movement may

[16]This is strictly true only in a two-commodity world. See Appendix 1.

be defined as the change in price between *A* and a point *C* directly above q_{2a} on the same indifference curve as *A*. The income effect is the change in price between *C* and *B*. According to these definitions, any movement along the compensated demand curve has a substitution effect but no income effect, any fall in the price of Q_2 has a positive income effect in a constant money-income demand curve, any finite deviation from equilibrium has a negative income effect in the production demand curve, and any deviation from the initial stock has a positive income effect in the traders' demand curve.

Community Indifference Curves

It has so far been assumed that community indifference curves exist, because this strong assumption dispenses with cumbersome qualifications that would impede the main argument. It would have been adequate merely to suppose the existence of a price-direction corresponding to every bundle of goods consumed. A price-direction need not be defined at every point in the (q_1, q_2)-plane but only at those points that could conceivably be attained by the mechanism postulated to cause movements along the demand curve. Whatever moves consumption from one point to another in the (q_1, q_2)-plane must have some determinate effect on the price direction even if it involves distribution effects among members of the community. This in itself, without any knowledge of whether changes make the community as a whole better off or worse off, is sufficient information for the construction of the demand curve. This is illustrated on Figure 9-13. Prices are indicated by little arrows as shown at points *A* and *B*. These price-directions need only be defined at each point on the price-consumption curve. The corresponding demand curve is continuous if the variation in price-directions along the price-consumption curve is continuous. The demand curve is downward sloping if the slope of the price-direction gradually decreases from left to right along the price-consumption curve. The compensated demand curve is meaningless if community

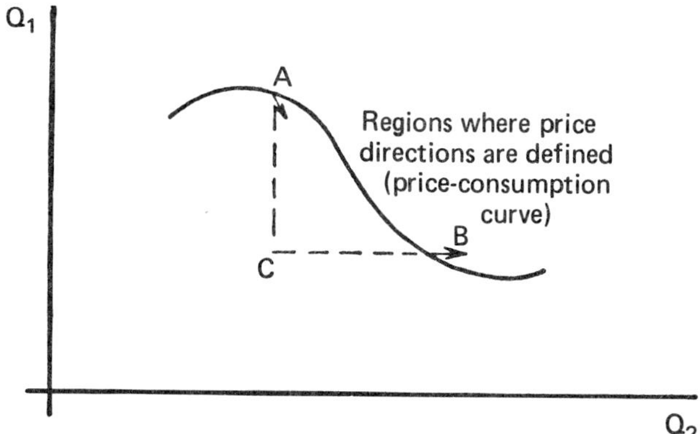

Figure 9-13

indifference curves are thought of in this way, but the remainder of the curves can be derived as above.[17]

Another approach to community price behavior is to imagine a community in which each member has identical tastes and owns an equal share of all productive resources. In this world a community indifference curve is an individual indifference curve magnified. It might be taken as a working hypothesis that the difference in the price behavior of an actual community and this hypothetical community is not sufficiently large to affect demand curves very much.[18]

APPENDIX 1

Extension from 2 to n Commodities and the Transformation from Relative to Absolute Prices

In an n-commodity world the subject of the demand curve, an individual consumer or a whole market, is assumed to possess a utility function

$$u(q_1 \ldots q_n). \tag{1}$$

Given any set of quantities $q_1, \ldots, q_n$, the vector of relative prices

$$\vec{P} \equiv \left(\frac{P_1}{\lambda} \cdots \frac{P_n}{\lambda}\right) \tag{2}$$

is determined by the relation

$$\frac{P_i}{\lambda} = u_i(q_1 \ldots q_n), \tag{3}$$

where P_i is the absolute money price and λ is any scalar. The price vector $\vec{P}$ at any point has the direction of the gradient of the utility function at that point.

A demand curve of the good Q_i is a relation with slope

$$\frac{dP_i(r)}{dq_i(r)} \tag{4}$$

defined over movements along the n-dimensional price-consumption curve

$$q_i = q_i(r) \tag{5}$$

for every $i = 1, \ldots, n$. Note that the demand curve dP_i/dq_i is related to the partial derivatives of the utility function by the equation

---

[17]This construction establishes a formal connection between the demand curve and the (q_1, q_2)-plane, but it leaves unsolved the more interesting problem of how the behavior of individuals aggregates to determine price.

[18]This would seem to be the line taken by H. Wold and L. Jureen. See *Demand Analysis*, *op. cit.*, p. 117.

(6) $$\frac{dP^i}{dq^i} = \frac{d(\lambda u_i)}{dq_i} = u_i \frac{d\lambda}{dq_i} + \lambda \sum_{j=1}^{n} u_{ij} \frac{dq_j(r)}{dq_i(r)}$$

where dq_j/dq_i is given by the equations of the price-consumption curve. This total differential expression is dominated by the partial differential u_{ii} if changes in r affect Q_i primarily, if the $u_{ij}(i \neq j)$ are small, or if the terms $u_{ij}(dq_j/dq_i)$ tend to cancel out.

This system is not yet determinate, for the parameter r sets relative prices only and is as yet consistent with any parameter λ. The transition from relative to absolute prices is a monetary phenomenon. Any consistent monetary theory might be used to tie down absolute prices. The simplest is the quantity theory of money.

(7) Suppose $$M = kY,$$

where M is the money supply assumed to be fixed, k is a constant, and Y is money income, defined as

(8) $$Y = \Sigma P_i q_i.$$

This equation may be used to pin down absolute prices, for by definition

(9) $$\lambda \equiv \frac{\Sigma u_i q_i}{\Sigma P_i q_i}.$$

To sum up: a system of equations underpinning a demand curve requires a utility function (1), a price-consumption curve (5), and a money equation connecting relative and absolute prices (7). Relative prices (3) are established by inserting into the utility function values consistent with the price-consumption curve. These are converted into absolute prices via the money equation. A demand curve (6) is a relationship between quantity available and price of some good defined over changes in the variable r of the price-consumption curve.

Consider some examples of how these equations work out. The price-consumption curve of the agricultural demand curve is

(5a) $$q_i = r \qquad q_j = \bar{q}_j \quad (i \neq j).$$

However much the quantity of Q_i varies other quantities are fixed. The slope of the demand curve for Q_i is

$$\frac{d(\lambda u_i(\bar{q}_1, \ldots, q_i, \ldots, \bar{q}_n))}{dq_i}$$

(9a) where $$\lambda = \frac{\sum_j u_j(\bar{q}_1, \ldots, q_i, \ldots, \bar{q}_n)}{\sum_j P_j q_j}$$

The production demand curve is more interesting. The subject of the demand curve is faced with a production possibility curve

$$g(q_1, q_2, \ldots, q_n) = 0. \tag{10}$$

At each output of Q_i, he maximizes utility with respect to all the other variables so that the price-consumption curve may be determined from the equations

$$q_i = r$$
$$(u_j)_{q_i=r} = \mu \cdot (g_j)_{q_i=r} \quad (i \neq j)$$
$$g(q_1, q_2, \ldots, q_n) = 0. \tag{5b}$$

The full demand curve for the commodity i can now be determined by means of equations (1) to (7).

The derivation of the constant-money income demand curve is simpler than the derivation of the other demand curves because one component in the derivation does the work of two. A man is given an income Y and allowed to buy $q_1, \ldots, q_n$ subject to prices $P_1, \ldots, P_n$. The demand curve of the good j traces out variations in q_j subject to variations in P_j only, when all $P_i (i \neq j)$ are held constant. The equations

$$P_j = \lambda u_j(q_1 \ldots q_n) \tag{5c}$$

$$\bar{P}_i = \lambda u_i(q_1 \ldots q_n) \quad (i = 1, \ldots, j-1, j+1, \ldots, n) \quad \bar{P}_i \text{ constant} \quad (i \neq j)$$

serve double duty as indicator of absolute prices and as the price-consumption curve subject to the parameter λ which is determined by the equation

$$P_i q_i = Y.$$

This last equation is the budget constraint. It plays a role in the derivation of the constant money-income demand curve similar to that played by the production possibility curve in the derivation of the production demand curve. The slope of the demand curve (this time q_i is the dependent variable) is

$$\frac{dq_i(P_i)}{d(P_i)} = \frac{\partial q_i}{\partial P_i}$$

for only one of $P_1, \ldots, P_n$ is allowed to vary at a time. The value of $\partial q_i / \partial P_i$ is given by the Stutsky equation.

The convexity of indifference curves ensures that the compensated demand curve is downward sloping in a two-good world. Unfortunately, this property does not always generalize to a world of more than two goods. There are types of movements $(dq_1 \ldots dq_n)$ along an indifference surface for which not all dP_i / dq_i are negative.

However, there is one important case in which dP_i / dq_i is always negative even in an n-commodity world. This is where the deviation $(dq_1 \ldots dq_n)$ changes the price P_i only leaving all other prices fixed. In this case

$$dP_j = u_j d\lambda + \lambda \sum_k u_{kj} dq_k = \delta_{ij} dP_i$$

yielding n equations with $n + 1$ unknowns. In addition since the deviation lies on an indifference surface

$$\sum_k u_k dq_k = 0.$$

This set of equation is exactly comparable to the set of equations 19.2 in the appendix to *Value and Capital* and the value of

$$\frac{dP_i}{dq_i} \text{ is exactly } \frac{U}{\lambda U_{ii}},$$

where U is the determinant

$$\begin{vmatrix} 0 & u_1 & . & . & . & u_n \\ u_1 & u_{11} & . & . & . & u_{n1} \\ . & . & . & . & . & . \\ . & . & . & . & . & . \\ u_n & u_{1n} & . & . & . & u_{nn} \end{vmatrix}$$

The slope dP_i/dq_i is necessarily negative because the term $U/\lambda U_{ii}$, the inverse of Hicks's substitution effect, is necessarily negative. The income effect fails to appear because the constancy of income ($\Sigma P_i X_i = M$) has been replaced by the constancy of utility ($\Sigma u_i dx_i = 0$).

In general it may be said that a demand curve is downward sloping (a) if the change in the quantities available does not deviate too much from a constant utility surface, and (b) if the change is such as to leave relatively invariant prices of goods other than the one to which the demand curve pertains.

APPENDIX 2

The "Welfare" Effects of an Income Tax and an Excise Tax

In his essay entitled as above,[19] Friedman contrasted his correct solution of this problem with an incorrect solution that is closely associated with the constant money-income demand curve. Friedman's argument can be pushed farther in a way that is directly relevant to his view of the Marshallian demand curve.

The top half of Figure 9-14 reproduces Figure 3 of Friedman's article partly relabelled to make it consistent with the rest of this paper. The production possibility curve represents the opportunities open to the community after certain resources have been allocated to public goods. An income tax will in perfect competition allow the community to pick the optimum output B. An excise tax on Q_2 creates a gap between the marginal rates of substitution of Q_1 for Q_2 in production (the slope of the line KL) and in use (the slope of the line IJ). Output is moved to the left along the production possibility curve, resting at a point A at which IJ is tangent to the indifference curve. The point A is necessarily inferior to the point B.

This argument can be logically transcribed to demand and supply curves. The bottom part of Figure 9-14 illustrates the supply curve, the production demand curve, and the compensated demand curve associated with the indifference curve passing through the point B. The loss in welfare in moving from B to A could be made up by giving the community an amount AA' of Q_1. The simple mathematical relationship between integrals and derivatives that ensured the equality between consumer's surplus as a distance on the q_1 axis and an area under a demand curve also ensures that the loss (in units of Q_1) resulting from the movement from B to A (the distance AA') is exactly equal to the area between the compensated demand curve and the supply curve over the interval on the

[19] Milton Friedman, *Essays in Positive Economics*, *op. cit.*, pp. 100–13.

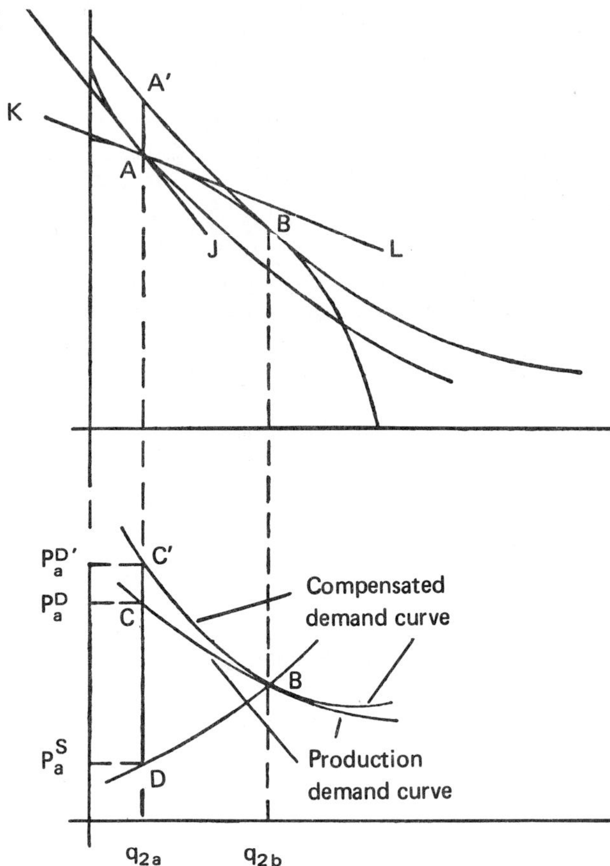

Figure 9-14

horizontal axis marked off by the projections of B and A. The welfare loss is the familiar triangle $C'BD$. Unfortunately the price corresponding to C' is not the market demand price of q_2 but a price that will in general be slightly higher. The market price of Q_2 is P_a^D indicated by a point on the production demand curve.

Friedman's proof of the inferiority (under certain specified assumptions) of the excise tax is logically equivalent to the proof appearing in Marshall's Principles (p. 468, Figure 31, eighth edition) provided Marshall's demand curve is interpreted as Friedman says it ought to be. Friedman in fact appears to have overlooked one strong reason for thinking that Marshall's demand curve was, or ought to have been, something like the compensated demand curve or the production demand curve. This is simply that Marshall put a supply curve and a demand curve on to the same diagram. This can be done with the production demand curve, the compensated demand curve, and even (though here the supply curve takes on a very special meaning) the traders' demand curve, but it is difficult to see how a supply curve can be made compatible with a constant income except where the production possibility curve is linear.

SECTION III. PRODUCTION AND COSTS

This section deals with the theory of supply, with attention being focused on production theory, including the production function and the determinants of demand for the factors of production, and the theory of costs, together with the cost curves of the firm. Initially there is an analysis of the concept of "the production function." Then, a linear programming model of the firm is compared with the marginal analysis model of the firm. The behavior of the firm in the short run under both the profit-maximizing and the wealth-maximizing approaches is discussed. Cost curves for the firm in the market period, the short run, and the long run are examined. And the relationships between a firm's short-run and long-run demands for a factor are considered.

Georgescu-Roegen analyzes the concept of the production process and discusses the two "commandments" of the economics of production. Naylor compares the Hicksian marginal analysis model of the multi-product, multi-factor firm with the linear programming model and delineates some of the differences between these two approaches. De Alessi demonstrates how relevant predictions about the short-run behavior of the firm may be derived from the wealth-maximizing (stock) approach instead of from the profit-maximizing (flow) approach, and he extends his analysis to the "uneconomic" regions of the production function. Maxwell emphasizes two "fundamental distinctions" in production theory and considers their implications for the output-expansion paths and cost curves of the firm for the market period, the short run, and the long run. Bishop demonstrates the derivation of the demand for a factor of production in both the short run (with one factor fixed and the other variable) and the long run (with both factors variable) and shows the relationships of factor demands in the short and long runs.

Georgescu-Roegen indicates that he chose his topic — the economics of production — not only for its own merits, but also to illustrate the importance of not disregarding "a basic requirement of science, namely, to have as clear an idea as possible about what corresponds in actuality to every piece of our symbolism." Initially, he comments briefly on the origin of "the production function" and indicates that two definitions of the production function have developed among economists.

Georgescu-Roegen seeks to clear up some of the ambiguity which has arisen because of the tendency of the economics profession to consider these two definitions as being "two completely equivalent ways" of representing any production process. He examines the concept of the production process, devoting particular attention to two categories of elements that are contained in such a process. He refers to these elements as "funds" and "flows."

Pointing out that one of the most important aspects of the economics of production is the minimization of periods of fund idleness, Georgescu-Roegen maintains that the only way to eliminate this type of idleness is by arranging the elementary production processes so that they take the form of a "factory system." He then determines the analytical representation of a factory process. He also indicates that there is a second kind of idleness which arises when the factory itself is not in operation a full day. In view of these two kinds of idleness, Georgescu-Roegen maintains that the economics of production reduces to "two commandments: first, produce by the factory system and, second, let the factory operate around the clock." He concludes by considering some of the difficulties and implications of following these two "commandments."

Naylor points out that, with the development of the simplex algorithm for solving linear programming problems, linear programming formed the basis for constructing an alternative model of the firm which was "quite different" from the conventional marginal analysis model employed by Hicks and others, both from the standpoint of the assumptions underlying such a model and its optimality conditions. He states that the literature dealing with the application of linear programming to the theory of the firm fails to spell out the precise differences between marginal analysis models and linear programming models of the firm in terms of their underlying assumptions and their optimality conditions and that his article is an attempt "to further delineate some of the differences" underlying these two approaches.

Naylor outlines the assumptions underlying the Hicksian model of the multi-product, multi-factor competitive firm and gives the optimality conditions for this model. Maintaining that most of the differences underlying the assumptions of marginal analysis and linear programming models of the firm are attributable to differences in their assumptions regarding the production function, Naylor includes a digression on "the production function."

He then states the assumptions underlying a linear programming model of the firm and formulates such a model. Utilizing the Kuhn-Tucker theorem, Naylor gives a detailed comparison of the optimality conditions of the linear programming model with those of the Hicksian model, concluding that the principal differences between the two lie in their assumptions and in the economic implications of their optimality conditions.

De Alessi maintains that the traditional approach to the short run as a period in which the quantities of some inputs cannot be varied "requires clarification." He reviews briefly the traditional short-run theory of the firm. De Alessi argues that it is "theoretically inadmissible" to consider the short run as a period in which some inputs cannot be varied and maintains that the extent of the variation of inputs in the short run will depend upon the relative costs and receipts of "all the alternative production strategies technologically available to the firm."

He then indicates how relevant predictions regarding the short-run behavior of the firm may be derived from the wealth-maximizing (stock) approach, which may be used to avoid some of the shortcomings of the traditional profit-maximizing (flow) approach.

De Alessi extends his analysis to the "uneconomic" regions of the production function and concludes that, if such regions exist, the wealth-maximizing models suggest that they are relevant for competitive as well as for monopolistic firms.

Maxwell seeks to show that "the possible situations in production theory are considerably more varied than the current literature would suggest and that the firm's cost curves consequently [are] less amenable to simple classification." Maxwell emphasizes two "fundamental distinctions" in production theory. One of these is that factor services are distinct from the factors of production themselves. Secondly, he distinguishes between the divisibility of the factors of production *in acquisition* and their divisibility *in use.* He argues that, given the production function, the basic determinant of the firm's cost curves is the degree of control which the firm has over the acquisition and use of factor *services.*

Taking into consideration these two distinctions, Maxwell determines the output-expansion paths for the firm under various situations. He covers the market period, the short run, and the long run and describes the cost curves for each of these time periods. He discusses some of the considerations which may lead to limitations of the firm's control of factor services and indicates that these considerations help to determine the shape and configuration of the firm's cost curves.

Bishop points to the lack in the literature of a "satisfactory but comparatively nontechnical treatment" of the relationships between a firm's short-run and long-run demands for a factor and seeks to bridge that gap in this article. Starting with the elementary case of a firm which produces a single product with two factors of production, Bishop briefly reviews the procedures for deriving the firm's cost curves and covers the profit-maximizing conditions for both the competitive and the monopolistic firm.

He then considers the short-run demand for a factor, with one factor of production being fixed and the other variable, supplementing the concepts of average and marginal revenue products with the concept of the "average net revenue product." Bishop next demonstrates the derivation of the long-run demand for a factor, with both factors of production being variable. The long-run demand for one factor is described with reference to a long-run variant of the factor's average net revenue product. Particular emphasis is given to the relationships of factor demands in the short and long runs. Bishop points out that his analysis, which has been limited to the case of only two factors, may be generalized to cover any number of factors.

In Appendix A, Bishop shows the determination of short-run and long-run factor demands when the firm has a constant demand elasticity for its product and a production function of the Cobb-Douglas type. In Appendix B, he looks at the determination of short-run and long-run factor demands when the firm has a constant demand elasticity and production is assumed to be subject to fixed coefficients.

10. THE ECONOMICS OF PRODUCTION*
RICHARD T. ELY LECTURE

Nicholas Georgescu-Roegen†

For the last twenty years or so I have singled myself out among my fellow econometricians for arguing with all the means at my disposal that not every element of the economic process can be related to a number and, consequently, that this process cannot be represented in its entirety by an arithmomorphic model. At the same time, I have insisted that in our haste to mathematize economics we have often been carried away by mathematical formalism to the point of disregarding a basic requirement of science, namely, to have as clear an idea as possible about what corresponds in actuality to every piece of our symbolism. Curiously, in the home of quantity, in the natural sciences, this position does not constitute a singularity. On the contrary, essentially the same words of caution have come from many a high authority in physics—such as Max Planck or Percy William Bridgman, for example.[1] But even some engineers have raised their voices against blind symbolism. The recent remarks by a well-known British engineer are worth quoting at length:

> Contrary to common belief it is sometimes easier to talk in mathematics than to talk in English; this is the reason why many scientific papers contain more mathematics than is either necessary or desirable. Contrary to common belief it is also often less precise to do so. For mathematical symbols have a tendency to conceal the physical meaning that they are intended to represent; they sometimes serve as a substitute for the arduous task of deciding what is and what is not relevant; .... It is true that mathematics cannot lie. But it can mislead.
>
> However, the dangers of over-indulgence in formula spinning are avoided if mathematics is treated, wherever possible, as a language into which *thoughts may only be translated after they have first been* [*clearly*] *expressed in the language of words*. The use of mathematics in this way is indeed disciplinary, helpful, and sometimes indispensable.[2]

The topic of this lecture—the economics of production—presents, I believe, sufficient interest by itself. But in choosing it, I have been guided also by the fact that it may serve as a substantial illustration of the harm caused by the blind symbolism that generally characterizes a hasty mathematization.

---

*From the *American Economic Review,* Vol. LX, No. 2 (May, 1970), pp. 1-9. Reprinted by permission of the publisher and the author.

†Nicholas Georgescu-Roegen, Distinguished Professor of Economics, Vanderbilt University.

[1]Max Planck, *The New Science* (New York: Meridan Books, 1959), pp. 43, 158-59; P. W. Bridgman, *The Logic of Modern Physics* (New York: Macmillan, 1949), p. 50.

[2]Reginald O. Kapp, *Towards a Unified Cosmology* (New York: Humanities, 1960), p. 111. My italics.

I

What has come to be known as "the production function" is quite an old item in the economist's analytical paraphernalia. As we may recall, it was introduced in 1894 by Wicksteed with one simple remark: "*the product being a function of the factors of production we have* $P = f(a, b, c, \ldots)$."[3] This paradigm of imprecision apparently sufficed to make us accept Wicksteed's simple symbolism as an adequate analytical representation of any production process and use it indiscriminately in every kind of situation. And as the usage of the vapid terms "input" and "output" became widespread, popular manuals came to treat the subject in an even more cavalier manner than Wicksteed's. A typical presentation is that the production function expresses symbolically the fact that "the output of the firm depends on its inputs."

But even consummate economists have accepted Wicksteed's formula without any ado. They only felt that the meaning of the variables involved ought to be explained. The greater number of such authors adopt the position that the formula shows the quantities of inputs (or of factors) necessary to produce a certain quantity of output (or of product). Accordingly, all symbols in a production function,

$$Q = F(X, Y, Z, \ldots), \tag{1}$$

stand for quantities.[4] Others conceive the same function as a relation between the inputs per unit of time and the output per unit of time; i.e., as a relation

$$q = f(x, y, z, \ldots), \tag{2}$$

in which all symbols stand for rates of flow.[5]

Curiously, no one seems to have been intrigued by the existence of these entirely distinct interpretations. Instead, many economists—including some analytical authorities—have used both definitions indifferently, sometimes even on the same page.[6] The undeniable inference is that the economic profession considers relations (1) and (2) as two completely equivalent ways of

---

[3]Philip H. Wicksteed, *The Co-ordination of the Laws of Distribution* (London: 1894), p. 4.

[4]For a small yet representative sample, see A. L. Bowley, *The Mathematical Groundwork of Economics* (Oxford: Kelley, 1924), pp. 28–29; J. R. Hicks, *The Theory of Wages* (London: Macmillan, 1932), p. 237; E. Schneider, *Theorie der Produktion* (Vienna: 1934), p. 1; A. C. Pigou, *The Economics of Stationary States* (London: Macmillan, 1935), p. 142; P. A. Samuelson, *Foundations of Economic Analysis* (Cambridge, Mass.: Harvard University Press, 1948), pp. 57–58; K. E. Boulding, *Economic Analysis* (3d ed.; New York: Harper and Row, 1955), p. 585; Sune Carlson, *A Study on the Pure Theory of Production* (New York: Kelley, 1956), p. 12; Ragnar Frisch, *Theory of Production* (Chicago: Rand, Inc., 1965), p. 41.

[5]G. Stigler, *The Theory of Competitive Price* (New York: Macmillan, 1942), p. 109; T. C. Koopmans, "Analysis of Production as an Efficient Combination of Activities," in *Activity Analysis of Production and Allocation*, edited by T. C. Koopmans (New York: Wiley, 1951), p. 35.

[6]E.g., Frisch, *op. cit.*, p. 43.

representing any production process whatsoever. Yet behind this belief there lies an analytical imbroglio which is easily brought to light.

We need only recall that the production function is a tool associated with a static process or, to use a more explicit expression, with a steady-going process. For such a process, the following relations

$$Q = tq,\ X = tx,\ Y = ty, \ldots \tag{3}$$

hold for any time interval t and for the quantities of product and of factors corresponding to that interval. With the aid of these relations and (2), relation (1) becomes

$$tf(x, y, z, \ldots) = F(tx, ty, tz, \ldots). \tag{4}$$

And since this relation must be true for any t, it follows, first, that f and F are one and the same function,

$$f(x, y, z, \ldots) \equiv F(x, y, z, \ldots), \tag{5}$$

and, second, that this function is homogeneous of the first degree. Therefore, the tacit presumption that the forms (1) and (2) are equivalent implies that the returns to scale must be constant in absolutely every production process.

Nothing, I believe, need be added to convince ourselves that this imbroglio is the direct consequence of our acceptance of Wicksteed's symbolism without first probing its validity as an analytical mirror of actuality. This conclusion raises a new and troublesome issue. Does either of the forms, (1) or (2), constitute an adequate representation of a process of production and, if so, what kind of process may be represented by it? For a start, let us try to examine it in its broad lines.

II

Before anything else, we should note that for no other branch of economics is the concept of process as essential as for the economics of production. But, widely used though the word "process" is in sciences and philosophy, the literature seems to offer no specific definition of it. Now and then, the concept is merely associated with change. However, change is a notoriously intricate notion which has kept philosophers divided into two opposing camps: one maintaining that all is only being; the other, that all is only becoming. Obviously, science can follow neither of these teachings. Nor can it, unfortunately, embrace Hegel's dialectical synthesis that being is becoming. Analytical science must distinguish between object and event. Consequently, it must embrace the so-called "vulgar" philosophy—according to which there are both being and becoming—and cling to it to the very end. The upshot is that science must find a way to represent a process analytically.

It is obvious that, for this purpose, we must retain one point of dialectics; namely, that change and, hence, process cannot be conceived otherwise than as a relation between some entity and its complement in the absolute whole. In viewing a living tree as a process we oppose that tree to everything else—to "its other," in Hegel's terminology. Only for the absolute whole—the universe in its eternity—has change no meaning: such a totality has no complement. The notion of partial process, therefore, implies some slits cut into the absolute whole. But as a long series of thinkers, from the ancient Anaxagoras to the modern Niels Bohr, have taught us, this whole is seamless.[7] However, in this case as in all others, analysis must proceed by some heroic simplifications and totally ignore their ultimate consequences.

The first heroic step is to divide actuality into two parts—one representing the partial process in point; the other, its environment (so to speak)—separated by a boundary consisting of an arithmomorphic void. For if the boundary would not be such a void, we would get three parts instead of two and, as is easily seen, we would be drawn into a dialectical infinite regress. So, all that exists in actuality at any moment must belong either to a process or to its environment. The basic element of the analytical picture of a process is, therefore, the boundary. No analytical boundary, no analytical process.

Now precisely because actuality is a seamless whole we can slice it wherever we may please. And Plato to the contrary,[8] actuality has no joints to guide a carver. As economists we know only too well the unsettled issue of where the natural boundary of the economic process lies. Only our particular purpose in each case can guide us in drawing the boundary of a process. So, every scientist slices actuality in the way that suits best his own objective—an operation that cannot be performed without some intimate knowledge of the corresponding phenomenal domain.

An analytical boundary, as conceived here, must consist of two components. Like a frontier, one component separates the process at any time from the rest of actuality, although we must not think that this frontier is necessarily geographical in nature or rigidly determined. Witness the process of thought itself or that of an acorn growing into an oak. The second component is the duration of the process, determined by the time moments at which the process we have in mind begins and ends. Naturally, these moments must be at a finite distance; otherwise we would not know all that has gone into the process or all that the process does. Nor must we allow them to coincide. For, to recall Whitehead's admonition,[9] a durationless

---

[7]See Fragment 8 in J. Burnet, *Early Greek Philosophy* (4th ed., London: Macmillan, 1930), p. 47; Niels Bohr, *Atomic Physics and Human Knowledge* (New York: Wiley, 1958), p. 10.

[8]Plato, *Phaedrus*, p. 265.

[9]Alfred North Whitehead, *An Enquiry Concerning the Principles of Natural Knowledge* (2d ed.; Cambridge, England: Macmillan, 1925), p. 2; also his *The Concept of Nature* (Cambridge, England: 1930), p. 57.

process, an event at an instant of time as a primary fact of nature, is nonsense.[10] We can then choose the time scale so that the process begins at $t=0$ and ends at $t=T$, with $T>0$. T is the duration of the process, but for a production process we may prefer, instead, Marx's term: the time of production.

The next point is truly crucial; in saying that a given analytical process begins at $t=0$ and ends at $t=T$ we must take the underscored words in their strictest sense. Before $t=0$ and after $t=T$, the analytical process is out of existence. That is, in conceiving such a process we must totally abstract from it what happens outside the duration we have assigned to the process. The mental operation is clear: an analytical process must be viewed as a hyphen between one *tabula rasa* and another.

Our next problem is to arrive at an analytical description of the happening, associated with a given process. Because of the principle, "No analytical boundary, no analytical process," analysis must renounce any hope of including in this description the happenings inside an analytical process. Indeed, in order to describe analytically what happens inside a process, we must divide it by a new boundary into two new processes to which the same rule will apply. And so on ad infinitum. The analytical description of a process, therefore, reduces to recording everything that crosses the boundary in either direction. In connection with this picture we can endow the terms input and output with quite precise meanings.

Analysis now needs to take another heroic step — to assume that the number of elements involved is finite and that every element is cardinally measurable (which implies that every element is a homogeneous entity). If $C_1, C_2, \ldots, C_m$ denote the distinct elements, the analytical description is complete if for every C_i we have determined two nondecreasing functions $F_i(t)$ and $G_i(t)$ over the closed interval $[0, T]$, the first function showing the cumulative output up to time t (inclusive). Any analytical process — whether in economics or any other domain — may therefore be represented graphically by a series of curves, as in Figure 10-1.

In a plastic image, the coordinates of an analytical process may be likened to continuously reported data of import and export, with one important detail. Since in describing a process analytically we must begin and end with a *tabula rasa*, this hall (in which we are now gathered) must be listed both as input and as output in the process consisting of the delivery of this lecture. In the analytical approach we are not interested in how this hall came into being or in its use before or after this lecture. However, we must recognize that, as the result of every use, the hall suffers some wear and tear, imperceptible though this may be. Similarly, in any production process the same person must be listed as a rested worker among inputs and as a tired worker among outputs. A tool, too, may go in new and come out used. But even

[10] All this does not mean that, in the next stage of our inquiry, we cannot arrive at the excluded cases by a passage to the limit.

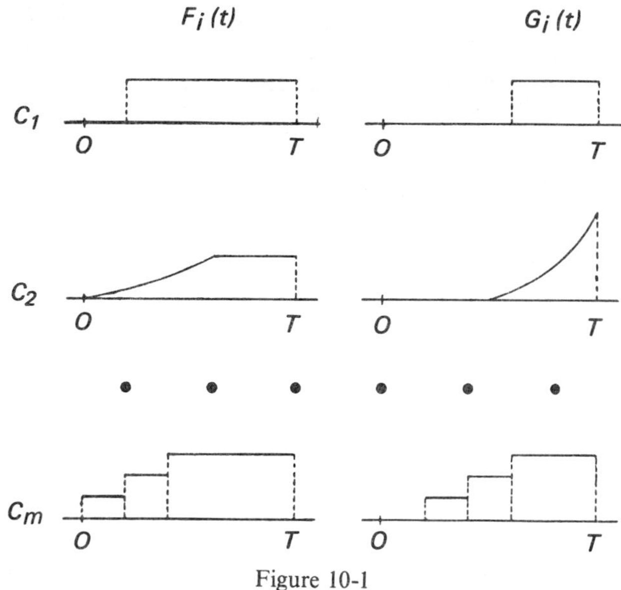

Figure 10-1

though we recognize the rested and the tired worker as being the same man, we must treat the former as a different element from the latter. Each element of an analytical process—as we have decided—must be completely homogeneous, a condition that does not always cover sameness.

These cases, of the worker and of the tool, raise a troublesome problem for the economist. The reason is that our material of study is the commodity. We slice the economic domain into units of production and units of consumption because at the boundaries thus drawn we can catch every commodity. Drawing a boundary in a glass plant between the melted glass furnace and the rolling machines would serve none of the economist's purposes; at this time, melted glass is not a commodity.[11] Briefly, the economist cannot afford to abandon his commodity fetishism any more than the chemist, for example, can renounce his fetishism of the molecule.

The difficulty, which at bottom is related to qualitative change, is that even though we cannot avoid including "tired worker" and "used tool" in the list of outputs of any production process, neither category fits the usual notion of commodity. Our entire analytical edifice would collapse if we were to accept the alternative position that the aim of economic production is to produce not only the usual products but also tired workers and used tools.

A new heroic step is needed to eliminate this difficulty. It consists of the familiar, old fiction of a process in which capital is maintained constant. The fiction does raise some analytical issues, for if all tools and all workers

[11]That technological innovations may change this situation is evidenced by ready-mix cement and brown-and-serve rolls, for example, which only recently have become commodities.

are to be maintained at a constant level of efficiency, any production process will have to include most of the enterprises and households in the world. Factually, however, the fiction is not more, not less reasonable than that of frictionless movement in mechanics. A simple glance at the activity inside a plant or a household suffices to convince us that efforts are constantly directed not toward keeping durable goods physically self-identical (which is quite impossible), but toward maintaining them in good working condition. And this is all that counts in production. The only factor we need neglect is the daily wear and tear of the worker. This is not too much to demand, since the worker is daily restored in the household.

The elements may now be divided into two relevant categories. In the first category we shall place those elements that appear as input and as output and are related by reason of sameness or of equality of quantity. A piece of Ricardian land, a motor, the amount of clover used as seed in growing clover seed (not clover fodder!), or a worker, illustrate this category. To elements such as these I propose to refer as funds so as to emphasize their economic invariableness. The other elements, which appear only as input or only as output, constitute the category of flows. Obviously since the fund elements are maintained, the process may be activated again provided that the necessary inflows are still forthcoming. Labeled variously as a static or as a stationary process, or, still, as a diagram of simple reproduction, this fiction constitutes the fundamental element in the analysis of production from the classical to the hypermodern school. Reproducible, however, seems to describe the process better. The analytical picture we have thus reached is worth stressing: in a reproducible process, the fund elements are the immutable agents that transform some input flows into output flows. No picture of a process—whether static or dynamic—is complete if it does not include both categories of elements.[12] And the essential difference between these categories calls for a different representation of the fund coordinates. A flow coordinate will continue to be represented, according to the case, by the cumulative input or the cumulative output; i.e., by a quantity of some substance. Because in case of a fund the input and the output are economically the same substance, the coordinate of a fund may be represented by the difference $F_i(t) - G_i(t)$. But to maintain a convenient symmetry with the flow coordinates, we may use instead the cumulative amount of that intangible entity usually called the service of the fund.

III

In the case of a production process, the elements may be classified into some fruitful categories. The inflows that are transformed by the agents may come either from nature or from other production processes; we shall denote

[12] A point on which I insisted long ago: cf. my article "Aggregate Linear Production Function and Its Applications to von Neumann's Model," in *Activity Analysis of Production and Allocation*, edited by T. C. Koopmans (New York: Wiley, 1951), pp. 100–01.

them generically by (R) and (I). There also are inflows, (M), earmarked for maintenance. The output flows consist of products, (Q), and waste, (W). Finally, the funds include Ricardian land (L), capital equipment (K), and—to use Marx's very appropriate term—labor power, (H). With these notations, the analytical representation of a reproducible process is

$$[\overset{T}{\underset{0}{R}}(t),\ \overset{T}{\underset{0}{I}}(t),\ \overset{T}{\underset{0}{M}}(t),\ \overset{T}{\underset{0}{Q}}(t),\ \overset{T}{\underset{0}{W}}(t);\ \overset{T}{\underset{0}{L}}(t),\ \overset{T}{\underset{0}{K}}(t),\ \overset{T}{\underset{0}{H}}(t)]; \tag{6}$$

that is, a set of functions, which defines a point in an abstract (functional) space.

This is a far cry from the notion inherited from Wicksteed, according to which a process is represented by a point in the ordinary (Euclidean) space. The superiority of (6) over the point representation needs no elaborate argument. In (6) we have a complete set of instructions on how to set up the corresponding process. The form also reminds us continuously that a process has a duration, a time of production. Nothing is missing from it.

The difference yields an entirely new form for the production function. Since by a production function we must still understand the set of all processes that transform the same input flows into an outflow of the same product, from (6) it follows that the production function must be a relation among functions, instead of numbers. This relation, which may be written after the old pattern as

$$\overset{T}{\underset{0}{Q}}(t) = \mathcal{F}[\overset{T}{\underset{0}{R}}(t),\ \overset{T}{\underset{0}{I}}(t),\ \overset{T}{\underset{0}{M}}(t),\ \overset{T}{\underset{0}{W}}(t);\ \overset{T}{\underset{0}{L}}(t),\ \overset{T}{\underset{0}{K}}(t),\ \overset{T}{\underset{0}{H}}(t)], \tag{7}$$

is what the mathematicians call a functional.

The results just reached call for numerous observations. Here, I can take up only a few and touch upon them briefly.[13]

First, the reason why I have excluded no element from the categories listed in (6), is that the scholar must never prejudge. Even an economist must first arrive at a complete description of a process and only then decide which elements may be left out because they are economically irrelevant. Nature does not indeed have a cashier's window where we may pay her for the elements (R); yet it would be utterly inept to ignore in the economics of production the fact that natural resources are neither inexhaustible nor uniformly distributed over the globe. The type of economic model now in vogue, which assumes that growth normally proceeds at a constant rate, simply blots out the most numerous and most critical cases—such as Somaliland or our own Appalachia, for instance. One may feel even more tempted to leave out the waste category on the ground that waste, by definition, has no value. But again, as we have come to recognize recently on an increasing scale, the existence of waste is not an innocuous aspect of the economic process.

[13]For greater details see Chapter IX in my forthcoming volume, *Entropy and the Economic Process* (Cambridge, Mass.: Harvard University Press, 1971).

Second, we should not fail to observe that, since a fund enters a reproducible process and comes out without any impairment of its economic efficiency, service is the only way by which it can participate in the production of the product. While it is true that the cloth — an inflow element — effectively passes into the coat, the same cannot apply to the needle—a fund element. And if one finds the needle in the coat just bought, it certainly is a regrettable accident. The point is that the problem of how the contribution of a fund affects the value of the product is not as directly simple as in the case of a flow factor.

Third, both the value of a fund's service and that of its maintenance flow must, in principle, be imputed to the value of the product. Contrary to Marx's teachings — which have gradually infiltrated the thinking of many a standard economist — there is no economic double counting in this. No worker, no lecturer, can discharge his duties by sending to the shop or to the classroom only that "definite quantity of muscle, nerve, brain, etc., [which] is wasted" during work — as Marx claimed.[14] When one works, one must be present with his entire fund of mental and physical capabilities. The same is true for all other funds: the bridge must be there in its full material existence before we can cross the river. If it were true that we could cross a river on the maintenance flow of a bridge or drive the maintenance flow of an automobile on the maintenance flow of a highway, there would be little financial difficulty in saturating the whole world with all the river crossings and automotive facilities. Economic development could be brought about everywhere with practically no waiting.

IV

As with almost everything else, among the various processes we may envisage in production there is one process that fits the epithet "elementary." It is the process by which every unit of the product — a single piece of furniture or a molecule of gasoline — is produced. The process is directly observable in the shop of a cabinetmaker, but it can be easily determined even in a large-scale enterprise. Whatever the product, one thing is certain about the elementary process. In relation to it, most of the funds are idle over large periods of time. The plow is needed only a few days during the whole production time of growing a corn plant; the same is true for the saw or the plane in the production of a table. There is no exception to this rule. And, I contend, one of the most important aspects of the economics of production is how to minimize these periods of fund idleness, whether we are thinking of man, capital equipment, or land.[15]

Now if only one table is demanded during the time of production, T, then

[14]Karl Marx, *Capital* (Chicago: 1932), Vol. I, p. 190.

[15]A period of idleness is characterized by the constancy of the corresponding fund coordinate.

obviously we need operate only one elementary process after another in succession. But if n tables, with $n > 1$, are demanded during T, then two alternatives are open to us. We may start n processes at the same time and repeat the operation when they are ended. This is the arrangement in parallel. The second arrangement is the arrangement in line, in which equal batches of processes are begun one after another at intervals equal to an aliquot part of T.

It is obvious that the production function of a system in which the elementary processes are arranged in parallel is obtained from (7) by multiplying every coordinate by n:

$$(8) \qquad [n\overset{T}{\underset{0}{Q}}(t)] = \mathcal{F}\{[n\overset{T}{\underset{0}{R}}(t)], \cdots, [n\overset{T}{\underset{0}{W}}(t)]; [n\overset{T}{\underset{0}{L}}(t)], \cdots\}.$$

The point that deserves to be stressed is that the arrangement in parallel offers little or no economic gain. Most kinds of fund factors are now needed in an amount n times as great as in the elementary process. In addition, the idleness of each such fund factor is *ipso facto* amplified by n. The only exceptions are the fund factors that —like a large bread oven, for instance— may accommodate several elementary processes simultaneously. But even though the capacity of such a fund factor would be more fully utilized, its idleness period would remain the same.

The situation completely changes for the arrangement in line. If we assume away any incommensurabilities among the time periods involved in the schedule of the elementary process—an inevitable assumption in practice —and if n is sufficiently large, then a number of processes can be arranged in line so that no fund is idle at any time.[16] The situation is vividly exemplified by an assembly line, in which every tool and every worker shift without interruption from one elementary process to the next. The arrangement in line, however, describes any factory. In a factory, therefore, the economy of time reaches its maximum. This conclusion opens an avenue of utmost importance. To explore it, we may begin by determining the analytical representation of a factory process.

In a first approach we may consider the entire physical plant as one monolithic fund, P. Over an arbitrary interval $[0, t]$, during which the factory process is in operation, the coordinate of this fund is the function Pt. Similarly, the coordinate of labor power is Ht. And if for the convenience of diction we assume that all flow elements are continuous, their coordinates, too, are represented by linear homogeneous functions. Thus (7) becomes:

$$(9) \qquad (\overset{t}{\underset{0}{q}}t) = \mathcal{G}[(\overset{t}{\underset{0}{r}}t), (\overset{t}{\underset{0}{i}}t), (\overset{t}{\underset{0}{m}}t), (\overset{t}{\underset{0}{w}}t); (\overset{t}{\underset{0}{P}}t), (\overset{t}{\underset{0}{H}}t)].$$

---

[16]The number of elementary processes that should be started each time is the smallest common multiple of the numbers of such processes that can be accommodated at the same time by each unit of the various funds. Batches should be started at intervals of T/d, d being the greatest common divisor of T and of the intervals during which the various funds are needed in an elementary process.

Let us note that this is a very special functional: first, every function involved in it depends upon a single parameter and, second, the value of t is entirely arbitrary. For these reasons, the functional degenerates into a point function.

There are two degenerate forms. The first is

$$q = \Theta(r, i, m, w; P, H). \tag{10}$$

This formula reminds us of one of the current interpretations mentioned in Section I; namely, that of relation (2). We should note, however, that Θ involves two dimensionally different categories of variables. The lower case symbols represent flow rates of some substances. The upper case symbols stand for the rates of service per unit of time. Strangely, however, these last rates do not involve the time element at all: P stands for the plant, and H, for the total labor power—briefly, for quantities of some substances. The second degenerate form is

$$Q = \Psi^{*}(R, I, M, W; \mathcal{P}, \mathcal{H}; t). \tag{11}$$

Here, the symbols in roman capital letters are again quantities of some substances; those in script letters are services, and t is the period with which these quantities and services are associated. The form (11), in turn, reminds us of relation (1); i.e., of the quantity interpretation of Wicksteed's formula. The most important difference is that Ψ^{*} includes time as an explicit variable.

This difference bears upon the earlier argument that Wicksteed's production function is homogeneous of the first degree. Actually, Ψ^{*} is such a function—as easily follows from the identities

$$Q = qt, \ldots, W = wt, \ \mathcal{P} = Pt, \ \mathcal{H} = Ht, \tag{12}$$

analogous to (3). There is then an intimate relation between (10) and (11); namely,

$$t\Theta(r, i, m, w; P, H) = \Psi^{*}(R, I, M, W; \mathcal{P}, \mathcal{H}; t). \tag{13}$$

Hence,

$$\Theta = [\Psi^{*}]_{t=1}. \tag{14}$$

The imbroglio created by (5) is thus resolved. Of course, this does not mean that the factory process operates with constant returns to scale. The homogeneity of Ψ^{*} corresponds to the tautology that if we double the time during which a factory works, then the quantity of every flow element and the service of every fund will also double. The issue of returns to scale pertains, instead, to what happens if the fund elements are doubled. The point may be made still clearer.

A superficial inspection of any operating plant suffices to reveal that P consists of some Ricardian land, R, some capital equipment, K, some technical inventories, S, and a special fund, Γ, usually called "goods in process." The last term is definitely a misnomer: half-tanned hides or partly wired radio sets, for example, are not goods. Process-fund seems a more exact term because Γ is in effect a becoming frozen in its various phases. If a photograph of Γ would be projected part by part, as if it were a movie, we would witness the actual change of some input flows into product and waste flows. In spite of this varied composition of any plant, what a given plant can do depends on its blueprint alone, which in turn involves only L and K. And since what a plant can do is shown by the flow rate of its product, we have a first relation

$$q^* = G^*(L, K). \tag{15}$$

A second relation expresses the fact that, given the plant, we require a certain labor power, H^*, if we want to obtain the flow rate q^*. Hence,

$$H^* = H^*(L, K). \tag{16}$$

Should we man the plant with less labor power than H^*, the product flow rate would also become smaller than q^*. To account for this rather common situation, we need to put

$$q = G(L, K, H) \leq q^*. \tag{17}$$

But the fact that this relation looks very familiar should not mislead us: as (17) is defined here, if $q<q^*$, q does not necessarily decrease (and ordinarily does not) when L and K are decreased while H is kept constant. Actually, the ratio q/q^* measures the percentage of capacity utilized if H is the labor power employed.[17]

The next relations are self-explanatory:

$$S = S(L, K, H), \qquad \Gamma = \Gamma(L, K, H). \tag{18}$$

There remain the relations binding the other flow elements. The case of the maintenance flow, m, is simple: its size must depend on the amount of equipment to be maintained and the labor fund employed. In addition, by virtue of the conservation law of matter and energy, m must be equal to w_1, the flow rate of wear-and-tear waste—burned or discarded lubricating oil, broken saw bands, and the like. Hence,

$$m = m(K, H), \qquad m = w_1. \tag{19}$$

---

[17]As an ordinal measure of the utilized capacity we may use H/H^*. On this point, see footnote 21.

The same conservation law applies to all other flows. For example, the wood contained in a piece of furniture together with the scrap and the sawdust must exactly account for the wood introduced into the production of that furniture. In the case of a factory system, this relationship yields

$$qt = g(rt, it, w_2t), \tag{20}$$

where w_2 is the flow rate of waste arising from transformation alone. Since (20) must be true for any t, the function g must be homogeneous of the first degree. To this function we may indeed apply the old-time tautology that "doubling the inputs doubles the output." The basic error in some arguments about the returns to scale is to apply this tautology to (17) instead of (20). If L, K, and H are doubled, q does not necessarily double even if we double at the same time all flow inputs. The new factory may be more efficient or more wasteful in using the input materials, which leads us to put

$$w_2 = w_2(L, K, H). \tag{21}$$

Relation (10) is thus decomposed into seven basic relations, listed from (17) to (21), which together constitute the general representation of a factory process.[18]

We should now note that the picture at which we have arrived is analogous to the inscription "60 watts" on an electric bulb. That is, it tells us what the factory can do, not what it has done, is doing, or, above all, will do. Like the inscription on the bulb, relation (17), for example, is true regardless of whether the factory works or is idle. To show what the factory does, we need an additional coordinate, which, under its various aspects, has deeply preoccupied Marx, but which, perhaps for easily understood reasons, is not found in the analytical tool box of the neoclassical economist. The coordinate is the time, δ, during which the factory works daily. The amount of the daily production, Q, follows immediately from (17):

$$Q = \delta G(L, K, H), \tag{22}$$

a relation which vindicates Marx's dear tenet that labor time measures value even though it has no value itself.[19]

V

So much for grounded-in-actuality symbolism. Let me devote my closing remarks to some of the object lessons of this symbolism.

[18]Obviously, this analytical description will have to be completed with additional relations if the particular factory process happens to involve other limitationalities.

[19]Marx, *op. cit.*, pp. 45, 588.

I have stressed the fact that in any elementary process every agent is idle over some definite periods that depend not on our choice or whim but on the state of the arts. I have also argued that we can, nonetheless, eliminate this kind of idleness completely and that there is only one way to achieve this: to arrange the elementary processes in a factory system. Because of this extraordinary property, the factory system deserves to be placed side by side with money as the two most fateful economic innovations for mankind. I say "economic" and not "technical" because the economy of time achieved by the factory system is independent of technology. Nothing prevents us from using the most primitive technique of cloth weaving in a factory system.

To be sure, there is a second kind of idleness, which depends entirely on our decision: it is the idleness of the factory itself if δ is shorter than a full day. In view of these two kinds of idleness, the economics of production reduces to two commandments: first, produce by the factory system and, second, let the factory operate around the clock.

The first commandment calls for two observations. Even though we can draw the blueprint of a factory for any elementary process whatsoever, not every such factory is economically advantageous. For example, we do not build transoceanic "Queens" by processes in line. The reason is that we can build a "Queen" more quickly than it is demanded in relation to time. The much extolled progress of the industrial revolution may not after all be due only to technological innovations. For these innovations as well as the increased specialization of labor could not have come about unless an increased demand had already induced most craft shops to introduce the system in line. There can be little doubt about it: the factory system was born in an artisan's workshop, not in a factory.

The second observation is that to operate an arrangement of elementary processes in line it is absolutely necessary that we have the freedom to start a process at any time of the day, of the week, and of the year. Unfortunately we do not always have this freedom. Seasonal variations—which result from the position of our planet relative to our main source of free energy, the sun—prevent us from adapting the factory system to a series of important productive activities. The most important instance is husbandry. For the overwhelming majority of localities, there is a very short and definite period of the year during which a corn plant, for instance, can be grown in the open space from seed. This is why farmers have to work their fields in parallel; that is, in a system of production that yields practically no economy of time. The global analytical representation of that system is (8), not (9). The upshot is that the open-air factories, about which socialist writers in particular have been continuously raving, will remain a utopian dream as long as we are unable to alter the orbit of the earth.

The association between agriculture and the idleness of all agents involved is by now a commonplace. Still, not much is known or even suspected about the importance of the related loss. Two simple illustrations may bring out this point. For the first, let us consider one of the exceptional localities—such as the Island of Bali—where, because of an almost constant climate throughout the year, rice could be grown in an open-air factory. In this case, every day the same number of hands would move over the fields with the same funds of plows, buffaloes, sickles, and flairs to plow, sow, harvest, and thresh. Every day the villagers would eat the rice sown that very day, as it were, and they would no longer have to bear the burden of the debts specific to agriculture. But most important of all, we would also discover that, without diminishing the old production at all, there would remain a substantial number of superfluous workers as well as a substantial stock of superfluous equipment—a palpable measure of the overcapitalization of farming in comparison with manufacturing. The second illustration pertains to the current technique by which chickens are raised in the United States. In fact, in this country there are no longer any chicken farms—even though the term continues to be used. Instead, there are chicken factories, with elementary processes arranged in line. The "chicken war" of yesteryear would not have come about if the difference between the old and the new techniques had not been so great as to exceed the shipping cost over the Atlantic plus the wage differential between this country and Europe.

But if not every production activity can be turned into a factory, we should at least try to render the idleness of the agents as small as possible in each particular case. In other words, to bring even a whole economy as near as possible to the functioning of a factory system should be the guiding thought of any planner at any level. In the activity of the countryside, the cottage industry propounded by the agrarians was one answer to this idea. In Romania (so I was told) tractors and drivers shuttle between the plain regions—where two crops are grown each year—and the hilly regions—where only one crop can be grown because of a shorter vegetation period. The necessary funds of tractors and drivers are thus substantially reduced at the cost of some gasoline, oil, and spare parts flows. Less costly solutions would be obtained by mixing several crops within the same locality, the crops being chosen so as to minimize idleness (and hence capital cost). Formally, the problem boils down to splicing graphic patterns with a minimizing condition—a problem of a special type of combinatorial analysis which, I am sure, will prove highly rewarding.

The second commandment is particularly relevant for the underdeveloped economies. In a rich country, it makes perfect sense to operate every factory with one shift, even if the shift be of six or four hours only. In a rich country, there also is no need for night shifts, except whenever technology imposes around-the-clock production. Briefly, in a rich country leisure is a commodity which people may prefer to higher income. Things are different in almost every underdeveloped country where—as every government pronouncement urges—the order of the day is not only development but rapid development. In such countries, the regimen of the eight-hour working day and the reluctance to use night shifts are anachronistic factors that work against the avowed aims.[20] There may be many reasons why planners as well as our planning theory have overlooked the simplest and the most direct lever of economic development; namely, the length of the working day. But one possible reason is that this element of the problem has been left out of the neoclassical representation of a production process. The same omission — we should note — vitiates also the familiar comparisons of the capital-output and capital-labor ratios computed from current satistical data. Since the theoretical apparatus ignores the working time, δ, the most sophisticated statistical agencies, too, have felt no need to include it in their usual collections. Thus, we are unable to obtain valid statistical estimates of K/q^* and K/H^*, the basic technical and theoretical elements.[21]

Another omission of the neoclassical representation is that, as a rule, only the funds (variously defined) are included in the production function. The fact that after a factory is built, production cannot go on unless the input flow factors are forthcoming, has thus been pushed away from the focus of attention. None other than an authority such as A. C. Pigou preached that "in a stationary state factors of production are stocks, unchanging in amount, out of which emerges a continuous flow, also unchanging in amount, of real income."[22] The omission of the input flow factors is not unrelated to the present race of all underdeveloped countries to build one factory after another without a thorough examination of the availability of the necessary flow inputs. I am confident that if the prospective economic plan of every country were realized by miracle overnight, we would discover that we have long since been planning for a world with an immense excess capacity of industrial production.

The thoughts I shared with you here may seem simple. Perhaps they are simple, once we have untangled the imbroglio hatched by blind symbolism. The economics of production, its elementary nature notwithstanding, is not a domain where one runs no risk of committing some respectable errors. In fact, the history of every science, including that of economics, teaches us that the elementary is the hotbed of the errors that count most.

[20] I may hasten to admit that (22) is only a first approximation formula: a factory working with one shift of ten hours will not produce 25 percent more than with a shift of eight hours. To take better account of facts, we should replace δ by a function of the number of shifts and the number of working hours of each shift. But this amendment does not affect in the least the validity of the statements just made.

[21] The difficulty is especially serious in the case of comparisons between two different industries. Even if we know that each industry has always used its full capacity, i.e., has worked with the corresponding H^*, the values of capital-labor ratios derived from the usual statistical data are neither comparable nor strictly relevant — unless we also know that both industries employed the same number of shifts. In fact, the Census of Manufactures provides no information on the number of shifts and on the percentage of utilized capacity.

[22] Pigou, *op. cit.*, p. 19.

11. THE THEORY OF THE FIRM: A COMPARISON OF MARGINAL ANALYSIS AND LINEAR PROGRAMMING*

Thomas H. Naylor†

Introduction

Prior to the development by George Dantzig [3] of the simplex algorithm for solving linear programming problems in 1947, the neoclassical model of the multi-product, multi-factor firm formulated by J. R. Hicks [8] was probably the most widely accepted mathematical model of the firm among economists. However, with the advent of the simplex method, economists were quick to recognize that linear programming could be used to construct an alternative model of the firm which was quite different from the conventional marginal analysis model used by Hicks and others both from the standpoint of the assumptions underlying such a model and the optimality conditions implied by the model. The first publication which took cognizance of the applicability of linear programming to the theory of the firm was Robert Dorfman's *Application of Linear Programming to the Theory of the Firm* [5]. In this important contribution to the literature on the theory of the firm Dorfman develops two alternative mathematical models of the firm, one using conventional marginal analysis and the other using linear programming. After a careful reading of Dorfman's work, it is possible to delineate some of the differences in the assumptions underlying his two models, but the notation which he uses in the linear programming model precludes the possibility of a detailed comparison of the optimality conditions of the two models.

A second contribution to this area of economic thought was not forthcoming until 1958 when Dorfman, Samuelson, and Solow collaborated to write *Linear Programming and Economic Analysis* [6]. Unfortunately however, the sections of this book which deal with the theory of the firm closely parallel Dorfman's original work and contribute little additional information in the way of comparisons of marginal analysis and linear programming as

*From *Southern Economic Journal*, Vol. XXXII, No. 3 (January, 1966), pp. 263–274. Reprinted by permission of the publisher and the author. The material contained in this article has also been reproduced in Thomas H. Naylor and John M. Vernon's *Microeconomic Theory and Decision Models of the Firm* (New York: Harcourt, Brace and World, 1969).

†Thomas H. Naylor, Professor of Economics, Duke University. This paper was presented at the Eastern Meeting of The Institute of Management Sciences in Rochester, N.Y., October 13–15, 1965.

alternative ways of viewing the theory of the firm. Although it has become popular to include a chapter on linear programming in recent textbooks on microeconomic theory and the theory of the firm such as Baumol [1], Boulding and Spivey [2], Henderson and Quandt [7], and Spencer and Siegelman [16], to mention only a few, none of these books have attempted to spell out the precise differences between marginal analysis models of the firm and linear programming models of the firm in terms of (1) their underlying assumptions and (2) their optimality conditions.

This paper represents an attempt to further delineate some of the differences underlying the marginal analysis and linear programming approaches to the theory of the firm. We begin with a verbal statement of the assumptions underlying the Hicksian model of the multi-product, multi-factor competitive firm. (The Hicksian model is assumed to be typical of a large class of marginal analysis models.) Next, we present a concise verbal summary of the optimality conditions of the Hicksian model for the purpose of a later comparison with the optimality conditions associated with linear programming models. This is followed by a verbal statement of the assumptions underlying a linear programming model of the firm. Since it is the production function which gives rise to the principal differences between the marginal analysis approach and the linear programming approach to the theory of the firm, an entire section of the paper is devoted to this topic. We then formulate a linear programming model of the firm using notation which lends itself to comparisons with the Hicksian model. Finally, with the aid of the Kuhn-Tucker theorem we attempt to achieve a detailed comparison of the optimality conditions of our linear programming model with the Hicksian optimality conditions.

The Hicksian Model of the Firm

The conventional marginal analysis model of the multi-product, multi-factor firm developed by J. R. Hicks [8] rests upon the following major assumptions [12]:

1. The firm possesses a productive process which is capable of transforming a maximum of m variable factors of production into p products. (There are no limitations on the availability of the factors.)
2. The prices of the firm's factors and products are fixed and known. (That is, perfect competition is assumed.)
3. The objective of the firm is to maximize profit subject to the technical constraints imposed by its production function.
4. A continuous production function exists (with nonzero first and second order partial derivatives) which relates the set of independent factor variables to the set of independent product variables.
5. The exact nature of the firm's production function has been predetermined by a set of technical decisions by the firm's engineers and technicians.
6. The firm's production function is characterized by: a decreasing marginal rate of technical substitution between any two factors; a decreasing marginal product for

all factor-product combinations; and an increasing marginal rate of product transformation between any two products.

7. Neither the factor prices, product prices, nor the parameters which determine the firm's production function will change over the time period which is being considered. (This is a static model.)

8. Neither the factor prices, product prices, nor the parameters which determine the production function are permitted to be random variables. (Complete certainty is assumed.)

Optimality Conditions for the Hicksian Model: An Economic Interpretation

The optimality conditions for the Hicksian model of the firm may be derived in a straightforward manner by use of the Lagrangian differential gradient method. These optimality conditions take the form of the following economic decision rules [8], [12]:

Rule 1. The price ratio of any two products must equal the marginal rate of product transformation between the two products.

Rule 2. The price ratio of any two factors must equal the marginal rate of technical substitution between the two factors.

Rule 3. The price ratio of any factor-product combination must be equal to the marginal product for the particular factor-product combination.

The Assumptions Underlying a Linear Programming Model of the Firm

Our linear programming model of the multi-product, multi-factor firm rests on the following set of assumptions:

1. The firm has p independent *activities* available, where an activity is defined as a particular way of combining a maximum of m variable factors with a maximum of n fixed factors for the production of a unit of output. A unit of output is analogous to a unit of product, but the firm may produce more than one product. Since a given product may be produced by several different activities each using different factor input ratios, the number of activities may exceed the number of products.

2. The prices of the firm's variable factors and products are fixed and known. (Perfect competition is assumed.)

3. The objective of the firm is to maximize profit subject to the constraints imposed by the nature of its activities and the amounts of fixed factors which are available.

4. Each activity is characterized by a set of ratios of the quantities of the factors to the levels of each of the outputs. These ratios are constant and independent to the extent to which each activity is used. (The firm's production functions are homogeneous of degree one, i.e., constant returns to scale are assumed) [5].

5. The firm is constrained in its selection of activity levels by its fixed endowments of certain resources (fixed factors) required to support the p activities. (The firm's fixed factors are perfectly divisible in use but there is an upper limit on the total quantity of each fixed factor available.)

6. Two or more activities can be used simultaneously, subject to the limitations of the fixed factors available to the firm, and if this is done, the quantities of the outputs and inputs will be the arithmetic sums of the quantities which would result if the activities were used separately [5].

7. The exact nature of the firm's activities has been predetermined by a set of technical decisions by the firm's engineers and technicians.

8. All of the firm's factors and products are perfectly divisible. (This assumption may, of course, be relaxed if one desires to formulate an integer linear programming model.)

9. Neither the factor prices, product prices, nor the coefficients which determine the firm's activities (input-output coefficients) will change over the time period which is being considered. (This is a static model.)

10. Neither the factor prices, product prices, nor the coefficients which determine the firm's activities are permitted to be random variables. (Complete certainty is assumed.)

The Production Function[1]

Since most of the differences underlying the assumptions of marginal analysis and linear programming models of the firm stem from differences in their assumptions regarding the production function, it seems appropriate to include a digression on "the production function." Before turning to a discussion of the production function it is necessary that we define explicitly what we mean by the terms "marginal analysis" and "linear programming."

Marginal analysis is concerned primarily with the process of making choices between alternative factor-product combinations considering infinitesimal changes in factor-product combinations. In order to apply marginal analysis to the economic theory of the firm it is necessary to reduce the problem of the firm to one of finding the optimal values of some objective function subject to a set of constraints. The objective function and the constraints must both be concave and continuous with nonzero first and second order partial derivatives. On the other hand, linear programming is concerned with problems involving the optimization of a *linear* objective function subject to a set of *linear* constraints imposed on the variables of the objective function.

The use of the production function as a schedule of technological possibilities has provided economists with a vast amount of information concerning the behavior of profit-maximizing firms. Under the assumptions of conventional marginal analysis (e.g., the Hicksian model of the firm [8]) the firm's production function is said to be a function of the quantities of fixed and variable factors which are used in the firm's production process. For any given factor quantities, the dependent variable represented by the function is usually defined as the maximum quantity of the particular product that can be produced, in a given state of technology, from the specified factor quantities. In the case of the multi-product, multi-factor firm, all products and factors are considered to be independent variables of the production function. The dependent variable is then defined as the maximum quantity of output of some arbitrarily selected product, attainable from the specified factor quantities along with the other specified product quantities. In

[1]For a comprehensive treatment of the properties of production functions see [13].

other words, the production function represents the results of the solution of an entire set of technical suboptimization problems [10].

There are at least two reasons for considering a level of abstraction in treating production functions which takes its starting point a little further back than is usually the case with marginal analysis models of the firm.[2] First, the concept of a production function becomes somewhat clumsy for production processes in which the number of factors of production and products is greater than the number of coefficients of production that are needed to differentiate one process from another. (An example of this phenomenon is a chemical process that can absorb some or all of its inputs only in fixed proportions.) Second, the definition of the production function implies that a physical maximization of output for given levels of input has already been achieved. Although in a market economy this physical maximization of output may be viewed as the first stage of a multi-stage problem, it is by no means a trivial prerequisite [10]. In essence this implies that the profit maximization problem of the firm is a two-stage problem. The first stage consists of deriving a prescription for achieving the physical maximization presupposed in the definition of the production function. That is, stage-one is equivalent to determining the technology for the firm. The second stage is merely the problem of maximizing total profit subject to the conditions imposed by the production function which resulted from the solution to the problem of stage-one.

It should be pointed out that the first of the firm's two decision problems can be solved independently of the second, but the second problem must either be solved simultaneously with the first problem or after the solution to the first problem has been obtained.

The distinction between the types of problems for which conventional marginal analysis and linear programming are best suited may be clarified by further examining the nature of the two different types of productive decision involves determining the use, if any, that the firm is to make of its fixed factors. That is, once technology is determined or has been fixed by the previous decisions, which products should be produced, and in what quantities firm must decide on the technology to be applied in the production of the set of product possibilities available to it. This involves determining the maximum quantity of output for each product variable attainable from specified factor quantities along with other specified product quantities. The second decision involves determining the use, if any, that the firm is to make of its fixed factors. That is, once technology is determined or has been fixed by the previous decisions, which products should be produced, and in what quantities should they be produced so as to maximize total profit? It should be remembered that at this point a decision to produce a particular set of products at a particular level of output automatically determines the level of factor usage for the firm, for the production function prescribes the exact proportions for each level of output for all possible product combinations.

[2]See Koopmans [10], pp. 69–70.

The Hicksian marginal analysis model of the firm is concerned only with the second type of decision problem of the firm, for it assumes that the firm's technological problem has already been solved. However, it is conceptually feasible to solve both of the firm's decision problems simultaneously with marginal analysis.[3] One variable must be introduced for each qualitatively different kind of factor and product and in turn these variables must be introduced into the production function. It is then possible, at least conceptually, to apply the optimality conditions of conventional marginalism to this new production function along with given product and factor prices and determine the profit maximizing levels for the firm's factors and products. This method is both artificial and extremely complex mathematically. However, it does at least consider the problem of the firm as one problem rather than as two distinct problems.

Dorfman has very concisely summarized some of the difficulties involved in attempting to solve the second of the firm's two decision problems by marginal analysis in modern industrial situations.

> Machinery, and especially the more advanced types, is likely to be inflexible with regard to the factors which must be combined with it and with regard to the rate and character of its output. Thus, when it has been determined to use a certain number of units of a specific machine, several of the other variables in the production function have been determined at the same time. It will not then be possible to move freely from point to point on the production surface except in an indirect manner.
>
> The type of decision which faces a firm using industrial processes is therefore essentially different from the decisions contemplated by marginal analysis. The firm may decide the extent to which to use each of the types of equipment it owns at any time. In that case any variation in the use of equipment implies simultaneous variation in the use of factors complementary to that equipment. The firm may choose among a number (generally finite) of ways of applying its equipment. Or it may select among a number of types of equipment offered for its purchase. All of these decisions differ in two respects from the kind of decisions treated by marginal analysis. First, they affect the quantities of a group of distinct inputs and outputs simultaneously. Second, the range of choice does not lie along a continuous scale, but involves selection among discrete alternatives. The effects of such decisions are therefore not adequately expressed by the theoretical operation of partial differentiation with respect to the quantities of separate inputs and outputs [5].

In other words the difficulty in solving the firm's second decision problem (profit maximization subject to the constraints imposed by the production function) stems from the fact that the solution of the firm's technological problem may yield a production function which does not possess such properties as continuity, concavity, and nonzero first and second order partial derivatives. Although marginal analysis may be quite suitable for solving the first type of decision problem (technological decisions), it may not be at all appropriate for solving the second type of decision problem in industrial

[3]See Dorfman [5], pp. 84–85.

environments similar to those outlined by Dorfman. Linear programming was devised specifically to circumvent the difficulties described by Dorfman in solving the firm's second-stage decision problem.

Linear programming can also be extended to treat both types of decision problems simultaneously.[4] This can be accomplished by considering each variation in technical proportions as a separate activity. Again, one gains the benefits of the treatment of the over-all problem of the firm by means of a unified theory, but the price is mathematical complexity.

By treating the firm's profit maximization problem as though it consisted of two dissimilar problems, one finds that the choice between linear programming and marginal analysis as a tool of analysis depends on which problem is being considered or, equivalently, which level of abstraction is desired. If the problem is "What technique should be applied for using a particular resource for the purpose adopted?" then marginal analysis is more suitable. If the question is "What use, if any, is to be made of a particular resource?" then linear programming is, perhaps, more appropriate [5].

In the final analysis the principal difference between the assumptions underlying marginal analysis models of the firm and linear programming models of the firm lies in the difference between the definition of the "production function" and the definition of an "activity." These salient differences have been summarized by Dorfman as follows,

> . . . the [activity] of linear programming is a more specifically defined concept than the production function of marginal analysis. Indeed, a production function is a family of [activities] which use the same factors and turn out the same products. If we compare any two points on a production surface, if the internal ratios of the inputs and outputs at the two points are the same they will represent different levels of the same [activity], otherwise they will represent different [activities]. The production function thus is a tool for exhibiting and comparing different but related [activities]. What it fails to present adequately is the consequence of using several [activities] in parallel, and such combinations of [activities] are characteristic of modern industry [5].

A Linear Programming Model of the Firm

Consider a firm that has p independent activities available, where an activity is defined as a particular way of combining a maximum of m variable factors with a maximum of n fixed factors for the production of a unit of output. We then let

(1) Z_k = the level of the kth activity, $(k = 1, \cdots, p)$

(2) X_{ik} = the total quantity of the ith variable factor required by the kth activity, $(i = 1, \cdots, m;\ k = 1, \cdots, p)$

[4]See Dorfman [5], p. 85.

(3) Y_{jk} = the total quantity of the jth fixed factor required by the kth activity, $(j = 1, \cdots, n; k = 1, \cdots, p)$

(4) Y_j = the quantity of the jth fixed factor which is currently available to the firm, $(j = 1, \cdots, n)$

(5) a_{ik} = the quantity of the ith variable factor required by one unit of the kth activity, $(i = 1, \cdots, m; k = 1, \cdots, p)$

(6) b_{jk} = the quantity of the jth fixed factor required by one unit of the kth activity, $(j = 1, \cdots, n; k = 1, \cdots, p)$

(7) P_k = the competitive price per unit of the kth activity, $(k = 1, \cdots, p)$.

(8) C_i = the competitive price per unit of the ith variable factor, $(i = 1, \cdots, m)$

(9) K_{jk} = the cost of converting one unit of the jth fixed factor for use in the kth activity, $(j = 1, \cdots, n; k = 1, \cdots, p)$.[5] These costs are assumed to be constant.

The firm's profit function may then be stated as follows,

$$(10) \qquad \pi = \sum_{k=1}^{p} P_k Z_k - \sum_{i=1}^{m} \sum_{k=1}^{p} C_i X_{ik} - \sum_{j=1}^{n} \sum_{k=1}^{p} K_{jk} Y_{jk}$$

By definition, in linear programming, each activity is characterized by certain ratios of the quantities of the factors to each other and to the levels of each of the outputs and is the result of a previous technical optimization decision. These ratios are defined to be constant and independent of the extent to which each activity is used. Hence, it becomes necessary to impose the following definitional constraints on our problem.

$$(11) \qquad X_{ik} = a_{ik} Z_k \quad (i = 1, \cdots, m; k = 1, \cdots, p)$$

$$(12) \qquad Y_{jk} = b_{jk} Z_k \quad (j = 1, \cdots, n; k = 1, \cdots, p).$$

These two constraints are tantamount to assuming that the firm's production functions are homogeneous of degree one. The firm is constrained in its selection of activity levels by its fixed endowments of certain resources required to support the p activities.

$$(13) \qquad \sum_{k=1}^{p} Y_{jk} \leq Y_j \quad (j = 1, \cdots, n)$$

Summarily, the mathematical problem of the firm is one of determining those values of Z_k, X_{ik}, and Y_{jk} which will maximize:

$$(14) \qquad \pi = \sum_{k=1}^{p} P_k Z_k - \sum_{i=1}^{m} \sum_{k=1}^{p} C_i X_{ik} - \sum_{j=1}^{n} \sum_{k=1}^{p} K_{jk} Y_{jk}$$

subject to:

---

[5]The nature of this type of conversion cost was first outlined by Professor Ralph W. Pfouts in [15].

(15)
$$X_{ik} = a_{ik}Z_k$$
$$(i = 1, \cdots, m;\ k = 1, \cdots, p)$$

(16)
$$Y_{jk} = b_{jk}Z_k$$
$$(j = 1, \cdots, n;\ k = 1, \cdots, p)$$

(17)
$$\sum_{k=1}^{p} Y_{jk} \leq Y_j \quad (j = 1, \cdots, n)$$

Although this constrained optimization problem can be solved by one or more variations of the simplex method [3 and 4], our principal concern here is not with the technique by which one would solve the problem, but rather how to interpret the solution in the light of existing economic theory. The Kuhn-Tucker theorem provides a convenient mathematical tool for describing the optimality conditions for our linear programming model of the firm. (For a formal statement of the Kuhn-Tucker theorem see [11, 14, and 15].)

Since both the objective function and the constraints in our linear programming model are linear, the concavity requirements of the Kuhn-Tucker theorem are automatically fulfilled. Next we must formulate the Lagrangian function for our model,

(18)
$$L = \pi + \sum_{j=1}^{n} u_j\left(Y_j - \sum_{k=1}^{p} Y_{jk}\right) + \sum_{i=1}^{m}\sum_{k=1}^{p} v_{ik}\,(X_{ik} - a_{ik}Z_k)$$
$$+ \sum_{j=1}^{n}\sum_{k=1}^{p} w_{jk}(Y_{jk} - b_{jk}Z_k)$$

(The symbols, u_j, v_{ik}, and w_{jk} denote Lagrangian multipliers.) The following conditions, (19) through (24), correspond to the Kuhn-Tucker necessary and sufficient conditions for a constrained maximum at Z_k^0, X_{ik}^0, Y_{jk}^0, u_j^0, v_{ik}^0, and w_{jk}^0.

(19a)
$$P_k \leq \sum_{i=1}^{m} v_{ik}a_{ik} + \sum_{j=1}^{n} w_{jk}b_{jk}$$
$$(k = 1, \cdots, p)$$

(19b)
$$-C_i \leq -v_{ik}$$
$$(i = 1, \cdots, m;\ k = 1, \cdots, p)$$

(19c)
$$w_{jk} - K_{jk} \leq u_j$$
$$(j = 1, \cdots, n;\ k = 1, \cdots, p)$$

(20)
$$\sum_{k=1}^{p} P_kZ_k^0 - \sum_{i=1}^{m}\sum_{k=1}^{p} C_iX_{ik}^0 - \sum_{j=1}^{n}\sum_{k=1}^{p} K_{jk}Y_{jk}^0 = \sum_{j=1}^{n}\sum_{k=1}^{p} u_jb_{jk}Z_k^0$$

(21a)
$$Z_k^0 \geq 0 \quad (k = 1, \cdots, p)$$

(21b)
$$X_{ik}^0 \geq 0$$
$$(i = 1, \cdots, m;\ k = 1, \cdots, p)$$

(21c)
$$Y^0_{jk} \geq 0$$
$$(j = 1, \cdots, n; k = 1, \cdots, p)$$

(22a)
$$\sum_{k=1}^{p} Y_{jk} \leq Y_j \quad (j = 1, \cdots, n)$$

(22b)
$$X_{ik} \geq a_{ik}Z_k$$
$$(i = 1, \cdots, m; k = 1, \ldots, p)$$

(22c)
$$Y_{ik} \geq b_{jk}Z_k$$
$$(j = 1, \cdots, n; k = 1, \cdots, p)$$

(23)
$$\sum_{j=1}^{n} u_j^0 Y_j = \sum_{j=1}^{n}\sum_{k=1}^{p} Y_{jk}u_j^0$$

(24a)
$$u_j^0 \geq 0 \quad (j = 1, \cdots, n)$$

(24b)
$$v^0_{ik} \geq 0$$
$$(i = 1, \cdots, m; k = 1, \cdots, p)$$

(24c)
$$w^0_{jk} \geq 0$$
$$(j = 1, \cdots, n; k = 1, \cdots, p)$$

Optimality Conditions for the Linear Programming Model: An Economic Interpretation

Having outlined a set of necessary and sufficient conditions for profit maximization for our linear programming model of the firm we now turn our attention to an economic interpretation of these results. In addition to providing an economic interpretation of the optimality conditions of our linear programming model we shall also compare these results with the economic interpretation of the optimality conditions of the Hicksian model of the firm.

Before interpreting the economic implications of the optimality conditions for the linear programming model it is necessary to define in economic terms the Lagrangian multipliers u_j, v_{ik}, and w_{jk}. These Lagrangian multipliers are the prices imputed to the firm's factors of production, i.e., the prices the firm would be willing to pay for a marginal unit of a particular factor. The marginal value imputed to the jth fixed factor is denoted by u_j. The marginal value imputed to the ith variable factor used in the kth activity is denoted by v_{ik}. The marginal value imputed to the jth fixed factor used in the kth activity is denoted by w_{jk}.

In analyzing the economic implications of (19a) it is impossible to come up with a relationship which is an exact analog to the familiar requirement of conventional marginalism that when optimum quantities of any two products are being produced the ratio of their prices must be equal to their rate of product transformation. The difficulty stems from the fact that the main emphasis of linear programming is placed on the "activity" rather than on particular products and factors. A particular product may be produced by several different activities each using different factor input ratios. Furthermore, the production of a single end-product may require several stages of production, each of which corresponds to a separate activity. Unless we specify which activities are associated with each of the different products produced by the firm, the rate of product transformation between any two products will not be defined. Since we have not chosen to assign each activity in our model to a particular product the rate of product transformation is not defined in our analysis. By assigning each activity to a particular product it would then be possible to define the rate of product transformation between any two products, but the mathematical complexity of the analysis would be increased considerably by the addition of a third subscript on each of the input-output coefficients (a_{ik} and b_{jk}).

Condition (19a) states that the price per unit of the kth activity must be less than or equal to the sum of the imputed costs of the fixed and variable factors used to produce one unit of the kth activity.[6] This is equivalent to stipulating that positive profits are not permitted for any activity of the given technology. Activities that are unprofitable under these imputed prices are not considered as claimants for the scarce resources in question [10]. This means that if the market price of the kth activity is less than its imputed price, the kth activity will not be utilized. Activities that break even are acceptable alternatives in combination with or as substitutes for those already in use [10]. That is, if the market price of the kth activity is equal to the imputed price of the fixed and variable factors used in its production, then the kth activity may be utilized at that level. Finally, activities that are profitable require the recalculation of the original linear programming problem with a technology into which they have been introduced [10]. Mathematically this implies that the profitable activity is introduced into the solution of the linear programming problem. As long as there exist profitable activities, the solution to the linear programming problem is not an optimum one. A recalculation will lead to a revision of the imputed prices of the factors and in general to changes in the levels of usage of the other activities included in the solution of the linear programming problem. In this manner the firm solves its internal allocation problem by a computational procedure that imitates the action of a competitive market with regard to resources not actually traded [10]. For this reason linear programming is considered to be an inward looking approach to the theory of the firm, while marginal analysis tends to be more of an outward looking approach.

Equation (19a) is actually an analog to the familiar result of marginal analysis in which optimality requires that marginal revenue (or price) be equated with marginal cost. In this case, if the price of the kth activity equals the

[6]Here we are using the term "imputed cost" to mean a valuation based on alternative factor uses *internal* to the firm. In conventional economic theory the term "imputed cost" usually refers to a valuation based on alternative factor uses *external* to the firm.

marginal imputed cost of the kth activity, the kth activity will be utilized at that level. If the price exceeds the marginal imputed cost the level of the kth activity will be increased until the price equals the marginal imputed cost, i.e., until an optimum level is reached. If the price is less than the marginal imputed cost, the activity will not be utilized. That is, the total profit will decrease if an unprofitable activity is introduced into the solution.

Condition (19b) states that if the ith variable is used by the kth activity the factor price must be equal to the marginal value imputed to the ith variable factor with regard to the kth activity. The competitive market analog of (19b) under marginal analysis is the requirement that the usage of a particular factor for a particular product be carried to the point where the price of the factor is just equal to the value of the marginal product for the particular product. If the price of the ith factor exceeds the marginal value imputed to the ith variable factor with regard to the kth activity, the factor will not be utilized by the kth activity. The market analog to this case stipulates that factors are not utilized at levels in which their factor costs exceed the value of their marginal product. If the price of the ith variable factor is less than the marginal value imputed to the ith variable factor with regard to the kth activity, then the level of usage of the ith factor in the kth activity should be increased. Furthermore, the condition of the Hicksian model that when optimum quantities of the variable factors are used in the production of a particular product, the ratio of their factor prices must be equal to their rate of technical substitution does not hold here, because the marginal rate of substitution is not defined in our linear programming model. The reason that the marginal rate of substitution is not defined again stems from the fact that we have not assigned product labels to the activities in our model. If we had assigned each activity to the production of one of the firm's products and if there were several activities capable of turning out the same product each with its own input proportions, then there would exist piecewise linear iso-product curves connecting corresponding points on the different activity rays and the slopes of these segments would be the marginal rates of substitution.

Condition (19c) states that the marginal value of the jth fixed factor used in the kth activity minus the marginal cost of converting one unit of the jth fixed factor into the kth activity must be less than or equal to the marginal value imputed to one unit of the jth fixed factor. There is no analog to this condition in the Hicksian model, for the Hicksian model contains no fixed factors of production. If the equality holds for (19c), then the jth fixed factor is being utilized at an optimum level with regard to the kth activity. If the inequality holds for (19c), then the jth fixed factor will not be utilized in the kth activity. Furthermore, if the direction of the inequality is reversed, then the firm should increase the level of usage of the jth fixed factor in the kth activity. If excess capacity exists in the jth fixed factor then, $w_{jk}-K_{jk} = 0$.

The familiar optimality requirement of marginal analysis that the price ratio of any factor-product combination must be equal to the marginal product for the particular factor-product combination is not discernible in our linear programming model. Although the term "value imputed to an activity" is analogous to the term "value of the marginal product" which is used in marginal analysis, the term "marginal product" is not defined under the assumptions of our linear programming model. Again this can be attributed to the fact that we have not specified which products are produced by the firm's different activities.

By utilizing equations (11) and (12) and the definition of profit per unit of the kth activity, condition (19) can also be expressed as

$$(25) \qquad P_k - \sum_{i=1}^{m} C_i a_{ik} - \sum_{j=1}^{n} K_{jk} b_{jk} \leq \sum_{j=1}^{n} u_j b_{jk} \qquad (k = 1, \cdots, p)$$

This is the mathematical formulation of the linear constraints of the so-called dual problem of linear programming which states that the profit per unit of the kth activity cannot exceed the imputed cost per unit of the kth activity. The dual problem of the firm may be expressed as follows:

$$(26) \qquad \text{Minimize } T = \sum_{j=1}^{n} u_j y_j$$

subject to:

$$(27) \qquad \sum_{j=1}^{n} u_j b_{jk} \geq P_k - \sum_{i=1}^{m} P_i a_{ik} - \sum_{j=1}^{n} K_{jk} b_{jk} \qquad (k = 1, \cdots, p)$$

The saddle point values $(Z_k^0, X_{ik}^0, Y_{jk}^0, u_j^0, v_{ik}^0, w_{jk}^0)$ of the Lagrangian function, L, possess the following interesting characteristics. The objective function, π, of the primal problem is maximized at Z_k^0, X_{ik}^0, Y_{jk}^0, while the objective function of the dual problem, T, is minimized at u_j^0, v_{ik}^0, w_{jk}^0, and $\pi^0 = T^0$. (The proof is omitted.)

The origin of the term "dual problem" lies in the symmetry of the mathematical statements of the two linear programming problems of the firm. The primal problem which is the main subject matter of this paper involves maximization, while the dual problem involves minimization. The former involves activity levels no greater than resources permit, the other an imputed price no lower than the amounts necessary to allocate all profits. The dual problem of the firm is to find prices for its scarce resources which will minimize the total imputed cost of these resources to the firm, and yet involve an imputed cost per unit of the kth activity which is no less than the profit per unit for the kth activity. The discussion of conditions (19a) and (19b) has indicated that through these two properties of the dual problem of linear programming the imputed prices provide criteria for decisions as to which activities are to be used by the firm. These criteria can also tentatively be applied to activities not represented in the technology from which the imputed prices were computed.

Condition (20) states that the firm's profits after paying the imputed costs to its scarce resources must be zero. This condition is analogous to the product exhaustion theorem of economic theory.

Conditions (21a) through (21c) are satisfied by the assumption of economic feasibility. Condition (22a) is merely a statement to the effect that the total usage of the jth fixed factor in the production of the firm's p activities cannot exceed the quantity of the firm's jth fixed factor which is currently available. The equalities will hold for (22b) and (22c), since they were defined accordingly. Condition (23) indicates that the values imputed to the scarce resources available to the firm must be equal to the value of the scarce resources used in manufacturing operations. Condition (23) is also analogous to the product exhaustion theorem of economic theory. Only in this case, it is the fixed factors which must be exhausted rather than the product. The Lagrangian multipliers are nonnegative by assumption.

For the purpose of comparison with the Hicksian marginal analysis model of the firm, the optimality conditions for our linear programming model of the firm may be summarized in the form of the following decision rules:

Rule 1. The unit price of each activity must be less than or equal to the sum of the imputed costs of the fixed and variable factors used to produce one unit of that activity.

Rule 2. For each variable factor — activity combination the unit price of the given variable factor must be greater than or equal to the marginal value imputed to the variable factor with regard to the given activity.

Rule 3. The cost of converting one unit of a given fixed factor for use in a given activity must be greater than or equal to the net marginal value imputed to the given fixed factor used in the given activity, i.e., the marginal value imputed to a unit of the given fixed factor used in the given activity minus the marginal value imputed to one unit of the fixed factor.

Rule 4. The firm's total profit after paying the costs of its scarce resources (fixed factors) must be equal to zero.

Rule 5. The total value imputed to the scarce resources available to the firm must be equal to the imputed value of the scarce resources used by the firm in manufacturing operations.

Conclusions

In this paper we have shown that there are a number of differences between conventional marginal analysis models of the firm and linear programming models of the firm. Our objective was to spell out in considerable detail exactly what some of these differences are. As a result of this investigation we have found that the principal differences between the two models lie in the assumptions underlying them and the economic implications of their optimality conditions. The Kuhn-Tucker theorem was found to be an extremely useful expository device for delineating the differences between the economic implications of the optimality conditions of the two models.

REFERENCES

[1] Baumol, William J. *Economic Theory and Operations Analysis.* Englewood cliffs, N.J.: Prentice-Hall, 1961.

[2] Boulding, Kenneth E., and W. Allen Spivey (eds.). *Linear Programming and the Theory of the Firm.* New York: Macmillan Co., 1960.

[3] Dantzig, George B. *A Procedure for Maximizing a Linear Function Subject to Linear Inequalities.* Washington, D.C.: Headquarters, U.S. Air Force, Comptroller, 1948.

[4] ———. *Linear Programming and Extensions.* Princeton, N.J.: Princeton University Press, 1963.

[5] Dorfman, Robert. *Application of Linear Programming to the Theory of the Firm.* Berkeley, Calif.: University of California Press, 1951.

[6] ———, Paul A. Samuelson, and Robert Solow. *Linear Programming and Economic Analysis.* New York: McGraw-Hill Book Co., 1958.

[7] Henderson, James M., and Richard E. Quandt. *Microeconomic Theory.* New York: McGraw-Hill Book Co., 1958.

[8] Hicks, J. R. *Value and Capital.* Oxford: Clarendon Press, 1939.

[9] Koopmans, Tjalling C. (ed.). *Activity Analysis of Production and Allocation.* New York: John Wiley & Sons, 1951.

[10] ———. *Three Essays on the State of Economic Science.* New York: McGraw-Hill Book Co., 1957.

[11] Kuhn, H. W., and A. Tucker. "Nonlinear Programming." *Proceedings of the Second Berkeley Symposium on Mathematical Statistics and Probability*, edited by J. Neyman. Berkeley, Calif.: University of California Press, 1951.

[12] Mauer, William A., and Thomas H. Naylor. "Monopolistic-Monopsonistic Competition: The Multi-Product, Multi-Factor Firm." *Southern Economic Journal* (July, 1964), pp. 38–43.

[13] Menger, Karl. "The Properties of the Production Function." *Economic Activity Analysis*, edited by O. Morgenstern. New York: John Wiley & Sons, 1954.

[14] Naylor, Thomas H. "A Kuhn-Tucker Model of the Multi-Product, Multi-Factor Firm." *Southern Economic Journal* (April, 1965).

[15] Pfouts, Ralph W. "The Theory of Cost and Production in the Multi-Product Firm." *Econometrica* (October, 1961), pp. 650–658.

[16] Spencer, Milton H., and Louis Siegelman. *Managerial Economics.* Homewood, Ill.: Richard D. Irwin, 1965.

12. THE SHORT-RUN REVISITED*

Louis De Alessi†

The theory of the firm has been the subject of voluminous literature. Nevertheless, some ambiguities and inconsistencies still persist. In particular, the traditional approach to the short-run as a period in which the quantities of some inputs cannot be varied[1] requires clarification. The failure to recognize explicitly that the adjustment of a firm to a change in market conditions depends upon the costs and receipts associated with the adjustment leads to a number of ambiguities, including some confusion regarding the regions of the production function that are empirically relevant.

Section I contains a brief statement of the traditional short-run theory of the firm; then, as a first approximation, the main implications regarding the paths of prices and of input proportions in the short-run are derived from higher level economic hypotheses. Section II indicates how the relevant predictions regarding the short-run behavior of the firm may be derived from the wealth-maximizing (stock) approach, avoiding some shortcomings of the traditional profit-maximizing (flow) approach. Section III extends the analysis to the "uneconomic" regions of the production function. Section IV contains a few concluding remarks.

I

Consider a competitive firm whose production function[2]

$$Z = f(a_1, a_2) \tag{1}$$

is hypothesized to be a single-valued, continuous function with continuous first- and second-order partial derivatives; all variables represent flows per unit time.[3] The parameter Z° defines a particular output isoquant, conforming to the usual requirement, with slope at a point equal to $-f_1/f_2$.

---

*From the *American Economic Review*, Vol. LVII, No. 3 (June, 1967), pp. 450–461. Reprinted by permission of the publisher and the author.

†Louis De Alessi, Professor of Economics, George Washington University. He acknowledges helpful comments by D. G. Davies, C. E. Ferguson, and J. S. McGee.

[1]For example, see [11, p. 41].

[2]The following exposition, equations (1) through (3), is standard in the literature. For example, see [6, Ch. 3].

[3]The traditional production function relates rates of input utilization to rates of output. As A. A. Alchian [1] has suggested, however, planned volume (V) of output (Contd.)

Let the firm purchase inputs a_1 and a_2 in perfectly competitive markets at constant prices p_1 and p_2. Total costs of production are given by the linear equation:

$$C = p_1 a_1 + p_2 a_2, \tag{2}$$

and the parameter C° defines a particular isocost with constant slope equal to $-p_1/p_2$.

Well known first-order conditions for cost minimization subject to an output constraint require that the input-output combination be on the locus of points (least cost path) where

$$\frac{f_1}{f_2} = \frac{p_1}{p_2}, \tag{3}$$

that is, where the ratio of the marginal products of the inputs is equal to the ratio of their prices.[4] In Figure 12-1, the least cost path is shown by *OE*.

Given the output demand function, the long-run equilibrium conditions for a profit-maximizing firm are easily obtained. Traditional statements of the theory then turn to the main problem at hand, the response of the individual firm to changes in circumstances (e.g., an increase in the demand for the output of the firm) that disrupt the equilibrium.[5] Let T measure the period from the instant of time some disturbance occurs to the instant of time a given adjustment is completed, where the adjustment may involve a change in input proportions as well as a change in the absolute quantity and in the form of the inputs utilized. The usual procedure is to consider adjustment periods or runs of progressively longer duration, where the longer the run, the more inputs the firm "can" vary and the greater the variation permitted in the quantity of any given input. In the two-input case, one short run may thus be shown by holding a_2 fixed at the initial equilibrium level (e.g., point 1 in Figure 12-1) and allowing a_1 to vary.

The purpose of distinguishing between runs of different length presumably is to explain the empirical observations that, the shorter the period T,

---

may be a crucial variable; this point, together with some shortcomings of the flow relative to the stock approach in the analysis of the firm, will be examined in subsequent sections of this paper.

[4]Fulfillment of second-order conditions implies that output isoquants are concave from above over the relevant range [6, p. 51].

[5]For the sake of brevity, the analysis in this paper is usually limited to the consequences associated with an increase in the demand for the output of the firm. The analysis, however, can be easily extended to include the consequences of a decrease in demand, of changes in the input supply function(s), and of changes in the firm's production function due to technological innovations.

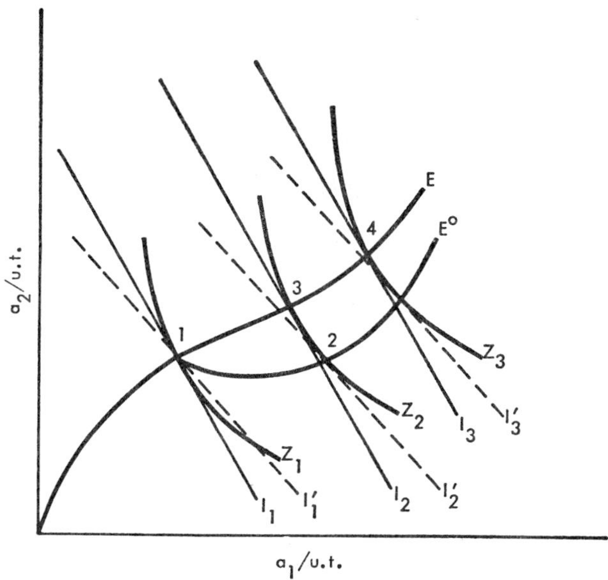

Figure 12-1

the higher is the cost of the change in output and the fewer the inputs that are varied. It follows that economic theory, *inter alia*, must yield implications consistent with this evidence. By defining the short-run as the time period in which some inputs cannot be varied, the desired implications regarding costs are obtained, e.g., [5, pp. 111–15]. This solution, however, avoids a crucial theoretical issue. Implications regarding the proportions in which factors are varied in a given market situation must also be derived from the theory. In particular, the statement that some inputs are held fixed during a given period must be interpreted as a falsifiable proposition implied by economic theory. The phenomenon in question may be identified (defined) as a short-run, but the definition in no sense substitutes for the hypothesis.

All factors of production are variable over any given time interval greater than zero. The rate at which different inputs in fact are varied over time in response to some change in market conditions must depend upon the relative costs and receipts of all the alternative production strategies technologically available to the firm.

As a first approximation, hypothesize that the closer an output program is moved to the present (the shorter the period T) the greater are the costs [1]. Applied to the sellers of the inputs, this proposition implies that as shorter T's are considered the input supply curves decrease (shift to the left) and the greater is the cost to the buyer of varying any given input. That is,

$$p_i = p_i(T),\ p'_i < 0, \qquad (i = 1, 2); \tag{4}$$

substituting[6] into equation (3) yields:

(5) $$\frac{f_1}{f_2} = \frac{p_1(T)}{p_2(T)}.$$

Equation (4) does not deny that each firm purchases its inputs competitively. The input supply curve facing the individual firm is still hypothesized to be perfectly elastic at the price associated with a particular T; however, the shorter the period the higher is the price intercept.

As shorter periods T are considered, not only do supply functions decrease, but the rates of shifting differ among at least some of the inputs. The ratio $p_1(T)/p_2(T)$ increases, remains the same, or decreases depending upon whether the rate of change in p_1 with respect to T is greater than, equal to, or less than the rate of change in p_2 with respect to T (in all cases, all isocosts shift to the left as shorter T's are considered).

Each firm is thus hypothesized to consult a family of sets of budget constraints, where each set contains all possible alternative budget constraints of a given slope associated with the particular run contemplated by the firm for the (possibly partial) adjustment. Presumably one family of sets is applicable to expansion and another is applicable to contraction. Given the iso-product map derived from the traditional production function, a least cost path exists for each input price ratio associated with each adjustment period T. Each short-run least cost path is discontinuous at the original equilibrium point (e.g., $1E°$ in Figure 12-1), since the firm presumably can continue to produce the current output at the current least cost.

Each short-run least cost path yields a short-run total cost curve. If diminishing returns prevail, the total cost curve (TC) for an increase in output during a particular short-run $T°$ would be similar to $TC°$ in Figure 12-2.[7] The longer the adjustment period T, the closer the short-run total cost curve approaches the long-run TC. Thus, the long-run TC (e.g., TC in Figure 12-2) is the boundary of all the short-run TC curves.

Economic theory also asserts that the shorter the time interval, the smaller is the price elasticity of the market demand for a commodity. Thus, even in the case of a firm selling its output under purely competitive conditions, different output prices will prevail during at least some of the different adjustment periods considered by the firm. The form of the function relating the

---

[6]Although the analysis developed in this paper is not dependent upon the validity of the following conditions, it may be presumed that eventually $p_i'=0$, and that $p_i''>0$ over at least part of the interval where $p_i'<0$.

[7]Note that the behavior of the individual firm is at issue. Thus, the *schedule* of input prices (where each price relates to a particular "run") is impounded in *ceteris paribus*. If expansion or contraction of all firms in the industry affects the schedules of input prices (input supply functions facing the industry are not perfectly elastic), then the firm's cost curves will shift accordingly.

The discontinuity in $TC°$ is associated with the approximation developed in this section and the two-dimensional nature of the diagram. A more complete statement of the appropriate cost surface is presented in Section II.

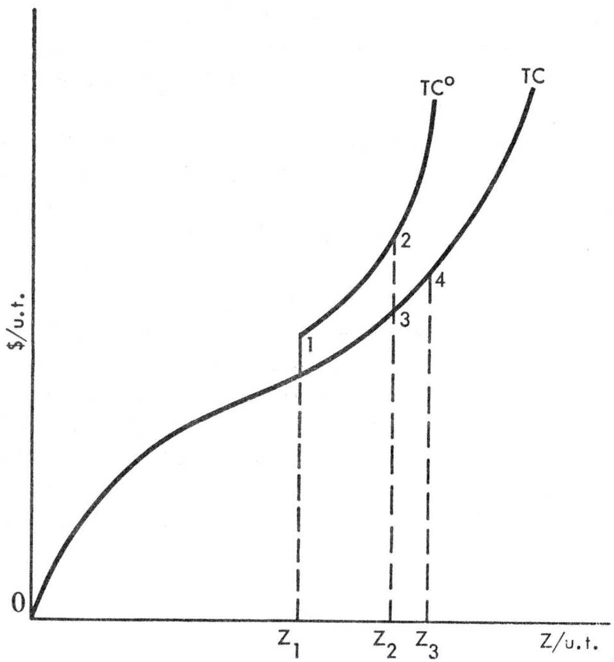

Figure 12-2

demand price per unit of output to T presumably has the same general properties attributed in equation (4) to the input price functions. It follows that a unique total revenue curve and a unique total cost curve may be associated with each run,[8] and the usual criteria may be used to derive the profit-maximizing program for each period.

The analysis developed in this section implies that the firm is induced to seek full adjustment over time rather than instantaneously, and to vary inputs in different proportions as longer T's are considered. In particular, the firm may *choose* to hold one or more inputs fixed during periods of partial adjustment. For example, suppose that a firm initially is producing under conditions of long-run equilibrium (e.g., point 1 in Figures 12-1 and 12-2), and that the demand for its output increases. Given the elasticity of this demand over time and the family of all short-run relative input prices, the profit-maximizing program during a particular short-run may be that associated with the input price ratio shown by I'_2 (Figure 12-1), and with point 2 (Figures 12-1 and 12-2) in particular. In this event, the firm would choose to hold a_2 fixed for a time. The long-run equilibrium output, for an unchanged *schedule* of input prices, would still be along OE (e.g., point 4 in Figures

[8]This approach yields the familiar implication that firms will specialize in the speed (time elapsed) of their responses to changes in market conditions.

12-1 and 12-2). It should be noted that, in the absence of any information regarding the relative costs of varying inputs in different proportions over different time periods, there is no a priori reason for predicting which factor, if any, will be held constant.[9]

It seems generally recognized that adjustment to a change in market conditions is not a free good. So far, the main assertion contained in this paper is that the extent of the adjustment depends upon the relevant costs and receipts. The traditional statement that the quantities of some inputs cannot be varied in the short-run implies a denial of the higher-level economic hypotheses that demand curves are negatively sloped (the lower the cost of changing the input mix, *ceteris paribus*, the quicker the full adjustment) and that supply curves are positively sloped (the quicker the full adjustment sought, *ceteris paribus*, the higher the cost of changing the input mix).

Similarity with traditional analysis, however, has been maintained by choosing the particular set of isocosts associated with a particular run, relating the short-run least cost path to the price per unit of output associated with that run, and identifying the profit-maximizing input-output combination.

II

The isoquant-based theory of the firm yields decision rules in terms of flows: under long-run competitive equilibrium, at the margin the rate of expenditures on all inputs is equal to the rate of receipts from the sale of the output, where presumably the rates in question remain constant indefinitely. When a disturbance occurs, *ceteris paribus*, the new long-run equilibrium flows may be derived and used to predict the long-run response of the firm. Under these circumstances, the present value of the constant rate of outlay given by each isocost and the present value of the constant rate of receipts associated with each output isoquant will yield present value total cost and total revenue curves with the same shape as the total cost and the total revenue curves given by the profit-maximizing model of traditional theory. Thus, application of the usual marginal rules to the stock (wealth) and to the flow (profit) models would yield the same predictions regarding the long-run behavior of the firm. As Alchian and others have emphasized, however, the crucial concept is the *wealth* effect of the alternative strategies considered by the firm; this must be so, since the firm can always alter the time pattern of the flows by either lending or borrowing.

---

[9]This conclusion does not seem to be inconsistent with observation. Without allowing empirical evidence to intrude, it might be granted that in some cases the short-run cost of varying the quantity of some types of labor is greater than the cost of varying some types of plants or equipment, while in other cases the opposite cost relationship prevails. For an example of empirical evidence inconsistent with the classical treatment of labor as a purely variable factor, see [9].

During the process of adjusting to a given disturbance, the pattern of flows for a given firm may be expected to vary from period to period. Predictions regarding the behavior of the firm in the (traditional) short-run are usually obtained by examining progressively longer "representative" short-runs of unspecified duration. Similarly, the short-run least cost paths derived in the preceding section may be useful pedagogically in deriving implications with respect to the nature of the short-run cost curves, and, in addition, to the short-run changes in input proportions. However, it must be recognized that the decision of the firm to adopt a particular input-output program during a particular time period can only be predicted by discounting to the present the flows associated with the alternative input-output programs for different periods, and then choosing the wealth-maximizing sequence of programs. That is, a rational firm must consider a multiperiod horizon in determining the input-output rates in a specific period; in particular, a firm owning resources must decide the intertemporal allocation of such resources.

A firm responding to a change in market conditions may be viewed as producing the adjustment involved in addition to the other product (Z) under consideration. The present value cost, C_p, of the adjustment may be hypothesized to be a function of (1) x, the rate at which the adjustment is undertaken, (2) V, the total planned adjustment, (3) T^*, the length of the interval between the time when the disturbance occurs and the time when the adjustment is begun, and (4) m, the length of the interval between the time when the adjustment is begun and the time when the adjustment is completed:[10]

$$C_p = f(x, V, m, T^*),\ C_p \geq 0, \tag{6}$$

where $f_x > 0, f_{xx} > 0, f_V > 0, f_{VV} < 0, f_{xV} < 0, f_{T^*} > 0$ [1]. The total quantity of the adjustment undertaken and its schedule over time would then be determined at the margin in conjunction with the present value of the receipts from the adjustment. In this construct, the long-run may be defined as the time period in which deferred changes in the quantity (and form) of each input used by the firm would not lead to a lower input price to the firm in present-value terms.

That is, the individual firm is hypothesized to adjust the quantity and the form of each input it uses until the present value of the marginal stream of outlays is equal to the present value of the marginal stream of receipts for each input. The firm chooses the least-cost mesh of the alternative input adjustments subject to a set of output constraints related to the elasticity over time of the demand for the firm's output. The wealth-maximizing solution thus yields the total planned change in the quantity and form of each

[10]The T^* used in this paper corresponds to the T used by Alchian [1]. Following Alchian, m is a dummy variable whose value is determined by the values assigned to x and to V, where $V = \int_{T^*}^{T^*+m} x(t)dt$ and x may vary over time.

input, the rate at which the change is undertaken, the instant of time when the change is begun, and the time period taken to complete it.[11] *Inter alia*, this approach yields information regarding the time period during which a specific input is held fixed and the schedule at which each input adjustment is phased into the production process.

The procedure outlined in the preceding paragraph would yield one point on the (flow) iso-product map for each period. The input-output program presumably will vary from period to period as the firm completes its adjustment, and may involve holding the rate of utilization of one or more inputs fixed during a given time period.[12]

These comments suggest that a particular input-output combination may appear to be irrational in terms of the flows prevailing in that period, and yet be the rational choice in terms of the wealth-maximizing model. Put more strongly, the flows prevailing in one time period do not provide, by themselves, sufficient information to determine the choice of the output program for that period [1]. Economists have obtained propositions regarding the short-run behavior of the firm from a model designed to predict long-run behavior under constant flows, but they have done so only at the cost of ignoring some relevant portions of economic theory.

III

The production function of a firm, according to one definition, ". . . shows the (maximum) quantity of product it [the firm] can produce for given quantities of each of the various factors of production it uses" [5, p. 123]. This definition has been taken to imply that a firm would not use additional quantities of a given input[13] beyond the economic region;[14] that is, output isoquants outside the relevant ridge lines would be straight lines parallel to their

---

[11]In the case of one type of labor, for example, the present value of the hiring and training costs would be related to the planned number of workers to be added to the labor force, the rate at which such individuals are to be hired and trained, and the instant of time when the hiring and training programs are to begin.

[12]J. Hirshleifer has suggested that a firm may choose to hold some inputs fixed in the short-run because of uncertainty regarding the permanence of the initial disturbance [7, p. 250]. The argument developed in this paper, although reinforced by the introduction of uncertainty, suggests that some inputs may be held fixed under conditions of certainty.

[13]As M. Friedman has pointed out, however, this presumes that the cost of discarding some units of this input is zero [5, pp. 130–131].

[14]The economic region is frequently defined (Rule I) as the range over which the marginal products (MP) of all inputs are greater than zero (and, possibly, equal to zero for some inputs); G. H. Borts and E. J. Mishan do so initially [3, p. 300]. Friedman [5, p. 130] and others, including Borts and Mishan later in the same article [3, p. 305], have noted that the maxim of rational behavior for a firm (Rule II) is to use such a combination of factors that the average product (AP) to each input separately is falling (or at least remains constant).

As Friedman and others recognize, these two rules yield the same answer only if the production function is homogeneous of degree one; then the locus of points (ridge line) where the AP of one input is maximum and the ridge line where the MP of the

respective axes [3, p. 304]. A second definition of the production function rests on the minimum factor quantities necessary for given outputs. On this definition, the segments of the output isoquants outside the ridge lines are taken to vanish [3, p. 304].

Recently Borts and Mishan have argued for a re-interpretation of the first definition. If a factor is taken to be fixed (and indivisible) during a given time period and if the firm sells its output under monopolistic conditions, then output isoquants supposedly have meaning in the uneconomic region for the fixed factor and are straight lines parallel to the axis in the uneconomic region for the variable factor.[15] Borts and Mishan conclude that ". . . it is logically inadmissible to construct a diagram in which in both uneconomic regions the iso-product curves are uniquely determined" [3, p. 307].

If "uneconomic" regions exist,[16] the flow analysis developed in Section I of this paper implies that a firm would not operate within them.[17] Since

---

other input is equal to zero coincide. If the production function is homogeneous of degree less than one, then the ridge lines for AP maximum are outside the ridge lines for $MP = 0$; if the production function is homogeneous of degree greater than one, the order of the ridge lines is reversed.

The two rules, of course, are not mutually exclusive. As Friedman concludes, "The point not to be exceeded is the point of vanishing (marginal) returns; the prudent man will seek to exceed the point of diminishing (average) returns" [5, p. 130].

If production functions are taken to be homogeneous of degree less than one, with degree one as the limit, satisfying the marginal conditions (operating in the range where the output isoquants are concave from above) is sufficient to insure that the AP of each input is either decreasing or constant.

Some economists, e.g., [10, p. 177], have suggested that the derivative of output, dZ (taken with respect to one of the inputs, when all inputs vary proportionately), first increases (increasing returns to scale) and then decreases (decreasing returns to scale). In the range of increasing returns to scale, application of rules I and II for rational behavior implies that the segments of the negatively sloped output isoquants outside the ridge lines for AP maximum would be in the "uneconomic" region of the production function.

Production functions yielding increasing returns to scale throughout are taken to be empirically irrelevant, since evidence purporting to support such functions has failed to allow for changes in the planned volume of output.

It may be useful to examine the form of the production function implied by Alchian's reformulation of the cost function. If planned volume (V) of output is held constant, the production surface with respect to the rate (x) of output exhibits decreasing returns to scale throughout. If the rate of output is held constant, the production surface with respect to V exhibits increasing returns to scale throughout. If V and x are taken to vary proportionately (the usual case, as suggested by Hirshleifer [7] and apparently accepted by Alchian [2, Ch. 21]), the production envelope at first exhibits increasing returns to scale and then decreasing returns to scale.

[15]Borts and Mishan [3, p. 307] argue that (i) if both factors are indivisible in the short period, the firm is restricted to a point within the economic region; (ii) if both factors are variable during the period in question, all choices must fall within the economic region.

[16]This paper is not concerned with the empirical question of whether "uneconomic" regions exist.

[17]As noted earlier, second-order conditions for profit maximization imply that the firm would operate in the range where iso-product curves are concave from above. Moreover, a firm (at least a competitive firm) would operate beyond the region of increasing returns to scale if such a region existed.

it has been suggested that a noncompetitive firm using an "indivisible" factor may in fact operate in one of the uneconomic regions in the short-run, the point deserves consideration.

The first issue to be examined is that of indivisibility.[18] Why should a factor be indivisible in the short-run? To take a standard example, consider a firm using tractors as one of the inputs. Following Friedman [5, pp. 131–32], suppose that tractors come in two sizes, with the tractor of size II being in some relevant sense "twice" the tractor of size I. Tractors presumably come in these two sizes, given the demand function for tractors, due to the lower unit cost associated with producing a larger planned volume of output (V) of each of the fewer models relative to the cost of producing a smaller V of each of a broader range of models [1]. A firm using tractors of size I, following some change such as an increase in the demand for its output, may well prefer to shift to an intermediate-size tractor at an intermediate price.[19] If the cost of an intermediate-size tractor produced to order is sufficiently high, however, the firm may choose to acquire more of the standard sizes. That is, the choice to acquire some inputs in lumps can be predicted, at least in some relevant cases, by cost considerations alone. It may seem that this argument, if acceptable, applies to "indivisibility in acquisition" and not to "indivisibility in use" [8, pp. 231–33]. But "divisibility" of all inputs in acquisition implies "divisibility" of all inputs in use, since a firm, at some cost, may always choose to modify the structure of its assets or change the form of its inputs.[20] The theory must be capable of predicting the revealed choice of a firm in the short-run, under specified circumstances, to vary some inputs in discrete quantities rather than in infinitesimally small quantities; it is not helpful to cloak in the name of indivisibility what is really a plea of ignorance.[21]

The second issue is whether a firm would ever operate in the uneconomic region. The usual argument asserts that a competitive firm ". . . can never produce in the uneconomic region. For if the price falls below the lowest

---

[18]The term "indivisibility" has been used to cover a variety of phenomena. For example some economists have used it to describe a factor which cannot be varied during a given interval of time, e.g., [3, p. 304]; some economists have also noted that ". . . indivisibility is necessary for economies of size or scale" [3, p. 305]. This paper is concerned with indivisibility as a short-run phenomenon.

[19]The "half-size man" to drive the "half-size tractor" [5, p. 132] apparently would not be a limit here. In any event I fail to see why, at some suitable price, the "half-size man" (in the technologically relevant sense) would not be forthcoming.

[20]The distinction between fixed and variable costs is also ambiguous. Whether a firm chooses to vary a particular cost depends upon the relative gains and losses of doing so. At some cost a contract can be broken (as any lawyer will gladly admit), a private radio network substituted for a telephone, and so on.

The only costs which legitimately (i.e., implied by economic theory) cannot be varied are "sunk" costs; such costs, of course, are irrelevant to the decision process.

[21]The preceding statements are not inconsistent with an alternative meaning of indivisibility. As Alchian suggests, the term may be interpreted to cover the phenomenon whereby more durable "dies" result in more than proportional increases in output potential [1, p. 29]. In this sense indivisibility is simply the name given to the sign of certain partial derivatives; it does not explain anything.

average variable cost (equals highest average return to the variable factor, given the factor price) it will incur negative quasi-rents"[22] [3, p. 305, footnote 2]. A firm facing a negatively sloped demand, however, apparently may do so: "All that is required in order to encompass the uneconomic region . . . is to regard some fixed amount of a factor . . . as being indivisible during the period in question" [3, p. 304].

If the concept of indivisibility is rejected as a short-run crutch, must output programs within the uneconomic region also be rejected? Given the argument developed in Section II, the answer seems to be negative. As the firm considers alternative adjustment periods, the present value cost of varying one input may be sufficiently greater than the present value cost of varying the other input(s) that the firm may choose to operate in one of the uneconomic regions during some limited time period. If wealth, rather than profit, is used as the relevant criterion, a competitive as well as a monopolistic firm may choose to operate for a time in the uneconomic region—particularly if it is granted that uncertainty may exist regarding the permanence of the change in circumstances inducing the adjustment in output.[23]

The preceding comments suggest that, for analytical purposes, it is necessary to show the uniquely determined iso-product curves in each uneconomic region.[24] Whether the firm will operate within any such region during a particular short-run can only be determined *after* allowing for the appropriate cost and revenue considerations. Furthermore, although at most one such region would be relevant in the two-input case, n-1 regions may be relevant in the n-inputs case.

The concept of a priori fixed, indivisible inputs is misleading. Among other things, such an approach masks the implication that a competitive firm may find it profitable to operate for a time within the uneconomic region.[25]

IV

The traditional approach to the short-run as a period in which some inputs cannot be varied is theoretically inadmissible. The substitution of a definition for the corresponding falsifiable hypothesis implied by economic theory masks some empirically relevant issues. In what proportion are inputs to be

---

[22]It should be noted that Borts and Mishan are working with a linearly homogeneous production function. Their statements would not be necessarily correct, even in the context of flow analysis, if, for example, the production function in question were homogeneous of degree less than one.

[23]R. H. Coase's suggestion that an input be considered ". . . as a right to perform certain (physical) actions" [4, pp. 43–44] is a promising point of departure for further investigations in this area.

[24]E.g., if the present-value cost of not using some resources is zero, the least cost path for these resources outside the relevant ridge lines would then be straight lines parallel to their respective axes.

[25]As Borts and Mishan point out, there is nothing necessarily uneconomic about operating in the uneconomic region.

varied in the short-run? Which inputs, if any, are to be held constant? Which regions of the production function are empirically relevant? Why?

The production function must specify which input-output combinations are technologically relevant; cost and revenue information alone can determine which combinations are economically relevant. If it is granted that variation in the input mix is not a free good, then the proportion in which inputs are varied in response to some change in market conditions will depend upon the relative costs and receipts of all the alternative production strategies technologically available to the firm. Moreover, traditional flow analysis yields propositions regarding behavior of the firm in the short-run only at the cost of some ambiguities. The wealth-maximizing model suggests that, if "uneconomic" regions exist, they are relevant for competitive as well as for monopolistic firms.

REFERENCES

[1] Alchian, A. A. "Costs and Outputs," in Abramovitz, M., *et al.* *The Allocation of Economic Resources: Essays in Honor of Bernard F. Haley.* Stanford, California: Stanford University Press, 1959.

[2] ———— and W. R. Allen. *University Economics.* Belmont, California: Wadsworth Publishing Co., 1964.

[3] Borts, G. H., and E. J. Mishan. "Exploring the 'Uneconomic Region' of the Production Function." *Review of Economic Studies*, Vol. IX (October, 1962), pp. 300–312.

[4] Coase, R. H. "The Problem of Social Cost." *Journal of Law and Economics*, Vol. III (October, 1960), pp. 1–44.

[5] Friedman, M. *Price Theory.* Chicago, Illinois: Aldine Publishing Co., 1962.

[6] Henderson, J. M., and R. E. Quandt. *Microeconomic Theory.* New York: McGraw-Hill Book Co., 1958.

[7] Hirshleifer, J. "The Firm's Cost Function: A Successful Reconstruction?" *Journal of Business*, Vol. XXXV (July, 1962), pp. 235–255.

[8] Machlup, F. *The Economics of Sellers' Competition.* Baltimore, Maryland: Johns Hopkins Press, 1952.

[9] Oi, W. Y. "Labor as a Quasi-Fixed Factor." *Journal of Political Economy*, Vol. LXX (December, 1962), pp. 538–555.

[10] Vickrey, W. S. *Microstatics.* New York: Harcourt, Brace and Co., 1964.

[11] Walters, A. A. "Production and Cost Functions: An Econometric Survey." *Econometrica*, Vol. XXXI (January-April, 1963), pp. 1–66.

13. PRODUCTION THEORY AND COST CURVES*

W. David Maxwell†

In elementary treatments of the theory of the firm we derive a set of cost curves to correspond to the situation in production theory typically called "the" short-run and another set to correspond to "the" long-run. In somewhat more advanced treatments we may indicate that there exists a much larger number of possible situations in production theory, depending upon such considerations as the "divisibility" and/or "adaptability" of factors of production, and that the firm's cost curves depend upon which of many possible assumptions are made about the physical nature of the factors of production.[1]

The present paper seeks to show that the possible situations in production theory are considerably more varied than the current literature would suggest and that the firm's cost curves consequently less amenable to simple classification.[2] After stressing two fundamental distinctions in production theory (neither original with the author), it is argued that the essential consideration is the degree of control of factor services possessed by the firm in a given production situation. Limitations of the firm's control of factor services may stem from indivisibilities in acquisition due to the physical characteristics of input, from the legal nature of the arrangements under which the firm purchases its input, from legal factors pertaining to the use of factor services, or from the nature of user costs. All these considerations affect the degree of control possessed by the firm and help to determine the shape and configuration of the firm's cost curves.

*From *Applied Economics*, Vol. I, No. 3 (August, 1969), pp. 211–224. Reprinted by permission of the publisher and the author.

†W. David Maxwell, Professor of Economics and Dean of the College of Liberal Arts, Texas A & M University.

[1]The classic article perhaps remains that of George Stigler, "Production and Distribution in the Short-Run," *Journal of Political Economy*, Vol. XLVII (1939), pp. 305–327. Reprinted in A. E. A., *Readings in the Theory of Income Distribution* (Philadelphia: Blakiston, 1949).

[2]For discussion of points similar or related to those developed herein see the following: A. A. Alchian, "Costs and Outputs," in M. Abramovitz, *et al. The Allocation of Economic Resources: Essays in Honor of Bernard F. Haley* (Stanford: Stanford University Press, 1959). Yuan-Li Wu and Ching-Wen Kwang, "An Analytical and Graphical Comparison of Marginal Analysis and Mathematical Programming in the Theory of the Firm," in K. E. Boulding and W. A. Spivey, *Linear Programming and the Theory of the Firm* (New York: Macmillan, 1960). Eirik Furubotn, "The Adaptability of Fixed Productive Services in the Short Run," *The Southern Economic Journal*, Vol. XXVIII (1962), pp. 329–339. W. Y. Oi, "Labor as a Quasi-Fixed Factor," *Journal of Political Economy*, Vol. LXX (1962), pp. 538–555. A. A. Walters, "Production and Cost Functions: An Econometric Survey," *Econometrica*, Vol. XXXI (1963), pp. 1–66. W. D. Maxwell, "Short-Run Returns to Scale and the Production of Services," *The Southern Economic Journal*, Vol. XXXII (1965), pp. 1–14.

TWO FUNDAMENTAL DISTINCTIONS

Factors of Production vs. Factor Services

Traditionally economists have divided the resources used in production into land, labor, capital and, sometimes, entrepreneurship, calling these the *factors of production or productive factors.* This is a somewhat arbitrary classification but it reflects the fact that there are inherent differences in productive factors such that one cannot be a perfect substitute for another. Land, labor, and capital differ in physical attributes, in the units in which they are measured, and in the roles that they play in production. Only within limits can more capital compensate for less land or more labor for less capital.

Distinct from the factors of production themselves are the *services yielded by these factors* or *factor services*, the contribution made by factors of production to the productive process. This distinction between productive factors and factor services reflects not only that there is a difference in the units in which productive factors are measured and the units in which they contribute to production but also that these units exist at different levels of abstraction.

Consider land. Not the land itself but something more abstract — the *services* of land — enters into the process of production. Moreover, while we have no readily available unit in which to measure the services of land, it is clear that any such unit would have a temporal dimension, for the services of land are yielded *through time.* Finally, it is apparent that at least some of the services of land are yielded *automatically* through time. The land upon which a refrigerator factory sits may contribute its services to the productive process for any portion of the 24 hours of the day or seven days of the week. Operation of the factory for only a portion of the day or week means that many of the services of land do not enter into production and are simply lost. Thus possession of a unit of land may be conceived of as possession of a stock of the services of land, these services being yielded through time, and all of which may or may not enter into the productive process.

The case of capital is similar but more complex. Capital is customarily measured and purchased in units appropriate to the form in which the capital exists. Thus, a farmer may purchase four hoes or four tractors and a textile manufacturer may purchase fifty looms or a building which he thinks of in terms of square feet of floor space and cubic feet of storage. But again, while hoes, tractors, looms, and buildings are tangible, we find no physical trace of hoes and tractors in carrots, or looms and buildings in sport shirts. Quite evidently something that we may call the *services* of capital enters into production — not capital itself.

Further, the services of capital, like those of land, are yielded through time. Also, as is true of the services of land, but to a lesser extent, some of the services of capital are yielded *automatically* through time.

To a considerable extent, *temporal substitution* of capital services is possible. Thus, in a given period machinery may be operated at a faster or slower rate, altering to some extent the distribution of its services through time, and buildings and/or machinery may be designed to last different periods of time. But in a going concern this type of substitution is limited, and future capital services may be at least as imperfect a substitute for present ones as are the services of other factors of production. Thus, as in the case of land, possession of a unit of capital may be conceived of as possession of a stock of factor services of a particular kind, these services being yielded through time, and all of which may or may not enter into production.

The definition of labor as a separate entity from its services is consistent with our earlier treatment of land and capital as different concepts from their respective services. It is immediately apparent, however, that the firm cannot purchase labor, so defined, (so long as slavery is not legal) and can only purchase labor services. The units in which we sometimes speak of these services (labor hours, man days, etc.) reflects a realization that the services of labor are yielded through time. Nonetheless, labor services, like other factor services, are intangible. Moreover, labor services are like capital services in that, while some temporal substitution is possible, some labor services are yielded automatically through time. If a worker is hired by the week, more-or-less of the labor services yielded may actually enter into production.

In this view factors of production are analogous to blocks of ice which, while they may be purchased in various sizes, melt through time yielding so many gallons of water per hour. The ice may sometimes be made to melt more, or less, rapidly but will melt at a certain rate, anyhow, regardless of whether or not the water is put to use. Purchase of a specific quantity of a factor constitutes the purchase of a specific quantity of factor services. An alternative conceptualization is that factor services are yielded only as they are used in production. This view preserves the distinction between factors and factor services and regards the latter as often being capable of being yielded (and used) at various rates. The major shortcoming of this approach, however, is that a given quantity of a factor is not necessarily coincident with a specific quantity of factor services. This deficiency may be remedied by the assumption that for any given quantity of the factor there is a maximum rate at which it may be made to yield its services and that there are thus available during any given period a maximum quantity of factor services coincident with the given quantity of the factor. If the rate at which the factor services are utilized in production is less than this maximum rate, this is equivalent (in the first view) to not using in production some of the services yielded during the period.

Divisibility in Acquisition vs. Divisibility in Use

An important related distinction is that between divisibility *in acquisition* and divisibility *in use*.[3] Since *factors* of production are purchased or hired

[3]F. Machlup, *The Economics of Sellers' Competition* (Baltimore: The Johns Hopkins Press, 1952), p. 231.

and factor *services* used in production, the distinction is thus basically a distinction between the divisibility of factors and the divisibility of factor services. *Factors* of production must often be purchased or hired in "lumps" and are thus typically far from completely divisible in *acquisition*. Further, factors of production must often be acquired in units which are not completely *compatible*. As noted above, such factors as buildings and land may yield many of their services throughout the twenty-four hours of the day. Yet the firm may be combining with these services the services of labor which are purchased for only eight hours of the day. Finally, the nature of the process of acquisition of factors is typically such that the firm must commit itself prior to the actual utilization of factor services in production.

Thus, indivisibility characterizes the *acquisition* of factors of production. They can often only be acquired in discrete "lumps," these "lumps" are often not completely compatible, and typically factors of production cannot be purchased at a rate simultaneous with the rate at which they yield factor services.

The *services* of factors of production are, however, far more divisible than the factors themselves, primarily because they are yielded through time. The indivisibility that characterizes the acquisition of factors imposes, in effect, an upper limit or constraint upon the quantity of services yielded during any period in which the quantity of factors is not changed, but does not prevent the use of *less* than this quantity of services in production. Millions of factories, stores, shops, etc., are closed during many hours of the day, providing ample evidence that we can use in production less than all of the services yielded by a building. And the fact that hours of operation differ widely, and have differed greatly through time, supports the contention that the *services* yielded by buildings are highly divisible up to the constraint imposed by the indivisibility of the units in which they are acquired. The same would, of course, be true of the services yielded by the land upon which the building stands.

Similarly, machinery, even if capable of operation at only one rate and consisting of only a single machine, may typically be operated for a variable proportion of the twenty-four hours of a day, so that the services it yields to production may be varied up to the constraint of the total quantity of services that it can yield to production. And given that the firm has acquired a specific quantity of labor, there is an upper limit to the quantity of labor services that may be utilized, but lesser quantities of labor service than this maximum may well enter into production.

Thus, it is typically the case that factor services are highly divisible up to the constraint imposed by the indivisibility of the units in which factors of production are acquired. Quite obviously, indivisibility in the *acquisition* of *factors* of production is not coincident with indivisibility in the *use* of the *services* of factors of production.[4]

---

[4]While the traditional theory of the firm does not distinguish indivisibility in use from indivisibility in acquisition (and thus attributes to the former the degree of indivisibility characterizing the latter), in many areas of business administration this error is not made. For example, Timms speaks explicitly of the firm's purchasing

THE PRODUCTION FUNCTION

The production function states mechanistically the (maximum) outputs that will result if different quantities of factor services are combined in a particular process. "Returns to proportion" refers to the results, in terms of output, of performing a specific operation with the production function. "What will be the result," the economist asks, "if we vary the quantity of the services of one factor only, while combining with the services of this factor a constant quantity of the services of all other factors?"

It should be noted that the question is not one of the *advisability* or *feasibility* of combining various quantities of labor services, for example, with a given quantity of the services of land. The question concerns only the nature of the results if the firm *were* to do so.

"Returns to scale," like "returns to proportion," refers to the results, in terms of output, of performing an operation with the production function but, needless to say, a different operation than that implied by returns to proportion. Again, it is true, however, that the question is not one of the advisability or feasibility of performing the operation but merely of the nature of the results if the operation were performed.

"What will be the result, in terms of output," the economist asks, "if all factor services are changed by a given percentage?" If the services of land, labor, and capital were increased by 10 percent, for example, would output increase by 10 percent, more than 10 percent, or less than 10 percent?[5]

Unfortunately while economists appear to agree on the question, there is far from agreement on the answer.[6] The area of disagreement can be reduced by careful consideration of the nature of the question. First of all, the question, as indicated earlier, is not an empirical one. It may well be that the firm *in reality* cannot change the quantity of all factor services by the same proportion. An inability to do so would automatically mean a change in the *proportions* in which factor services are combined and a violation of the conditions of the question. It would also automatically mean that any type of result, in terms of output, is acceptable but irrelevant—for there is no dispute that there can be any type of returns *to proportion.* The question requires that the proportions between the various types of factor services remain unchanged throughout the (conceptual) operation.

"inventories" of physical facilities, raw materials, and human skills, while implying the greater divisibility in the use of factor services in stressing the necessity of avoiding idle labor time, machine time, waiting lines, etc. In the traditional theory of the firm factor services *purchased* are factor services *used* just as output produced is output sold. (Timms, Howard L., *The Production Function in Business* [Homewood, Illinois: Richard D. Irwin, 1966]).

[5]More technically, if $P = f(a, b)$ where P is output and a and b are the quantities of services of factors A and B, respectively, returns to proportion refers to the behavior of P when the partial derivative $\gamma P / \gamma a$ or $\gamma P / \gamma b$ is taken, whereas returns to scale refers to the effect upon P of multiplying a and b by the same positive constant λ.

[6]For a summary of the arguments see Edward H. Chamberlin, *The Theory of Monopolistic Competition* (6th ed.; Cambridge, Massachusetts: Harvard University Press, 1950), pp. 235–244.

Similarly, we must be careful to note that the operation specified by returns to scale requires the same proportionate change in *all* factor *services*. Thus, the fact that the same size management may be able to as easily supervise a larger as a smaller enterprise is again irrelevant. If, at both the larger and smaller outputs *all* the *services* of management were entering into production then, quite obviously, the *proportion* of these factor services to all others has altered — violating the conditions of the question. If, at the larger output, a greater quantity of management *services* enter into production, the operation requires that the percentage increase in these services that enter into production be no more nor less than that of the other types of factor services. Unfortunately since factor services are intangible and we have no independent measure of them, we cannot specify, in reality, that the quantity of management services entering into production has, or has not, increased by a specific percentage. Thus, if output *were* to increase by a percentage other than the percentage increase in all other types of factor services and if we were attempting to attribute this result to the services of management, we would either have to conclude that the quantity of management services entering into production had changed by other than the specified percentage or we would be faced with the quite impossible task of establishing that this was not indeed the case.

The productive process is assumed to remain unchanged during the conceptual operation posed by "returns to scale." The meaning of this assumption, however, is far from clear. All economists would agree that "the state of the arts" or technology is given any such operation as that posed by returns to scale. But is it not undeniably true that some techniques can be used at some scales of production and not at others — that specialization of workers, e.g., can occur at some scales of output and not at others? And does this not yield increasing returns to scale? Those who argue not can contend either that the production function has been altered in such instances or that in such instances a ten percent change in the factor is not, and cannot be shown to be, a 10 percent change in the quantity of that factor's *services* entering into production. Thus, a result other than proportionate change in output is again indicative of an alteration in the proportion in which factor services are combined.

Finally, questions arise in instances in which the units in which output is measured are not homogeneous. In making barrels, e.g., twice as much wood can be used to make a barrel with more than twice as much volume. Similarly, twice as many feet of fence can enclose more than twice as many acres. Critics can reply that the units in which output is measured must be homogeneous and that the conditions of the question require, by analogy, that barrels of the same size be produced and plots of equal size be enclosed. Alternatively they can argue in terms of factor *services*, as before.

In the heat of the argument it is easy to lose sight of the fact that no one would expect returns to scale not to be comingled in reality with returns to proportion. Since the latter can, it is agreed, result in increasing or decreasing returns it is probably best to regard what appear to be returns to scale other than constant as attributable to changes in the proportions in which factor services are combined.

In the present paper, a linear homogeneous production function is assumed implying, of course, constant returns to scale. The "classical" type of returns to proportion is assumed; i.e., output increases at an increasing rate over some range of input, followed by a range in which output continues to rise but at a decreasing rate, followed by a range in which output decreases, as larger quantities of the services of one factor of production are combined with a given quantity of the services of other factors.

Output-Expansion Paths

Given rationality, and given a linearly homogeneous production function of the type described in the previous section, the next task is to determine the optimal combinations of factor-service inputs that the firm should use in producing the various outputs that it can produce in a given production situation. In other words the next task is to determine, for various situations, the nature of the firm's output-expansion path. As this implies, we are not concerned with the equilibrium output of the firm. Prior to the selection of a particular output the firm must determine the best way of producing various outputs. Similarly, the revenues associated with the sale of various outputs are not under consideration but the factors affecting the costs of these outputs are.

The Market Period. The term "market period" may be used to describe a set of situations characterized by indivisibility in the acquisition of all factor services. The market period may have been chosen merely because it is desired to analyze separately those decisions pertaining to the utilization (but not acquisition) of factor services. Or it may have been chosen to describe a situation in which the firm has entered into contractual arrangements that specify that the firm will purchase during the period certain quantities of all inputs, these quantities not readily subject to change.[7] These contractual arrangements may specify that certain quantities of input will be purchased at a stipulated price or that the firm will purchase all of the output of suppliers. In the latter case, however, the purchasing firm must have a fairly accurate estimate of the quantities that it has committed itself to purchase. Or the physical characteristics of the factors may be such that they can only be purchased in blocks or lumps yielding up to some maximum quantity of factor services, and the firm has already purchased, or committed itself to purchase, a specified number of such lumps or blocks of each. Or this situation may have been chosen simply as the logical beginning of a conceptual continuum of situations through time.

---

[7]For example, the firm may have already determined its "economic order quantities" for all inputs and entered into contracts based upon these order sizes. (See Timms, *op. cit.*, p. 533).

Thus, the market period, for whatever reason chosen, is a situation in which the firm has surrendered a great deal of its control over its inputs. In terms of *acquisition* the decisions have been made. There remain only decisions concerning factor-service utilization. The firm has acquired certain quantities of land, labor, and capital and can secure no more during this period, nor can it act as a seller of factors of production or utilize the factor services at its command in any productive process other than that particular one to which the production function refers.

Since indivisibility in acquisition does not imply an equal degree of indivisibility in use, let it be assumed that factor services are divisible in use, in the sense that factor services may be excluded from production if rationality so dictates. Let it also be assumed of all factor services other than those that give rise to user cost that no intertemporal substitution of factor services is possible in the market period; i.e., that the factor services at the command of the firm (except those giving rise to user costs) during this period can only be utilized in this period. Finally, let it be assumed initially that user costs are zero; i.e., that the use in production of more rather than less (or less rather than more) of the available quantities of factor services occasions no additional costs to the firm.

Given the situation just described, what are the best factor-service combinations to use in producing the various outputs that the firm can produce? In Figure 13-1 it is assumed that the firm has at its disposal OY of capital services

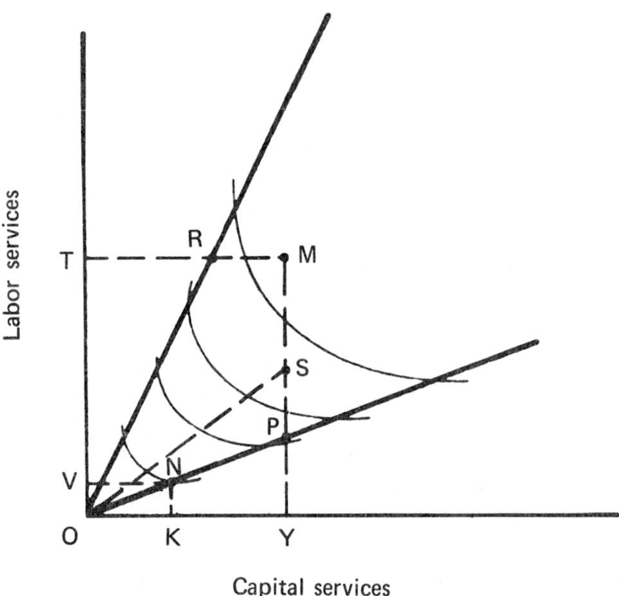

Figure 13-1

and *OT* of labor services and that labor and capital are the only factors of production. Point *M* represents the maximum output that can be produced. The range of possible combinations is bounded by the rectangle *OTMY*, however, so that there is no unique output-expansion path connecting *O* and *M*. Any output other than that represented by *M* could be produced by any of the factor service combinations within the rectangle *OTMY* which yield that output (as shown by the relevant isoquant).

In this situation the proportion *OT*/*OY* could be maintained for all outputs, and alterations in output would occur only by changes in scale. Alternatively, the output-expansion path could be *YM* or *TM* in which cases there would be only returns to proportion. All other output-expansion paths connecting *O* and *M* would reflect a mixture of returns to proportion and returns to scale. Thus, in the market period, there can be returns to scale, returns to proportion, or a mixture of the two.

So long as user costs are not introduced the decision-making process of the firm is a relatively simple one in the market period. There is one, and only one, combination of factor services that will yield the maximum output, but there is a wide range of combinations of factor services which will yield any smaller output that the firm might choose to produce. A decision to use less than the total available stocks of either or both types of factor services is simultaneously, however, a decision to preclude from entry into production some of the available factor services. Thus, while there is no unique output-expansion path, the choice of any specific output-expansion path implies that—for any output other than that which use of all factor services would yield—specific quantities of the available factor services are being excluded from production.

The assumption of (positive) user costs confines the output-expansion path to the "economic" region of the rectangle *OTMY*. If these costs are constant (and positive) per unit of labor services but are not incurred with respect to capital services, the output-expansion path becomes *OPM*. In producing the output represented by the isoquant on which *N* is a point, for example, the least costly way of doing so is to use *OV* of the available labor services. The corresponding user cost assumption with respect to capital services (only) yields the output-expansion path *ORM*. The corresponding user cost assumption with respect to both inputs yields an output-expansion path such as *OSM*, the "returns to scale" portion of the path being determined by tangencies of iso-user-cost lines to isoquants. The point *S*, of course, could coincide with *M* or lie to the left of *M* on the *RM* portion of the labor-services constraint.

Thus, in situations in which decisions concerning the acquisition of all factor services have been made but in which the firm retains complete control over the use of these services, the output-expansion path is not unique (assuming also that no intertemporal substitution of factor services is possible). If the firm does not have complete control over the use of factor services but is instead limited by the necessity of incurring positive user costs if factor services are used in production, output-expansion paths are confined to that portion of the "economic" region of the production surface lying within the constraints imposed by surrender of control over acquisition and are uniquely determined. If user costs are incurred in the use of only one of the inputs the output-expansion path proceeds along one of the two ridge lines until the constraint is met, after which (in terms of output) it is characterized by returns to proportion. If user costs are incurred in the use of both inputs the output-expansion path may be linear throughout (if neither contraint is met before the maximum output is reached) or linear for only a portion of its range. All output-expansion paths have a terminus at the maximum output (assuming *M* to lie within the ridge lines).[8]

The Short-Run. The short-run is similar to the market period except that with respect to at least one of its major inputs (but not all) the firm has a greater degree of control. The services of at least one factor are divisible in acquisition as well as in use while those of at least one other factor are divisible only in use. There is thus a maximum quantity of factor services of one or more types available (or maximum rates at which one or more factors yield their services) but no such constraint with respect to the services of at least one of the other factors of production. It is again assumed that stocks of factor services which have already been acquired can only be utilized in the productive process to which the production function refers and, initially, that the use in production of more rather than less (or less rather than more) of such services occasions the firm no additional cost. No intertemporal substitution of factor services is possible, and factor services may be excluded from production if rationality so dictates. The situation is thus analogous to that of a firm which has leased a specific quantity of capital for a given period of time but can vary the quantity of labor services it purchases, and uses, at will.

Assume in terms of Figure 13-2 that the firm has at its disposal *OY* of capital services and that capital is referred to as the "fixed" factor. Assume that labor is the only other factor of production and that the firm can purchase and use various quantities of labor services — so that labor may be referred to as the "variable" factor.[9]

In this situation the output-expansion path proceeds from *O* along the ray of which *OP* is a segment until the output corresponding to *P* is attained, after which the output-expansion path proceeds across the surface along the line on which *M* is a point. Thus, the range of output from *O* to *P* is characterized

[8]The assumptions that: (a) no intertemporal substitution of factor services is possible, (b) that the firm cannot act as a seller of factor services, and (c) that there is only one productive process in which factor services at the command of the firm can be used can each be relaxed and treated in a manner similar to that accorded user costs. If intertemporal substitution of factor services is possible the present value of such services (if so used) can be treated as the present user cost. Similarly, the opportunity cost of factor services devoted to this process that could be used in other processes in this or other firms can be treated as user cost.

[9]The firm may have "blanket order" contracts with one or more of its suppliers for the purchase of one or more (but not all) inputs. (See Timms, *op. cit.*, p. 579).

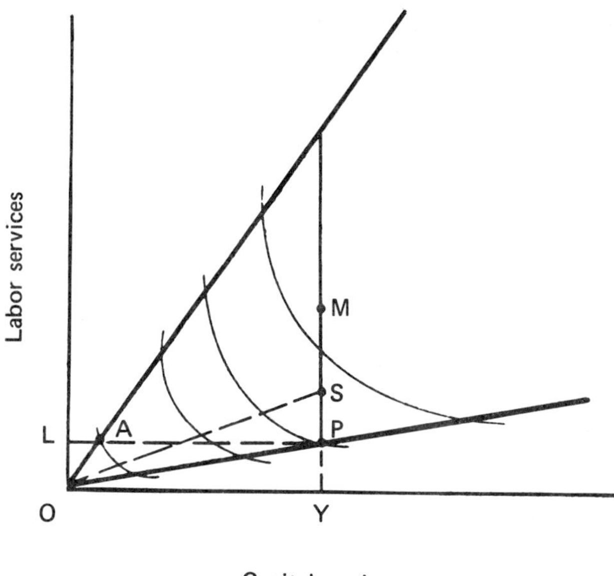

Figure 13-2

by returns to scale, greater outputs than that corresponding to *P* being the result of varying the proportion of labor services to the maximum available quantity of capital services. Thus, the short-run output-expansion path is characterized by returns to scale and returns to proportion, the latter following the former in terms of output. In producing outputs smaller than that to which *P* refers, systematic exclusion from production of some of the available capital services occurs. In producing the output to which *P* corresponds the firm purchases and uses *OL* of labor services and uses all of its available capital services (*OY*). Rational production of outputs greater than that to which *P* refers requires the combining of more than *OL* of labor services with *OY* of capital services and thus again, requires no exclusion from entry into production of any of the available capital services.

Thus, along *OP* the marginal product of capital services is zero and the marginal and average products of labor services are equal and constant.[10] Reasonably enough, the firm is maximizing the output per unit from the services of the factor for which it must pay as it uses, by combining with them other factor services (for which it has already paid) only so long as the latter contribute positively to production. The marginal product of capital services, equal to zero, at *P*, rises for greater outputs along the "returns to proportion" portion of the output-expansion path, while the marginal and average product

[10]Along *OP* the marginal product of labor services is the ratio of the differential of output to the differential of labor services. On the remainder of the output-expansion path the marginal product of labor services is the more familiar partial derivative of output with respect to labor services.

of labor services decline. At the point at which the marginal product of labor services equals zero, the marginal product of capital services (which has already begun to decline) equals its average product.

Under our assumptions, the output-expansion path is linear from *O* to *P* and curvilinear thereafter. There is a unique output-expansion path, a portion of which (*OP* in Figure 13-2) implies a specific type of cost-minimizing behavior on the part of the firm. For at each input of labor services over this portion of the path, the firm must determine the correct amount of the available capital services *not* to use. That part of the output-expansion path characterized by returns to proportion does not, of course, require this type of decision.

Alteration of the assumptions so as to permit the introduction of (positive) user costs with respect to labor services (only) does not affect the output-expansion path (although it will affect the firm's cost curves). If, however, positive linear user costs are assumed with respect to the use of capital services (or capital services and labor services) an output-expansion path such as that on which lie the points *OSM* in Figure 13-2 is generated. *S* could, of course, lie above *M* but at whatever point the output-expansion path encountered the capital services constraint further output would be characterized by returns to proportion and the output-expansion path would proceed along the constraint.

Thus, in the short-run some of the decisions concerning the acquisition of factor services have been made and others have not. The firm has complete control over the use of factor services (if there are no user costs), no control over the acquisition of the services of at least one factor, and complete control of the acquisition of at least one other factor. The introduction of user costs implies a loss of some control of the use of the services of one or all factors.[11]

The Long-Run. In the market period it is assumed that all factor services are indivisible in acquisition but divisible in use. In the short-run it is assumed that the services of at least one factor of production are divisible in acquisition and in use and that the services of at least one factor are indivisible in acquisition but divisible in use. In the long-run it is assumed that the services of *all* factors of production are divisible in acquisition and in use. Thus, the long run is the logically limiting case of a progression of cases that can be conceived of in terms of the number of factors whose services are divisible in acquisition, as well as in use. No problem of excluding factor services from entry into production arises. Similarly there is no problem of intertemporal substitution of factor services since factor services are either only acquired as used or resold if in excess.[12]

---

[11]Again relaxation of assumptions concerning intertemporal substitution, alternative processes, and resale of factor services yields essentially the same analysis as that arising from the introduction of positive user costs (cf. footnote 8, p. 244).

[12]For similar reasons, no problem exists concerning alternative processes in which factor services used in this process could be used.

The long run is analogous to a situation in which the firm has an arrangement with suppliers to provide any quantity of factor services upon demand. The firm can thus vary the quantity of all the factor services that it purchases at will. The firm's control over acquisition is hindered solely by the necessity of paying the agreed-upon factor prices.

In the market period there is no unique output-expansion path (so long as user costs are zero) because, in effect, the services of all factors of production are free up to the constraints of the quantities previously acquired. In the short-run there is a unique output-expansion path because, in essence, the services of at least one factor are *not* free. Since this need be true of the services of only one factor, the long-run output-expansion path is also unique. Since a minimum of one constraint is needed to determine a maximum physical output, there exists a terminal point on the market-period and short-run expansion paths but no such terminus on the long-run expansion path (so long as the assumption of constant returns to scale is maintained). Alteration of the assumptions so as to permit the introduction of user costs does not affect the long-run output-expansion path in any basic way, since iso-cost lines would simply in this case include both types of factor-service cost, the cost of use as well as the cost of acquisition. The long-run output-expansion path can therefore be depicted as in Figure 13-3 assuming the cost per unit of factor services to be constant.

The Market Period. So long as we maintain the assumption, for the market period, that there are no user costs, all of the costs of the firm are fixed

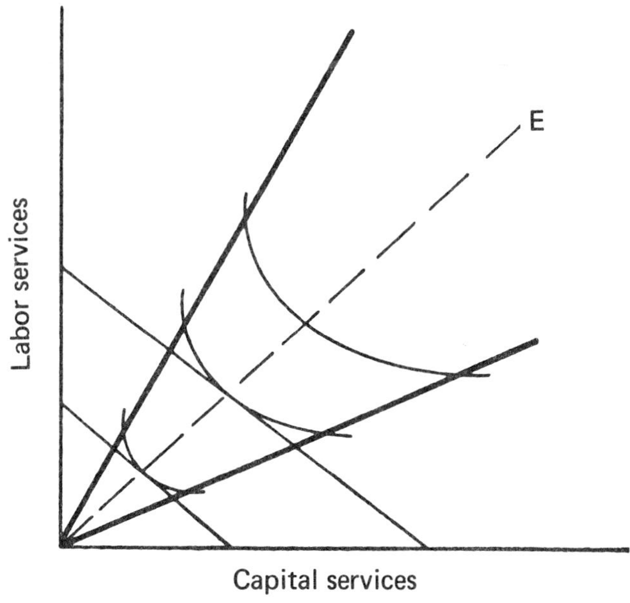

Figure 13-3

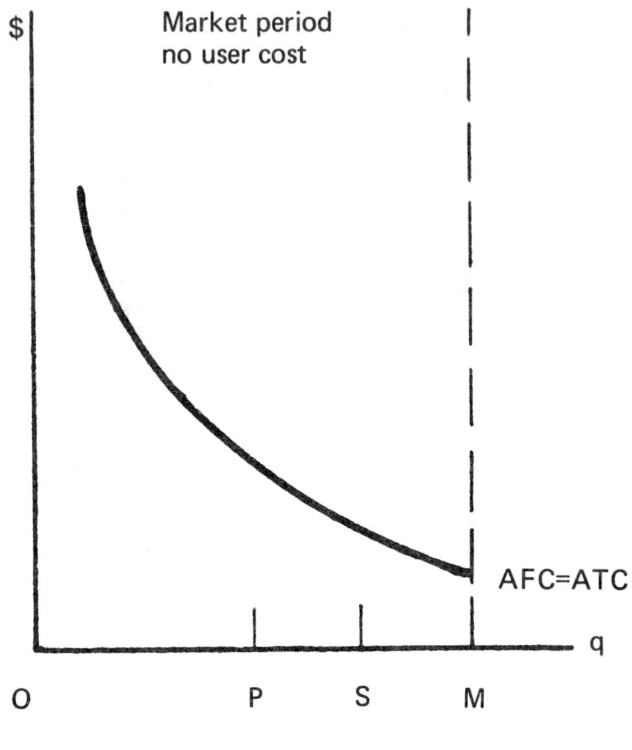

Figure 13-4

costs. In this case there is no relationship between the production function and the firm's costs. Marginal and average variable costs are zero and average fixed cost identical with average total cost for the range of output that the firm can produce (Figure 13-4). If positive user costs are assumed (constant per unit of input) with respect to one input, marginal cost and average variable cost are equal and constant over the range of output characterized by returns to scale (*OP* in Figures 13-1 and 13-5). The remainder of the range of possible outputs (*PM*) is characterized by returns to proportion, equal increases in user costs being accompanied by less than proportionate increases in output, and equal increases in output occasioning more than proportionate increases in user costs. Marginal and average variable costs thus increase with output. If positive user costs (constant per unit of input) are assumed for all inputs the range of constancy and equality of marginal and average variable costs is increased (*OS* in Figures 13-1 and 13-6) so as to encompass a larger portion, or all of the range of possible outputs *OM*.

Thus, when the firm has no further control over acquisition but is completely unhampered in its use of previously acquired factor services (up to the constraints of the quantities acquired) marginal cost and average variable cost are constant, equal, and zero throughout the range of possible outputs. When

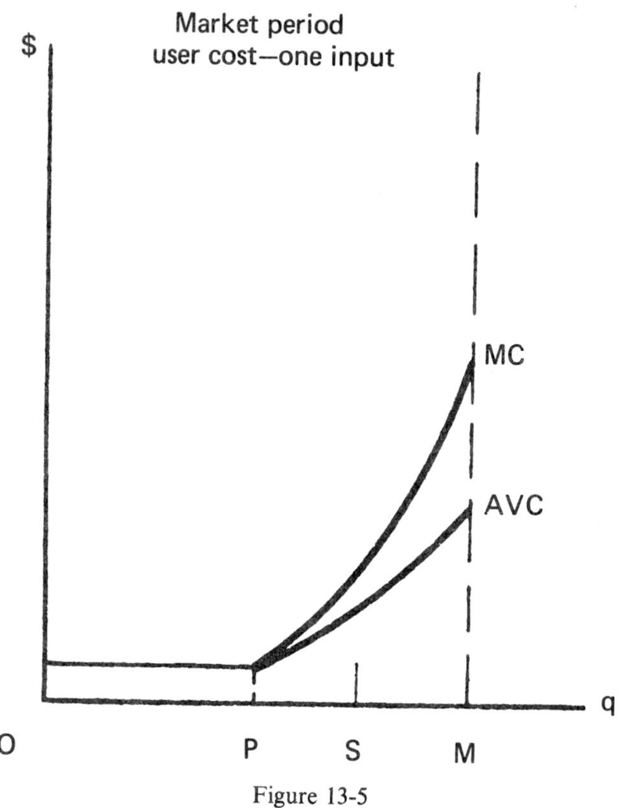

Figure 13-5

positive user costs exist, marginal and average variable costs reflect the combined effect of the nature of these user costs as a function of input, the nature of returns to scale in the production function, and the nature of returns to proportion (if operation in the range of returns to scale does not encompass the range of possible outputs). Consequently, a vast range of shapes and configurations of the firm's cost curves is conceptually possible.

The Short-Run. Even in the traditional short-run a considerable number of shapes and configurations of the firm's cost curves is possible, depending primarily upon what assumptions are made concerning factor supply functions. This number is limited in traditional analysis, however, by the assumption that the services of the fixed factor are completely indivisible in use—that all of the services of the fixed factor must be combined with each quantity of the services of the variable. While conceivable as a limiting case, this is obviously a poor choice of assumptions for the "representative" firm. Except for such instances as blast furnaces the traditional assumption does not hold. Assuming instead that the firm can prevent entry into production of factor services, the marginal productivity of which is negative, the short-run is characterized by returns to scale as well as returns to proportion.

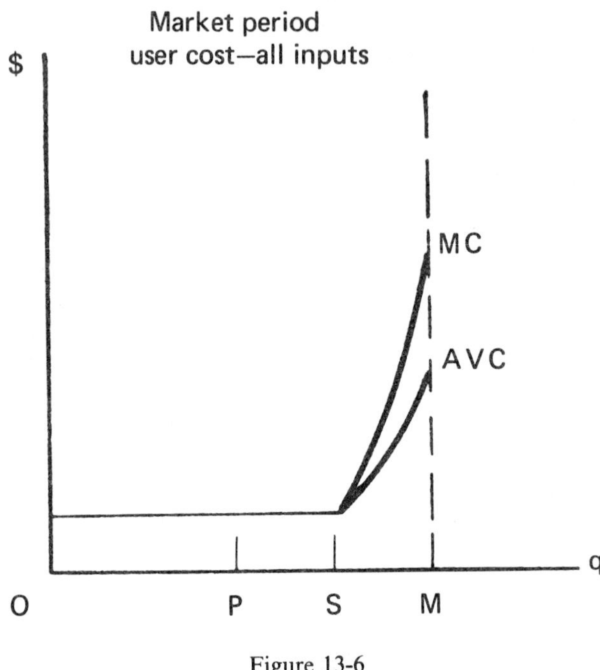

Figure 13-6

Given constant factor-service prices and a linearly homogeneous production function of the type described in the second section of this paper, and also assuming that user costs are zero, marginal cost and average variable cost are constant and equal over the range of output characterized by returns to scale (*OP* in Figures 13-2 and 13-7). Larger outputs are characterized by returns to proportion and marginal and average variable costs increase. If positive user costs are assumed (constant per unit of input) for the variable input, marginal and average variable costs are again constant over the same range of output (*OP* in Figures 13-2 and 13-8), rising thereafter. If user costs (positive and constant per unit of input) are assumed for the services of the fixed (in acquisition) factor or for all inputs, the range of constancy and equality of marginal and average variable costs is increased (*OS* in Figures 13-2 and 13-9).

Thus, when the firm has control over the acquisition of some factors, no control over the acquisition of others, and complete freedom in the use of factor services, marginal and average costs reflect over some range the nature of returns to scale and the conditions of factor supply. For larger outputs the influence of returns to scale is supplanted by that of returns to proportion. If user costs are assumed for the services of the variable factor the two ranges of output are unaffected in magnitude but the cost curves affected (in level and configuration) by the nature of user costs as a function of input. If the firm is hampered in its use of the services of the fixed or all factors by user costs, the range of output affected by the nature of returns to scale is increased.

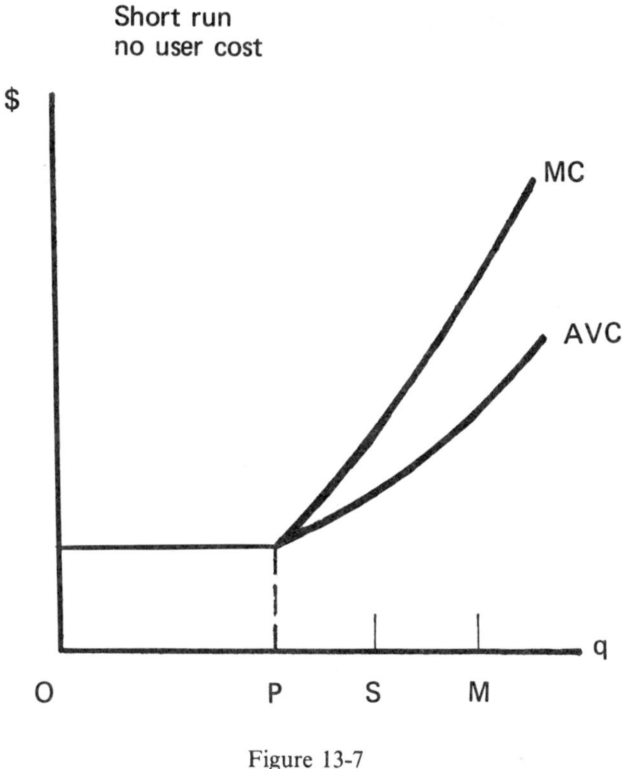

Figure 13-7

A large variety of types of cost behavior can therefore occur in the short-run, all of which are affected by returns to scale.

The Long-Run. If a firm can acquire any quantities of factor services that it wishes; i.e., if there is complete divisibility in acquisition, the cost curves of the firm reflect only the nature of returns to scale and the combined effect of factor-service supply and user cost functions. Given constant returns to scale, and factor-service prices and user costs the combined effect of which is constant per unit of input, long-run marginal and average costs are equal and constant (Figure 13-10), so long as external economies and diseconomies are not considered.

CONCLUSIONS

Given the production function, the basic determinant of the firm's cost curves is the degree of control the firm possesses over the acquisition and use of factor services. The market period may be viewed as a situation in which the firm has sacrificed all of its control over factor-service acquisition, the

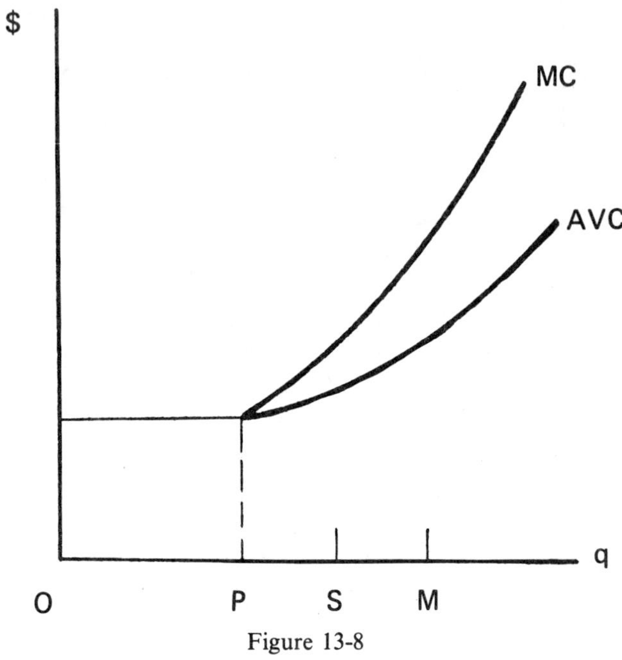

Figure 13-8

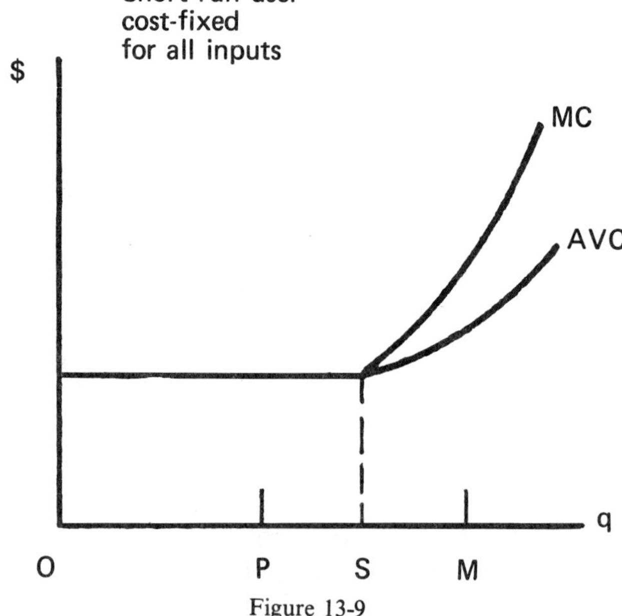

Figure 13-9

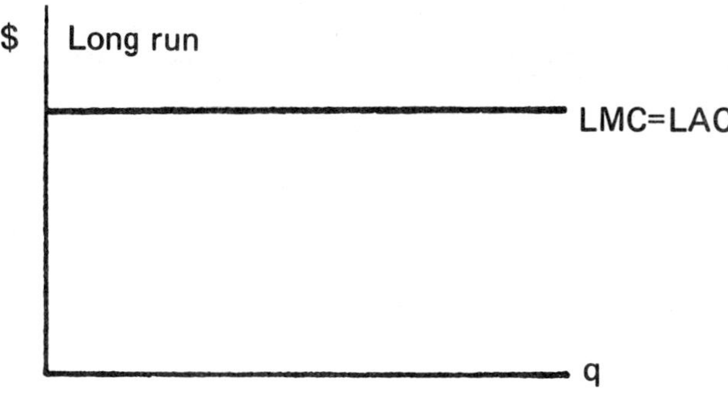

Figure 13-10

short-run as a situation in which all control over acquisition has been sacrificed with respect to one or more but not all inputs, and the long-run as a situation in which only the necessity of paying factor-service prices hampers control of acquisition. Control over the use of factor services is much greater than indivisibilities in acquisition might suggest but may be restricted by user costs. Viewed in the framework, the traditional treatment of short-run costs as reflecting only returns to proportion is quite misleading and seriously inadequate.

14. A FIRM'S SHORT-RUN AND LONG-RUN DEMANDS FOR A FACTOR*

Robert L. Bishop†

Fundamental as the concepts are, there does not seem to exist in the literature a satisfactory but comparatively nontechnical treatment of the relationships between a firm's short-run and long-run demands for a factor, even in the most elementary static context.[1] The standard textbooks regularly slide over the topic altogether; and even when it is treated in a comparatively nontechnical manner, as by Mrs. Robinson in *The Economics of Imperfect Competition* (1933), the discussion is marred by some serious gaps in the exposition, some irrelevancies, and even some confusions. An effort will be made here to remedy the situation.

Some Preliminaries

Consider first the elementary case of a firm that produces a single product with just the two factors, labor and land. We designate the quantity of output as q, the factor quantities as L and T, the price of the product as p, the wage and rent rates as w and r, and total revenue, cost, and profit as R, C, and π. The basic data are then: the production function, $q = q(L, T)$; the demand-price function, $p = p(q)$, from which is immediately derived the total-revenue function, $R = R(q)$; and the supply-price functions of the factors, $w = w(L)$ and $r = r(T)$, such that total cost is $C = w(L)L + r(T)T = C(L, T)$.[2]

As implied by the familiar type of isoquant map in Figure 14-1, it is assumed initially that the production function and its first derivatives are continuous

*From *Western Economic Journal*, Vol. V, No. 2 (March, 1967), pp. 122–140. Reprinted by permission of the publisher and the author.

†Robert L. Bishop, Professor of Economics and Dean of the School of Humanities and Social Science, Massachusetts Institute of Technology.

[1]To be sure, the present subject matter is treated very well, though quite abstractly, by P. A. Samuelson in his *Foundations of Economic Analysis* (Cambridge, Mass.: Harvard University Press, 1947), pp. 36–39, 45–46, and 57–89. My own discussion is intended for those to whom Samuelson's technical apparatus is rather forbidding, or as a preparatory step toward an understanding of his analysis. On the other hand, even his discussion skips over some features that are more explicitly treated here. Similar comments also apply to the analysis by J. R. Hicks, *Value and Capital* (New York: Oxford University Press, 1939), pp. 89–98 and 320–23, though his discussion is limited to the case of a purely competitive firm and is rather awkward in a number of respects.

[2]It would also be acceptable to make the more general (though usually unnecessary) assumption that $w = w(L, T)$ and $r = r(L, T)$; for that would still be consistent with the general relationship whereby $C = C(L, T)$.

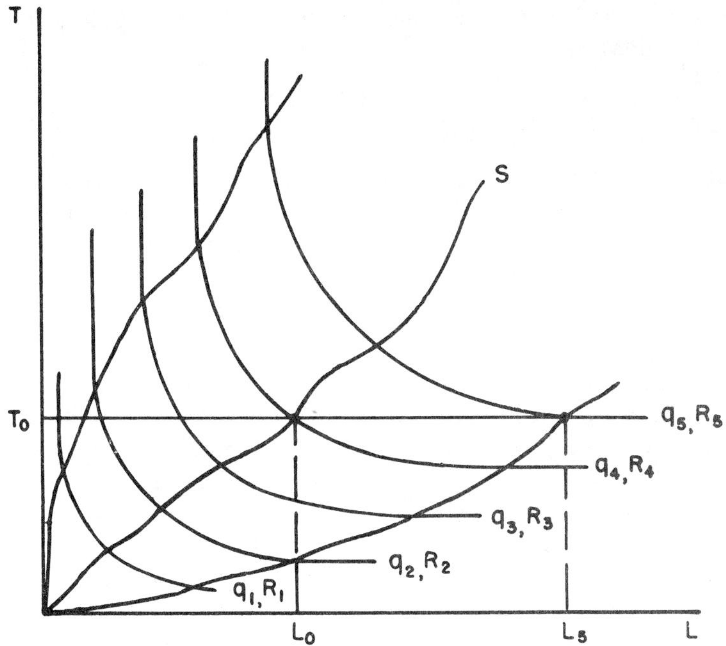

Figure 14-1

and that the isoquants are concave from above in the central region where the factors are substitutable.[3] It is further assumed that production is subject to economies of scale in a range of low outputs and, thereafter, to diseconomies (as reflected by the unequal spacing of the selected isoquants, which are assumed to correspond to outputs, such as $q_1 = 100$, $q_2 = 200$, . . ., $q_5 = 500$).

Even though extremely well known, the procedures for deriving the firm's cost curves may be noticed in passing, so that they may be compared and contrasted with the procedures for determining the factor demands. To determine the firm's long-run costs, one would first add to Figure 14-1 the relevant isocost curves (which are assumed to be smoothly continuous, though not necessarily linear), and then connect up the points of tangency between isoquants and isocost curves to yield the scale locus or expansion path, such as the curve S in the diagram. Since the slopes of isoquants and isocost curves are, respectively, $(dT/dL)_{\bar{q}} = -(\partial q/\partial L)/(\partial q/\partial T)$ and $(dT/dL)_{\bar{C}} = -(\partial C/\partial L)/(\partial C/\partial T)$, we

[3]In place of the more popular but questionable assumption of backward-bending isoquants beyond the ridge lines, it is assumed here that the isoquants are then merely parallel to the axis of the redundant factor. Since the production function depicts the *maximum* attainable output for any given available quantities of the factors, the isoquants are properly depicted as backward-bending only when (1) the mere presence of a redundant factor quantity necessarily depresses the output and (2) the redundant quantity is not costlessly disposable. This might be the case with labor, but hardly with land.

thereby have as the familiar first-order condition for producing any given output at minimum total cost:[4]

$$\frac{\partial q/\partial L}{\partial q/\partial T}=\frac{\partial C/\partial L}{\partial C/\partial T}\text{ or }\frac{\partial q/\partial L}{\partial C/\partial L}=\frac{\partial q/\partial T}{\partial C/\partial T}=\frac{dq}{dC}\text{ or }\frac{\partial C/\partial L}{\partial q/\partial L}=\frac{\partial C/\partial T}{\partial q/\partial T}=\frac{dC}{dq}.$$

Alternatively, designating the factors' marginal physical products as MPP_L and MPP_T, their marginal costs as MC_L and MC_T, and marginal cost of the product as MC, we may write the last of these three variants as:

$$\frac{MC_L}{MPP_L}=\frac{MC_T}{MPP_T}=MC.$$

In other words, even before we obtain the firm's total cost curve by plotting the isocost values C against the isoquant values q that are associated along the scale locus, we already have the total cost curve's slope, or the marginal cost $MC = dC/dq$, from the indicated relationship of each factor's marginal cost and marginal physical product.

Similarly, to illustrate the special type of short-run total cost curve when the quantity of land is fixed at a level such as T_0 and only labor is variable, we need only plot the values of C and q that are associated along the horizontal locus at T_0. Where $r_0 = r(T_0)$, there is then a fixed cost of r_0T_0 and a variable cost of $w(L)L$, yielding a short-run total cost that is greater than the long-run total cost for every output except the one that is produced with L_0 and T_0, at the common point of the long-run and short-run scale loci. At the output corresponding to that point, owing to the continuous slopes, the long-run and short-run total cost curves are tangent; so the long-run and short-run marginal costs are equal. Both there and elsewhere on the short-run total cost curve, the short-run marginal cost is equal to just MC_L/MPP_L, while the corresponding expression MC_T/MPP_T is irrelevant owing to the fixity of T. Furthermore, since short-run total cost is tangent to long-run total cost from above and, therefore, has an algebraically higher second derivative at that point, the short-run marginal cost has the algebraically greater slope and thus cuts the long-run marginal cost from below. On the other hand, the long-run and short-run average costs, like the total costs, are tangent at their common point. The implied "envelope" relationships of long-run total and average costs to their numerous alternative short-run counterparts, together with the intersecting relationships of the long-run and short-run marginal costs, should be borne in mind; for analogous relationships will be developed for the relevant factor-productivity curves.

When the revenue function $R = R(q)$ and its first derivative dR/dq (or the marginal revenue MR) are likewise continuous, the profit-maximizing equilibrium of the firm then rests on the first-order condition, $MR = MC$. Thus,

[4]Appropriate second-order conditions will be taken for granted throughout, since they are usually obvious enough in the geometrical representations of equilibrium that will be used. Similarly, the possibility of multiple local maxima or minima will also be ignored, also in the interest of avoiding any unnecessary lengthening of the discussion.

substituting MR for MC in the above cost-minimizing conditions for any given output in the long run, we get:

$$\frac{MC_L}{MPP_L} = \frac{MC_T}{MPP_T} = MR \quad \text{or} \quad \frac{\partial C/\partial L}{\partial q/\partial L} = \frac{\partial C/\partial T}{\partial q/\partial T} = \frac{dR}{dq}.$$

Alternatively, defining the marginal revenue product of a factor (MRP) as its marginal physical product (MPP) times the marginal revenue (MR), we may state these profit-maximizing conditions as:

$$MRP_L(= MPP_L \cdot MR) = MC_L \quad \text{or} \quad \frac{\partial R}{\partial L}\left(= \frac{\partial q}{\partial L} \cdot \frac{dR}{dq}\right) = \frac{\partial C}{\partial L}$$

$$MRP_T(= MPP_T \cdot MR) = MC_T \quad \text{or} \quad \frac{\partial R}{\partial T}\left(= \frac{\partial q}{\partial T} \cdot \frac{dR}{dp}\right) = \frac{\partial C}{\partial T}$$

The Short-Run Demand for a Factor

In contrast to the procedure for a cost-curve derivation, the first step in deriving a factor demand is to combine the production function $q = q(L, T)$ and the revenue function $R = R(q)$ in such a way as to express R as a function of L and T. This involves merely the concept of a function of a function:

$$R = R[q(L, T)] = R^*(L, T).$$

In other words, to each q (such as $q_1, q_2, \ldots, q_5$) there corresponds a unique magnitude of R (designated respectively in Figure 14-1 as $R_1, R_2, \ldots, R_5$). In this manner, the isoquant map is readily converted to an iso-revenue-curve map, consisting of the contours of the three-dimensional surface that corresponds to the function $R = R^*(L, T)$. The various revenue-product concepts are then directly derivable from this revenue function.

In the particular short run when the quantity of land is again fixed at T_0, the total revenue, R, as a function of the only variable factor, L, is then determined from the cross-section of the revenue surface in the plane perpendicular to the LT-plane along the line at T_0. The resulting curve is labelled $R^*(L, T_0)$ in Figure 14-2. In the special case when the firm sells its product in a purely competitive market, at a constant price, this total-revenue curve would correspond exactly to the total-physical-product curve that is similarly derivable from the surface that corresponds to the production function, with merely the scalar substitution of R for q on the vertical axis. When price and marginal revenue are both decreasing functions of q, however, the curve $R^*(L, T_0)$ will be a correspondingly deformed version of $q(L, T_0)$. Indeed, if MR were to reach zero at an output smaller than q_5 (producible with L_5, T_0), $R^*(L, T_0)$ would reach its peak at a smaller labor quantity than L_5, rather than at that quantity (as actually assumed in the construction of Figure 14-2).

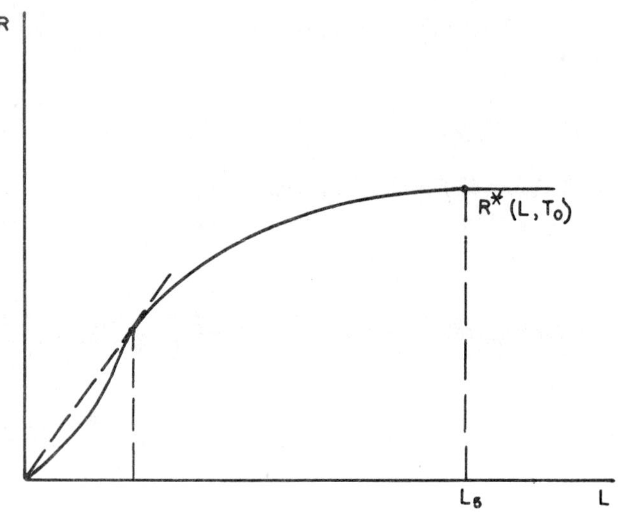

Figure 14-2

The average and marginal revenue products, as derived from the total-revenue schedule of Figure 14-2, are shown in Figure 14-3. These concepts, together with their relationships to average or marginal physical product and average or marginal revenue, are thus:[5]

$$ARP_L = APP_L \cdot AR \qquad \text{or} \qquad \frac{R}{L} = \frac{q}{L} \cdot \frac{R}{q},$$

$$MRP_L = MPP_L \cdot MR \qquad \text{or} \qquad \frac{\partial R}{\partial L} = \frac{\partial q}{\partial L} \cdot \frac{dR}{dq}.$$

These two curves are then sufficient, in conjunction with the average and marginal costs of labor (AC_L and MC_L), to determine the firm's short-run equilibrium. Provided that AC_L does not lie everywhere above ARP_L, the equilibrium labor quantity is determined where MC_L cuts MRP_L from below. Accordingly, for various alternative constant wage rates (with horizontal $AC_L \equiv MC_L$), the short-run demand for labor coincides with MRP_L in the range below ARP_L, and it coincides with the vertical axis for higher wage rates (being subject to a two-point indeterminacy when the wage rate is precisely w_0, at the level of maximum ARP_L).

[5]As with $R^*(L, T_0)$ and $q(L, T_0)$, the ARP_L and MRP_L curves will differ from the respective APP_L and MPP_L curves only as to scale when $AR \equiv MR$. When APP_L has the "normal" shape of an inverted *u*, ARP_L will too, provided that AR is not too sharply decreasing. With decreasing AR, however, ARP_L will reach its peak at a lower level of L than APP_L; and with sharply decreasing AR, ARP_L may be everywhere decreasing. Similar remarks apply to the comparative shapes of MRP_L and MPP_L with reference to that of MR.

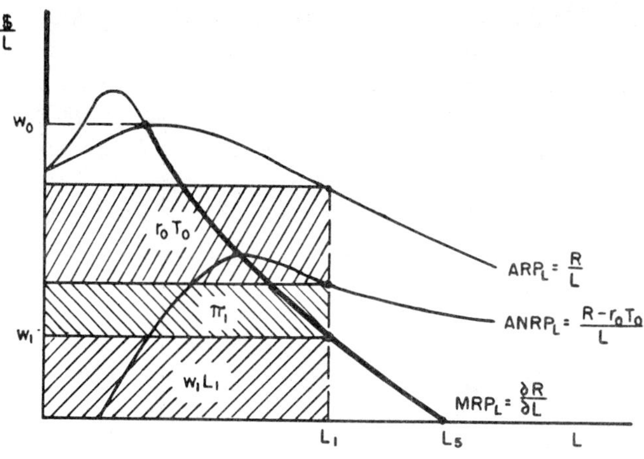

Figure 14-3

In order to show how the net revenue over and above the variable labor cost is divided between the fixed land cost and profit, it is necessary to add to Figure 14-3 the type of schedule that may be called the "average net revenue product of labor" ($ANRP_L$). This is defined as $ARP_L = R/L$ minus the fixed land cost per unit of labor, $r_0 T_0 / L$, such that:

$$ANRP_L = \frac{R - r_0 T_0}{L}.$$

Since this differs from the ARP_L curve only by the rectangular hyperbola corresponding to $r_0 T_0/L$, MRP_L has the same type of marginal-to-average relationship to $ANRP_L$ that it has to ARP_L. Indeed, in view of the constant value of $r_0 T_0$, $MRP_L = \partial R / \partial L$ may be regarded interchangeably as the "marginal net revenue product," $MNRP_L = \partial(R - r_0 T_0) / \partial L$.

In Figure 14-3, for example, when the wage rate is the constant w_1 and the equilibrium labor quantity is L_1, total revenue and its components correspond to a series of rectangles with a base of L_1 and varying heights. Thus, total revenue R corresponds to the rectangle up to ARP_L; total wages $w_1 L_1$ to the rectangle up to $w_1 = MRP_L$; total rent $r_0 T_0$ to the rectangle between ARP_L and $ANRP_L$; and profit π_1 to the remaining rectangle between $ANRP_L$ and MRP_L.

The Long-Run Demand for a Factor

In the long-run, when T is variable as well as L, the firm has a choice among all of the different pairs of short-run $ANRP_L$ and MRP_L curves that correspond to the different possible quantities of T. All such $ANRP_L$ curves then have an upper envelope, which may be called the "long-run average net revenue product of labor," $LR\text{-}ANRP_L$. Such a curve is shown in Figure 14-4, along with two sample $ANRP_L$ curves corresponding respectively to the land quantities T_1 and T_2. The labor quantities at which these short-run curves are tangent to the long-run curve are similarly designated as L_1 and L_2, respectively. At any specified labor quantity such as L_1, notice that the relevantly associated land quantity T_1 is the one for which $R - rT$ and $ANRP_L = (R - rT)/L_1$ are maximized. This is so because, irrespective of the cost of L_1 (namely, w_1L_1), the maximizing of profit at that labor quantity (namely, $\pi = R\text{-}rT\text{-}w_1L_1$) obviously calls for the maximizing of $R - rT$.[6]

With respect to $LR\text{-}ANRP_L$ as an average, the associated marginal curve is then designated as $LR\text{-}MNRP_L$.[7] Just as with long-run and short-run marginal costs, $LR\text{-}MNRP_L$ intersects each successively relevant MRP_L (or $MNRP_L$) curve at the same labor quantity where the associated $ANRP_L$ curve is tangent to $LR\text{-}ANRP_L$. This is illustrated in Figure 14-4 at L_1 and L_2, with reference to $MRP_L(T_1)$ and $MRP_L(T_2)$.

As to the shapes of the $LR\text{-}ANRP_L$ and $LR\text{-}MNRP_L$ curves, it should be noticed that these functions depend on these data: (1) the production function, $q = q(L, T)$; (2) the revenue function, $R = R(q)$; and (3) the supply-price function of land, $r = r(T)$. When those three functions are all continuous (as a sufficient condition, though not a necessary one), so will $LR\text{-}ANRP_L$ be; and when their first derivatives are also continuous, $LR\text{-}MNRP_L$ will be a continuous function as well (with a surely continuous first derivative if the underlying functions have continuous second derivatives). $LR\text{-}ANRP_L$ and $LR\text{-}MNRP_L$ will then have the inverted-*u* shapes illustrated in Figure 14-4 as a reflection of the successive economies and diseconomies of scale assumed earlier, provided that AR and MR do not decrease too sharply as functions of q and provided

---

[6]Mathematically, when we are given total revenue $R^*(L, T)$ and total land cost $r(T)T$, the first-order condition for maximizing $R\text{-}rT$ for any specified L is:

$$\frac{\partial(R - rT)}{\partial T} = 0.$$

This is an equation in L and T that may be visualized in the form of $T = T(L)$. Then, substituting that function of L in place of T in $R^*(L, T) - r(T)T$, we obtain that net revenue simply as a function of L. It is this function, when differentiated with respect to L, that yields the concept in the next paragraph of the text, $LR\text{-}MNRP_L$. For an illustrative determination of both of these functions in a computationally tractable case, see Appendix A.

[7]Mathematically, as implied in the preceding footnote, $LR\text{-}MNRP_L$ may be visualized as the simple derivative $d(R\text{-}rT)/dL$ of net revenue as a function of L, namely $R^*[L, T(L)] - r[T(L)]T(L)$. Here, of course, $T = T(L)$ again reflects the appropriate variation of T with respect to L. Alternatively, when that function has a continuous first derivative dT/dL, $MNRP_L$ can also be represented as the total derivative of the net revenue $R^*(L, T) - r(T)T$ with respect to L:

$$\frac{d(R - rT)}{dL} = \frac{\partial(R - rT)}{\partial L} + \frac{\partial(R - rT)}{\partial T} \cdot \frac{dT}{dL}.$$

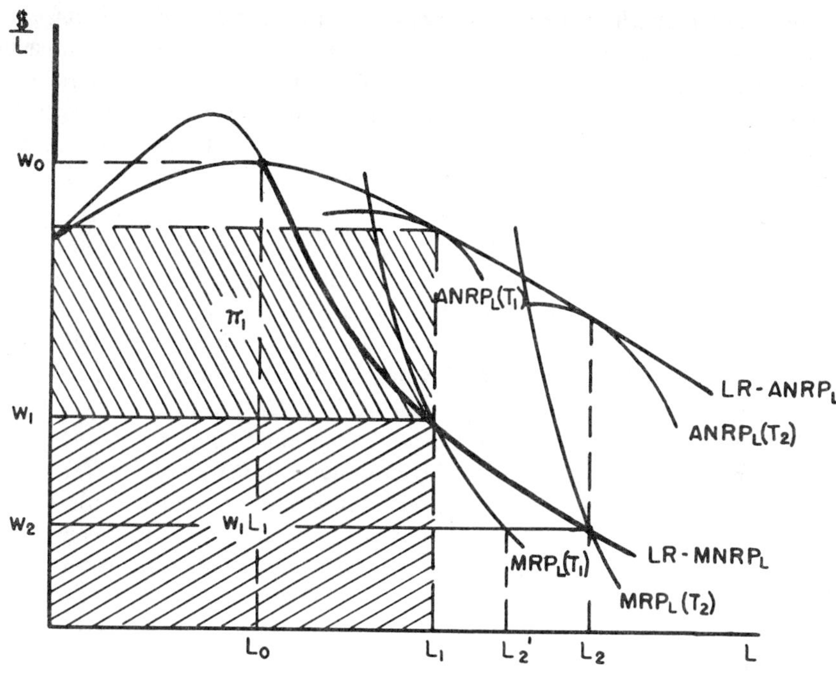

Figure 14-4

that $r = AC_T$ and MC_T do not increase too sharply as functions of T (in the "normal" case where q and T vary in the same direction as L).[8] On the other hand, decreasing AR and MR and increasing AC_T and MC_T (still in the same "normal" case) will cause $LR\text{-}ANRP_L$ and $LR\text{-}MNRP_L$ to reach their respective peaks at lower levels of L than they otherwise would. As the indicated qualifications suggest, however, it is difficult to formulate generalizations as to the shapes of those curves to cover any and all conceivable cases.

Now as far as the long-run equilibrium of the firm is concerned, this is determined with reference to $LR\text{-}ANRP_L$ and $LR\text{-}MNRP_L$ in the same way that short-run equilibrium (with fixed T) is determined with reference to ARP_L and MRP_L. That is to say, provided that AC_L does not everywhere exceed $LR\text{-}ANRP_L$, the long-run equilibrium quantity of L is determined where MC_L intersects $LR\text{-}MNRP_L$ from below. Or when the wage rate is independent of L, the firm's long-run demand for labor coincides with the vertical axis down to the level where $LR\text{-}ANRP_L$ is a maximum and thereafter coincides with $LR\text{-}MNRP_L$ (again with a two-point indeterminacy at the critical wage rate where the discontinuity occurs).

Thus, at the critical wage rate w_0 in Figure 14-4, the firm can make only a zero profit, whether it hires L_0 (and the correspondingly appropriate T_0) or

[8]For other possible patterns, see pp. 264-267.

does not produce at all. Or if it confronts a constant wage rate of w_1, it employs L_1 (and T_1). It then receives a net revenue of $R - r_1T_1$, equal to the area of the rectangle with a base of L_1 and a height determined by $LR\text{-}ANRP_L$ or $ANRP_L(T_1)$ at L_1. In turn, that rectangle is divided into two others with the same base: one that corresponds to the total wage cost of w_1L_1 and another that corresponds to the total profit π_1.

When $LR\text{-}MNRP_L$ is itself continuous, its intersection with the successively relevant short-run schedules of MRP_L is a necessary relationship as long as the basic revenue function $R = R^*(L, T)$ has continuous first derivatives, so that MRP_L is always determinate. There is another basic possibility, however, that each MRP_L schedule may exhibit a vertical discontinuity at precisely the critical labor quantity, even though $LR\text{-}MNRP_L$ remains continuous. This is so when, with the first derivative of $R = R(q)$ still continuous, the first derivatives of $q = q(L, T)$ are discontinuous and hence indeterminate on the relevant scale locus, even though q remains a smoothly continuous function of L and T when those factors are suitably varied together. This is most conveniently illustrated in the case of fixed coefficients, where efficient production calls for $L = aq$ and $T = bq$, irrespective of the relative marginal costs of the factor. In turn, this means that: (1) each isoquant is L-shaped (implying nonsubstitutability of the factors); (2) the "corners" of all isoquants lie on a straight line from the origin (with a slope of $dT/dL = b/a$, reflecting the fixed proportionality of the factors); and (3) the output $q = L/a = T/b$ is also proportional to both factor quantities along the scale line.[9] In that event, when $L < (a/b)T$, $APP_L \equiv MPP_L \equiv 1/a$; and when $L > (a/b)T$, $APP_L = q/L = T/bL$ (a rectangular hyperbola for given T) and $MPP_L = 0$; but when $L = (a/b)T$, $APP_L = 1/a$ and MPP_L is indeterminate, since it is then falling discontinuously from $1/a$ to 0 — and similarly for APP_T and MPP_T according as $T \gtreqless (b/a)\, L$. Accordingly, $MRP_L = MPP_L \cdot MR$ and $MRP_T = MPP_T \cdot MR$ are similarly indeterminate when $T/L = b/a$. In that event, of course, the short-run demand for a factor, with the other factor fixed, is perfectly inelastic in the relevant range. Nevertheless, when T and L are varied together in just the appropriate ratio, $LR\text{-}MNRP_L$ and $LR\text{-}MNRP_T$ are still determinate, somewhere in the vertically discontinuous range of MRP_L or MRP_T respectively.[10]

---

[9]Notice that condition (1) can exist without (2) and (3), since the scale locus may be curvilinear even though all isoquants are L-shaped. Similarly, conditions (1) and (2) can exist without (3), since output (in the third dimension of the production surface) may be subject to economies or diseconomies of scale even though the scale locus through the corners of L-shaped isoquants is linear from the origin in the LT-plane of the isoquant map. Only when all three conditions exist together do we have, in addition to nonsubstitutability of the factors, a homogeneous production function of first degree. On the other hand, nonsubstitutability alone is sufficient to render MPP_L and MPP_T indeterminate on the scale locus.

[10]For an illustrative calculation of the relevant long-run and short-run revenue-product functions in such a case, see Appendix B.

This exposition may be briefly compared with Mrs. Robinson's. She begins with this definition (p. 236): "The *marginal physical productivity* of labour is the increment of output caused by employing an additional unit of labour with a fixed expenditure on other factors." This is open to several criticisms. First, it is not a purely "physical" concept, since it involves the supply functions (the pecuniary costs) of the "other factors" (when there is more than one). Second, her avoidance of the alternative specification of a fixed *quantity* of each other factor, together with the discreteness of the "increment of output" from an additional "unit" of labor, leads to a continuing ambivalence as to whether or not the factors can be treated as continuously substitutable.[11] Thus, she makes the essentially misleading, if not erroneous, comment (p. 236, footnote): "Marginal productivity in the short period, when the other factors are fixed not only in amount but in form, will be very different from marginal productivity in the long period."[12] Several pages later, however, after defining "marginal net productivity" (analogous to $LR\text{-}MNRP_L$) as (p. 239) "the marginal gross productivity caused by employing an additional man with the appropriate addition to other factors, less the addition to the cost of other factors," she implicitly assumes continuous substitutability in concluding (pp. 240–41), subject to the assumption that the changes in factor quantities are "small," that "the marginal net productivity of labour is equal to the marginal productivity of labour." On the other hand, the demonstration of that conclusion is neither clear nor conclusive. In particular, there is no reference to the tangency relationship of the long-run and short-run total (or average) curves, nor to the intersecting relationship of the long-run and short-run marginal curves. The relationships of factor demands in the short and long runs are thus not treated at all.[13]

---

[11]This also carries over, of course, to her definition of the concept analogous to MRP_L (p. 237): "*Marginal productivity* is the increment of value of the total output caused by employing an additional man, the total value of other factors remaining unchanged. That is to say, it is the marginal physical productivity multiplied by the marginal revenue . . ."

[12]Although the long-run and short-run marginal productivities in derivative form differ, of course, as schedules, their magnitudes are necessarily the same in any given long-run equilibrium whenever both are determinate. Thus, even though they may "differ" in the sense that the one is determinate while the other is not, they are never both determinate and different.

[13]Mrs. Robinson also makes use of some gross-productivity concepts which make no appearance in the present exposition. Their definitions, subject to the specification that "A given amount of labour is now conceived to be working with that amount of the other factors which would actually be employed with that amount of labour," are (p. 239):

> *Average gross productivity* is the average value of output per man. It is the total value of output divided by the number of men employed.
>
> *Marginal gross productivity* is the increment of value of output caused by employing an additional man with the appropriate addition to other factors. It bears to average gross productivity the ordinary relationship of marginal to average values.

Although average gross productivity equals R/L, it is unlike ARP_L as a schedule (as on p. 246), because of the specification of an appropriate variation of other factors. For the same reason marginal gross productivity bears no relationship at all to any concept used here. (Contd. on next page.)

Further Implications of Long-Run Adjustments

When the wage rate (more generally, MC_L) is reduced, as from w_1 to w_2 in Figure 14-4, that diagram illustrates the increase of labor quantity in the short-run (from L_1 to L_2'), the greater such increase in the long run (from L_1 to L_2), and the similar increases of both the net revenue $R - rT$ and the profit π (both such increases being likewise greater in the long run than in the short run). As alternative possibilities, on the other hand, there need not be any change of L in the short run (as in the above case of fixed coefficients); and as we shall see, there is another type of limiting case in which there may be no further change of L, $R - rT$, or π as between the short run and the long. One should not jump to conclusions, however, as to the long-run changes in T or q (as Mrs. Robinson does in her implicit theorizing about the "appropriate" changes of the "other factors"). Although it is perhaps "normal" for these to change in the same direction as L, such results are by no means necessary ones.

Whether L increases or not in the short run, its long-run increase must be, if anything, greater — irrespective of the concurrent changes, if any, of T and q. This is so whether L and T are complementary, rival, or (as the borderline possibility) neutral, whether MR is constant as in a purely competitive product market or (presumably) decreasing as under monopoly,[14] and whether AC_T and MC_T are constant or variable. The grounds for this assertion may now be explored.

In the physical sense, L and T are defined as complementary or rival according as $\partial^2 q/\partial L \partial T \equiv \partial^2 q/\partial T \partial L$ is positive or negative — that is to say, according as an increase of L would raise or lower $MPP_T = \partial q/\partial T$ and, equivalently, according as an increase of T would raise or lower $MPP_L = \partial q/\partial L$.[15] Complementarity, to be sure, is the more "normal" relationship, especially when there are just two factors; but a rival relationship is also possible even then.[16]

On the other hand, Mrs. Robinson's "average net productivity" is equivalent to $LR\text{-}ANRP_L$, just as her "marginal net productivity" corresponds to $LR\text{-}MNRP_L$. As this implies, I cannot agree altogether with Samuelson when he characterizes Mrs. Robinson's "use of marginal net productivity curves" as "improper," on the alleged grounds that her "reasoning is mathematically circular" (*Foundations*, *op. cit.*, p. 75, footnote.). It seems to me, rather, that Mrs. Robinson does handle in an essentially correct (though excessively casual) manner the critical matter of the "appropriate" adjustment of the other factors in the construction of her net productivity curves (pp. 239–40). Indeed, as far as the long-run demand for a factor is concerned, my own exposition merely supplies a somewhat firmer foundation for her end-results.

[14] I shall continue to neglect the rather unlikely possibility that a monopolist may be in equilibrium where a rising (or horizontal) segment of a marginal-revenue curve may be cut by a more sharply rising marginal-cost curve.

[15] The identity of the second-order cross-derivatives is subject to the assumption that they are continuous. Even if $\partial q/\partial L$ and $\partial q/\partial T$ have "kinks" (or discontinuities of slope), however, the ensuing discussion could be appropriately modified to take care of such complications, since the implied direction of movement away from any such kink-point is consistently unique. A similar assumption is also applicable to the subsequent references to $\partial^2 R/\partial L \partial T \equiv \partial^2 R/\partial T \partial L$.

[16] It is a familiar property of any two-factor homogeneous production function of first degree with normally curved isoquants that the factors must be complementary. With

Now the question as to whether L and T change in the same direction or oppositely when MC_L is changed depends in part on their physical complementarity or rivalry, but it also depends on whether marginal revenue is constant or decreasing. That is to say, it depends on the sign of $\partial^2 R/\partial L \partial T \equiv \partial^2 R/\partial T \partial L$, which in turn depends on whether $\partial R/\partial T = (\partial q/\partial T)(dR/dq)$ — or $MRP_T = MPP_T \cdot MR$ — rises or falls as L is increased. Thus, in response to a reduction of MC_L, as L is increased with T constant (as along a short-run curve such as $MRP_L(T_1)$ in Figure 14-4), the alternative movement along $LR\text{-}MNRP_L$ calls for an increase of T if the increased L raises MRP_T or a decrease of T if MRP_T is lowered.

In either case, however, the appropriate adjustment of T calls for a further *increase* of L. This follows from the symmetry whereby, given the effect of increased L on MRP_T, the effect of increased T on MRP_L must be the same — or, equivalently, the effect of decreased T on MRP_L must be opposite. Thus, when the increased L raises MRP_T, the induced increase of T raises MRP_L and therefore leads to a further increase of L; or, when the increased L lowers MRP_T, the induced decrease of T also raises MRP_L and therefore also leads to a further increase of L. This is why the long-run demand for a factor (with other factors variable) is always, if anything, more elastic than any corresponding short-run demand (with at least some of the other factors fixed).

As a limiting possibility, however, the two such demands may also have the same elasticity. This would be illustrated in the present context if, whether at just a point or even over a finite range, $\partial^2 R/\partial L \partial T \equiv \partial^2 R/\partial T \partial L$ is precisely zero. Thus, if MRP_T is wholly unaffected over the range of a finite increase of L, there will be no adjustment of T even in the long run; so the long-run demand for L will coincide with the short-run demand in the indicated range.[17]

When the firm sells its product in a purely competitive market, so that MR is constant, the effect of an increase of L on $MRP_T = MPP_T \cdot MR$ must obviously be in the same direction as its effect on MPP_T; so the long-run effect

n factors, moreover, even though there may be rivalry among as many as $n - 1$ of them, there is a sense in which complementarity must still be predominant. As this suggests, if a production function does not differ too sharply from a first-degree homogeneous one in a relevant range, complementarity will still be more likely than rivalry.

This is especially so in a range of increasing or not-too-sharply decreasing marginal returns to scale (alternatively, falling or not-too-sharply rising marginal costs), at least when scale loci (for constant factor prices) are positively sloped on the isoquant map. For example, if two factors were everywhere neutral, there would be pronounced decreasing returns to scale in the range where both marginal products are decreasing. Then, for the same isoquant map, any softening of the decreasing returns to scale would make the factors complementary. In a range where scale loci are negatively sloped, however, decreasing marginal productivity for both factors requires them to be rival. That is to say, if the two factors were neutral in such a case, one of them would have to exhibit increasing marginal productivity; so if that feature is to be avoided, the factors have to be rival.

[17]It is also possible for both such demands to be perfectly inelastic, if (1) the factors are nonsubstitutable, at least within the range of the specified change of MC_L, and (2) MR is vertically discontinuous within the corresponding range of the implied change in long-run MC (as a reflection of a kinked demand).

on T will then depend exclusively on the physical complementarity or rivalry of the factors. When the firm is a monopolist, however, and MR declines as output is increased, it is possible for an increase of L to be accompanied by a decrease of T even though the factors are complementary in the physical sense; for, if there is a sharp enough decline of MR as L and q are increased with T constant, MRP_T may well be lowered even though MPP_T is raised, with the result that T is then reduced in the long run. Even when the factors are very strongly (though not perfectly) complementary, this will always be the case if, with a kinked demand and a vertically discontinuous MR, the reduction of MC_L does not alter the equilibrium output; for the long-run adjustment will then consist only of a substitution of L for T.

In a broad class of instances where a reduction of MC_L leads to a reduction of T, there is at least no perverse implication as to the effect on the firm's output. Thus, just as output always goes up when L and T are both increased, so will it also go up when there is only a mild decrease of T relative to the increase of L. It is also possible, however, that T may be reduced so much that output will actually fall. In the case where w and r are both independent of the factor quantities purchased, this will be so when labor is a "regressive" factor — such that, when output is increased along a scale locus, L is reduced at the same time that T is increased (analogously to the phenomenon of an "inferior good" in consumer-equilibrium analysis).[18] In this case, in other words, an increase of w has the perverse effect of lowering the firm's marginal-cost curve in the relevant range, with the result that the equilibrium output is increased (despite the fact that the total-cost and average-cost curves are, of course, raised).[19]

The demonstration of this conclusion involves somewhat more sophisticated analysis than that needed so far, but the logic is still reasonably straightforward. It concerns two basic functions:

$$C = C\,(q; w, r), \text{ and } L = L\,(q; w, r).$$

The first reflects the minimum total cost at which any given output can be produced, subject to specified values of the parameters w and r; and the second is a companion function reflecting the quantity of labor that is then used in such a cost-minimizing situation. We are interested in these two partial derivatives of the first function: $\partial C/\partial q$, which is the marginal cost MC (again with given w and r); and $\partial C/\partial w$, which reflects the effect of a wage-rate change on the

[18]In contrast to the "normal" positive slope of the scale locus S illustrated in Figure 14-1, that slope is negative when a factor is regressive. When L is the regressive factor, as in the case to be considered here, the scale locus bends toward the T-axis as output is increased. The term "regressive" was first used in this sense by Hicks, *op cit.*, p. 93. He was also the first to prove the proposition stated.

[19]Naturally, MC cannot shift oppositely to C and AC at all outputs, any more than a factor can be everywhere regressive; even if regressive whenever it is used with positive T, L would have to be "normal" where the scale locus coincided with the L-axis. On the other hand, in a range where the total-cost curve's slope is lowered as the curve itself shifts upward, MC shifts downward.

total cost of a given output (also with given r). Both are, of course, positive. Further partial differentiation of either of them (the first with respect to w or the second with respect to q) then yields, under the appropriate continuity assumptions, the equivalent second-order cross-derivatives, $\partial^2 C/\partial w \partial q \equiv \partial^2 C/\partial q \partial w$. Since the former, which may also be written as $\partial(\partial C/\partial q)/\partial w$, shows the effect on MC of a change of w, it has a positive value when a change of wage rate has the normal effect of shifting MC in the same direction, but a negative value when the effect on MC is perverse.

Now to relate that phenomenon to the regressiveness of labor, notice first that $\partial L/\partial q$ (from the second of the basic functions) reflects the change of L that is associated with a change of q, along the scale locus (with constant w and r). Notice also that, for an indefinitely small change of w, $\partial C/\partial w = L$, as a reflection of the fact that in the immediate vicinity of a given point, the effect of a wage-rate change on total cost is proportional to the quantity of labor being used.[20] Accordingly, differentiating both $\partial C/\partial w$ and L with respect to q yields: $\partial(\partial C/\partial w)/\partial q$ (or $\partial^2 C/\partial q \partial w$) $= \partial L/\partial q$.[21] That equality then proves our proposition; for when $\partial L/\partial q < 0$ (labor being regressive), it is also implied that $\partial^2 C/\partial q \partial w \equiv \partial^2 C/\partial w \partial q < 0$ (MC shifts in a direction opposite to that of the change in w). Finally, then, since the equilibrium output falls or rises according as MC shifts upward or downward, we have the perverse result that, when labor is a regressive factor, output rises or falls according as the wage rate is increased or decreased.

Extension To N Factors

Although the foregoing discussion has been limited to the case of just two factors, there is no essential novelty when the analysis is generalized to embrace any number of factors. Thus, in a short run when only one factor is variable, the construction of curves analogous to ARP_L and MRP_L is exactly the same as before, and $ANRP_L$ requires only the subtraction of the sum of all fixed costs in its numerator. Similarly, when two factors are variable, with the other $n - 2$ factors fixed, the relevant short-run revenue-product curves of either of the variable factors are closely analogous to those that appeared as long-run curves in the preceding discussion, when there were only two variable factors even in the long run.

Then, when there are three variable factors (either because there are only that many even in the long run or because all other factors are fixed),

---

[20]Naturally a small but finite change of w has slightly different effects on both L and C (1) in a short run when T is fixed and (2) in the long run when T is variable but r is fixed. As with the tangency relationship of a short-run total cost to its envelope of long-run total cost, however, those differences vanish in the limit, as the change in w is visualized to become indefinitely small (in the course of evaluating a derivative such as $\partial C/\partial w$).

[21]For a rigorous proof of this critical relationship, see Samuelson, *Foundations*, *op. cit.*, pp. 63–66.

the net-revenue-product curves of any one of them are derived subject to a maximizing of that factor's total net revenue product (or the corresponding average, *ANRP*), through an appropriate variation of both of the other variable factors for successively stipulated quantities of the one. And so on, when there are four or more variable factors. The reader can supply the appropriate modifications when there are n factors, $n-m$ of which may be fixed in any particular short run.

APPENDIX A

In order to illustrate the determination of $LR\text{-}ANRP_L = (R - rT)/L$ and $LR\text{-}MNRP_L = d(R - rT)/dL$, let us make the tractable assumptions that: (1) the production function is of the Cobb-Douglas type, $q = aL^kT^{1-k}$, where $a > 0$ and $0 < k < 1$; (2) the product's demand-price function is $p = bq^{n-1}$, where $0 < n \leq 1$, such that the constant demand elasticity is $E_{qp} = (dq/dp)(p/q) = -1/(1-n)$ and $R = bq^n$; and (3) the rent rate r is a constant.

Total revenue as a function of L and T is then $R = b(aL^kT^{1-k})^n = a^nbL^{nk}T^{n-nk}$, so that:

$$R - rT = a^nbL^{nk}T^{n-nk} - rT.$$

To maximize this function with respect to T, for any given L,

$$\frac{\partial(R - rT)}{\partial T} = n(1-k)a^nbL^{nk}T^{n-nk-1} - r = 0;$$

whence

$$T = \left[\frac{n(1-k)a^nb}{r}\right]^{\frac{1}{1-n+nk}} L^{\frac{nk}{1-n+nk}}$$

Since this equation indicates the appropriate value of T for any given L, substituting it in the above expression for $R - rT$ yields that net revenue as a function of just L:

$$R - rT = (a^nb)^{\frac{1}{1-n+nk}}\left[\frac{n(1-k)}{r}\right]^{\frac{n-nk}{1-n+nk}}(1-n+nk)L^{\frac{nk}{1-n+nk}}$$

To simplify that expression, let us substitute

$$s = (a^nb)^{\frac{1}{1-n+nk}}\left[\frac{n(1-k)}{r}\right]^{\frac{n-nk}{1-n+nk}}(1-n+nk),$$

and

$$t = \frac{1-n}{1-n+nk},$$

noting that $s > 0$ and $0 \leq t < 1$. It then follows that:

$$R - rT = sL^{1-t}; \qquad \frac{R - rT}{L} = sL^{-t}; \qquad \text{and } \frac{d(R - rT)}{dL} = (1-t)sL^{-t}.$$

Since, when $n < 1$ and $0 < t < 1$, $LR\text{-}MNRP_L$ is everywhere equal to the fraction

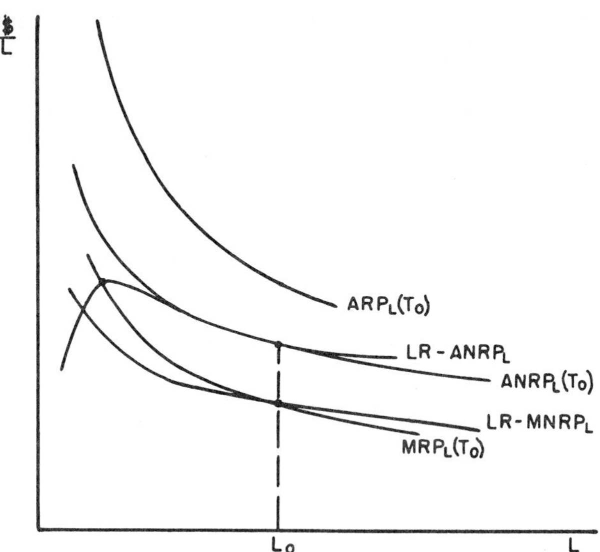

Figure 14-5

$(1 - t)$ of $LR\text{-}ANRP_L$, as illustrated in Figure 14-5,[22] $LR\text{-}MNRP_L$ reflects the firm's long-run demand for labor for all positive values of w and L. Furthermore, the elasticity of the demand for labor is the constant $E_{Lw} = (dL/dw)(w/L) = -1/t = -(1 - n + nk)/(1 - n)$. Provided that $n < 1$, this is less than the product-demand elasticity in absolute value, since $E_{Lw} = (1 - n + nk)E_{qp}$. Both demands are, however, relatively elastic.[23]

The limiting case of a purely competitive product market is implied when $n = 1$ and $t = 0$. In that event, $LR\text{-}ANRP_L$ and $LR\text{-}MNRP_L$ are both equal to the same constant:

$$\frac{R - rt}{L} = \frac{d(R - rT)}{dL} = s = k(ab)^{\frac{1}{k}}\left(\frac{1 - k}{r}\right)^{\frac{1-k}{k}}.$$

[22]For the specific illustrative values on which the curves in Figure 14-5 are based, see footnote 25.

[23]The relationship of the absolute values of these elasticities may be expressed in another way. Thus, $|E_{qp}| = 1/(1 - n)$ and $|E_{Lw}| = (1 - n + nk)/(1 - n)$. Then, since

$$|E_{Lw}| = 1 + \frac{nk}{1 - n} \text{ and } |E_{qp}| - 1 = \frac{n}{1 - n},$$

it follows that:

$$|E_{Lw}| = 1 + k(|E_{qp}| - 1).$$

In other words, $|E_{Lw}|$ exceeds unity only by the fraction k of the amount by which $|E_{qp}|$ exceeds unity. The parameter k also represents the fraction of total cost that is represented by wages. We have here, therefore, an illustration of the familiar generalization that the elasticity of demand for a factor is the greater, (1) the greater is the elasticity of product demand and (2) the greater is the outlay on that factor as a fraction of total cost.

Since the demand for labor is then perfectly elastic, the equilibrium quantity of labor is indeterminate when the wage rate w is a constant at the critical level. This is merely the reflection of the corresponding indeterminacy of the purely competitive firm's equilibrium output when it produces at constant returns to scale and faces constant factor prices that imply a coincidence of $AC \equiv MC$ with $AR \equiv MR$.

When the quantity of land is fixed at T_0 and only labor is variable, the determination of the short-run functions, $ARP_L = R/L$, $ANRP_L = (R - rT_0)/L$, and $MRP_L = \partial R/\partial L$, may also be illustrated. Given T_0, it is related to the long-run-equilibrium quantity of labor L_0 as above:

$$T_0 = \left[\frac{n(1-k)a^n b}{r}\right]^{\frac{1}{1-n+nk}} L_0^{\frac{nk}{1-n+nk}}$$

This may then be substituted in the expressions for $R = a^n bL^{nk}T_0^{n-nk}$ and $R - rT_0 = a^n bL^{nk}T_0^{n-nk} - rT_0$ in order to convert them into functions of just L and L_0:

$$R = (a^n b)^{\frac{1}{1-n+nk}} \left[\frac{n(1-k)}{r}\right]^{\frac{n-nk}{1-n+nk}} L_0^{\frac{n^2k(1-k)}{1-n+nk}} L^{nk},$$

$$R - rT_0 = (a^n b)^{\frac{1}{1-n+nk}} \left[\frac{n(1-k)}{r}\right]^{\frac{n-nk}{1-n+nk}} L_0^{\frac{n^2k(1-k)}{1-n+nk}} \left[L^{nk} - n(1-k)L_0^{nk}\right].$$

We now employ these simplifying substitutions:

$$u = (a^n b)^{\frac{1}{1-n+nk}} \left[\frac{n(1-k)}{r}\right]^{\frac{n-nk}{1-n+nk}} L_0^{\frac{n^2k(1-k)}{1-n+nk}}$$

$$v = 1 - nk,$$

$$z = n(1-k)L_0^{nk},$$

noting that $u > 0$, $0 < v < 1$, and $z > 0$.

It then follows that:

$$R = uL^{1-v}, \qquad R - rT_0 = u(L^{1-v} - z),$$

$$\frac{R}{L} = uL^{-v}, \qquad \frac{R - rT_0}{L} = u(L^{-v} - zL^{-1}), \text{ and } \frac{\partial R}{\partial L} = (1-v)uL^{-v}.$$

As illustrated in Figure 14-5, MRP_L is everywhere equal to the fraction $(1 - v)$ of ARP_L; so MRP_L reflects the short-run demand for labor for all positive values of w and

L. On the other hand, MRP_L intersects $ANRP_L$ at the latter's maximum point; so the firm's profit is negative or positive according as w is above or below that level.[24]

This short-run demand for labor has an elasticity of $e_{Lw} = -1/v = -1/(1 - nk)$. In absolute value, it is always greater than unity and finite (even in a purely competitive product market, when $n = 1$), but less than the corresponding long-run elasticity.[25]

APPENDIX B

Production is assumed to be subject to fixed coefficients, such that the efficient factor quantities for any specified output are $L = (1/h)q$ and $T = (1/k)q$, where h and k are positive constants. More generally, for any specified L and T, q is equal to hL or kT, whichever is the smaller.[26] Provided that $T = (h/k)L$, however, we may specify that $q = hL$. It is also convenient to define $a = h/k$, so that the efficient factor proportionality may be designated as $T = aL$. It is further assumed (as in Appendix A) that $R = bq^n$, where $0 < n \leq 1$; but it is now assumed that the rent rate $r = f + gT$, where the constants f and g are nonnegative.[27]

Accordingly, when $T = aL$, it is implied that $R = b(hL)^n$ and $rT = fT + gT^2 = f(aL) + g(aL)^2$, such that:

$$R - rT = bh^nL^n - afL - a^2gL^2.$$

---

[24]The intersection point of MRP_L and $ANRP_L$ is at the labor quantity:

$$L = \left(\frac{n - nk}{1 - nk}\right)^{\frac{1}{nk}} L_0 \leq L_0 \text{ according as } n \leq 1.$$

[25]The five curves in Figure 14-5 reflect values of $k = 2/3$ and $n = 3/4$. In turn, these imply that:

$$t = \frac{1 - n}{1 - n + nk} = \frac{1}{3}, \quad v = 1 - nk = \frac{1}{2},$$

$$E_{qp} = -\frac{1}{1 - n} = -4, \quad E_{Lw} = -\frac{1}{t} = -3, \quad E_{Lw} = -\frac{1}{v} = -2.$$

It is further implied that $LR\text{-}MNRP_L = (2/3)LR\text{-}ANRP_L$ and $MRP_L = (1/2)ARP_L$. Then, since $ANRP_L$ is tangent to $LR\text{-}ANRP_L$ at the labor quantity (L_0) where MRP_L and $LR\text{-}MNRP_L$ intersect, the rest of the $ANRP_L$ curve is determined from the fact that it differs from the ARP_L curve only by a rectangular hyperbola. From the preceding footnote, it is also established that the peak of $ANRP_L$ occurs at $L = (1/4)L_0$. Values of a, b, r, and hence s have only scalar implications for the long-run curves — as, in addition, do L_0 and hence u for the short-run curves.

[26]This also implies that the production function can be written as:

$$q = \frac{hL + kT - |hL - kT|}{2}.$$

[27]It would also be acceptable to allow g to be negative, but only within a limited range of values of T; for the marginal cost of that factor would then be negative when $T > -f/2g$.

It then follows that $LR\text{-}ANRP_L$ and $LR\text{-}MNRP_L$ are, respectively:

$$\frac{R - rT}{L} = bh^n L^{n-1} - af - a^2 gL,$$

$$\frac{d(R - rT)}{dL} = nbh^n L^{n-1} - af - 2a^2 gL.$$

Clearly $LR\text{-}ANRP_L$ is never less than $LR\text{-}MNRP_L$. Therefore, when $n < 1$, $LR\text{-}MNRP_L$ reflects the firm's long-run demand for labor for $w \geq 0$ (and with a finite L demanded even when $w = 0$, provided only that f and g are not both zero). Furthermore, the elasticity of labor demand E_{Lw} is smaller in absolute value than the elasticity of product demand $E_{qp} = -1/(1 - n)$; for the two would merely be equal if land were a free good, with $f = g = 0$, whereas E_{Lw} is lower in absolute value the higher are f and g.

In the short run when the quantity of land is fixed at T_0, such that the long-run equilibrium quantity of labor is $L_0 = T_0/a$, we again have $q = hL$ as long as $L \leq L_0$, but with $q = hL_0$ when $L \geq L_0$. This is still a continuous function, but with a discontinuity of slope at L_0, where $MPP_L = \partial q/\partial L$ falls discontinuously from h to 0. Similarly, it is now implied that $R = bh^n L^n$ when $L \leq L_0$ and $R = bh^n L_0^n$ when $L \geq L_0$. The fixed land cost is $r_0 T_0 = afL_0 + a^2 gL_0^2$. Accordingly, ARP_L and $ANRP_L$ have discontinuities of slope at L_0; for, when $L \leq L_0$,

$$\frac{R}{L} = bh^n L^{n-1} \quad \text{and} \quad \frac{R - R_0 T_0}{L} = bh^n L^{n-1} - (afL_0 + a^2 gL_0^2)L^{-1},$$

and, when $L \geq L_0$,

$$\frac{R}{L} = bh^n L_0^n L^{-1} \quad \text{and} \quad \frac{R - r_0 T_0}{L} = (bh^n L_0^n - afL_0 - a^2 gL_0^2)L^{-1}.$$

On the other hand, MRP_L is itself discontinuous at L_0, since:

$$\frac{\partial R}{\partial L} = nbh^n L^{n-1} \text{ when } L < L_0, \text{ and } \frac{\partial R}{\partial L} = 0 \text{ when } L > L_0.$$

In the special case where $n = 1$ and $g = 0$ (with a purely competitive product market and a constant $r = f$— with $bh > af$), $LR\text{-}ANRP_L$ and $LR\text{-}MNRP_L$ are constant and equal:

$$\frac{R - rT}{L} = \frac{d(R - rT)}{dL} = bh - af.$$

Thus, when w is a constant at the critical level, the firm's equilibrium labor quantity and output are again indeterminate, owing to the first-degree homogeneity of the production function. In the short run, labor demand is also perfectly elastic at $w = bh$ where $L < L_0$, but perfectly inelastic at L_0 for $w < bh$, since:

$$\frac{R}{L} = \frac{\partial R}{\partial L} = bh \text{ when } L < L_0, \text{ and } \frac{\partial R}{\partial L} = 0 \text{ when } L > L_0.$$

Where $n = 1$ and $g > 0$ (again with a purely competitive product market but monopsony in the market for land — and again with $bh > af$), the long-run demand for labor ($LR\text{-}MNRP_L$) is linearly downward-sloping and less than the likewise linearly downward-sloping $LR\text{-}ANRP_L$ for $L > 0$:

$$\frac{R - rT}{L} = bh - af - a^2 gL,$$

$$\frac{d(R - rT)}{dr} = bh - af - 2a^2 gL.$$

In the short run, however, ARP_L and MRP_L are exactly the same as in the preceding case.

SECTION IV. MARKET STRUCTURE: COMPETITION AND MONOPOLY

Section IV examines the market structures of competition and monopoly. Attention is also focused on the "nature of the firm" in a market economy, the concept of "industry," and the measurement of welfare losses from monopoly.

In his article, Coase discusses why a firm emerges in an exchange economy and explains some of the functions of the firm. By tracing the evolution of the concept of competition, McNulty discusses some of the reasons for the confusion associated with the meaning of competition in economic theory. Olson and McFarland offer an explanation of why some economists reject the concepts of "pure monopoly" and "industry." Further, they provide theoretical definitions for these two concepts and argue that they are important components of the theory of market structure. Comanor and Leibenstein analyze the implications for the measurement of welfare losses from monopoly of their hypothesis that competition results in lower costs (an increase in "X-efficiency") as well as lower prices.

In his article, Coase states that while economists view the price mechanism as a coordinating instrument, they likewise see the "entrepreneur" as performing a coordinating function. Coase indicates that the purpose of this article is to bridge the apparent gap in economic theory "between the assumption (made for some purposes) that resources are allocated by means of the price mechanism and the assumption (made for other purposes) that this allocation is dependent on the entrepreneur-co-ordinator."

Coase approaches this problem and the related one of defining a "firm" by discussing why a firm emerges in a specialized exchange economy. He argues that the main reason it is profitable to establish a firm is that there is a cost of using the price mechanism; Coase discusses some examples of this type of cost. Firms emerge, then, because it is possible to save certain marketing costs by "forming an organization and allowing some authority (an 'entrepreneur') to direct the resources." According to Coase, a firm "consists of the system of relationships which comes into existence when the direction of resources is dependent on an entrepreneur."

Coase reviews some of the explanations advanced by other economists as to why firms develop and indicates why the reasons he has offered are preferable. In answer to the question about whether his concept of the firm fits in with that existing in the real world, he concludes that his definition is one which "approximates closely" the firm as it is considered in the real world.

McNulty's purpose is to examine some of the factors which have contributed to the failure of economists to define competition adequately and to point out some specific shortcomings of the economic concept of competition for both analysis and policy. In looking at the meaning of competition, McNulty states that most generally it is considered as the opposite of monopoly, a view which has led to a great deal of confusion concerning the relationship between economic efficiency and business behavior. He argues that a concept of economic competition which is to be significant for economic policy should relate to patterns of business behavior which "might reasonably be associated with the verb 'to compete'."

McNulty discusses in some detail the evolution of the concept of competition, pointing out that the classical economists considered competition as an "ordering force" which resulted in allocative efficiency in the use of resources. On the other hand, the neoclassicists contributed the idea of competition as "itself a market structure." McNulty maintains that these two "fundamentally different" ways of looking at competition have been of considerable importance in explaining the ambiguity associated with the meaning of competition.

McNulty identifies the major weaknesses of the concept of competition which have persisted in economic theory and discusses their relevance for economic analysis and policy. While he does not deny the analytical usefulness of competition when it is treated as a market structure, McNulty suggests the importance of a "reformulation and expansion" of the concept of competition which would restore it to "what it was at the hands of Adam Smith: a disequilibrium, behavioral concept which is meaningful and relevant in terms of the contemporary pattern of economic life."

Pointing out that some economists reject the concept of "pure monopoly" and the concept of "industry," Olson and McFarland state that their article is designed to show that these two concepts "can be given precise theoretical definitions" and to argue that they "deserve prominent places in the theory of market structure."

The authors maintain that the rejection of the concepts of monopoly and industry are primarily attributable to an "excessive concern" for the elasticity of the demand curve facing the firm and the cross-elasticity of demand between firms. Their basic objection to the use of elasticity and cross-elasticity is that it leads to a neglect of the two basic determinants of market structure, which are the number of firms in the market and the degree of closeness or remoteness of substitution among the products of the different firms in the market.

In considering the number of firms, the authors point out that the extent to which a firm must consider the effects of its actions on "the state of the market" is a much more significant factor in distinguishing types of market structure than are the elasticity or cross-elasticity of demand. In the pure monopoly situation, the firm *is* the group, and the effect of its action on the market is so great that it alone determines the price. In looking at substitution among products, the authors do not accept Chamberlin's idea that there is a continuous chain of substitution linking all products. Instead, they argue that "all goods are stretched out along a continuum," ranging from some goods which are perfect substitutes to those goods which have no close substitutes. Olson and McFarland maintain that groups of firms which produce a set of products "with no close, competitive substitutes" should be called "industries."

Olson and McFarland conclude by giving reasons to support their argument that the concept of pure monopoly and the concept of industry in monopolistic competition are logically implicit in most modern writings on market structure.

Comanor and Leibenstein point out that in estimating the welfare losses from monopoly, it has been commonly assumed that inputs are used as efficiently in monopoly as they are in competitive markets. However, Comanor and Leibenstein maintain that monopoly will affect costs as well as prices; accordingly, the welfare loss from monopoly should include the reduction in "X-efficiency," as well as the loss from allocative inefficiency. A shift from monopoly to competition, then, has two possible effects—the elimination of monopoly rents and the reduction of unit costs.

If a shift from monopoly to competition reduces costs as well as prices, what are the welfare losses which are due to monopoly? In examining this question, Comanor and Leibenstein maintain that the actual degree of allocative inefficiency "may be very much larger" than previously calculated. Then, to this larger sum it is necessary to add the volume of X-inefficiency for the monopolistically used inputs to arrive at the total welfare loss from monopoly. The authors compare the traditional measure of the allocative inefficiency attributable to monopoly with the full measure of inefficiency associated with their hypothesis that competition affects costs as well as prices.

In their concluding section, Comanor and Leibenstein look at the relationship between the theory of the second best and the welfare gains resulting from a shift from monopoly to competition in a single industry. They conclude that there is more likely to be a welfare gain from such a shift when there is an increase in X-efficiency (a reduction in costs) as well as lower prices.

15. THE NATURE OF THE FIRM*

R. H. Coase†

Economic theory has suffered in the past from a failure to state clearly its assumptions. Economists in building up a theory have often omitted to examine the foundations on which it was erected. This examination is, however, essential not only to prevent the misunderstanding and needless controversy which arise from a lack of knowledge of the assumptions on which a theory is based, but also because of the extreme importance for economics of good judgment in choosing between rival sets of assumptions. For instance, it is suggested that the use of the word "firm" in economics may be different from the use of the term by the "plain man."[1] Since there is apparently a trend in economic theory towards starting analysis with the individual firm and not with the industry,[2] it is all the more necessary not only that a clear definition of the word "firm" should be given but that its difference from a firm in the "real world," if it exists, should be made clear. Mrs. Robinson has said that "the two questions to be asked of a set of assumptions in economics are: Are they tractable? and: Do they correspond with the real world?"[3] Though, as Mrs. Robinson points out, "more often one set will be manageable and the other realistic," yet there may well be branches of theory where assumptions may be both manageable and realistic. It is hoped to show in the following paper that a definition of a firm may be obtained which is not only realistic in that it corresponds to what is meant by a firm in the real world, but is tractable by two of the most powerful instruments of economic analysis developed by Marshall, the idea of the margin and that of substitution, together giving the idea of substitution at the margin.[4] Our definition must, of course, "relate to formal relations which are capable of being *conceived* exactly."[5]

I

It is convenient if, in searching for a definition of a firm, we first consider the economic system as it is normally treated by the economist. Let us

---

*From *Economica*, N. S., Vol. IV, Nos. 13–16 (1937), pp. 386–405. Reprinted by permission of the publisher and the author.

†R. H. Coase, Professor of Economics, University of Chicago.

[1]Joan Robinson, *Economics is a Serious Subject* (Cambridge, England: W. Heffer and Sons, Ltd., 1932), p. 12.

[2]See N. Kaldor, "The Equilibrium of the Firm," *Economic Journal* (March, 1934).

[3]Robinson, *op. cit.*, p. 6.

[4]J.M. Keynes, *Essays in Biography* (London: Macmillan and Co., 1933), pp. 223–4.

[5]L. Robbins, *Nature and Significance of Economic Science* (New York: Macmillan, 1932), p. 63.

consider the description of the economic system given by Sir Arthur Salter.[6] "The normal economic system works itself. For its current operation it is under no central control, it needs no central survey. Over the whole range of human activity and human need, supply is adjusted to demand, and production to consumption, by a process that is automatic, elastic and responsive." An economist thinks of the economic system as being co-ordinated by the price mechanism and society becomes not an organization but an organism.[7] The economic system "works itself." This does not mean that there is no planning by individuals. These exercise foresight and choose between alternatives. This is necessarily so if there is to be order in the system. But this theory assumes that the direction of resources is dependent directly on the price mechanism. Indeed, it is often considered to be an objection to economic planning that it merely tries to do what is already done by the price mechanism.[8] Sir Arthur Salter's description, however, gives a very incomplete picture of our economic system. Within a firm, the description does not fit at all. For instance, in economic theory we find that the allocation of factors of production between different uses is determined by the price mechanism. The price of factor *A* becomes higher in *X* than in *Y*. As a result, *A* moves from *Y* to *X* until the difference between the prices in *X* and *Y*, except in so far as it compensates for other differential advantages, disappears. Yet in the real world, we find that there are many areas where this does not apply. If a workman moves from department *Y* to department *X*, he does not go because of a change in relative prices, but because he is ordered to do so. Those who object to economic planning on the grounds that the problem is solved by price movements can be answered by pointing out that there is planning within our economic system which is quite different from the individual planning mentioned above and which is akin to what is normally called economic planning. The example given above is typical of a large sphere in our modern economic system. Of course, this fact has not been ignored by economists. Marshall introduces organization as a fourth factor of production; J. B. Clark gives the co-ordinating function to the entrepreneur; Professor Knight introduces managers who co-ordinate. As D. H. Robertson points out, we find "islands of conscious power in this ocean of unconscious co-operation like lumps of butter coagulating in a pail of buttermilk."[9] But in view of the fact that it is usually argued that co-ordination will be done by the price mechanism, why is such organization necessary? Why are there these "island of conscious power"? Outside the firm, price

---

[6]This description is quoted with approval by D. H. Robertson, *Control of Industry* (London: Nisbet, 1930), p. 85, and by Professor Arnold Plant, "Trends in Business Administration," *Economica* (February, 1932). It appears in *Allied Shipping Control*, pp. 16–17.

[7]See F. A. Hayek, "The Trend of Economic Thinking," *Economica* (May, 1933).

[8]See F. A. Hayek, *op. cit.*

[9]D. H. Robertson, *op. cit.*, p. 85.

movements direct production, which is co-ordinated through a series of exchange transactions on the market. Within a firm, these market transactions are eliminated and in place of the complicated market structure with exchange transactions is substituted the entrepreneur-co-ordinator, who directs production.[10] It is clear that these are alternative methods of co-ordinating production. Yet having regard to the fact that if production is regulated by price movements, production could be carried on without any organization at all, well might we ask, why is there any organization?

Of course, the degree to which the price mechanism is superseded varies greatly. In a department store, the allocation of the different sections to the various locations in the building may be done by the controlling authority or it may be the result of competitive price bidding for space. In the Lancashire cotton industry, a weaver can rent power and shop-room and can obtain looms and yarn on credit.[11] This co-ordination of the various factors of production is, however, normally carried out without the intervention of the price mechanism. As is evident, the amount of "vertical" integration, involving as it does the supersession of the price mechanism, varies greatly from industry to industry and from firm to firm.

It can, I think, be assumed that the distinguishing mark of the firm is the supersession of the price mechanism. It is, of course, as Professor Robbins points out, "related to an outside network of relative prices and costs,"[12] but it is important to discover the exact nature of this relationship. This distinction between the allocation of resources in a firm and the allocation in the economic system has been very vividly described by Mr. Maurice Dobb when discussing Adam Smith's conception of the capitalist:

> . . . It began to be seen that there was something more important than the relations inside each factory or unit captained by an undertaker; there were the relations of the undertaker with the rest of the economic world outside his immediate sphere . . . the undertaker busies himself with the division of labour inside each firm and he plans and organises consciously,

but

> . . . he is related to the much larger economic specialisation of which he himself is merely one specialised unit. Here, he plays his part as a single cell in a larger organism, mainly unconscious of the wider role he fills.[13]

---

[10]In the rest of this paper I shall use the term entrepreneur to refer to the person or persons who, in a competitive system, take the place of the price mechanism in the direction of resources.

[11]*Survey of Textile Industries*, p. 26.

[12]Robbins, *op. cit.*, p. 71.

[13]Maurice Dobb, *Capitalist Enterprise and Social Progress* (London: George Routledge and Sons, Ltd., 1925), p. 20. Cf., also, Henderson, *Supply and Demand* (New York: Harcourt, Brace and Co., 1922), pp. 3–5.

In view of the fact that while economists treat the price mechanism as a co-ordinating instrument, they also admit the co-ordinating function of the "entrepreneur," it is surely important to inquire why co-ordination is the work of the price mechanism in one case and of the entrepreneur in another. The purpose of this paper is to bridge what appears to be a gap in economic theory between the assumption (made for some purposes) that resources are allocated by means of the price mechanism and the assumption (made for other purposes) that this allocation is dependent on the entrepreneur-co-ordinator. We have to explain the basis on which, in practice, this choice between alternatives is effected.[14]

II

Our task is to attempt to discover why a firm emerges at all in a specialized exchange economy. The price mechanism (considered purely from the side of the direction of resources) might be superseded if the relationship which replaced it was desired for its own sake. This would be the case, for example, if some people preferred to work under the direction of some other person. Such individuals would accept less in order to work under someone, and firms would arise naturally from this. But it would appear that this cannot be a very important reason, for it would rather seem that the opposite tendency is operating if one judges from the stress normally laid on the advantage of "being one's own master."[15] Of course, if the desire was not to be controlled but to control, to exercise power over others, then people might be willing to give up something in order to direct others; that is, they would be willing to pay others more than they could get under the price mechanism in order to be able to direct them. But this implies that those who direct pay in order to be able to do this and are not paid to direct, which is clearly not true in the majority of cases.[16] Firms might also exist if purchasers preferred commodities which are produced by firms to those not so produced; but even in spheres

---

[14]It is easy to see when the State takes over the direction of an industry that, in planning it, it is doing something which was previously done by the price mechanism. What is usually not realized is that any business man in organizing the relations between his departments is also doing something which could be organized through the price mechanism. There is therefore point in Mr. Durbin's answer to those who emphasize the problems involved in economic planning that the same problems have to be solved by business men in the competitive system. (See "Economic Calculus in a Planned Economy," *Economic Journal* [December, 1936]). The important difference between these two cases is that economic planning is imposed on industry while firms arise voluntarily because they represent a more efficient method of organizing production. In a competitive system, there is an "optimum" amount of planning!

[15]Cf. Harry Dawes, "Labour Mobility in the Steel Industry," *Economic Journal* (March, 1934), who instances "the trek to retail shopkeeping and insurance work by the better paid of skilled men due to the desire (often the main aim in life of a worker) to be independent" (p. 86).

[16]None the less, this is not altogether fanciful. Some small shopkeepers are said to earn less than their assistants.

where one would expect such preferences (if they exist) to be of negligible importance, firms are to be found in the real world.[17] Therefore there must be other elements involved.

The main reason why it is profitable to establish a firm would seem to be that there is a cost of using the price mechanism. The most obvious cost of "organizing" production through the price mechanism is that of discovering what the relevant prices are.[18] This cost may be reduced but it will not be eliminated by the emergence of specialists who will sell this information. The costs of negotiating and concluding a separate contract for each exchange transaction which takes place on a market must also be taken into account.[19] Again, in certain markets, e.g., produce exchanges, a technique is devised for minimizing these contract costs; but they are not eliminated. It is true that contracts are not eliminated when there is a firm but they are greatly reduced. A factor of production (or the owner thereof) does not have to make a series of contracts with the factors with whom he is co-operating within the firm, as would be necessary, of course, if this co-operation were as a direct result of the working of the price mechanism. For this series of contracts is substituted one. At this stage, it is important to note the character of the contract into which a factor enters that is employed within a firm. The contract is one whereby the factor, for a certain remuneration (which may be fixed or fluctuating), agrees to obey the directions of an entrepreneur *within certain limits.*[20] The essence of the contract is that it should only state the limits to the powers of the entrepreneur. Within these limits, he can therefore direct the other factors of production.

There are, however, other disadvantages — or costs — of using the price mechanism. It may be desired to make a long-term contract for the supply of some article or service. This may be due to the fact that if one contract is made for a longer period, instead of several shorter ones, then certain costs of making each contract will be avoided. Or, owing to the risk attitude of the people concerned, they may prefer to make a long rather than a short-term contract. Now, owing to the difficulty of forecasting, the longer the period

---

[17] G. F. Shove, "The Imperfection of the Market: a Further Note," *Economic Journal* (March, 1933), p. 116, note I, points out that such preferences may exist, although the example he gives is almost the reverse of the instance given in the text.

[18] According to N. Kaldor, "A Classificatory Note of the Determinateness of Equilibrium," *Review of Economic Studies* (February, 1934), it is one of the assumptions of static theory that "All the relevant prices are known to all individuals." But this is clearly not true of the real world.

[19] This influence was noted by Professor Usher when discussing the development of capitalism. He says: "The successive buying and selling of partly finished products were sheer waste of energy." (*Introduction to the Industrial History of England* [London: G. C. Harrap and Co., Ltd., 1921], p. 13). But he does not develop the idea nor consider why it is that buying and selling operations still exist.

[20] It would be possible for no limits to the powers of the entrepreneur to be fixed. This would be voluntary slavery. According to Professor Batt, *The Law of Master and Servant* (New York: Pitman Publishing Co., 1929), p. 18, such a contract would be void and unenforceable.

of the contract is for the supply of the commodity or service, the less possible, and indeed, the less desirable it is for the person purchasing to specify what the other contracting party is expected to do. It may well be a matter of indifference to the person supplying the service or commodity which of several courses of action is taken, but not to the purchaser of that service or commodity. But the purchaser will not know which of these several courses he will want the supplier to take. Therefore, the service which is being provided is expressed in general terms, the exact details being left until a later date. All that is stated in the contract is the limits to what the persons supplying the commodity or service are expected to do. The details of what the supplier is expected to do are not stated in the contract but are decided later by the purchaser. When the direction of resources (within the limits of the contract) becomes dependent on the buyer in this way, that relationship which I term a "firm" may be obtained.[21] A firm is likely therefore to emerge in those cases where a very short term contract would be unsatisfactory. It is obviously of more importance in the case of services — labor — than it is in the case of the buying of commodities. In the case of commodities, the main items can be stated in advance and the details which will be decided later will be of minor significance.

We may sum up this section of the argument by saying that the operation of a market costs something and by forming an organization and allowing some authority (an "entrepreneur") to direct the resources, certain marketing costs are saved. The entrepreneur has to carry out his function at less cost, taking into account the fact that he may get factors of production at a lower price than the market transactions which he supersedes, because it is always possible to revert to the open market if he fails to do this.

The question of uncertainty is one which is often considered to be very relevant to the study of the equilibrium of the firm. It seems improbable that a firm would emerge without the existence of uncertainty. But those, for instance, Professor Knight, who make the *mode of payment* the distinguishing mark of the firm — fixed incomes being guaranteed to some of those engaged in production by a person who takes the residual, and fluctuating, income — would appear to be introducing a point which is irrelevant to the problem we are considering. One entrepreneur may sell his services to another for a certain sum of money, while the payment to his employees may be mainly or wholly a share in profits.[22] The significant question would appear to be why the allocation of resources is not done directly by the price mechanism.

---

[21]Of course, it is not possible to draw a hard and fast line which determines whether there is a firm or not. There may be more or less direction. It is similar to the legal question of whether there is the relationship of master and servant or principal and agent. See the discussion of this problem presented later.

[22]The views of Professor Knight are examined later in more detail.

Another factor that should be noted is that exchange transactions on a market and the same transactions organized within a firm are often treated differently by Governments or other bodies with regulatory powers. If we consider the operation of a sales tax, it is clear that it is a tax on market transactions and not on the same transactions organized within the firm. Now since these are alternative methods of "organization"—by the price mechanism or by the entrepreneur—such a regulation would bring into existence firms which otherwise would have no *raison d'être*. It would furnish a reason for the emergence of a firm in a specialized exchange economy. Of course, to the extent that firms already exist, such a measure as a sales tax would merely tend to make them larger than they would otherwise be. Similarly, quota schemes, and methods of price control which imply that there is rationing, and which do not apply to firms producing such products for themselves, by allowing advantages to those who organize within the firm and not through the market, necessarily encourage the growth of firms. But it is difficult to believe that it is measures such as have been mentioned in this paragraph which have brought firms into existence. Such measures would, however, tend to have this result if they did not exist for other reasons.

These, then, are the reasons why organizations such as firms exist in a specialized exchange economy in which it is generally assumed that the distribution of resources is "organized" by the price mechanism. A firm, therefore, consists of the system of relationships which comes into existence when the direction of resources is dependent on an entrepreneur.

The approach which has just been sketched would appear to offer an advantage in that it is possible to give a scientific meaning to what is meant by saying that a firm gets larger or smaller. A firm becomes larger as additional transactions (which could be exchange transactions co-ordinated through the price mechanism) are organized by the entrepreneur and becomes smaller as he abandons the organization of such transactions. The question which arises is whether it is possible to study the forces which determine the size of the firm. Why does the entrepreneur not organize one less transaction or one more? It is interesting to note that Professor Knight considers that:

> . . . the relation between efficiency and size is one of the most serious problems of theory, being, in contrast with the relation for a plant, largely a matter of personality and historical accident rather than of intelligible general principles. But the question is peculiarly vital because the possibility of monopoly gain offers a powerful incentive to *continuous and unlimited* expansion of the firm, which force must be offset by some equally powerful one making for decreased efficiency (in the production of money income) with growth in size, if even boundary competition is to exist.[23]

[23]Frank Knight, *Risk, Uncertainty and Profit*, Preface to the Re-issue (London School of Economics Series of Reprints, No. 16, 1933).

Professor Knight would appear to consider that it is impossible to treat scientifically the determinants of the size of the firm. On the basis of the concept of the firm developed above, this task will now be attempted.

It was suggested that the introduction of the firm was due primarily to the existence of marketing costs. A pertinent question to ask would appear to be (quite apart from the monopoly considerations raised by Professor Knight), why, if by organizing one can eliminate certain costs and in fact reduce the cost of production, are there any market transactions at all?[24] Why is not all production carried on by one big firm? There would appear to be certain possible explanations.

First, as a firm gets larger, there may be decreasing returns to the entrepreneur function, that is, the costs of organizing additional transactions within the firm may rise.[25] Naturally a point must be reached where the costs of organizing an extra transaction within the firm are equal to the costs involved in carrying out the transaction in the open market, or, to the costs of organizing by another entrepreneur. Secondly, it may be that as the transactions which are organized increase, the entrepreneur fails to place the factors of production in the uses where their value is greatest, that is, fails to make the best use of the factors of production. Again, a point must be reached where the loss through the waste of resources is equal to the marketing costs of the exchange transaction in the open market or to the loss if the transaction was organized by another entrepreneur. Finally, the supply price of one or more of the factors of production may rise, because the "other advantages" of a small firm are greater than those of a large firm.[26] Of course, the actual point where the expansion of the firm ceases might be determined by a combination of the factors mentioned above. The first two reasons given most probably correspond to the economists' phrase of "diminishing returns to management."[27]

---

[24]There are certain marketing costs which could only be eliminated by the abolition of "consumers' choice" and these are the costs of retailing. It is conceivable that these costs might be so high that people would be willing to accept rations because the extra product obtained was worth the loss of their choice.

[25]This argument assumes that exchange transactions on a market can be considered as homogeneous; which is clearly untrue in fact. This complication is taken into account later.

[26]For a discussion of the variation of the supply price of factors of production to firms of varying size, see E. A. G. Robinson, *The Structure of Competitive Industry* (London: Cambridge University Press, 1931). It is sometimes said that the supply price of organizing ability increases as the size of the firm increases because men prefer to be the heads of small independent businesses rather than the heads of departments in a large business. See Jones, *The Trust Problem* (New York: Macmillan Co., 1927), p. 531, and Macgregor, *Industrial Combination* (London: George Bell and Sons, 1906), p. 63. This is a common argument of those who advocate Rationalization. It is said that larger units would be more efficient, but owing to the individualistic spirit of the smaller entrepreneurs, they prefer to remain independent, apparently in spite of the higher income which their increased efficiency under Rationalization makes possible.

[27]This discussion is, of course, brief and incomplete. For a more thorough discussion of this particular problem, see N. Kaldor, "The Equilibrium of the Firm," *Economic Journal* (March, 1934), and E. A. G. Robinson, "The Problem of Management and the Size of the Firm," *Economic Journal* (June, 1934).

The point has been made in the previous paragraph that a firm will tend to expand until the costs of organizing an extra transaction within the firm become equal to the costs of carrying out the same transaction by means of an exchange on the open market or the costs of organizing in another firm. But if the firm stops its expansion at a point below the costs of marketing in the open market and at a point equal to the costs of organizing in another firm, in most cases (excluding the case of "combination"[28]), this will imply that there is a market transaction between these two producers, each of whom could organize it at less than the actual marketing costs. How is the paradox to be resolved? If we consider an example the reason for this will become clear. Suppose *A* is buying a product from *B* and that both *A* and *B* could organize this marketing transaction at less than its present cost. *B*, we can assume, is not organizing one process or stage of production, but several. If *A* therefore wishes to avoid a market transaction, he will have to take over all the processes of production controlled by *B*. Unless *A* takes over all the processes of production, a market transaction will still remain, although it is a different product that is bought. But we have previously assumed that as each producer expands he becomes less efficient; the additional costs of organizing extra transactions increase. It is probable that *A*'s cost of organizing the transactions previously organized by *B* will be greater than *B*'s cost of doing the same thing. *A* therefore will take over the whole of B's organization only if his cost of organizing *B*'s work is not greater than *B*'s cost by an amount equal to the costs of carrying out an exchange transaction on the open market. But once it becomes economical to have a market transaction, it also pays to divide production in such a way that the cost of organizing an extra transaction in each firm is the same.

Up to now it has been assumed that the exchange transactions which take place through the price mechanism are homogeneous. In fact, nothing could be more diverse than the actual transactions which take place in our modern world. This would seem to imply that the costs of carrying out exchange transactions through the price mechanism will vary considerably as will also the costs of organizing these transactions within the firm. It seems therefore possible that quite apart from the question of diminishing returns the costs of organizing certain transactions within the firm may be greater than the costs of carrying out the exchange transactions in the open market. This would necessarily imply that there were exchange transactions carried out through the price mechanism, but would it mean that there would have to be more than one firm? Clearly not, for all those areas in the economic system where the direction of resources was not dependent directly on the price mechanism could be organized within one firm. The factors which were discussed earlier would seem to be the important ones, though it is difficult to say whether "diminishing returns to management" or the rising supply price of factors is likely to be the more important.

---

[28]A definition of this term is given later.

Other things being equal, therefore, a firm will tend to be larger:

(a) the less the costs of organizing and the slower these costs rise with an increase in the transactions organized;

(b) the less likely the entrepreneur is to make mistakes and the smaller the increase in mistakes with an increase in the transactions organized;

(c) the greater the lowering (or the less the rise) in the supply price of factors of production to firms of larger size.

Apart from variations in the supply price of factors of production to firms of different sizes, it would appear that the costs of organizing and the losses through mistakes will increase with an increase in the spatial distribution of the transactions organized, in the dissimilarity of the transactions, and in the probability of changes in the relevant prices.[29] As more transactions are organized by an entrepreneur, it would appear that the transactions would tend to be either different in kind or in different places. This furnishes an additional reason why efficiency will tend to decrease as the firm gets larger. Inventions which tend to bring factors of production nearer together, by lessening spatial distribution, tend to increase the size of the firm.[30] Changes like the telephone and the telegraph which tend to reduce the cost of organizing spatially will tend to increase the size of the firm. All changes which improve managerial technique will tend to increase the size of the firm.[31] [32]

It should be noted that the definition of a firm which was given above can be used to give more precise meanings to the terms "combination" and

---

[29]This aspect of the problem is emphasized by N. Kaldor, *op. cit.* Its importance in this connection had been previously noted by E. A. G. Robinson, *The Structure of Competitive Industry, op. cit.*, pp. 83–106. This assumes that an increase in the probability of price movements increases the costs of organizing within a firm more than it increases the cost of carrying out an exchange transaction on the market—which is probable.

[30]This would appear to be the importance of the treatment of the technical unit by E. A. G. Robinson, *op. cit.*, pp. 27–33. The larger the technical unit, the greater the concentration of factors and therefore the firm is likely to be larger.

[31]It should be noted that most inventions will change both the costs of organizing and the costs of using the price mechanism. In such cases, whether the invention tends to make firms larger or smaller will depend on the relative effect on these two sets of costs. For instance, if the telephone reduces the costs of using the price mechanism more than it reduces the costs of organizing, then it will have the effect of reducing the size of the firm.

[32]An illustration of these dynamic forces is furnished by Maurice Dobb, *Russian Economic Development* (New York: E. P. Dutton and Co., 1928), p. 68. "With the passing of bonded labour the factory, as an establishment where work was organised under the whip of the overseer, lost its *raison d'être* until this was restored to it with the introduction of power machinery after 1846." It seems important to realize that the passage from the domestic system to the factory system is not a mere historical accident, but is conditioned by economic forces. This is shown by the fact that it is possible to move from the factory system to the domestic system, as in the Russian example, as well as vice versa. It is the essence of serfdom that the price mechanism is not allowed to operate. Therefore, there has to be direction from some organizer. When, however, serfdom passed, the price mechanism was allowed to operate. It was not until machinery drew workers into one locality that it paid to supersede the price mechanism and the firm again emerged.

"integration."[33] There is a combination when transactions which were previously organized by two or more entrepreneurs become organized by one. This becomes integration when it involves the organization of transactions which were previously carried out between the entrepreneurs on a market. A firm can expand in either or both of these two ways. The whole of the "structure of competitive industry" becomes tractable by the ordinary technique of economic analysis.

III

The problem which has been investigated in the previous section has not been entirely neglected by economists and it is now necessary to consider why the reasons given above for the emergence of a firm in a specialized exchange economy are to be preferred to the other explanations which have been offered.

It is sometimes said that the reason for the existence of a firm is to be found in the division of labor. This is the view of Professor Usher, a view which has been adopted and expanded by Mr. Maurice Dobb. The firm becomes

> . . . the result of an increasing complexity of the division of labour. . . . The growth of this economic differentiation creates the need for some integrating force without which differentiation would collapse into chaos; and it is as the integrating force in a differentiated economy that industrial forms are chiefly significant.[34]

The answer to this argument is an obvious one. The "integrating force in a differentiated economy" already exists in the form of the price mechanism. It is perhaps the main achievement of economic science that it has shown that there is no reason to suppose that specialization must lead to chaos.[35] The reason given by Mr. Maurice Dobb is therefore inadmissible. What has to be explained is why one integrating force (the entrepreneur) should be substituted for another integrating force (the price mechanism).

The most interesting reasons (and probably the most widely accepted) which have been given to explain this fact are those to be found in Professor Knight's *Risk, Uncertainty and Profit.* His views will be examined in some detail.

Professor Knight starts with a system in which there is no uncertainty:

> . . . acting as individuals under absolute freedom but without collusion men are supposed to have organised economic life with the primary and

---

[33]This is often called "vertical integration," combination being termed "lateral integration."

[34]Maurice Dobb, *op. cit.*, p. 10. Professor Usher's views are to be found in his *Introduction to the Industrial History of England, op. cit.*, p. 1–18.

[35]Cf. J. B. Clark, *Distribution of Wealth* (New York: Macmillan Co., 1900). p. 19, who speaks of the theory of exchange as being the "theory of the organisation of industrial society."

> secondary division of labour, the use of capital, etc., developed to the point familiar in present-day America. The principal fact which calls for the exercise of the imagination is the internal organisation of the productive groups or establishments. With uncertainty entirely absent, every individual being in possession of perfect knowledge of the situation, there would be no occasion for anything of the nature of responsible management or control of productive activity. Even marketing transactions in any realistic sense would not be found. The flow of raw materials and productive services to the consumer would be entirely automatic.[36]

Professor Knight says that we can imagine this adjustment as being "the result of a long process of experimentation worked out by trial-and-error methods alone," while it is not necessary "to imagine every worker doing exactly the right thing at the right time in a sort of 'pre-established harmony' with the work of others. There might be managers, superintendents, etc., for the purpose of co-ordinating the activities of individuals," though these managers would be performing a purely routine function, "without responsibility of any sort."[37]

Professor Knight then continues:

> With the introduction of uncertainty—the fact of ignorance and the necessity of acting upon opinion rather than knowledge—into this Eden-like situation, its character is entirely changed. . . . With uncertainty present doing things, the actual execution of activity, becomes in a real sense a secondary part of life; the primary problem or function is deciding what to do and how to do it.[38]

This fact of uncertainty brings about the two most important characteristics of social organization.

> In the first place, goods are produced for a market, on the basis of entirely impersonal prediction of wants, not for the satisfaction of the wants of the producers themselves. The producer takes the responsibility of forecasting the consumers' wants. In the second place, the work of forecasting and at the same time a large part of the technological direction and control of production are still further concentrated upon a very narrow class of producers, and we meet with a new economic functionary, the entrepreneur. . . . When uncertainty is present and the task of deciding what to do and how to do it takes the ascendancy over that of execution the internal organisation of the productive groups is no longer a matter of indifference or a mechanical detail. Centralisation of this deciding and controlling function is imperative, a process of "cephalisation" is inevitable.[39]

The most fundamental change is:

---

[36] Frank Knight, *Risk, Uncertainty and Profit* (New York: Houghton Mifflin Co., 1921), p. 267.

[37] *Ibid.*, pp. 267–8.

[38] *Op. cit.*, p. 268.

[39] *Op. cit.*, pp. 268–95.

> . . . the system under which the confident and venturesome assume the risk or insure the doubtful and timid by guaranteeing to the latter a specified income in return for an assignment of the actual results. . . . With human nature as we know it it would be impracticable or very unusual for one man to guarantee to another a definite result of the latter's actions without being given power to direct his work. And on the other hand the second party would not place himself under the direction of the first without such a guarantee. . . . The result of this manifold specialisation of function is the enterprise and wage system of industry. Its existence in the world is the direct result of the fact of uncertainty.[40]

These quotations give the essence of Professor Knight's theory. The fact of uncertainty means that people have to forecast future wants. Therefore, you get a special class springing up who direct the activities of others to whom they give guaranteed wages. It acts because good judgment is generally associated with confidence in one's judgment.[41]

Professor Knight would appear to leave himself open to criticism on several grounds. First of all, as he himself points out, the fact that certain people have better judgment or better knowledge does not mean that they can only get an income from it by themselves actively taking part in production. They can sell advice or knowledge. Every business buys the services of a host of advisers. We can imagine a system where all advice or knowledge was bought as required. Again, it is possible to get a reward from better knowledge or judgment not by actively taking part in production but by making contracts with people who are producing. A merchant buying for future delivery represents an example of this. But this merely illustrates the point that it is quite possible to give a guaranteed reward providing that certain acts are performed without directing the performance of those acts. Professor Knight says that "with human nature as we know it it would be impracticable or very unusual for one man to guarantee to another a definite result of the latter's actions without being given power to direct his work." This is surely incorrect. A large proportion of jobs are done to contract, that is, the contractor is guaranteed a certain sum providing he performs certain acts. But this does not involve any direction. It does mean, however, that the system of relative prices has been changed and that there will be a new arrangement of the factors of production.[42] The fact that Professor Knight mentions that the "second party would not place himself under the direction of the first without such a guarantee" is irrelevant to the problem we are

[40] *Op. cit.*, pp. 269–70.

[41] *Op. cit.*, p. 270.

[42] This shows that it is possible to have a private enterprise system without the existence of firms. Though, in practice, the two functions of enterprise, which actually influences the system of relative prices by forecasting wants and acting in accordance with such forecasts, and management, which accepts the system of relative prices as being given, are normally carried out by the same persons, yet it seems important to keep them separate in theory. This point is further discussed later.

considering. Finally, it seems important to notice that even in the case of an economic system where there is no uncertainty Professor Knight considers that there would be co-ordinators, though they would perform only a routine function. He immediately adds that they would be "without responsibility of any sort," which raises the question by whom are they paid and why? It seems that nowhere does Professor Knight give a reason why the price mechanism should be superseded.

IV

It would seem important to examine one further point and that is to consider the relevance of this discussion to the general question of the "cost-curve of the firm."

It has sometimes been assumed that a firm is limited in size under perfect competition if its cost curve slopes upward,[43] while under imperfect competition, it is limited in size because it will not pay to produce more than the output at which marginal cost is equal to marginal revenue.[44] But it is clear that a firm may produce more than one product and, therefore, there appears to be no *prima facie* reason why this upward slope of the cost curve in the case of perfect competition or the fact that marginal cost will not always be below marginal revenue in the case of imperfect competition should limit the size of the firm.[45] Mrs. Robinson[46] makes the simplifying assumption that only one product is being produced. But it is clearly important to investigate how the number of products produced by a firm is determined, while no theory which assumes that only one product is in fact produced can have very great practical significance.

It might be replied that under perfect competition, since everything that is produced can be sold at the prevailing price, then there is no need for any other product to be produced. But this argument ignores the fact that there may be a point where it is less costly to organize the exchange transactions of a new product than to organize further exchange transactions of the old product. This point can be illustrated in the following way. Imagine, following von Thunen, that there is a town, the consuming center, and that industries are located around this central point in rings. These conditions are illustrated in the following diagram in which *A*, *B* and *C* represent different industries.

[43]See N. Kaldor, *op. cit.,* and E. A. G. Robinson, "The Problem of Management and the Size of the Firm," *op. cit.*

[44]Mr. Robinson calls this the Imperfect Competition solution for the survival of the small firm.

[45]Mr. Robinson's conclusion, *op. cit.*, p. 249, footnote 1, would appear to be definitely wrong. He is followed by Horace J. White, Jr., "Monopolistic and Perfect Competition," *American Economic Review* (December, 1936), p. 645, footnote 27. Mr. White states, "It is obvious that the size of the firm is limited in conditions of monopolistic competition."

[46]Joan Robinson, *Economics of Imperfect Competition* (New York: St. Martins Press, 1934).

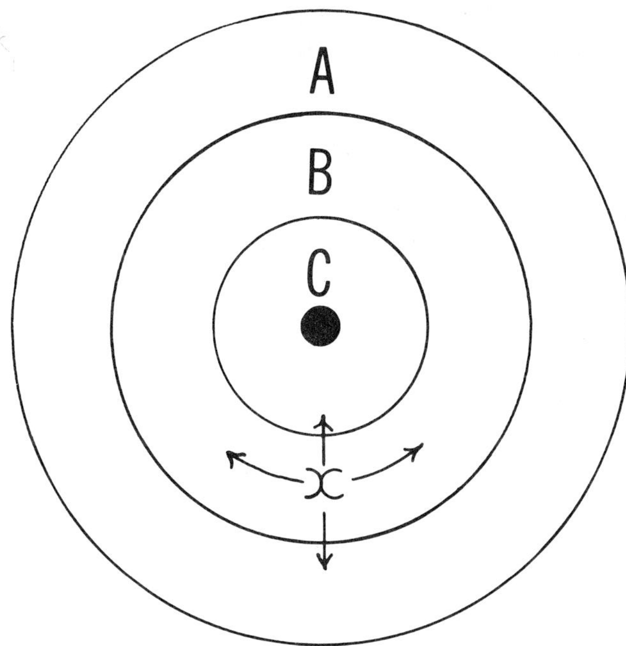

Figure 15-1

Imagine an entrepreneur who starts controlling exchange transactions from *x*. Now as he extends his activities in the same product (B), the cost of organizing increases until at some point it becomes equal to that of a dissimilar product which is nearer. As the firm expands, it will therefore from this point include more than one product (*A* and *C*). This treatment of the problem is obviously incomplete,[47] but it is necessary to show that merely proving that the cost curve turns upwards does not give a limitation to the size of the firm. So far we have only considered the case of perfect competition; the case of imperfect competition would appear to be obvious.

To determine the size of the firm, we have to consider the marketing costs (that is, the costs of using the price mechanism), and the costs of organizing of different entrepreneurs and then we can determine how many products will be produced by each firm and how much of each it will produce. It would, therefore, appear that Mr. Shove[48] in his article on "Imperfect Competition"

[47]As has been shown above, location is only one of the factors influencing the cost of organizing.

[48]G. F. Shove, "The Imperfection of the Market," *Economic Journal* (March, 1933), p. 115. In connection with an increase in demand in the suburbs and the effect on the price charged by suppliers, Mr. Shove asks ". . . why do not the old firms open branches in the surburbs?" If the argument in the text is correct, this is a question which Mrs. Robinson's apparatus cannot answer.

was asking questions which Mrs. Robinson's cost curve apparatus cannot answer. The factors mentioned above would seem to be the relevant ones.

V

Only one task now remains; and that is, to see whether the concept of a firm which has been developed fits in with that existing in the real world. We can best approach the question of what constitutes a firm in practice by considering the legal relationship normally called that of "master and servant" or "employer and employee."[49] The essentials of this relationship have been given as follows:

> (1) The servant must be under the duty of rendering personal services to the master or to others on behalf of the master, otherwise the contract is a contract for sale of goods or the like.
>
> (2) The master must have the right to control the servant's work, either personally or by another servant or agent. It is this right of control or interference, of being entitled to tell the servant when to work (within the hours of service) and when not to work, and what work to do and how to do it (within the terms of such service) which is the dominant characteristic in this relation and marks off the servant from an independent contractor, or from one employed merely to give to his employer the fruits of his labour. In the latter case, the contractor or performer is not under the employer's control in doing the work or effecting the service; he has to shape and manage his work so as to give the result he has contracted to effect.[50]

We thus see that it is the fact of direction which is the essence of the legal concept of "employer and employee," just as it was in the economic concept which was developed above. It is interesting to note that Professor Batt says further:

> That which distinguishes an agent from a servant is not the absence or presence of a fixed wage or the payment only of commission on business done, but rather the freedom with which an agent may carry out his employment.[51]

We can, therefore, conclude that the definition we have given is one which approximates closely to the firm as it is considered in the real world.

Our definition is, therefore, realistic. Is it manageable? This ought to be clear. When we are considering how large a firm will be the principle of marginalism works smoothly. The question always is, will it pay to bring an extra

[49]The legal concept of "employer and employee" and the economic concept of a firm are not identical, in that the firm may imply control over another person's property as well as over their labor. But the identity of these two concepts is sufficiently close for an examination of the legal concept to be of value in appraising the worth of the economic concept.

[50]Batt, *op. cit.*, p. 6.

[51]*Op. cit.*, p. 7.

exchange transaction under the organizing authority? At the margin, the costs of organizing within the firm will be equal either to the costs of organizing in another firm or to the costs involved in leaving the transaction to be "organized" by the price mechanism. Business men will be constantly experimenting, controlling more or less, and in this way, equilibrium will be maintained. This gives the position of equilibrium for static analysis. But it is clear that the dynamic factors are also of considerable importance, and an investigation of the effect changes have on the cost of organizing within the firm and on marketing costs generally will enable one to explain why firms get larger and smaller. We thus have a theory of moving equilibrium. The above analysis would also appear to have clarified the relationship between initiative or enterprise and management. Initiative means forecasting and operates through the price mechanism by the making of new contracts. Management proper merely reacts to price changes, rearranging the factors of production under its control. That the business man normally combines both functions is an obvious result of the marketing costs which were discussed above. Finally, this analysis enables us to state more exactly what is meant by the "marginal product" of the entrepreneur. But an elaboration of this point would take us far from our comparatively simple task of definition and clarification.

16. ECONOMIC THEORY AND THE MEANING OF COMPETITION*

Paul J. McNulty†

There is probably no concept in all of economics that is at once more fundamental and pervasive, yet less satisfactorily developed, than the concept of competition. Although the hesitancy and inconsistency which has characterized the history of American competitive policy is doubtless partly due, as is often emphasized, to the fact that competition is, in our system, a political and social *desideratum* no less than an economic one, with some possible resulting conflict between these various values,[1] surely it is due also to the failure of economists adequately to define competition. Not the least among the many achievements of economic science has been the ability to erect a rigorous analytical system on the principle of competition — a principle so basic to economic reasoning that not even such powerful yet diverse critics of orthodox theory as Marx and Keynes could avoid relying upon it — without ever clearly specifying what, exactly, competition is. The purpose of this paper is to examine some of the factors which account for this curious development, and to indicate some specific inadequacies of the economic concept of competition both for analysis and for policy.

I

Probably the most general tendency concerning the meaning of competition in economic theory is to regard it as the opposite of monopoly. An unfortunate result of this way of thinking has been no little confusion concerning the

*From *Quarterly Journal of Economics*, Vol. LXXXII, No. 4 (November, 1968), pp. 639–656. Reprinted by permission of the publisher and the author.

†Paul J. McNulty, Associate Professor, Graduate School of Business, Columbia University. The author is indebted to his colleague, Maurice Wilkinson, for a number of helpful suggestions and comments. Needless to say, the author is solely responsible for the views expressed herein. He also wishes to acknowledge the financial support provided by the faculty research fund of the Graduate School of Business, Columbia University.

[1]"It is possible, because of its indirect social or moral effect, to prefer a system of small producers, each dependent for his success upon his own skill and character, to one in which the great mass of those engaged must accept the direction of a few." *United States* v. *Aluminum Company of America*, 148 F. 2d 416 (1945). "Of course, some of the results of large integrated or chain operations are beneficial to consumers . . . But we cannot fail to recognize Congress' desire to promote competition through the protection of viable, small, locally owned businesses. Congress appreciated that occasional higher costs and prices might result from the maintenance of fragmented industries and markets. It resolved these competing considerations in favor of decentralization." *Brown Shoe Co.* v. *United States*, 370 U.S. 294 (1962).

relationship between economic efficiency and business behavior. There is a striking contrast in economic literature between the analytical rigor and precision of competition when it is described as a market structure, and the ambiguity surrounding the idea of competition whenever it is discussed in behavioral terms. Since, as Hayek has rightly noted, "the law cannot effectively prohibit states of affairs but only kinds of action,"[2] a concept of economic competition, if it is to be significant for economic policy, ought to relate to patterns of business behavior such as might reasonably be associated with the verb "to compete." That was the case with the competition which Adam Smith made the central organizing principle of economic society in the *Wealth of Nations*, and with the competition whose effects Cournot, in the first formal statement of the idea of "perfect" competition, could accurately claim to be "realized, in social economy, for a multitude of products, and, among them, for the most important products."[3] Whether it was seen as price undercutting by sellers, the bidding up of prices by buyers, or the entry of new firms into profitable industries, the fact is that competition entered economics as a concept which had empirical relevance and operational meaning in terms of contemporary business behavior. Yet on the question of whether such common current practices as advertising, product variation, price undercutting, or other forms of business activity do or do not constitute competition, modern economic theory offers the clarification that they are "monopolistically" competitive. While this is a useful way of illustrating the truth that most markets are in some degree both controlled and controlling, it is less useful as a guide in implementing a policy, such as our antitrust policy, which seeks at once to restrain monopoly and promote competition. It is too late in the history of economics, and it is surely not in any way here the purpose, to de-emphasize the truly monumental character of E. H. Chamberlin's great achievement a generation ago[4] in reconciling economic theory with the undeniable fact that much of the business world was really a mixture of competition and monopoly, as those concepts were then defined in economics, which fitted neither of those traditional economic models of business enterprise. But it is not, perhaps, too late to suggest that the traditional distinction between competition and monopoly was, in a fundamental sense, inappropriate to begin with, and that the merging of the concepts in a theory of monopolistic competition, while representing a profound improvement over the simplicity of the older classification, and giving microeconomics a new vitality almost comparable to that which Keynes was at the same time bringing to employment theory, has, nonetheless, allowed us to avoid defining a concept of competition, *as distinct from the concept of a competitive market*, which

[2]F. A. Hayek, *The Constitution of Liberty* (Chicago: University of Chicago Press, 1960), p. 265.

[3]Augustin Cournot, *Researches into the Mathematical Principles of the Theory of Wealth*, translated by Nathaniel T. Bacon (New York: Macmillan, 1929), p. 90.

[4]Edward H. Chamberlin, *The Theory of Monopolistic Competition* (Cambridge, Mass.: Harvard University Press, 1956).

is at once relevant and adequate both for economic analysis and for economic policy.

Clearly, the failure to distinguish between the idea of competition and the idea of market structure is at the root of much of the ambiguity concerning the meaning of competition. As far as market structure, conceived of in terms of the paucity or plethora of sellers (buyers), is the appropriate focus of analysis, consistency would suggest relying on terms such as monopoly (sony), duopoly, triopoly, oligopoly, polypoly, and, perhaps, a newly-coined term ending in "poly," the prefix of which means an indefinitely large number.[5] Such a classification, although it would add to an already cumbersome body of technical jargon, would nonetheless retain for market taxonomy the analytical usefulness it currently possesses, while having the further advantage of eliminating much of the confusion that now exists between competition and monopoly. As it is, it is one of the great paradoxes of economic science that every *act* of competition on the part of a businessman is evidence, in economic theory, of some degree of monopoly power, while the concepts of monopoly and perfect competition have this important common feature: both are situations in which the possibility of any competitive behavior has been ruled out by definition.

That perfect competition is an ideal state, incapable of actual realization, is a familiar theme of economic literature. That for various reasons it would be less than altogether desirable, even if it were attainable, is also widely acknowledged. But that perfect competition is a state of affairs quite incompatible with the idea of any and all competition has been insufficiently emphasized. It is this last feature of perfect competition, and not, as is sometimes incorrectly claimed, its high level of abstraction or the "unreality" of its assumptions, which limits its usefulness, especially for economic policy. What needs more stress than it has generally received is not the inescapably abstract and "unreal" nature of theory but, rather, the fact that while all other forms of competition represent, in economic theory, an *admixture* of monopoly and competition, perfect competition itself means the *absence* of competition in quite as compete a sense, although for different reasons, as does pure monopoly. Monopoly is a market situation in which intra-industry competition has been defined away by identifying the firm as the industry. Perfect competition, on the other hand, is a market situation which, although itself the *result* of the free entry of a large number of formerly competing firms, has evolved or progressed to the point (of equilibrium) where no *further* competition within the industry is possible, or, in the words of A. A. Cournot, its intellectual parent, to the point where "the effects of competition have reached their limit."[6] It is for this reason that Frank Knight can

[5]Professor Machlup has employed a classification along these lines, adding the term"pliopoly" (more sellers) to cover the condition of free entry. Fritz Machlup, *The Economics of Sellers' Competition* (Baltimore: The Johns Hopkins Press, 1952), Chapter 4.

[6]Cournot, *op. cit.*, p. 90.

correctly stress, as he often has, that perfect competition involves "no presumption of psychological competition, emulation, or rivalry,"[7] and can rightly assert that " 'atomism' is a better term for the idea."[8] Perfect competition, the only clearly and rigorously defined concept of competition to be found in the corpus of economic theory, which is free of all traces of business behavior associated with "monopolistic" elements, means simply the *existence* of an indefinitely large number of noncompeting firms. Economists have sometimes criticized American competitive policy for its not infrequently manifested tendency over the years to identify the maintenance of competition with the maintenance of competitors. But economic theory offers no clear guide for distinguishing between them. To the extent that we look to economics for an answer to the question "What are the advantages of competition over monopoly?," we ought also to be able to look to economics for an answer to the question "How may a business firm be expected to compete without monopolizing?" And the critical reader will search economic literature in vain for a clear answer to that question.

An analysis of the ambiguities and weaknesses of the competitive concept confirms the correctness of Schumpeter's assertion (despite the apparently widely held contemporary view to the contrary) that in economics "modern problems, methods and results cannot be fully understood without some knowledge of how economists have come to reason as they do."[9] In order fully to understand how our thinking on competition has come to be what it is, it is necessary, then, to examine briefly the emergence and evolution of the concept within the larger framework of the historical development of economic science.

II

Although competition, as we noted earlier, has usually been conceived of as being in general the opposite of monopoly, the conception has taken two basic, and fundamentally different, forms. On the one hand, it has been the "force" which, by equating prices and marginal costs, assures allocative efficiency in the use of resources. Competition in this sense is somewhat analogous to the force of gravitation in physical science; through competition, resources "gravitate" toward their most productive uses, and, through competition, price is "forced" to the lowest level which is sustainable over the long run. Thus viewed, competition assures order and stability in the economic world much as does gravitation in the physical world. But competition has also been conceived of in a second way, as a descriptive term characterizing a particular (idealized) situation. The concept of perfect competition, for example, to continue the comparison with physical science, is analogous not to

[7]Frank H. Knight, "Immutable Law in Economics: Its Reality and Limitations," *American Economic Review*, Vol. XXXVI (May, 1946), p. 102.

[8]*Loc. cit.*

[9]Joseph A. Schumpeter, *History of Economic Analysis* (New York: Oxford University Press, 1954), p. 6.

the principle of gravitation but rather to the idea of a perfect vacuum; it is not an "ordering force" but rather an assumed "state of affairs" — one which, although an "unrealistic," — indeed, unrealizable, — abstraction, is nonetheless a useful analytical device. That competition has been conceived of in these two quite different ways is of no small importance in explaining the ambiguity and confusion which has surrounded the concept.

It was the conception of competition as an ordering force which dominated classical economics. When Adam Smith spoke of competition, it was in connection with the forcing of market price to its "natural" level[10] or to the lowering of profits to a minimum.[11] It was not competition and monopoly per se, or as market models, which Adam Smith contrasted, but rather the level of prices resulting from the presence or absence of competition as a regulatory force.[12] Indeed, so unsystematic was any association between the idea of competition and that of market structure for Adam Smith that he applied the term to duopoly almost exactly as he did to a market in which a larger number of firms operated. If the capital sufficient to satisfy the demand for groceries in a particular town "is divided between two different grocers," he wrote, "their competition will tend to make both of them sell cheaper, than if it were in the hands of one only."[13] Although Smith and the classical economists generally acknowledged that competition was more effective with a larger number than with a smaller number of competitors, competition was viewed as a price-determining force operating in, but not itself identified as, a market. On this, Ricardo was explicit:

> In speaking, then, of commodities, of their exchangeable value, and of the laws which regulate their relative prices, we mean always such commodities . . . on the production of which *competition operates* without restraint.[14]

And John Stuart Mill wrote:

> So far as rents, profits, wages, prices, are determined by competition, laws may be assigned for them. Assume competition to be their exclusive regulator and principles of broad generality and scientific precision may be laid down, according to which they will be regulated.[15]

---

[10]Adam Smith, *The Wealth of Nations* (New York: Modern Library, 1937), pp. 56–7.

[11]*Ibid.*, p. 87.

[12]"The price of monopoly is upon every occasion the highest which can be got. The natural price, or the price of free competition, on the contrary, is the lowest which can be taken . . . for any considerable time together." *Ibid.*, p. 61.

[13]*Ibid.*, p. 342.

[14]David Ricardo, *The Principles of Political Economy and Taxation* (London: J. M. Dent, 1955), p. 6, emphasis added.

[15]John Stuart Mill, *Principles of Political Economy*, Vol. I (New York: D. Appleton, 1864), p. 306.

The "perfection" of the concept of competition, that is, the emergence of the idea of competition as itself a market structure, was a distinguishing contribution of neoclassical economics. The groundwork for this development was laid by Cournot, whose interest was in specifying, as rigorously as possible, the *effects* of competition. According to him, the effects of competition had reached their limit when the output of each firm was "inappreciable" with respect to total industry output, and could be subtracted from the total output "without any appreciable variation resulting in the price of the commodity."[16] This implied a very large number of sellers, but Cournot was not much more explicit on the subject of market structure, and it was only with Jevons[17] and Edgeworth[18] in the late nineteenth century, that the actual wedding of the concepts of competition and the market was effected, leading ultimately, after refinements by J. B. Clark[19] and Frank Knight,[20] to the concept of perfect competition as we know it today.[21] As Stigler has rightly stressed, "the merging of the concepts of competition and the market was unfortunate, for each deserved a full and separate treatment."

> A market is an institution for the consummation of transactions. It performs this function efficiently when every buyer who will pay more than the minimum realized price for any class of commodities succeeds in buying the commodity, and every seller who will sell it for less than the maximum realized price succeeds in selling the commodity. . . . A market may be perfect and monopolistic or imperfect and competitive. Jevons' mixture of the two has been widely imitated by successors, of course, so that even today a market is commonly treated as a concept subsidiary to competition.[22]

Although we can agree that "the merging of the concepts of competition and the market was unfortunate," it is probably more accurate to say that competition has been conceived of as a concept subsidiary to that of the market rather than the other way around. In fact, Jevons' "mixture" of the concepts may be viewed as a development which was thoroughly in the tradition of, and indeed, perhaps only a logical consequence of, the historical tendency on the part of economists to identify competition as entirely a phenomenon of exchange. For, if the classical economists did not, like their neoclassical successors, identify competition with a *particular* market structure, they did nonetheless conceive of it as taking place exclusively *in* the

---

[16]Cournot, *op. cit.*, p. 90.

[17]W. Stanley Jevons, *The Theory of Political Economy* (4th ed.; London: Macmillan, 1911).

[18]F. Y. Edgeworth, *Mathematical Psychics* (London: C. Kegan Paul, 1881).

[19]J. B. Clark, *The Distribution of Wealth* (New York: Macmillan, 1900).

[20]Frank H. Knight, *Risk, Uncertainty and Profit*, Series of Reprints of Scarce Tracts, No. 16 (London: London School of Economics and Political Science, 1933).

[21]George J. Stigler, "Perfect Competition, Historically Contemplated," *Journal of Political Economy*, Vol. LXV (February, 1957), pp. 1–17.

[22]*Ibid.*, p. 6.

various markets in which the business firm was operating. Competition, that is, was never related in any systematic way to the technique of production within, or to the organizational form of, the business firm itself. The concept has thus been divorced, since the earliest days of scientific economic analysis, from a major area or facet of economic activity.

Economic goods and services possess, broadly speaking, two characteristics: quality and price. In a free enterprise economy, moreover, there are two primary institutions through which resources are organized, transformed, and channeled for ultimate consumption as goods or services: the private business firm and the market. These institutions correspond to the two characteristics possessed by economic goods. Production, or the determination of physical form, or quality, takes place within the business firm; exchange, or the determination of economic value, or price, within the various markets in which the firm operates. However, although economic activity encompasses both production and exchange, the concepts of competition has been generally associated only with the latter. The operations of the business firm, except for the exchange relationships associated with its purchase or sale of a factor, product, or service, have not traditionally come within the meaning of competition nor, indeed, have they been a part of economic theory generally. In economic analysis, one firm is seen as differing from another only with respect to the kind of product or factor market in which it buys or sells, and the economic system as a whole is seen not as a complex set of varied and changing institutions but, rather, the process of buying and selling is isolated as the critical element of economic activity and the economy is viewed as simply "a system of interrelated markets."[23] In short, as Allyn Young once put it, "for system's sake, the whole material equipment of human living is recast in molds fashioned after the notions of catallactics."[24]

Both the dominance of exchange, and hence of price, in economic theory generally, and the limitation of the concept of competition specifically to the firm's external relationships in the market, relate to the way in which competition entered economics and came to occupy the position of primacy which it has held in the science ever since the work of Adam Smith. In one sense Smith was, and in another sense he was not, the great "prophet of competition"[25] that historians of the subject have often made him appear to be. Smith was a prophet of competition in that he did for the concept what no others before him did so effectively: he made it literally a general organizing principle of economic society and of economic analysis. No writer before Smith presented so effectively the conception of competition as a force which,

---

[23]Lloyd G. Reynolds, *The Structure of Labor Markets* (New York: Harper, 1951), p. 1.

[24]Allyn A. Young, "Some Limitations of the Value Concept," *Quarterly Journal of Economics*, Vol. XXV (May, 1911), p. 424.

[25]John Maurice Clark, *Competition as a Dynamic Process* (Washington: The Brookings Institution, 1961), p. 24.

operating in an atmosphere of "perfect liberty," would lead self-seeking individuals unconsciously to serve the general welfare. In a sense, Smith did for economics, through the principle of competition, precisely what he himself credited Newton with having done for physics and astronomy through the principle of gravity; "the discovery of an immense chain of the most important and sublime truths, all closely connected together, by one capital fact, of the reality of which we have daily experience."[26] But while Smith gave to competition an intellectual and ideological significance it had never had before, neither its specific economic meaning, nor its particular analytical function, was original with him. On the contrary, he incorporated into the *Wealth of Nations* a concept of competition already well developed in the economic literature of his time. That concept was a behavioral one, the essence of which was the effort of the individual seller to undersell, or the individual buyer to outbid, his rivals in the marketplace, and had earlier been employed and developed by a number of writers including Cantillon, Turgot, Hume, Steuart, and others, in their various efforts to explain how price was, in a free market, ultimately forced to a level which would just cover costs, that is, to the lowest level which would be sustainable over the long run.[27] Thus, although Smith played a major role in making the principle of competition quite literally the *sine qua non* of economic analysis, to the extent that Ricardo would later contemplate only cases in which "competition operates without restraint,"[28] and John Stuart Mill would go on to assert that "only through the principle of competition has political economy any pretension to the character of a science,"[29] he contributed little, if anything, to its economic meaning.

Had the concept of competition in fact been, as is often implied, a major contribution of Adam Smith, or had he added significantly to its economic meaning, there is some reason, indeed, to suppose that economic theory would have produced at an early date a concept of competition not unlike that later called for by Schumpeter, that is, competition associated with internal industrial efficiency and with the development of "the new technology, the new source of supply, [and] the new type of organization."[30] For Smith after all, writing in the environment of the English industrial revolution, was eminently aware of the importance of dynamic changes in productive technique and industrial organization, which he somewhat loosely termed "the division of labor." It was precisely the productive and organizational relationships within the business enterprise and not, as with the physiocrats, the natural fertility of the soil, or, as with the mercantilists, exchange in the market per se, which

[26]Adam Smith, "The History of Astronomy," *The Works of Adam Smith, LL.D.*, Vol. V, edited by Dugald Stewart (Aalen: Otto Zeller, 1963), pp. 189–90.

[27]Paul J. McNulty, "A Note on the History of Perfect Competition," *Journal of Political Economy*, Vol. LXXV (August, 1967), Part I, pp. 395–99.

[28]Ricardo, *op. cit.*, p. 6.

[29]Mill, *op. cit.*, p. 306.

[30]Joseph A. Schumpeter, *Capitalism, Socialism and Democracy* (New York: Harper and Row, 1962), p. 84.

was for Adam Smith the ultimate source of economic surplus and the essential basis of economic activity. But having opened the *Wealth of Nations* with an uncommonly strong tribute to the idea of division of labor and the associated productive efficiency to be found within the contemporary business firm, Smith curiously failed to relate productive technique to the concept of competition, the central organizing principle upon which, according to him, society could safely in most cases depend. At one point, it is true, he did speak of "the competition of producers who, in order to undersell one another, have recourse to new divisions of labour, and new improvements of art, which might never otherwise have been thought of."[31] But this was little more than a passing comment, and came only in Book V, well after his extended, but separate, discussions of competition and division of labor in Book I. Moreover, the "recourse to new divisions of labour and new improvements of art" were clearly subsidiary aspects of his concept of competition, the essence of which was the effort to undersell in the market by lowering price. As division of labor was limited by the extent of the market, so its analysis in terms of the organization of production within the business firm came to be circumscribed, even for Adam Smith, by the analysis of the firm's external market relationships. Not the essence of the industrial revolution — the changing mode of production — but rather, the mercantilists' overriding concern with price, continued, with Smith, to be the central theme of economic analysis. The division of labor came, with his successors, to be "given" as "the state of the arts," changes in which were ruled out through the use of the "pound of *ceteris paribus*," and competition continued to be consistently viewed in terms of exchange relationships between existing and unchanging economic units.[32]

Although the classical economists thus viewed competition as exclusively a market process, the neoclassical development of the concept of perfect

[31]Smith, *op. cit.*, p. 706.

[32]This is not to suggest that the leading neoclassical economists were unaware of the dynamic aspects of competition. Their failure was in their inability to integrate these aspects systematically into their economic theory. J. B. Clark, for example, in *The Essentials of Economic Theory — as Applied to Modern Problems of Industry and Public Policy* (New York: Macmillan, 1915), a volume on economic dynamics which followed his static analysis of *The Distribution of Wealth*, and which made it clear that he was eminently aware of the significance of the changing mode of production, spoke of "the competition which is active enough to change the standard shape of society rapidly — that, for example, which spurs on mechanical invention" (p. 198), and of those situations in which "competition has reduced the establishments in one subgroup to a half dozen or less" (p. 201). But it was Clark's static analysis of perfect competition, and not his observations on economic change, or on the dynamic aspects of competition, which had a permanent effect on the development of economic theory. Marshall, too, took a quite realistic view of competition. But (and perhaps for that very reason) Marshall's impact on the development of the concept of competition, in contrast to his impact on economics generally, was minimal. Indeed, as Stigler has noted (*op. cit.*, p. 9), Marshall's "treatment of competition was much closer to Adam Smith's than to that of his contemporaries, . . . [and was] almost as informal and unsystematic."

competition as itself a market structure nonetheless represented a sharp discontinuity in the development of social thought, for, although competition, according to the older view, took place exclusively within the market, the latter was always seen as allowing for individual initiative in buying and selling. That is, although the classical economists largely ignored the entrepreneurial function as far as it was concerned with operations within the business enterprise, their concept of competition was a disequilibrium one of market activity, with price a variable from the standpoint of the individual firm. Perfect competition, on the other hand, is an equilibrium situation in which price becomes a parameter from the standpoint of the individual firm and no market activity is possible. Thus, the classical concept of competition as a guiding force, to which we earlier referred, is not only different from that of the neoclassical concept of competition as a state of affairs; the two are incompatible in a fundamental sense, reflecting precisely the difference between a condition of equilibrium and the behavioral pattern leading to it. As Hayek has rightly noted, the idea of perfect competition

> . . . throughout assumes that state of affairs already to exist which, according to the truer view of the older theory, the process of competition tends to bring about (or to approximate) . . . [and] if the state of affairs assumed by the theory of perfect competition ever existed, it would not only deprive of their scope all the activities which the verb 'to compete' describes but would make them virtually impossible.[33]

Thus, the single activity which best characterized the meaning of competition in classical economics — price cutting by an individual firm in order to get rid of excess supplies — becomes the one activity impossible under perfect competition. And what for the classical economists was the single analytical function of the competitive process — the determination of market price — becomes, with perfect competition, the one thing unexplained and unaccounted for.[34] The perfection of competition thus drained the concept of all behavioral content, so that, using perfect competition as a standard, even price competition, the essence of the competitive process for Adam Smith, is imperfect or monopolistic. That perfect competition has come to be "a rigorously defined concept"[35] is not to be denied. But the result of that rigorous definition is that the verb "to compete" has no meaning in economic

---

[33]F. A. Hayek, *Individualism and Economic Order (Chicago: University of Chicago Press, 1948), pp. 92, 96.*

[34]As Arrow has pointed out, "there exists a logical gap in the usual formulation of the theory of the perfectly competitive economy, . . . [in that] there is no place for a rational decision with respect to prices as there is with respect to quantities." Kenneth J. Arrow, "Towards a Theory of Price Adjustment," in Moses Abramovitz, *et al.*, *The Allocation of Economic Resources* (Stanford, Calif.: Stanford University Press, 1959), p. 41.

[35]Stigler, *op. cit.*, p. 11.

theory except in connection with activities which are also in some sense "monopolistic." Indeed, the perfectly competitive firm itself is but "a monopolist with a special environment."[36]

III

Some of the ambiguity concerning the relationship between the idea of perfect competition and business behavior might perhaps have been avoided if Cournot had not designated as "the hypothesis of unlimited competition" the very state of affairs which he had earlier characterized as that in which "the effects of competition have reached their limit."[37] But the classical, behavioral, "imperfect" concept of (price) competition itself possessed certain inherent weaknesses, which have persisted in economic theory to the present day. The remainder of this paper will be concerned with identifying what seem to be the most important of these, and with indicating their relevance for economic analysis and policy.

One fundamental deficiency of competition as the concept has been employed in economic theory is that it has never been related in a systematic way to costs of production. There has been a curious dichotomy in economic science in the assumption that self-interest alone will insure that the businessman will work optimally in the interests of society within the business enterprise, or in his *administration* of owned or hired resources and factors of production, while without the enterprise, in his *buying and selling* of factors or products in the market, either an "invisible hand" of competition, or a "visible hand" of public policy, is needed to insure efficiency. Although Adam Smith observed that monopoly "is a great enemy to good management, which can never be universally established but in consequence of that free and universal competition which forces everybody to have recourse to it for the sake of self-defence,"[38] his successors failed systematically to relate competition to the search for cost reduction or to "good management" generally. On the contrary, the competitive and monopolistic firms of economic theory differ only with respect to the *demand* curves they face, and the single analytical function of competition has been to get price down to the level of marginal cost. "Under free competition," as Senior wrote, "cost of production is the regulator of price."[39] But the question remains: what is the regulator of cost? Economic theory stresses the optimality of the equation of price and marginal cost. There is nothing in this equation, however, if marginal cost is higher than need be due to internal inefficiencies, and there is reason, indeed, to suppose that the latter is not infrequently the case. Chandler's research in the history of American business administration points

[36]Arrow, *op. cit.*, p. 45.

[37]Cournot, *op. cit.*, pp. 90–91.

[38]Smith, *op. cit.*, p. 147.

[39]Nassau W. Senior, *An Outline of the Science of Political Economy* (New York: Augustus M. Kelly, 1951), p. 102.

up the significance of the search for cost-reducing methods *within the company itself* as one of the significant forces shaping the reorganization of American industry around the turn of the century. The 1901 Annual Report of the National Biscuit Company, for example, highlighted the company's dissatisfaction with its earlier policies of price competition and acquisition of competitors.

> The first meant a ruinous war of prices and a great loss of profits; the second, constantly increased capitalization. . . . We soon satisfied ourselves that within the company itself we must look for success.
>
> We turned our attention and bent our energies to improving the internal management of our business, to getting full benefit from purchasing our raw materials in large quantities, to economizing the expenses of manufacture, to systematizing and rendering more effective our selling department, and above all things and before all things to improving the quality of our goods and the conditions in which they should reach the customer.[40]

There is, of course, nothing in this list of undertakings which is inconsistent with the postulates of economic theory. On the contrary, the trouble is precisely that economic theory assumes the company should have been doing those things all along. To say that this company was not operating in a fully (or even moderately) competitive market is not to eliminate the problem. The fact is that there is no explanation even in the theory of the perfectly competitive firm for the minimization of costs; the latter is merely assumed. If all firms are equally inefficient in internal administration, a perfectly competitive equilibrium could involve a welfare loss not less significant than any which might result from market imperfections.

That there may currently be considerable room for increased efficiency within business enterprises is suggested by the evidence Leibenstein has summarized concerning the existence of what he calls "X-inefficiencies," — those which, unlike "allocative inefficiencies," stem not from imperfections in the structure of the market but rather from the fact that "for a variety of reasons people and organizations normally work neither as hard nor as effectively as they could."[41] If economic efficiency is truly a goal of competitive policy, and if Leibenstein is correct that "in a great many instances the amount to be gained by increasing allocative efficiency is trivial while the amount to be gained by increasing X-efficiency is frequently significant,"[42] the desirability of a new dimension in American competitive policy no less than in the economic concept of competition— one which will relate to principles of managerial science as well as to those of market taxonomy — is apparent.

Another fundamental weakness of the competitive concept, and one not unrelated to the above discussion, has been its consistent failure to relate to

---

[40]Alfred D. Chandler, Jr., *Strategy and Structure* (Cambridge, Mass.: The Massachusetts Institute of Technology Press, 1962), p. 33.

[41]Harvey Leibenstein, "Allocative Efficiency vs. 'X-Efficiency,' " *American Economic Review*, Vol. LVI (June, 1966), p. 413.

[42]*Ibid.*

economic growth. In this respect, competition seems never to have fully recovered from the influence of Ricardo, who, in a letter to Malthus, once wrote:

> Political Economy you think is an enquiry into the nature and causes of wealth — I think it should rather be called an enquiry into the laws which determine the division of the produce of industry amongst the classes who concur in its formation. . . . Every day I am more satisfied that the former enquiry is vain and delusive, and the latter only the true object of science.[43]

The analytical refinement of the concept of competition, from the work of Cournot to that of Frank Knight, is at one with this general point of view. Edgeworth's definition of a "perfect field of competition," for example, ran entirely in terms of contracting and recontracting over the division of an existing and unchanging quantity of economic resources.[44] Although economic theory is no longer coterminous with price theory, and although the question of allocative efficiency now seems, indeed, to be of less urgency and relevance than that of economic growth (the precise relationship between the two being, apparently, a matter of considerable uncertainty), the concept of competition has been only partially transformed from one of pure catallactics to one more closely related to the question of economic change. It is true that the beginnings of such a transformation are to be found in Chamberlin's reformulation, especially in his analysis of the product as a variable, his attention to sales effort, and in his general emphasis on commodities as "the most volatile things in the economic system."[45] But the focus of the Chamberlinian analysis is still allocative efficiency, and much more needs to be done by way of systematically relating product and sales competition to economic change and growth. Moreover, Chamberlin's emphasis on variability of the product needs to be complemented by an increased emphasis on the variability of the form of the business firm itself and of the conditions under which commodities are produced and distributed — the latter being, perhaps, hardly less "volatile" than commodities themselves, and undoubtedly of no less significance for the overall growth process.

It was precisely during the years when the concept of competition was being analytically refined by becoming more and more closely identified with the atomistic market at the hands of Jevons, Edgeworth, J. B. Clark, and Knight,[46] that the industrial structures of the advanced economies of the world were taking shape, largely through changes in organizational forms which had little to do with price competition except in terms of the search for ways to avoid it. The analysis of these changes — indeed, the whole question of economic growth — was by that time largely becoming the province

---

[43]Piero Sraffa (ed.), *Works and Correspondence*, Vol. VIII (Cambridge, England: Cambridge University Press, 1958), p. 278.

[44]Edgeworth, *op. cit.*, pp. 17–19.

[45]*Towards a More General Theory of Value* (New York: Oxford University Press, 1957), p. 114.

[46]Stigler, *op. cit.*

of the newly emerging discipline of economic history, which has necessarily had to give a broader meaning to competition than that traditionally associated with economic theory. The theorist cannot, for example, view the transformation of (say) the meat-packing industry in the United States during those years as a "competitive" development, for it was a movement which resulted in a market structure dominated by a "Big Four" or "Big Five"—results exactly opposite to those specified by Cournot. The historian, on the other hand, can—indeed, must—view this development as an adaptive response on the part of Armour, Morris, Cudahy, and Schwarzschild and Sulzberger, who, faced with the innovations in production and marketing introduced by Gustavus Swift, "had to build similarly integrated organizations" if they were "to compete effectively."[47] It is well known that the essence of industrialization and economic growth is a changing production function and the development of new products, techniques, and forms of business organization. What has been lacking is any systematic effort to relate these changes to the concept of competition. The separation of so central a concept of economic theory from much of the analysis of our most pressing economic problem is unfortunate. Clearly, the time has come to incorporate into *the mainstream of economic theory* (as distinct from monographs on "new" or "workable" competition recurrently emerging in the specialized literature of industrial organization) a concept of competition closer to that occasionally suggested by Adam Smith and strongly advocated by Schumpeter—competition associated with new "divisions of labor" within the business firm and in the industrial structure generally, and one that is more closely allied with concepts of "internal, especially technological, efficiency."[48] It is unfortunate that Schumpeter's defense of monopoly and big business has tended to overshadow his insights into the competitive process, insights which extended beyond those of even Chamberlin because they included an appreciation of the importance of changing methods of production and forms of industrial organization. Although Schumpeter was probably wrong, as recent evidence suggests,[49] in his assertion that "the large scale establishment . . . has come to be the most powerful engine of progress and in particular of the long-run expansion of total output,"[50] he seems less likely to be mistaken in his insistence that, at least from the standpoint of economic growth,

> . . . it is not . . . [price] competition which counts but the competition from the new commodity, the new technology, the new source of supply, the new type of organization . . . competition which commands a decisive cost or quality advantage and which strikes not at the margin of the profits

[47]Chandler, *op. cit.*, p. 26.

[48]Schumpeter, *op. cit.*, p. 106.

[49]F. M. Scherer, "Firm Size, Market Structure, Opportunity, and the Output of Patented Inventions," *American Economic Review*, Vol. LV (Part I, December, 1965), pp. 1097–1125.

[50]Schumpeter, *op. cit.*, p. 106.

and the outputs of the existing firms but at their foundations and their very lives.[51]

Finally, a persistent weakness of the concept of competition has been the tendency of economists to minimize, ignore, or deny, its externally interdependent nature, that is, the extent to which the competition of one economic unit tends to affect the economic position of others, and thus, the overall industrial structure. Despite the etymology of the verb (literally, "to seek together"), to compete, in economic theory, has generally meant to act independently. "The meaning of 'competition,' " Frank Knight has written, is simply that the competing units "are numerous and act independently."[52] Even the literature of the so-called "new" or "workable" competition reflects the influence of this way of thinking.[53] This emphasis on independence has meant a close conceptual connection between competition, on the one hand, and both economic rationality and economic freedom, on the other. Thus Henry Moore, in his classic categorization of the various meanings given to competition in economic theory concluded that "the essential meaning of the term" is that "every economic factor seeks and obtains a maximum net income,"[54] and Knight, on another occasion, wrote: "What competition actually means is simply the freedom of the individual to 'deal' with any and all other individuals and to select the best terms as judged by himself, among those offered."[55]

The trouble with this view is that it fails to specify *how* the competing units act, either in terms of securing a "maximum net income" or in "dealing" with "any and all other individuals." Moreover, it ascribes to the competing unit altogether too passive a pattern of behavior. Rather than merely "selecting" the best terms among those offered, a competitor may well choose to try to twist the terms of trade to his own advantage. In this respect, as Morris Copeland has rightly noted, "competition frequently means discrimination."

In fact a competitor that gets ahead in an industry may do so in substantial part by developing business connections, i.e., arrangements that give him preferential treatment in terms of financing, in terms of purchase,

---

[51]*Ibid.*, p. 84.

[52]Knight, "Immutable Laws in Economics," *op. cit.*, p. 102.

[53]In his last major work, J. M. Clark shifted his emphasis from "workable" to "effective" competition, and then went on to say:

> For the competition to be effective, *the crucial thing seems to be that prices be independently made* under conditions that give some competitors an incentive to aggressive action that others will have to meet, whenever prices are materially above the minimum necessary supply prices at which the industry would supply the amounts demanded of the various grades and types of products it produces.

Competition as a Dynamic Process, *op. cit.*, p. 18, emphasis added.

[54]Henry L. Moore, "Paradoxes of Competition," *Quarterly Journal of Economics*, Vol. XX, No. 4 (February, 1906), p. 213.

[55]"The Meaning of Freedom," *Ethics*, Vol. LII (October, 1941), p. 103.

> in access to market information, in the award of private contracts, even preferential treatment in the administration of a public office.[56]

Implicit in Professor Copeland's view of competition is the realistic notion that some competitors may be better *able* to compete than others. Such a difference in competitive ability would allow for differential growth and profit rates among the firms within an industry—variables to which the Jevonian "Law of Indifference" need not, apparently, apply even in an otherwise conceptually perfect market. Moreover, competition which involves the active effort to improve the terms on which one trades, rather than the merely passive selection of the best terms available, may well be, in fact, competition for a position of monopoly power—a not unrealistic view of the actual competitive process in the light of our industrial history. To compete for monopoly power is not, of course, necessarily to realize it. But to the extent that the result, not to say the purpose, of economic competition is a changed environment in which that competition proceeds, the case is strengthened for distinguishing between, rather than identifying, the idea of competition and that of market structure.

IV

A promising, if not yet altogether satisfying, new dimension has been suggested for microeconomics in recent years in the various efforts to develop a "behavioral theory of the firm," in which analysis would go beyond that of the traditional determinate equilibrium toward which the business firm is assumed to be perfectly adapting in a world of no uncertainty, to include also "at least some description of the processes and mechanisms through which the adaptation takes place."[57] The reformulation and expansion of the concept of competition would appear to be an important, if yet underemphasized, part of that general task. To the degree that that effort is successful, it seems reasonable to predict that the idea of the market and that of competition may increasingly come to be separately identified, and competition itself may be, once again, what it was at the hands of Adam Smith: a disequilibrium, behavioral concept which is meaningful and relevant in terms of the contemporary pattern of economic life.

---

[56]M. A. Copeland, "Institutionalism and Welfare Economics," *American Economic Review*, Vol. XLVIII (March, 1958), p. 13.

[57]H. A. Simon, "Theories of Decision-Making in Economics," *American Economic Review*, Vol. XLIX (June, 1959), p. 256.

17. THE RESTORATION OF PURE MONOPOLY AND THE CONCEPT OF THE INDUSTRY*

Mancur Olson and David McFarland†

Introduction

This paper is designed to show that the concept of "pure monopoly" and the concept of "industry" can be given precise theoretical definitions, and to argue that these concepts, which some modern economists reject, deserve prominent places in the theory of market structure. These concepts have been wrongly rejected, this article argues, because an excessive reliance on elasticity and cross-elasticity of demand has obscured important aspects of market structure theory.

Some theorists have used the following four categories in their analyses of market structure: (1) pure competition, (2) monopolistic competition with the "large group," (3) oligopoly with a homogeneous product, and (4) oligopoly with a differentiated product. Pure monopoly, evidently at the opposite pole from pure competition, is sometimes either not listed as a market category or is reserved for the completely unrealistic case of a firm that controls the entire supply of *every* product, including leisure.[1]

Before the advent of the theory of monopolistic competition many economists thought any firm facing a significantly declining demand curve was a monopolist.[2] The slope of the demand curve alone distinguished monopoly,

*From *Quarterly Journal of Economics*, Vol. LXXVI, No. 4 (November, 1962), pp. 613–631. Reprinted by permission of the publisher and the authors.

†Mancur Olson, Professor of Economics, University of Maryland, and David McFarland, Professor of Economics, University of North Carolina at Chapel Hill. The authors are indebted to several of their colleagues at Princeton University and at the U.S. Air Force Academy for helpful criticism, especially Professors Jesse Markham, Richard Quandt, Lee Baldwin, Aldrich Finegan, Colonel Wayne Yeoman and Captain Edward Claiborn. None of the critics is responsible for any errors. Both authors are on the faculty of economics at Princeton University, but Lt. Olson is on military leave, stationed at the Department of Economics at the Air Force Academy, which he thanks for generous encouragement of this project. The authors also thank the Princeton University Research Fund for support.

[1]This general approach to market structure stems mainly from Professor Chamberlin, who first restricted the idea of pure monopoly, that is monopoly unmixed with competition, to the case of a firm that controls the output of every economic good. See Edward H. Chamberlin, *The Theory of Monopolistic Competition* (6th ed.; Cambridge, Mass.: Harvard University Press, 1950), pp. 63, 64, 68, 208, and E. H. Chamberlin, *Towards a More General Theory of Value* (New York: Oxford University Press, 1957), p. 79–81.

[2]There are some who still regard a monopolist as any firm with a downward sloping demand curve. See, for example, Abba P. Lerner, "The Concept of Monopoly and the Measurement of Economic Power," *Review of Economic Studies*, Vol. I (1934), pp. 157–75, and George Stigler, *Theory of Price* (New York: Macmillan, 1952), p. 206.

the unusual, from competition, the usual, type of market structure. Once product differentiation was recognized, the competition faced by a firm with a declining demand curve from firms selling similar, but not identical, products, could no longer be ignored. The pervasiveness of competition among products and therefore of firms with declining demand curves implied that typically firms were in part competitive, in part monopolistic, and that there could be no purely monopolistic pole unless it was the firm with an absolutely inelastic demand curve.[3] But this was immediately recognized as absurd, since a firm, however monopolistic, will always use an elastic part of its demand curve if it maximizes profits.[4] So Professor Chamberlin argued that the idea of pure or traditional monopoly had no counterpart in reality, and that in practice monopoly was always blended with competition.[5] Many other economists have followed him in denying the existence of pure or complete monopoly; Mr. Kaldor, for example, claimed that the complete independence of a firm, or pure monopoly, "is not even conceivable, since it would conflict with our basic assumptions about the nature of human wants."[6] Though Professor Triffin defines a concept of pure monopoly, he says that the required "assumptions are totally unrealistic."[7]

The usual argument against the real-world existence of pure monopoly rests on the universality of substitution among products; all products have substitutes of some sort, often highly imperfect substitutes to be sure, but practically significant substitutes nonetheless. If the price of any product goes up some buyers will decide to spend their money on other products or substitute leisure for goods, so there will always be some substitution among products. And so long as there is substitution, a firm does not have a pure monopoly unless it controls the supply of all products. Certainly everyone takes it for granted that any firm selling a product for which there is no perfect substitute has some monopoly power, but this element of monopoly, Chamberlin would argue, is blended with and limited by the competition of other products.

The competition among products also makes the concept of the "industry" theoretically meaningless, according to Chamberlin, Triffin, and many other students of market structure. Just as the product sold by a given firm in monopolistic competition has more or less perfect substitutes, so each of these substitute products also has its substitutes, and so on, with the result that all goods are directly or indirectly connected with one another in an endless chain of substitution. And it seems theoretically arbitrary and unhelpful simply to

[3]Or perhaps a firm with a demand of unit elasticity throughout. This is, however, a dubious definition, since any firm with positive marginal costs will, if it maximizes profits, use a segment of its demand curve which has an elasticity greater than unity.

[4]Nicholas Kaldor, "Professor Chamberlin on Monopolistic and Imperfect Competition," *Quarterly Journal of Economics*, Vol. LII (May, 1938), pp. 526–27.

[5]Chamberlin, *Monopolistic Competition*, *op. cit.*, pp. 63, 64, 68, 208.

[6]Kaldor, *op. cit.*, p. 526.

[7]Robert Triffin, *Monopolistic Competition and General Equilibrium Theory* (Cambridge, Mass.: Harvard University Press, 1940), p. 132.

assume, as Mrs. Robinson did, that there are somewhere "gaps" in this chain of substitution that justify treating the areas between these gaps as separate industries.

Despite the plausibility and popularity of the foregoing objections to the concept of complete or traditional monopoly and the concept of industry, these concepts are nonetheless often used. Economists commonly use the words "monopoly" and "industry" without qualification in empirical work. In textbooks and classroom lectures these concepts are often employed, not because they have theoretical validity, but probably because they are convenient, and because it seems esthetically and intuitively natural that there should be a concept of pure monopoly as the polar opposite of pure competition. It is unfortunate that concepts with such general usefulness, both in everyday conversation and in the teaching of economic theory, should have no generally accepted theoretical definition, and should even be thought incapable of being defined in a theoretically meaningful way.[8] Triffin states this view most clearly.

> . . . To summarize, it is now evident that monopolistic competition robs the old concept of industry (and also the Chamberlinian group) of any theoretical significance. . . . The theoretical problem is the problem of general competitiveness between goods. . . . every firm competes with all other firms in the economy, but with different degrees of closeness. . . . When competition is discussed in general abstract terms, we may just as well make the group (or industry) co-extensive with the whole economic collectivity. . . . It is never useful to speak of "industries" or "groups" in a general, abstract way. . . . In the general pure theory of value, the group and the industry are useless concepts. The new wine of monopolistic competition should not be poured into the old goatskins of particular equilibrium methodology.[9]

There are no doubt some who would follow Mrs. Robinson in assuming that there are always gaps in the chain of substitution, and thus a basis for definitions of "pure" monopoly and industry. Still others deny that there is any validity in either the theory of imperfect competition or the theory of monopolistic competition, and accept Marshall's explanation of "industry" and "monopoly."

These approaches will not be accepted in this paper. Nothing can be gained by *arbitrarily* assuming gaps in the chain of substitution, nor by denying the ubiquity and importance of substitution among products. Here the usual approach to monopolistic competition will be followed, and there will be an attempt to show that, given the assumptions of that theory, the acceptance of the pure monopoly and industry concepts is logically necessary. These two

---

[8]P. W. S. Andrews, "Industrial Analysis in Economics—With Especial Reference to Marshallian Doctrine," in T. Wilson and P. W. S. Andrews (eds.), *Oxford Studies in The Price Mechanism* (Oxford: Clarendon Press, 1951), pp. 139–40.

[9]Triffin, *op. cit.*, pp. 88, 89.

concepts are not only compatible with the usual modern analysis of market structure, but are logically entailed by that analysis.

The fact that pure monopoly and the industry belong in the theory of monopolistic competition has been overlooked apparently because the concepts of elasticity of demand and cross-elasticity of demand have confused most discussions of market structure. This article will argue that a misplaced emphasis on elasticity and cross-elasticity of demand has led to neglect of the traditional interest in the number of firms in the market, and has obscured a necessary distinction between the near or competitive and remote or non-competitive character of market substitution among the products of different firms, and has thus hidden an important difference between various market structures.

The Number of Firms

Whatever else a pure monopoly might involve, it clearly does not involve large numbers. A monopolist is a single seller and is at the opposite pole from an industry with a large number of sellers. It will then be useful to begin by considering the features that distinguish the workings of a market with many firms from a monopoly.

The most important distinguishing feature of a market with a large number of firms, whether there is pure competition or monopolistic competition in the large group, is that the individual firms in such a market have an incentive to act in opposition to the interests of the group or industry, even to the extent that in equilibrium there are no profits. Consider first a purely competitive industry, and assume (if only for the sake of simplicity) that the firms have zero marginal costs.[10] In such a case it would pay each firm to increase its output as long as its elasticity of demand is greater than unity, for when the demand is elastic any increase in output will bring an increase in revenue. Since the elasticity of demand for the firm is always a multiple of the elasticity for the industry, increases in output will continue to be profitable for each individual firm even after the industry is on the inelastic portion of its demand curve, and the total revenue of all firms taken together is decreasing. This process continues until, in equilibrium, there are no profits. If as usual there are positive marginal costs, the price will be greater than zero, but in any event in equilibrium no firm realizes profits.

Thus, all of the firms are worse off than if they had not tried to maximize profits by increasing output. There was a time when this was not understood. Some economists seem to have thought that in a situation of the kind described above firms would not increase output, on the ground that the result of such behavior would be lower profits for all of them, which contradicts the assumption of the rational pursuit of self-interest upon which economic theory rests. J. M. Clark, for instance, said that, "if all the competitors followed suit

[10]Assume also that there is no entry or exit of firms.

the moment any (price) cut was made, each would gain his quota of the resulting increase in output, and no one would gain any larger proportion of his previous business than a monopoly would gain by a similar cut in prices. Thus, the competitive cutting of prices would naturally stop exactly where it would if there was no competition."[11] Accordingly, Clark concludes that a competitive market will function properly only if each firm has a very slight degree of monopoly power. As Professor Knight points out, "there does seem to be a certain Hegelian contradiction in the idea of perfect competition after all."[12]

This view is now known to be mistaken.[13] It does not follow, because every firm would lose from increasing its output as a result of the fall in price, that no firm would increase its output in a competitive market. For whenever numbers are large each firm is so small that it can ignore the effect of its output on price in the market as a whole. Each firm finds it advantageous to increase output to the point where marginal cost equals price and to ignore the effects of its extra output on price, and therefore on the group interest. True, the net result is that all firms are worse off, but not because any firm has failed to act in its own self-interest. If a firm, foreseeing the fall in price resulting from the increase in industry output, were to restrict its own output, it would lose more than ever, for the price it received would fall quite as much in any case and it would have a smaller output as well. A firm that reduces its output in a market with large numbers gets only a small share of any extra revenue accruing to the industry because of that reduction in output.

The nature of the mistake Clark and other economists apparently made in an earlier day is now widely understood. Economists today recognize that if all of the firms in an industry with a large number of firms are maximizing profits, the profits for the industry as a whole will be less than they could be if the firms did not individually seek to maximize profits. And all would agree that this theoretical conclusion fits the facts for markets characterized by large numbers.

What we have been saying about pure competition also applies to the "large group" case in monopolistic competition, where, as is well known, profits are zero in equilibrium and the average cost curve is tangent to the average revenue curve.[14] For in the large group case, by definition, each firm is so small in relation to the group that it can ignore the effects of increases in its own output on the group. Accordingly, it pays each firm to increase its output as much as its own, relatively elastic, demand curve would dictate, and ignore the generally adverse effects its increase in output would have on the group

[11] J. M. Clark, *The Economics of Overhead Costs* (Chicago: University of Chicago Press, 1923), p. 417.

[12] Frank H. Knight, *Risk, Uncertainty and Profit* (Boston: Houghton Mifflin, 1921), p. 193.

[13] See Chamberlin, *Monopolistic Competition, op. cit.*, p. 4.

[14] Of course, entry or exit of firms may be required to achieve an equilibrium with the tangency condition, and Chamberlin's "uniformity" and "symmetry" assumptions must also be granted. See *Monopolistic Competition, op. cit.*, pp. 81–100.

as a whole because of the lower elasticity of the demand curve facing the group as a whole.[15] Since the individual firm would continue to increase output until its marginal revenue equaled marginal cost, and since the elasticity of the demand curve facing the group as a whole is less elastic than that facing a given firm, the marginal revenue to the group as a whole will be less than the marginal cost, and the group as a whole will therefore be worse off when individual firms increase output to the point where individual profits are maximized.[16]

Therefore in any market with large numbers, whether the product be homogeneous or differentiated, whether each firm faces a perfectly elastic or a sloping demand curve, the firms act in opposition to their common interest in higher profits for the group. with the result that in equilibrium there are no profits. This paradoxical consequence comes about because the effects of the individual firm's actions are so small in relation to the market that no one firm in the industry is significantly affected by them.

The very absence of this condition has always been used to describe oligopoly. In an oligopolistic market, by definition, a firm's action will significantly affect competing firms, so a firm has to take other firms' reactions into account in making its own decisions. In an oligopolistic market, as is well known, if one firm increases its output and cuts its price, this will have a noticeable effect on other firms in the group, and may induce them also to cut prices and increase output, leaving all of the firms including the one which first cut its price worse off than before. Foreseeing this, the first firm may not cut price, and the oligopolistic industry may in equilibrium have positive profits because the firms may have an incentive to forego actions not consistent with the interests of the group.

In an oligopolistic market, as in the markets with large numbers, the product may be homogeneous or differentiated. The usual market categories, then, can be distinguished by two criteria: (1) whether any individual firm in the group is large enough to have a perceptible effect on the fortunes of the group as a whole or any other firm in the group, and (2) whether the products sold by the firms in the group are homogeneous or differentiated. The first criterion distinguishes oligopoly from pure competition and monopolistic competition in the large group, both of which we will here describe as types of "atomistic competition." The second criterion distinguishes both atomistically competitive and oligopolistic markets into two sub-cases according to whether the product is homogeneous or differentiated. The elasticity and cross-elasticity of demand need not play any role in the derivation of the different types of market structure.

---

[15]This is Chamberlin's "demand curve for the general class of product," of which his *DD* curve is a "fractional part." (*Monopolistic Competition, op. cit.*, p. 90.) While there are practical objections to the general use of such a demand curve, these objections do not apply to its use for this particular purpose. The point here is simply that the individual firm absorbs only a small part of any loss to the group that results when it increases its output, but gets all of the gain from the extra output.

[16]See William Baumol, *Welfare Economics and the Theory of the State* (Cambridge, Mass.: Harvard University Press, 1952), pp. 108–18.

The extent to which a firm must consider the effects of its actions on the state of the market is a much more significant factor in distinguishing types of market structure than the elasticity or cross-elasticity of demand. The analysis in this paper has progressed from the case where the firm's actions have no perceptible effect on the market or on any other firm, to the case where the effects of its actions on the market are great enough so that other firms may react to its changes in output. Why not include the remaining category: the case where the effect of a firm's action on the market is so great that it alone determines the state of the market? That is the case where the "group" is composed of only one firm, where there is only one seller in the market, where a firm's effect on the market and its effect on itself are exactly the same, and where it alone determines the price. In such a case the firm can ignore the reactions of other firms entirely, not because it is so small that the effects of its actions are not perceived by others, but because the firm is so large that it alone absorbs all of the effects of its actions on the market. Here the firm *is* the group, and there is obviously no possibility that the firm will act in opposition to the group interest. This situation surely should be called "pure monopoly."

Substitution Among Products

Some readers may, at this point, feel that this conclusion is only a verbal illusion, but the following pages will perhaps persuade them that this judgment was premature. The market category of pure monopoly can have empirical content in spite of the ubiquity of substitution of one product for another and of competition among different products. This conception of pure monopoly requires *no assumptions* about competition among products, and the definition of the market, *that are not also required for models of perfectly competitive markets.* The theory of perfect competition implicitly assumes that, when the price of the product of the perfectly competitive industry changes, there are no reactions from particular firms or groups of firms outside the industry. The simple supply and demand model in perfect competition reveals this most clearly. Suppose that an invention lowers marginal costs in a perfectly competitive industry so that the output of that industry increases and price falls, by amounts that could be computed given the change in marginal costs and the elasticity of demand. If this fall in price perceptibly affects the fortunes of any firms outside of the industry, or any other industry, presumably that firm or industry would have an incentive to change its output and price. Then the industry whose supply curve had shifted in the first place would find that its demand curve had also shifted, thus emasculating supply and demand analysis. Some models of oligopoly with a homogeneous product would face a similar problem. If Cournot's famous mineral springs had produced a product with a close and competitive, but imperfect, substitute, his analysis would be vitiated.

In ordinary Marshallian models of perfect competition, as well as in many other market models, it is usually assumed that the prices of other, substitute products are constant, and this is possible only if there is no significant interdependence between the demand curve of the firm or the industry considered and any other demand curve. If there is such interdependence and other prices change, the elementary conclusions of supply and demand analysis need not hold. Thus, there can be no question but that the ordinary Marshallian supply and demand model assumes that the demand for the product in question is held independent of the price or output of any other single product.[17]

But what is sauce for the perfectly competitive goose is also sauce for the purely monopolistic gander. There is nothing in the order of the universe to suggest that a product produced by one firm alone could not enjoy a demand curve that is unaffected by the price or output of any other product, if a product produced by a small or large number of firms can have such a stable demand curve. The conclusion is that, if the model of perfect competition is to be retained, the category of pure monopoly must be allowed. And surely most economists would concede that the partial equilibrium model of perfect competition is occasionally useful.

Nor is the concept of pure monopoly any less plausible than the concept of the large group in monopolistic competition. It is no more probable that there should be a large number of firms producing goods so similar, yet not identical, that the price-output decision of any one of these firms should have no noticable affect on *any one* other firm (as is assumed in the large group case), than that a firm should produce a product that had no single close or competitive substitute, so *no one* other firm would react to its price-output decisions (as is assumed in the pure monopoly case). It is no more likely that a firm should find, when it increases its sales, that the extra revenue it acquires should come because consumers spend less on a whole series of similar, competitive products, than that it should find that its increased sales imply that consumers spend less on a whole range of different noncompetitive products.

The contrast between what is usually called monopolistic competition in the large group, and pure monopoly, resolves the paradox between the fact that the substitution among products is always present and important, and the fact that there can be pure monopolies and perfectly competitive industries. For while every economic good shares the consumers' dollars, directly or indirectly, with every other economic good, and every economic good is therefore a possible substitute for every other economic good, it by no means follows that any given good is necessarily a close or competitive substitute for any other particular good, or that the demand for it will be affected by the price of that other good. This does not mean that there are "arbitrary" gaps in the chain of substitution. Not at all. It is no more arbitrary to assume that a particular firm's product has many distant or noncompetitive substitutes,

[17]Alfred Marshall, *Principles of Economics* (8th ed.; London: Macmillan, 1920), p. 100.

but no close or competitive substitutes, than it is to assume that it has many close, competitive substitutes, but no identical, perfect substitutes. In the real world, presumably particular goods have different types of substitutes. Some have many close substitutes (those produced in the large group of monopolistic competition), some have a few close substitutes (those produced in oligopoly with a differentiated product), some have no close or competitive substitutes (and are produced by perfectly competitive industries or pure monopolists). All goods have substitutes, but some have closer substitutes than others. There is surely nothing "arbitrary" in this assumption.[18]

When a firm is a pure monopolist, i.e., selling a good that has only distant, noncompetitive substitutes, it can, of course, lower the price of its product without danger of retaliation from any other firm. For though its lower price will bring about the substitution of its product for other products produced in the economy, no *one* other firm will be perceptibly affected by this substitution or find that its subjective demand curve has shifted, so there will be no oligopolistic reaction. This argument is analogous to that of the perfectly competitive model, in which a firm ignores the effect of its output on price and acts as though it faced an infinitely elastic demand curve, because its effect on price is not perceptible to it. It does, however, have an impact on price, just as any action by the pure monopolist has an impact on the rest of the economy. The essential point in both cases is that this impact is diffused over so many firms that no one firm perceives it, and accordingly, no firm's subjective demand curve is affected.

But if we unearth the concept of pure monopoly, we must also exhume its historic partner, the concept of industry. For the same arguments that have shown the possibility of pure monopoly and pure competition have also shown the possibility of the concept of industry. The concept of industry lost favor because of Chamberlin's insistence that competition among products was ubiquitous, that there was a continuous chain of substitution linking all products. But as has been shown, the most general view of the process of substitution requires that we do *not* assume that *every* product must necessarily have at the same time *every* type of substitute—very close substitutes and moderately close substitutes, as well as distant, noncompetitive substitutes. That would be arbitrary. Instead it should be assumed that all goods are stretched out along a continuum: some have perfect substitutes, some have many close substitutes, some have a few close substitutes, and some have no close substitutes. Groups of firms that produce a set of products with no close, competitive substitutes have usually been called "industries." And that is as it should be. Moreover, there is no more reason to expect that the concept of industry should apply any more to very large groups of firms, as in perfect competition, than to assume that it should apply to small groups of firms, or to a single firm. There is no necessary connection between the number of firms that sell a product and the closeness of the substitutes for the product.

[18]Pure monopoly cannot, of course, be maintained over a long period unless there are obstacles to the entry of new firms.

If an invention changed the shape of the cost curves and enabled, say, a half dozen firms to take over what had been a perfectly competitive industry, these six firms would constitute an industry, just as the perfectly competitive firms they replaced had done. If in turn one of these six oligopolistic firms was to take over the other five, and to produce by itself all that the other five, and the perfect competitors that preceded them, had produced, this one firm would be a pure monopolist. It would be the only firm in the industry. A simple example of this kind shows that there is not now, nor was there ever, any reason to assume that the concept of industry was appropriate in pure competition but inappropriate in monopolistic competition. If an economist uses the concept of industry in the study of pure competition, he is by any logical procedure required to allow the concept of industry in the theory of monopolistic competition.

Elasticity and Cross-Elasticity of Demand

The confusions in economic writing about the concept of monopoly and the concept of industry probably stem primarily from an excessive concern for the elasticity of the demand curve facing the firm and for the cross-elasticity of demand between firms. The concern with elasticities goes back at least to Sraffa's classic article:

> The extreme case, which may properly be called "absolute monopoly," is that in which the elasticity of the demand for the products of a firm is equal to unity; in that case, however much the monopolist raises his prices, the sums periodically expended in purchasing his goods are not even partially diverted into different channels of expenditures, and his price policy will not be affected at all by the fear of competition from other sources of supply. So soon as this elasticity increases, competition begins to make itself felt, and becomes ever more intense as the elasticity grows, until to infinite elasticity in the demand for the products of an individual undertaking a state of perfect competition corresponds.[19]

It is in the attempt to understand monopoly or pure monopoly that the elasticity of demand causes the most difficulty. Take for example the following approach, which was suggested (though not finally adopted) by Professor Machlup, and which is implicit in most of the discussions of the degree of monopoly:

> Monopolistic competition would then comprise the cases of closer substitutes and more elastic demand curves, while monopoly would comprise those of remote substitutes and steeper demand curves.[20]

---

[19]Piero Sraffa, "The Laws of Diminishing Returns Under Competitive Conditions," *Economic Journal*, Vol. XXXVI (December, 1926), p. 545.

[20]Fritz Machlup, "Monopoly and Competition: A Classification of Market Positions," *American Economic Review*, Vol. XXVII (September, 1937), p. 448.

This approach is also basic to most of the literature on the "degree of monopoly,"[21] and is very strong in Mrs. Robinson's writing.

> Competition will be more perfect the smaller is the ratio of the output of one firm to the output of the industry, and more perfect the greater is the elasticity of the total demand curve. At first sight it may appear strange that the degree of competition *within* an industry should be affected by the elasticity of the total demand curve. But after all it is natural that this should be so. For the form of the demand curve represents the degree of competition between the product of this industry and other commodities. The stronger the competition from substitutes for this commodity the smaller the degree of competition within the industry necessary to secure any given elasticity of demand for each separate producer.[22]

Once this focus on the elasticity of demand is accepted, there is no possibility of any but arbitrary designations of the industry or monopoly.[23] Except for the distinction between perfect and "imperfect" competition, distinctions among market structures are only questions of degree, the degree depending on the elasticity of demand. But the elasticity of demand is ordinarily different for every point on the demand curve, so if cost conditions for a given firm change and the firm charges a different price, the elasticity of demand can change without any necessary change in the number or type of competitors a firm faces. Moreover, the elasticity of demand for a particular good, in some cases, depends on the extent to which leisure would be substituted for that good. Or it might depend partly on the importance of a particular product in the budget of the consumer, and thus the extent to which his income would allow him to purchase a constant amount of that product when its price rises. A fall in the price of a good affects the demand for that good and for other goods by means both of an income effect and a substitution effect.[24] To the extent that the income effect determines the elasticity of demand, it is clear that the elasticity of demand is not a measure of the amount of rivalry or competition among firms or the degree of monopoly. It is not even a measure of how good a substitute one product is for another. It follows that Mrs. Robinson is not correct in saying that "the form of the demand curve represents the degree of competition between the product of (an) industry and other

---

[21]For example: K. W. Rothschild, "The Degree of Monopoly," *Economica*, Vol. IX (February, 1942), and Abba P. Lerner, "The Concept of Monopoly and the Measurement of Monopoly Power," *Review of Economic Studies*, Vol. I (1934).

[22]Joan Robinson, "What is Perfect Competition?" *Quarterly Journal of Economics*, Vol. XLIX (November, 1934), p. 116.

[23]Ralph W. Pfouts and C. E. Ferguson, "Market Classification Systems in Theory and Policy," *Southern Economic Journal*, Vol. XXVI (October, 1959), p. 118. These authors state that, "a satisfactory theoretical system cannot be constructed on the basis of demand elasticity coefficients alone." We would add that neither elasticity nor cross-elasticity is necessary.

[24]J. R. Hicks, *Value and Capital* (Oxford: Clarendon Press, 1953), Chapters II and III, esp. p. 48.

commodities."[25] For these reasons, among others, it is evident that there need be little relation between the elasticity of demand for a firm and the number or importance of its rivals or competitors.

The cross-elasticity of demand, in turn, is in part determined by the elasticity of demand, so the foregoing arguments to a degree also weaken the concept of cross-elasticity of demand as a measure of the amount and kind of competition among firms.

The basic objection to the concept of cross-elasticity, however, is that it causes neglect of the two basic determinants of market structure: the degree of closeness or remoteness of substitution among products and the number of firms in the relevant group or industry. The concept of cross-elasticity and, for that matter, the concept of elasticity lead to neglect of the two elements which this paper argues are fundamental to an understanding of market structure.

The coefficient of cross-elasticity neglects the closeness or remoteness of substitution among products most glaringly when it is used to classify pure competition and pure monopoly. The cross-elasticity of demand between a pure monopolist and any other firm is obviously zero, for the output or price of the pure monopolist will not be noticeably affected by the output or price of any other firm. Similarly, in pure competition, as several previous writers have pointed out,[26] the cross-elasticity of any pure competitor, i, with any other firm, j, will be zero, at least so long as the rising marginal costs essential to pure competition are recognized. The output, q_i, of any firm i in pure competition will not be significantly affected by the price, p_j, of any firm j: in short $p_j dq_i / q_i dp_j$ is zero. Even if firm j should reduce its prices to deprive other firms of sales, it would because of its rising marginal costs be unable to satisfy the demand at the lower prices, so the sales of firm i would not be perceptibly affected.[27] In pure competition by definition no firm is large enough to influence perceptibly the sales of any other firm.

---

[25]Robinson, *op. cit.*, p. 116.

[26]For example, E. F. Beach, "Triffin's Classification of Market Positions," *Canadian Journal of Economics and Politics*, Vol. IX (February, 1943), pp. 69–74; William Fellner, *Competition Among the Few* (New York: A. Knopf, 1949), pp. 50–54; A. G. Papandreou, "Market Structure and Monopoly Power," *American Economic Review*, Vol. XXXIX (September, 1949), pp. 883–97, esp. p. 889; Chamberlin, *More General Theory, op. cit.*, pp. 79–81; and William Fellner, "Comment," *American Economic Review*, Vol. XLIII (December, 1953), pp. 898–910.

[27]There are to be sure some, like Professor Bishop, who argue that the rising marginal cost curves essential to pure competition should not be considered in a discussion of the cross-elasticities of *demand*, and that there is therefore some reason for holding that the cross-elasticity of demand in pure competition is not after all zero. If one perfectly competitive firm shades its price, and there is no limit to the amount it can profitably sell at that lower price, the sales of other firms in the industry at their old price will fall to zero, so the cross-elasticity of demand is allegedly infinite in pure competition. This argument is not however very helpful, for the interest in cross-elasticities is due to the hope that they could help explain how firms act in different situations. How firms act in turn depends upon the effect of alternative courses of action upon

(Contd.)

The cross-elasticity of demand of a pure monopolist is zero because he produces a product that has a great many more or less equally distant, noncompetitive substitutes. Because the number of firms producing distant substitutes is so great, no *one* of them will be noticeably affected when the pure monopolist changes his price or output. When a pure monopolist changes his price-output policy, the aggregate effect on other firms may be sizeable; the total amount of substitution of other products for its product when its price rises may be considerable. But the crucial consideration is that no other one firm perceives this change because the number of firms involved is so large.

The cross-elasticity of a purely competitive firm is also zero because it produces a product that has so many very close or identical substitutes. Because the number of firms producing very close or identical substitutes is so great no *one* of them will be noticeably affected when the pure competitor changes his price or output. If the pure competitor should attempt to raise his price unilaterally, the amount of substitution of the outputs of other firms for his firm's output will be considerable, since these other substitutes are virtually identical. But the crucial consideration is that no other one firm perceives any change because the number of firms involved is so large.

Though the cross-elasticities of demand of the pure competitor and the pure monopolist are the same, no one suggests that a pure monopolist and a pure competitor are in identical situations. In apparently suggesting that they are, the concept of cross-elasticity shows that it is not an adequate device for distinguishing market structures. The concept gives this misleading result because it ignores the distinction between near or competitive and remote or noncompetitive substitution. It neglects the fact that when the pure monopolist raises his price the consumer has no alternative except to pay that higher price and reduce his consumption of other things, or else spend his money on something quite different and forego the good sold by the pure monopolist. The pure competitor cannot raise his price above the competitive level because many other firms produce competitive substitutes for his product; the pure monopolist can raise his price above the competitive level because the only type of substitution that can take place is distant, noncompetitive substitution. The distinction between competitive and noncompetitive substitution thus accounts for the vast difference between pure monopoly and pure competition which the concept of cross-elasticity neglects.

The basic point of the foregoing analysis does not in fact depend upon the assumption, questioned by some economists,[28] that the cross-elasticity of

their profits, and a firm's profits depend on its cost conditions as well as upon its demand curve. In any penetrating analysis, then, the cost conditions must not be ignored. And if they are not, there can be no question that the relevant cross-elasticity for a pure competitor is zero, just as it is for a pure monopolist. See Robert L. Bishop, "Elasticities, Cross-Elasticities, and Market Relationships," *American Economic Review*, Vol. XLII (December, 1952), pp. 779–803; William Fellner, "Comment," Edward H. Chamberlin, "Comment," and Robert L. Bishop, "Reply," *American Economic Review*, Vol. XLIII (December, 1953), pp. 898–924.

[28]Triffin is one of these economists: *op. cit.*, pp. 105, 133–41.

demand in pure competition is zero and thus the same as that of a pure monopolist. The fundamental point is that the cross-elasticity of demand neglects the fundamental distinction between competitive and noncompetitive substitution, and that point is valid whatever the cross-elasticity of demand in pure competition might be. A comparison of pure or traditional monopoly with the large group in monopolistic competition makes this clear. The cross-elasticity of demand in both cases is everywhere known to be zero. Yet these two market structures are hardly identical. In the case of pure monopoly a firm sells a product that has many remote, noncompetitive substitutes. In the large group in monopolistic competition a firm sells a product that has many close and competitive substitutes. Because the effects of the actions of either a pure monopolist or a monopolistic competitor in the large group are spread out more or less evenly over a large number of firms, so that none will react to those actions, the cross-elasticity of demand in both cases is zero. But this means only that both the pure monopolist and the monopolistic competitor in the large group have in common nothing more than that neither is the same as oligopoly.

There can be no doubt that the pure monopolist and the monopolistic competitor in the large group are in decidedly different situations. This would be true even if the two had not only the same cross-elasticity of demand but also the same elasticity of demand. These two concepts, even when used together, are not sufficient to distinguish all different market structrues. The monopolistic competitor in the large group would often have more reason to emphasize selling costs and product variation than the pure monopolist. Because the monopolistic competitor in the large group has many close, competitive substitutes, and the pure monopolist has none, the former may well gain more by making improvements in his product, or by making customers believe that he has made such improvements, than the latter. The monopolistic competitor in the large group will sometimes also have an incentive to merge with or buy out some of his competitors to increase his market power, but the pure monopolist has no such incentive. The monopolistic competitor struggles against a large group of rival firms, while the pure monopolist is concerned only with the fact that when he raises his price some consumers will decide to forego his product to maintain their purchases of a wide range of much different products. The monopolistic competitor in the large group competes, the pure monopolist does not. All these differences between the monopolistic competitor in the large group and the pure monopolist can exist even when the cross-elasticity of demand and the elasticity of demand are the same for both of them. If these two concepts do not, even when used together, reveal such an important distinction as that between pure monopoly and monopolistic competition in the large group, they surely should be called into question.[29]

---

[29]Chamberlin has recently, in contrast with his earlier writing, used elasticity and cross-elasticity to classify market structures and has seemingly attempted to put the (Contd.)

The concepts of elasticity and cross-elasticity of demand also fail to take account of the decisive importance of the number of firms to the type of market structure, a factor that has been recognized for centuries. It was shown above that there need be no relation between a firm's elasticity of demand and the number or importance of its rivals or competitors. The cross-elasticity of demand can also neglect the relationship between the number of firms and the amount of competition. Consider for example a market in which there is product differentiation and only a relatively small number of firms: a market characterized by oligopoly with a differentiated product. The cross-elasticity of demand of a firm in such a market with any other firm in that market will be finite and greater than zero: the price or output changes of one firm in the group will have some finite impact on the price or output of another firm in that group. Now suppose that new firms enter the market, but that the degree of difference between the products — the degree of product differentiation — remains unchanged. With a larger number of competitors in the market, the influence of any one firm on any one other firm in the group will become less, so the cross-elasticity of demand will become smaller. In short the cross-elasticity of demand will suggest that the amount of competition is becoming less just as the number of competitors in the market and the amount of competition is increasing. The concept of cross-elasticity also obscures the importance of the number of firms to the type and amount of competition by putting pure monopoly, involving only one firm, and monopolistic competition in the large group, involving many firms, into the same category because they both involve zero cross-elasticities.

Thus the concept of cross-elasticity can neglect the importance of the number of firms to the amount and kind of competition in a market. And as earlier sections of this article revealed, the size of the group is decidedly important, particularly in that it determines the relationship between the interest of the individual firm and the interest of the group as a whole.

Conclusion

The point then is that the concepts of elasticity and cross-elasticity of demand often lead to the neglect of the two most important factors distinguishing the various market structures: (1) the number of firms in the market, and

traditional concept of monopoly inside the large group case in monopolistic competition. By this approach he seems to us to be doing violence to the richness of distinction implicit in his own original contribution. Admittedly most economists, who rely on elasticity and cross-elasticity of demand in their classifications of market structure, are logically required to take their concept of monopoly in hand and follow Chamberlin into the large group. But if this paper is correct, and other criteria for distinguishing market structures are appropriate, a distinction between traditional, complete, pure monopoly and the large group in monopolistic competition must be allowed. For Chamberlin's side of the argument see his *Towards a More General Theory, op. cit.*, pp. 78–84, and his "Elasticities, Cross-Elasticities, and Market Relationships: Comment," *op. cit.*, esp. pp. 911–12.

(2) the closeness or competitiveness and remoteness or noncompetitiveness of the substitution among the products of the different firms in that market. Economists have known since the dawn of economic thought that the number of firms was a determinant of the amount of competition in a market, and they have sensed, at least since the early thirties, that the closeness or remoteness of the substitution among the products of the different firms in the market also affected the quantity and character of the competition in that market. But an excessive preoccupation with the elasticity and cross-elasticity of demand seems to have led to the neglect of these more obvious and fundamental determinants of market structure. This preoccupation is the more unfortunate because the number of firms and the closeness or remoteness of the substitution among the products they sell are by themselves sufficient to classify the various market structures.

Most important, a consideration of the question of numbers and of the competitiveness or noncompetitiveness of substitution makes it clear that the concept of pure monopoly and the concept of industry can be given the simple and sensible definitions that many economists have denied them. Economists have not infrequently been led by the elasticity and cross-elasticity of demand to neglect the most basic and elementary variables affecting market structure, and from there into denying the practical possibility and theoretical specificity of the industry and pure monopoly. The concept of industry in pure competition, which is everywhere acknowledged, is based on assumptions that are perfectly parallel to those required for the concept of industry in monopolistic competition, which is often denied. Yet the methodological inconsistency in granting the concept in the one case but not the other has not generally been recognized. Similarly, some writers have granted the practical existence of pure monopoly, but denied the practical possibility of the industry anywhere except in pure competition, or vice versa. This again is inconsistent. If there is a pure monopoly, it can control an industry; if there is an industry, it can be held by one firm. A moment's reflection about the two elementary determinants of market structure brought out in this article should make clear that if there can be a large number of purely competitive firms in an industry, it is at least possible that sometime there could be only a few firms, or only one firm, in that industry; and that if the required assumption about the remoteness of the substitutes of a product sold by a perfectly competitive industry can be granted, it is also proper to grant the same assumption about noncompetitive substitutability in monopolistic competition, and therefore to give the pure monopoly and the industry a central place in monopolistic competition. The concept of pure monopoly and the concept of industry in monopolistic competition are accordingly implicit in most modern discussions of market structure.

18. ALLOCATIVE EFFICIENCY, X-EFFICIENCY AND THE MEASUREMENT OF WELFARE LOSSES*

William S. Comanor and Harvey Leibenstein†

In estimating the loss from monopoly,[1] it has been common to assume that inputs are used as efficiently as in competitive markets. The presumed reason for this assumption is that firms have a clear interest in minimizing costs per unit of output. While the "carrot" of greater profits may well be a major determinant of firm behavior, the competitive "stick" may be equally important, and to this extent, monopoly will affect costs as well as prices. In this context, the welfare loss from monopoly should include the reduction in what one of the authors has called "X-efficiency"[2] as well as the extent of allocative inefficiency, and therefore, the combined welfare loss from monopoly may be very much larger than the usually calculated loss.

Competition may have an important impact on costs because it serves as a major source of disciplinary pressure on firms in the market, which, to a greater or lesser degree, affects all firms in competitive industries. In the first place, the process of competition tends to eliminate high-cost producers, while the existence of substantial market power often allows such firms to remain in business. This is due to the oft-noted fact that the high price-cost margins, which are established by firms with substantial market power, often serve as an umbrella which protects their high-cost rivals. Second, the process of competition, by mounting pressures on firm profits, tends to discipline managements *and employees* to utilize their inputs, and to put forth effort, more energetically and more effectively than is the case where this pressure is absent.[3] Thus, a shift from monopoly to competition has two possible effects: (1) the elimination of monopoly rents, and (2) the reduction of unit costs.[4]

*From *Economica*, N.S., Vol. XXXVI, No. 143 (August, 1969), pp. 304–309. Reprinted by permission of the publisher and the authors.

†William S. Comanor, Associate Professor of Economics, Stanford University, and Harvey Leibenstein, Andelot Professor of Economics and Population, Harvard University.

[1]In this paper it is recognized that monopoly does not depend entirely on the size distribution of firms but rather rests on the entire set of factors which permits firms to behave differently from what would be enforced in purely competitive markets with similar cost and demand conditions.

[2]Harvey Leibenstein, "Allocative Efficiency vs. 'X-Efficiency,' " *American Economic Review*, Vol. LVI (1966), pp. 392–415.

[3]Cf. R. M. Cyert and J. G. March, *A Behavioral Theory of the Firm* (Englewood Cliffs, N.J.: Prentice-Hall, Inc., 1963), where the related concept of "organizational slack" is used to describe the process whereby costs rise above minimum levels.

[4]The hypothesized cost effect of competition is not original to this article but originated as long ago as 1897 in an article in the *Atlantic Monthly* of that year by A. T.

Although both of these effects should be included in estimating the welfare losses which result from monopoly, in fact, frequently only the first has been examined. By assuming that actual costs equal minimum costs, Harberger[5] and others have estimated the welfare loss which results from monopoly by calculating approximately the total consumer surplus which is lost. This is illustrated in Figure 18-1 by the triangle ABC where this area equals $\frac{1}{2}\Delta p \Delta q$, where Δp is the difference between price and actual unit costs and Δq is the corresponding difference in quantities. It is in these computations where actual costs are assumed to represent economic costs, for Δp is also considered to represent the difference in price between monopolistic and competitive equilibrium.

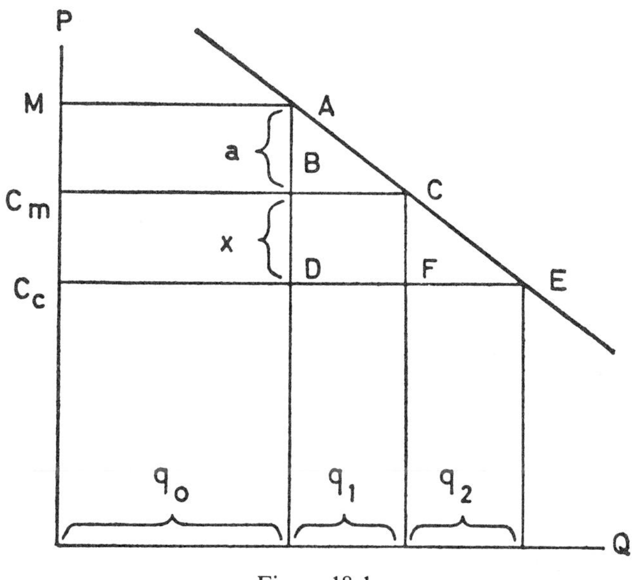

Figure 18-1

Now let us suppose that a shift from monopoly to competition not only lowers price but also lowers costs (i.e., increases X-efficiency). What are the welfare losses under these circumstances which are due to monopoly? We show below that there is a simple mathematical relation, in the case of linear demand functions, which relates the full reduction in allocative efficiency to

---

Hadley. See Oliver E. Williamson, "A Dynamic Stochastic Theory of Managerial Behavior," in A. Phillips and O. Williamson (eds.), *Prices: Issues in Theory, Practice and Public Policy*, p. 23. A more recent statement of this hypothesis was made by Tibor Scitovsky in "Economic Theory and the Measurement of Concentration," in National Bureau of Economic Research, *Business Concentration and Price Policy* (Princeton: Princeton University Press, 1955), pp. 106–8.

[5]Arnold Harberger, "Monopoly and Resource Allocation," *American Economic Review, Papers and Proceedings*, Vol. XLIV (1954), pp. 77–92.

that estimated under the limiting assumption noted above. The important implication of our result is that the actual degree of *allocative inefficiency* may be very much larger than the level as heretofore calculated. Furthermore, to this larger sum must be added the volume of *X-inefficiency* for the monopolistically used inputs to obtain the total welfare loss from monopoly.

I

In Figure 18-1, we assume that a shift from monopoly to competition will reduce the monopoly rent per unit of output by a units but that it will reduce unit costs by x units. On this basis, we can distinguish the various components of welfare loss which result from monopoly. W_a is the partial welfare loss which results from allocative inefficiency associated with monopoly, and is illustrated by the triangle ABC in Figure 18-1. This is the standard measure of the welfare loss which has been calculated in earlier studies. W_{ax}, on the other hand, describes the full measure of allocative inefficiency which results from monopoly under the view that competition affects the level of costs as well as prices. It is measured by the triangle ADE. At the same time, W_x is the welfare loss from X-inefficiency resulting from monopoly, and refers to the higher costs used to produce the restricted level of output. This loss has no allocative component since it is concerned with no change in output levels, and is the rectangle $C_m C_c DB$.

The quantity a is the price-cost margin which exists under monopoly, while the quantity x is the cost difference between monopoly and competition; q_1 is the difference in quantity which results from a shift from monopoly to competition exclusive of the cost effect, while q_2 is the difference in quantity directly associated with the cost reduction. Now let X equal the cost difference in units of a, i.e., X is equal to x/a, which is the ratio of the cost difference to the price-cost margin under monopoly.

As indicated above, $W_a = aq_1/2$, while

$$W_{ax} = (a + Xa)(q_1 + q_2)/2. \tag{1}$$

We can then note that the total welfare loss which results from the allocative inefficiency due to monopoly is some multiple of the welfare loss as measured earlier, and this factor is indicated by

$$\frac{W_{ax}}{W_a} = \frac{aq_1 + aq_2 + Xaq_1 + Xaq_2}{aq_1}, \tag{2}$$

and hence[6]

$$W_{ax}/W_x = (1 + X)^2. \tag{3}$$

[6]We note that $q_2/q_1 = x/a = X$, by similar triangles. Therefore $W_{ax}/W_a = 1 + 2X + X^2$.

This relationship implies that where the cost difference due to monopoly is large relative to the price-cost margin, the loss in allocative inefficiency may be far greater than the allocative loss as usually measured. For example, in the diagram above, it is assumed that the monopoly rent and the cost effect are equal, and as a consequence W_{ax} is four times the usual measure of welfare loss. If, on the other hand, the ratio of x to a were three, then we would need to multiply the conventional welfare loss by a factor of sixteen.

A numerical example may illustrate the implications of this relationship. Suppose that actual costs are 6 percent below the monopoly price, and that one-half of the total output of the economy is produced in monopolized sectors. If the price elasticity were equal to two, the welfare loss W_a would be approximately 0.18 percent of the net national product. Now suppose that the cost-effect differential is 18 percent, which does not appear to be an impossible figure. In that case, the full allocative welfare loss W_{ax} is nearly 3 percent of the net national product—a not insubstantial sum.

The pure X-efficiency effect, apart from the allocative effect, is, of course, likely to be the largest of all. In the numerical illustration above, the welfare loss W_x would be one-half of 18 percent, i.e., 9 percent, of the net national product. Furthermore, it should be noted that in fact W_x is likely to be even larger relatively to W_{ax}, since we have assumed a high price-elasticity of demand.

II

The usual estimates of W_a ignore the problems associated with the theory of the second best, for they indicate only the welfare gain associated with a single change from monopolistic to competitive equilibrium. On this account, they have few policy implications where policy necessarily demands piecemeal and partial measures. A shift, for example, from monopoly to competition in some industries may not improve welfare if the resources allocated to the newly-competitive industry are drawn from uses where they are currently in insufficient supply. In some circumstances, the value of the additional resources used in a newly competitive industry may conceivably have been higher in the industries where they had been previously allocated. Thus, second-best considerations may make it difficult to determine whether a shift to a greater degree of competition in a particular industry represents a true improvement in allocative efficiency. In the case, however, where there is a reduction in costs as well, and thereby an improvement in X-efficiency, it becomes far easier to conclude that a shift from monopoly to competition in a single industry represents a welfare gain.

Returning to the numerical example of the previous section, we determined that W_x was 9 percent of net national product. Such gains represent a clear improvement in welfare since they do not depend on a re-allocation of resources. More units of output for particular goods can be produced without reducing the output of other goods in the economy. Furthermore, even if the allocative effect of a single industry shift from monopoly to competition were negative, this gain would represent a positive counter-weight.

Second-best results depend on the structure of inter-relationships among sectors in the economy and focus on the traditional general equilibrium conclusion that "everything depends on everything else." While this conclusion is qualitatively correct, it ignores quantitative considerations. The magnitude of the second-best problem for specific sectors depends on the degree of interdependence among industries, the degree of monopoly in sectors related to the one at issue, as well as the structure of input-output relationships. Quantitatively important second-best considerations may depend on a small set of related industries rather than all others, and thereby policy judgments may demand a *specific* rather than a *general* theory of the second best. In such circumstances, it might be possible to estimate the gain or loss in allocative efficiency from a shift from monopoly to competition, and if the latter, to compare it with the clear gain in X-efficiency. In any event, since the X-efficiency improvement may be large and represents a clear gain, we should have confidence that changes which represent both allocative and cost-differential effects are far more likely to represent positive welfare gains as compared to those where only the re-allocation of resources is concerned.

One further point should be noted. Because of the higher costs which are assumed to exist under monopoly, the increase in output with competition demands only a partial re-allocation of resources. In Figure 18-1, xq_0 denotes the volume of redundant inputs under monopoly which could be used to produce xq_0/C_c additional units of output. At the same time, the percentage increase in output, due to a shift from monopoly to competition, is $(q_1 + q_2)/q_0$, which equals

$$(a + x)e/M, \tag{4}$$

where e is the absolute value of the elasticity of demand.[7] Then, the increase in output from re-allocated inputs, expressed as a proportion of original output, is

$$\frac{(a + x)e}{M} - \frac{x}{C_c}, \tag{5}$$

which equals[8]

[7]This elasticity represents the average value between points A and E such that

$$e\frac{\Delta p}{p} = \frac{\Delta q}{q}.$$

[8]This can be seen by expanding the second term of expression (5):

$$\frac{x}{C_c} = \frac{xM}{MC_c} = \frac{x(C_c + a + x)}{MC_c} = \frac{x}{M} + \frac{x(a + x)}{MC_c}.$$

$$(6) \qquad \frac{ae + x(e-1)}{M} - \frac{x(a+x)}{MC_c}.$$

The extent to which inputs have to be re-allocated depends on the degree to which e is close to unity, and the ratio of x to a (i.e., the value of X). This can be seen by considering the proportion of the total increase in output which must be produced from re-allocated inputs. Dividing both terms in (6) by (4) gives the following expression:

$$(7) \qquad 1 - \frac{x}{(a+x)e} - \frac{x}{C_c e}.$$

In industries where demand is relatively inelastic, no increase in inputs may be required, and it may even be the case that output is increased while the total volume of imports is reduced. In the latter situation, expression (7) will be negative. And here no second-best problem will arise.

From this analysis it appears that there may be many cases where the clear welfare gain associated with the cost effect of competition is a significant counteracting element to the possible loss on "second best" grounds from the re-allocation of inputs. The likelihood of an improved welfare position resulting from a single industry shift from monopoly to competition would seem thereby to be greatly enhanced.

SECTION V. MARKET STRUCTURE: MONOPOLISTIC COMPETITION AND OLIGOPOLY

Section V is concerned with the market structures of monopolistic competition and oligopoly. While the articles in this section provide a review of the essential elements of the traditional theory dealing with these two market structures, they also represent important additions to this body of theory.

Demsetz discusses the shortcomings of the usual treatment of "demand-increasing costs" in the large numbers case of monopolistic competition and provides a beginning for rebuilding a model of monopolistic competition which analyzes the phenomenon of differentiation. Furubotn develops a stock-flow model of monopolistic competition which provides an optimal price-output guide when the firm's demand schedule is influenced by its cumulative past sales and when its objective is to maximize the yield on its fixed capital. Pointing out that the focus of oligopoly theory has shifted to entry-prevention models, Bhagwati examines the effects of potential competition on the theory of oligopolistic pricing. Shubik analyzes the effects of product differentiation and the number of firms on the noncooperative oligopoly equilibrium price and relates this equilibrium to that of pure competition. Schuster extends and modifies the findings contained in Baumol's recent contribution to the development of a theory of product differentiation.

In an earlier article dealing with monopolistic competition, Demsetz demonstrated that the large numbers case "cannot generate the famous excess capacity theorem insofar as advertising expenditures are the cause of differentiation." The first part of this article extends the analysis to include any "demand-increasing costs." Demsetz concludes that equilibrium at the low point of the relevant cost curve is consistent with the large numbers case of monopolistic competition whatever the general cause of differentiation.

In the second section, Demsetz seeks "to lay bare" the implicit assumptions in the assertion that product differentiation leads to an inefficient equilibrium (in the welfare sense) in the large numbers case. Demsetz' analysis shows that a strong case can be made for the possibility of an efficient solution, in the welfare sense, to the production problem in monopolistically competitive markets.

Demsetz maintains that his rejection of the excess capacity theorem in the first section of this article has left a monopolistic competition model which is "empty with regard to empirically testable statements." His objective in the third section is to suggest an approach for generating empirically testable statements about the comparative statics of monopolistic competition. He emphasizes that he is attempting "to begin rebuilding a model that seeks to analyze the common phenomenon of differentiation."

Furubotn points out that under the conventional static theory of monopolistic competition a firm producing a differentiated product will achieve short-run equilibrium through equalization of instantaneous marginal cost and marginal revenue. However, when the firm's cost or revenue functions shift systematically over time, there is "serious doubt" as to the usefulness of the standard marginal rules. Under these conditions, "a new explanation of optimizing behavior is called for."

Furubotn's stock-flow model is a "simple dynamic extension" of the basic model of monopolistic competition. Instead of trying to maximize one-period profits, the objective of the firm in Furubotn's model is to maximize the *yield* of the capital investment over the entire planning period. Furubotn introduces a dynamic demand relation which shows demand in any period as a function not only of the usual price-income variables but also of the cumulative output produced by the firm over some past time interval.

Based on his analysis, Furubotn emphasizes that when cumulative output has any influence on the position of the firm's demand schedule, there is, in general, no reason to equate marginal cost to marginal revenue in each period. He concludes by demonstrating that his model has practical significance since the demand of many monopolistically competitive firms is related to the aggregate of past sales.

Bhagwati points out that the focus of oligopoly theory has shifted toward entry-prevention models as a result of the recent work of Sylos Labini and J. S. Bain, especially after its formalization by Franco Modigliani. Bhagwati examines the entry-prevention approach, relating it to the traditional approaches to the analysis of oligopoly behavior.

Bhagwati maintains that "the really fundamental innovation" in oligopoly theory came with the realization that oligopoly theory must deal with "potential" competition as distinct from "actual" competition (with firms *already* in the industry). This shift of focus also means, according to Bhagwati, that profit maximization must be reinterpreted. In this sense, firms already in an industry will have a choice between either maximizing profits in the short run or maximizing the value of profits over the long run "*taking into account the repercussions on entry, and hence on future profitability, of any price policy pursued in the short period*"—the latter is the "hallmark" of the new approach to oligopoly theory.

How does potential competition affect the price policy of a firm? In his analysis of this problem, which is primarily concerned with the level of the entry-prevention price, Bhagwati examines the Harrod strategy, the Andrews strategy, and the SBM strategy (the Sylos-Bain model, as presented by Modigliani).

Bhagwati points out that much of the analysis made with the entry models assumes a *given* demand curve for the industry. In the concluding sections, he incorporates the effects of growing demand into the entry models and discusses some of the implications.

Shapley and Shubik have analyzed the behavior of the noncooperative equilibrium (with price as the strategic variable utilized by each firm) in a model of an oligopolistic market with n firms selling symmetrically differentiated products under the condition that the number of firms becomes arbitrarily large. In this article, Shubik examines the implications of this model concerning the "nature of product differentiation and the different ways in which the concept of 'the number of firms in a market becomes large.' "

Initially, Shubik discusses how the effect of numbers (specifically, the effect of a greater number of competitors in the market) can be analyzed in an economic model.

In looking at the role of product differentiation and the number of firms, Shubik concludes that when the market is growing and "a few more" substitute products appear, it "is not unreasonable that the substitutes remain apart." However, when the number of substitutes becomes large, "it is likely that in some sense they become closer substitutes for each other."

Shubik discusses the noncooperative oligopoly equilibrium with price as the independent variable. He concludes that when all products are gross substitutes and there is continuous differentiation among them, the noncooperative price may decrease with new entrants but it will not approach the competitive market equilibrium "if the substitutes do not pack together."

How many competitors constitute "many competitors" in an oligopolistic market? Shubik concludes by discussing this question and by providing some numerical examples to demonstrate the conditions affecting the convergence (or failure of convergence) of the oligopoly price with the competitive price.

Schuster's article is designed to "extend" and "modify" the findings contained in Baumol's recent contribution toward the development of what might be called a theory of product differentiation. Briefly stated, Baumol's conclusion is that the optimal strategy of the firm introducing a new product is to provide it with a combination of characteristics similar to those of some other product already on the market, rather than to differentiate it as much as possible from any rival product. The reasoning behind this strategy, which is diametrically opposed to traditional theory, is that the greater the similarity of the new product to one already on the market, the greater will be the demand for the new product since it will be considered as a close substitute for the rival product.

Schuster maintains that through a relaxation of some of Baumol's "very stringent assumptions" his theorem can be "reconciled with and integrated into the traditional theory of competition." In this context, he critically examines Baumol's three main assumptions and makes recommendations for their modification.

What are the results of Schuster's analysis? Since the new product has a greater likelihood of drawing demand from other lines of consumption when there is a greater degree of differentiation between it and its close rival products, and since the danger of retaliation (and a possible ensuing costly price or quality war) is lower when the new product is attracting demand from outside the industry, Schuster maintains that "the firm's objective will be a high degree of product differentiation rather than a combination of characteristics similar to that of some existing product."

19. THE WELFARE AND EMPIRICAL IMPLICATIONS OF MONOPOLISTIC COMPETITION*

Harold Demsetz†

This paper has three basic objectives. One is to extend some earlier work [5, pp. 21–30] on the subject of monopolistic competition which contained a demonstration that the large numbers case cannot generate the famous excess capacity theorem in so far as advertising expenditures are the cause of differentiation. In part one of this paper the demonstration is extended to include any "demand-increasing cost," such as expenditures on product quality and on firm location.

The second objective of this paper is to lay bare the implicit assumptions involved in the assertion that product differentiation leads to an inefficient equilibrium (in the welfare sense) in the large numbers case. These implicit assumptions are shown to be inconsistent with those usually made in economics. A further objective of the second section is to point out some doubts and suspicions about the extensive use of the demand curve in drawing conclusions about efficiency.

The general rejection of the excess capacity theorem contained in the first part of this paper makes the monopolistic competition model empty with respect to empirically testable content.[1] None the less, the model attempts to deal with a common phenomenon and should not be discarded hastily. The third objective of this paper is to suggest what looks like a fruitful technique for generating empirically testable statements about the comparative statics of monopolistic competition.

A General Rejection of the Excess Capacity Theorem

In this section we demonstrate that full-capacity equilibrium is consistent with the assumptions of monopolistic competition. Our demonstration rests on explicit recognition of the interdependence of differentiation costs and rates of output. This differs from the usual treatments of the subject, which

*From *Economic Journal*, Vol. LXXIV, No. 295 (September, 1964), pp. 623–641. Reprinted by permission of the publisher and the author.

†Harold Demsetz, Professor of Business Economics, University of Chicago.

[1]In a recent paper [1] G. C. Archibald comments on the general lack of empirical content in the Chamberlin model. Archibald, however, states that the excess-capacity theorem remains valid for those cases in which advertising is not the cause of differentiation. In this respect the conclusion of this paper differs from Archibald's: the excess capacity theorem is shown to be generally invalid for all causes of differentiation in the present paper.

show the equilibrium with optimal amounts of differentiation costs already determined in prior analysis.[2]

The mathematics of the Chamberlinian monopolistic competition equilibrium can be put quite simply. We define the following variables and relations.

$$\text{Revenue} = R = R(q, dic), \text{ Cost} = C = C(q, dic). \tag{1}$$

Where q is the quantity variable and *dic* represents all demand-increasing costs, such as expenditures on advertising, product quality, and location.

$$\text{Average Revenue} = R/q \text{ and Average Cost} = C/q. \tag{2}$$

Using subscripts to indicate partial differentiation, we have the following marginal conditions for profit maximization.

$$R_q = C_q,\ R_{dic} = C_{dic} \tag{3}$$

and for a zero profit "group equilibrium," we have

$$R = C \text{ or } R/q = C/q. \tag{4}$$

Writing out the first part of (3), we have

$$R_q = R/q + q(R/q)_q = C/q + q(C/q)_q = C_q. \tag{5}$$

Using (4), we reduce (5) to

$$(R/q)_q = (C/q)_q < 0. \tag{6}$$

The last inequality, which gives the negative slope to the average cost curve (the excess capacity theorem), holds by virtue of the requirement that demand curves are negatively sloped, *i.e.*, that $(R/q)_q$ is less than zero.

The difficulty with the above mathematical proof and its geometric counterpart is that C/q (and R/q) are shown decreasing only on the assumption that all variables influencing average cost and average revenue other than quantity are *held constant* (at their profit maximizing levels). This is strikingly at odds with traditional production theory, which derives the average cost *curve* by allowing the entrepreneur to vary the quantities of all inputs optimally. The Chamberlin treatment of monopolistic competition does, indeed, allow us to derive the equilibrium values of price, cost, and quantity by selecting the set of these variables that simultaneously satisfies the above marginal, *partial* conditions. But the analysis gives us no information about price and cost at rates of output other than that which maximizes profit, and this is precisely the information needed to show that the average cost curve falls (remains level or rises) to the right of the equilibrium rate of output.

[2]However, Norman S. Buchanan [2, pp. 537–57] presents an analysis of differentiation costs similar to that presented here in that price and quantity produced are allowed to vary simultaneously with selling cost. However, he does not examine the probable shape of the locus of best selling cost-price combinations, nor does he consider the implications of such a locus for equilibrium.

In positive economics, economists are interested in the slope and shift properties of the cost curve that will be sought out by a manager acting according to the assumptions of the economist's model, in this case the profit maximization assumption. The theory of monopolistic competition, in its inception, was concerned with the nature of the solution to the production problem that would be selected by managers in a world that was viewed as monopolistically competitive. The excess capacity theorem must pertain to cost curves, as managers could be thought to see the curves, and managers do view demand-increasing costs as variables to be varied as planned output varies. To prove the case of excess capacity in the sense of positive economics (we shall defer until the next section our discussion of the welfare aspects), it is necessary to show that at the equilibrium output rate the total derivative of average cost with respect to output rate is negative. The sign of this total derivative cannot be deduced from the Chamberlinian assumptions, as is shown in the following, where we indicate the total derivative by a prime.

$$(1^*) \qquad R/q = R^*(q, \text{dic}) \text{ and } C/q = C^*(q, \text{dic})$$

using our previous notation to define the average revenue and average cost curves and using the asterisk to distinguish the relations defining the averages from those defining the totals.

Taking the total derivatives with respect to q, we have

$$(2^*) \qquad (R/q)' = R_q^* + R_{dic}^*\,(dic)' \text{ and } (C/q)' = C_q^* + C_{dic}^*\,(dic)'$$

The proof given earlier shows only that R_q^* and C_q^* are negative. This deduction is insufficient to further deduce that $(R/q)'$ and $(C/q)'$ are negative, since R_{dic}^* and C_{dic}^* are necessarily positive (given that demand-increasing costs are both demand increasing and costs) and since $(dic)'$ is plausibly positive over some output rates. A positive $(dic)'$ indicates that managers will find their most profitable course to be one that associates higher levels of *dic* with higher rates of output, a not unlikely pattern. We do not require $(dic)'$ to be positive at all output rates to reject the excess capacity theorem. We require only that it not be negative for all output rates. (The second-order conditions for the profit-maximization problem are traced through in the Appendix.)

Demand-increasing costs are generally classified into the three categories: promotional costs, product quality costs and location costs. The meaning of a positive $(dic)'$ is fairly obvious for the first two categories; a positive $(dic)'$ implies that managers find their most profitable strategy to be one that associates larger rates of expenditures on promotional and/or quality enhancing inputs with larger rates of output. Should the seller consider selling larger output rates, there is no reason to suppose he would not find it profitable to raise the rates of expenditure on promotional and/or quality inputs if this allows him to secure a more than compensating increase in the price his product will fetch. There is nothing that excludes this possibility in the monopolistic competition model.

Spatial differentiation must be treated in the same way as promotional and quality differentiation. We must not view the firm as having a fixed location any more than we view its expenditures on promotion and quality as fixed amounts. Location must be treated as a variable in the model. Our seller is viewed as facing a schedule of locations which he must consider in determining the optimal combination of price, location and quantity. We are entitled to presume that locations offering better potentialities to the seller can be had only if the seller is willing to buy or rent these locations at higher prices than he need pay for inferior locations. In this case, a positive $(dic)'$ implies that the seller finds his most profitable course to be the purchase or rent of increasingly superior locations if he considers selling larger rates of output.

Chamberlin's demonstration implies that $C_q{}^*$ is negative because the conventional demand curve is negatively sloped (*i.e.*, $R_q{}^*$ is negative). But the seller, by varying his demand-increasing inputs, can shift the conventional demand curve so that price need not fall as he sells at larger output rates. This will hold if the behavior of buyers is such that the absolute value of $R_q{}^*$ is less than or equal to $R_{dic}{}^* \, (dic)'$. In particular, these two magnitudes may be equal to each other in absolute value at the equilibrium output rate. (That this may not simply be fortuitous will be shown in the third section of this paper.) If such be the case, the slope of the profit-maximizing price path (to be distinguished from the slope of the conventional demand curve) will be zero at the equilibrium output rate. Since we require a zero-profit group equilibrium, this implies that the slope of the relevant average cost curve (the cost curve containing varying amounts of *dic*) also will be zero at the equilibrium output rate. We shall look at the geometry of our argument in the second section of this paper, where implications for welfare economics will be discussed. The conclusion reached here is that equilibrium at the low point of the relevant cost curve is consistent with the large numbers case of monopolistic competition whatever the general cause of differentiation.

Efficiency and Inefficiency in Monopolistic Competition

In this part of the paper we are concerned with the welfare implications of our model, which assumes free entry and varying amounts of *dic*. To do this, we first consider the geometry of the Chamberlinian solution and contrast this with the geometry of our solution. This procedure will set before the reader two alternative sets of curves from which he can derive differing statements about efficiency. We will argue in favor of that set which allows an efficient solution to the allocation problem and proceed to show that this argument contains serious implications about the inadmissibility of the conventional demand curve in welfare economics.

Chamberlin's zero profit group equilibrium is shown in Figure 19-1. That this is an equilibrium, Chamberlin shows as follows. Let the firm keep its

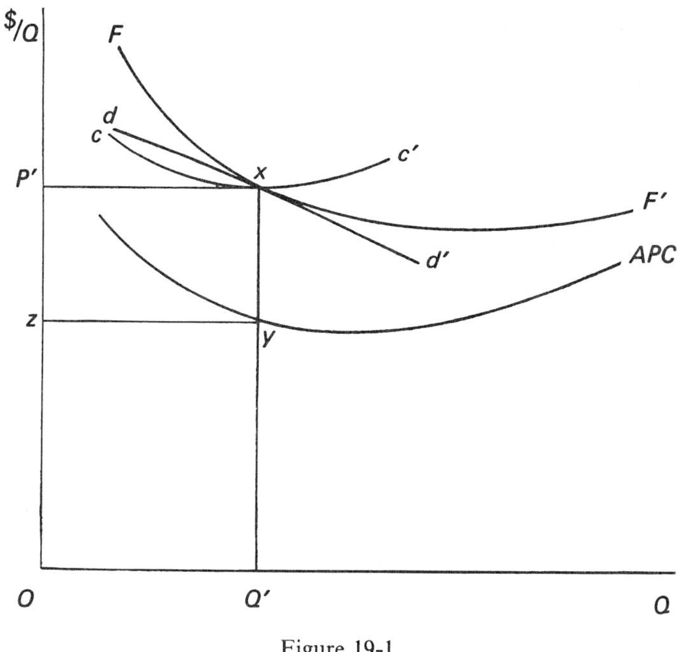

Figure 19-1

price constant and optimally vary selling cost so as to sell rates of output different from Q', the equilibrium output rate. The curve of combined average production and average selling cost so obtained is indicated cc' (where APC is the average production cost). If Q' is to be a true equilibrium it follows that cc' must everywhere be above the price line P', except at output rate Q', where it is just tangent. If this were not so, the firm could convert zero profits to positive profits by changing selling cost while keeping price constant.

Suppose the seller keeps selling cost constant, as shown by curve FF', and considers selling other output rates by changing price. With selling cost constant, the price-quantity relation is given by the demand curve dd', which must everywhere lie beneath the combined cost curve, FF', except at Q', where dd' and FF' are tangent. If dd' intersected FF' it would appear to the firm that positive profits could be obtained by varying price while keeping selling cost constant. If the firm is to be in equilibrium, the firm must view its position as one from which no improvement is possible through a change of any of its inputs or a change of its price. Hence, the equilibrium output rate, price, and selling cost must be those indicated by Q', P' and the rectangle $P'xyz$, respectively.

Our criticism of Chamberlin is that none of the curves in Figure 19-1 has any relevance for points other than P', Q'. If a seller were to consider selling more or less than Q', he would consider changing both price and selling cost (*dic*) simultaneously. Since all the curves in Figure 19-1 assume that either price or selling cost is held constant for output rates different from Q', none depict the true cost and revenue expansion paths.

Let us redraw parts of Figure 19-1 in Figure 19-2 (the redrawn portions are shown as dotted curves) and simply construct relevant cost and revenue curves that do not violate any of Chamberlin's assumptions and yet that convert P', Q' into an equilibrium at the low point of the relevant curves. In Figure 19-2 consider output rate Q_1. If the seller should consider selling at this rate, he might very well decide that the best thing he can do is to reduce *dic* from the level he chose when considering output rate Q'. Since Q_1 is less than Q', this does not seem unreasonable. The reduction in selling expenditures implies that he can sell output rate Q_1 only at lower prices than indicated by the *dd'* curve, which is based on constancy of *dic*. The best the seller may be able to do when selling Q_1 with reduced selling expenditure is to charge the price P_1. This will be profitable so long as the required reduction in price ($dd' — MAR$ at output rate Q_1) is less than the reduction in average cost ($FF' — ATC$ at output Q_1). If this is so, and there is nothing in the assumptions of monopolistic competition that prohibits it, the relevant *ATC* curve will be lower than the *FF'* curve to the left of output rate Q'.

Should the seller consider selling output rate Q_2, there is no reason to suppose he would not find it profitable to raise *dic* so as to secure a more than compensating increase in price from the price allowed by curve *dd'*. Again, there is nothing to prohibit this in the monopolistic competition model. In this case the relevant *ATC* curve will be above the *FF'* curve to the right of

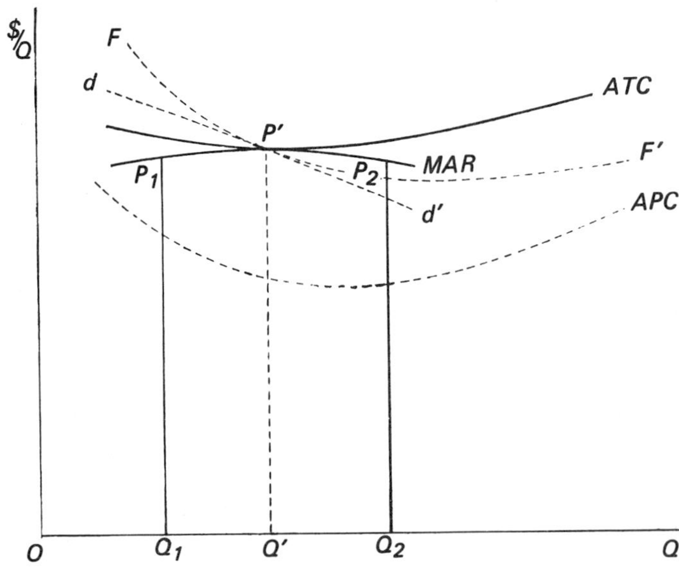

Figure 19-2

Q' and the relevant price will be above that allowed by the dd' curve. Connecting the relevant prices with a *mutatis mutandis* average revenue curve, (MAR), we have a price path for output rates other than Q' that is meaningful if the seller is allowed to vary *dic*. Likewise, the ATC curve gives the per unit cost expansion path for output rates other than Q' with price and *dic* allowed to vary optimally. It is entirely possible for Chamberlin's equilibrium point to appear at the low point of the relevant (for positive economics) average total cost curve, as we have already concluded mathematically.

We shall want to look at some price-marginal-cost comparisons to examine the efficiency of the equilibrium in the special case that has been constructed in Figure 19-2. In Figure 19-3 the MAR and dd' curves are redrawn with their respective associated marginal curves, MMR and mr. Also drawn is the marginal-cost curve associated with ATC, labelled MMC, and the marginal-cost curve associated with FF', labelled mc. The cost and revenue curves that are relevant from the viewpoint of positive economics are MMC and MAR, since these reflect the seller's ability to vary all inputs. Quite clearly, profit maximization and free entry combine in this special case to produce an equilibrium such that price $(P') = MMR = MMC$. It would appear that the usual criterion for efficiency, price = marginal cost, is met by our special case.

However, an examination of those curves irrelevant from the viewpoint of positive economics, mr and mc, reveals that price is greater than marginal cost, so that inefficiency would seem to be the equilibrium outcome. Which set of curves is relevant for welfare economics?

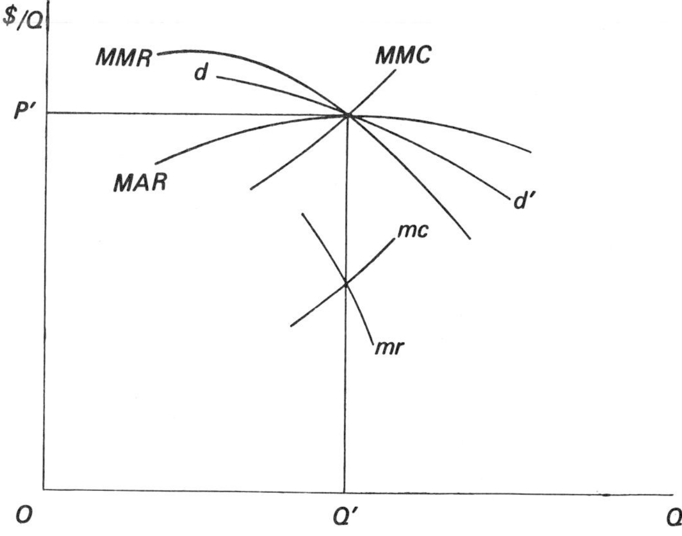

Figure 19-3

In support of those curves producing the efficient solution, one can argue that consumers are willing to pay a higher price for more expenditures on differentiation-producing costs (location, quality, and promotional costs). Therefore, consumers derive some utility from these cost expenditures, and they are properly included in the welfare economist's marginal-cost curve.

The contrary argument goes something like this. Situations are frequently found where consumers care very little which product variant they obtain and where a reduction in available brands would cause little remorse. Here customers distribute themselves among products perhaps randomly to begin with, and then often remain with their choice as a matter of habit or inertia. Each producer manages to keep himself in the market, but a reduction in the number of items would be welcomed if it yielded a significant reduction in cost.

My own preference lies with the first argument because the second is based on assumptions that are either inconsistent with the usual assumptions of economic theory or are inconsistent with the monopolistic competition model. It is difficult to envisage a long-run situation in which buyers do not really want differentiated products while at the same time these products are forced on them, especially if non-differentiated products can be produced at lower cost. The model is one of free entry with large numbers of firms. If enough customers would rather have a non-differentiated product at a lower price, sellers would find it to their advantage to offer this product-price combination to customers. The above argument must implicitly and incorrectly assume entry restrictions or, alternatively, it must assume that customers really do not know what is good for them, that they should not prefer differentiated products even though they do. This assumption runs counter to that usually made in welfare economics. Aside from such items as externalities, which for institutional reasons are beyond capture in the market-place, welfare economics generally assumes that individuals do know what is best for themselves. While such is not true for all buyers all of the time, the converse assumption, that buyers do not know what is best for themselves, would undermine all of welfare economics. Moreover, the converse assumption would lead to policy recommendations that err in the opposite direction, for many of us a more serious direction in which to err.

Consistency of treatment implies that as long as we are dealing with free entry and large numbers, the proper measures for welfare economics are those that include differentiation costs and those that reflect the prices that buyers are willing to pay for differentiated products. These are the *MAR*, *ATC*, *MMC* and *MMR* curves of our diagrams and the total derivatives discussed in the first part of this paper. Our argument proceeds on the assumption that these are the relevant magnitudes for welfare economics.

This argument casts suspicion on the use of the conventional demand curve in welfare economics.[3] The conventional demand curve is largely irrelevant

[3] The applicability of this argument to the use of the demand curve in welfare economics was first suggested to me by Armen A. Alchian.

for welfare problems concerning free-entry-large-number markets, in which demand-increasing costs play a significant role. Indeed, only one point on each such demand curve is relevant, namely, the point of intersection with the *MAR* curve. If an economist were interested in measuring the welfare loss or gain involved in producing alternative output rates, he need concern himself with the differences between the *MAR* curve, which traces out the relevant price path, and the *MMC* curve, which gives the relevant marginal cost path. He should not generally measure the differences between the *MMC* curve and different points on a given demand curve.

The impact of this can be seen by considering the extreme case pictured in Figure 19-4. Consider output rate Q' and the conventional demand curve dd'. This is the demand curve traced out by varying price while holding *dic* fixed. In our diagram and by our preceding argument Q' is efficient. Should the welfare economist wish to pass judgment on the efficiency of Q, he would be led astray by a comparison of p, the height of $d'd'$ with that of *MMC* at Q. Indeed, in our extreme example he would judge Q inefficient, whereas the relevant comparison, between *MAR* (or *dd*) at Q and *MMC*, indicates that Q is efficient.[4]

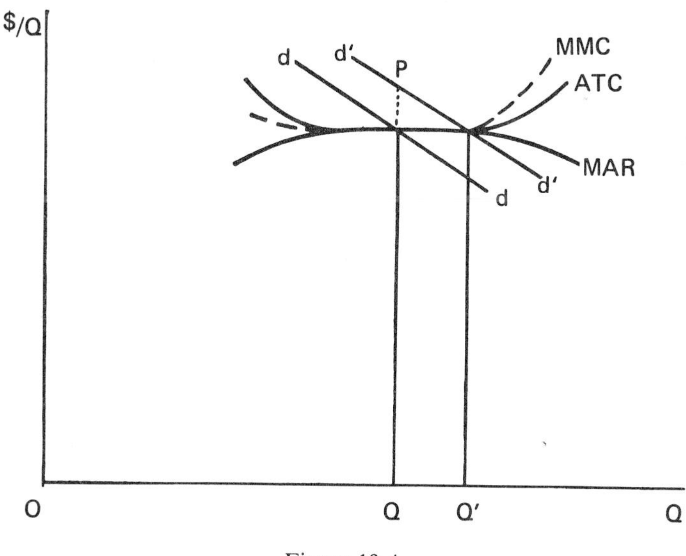

Figure 19-4

[4]The relevancy of *MAR* can be made quite explicit here. In a sense, free entry asks the following question of buyers. If we are to reduce output to Q, would you prefer that we keep *dic* constant and charge the price indicated by dd', or would you prefer that we reduce *dic* and charge the price indicated by *dd*? The fact that buyers make the latter prospect more profitable for sellers to pursue (*i.e.*, the latter prospect is on the *MAR* curve) indicates that they prefer it and that it would be a mistake to look at dd' when judging the efficiency of Q.

The irrelevance of all points on conventional demand curves except those which also lie on the *MAR* curve is a conclusion that follows irrespective of the efficiency of the particular equilibrium example we are considering. However, the efficient equilibrium that has been our example should not be looked upon as an improbable possibility. Market forces operate so as to significantly increase the probability that the long-run equilibrium is an efficient one. This will be developed in the final section of this paper.[5]

The Deduction of Empirically Testable Statements About Monopolistic Competition

Our rejection of the excess capacity theorem in the first section of this paper has left us with a model that is empty with regard to empirically testable statements, and our discussion of the model's welfare implications also left us with the impression that "anything is possible." The purpose of this section is to suggest some assumptions that look promising in deriving meaningful conclusions for positive economics and, incidentally, for welfare economics. It is to be emphasised that, in distinction to the first two parts, this part of the paper is not meant to be conclusive; rather, we attempt here to begin rebuilding a model that seeks to analyze the common phenomenon of differentiation. The following discussion is couched primarily within the framework of positive economics. In this framework we will examine the implications of some assumptions about how entry affects our *MAR* and *ATC* curves and how contractual arrangements among sellers will affect the group equilibrium.

There are two problems in the derivation of refutable theorems from the monopolistic competition model. The first is that the long-run equilibrium output rate associated with any given long-run average cost curve is ambiguously located with reference to the low point of the cost curve. We have met this ambiguity in the first two sections of this paper. The second is associated with entry and exit from an industry. What happens to the position of a firm's long-run cost curve when entry or exit takes place?

The important effects of entry can be deduced with the aid of some reasonable assumptions, but before introducing these, it is necessary to look more deeply into the underlying determinants of the *ATC* and *MAR* curves than was required above. Some tools for doing this can be found in my earlier paper on the subject [5]. Since I cannot count on the reader's familiarity with these tools, a summary review is necessary.

Consider a particular rate of output, say Q_1, and with each different possible price for Q_1 associate the minimum demand-increasing cost required to

---

[5]In his more recent work on value theory [3, p. 98] Chamberlin expresses some doubts about inferring inefficiency from excess capacity. Essentially, he argues that excess capacity may be justified by the desirability of product heterogeneity. However, Chamberlin's remarks are permissive of efficiency rather than conclusive and do not provide a framework for analyzing the problem or its implications for the use of demand curves in welfare economics.

sell Q_1. Starting from zero *dic*, small increments in *dic* would probably allow the seller to raise price considerably and still sell all of Q_1. As more and more *dic* is incurred, such incremental changes in *dic* become less efficient as a substitute for price decreases, so that small positive price increments require large additions to *dic* if Q_1 is to be sold. This is illustrated by isoquant Q_1 in Figure 19-5. Isoquant Q_0 represents a smaller rate of output and isoquant Q_2 a larger rate of output than Q_1. The maximum price at which each quantity can be sold with no *dic* is given by the points at which such isoquants touch the price axis.

For each quantity, as price is increased, the seller earns a larger total revenue. Total revenue is proportional to price, the exact proportionality depending upon the quantity considered. If from the total revenue curve associated with a particular quantity and various prices the cost of production is deducted, the optimal price—*dic* combination will be given by that point for which total revenue net of production cost exceeds *dic* by the greatest amount. For example, consider Q_1. At a price $P = 0$, zero total revenue is earned, and when production costs are deducted a net loss results. This net loss is indicated by C_1 as negative revenue on the vertical axis. As price is increased, revenue curve R_1 is traced out. The optimal price—*dic* combination for output rate Q_1 is located where the algebraic difference between R_1 and isoquant Q_1 is greatest. If this combination involves positive *dic* it will be determined by equality between the slope of R_1, which is Q_1, and the slope of isoquant Q_1,

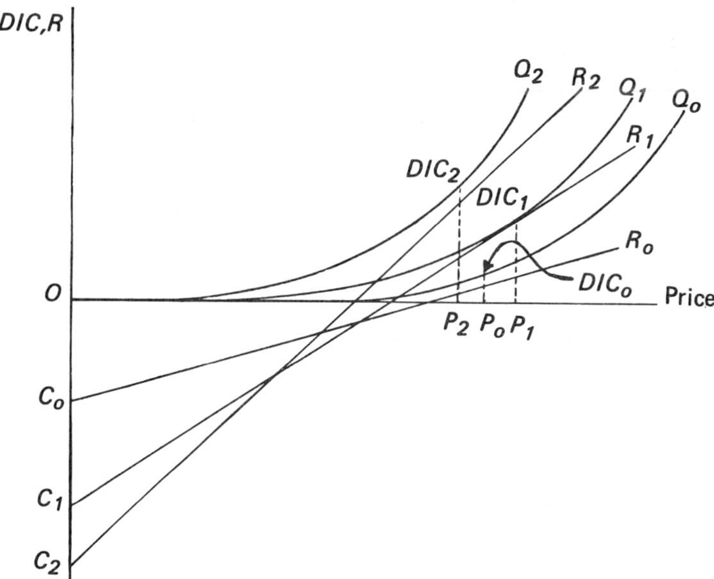

Figure 19-5

which is the marginal rate of substitution between *dic* and price. The optimal combination for quantity Q_1 is P_1 and dic_1, a zero profit solution.

Since Q_0 is less and Q_2 more than Q_1, revenue curve R_0 must have a higher vertical intercept, indicating lower production cost, and R_2 a lower vertical intercept, indicating higher production cost than the intercept of R_1.

There is nothing in the nature of monopolistic competition which prevents the price path, P_0, P_1, P_2 from tracing out an inverted U in relation to quantity. We assume such a path and also assume that the corresponding average total cost curve, defined by $(dic_0 - C_0)/Q_0$, $(dic_1 - C_1)/Q_1$, $(dic_2 - C_2)/Q_2$ and with C_i negative, reaches its low point at quantity Q_1. The zero profit equilibrium, P_1, dic_1, Q_1, maps into an ATC and MAR graph as does P', Q' in Figure 19-2. The assumption of equilibrium at the low point of average total cost remains merely an assumption at this point, but it is a convenient reminder of the possibility.

The following assumptions are useful in analyzing the effects of entry and exit. (1) The larger the number of firms, the more complete the commodity spectrum and the closer the substitutes offered to consumers. (2) The closer the substitute relation and more complete the commodity spectrum, the more difficult (expensive) it is for a seller to differentiate his product. These assumptions allow us to establish the direction of shift in isoquants.[6]

A seller can sell a given quantity after entry only if he asks a lower price and/or incurs a higher *dic* than was necessary before entry. Should he offer the same price-*dic* combination after entry as before entry, the seller will lose marginally satisfied buyers to new offerings of close substitutes. Therefore, each isoquant will be displaced in a north-westerly direction as a result of entry and in a south-easterly direction as a result of exit.

Assumption 2 can be interpreted so as to imply restrictions on the slope of each post-entry isoquant as compared with its pre-entry counterpart. For any particular *dic* the seller will need to accompany any given positive price increment with larger increments in *dic* after entry than was necessary before entry if he is to remain on the same isoquant. This is attributable to the existence of closer substitutes post-entry, to which buyers can shift when confronted by a price increase. For any particular price the seller will find that a given increment in *dic* will allow him to increase price by less after entry than before entry. Again, this is attributable to the greater difficulty of achieving any degree of buyer preference when the buyer is confronted by a large spectrum of closer substitutes. Our two assumptions associate a north-westerly shift in each segment of any isoquant and an increase in the marginal rate of substitution between price and *dic* with entry.

These shifts and changes of slope are indicated in Figure 19-6 where two isoquants for quantity Q_1 are shown. Isoquant Q_1 gives the pre-entry position

---

[6]The evidence I have found in analyzing prices and market shares in the development of the frozen orange concentrate industry in the United States is consistent with the assumptions used here [4, pp. 22–33].

and isoquant Q_1' the post-entry position. We interpret the greater availability of closer substitutes and the more complete spectrum of offerings to imply that isoquant Q_1' has greater slopes at an above point B than has isoquant Q_1 at point A.

The opposite, of course, is true for an exit of firms. Isoquant Q_1' is to be interpreted as a pre-exit isoquant and Q_1 as a post-exit isoquant.

If the reader is willing to consider assumptions 1 and 2 and the geometric interpretation that I have given to them it is quite easy to assess the effects of entry and exit on the *ATC* and MAR curves. It will be shown that entry shifts the *ATC* curve down by reducing the optimal amount of *dic* associated with any given rate of output and, simultaneously, shifts the *MAR* curve down by reducing the optimal price associated with any given rate of output. Entry affects these curves as would be expected from the content of these curves in the extreme case of perfect competition. As the number of firms grows and, presumably, as competition increases, the *ATC* and *MAR* curves move closer to the average production cost curve.

The effects of entry and exit on the *ATC* and *MAR* curves can be readily deduced from Figure 19-6. The pre-entry situation is shown by isoquant Q_1 and revenue curve R_1. The optimal combination of price and *dic* is represented by point A (a positive profit situation). Entry takes place and affects Q_1 as stated above, shifting it to a position such as Q_1'. The new optimal combination of price and *dic* for quantity Q_1, call it A', must be below point B on isoquant Q_1' by virtue of the fact that all points above and including B have greater slope than A and, hence, greater slope than R_1. The implication that the new optimal combination involves a smaller amount of *dic* and a

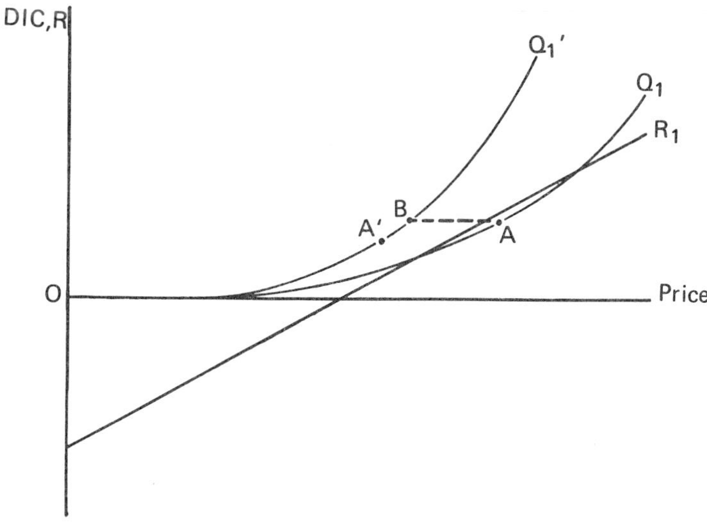

Figure 19-6

lower price is readily extended to all isoquants, since we have made no special assumptions regarding the choice of isoquant. Conversely, if we had started with isoquant Q_1' and revenue curve R_1 and considered the effect of an exit of firms, the post-exit optimal combination would be at A and would represent a higher price and greater *dic* than the pre-exit optimal combination.

The interpretations we have given to assumptions 1 and 2 have allowed us to move a long way towards giving empirical content to monopolistic competition, since the use of the model in generating comparative-static implications requires that we know how entry and exit affect the ATC and MAR curves. We have not yet gone the whole distance, however.

To remove all ambiguity from the outcome of most comparative-static experiments, it is necessary to come to grips with our first problem. Where on the ATC curve, with reference to the low point, will be the long-run profit-maximizing rate of output? In monopolistic competition it would seem from our previous discussion that tangency between the MAR curve and the ATC curve can take place to the left, to the right, or directly at the low point of the cost curve. If the equilibrium should be to the left or right, the outcome of any comparative-static experiment would be ambiguous.

For example, a per unit tax levied on sellers will generate losses, and losses cause an exit of firms. This exit raises the ATC and the MAR (net of tax) curves from their pre-exit, post-tax levels. This process continues until a new

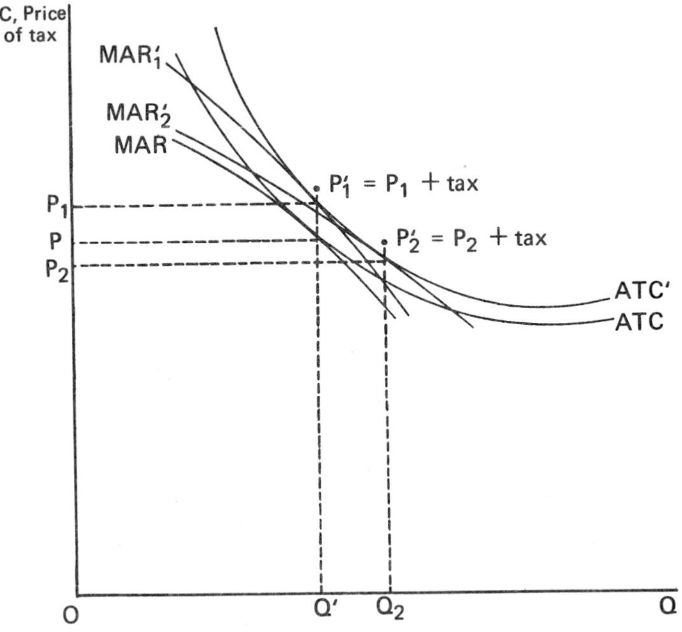

Figure 19-7

tangency is reached. Whether or not this new tangency involves a higher price to buyers and more *dic* to sellers depends on how far the new equilibrium has shifted to the left or right of the old equilibrium. Since this shift cannot be ascertained from anything we have said up to this point, the results are ambiguous.

This problem is illustrated in Figure 19-7 for an equilibrium position to the left of the low point of the initial *ATC* curve. *ATC* represents the optimal combinations of production and *dic* before the tax and before the reduction in number of firms. *MAR* shows the optimal price-quantity relation (given optimal *dic*) before the tax. The downward shift in *MAR* caused by the tax levy results in losses and leads to an exit of firms, which raises the depressed *MAR* curve; this curve could validly move to MAR_1' or MAR_2', so that when the tax is added to calculate the price to buyers it may be less than the initial price, *P*, as is P_2', or more than *P*, as is P_1'. The same sort of ambiguity can be shown for an equilibrium position to the right of the low point of the *ATC* curve.

There are two ways to remove this ambiguity. First, we may make further assumptions about how isoquants shift when the number of firms in an industry changes. It seems to me that this is an unsatisfactory direction in which to proceed. Placing additional restrictions on the shifts of isoquants requires a quantitative knowledge that cannot be supposed and that would not readily be accepted by most economists.

Second, we can inquire if there is any reason or evidence that would lead us to expect equilibrium to be at only the low point of the *ATC* curve. If this is the expected outcome, all ambiguities are removed, both with respect to positive economics and with respect to welfare economics. Having ascertained the direction of shift in the *ATC* and *MAR* curves, we can make very clear predictions as to the effect of any comparative-static experiment on price and *ATC* if we also know that equilibrium will be at the low point of the *ATC* curve. Further, if we are willing to accept the argument that the *MAR* and *ATC* curves are, indeed, the relevant ones for welfare economics in a free-entry, large-numbers context, efficiency of equilibrium follows from a tangency solution at the low point of *ATC*.

Let us suppose first that the *MAR* curve has some point or segment that has zero slope. (We also assume, without question, that the second derivative of the *MAR* curve never alternates in sign.) If such be the case, equilibrium to the right or left of the low point will be unstable and not a true equilibrium. Tangency to the left of the low point implies the presence of market pressures leading to mergers of firms producing different brands, so as to take advantage of whatever input indivisibilities are causing the *ATC* curve to be negatively sloped. Likewise, tangency to the right of the low point will generate pressures leading to "spin-off," since two or more firms replacing a single firm will be able to produce at lower per unit cost.[7] But, positive profits will induce

[7]To the extent that the economies or diseconomies of scale are unique to particular brands, mergers and spin-offs will not yield the cost advantages claimed above.

further entry, etc., until it is no longer possible to profitably spin-off or merge. This can take place only when equilibrium is neither to the right nor left of the low point of the cost curve. Hence, a zero slope at some point in a well-behaved *MAR* curve implies equilibrium at the lower point of the *ATC* curve.[8]

While we have talked in terms of the *ATC* curve, we can also expect contractual arrangements to lead to rationalization of the resources allocated to the various components of *ATC*. For example, suppose average *dic* continues to decline for output rates greater than required to reach the low point of average production cost. Firms would find it to their advantage to pool their selling activities through some intermediary, or merge their selling activities to a different degree than is required to rationalize production costs. Of course, there are costs associated with, say, different firms hiring a common advertising agency, and these must be taken into account in measuring the profitability of rationalization.

Let us now consider the possibility of the *MAR* curve possessing this slope characteristic.[9] Quite clearly, the *MAR* curve cannot always be positively sloped, for this means that it will be most profitable for sellers to charge continuously higher prices if they are to sell at higher output rates. The *MAR* curve must turn down sooner or later. However, it is not unreasonable to expect the *MAR* curve to be positively sloped for small output rates. It is not implausible that sellers considering changes in output rate from very small rates to slightly larger ones will find it profitable to raise price, or, at least, not to lower price, at the same time that they increase their expenditures on promotion, quality, and/or location.

A common observation about firms selling in markets that can be classified as monopolistically competitive is that, if these markets are stable, firms generally seek to expand sales by increasing *dic* and maintaining price. This would seem to suggest that many firms in many monopolistically competitive industries behave as if the portion of the *MAR* curve on which they are located is horizontal. This does not imply that firms do not find it desirable to decrease or increase price at certain times, rather, this implies that these occasions are most often associated with conditions of decreasing or increasing demand for the industry's "product" and, hence, with shifting isoquant maps. Given stable demand conditions and stability in the number of firms in the industry, we most often observe that attempts to shift market share are associated with changes in *dic* and not with changes in price. This often observed phenomenon has given rise to theories of "non-maximizing" behavior, but such behavior is consistent with profit-maximizing behavior if the *MAR* curve is horizontal in the relevant range.

---

[8]Donald Dewey [6, pp. 24–33] makes this rationalization argument, but he deals only with a completely homogeneous product.

[9]Indeed, the *MAR* curve must possess this slope characteristic if long-run equilibrium is to be stable with regard to a cessation of mergers or spin-offs and entry.

(In a dynamic context, sellers can be expected to exert considerable ingenuity to prevent the *MAR* curve from declining to the right of their particular output rates, for a decline means that sales expansion depends increasingly on easily imitated price concessions.)

The assumption of a horizontal section of the *MAR* curve and freedom of contract together imply equilibrium at or near the low point of the *ATC* curve, depending on the degree to which scale economies or diseconomies unique to particular brands are present. Equilibrium at the low point of the *ATC* curve, together with the indicated shifts in *ATC* and *MAR* associated with a change in the number of firms in the industry, allow us to derive a full range of comparative-static deductions with our modified monopolistic-competition model. These deductions are too numerous and lengthy to include in this paper, but, as an example, we can finish our tax problem.

In the tax problem our typical firm can now be viewed as starting from a zero-profit equilibrium at the low point of its *ATC* curve. The levying of the tax causes losses to be incurred by firms in the industry. This leads to an exit of firms, which in turn shifts the *MAR* curve upward and also shifts the *ATC* curve upward (by increasing the optimal amounts of *dic*). These shifts continue until the *MAR* curve (net of the tax) is just tangent to the *ATC* curve at the low point of the latter. The new equilibrium involves: (1) a higher net and gross price than before the tax; (2) a larger amount of *ATC* per unit than before the tax; (3) a smaller number of firms; and (4) a rate of output per firm that is not necessarily the same as the pre-tax rate of output but that is necessarily a minimum *ATC* rate of output.

Conclusions

In this paper I have tried to demonstrate the acceptability of the following statements:

1. Monopolistic competition arising from advertising, quality, or spatial differentiation does not imply excess capacity.
2. In industries characterized by large numbers of firms, easy entry and significant expenditures on demand-increasing costs the use of the conventional demand curve by welfare economists to draw conclusions about the efficiency of various output rates is open to serious suspicion. Strong cases can be made for not using conventional demand curves and for the possibility of an efficient solution (in the welfare sense) to the production problem in monopolistically competitive markets.
3. Granted two rather reasonable assumptions about the effects of entry and exit, we are able to predict the direction of shift of the revenue and cost curves relevant for positive economics.
4. For the plausible case where the *MAR* curve has a horizontal section, freedom of contract to merge or spin-off implies equilibrium at the low point of the *ATC* curve (subject to some reservations). This low point can be thought of solely as the "best compromise" among given low points of various sub-parts of average cost, such as

production cost and *dic*. However, it is also a best compromise in the sense that rationalization among firms and through, say, advertising agencies, will have produced the lowest levels of these sub-part costs consistent with the constraint imposed by the cost of rationalization itself.

5. Conclusions (3) and (4) together imply that a full range of comparative static deductions can be made with a modified monopolistic competition model.

APPENDIX

We employ the following notation to derive the profit maximization conditions.

P = Profit
$\overline{AR}$ = Average revenue = price
$\overline{AC}$ = Average total cost
q = Quantity
dic = Demand-increasing cost

Subscripts indicate partial differentiation.

(1) $$P = q(\overline{AR} - \overline{AC}) \text{ where } \overline{AR} = f(q, dic), \overline{AC} = g(q, dic).$$

Our first-order maximization conditions are:

(2) $$P_q = \overline{AR} - \overline{AC} + q(\overline{AR}_q = \overline{AC}_q) = 0$$

(3) $$P_{dic} = q(\overline{AR}_{dic} - \overline{AC}_{dic}) = 0.$$

Since group equilibrium implies $\overline{AR} = \overline{AC}$ and since $q > 0$, these conditions can be rewritten as:

(2′) $$\overline{AR}_q = \overline{AC}_q < 0$$

by the negative slope of the conventional demand curve.

(3′) $$\overline{AR}_{dic} = \overline{AC}_{dic} > 0$$

by the definition of *demand-increasing cost*.

The first two of our second-order conditions are:

(4) $$P_{qq} = 2(\overline{AR}_q - \overline{AC}_q) + q(\overline{AR}_{qq} = \overline{AC}_{qq}) < 0$$

(5) $$P_{dicdic} = q(\overline{AR}_{dicdic} - \overline{AC}_{dicdic}) < 0.$$

Using our first-order conditions and the fact that $q > 0$, we can reduce these to

$$(4') \qquad \overline{AR}_{qq} < \overline{AC}_{qq}$$

$$(5') \qquad \overline{AR}_{dic\,dic} < \overline{AC}_{dic\,dic}$$

It is to be noted that (4′) is consistent with the shapes of the conventional demand curves and FF' cost curves we have been using and that (5′) is consistent with the shape of the isoquant map we have been using, since each isoquant exhibits a positive $\overline{AC}_{dic\,dic}$ and a negative $\overline{AR}_{dic\,dic}$.

The last of our second-order conditions, $P_{qq}P_{dic\,dic} - P_{qdic}{}^2 > 0$, after using our first-order and positive q conditions, can be written as follows:

$$(6) \qquad (\overline{AR}_{qq} - \overline{AC}_{qq})\,(\overline{AR}_{dic\,dic} - \overline{AC}_{dic\,dic}) - (\overline{AR}_{qdic} - \overline{AC}_{qdic})^2 > 0.$$

This condition is satisfied by the geometry of our ATC and MAR curves. These separate in a manner that guarantees the equilibrium is one of profit maximization and not a saddle point.

We note finally that none of the first- or second-order conditions are violated by our assumptions and that $\overline{AR}_{dic}$ and $\overline{ATC}_{dic}$ can take on positive, zero or negative values. Hence, a profit-maximizing equilibrium is consistent with the shape we have given to the MAR curve.

REFERENCES

[1] Archibald, G. C. "Chamberlin Versus Chicago." *Revue of Economic Studies* (October, 1961).

[2] Buchanan, Norman S. "Advertising Expenditures: A Suggested Treatment." *Journal of Political Economy* (August, 1942).

[3] Chamberlin, E. H. *Towards a More General Theory of Value.* New York: Oxford University Press, 1957.

[4] Demsetz, H. "The Effect of Consumer Experience on Brand Loyalty and the Structure of Demand." *Econometrica* (January, 1962).

[5] ———. "The Nature of Equilibrium in Monopolistic Competition." *Journal of Political Economy* (February, 1959).

[6] Dewey, Donald. "Imperfect Competition No Bar to Efficient Production." *Journal of Political Economy* (February, 1958).

20. A STOCK-FLOW MODEL OF MONOPOLISTIC COMPETITION: THE SHORT-RUN CASE*

Eirik G. Furubotn†

The elementary theory of monopolistic competition indicates that a firm producing a differentiated product will reach short-run equilibrium at an output where marginal cost equals marginal revenue.[1] Price is set at a level consistent with the output solution, and instantaneous profits are maximized. A major difficulty with this approach is, of course, that the production problem is conceived in purely static terms. Once we recognize the possibility of the firm's cost or revenue functions shifting systematically over time, serious doubt is cast on the usefulness of the marginal cost = marginal revenue rule as a practical policy guide,[2] and a new explanation of optimizing behavior is called for.

The present paper will focus on a simple dynamic extension of the basic model of monopolistic competition.[3] The plan is to replace the normal flow-flow production function with a stock-flow variant, and to introduce an unorthodox demand relation that shows demand in any period as a function not only of the usual price-income variables but, also, of the cumulative output produced by the firm over some past time interval. In the short-run, aggregate production costs vary with the rate of output maintained at each period over the capital stock's finite lifespan;[4] yet, insofar as cumulative output influences demand conditions, the firm must also consider, at each moment, the effect of today's output decision on tomorrow's demand and price.

A possible conflict can arise, then, between the price-output policy that appears best from the standpoint of instantaneous cost-revenue calculations, and the policy that leads to the most favorable sequence of net revenues over

*From *Western Economic Journal*, Vol. VIII, No. 1 (March, 1970), pp. 37–46. Reprinted by permission of the publisher and the author.

†Eirik G. Furubotn, Professor of Economics, Texas A & M University.

[1]Even in more advanced discussions of the theory, it is customary to retain the static viewpoint and speak of solutions that are, in effect, modified statements of the $MC = MR$ rule. For example, see [10] and [11].

[2]The need to reconsider the traditional theory of the firm is widely recognized and can be supported by several lines of argument. The nature of the criticisms raised against the standard marginalist model is suggested in [1], [2, pp. 1–17], [6], [16], [17], [18], [19], [22, pp. 381–84], [23].

[3]The model being developed here retains most of the assumptions used in the elementary theory of monopolistic competition. Thus, the approach is essentially deterministic and avoids any explanation of how expectations are formed; similarly, no consideration is given to such matters as inventory policy, capital replacement, maintenance outlays, sale or conversion of equipment [9, pp. 27–31], multiple products, etc.

[4]Following the usual practice, we merely assume that one factor is fixed in the short run. Although no attempt is made to discuss the reasons for capital fixity, economic explanations are possible. See [7], [9], [14].

time and maximizes the yield of capital. Under reasonable assumptions about the real world, the standard marginal rules do not, in general, point to the optimal price-output program for a monopolistically competitive firm. To explore the problem of optimization over time, analysis must be conducted in terms of a stock-flow system of the general type noted above.

I

Consider a firm operating with one current input (x) and one capital input (K) subject to the stock-flow production function,

$$q_{jt} = G_t(x_t, K_0) \qquad t = 1, 2, \ldots, T. \tag{1}$$

Here, q_{jt} represents the flow of commodity output in any period, x_t is the flow of a "variable" productive service like labor, and K_0 the stock of real capital equipment present. The capital stock, which is continuously variable, is assumed to have a durability of precisely T periods; at the end of the T-th period the equipment is completely worn out, but physical depreciation does not affect the input's productive powers during its lifespan over periods 1, 2, . . ., T. Investment is of the point-input — multipoint-output type. Thus, when an initial act of investment is undertaken, units of the capital good are put in place at the beginning of the "first" period and, thereafter, no further investment is made until the end of period T is reached. For purposes of the present demonstration, however, the problem of capital replacement need not be considered; the planning interval is taken to be coextensive with the lifespan of the capital stock.[5]

In the short-run period, the firm has already chosen the capital stock (K_0) and, under our assumptions, must live with the capital decision for a finite interval of time into the future (say T periods). Then, a certain (nonnegative) quantity of the variable input is employed each period ($x_1, x_2, \ldots, x_T$) to work with the fixed capital stock, and an output stream ($q_{j1}, q_{j2}, \ldots, q_{jT}$) emerges. The flow of output each period takes the form of the distinctive commodity j sold by the monopolistically competitive firm.

To limit complications, we assume that the firm expects the market rate of interest (i) that holds at the beginning of the first period to remain unchanged over the T periods to the planning horizon. A simple optimization model can now be established which runs parallel with that used in static neoclassical analysis. But instead of maximizing the conventional net revenue or profit equation, the firm's objective is one of maximizing the *yield* of the capital investment over the T-period planning interval. By definition, the yield (π) of capital installed at the beginning of period 1 is given by the difference between

[5] The assumption that the planning horizon is only T periods seems justified if the market for the firm's product is not expected to last much beyond the life of the capital equipment. Since the course of product innovation cannot normally be foreseen, serious long-term investment planning is not feasible.

the present value of the anticipated net revenue stream (inclusive of depreciation) and the initial outlay made on the capital stock [24, pp. 264–68].

The firm with fixed capital equipment already in place, and faced with a particular forecast of market conditions, may find itself possessed of a non-optimal capital stock. In the short-run, little can be done about this situation; indeed, the firm may be forced to accept immediate capital loss, or acquiesce to a negative yield until such time as the fixed plant is worn out at the end of the T-th period. But whatever its short-run position, the firm can attempt to adjust its employment of the variable input over time so as to make π as large as possible.

For the case where only one form of variable input exists and time is a discrete variable, the basic expression for yield reduces to:

$$\pi=\sum_{t=1}^{T}\{[(p_{jt})G_t(x_t,\, K_0)-r_t x_t](1+i)^{-t}\}-Z_0K_0 \tag{2}$$

$$t=1,\,2,\,\ldots,\,T.$$

If the variable input is sold on a perfectly competitive market, the firm knows the going price of this input (r_1) for the first period and, by assumption, can make single-valued price estimates ($r_2, r_3, \ldots, r_T$) for all subsequent periods to the planning horizon. Then, since the capital stock, the original investment outlay (Z_0K_0), and the unchanging interest rate are all given, yield depends on the variables: x_t, p_{jt}.

But further simplification is possible; the commodity prices p_{jt} are functions of the current inputs: $x_1, x_2, \ldots, x_T$. Assuming the monopolistic competitor estimates a single demand schedule for each period through T, and recognizes the role cumulative output plays in shaping demand, the respective demand relations can be represented as

$$p_{jt}=F_t\,(q_{jt},\, S_{jt}) \qquad t=1,\,2,\,\ldots,\,T \tag{3}$$

where S_{jt} is the cumulative total of past sales at the beginning of the t-th period.[6]

$$S_{jt}=\sum_{k=0}^{t-1} q_{jk}+s. \tag{4}$$

Since the standard demand curve has a unique inverse, price is expressed as a function of quantity (q_{jt}) and the stock level (S_{jt}). We assume that other variables capable of influencing the firm's demand are held constant for the period of the analysis — or are regarded as constant by the firm making the demand projections [12, pp. 192–95].

As system (4) has been written, the past output that is significant for demand at any time t consists of some historical aggregate of sales s (which can

[6]For notational convenience, the symbol S_{jt} is used instead of $S_{jt\text{-}1}$.

be zero) plus the sum of the firm's output from the beginning of accounting period one through the end of the $t-1$ period (i.e., $s+q_{j1}+q_{j2}+\ldots+q_{jt-1}$). But, while convenient, the particular arrangement adopted in (3)–(4) is not essential to the general model being developed here. Alternate formulations showing current demand to be a function of aggregate sales in a certain past period or sequence of periods would be equally satisfactory [8,.pp. 104-10], [19, p. 206]. The basic requirement is that the scheme establish a systematic connection between economic decisions in successive time periods.

Accepting the original interpretation of (3)–(4), we must decide next about the direction of influence of the variables q_{jt}, S_{jt}. For the usual reasons, the price of commodity j in any period t is taken to vary inversely with the quantity of j sold in that period ($\partial p_{jt}/\partial q_{jt}<0$). On the other hand, the variable S_{jt} can be viewed as exerting either a positive or a negative effect on price (i.e., $\partial p_{jt}/\partial S_{jt}>0$ or $\partial p_{jt}/\partial S_{jt}<0$). In other words, depending on the economic situation envisioned, cumulative past sales can contribute to the growth of demand over time and the progressive rightward shift of the demand schedule or, conversely, to the decay of demand and the leftward shift of the schedule. There are plausible grounds for believing that both hypotheses apply to the circumstances of the monopolistically competitive firm over different portions of its lifespan. Economic justification of the respective hypotheses will be taken up in Section III; for the immediate development of the model, we proceed on the assumption that $\partial p_{jt}/\partial S_{jt}>0$, $t=1, 2, \ldots, T$.

Given (1), it is obvious that the equations of system (3) involve one or more of the inputs x_t as independent variables. For example, the price of commodity j in the first period (p_{j1}) depends on x_1; similarly, p_{j2} depends on x_1, x_2; and so on. Having these expressions in x_t, it becomes possible to substitute for p_{jt} in equation (2). Then, the yield π appears as a function of x_t, $t=1, 2, \ldots, T$; and of certain parameters reflecting the unique demand and production conditions confronting the firm. For convenience, (2) may now be written in the general form:

$$\pi=\phi\,(x_1, x_2, \ldots, x_T;\ i, r_1, r_2, \ldots, r_T, K_0, s, \ldots). \tag{5}$$

To determine the optimal employment levels of the variable input in periods 1, 2, . . ., T, maximize (5) with respect to the variables x_t. In the simple case considered here, the first-order conditions emerge as:

$$\partial\pi/\partial x_t=\phi_t\,(x_1, x_2, \ldots, x_T;\ i, r_1, r_2, \ldots, r_T, K_0, s, \ldots)=0 \qquad t=1, 2, \ldots, T. \tag{6}$$

System (6) is made up of T equations in T unknowns (and the various parameters). The cumulative output term embedded in the demand relations (3) insures the appearance of all the variables $x_1, x_2, \ldots, x_T$ in *each* equation of (6), indicating the interdependence of the input solutions. Since the optimal level of the variable input in any one period depends on x_t in all other periods, the system (6) must be solved simultaneously.

The general assumptions made about the demand and production relations suggest that the yield function (5) is well behaved mathematically and has an internal maximum.[7] Thus, the second-order conditions should be met without difficulty.[8] Simultaneous solution of the first-order equations in (6) can be expected to yield a unique and economically meaningful equilibrium value for each of the T variables of concern (say $X_1, X_2, \ldots, X_T$). In other words, we are able to determine the optimal amount of the cooperating variable input (X_t) to be used at each period over the life of the fixed capital stock.

Once the optimal input values X_t are known, they can be inserted into the stock-flow production function (1) and the ideal output stream $Q_{j1}, Q_{j2}, \ldots, Q_{jT}$ can be determined. If there is confidence that reliable estimates have been made for the parameters of the system, the firm should produce the succession of outputs Q_{jt} dictated by the optimal input stream and sell these outputs at the equilibrium prices $(P_{j1}, P_{j2}, \ldots, P_{jT})$ required by (3).[9] Given the information available to the firm at the beginning of the first period, this price-output program (P_{jt}, Q_{jt}) represents the best choice to maximize yield.[10]

II

Like the conventional (static) analysis, the dynamic theory must take cognizance of the fact that the firm is never compelled to maintain production of commodity j. Under the assumption normally adopted for the static short-run case, the firm will cease production in any period when the commodity price obtainable is less than the average variable cost. By analogy, in the present situation the firm will not produce commodity j at *any* date in the planning interval if the expected yield is negative and less than $-Z_0 K_0$. When yield is just equal to $-Z_0K_0$, the firm can recover nothing more than the present value of the outlays made on the variable input and, therefore, such an operating position represents the theoretical limit to the firm's willingness to produce. When conditions are such that $-Z_0K_0 < \pi < 0$, the firm is unable to earn the going rate of return (i) and/or recoup all of its original investment (Z_0K_0). Finally, when $\pi \geqslant 0$, the firm earns an average rate of return over the planning interval that is, respectively, equal to or greater than the market rate of interest.

---

[7]It is generally assumed that, in the short run, the law of diminishing marginal productivity is operative. Such lessening of the variable input's physical productivity must set an upper limit on profit, given fixity of all parameters.

[8]Since the second-order conditions do not raise any special problems of economic interpretation here, they are omitted.

[9]That is, the prices (P_{jt}) can be discovered by substituting the known values for Q_{jt} in (3)–(4).

[10]As time elapses, the firm comes into possession of additional market information and may wish to revise the original price-output program (P_{jt}, Q_{jt}). Thus, a succession of optimal programs may be determined over time. Such a possibility, however, does not alter our conclusion concerning the $MC = MR$ rule [3, p. 121].

If production is justified ($\pi \geqslant -Z_0K_0$), another question concerns the production rates at individual periods through T. In our simple case, the analysis is straightforward. Assuming demand grows with cumulative output, the firm will find it advantageous to maintain a positive output rate at each period. Clearly so long as market conditions improve with greater aggregate output and the interest rate is positive, the firm's yield can only be decreased by the cessation of production at any period in the planning interval. If production is worth undertaking at all, it should be continued over the whole lifespan of the capital stock.

The characteristics of the production function and the demand shift relation influence the ideal level of output for each period; and, in general, we can expect the ideal output to vary from period to period. The possibility of a changing output rate over time does not mean, though, that the usual static optimizing rules apply at each cross-section of time. In particular, we should recognize that production need not be halted when the instantaneous or one-period average variable cost is greater than the contemporaneous commodity price: i.e., $p_{jt} < r_t x_t / G_t(x_t, K_0)$.

The desirability of undertaking production in any period is determined exclusively on the basis of the contribution such action makes to yield. But given the nature of the model, the contribution to yield can only be calculated by considering the effects of one period's production on the events of other periods. Theoretically, at least, a loss incurred at any cross-section of time can be more than made up by the gain induced in another period or periods, and conversely.[11] At any period t, the instantaneous profit will decline if output is pushed beyond the level (a_{jt}) where $MC_t = MR_t$ to a higher level like Q_{jt}. However, what appears as "excess" output ($Q_{jt} - a_{jt}$) from the one-period standpoint has other significance. The "excess" output has the effect of shifting the firm's demand curve further to the right in the next period ($t + 1$) than it would otherwise have gone. In brief, the demand shift is greater than the shift that would have occurred under the strategy of equating MC_t to MR_t. And if the expansion of demand induced by the "excess" output $Q_{jt} - a_{jt}$ is substantial, the profitability of the firm's operations in period $t + 1$ will be enhanced correspondingly. Then the "extra" profit obtainable in $t + 1$ (and subsequent periods) can be more than sufficient to compensate for the profit "loss" incurred in period t. The best production plan here is one that involves violation of the standard marginal conditions in period t.

To determine the degree of divergence from the one-period rule ($MC_t = MR_t$) justified in any given case, we must have detailed information on the quantitative characteristics of the system. Nevertheless, it is easy to see from the structure of the model why the attempt to maximize one-period profit is,

[11]The case for violating the traditional marginal rules breaks down under conditions of perfect competition. The individual firm is too small to generate a significant intertemporal shift in the market demand schedule and, furthermore, is unable to appropriate any important gain from the demand shift that does occur.

in general, an unsatisfactory policy. A firm possessed of durable capital has to think of how the capital stock can best be utilized over the *whole* planning period; thus, yield represents a logical index to consider. Of course, when demand grows steadily with cumulative output, there can be good reason for the monopolistically competitive firm to try to *accelerate* the growth rate. By taking action that improves demand conditions during the lifespan of the capital stock, the firm will tend (*ceteris paribus*) to enlarge the yield from the initial investment. But insofar as there are costs associated with demand acceleration, the potential gains from manipulating the growth of demand have to be balanced against the costs of achieving the favorable changes. A systematic procedure for making precisely this type of assessment was discussed in connection with the yield maximization problem—equations (5), (6). The marginal principle remains valid when the focus is on the yield π, but the objective is to maximize a function (5) involving variables attached to different points in time.[12]

If the maximizing solution via (6) gives a value for π that is consistent with active operation of the firm, output will be greater than zero in all of the periods 1, 2, . . ., T. But then having the optimal employment levels for the variable input (X_t, $t=1, 2, \ldots, T$), it is possible to establish the ideal one-period magnitudes for: (1) marginal cost and (2) marginal revenue at each date over the planning interval. By definition, the equilibrium marginal cost at any period t must be: $(r_t)/(\partial q_{jt}/\partial X_t)$. Further, since total revenue at t (*i.e.*, $p_{jt}\, q_{jt}$) is a function of the variables $x_1, x_2, \ldots, x_t$, marginal revenue is also a function (say M_t) of these variables and, when yield is being maximized, MR_t must be given by: $M_t\,(X_1, X_2, \ldots, X_t)$. The basic conclusion can, then, be expressed as follows. If yield is to be maximized under conditions where $\partial p_{jt}/\partial S_{jt}>0$, $t=1, 2, \ldots, T$, there is no a priori reason to expect the equality of marginal cost and marginal revenue at any cross-section of time except T.[13] Rather, the optimizing condition at one or more periods is likely to be:

$$(7) \qquad (r_t)/(\partial q_{jt}/\partial X_t)>M_t(X_1, X_2, \ldots, X_t) \qquad t\neq T.$$

In general, one-period profit maximization is not consistent with yield maximization because we can always conceive of a set of parameters for the system such that the gains from shifting the demand curve of period $t+1$ (via output expansion in t beyond $MC_t=MR_t$) exceed the costs incurred at t in generating the extra $t+1$ shift.

[12]If the accounting period is assumed to be the same as the planning interval, the marginal cost = marginal revenue rule reappears in somewhat different guise. The procedure outlined in the paper determines the particular set of one-period outputs that makes the yield a maximum. In effect, this result is accomplished by equating the (discounted) "marginal revenue" considered over the interval 1, 2, . . ., T to the corresponding "marginal cost" over this period.

[13]When the planning horizon is fixed at T, the operating rule for the T-th period must be: $MC_T=MR_T$, because the firm has no interest in the level of market demand in period $T+1$. See [19, p. 210].

III

The practical significance of the optimization model described above depends on whether the special demand relation (3) has much applicability to the real world. For clearly, if demand is typically unrelated to the aggregate of previous sales, there is little scope for unorthodox price-output policy. We must inquire, then, into the likelihood of the firm's encountering demand changes of the self-generating type.

In the case of a newly introduced product, empirical evidence does suggest that the market for the commodity at any period is related to the aggregate sales in a previous period or succession of periods.[14] By the nature of the situation, learning plays a major role in new product acceptance; and since the opportunities for community understanding of the attractions and technical properties of a new product tend to improve with cumulative sales, the latter must be a key variable [5], [12], [20], [21]. Professor Duesenberry has developed an ingenious emplanation of market growth which places less stress on simple learning than on the demonstration effect and a self-generating shift in preferences over time [8, p. 105]. He argues that if each individual's preferences at time t are dependent on the actual purchases made by other individuals at $t - 1$, the basis for progressive movement of demand exists.

This general conclusion is important because the monopolistically competitive firm, which is the focus of our interest in the present paper, is precisely the type of organization that must be concerned with product differentiation and innovation. The firm recognizes that such monopoly power as it may possess rests on the distinctive qualities of its output and, further, that there is need for periodic redesign of the product so that quality competition from rivals can be met.[15] For a wide range of monopolistically competitive firms, we can anticipate continual change or modification in the products marketed. Hence, a given firm must often be in the situation described in the model—i.e., observing the demand for a recently introduced product growing over time.

Of course, a monopolistic competitor need not face an expanding market. A growing aggregate of sales may be associated with shrinking sales opportunities. For example, as the firm's cumulative output becomes larger, the product may appear more and more commonplace and, thus, become progressively less attractive to consumers. We have the reverse of the situation discussed by Duesenberry; now, in effect, familiarity breeds contempt. Instead of approaching a finite saturation level through a gradual process of

[14]Although there may not be complete agreement on the underlying causes of the product life cycle, there is definite evidence that such a cyclical pattern exists. After careful testing of the life cycle model, Cook and Polli conclude: ". . . While the overall performance of the model leaves some questions as to its general applicability, it is clearly a good model of sales behavior in certain market situations—especially so in the case of different product forms competing for essentially the same market segment within a general class of products" [5, p. 400].

[15]This is a familiar theme in the literature of monopolistic competition. See, for example, [3, pp. 12–25], [4, pp. 145–49], [15].

sales expansion per period, the market shows continuing decay, and the firm's demand schedule shifts to the left over time.[16]

Another possible explanation for the existence of an inverse relation between cumulative sales and current demand can be found in the tendency of members of an industry (i.e., product group) to engage in quality competition. Although a firm introducing a new product need not fear direct or instantaneous reaction from rivals in the group, *sustained success* by the new product (where sustained success is defined in terms of the cumulative amount sold over a given time interval) is likely to provoke imitation by rivals. The particular characteristics that give the new product special appeal will tend to be matched through product changes instituted by other firms, and the market for the original product will then shrink correspondingly.[17] Thus, to the extent decisions to imitate a new product are influenced by the history of its sales, the demand for the product at any cross-section of time may be viewed as some decreasing function of cumulative output.

Many alternative patterns for the growth and/or decay of demand are conceivable.[18] For example, a firm having fixed capital equipment might enjoy a growing market for a newly-designed product over a certain portion of the capital stock's lifespan and a deteriorating market over the remaining time. Formal analysis of this and other more complex cases is feasible [19, pp. 207–11] but, for purposes of the present discussion, the details need not be explored. It is sufficient to re-emphasize that unless cumulative output exerts no influence whatsoever on the position of the firm's demand schedule, there is, in general, no reason to equate marginal cost to marginal revenue each period. When the market is self-generating upward, yield maximization may require that $MC_t > MR_t$ in one or more periods over the range $1, 2, \ldots, T-1$; on the other hand, when demand is diminishing with cumulative output, optimal adjustment may require $MC_t < MR_t$ in certain of these periods. Because intertemporal relations have central importance in the optimization process, independently formed one-period solutions are unsatisfactory. Rational assessment of price-output policy depends on the use of an objective function like (5) that insures proper perspective of the costs and revenues accruing over the whole planning interval. Regardless of the mathematical forms of the dynamic demand relation (3) and the production function (1), an optimal price-output strategy can be determined with the aid of the procedure developed in Section I. Thus, the monopolistically competitive firm has both the incentive and the capacity to regulate output in a deliberate effort to alter the timing of demand and increase the yield earned by capital.

---

[16]All firms in the product group may face shrinking demand in the case where the general type of product is becoming progressively less fashionable over time.

[17]We can assume that price (quantity) variations undertaken by one firm will be matched immediately by others. Product quality, however, will not be changed instantly.

[18]Duesenberry's linear model represents one variant [8, pp. 104–10]. See also [19, p. 208].

REFERENCES

[1] Andrews, P. W. S. *On Competition in Economic Theory.* London: St. Martin Press, 1964.

[2] Boulding, K. E. "The Present Position of the Theory of the Firm," in Boulding, K. E., and W. A. Spivey (eds.). *Linear Programming and the Theory of the Firm.* New York: Macmillan, 1960.

[3] Brems, H. *Product Equilibrium Under Monopolistic Competition.* Cambridge, Mass.: Harvard University Press, 1951.

[4] Chamberlin, E. H. *The Theory of Monopolistic Competition.* Cambridge, Mass.: Harvard University Press, 1948.

[5] Cyert, R. M., and J. G. March. *A Behavioral Theory of the Firm.* Englewood Cliffs, N.J.: Prentice-Hall, 1963.

[6] De Alessi, L. "The Short-Run Revisited." *American Economic Review*, Vol. LVII (June, 1967), pp. 450–61.

[7] Duesenberry, J. S. *Income, Saving and the Theory of Consumer Behavior.* Cambridge, Mass.: Harvard University Press, 1952.

[8] Furubotn, E. G. "Investment Alternatives and the Supply Schedule of the Firm." *Southern Economic Journal*, Vol. XXXI (July, 1964), pp. 21–37.

[9] ———. "Quality Control, Expected Utility, and Product Equilibrium." *Western Economic Journal*, Vol. VII (March, 1969), pp. 9–26.

[10] Hadar, J. "On the Predictive Content of Models of Monopolistic Competition." *Southern Economic Journal*, Vol. XXXVI (July, 1969), pp. 67–73.

[11] Henderson, J. M., and R. E. Quandt. *Microeconomic Theory.* New York: McGraw-Hill, 1958.

[12] Kotler, P. "Behavioral Models for Analyzing Buyers." *Journal of Marketing*, Vol. XXIX (October, 1965), pp. 37–45.

[13] Lucas, R. E., Jr. "Adjustment Costs and the Theory of Supply." *Journal of Political Economy*, Vol. LXXV (August, 1967), pp. 321–34.

[14] Reichardt, R. "Competition Through the Introduction of New Products." *Zeitschrift für Nationalökonomie*, Vol. XXII (May, 1962), pp. 41–84.

[15] Thompson, R. G., and M.D. George. "Optimal Operations and Investments of the Firm." *Management Science*, Vol. XV (September, 1968), 49–56.

[16] Thompson, R. G. "Discussion: The Potential Role of Control Theory." *American Journal of Agricultural Economics*, Vol. LI (May, 1969), pp. 404–408.

[17] Turvey, R. "Marginal Cost." *Economic Journal*, Vol. LXXIX (June, 1969), pp. 204–25.

[18] Wan, H. Y., Jr. "Intertemporal Optimization with Systematically Shifting Cost and Revenue Functions." *International Economic Review*, Vol. VII (May, 1966), pp. 204–25.

[19] Wasson, C. R. "What Is 'New' about a New Product?" *Journal of Marketing*, Vol. XXV (July, 1960), pp. 52–56.
[20] ———. "How Predictable Are Fashion and Other Product Life Cycles?" *Journal of Marketing*, Vol. XXXII (July, 1968), pp. 36–43.
[21] Weintraub, S. *Price Theory*. New York: Pitman, 1949.
[22] Whitin, T. M. "Dynamic Programming Extensions to the Theory of the Firm." *Journal of Industrial Economics*, Vol. XVI (April, 1968), pp. 81–98.
[23] Wijkman, P. M. "The Marginal Efficiency of Capital and of Investment: A Didactic Exercise." *Swedish Journal of Economics*, Vol. LXVII (December, 1965), pp. 263–78.

21. OLIGOPOLY THEORY, ENTRY-PREVENTION, AND GROWTH*

Jagdish N. Bhagwati†

1. The focus of the theory of oligopoly has been shifted towards entry-prevention models since the recent work of Sylos Labini and Bain, especially after its brilliant formalization by Franco Modigliani.[1] This paper examines the entry-prevention approach critically, while relating it to the traditional approaches to the analysis of oligopoly behavior. The analysis is also extended to incorporate the phenomenon of "growth of firms."

2.1. Traditional oligopoly theory was founded on two basic assumptions: (1) each firm maximizes its profits; and (2) each firm concerns itself with the repercussions of its action on the behavior of other firms *already* in the industry, firms which could be described as actual rivals. The former assumption was universal and extended to all market structures. The latter assumption, of interdependence among firms, was supposed to be the hallmark distinguishing oligopoly theory (the "small group" case) from the traditional competitive theory (the "large group" case).[2]

2.2. Under the perfectly competitive structure, the firm is assumed to act as if an infinitesimal "cut" in its price will enable it to sell as much as it likes and an infinitesimal "raise" will lose it its entire sales. This follows from the

*From *Oxford Economic Papers*, N. S., Vol. XXII, No. 3 (November, 1970), pp. 297–310. Reprinted by permission of the Clarendon Press, Oxford, and the author.

†Jagdish N. Bhagwati, Professor of Economics, Massachusetts Institute of Technology. The author is grateful to G. C. Archibald, W. M. Gorman, Ian Little, Harry Johnson, Walter Eltis, and N. Kaldor for helpful comments on earlier drafts of this paper.

[1]Franco Modigliani, "New Developments in the Oligopoly Front," *Journal of Political Economy*, Vol. LXVI, No. 2 (June, 1958), pp. 215–32; Sylos Labini, *Oligopolio e progresso tecnico* (Milan: Guiffre, 1957); and J. S. Bain, *Barriers to New Competition* (Cambridge, Mass.: Harvard University Press, 1956). Two earlier commentators on Modigliani's paper are: F. Fisher, "New Developments on the Oligopoly Front: Cournot and the Bain-Sylos Analysis," *Journal of Political Economy*, Vol. LXVII, No. 4 (August, 1959), pp. 410–13, and D. E. Farrar and C. F. Phillips, Jr., "New Developments on the Oligopoly Front: A Comment," *Journal of Political Economy*, Vol. LXVII, No. 4 (August, 1959), pp. 414–17.

[2]It should thus be emphasized that the distinction between the small and the large group cases is a matter, *not* of numbers, but of the pattern of behavior that characterizes the firm.

fact that it is assumed to be atomistic in relation to the industry and hence, the effects of its action will be "spread over many sellers" and hence, provoke no attempt on their part to alter their prices in response to this firm's action. Oligopoly theory departs from competitive theory basically in so far as each oligopolistic firm is *conscious* of the impact of its decisions on the economic behavior of its rivals. Under this view, the solution to the oligopolistic system would be quite different from the competitive solution unless each firm, in reaching its policy decision, assumed that the rival firms would keep their prices unchanged (so that the demand curve for each firm becomes infinitely elastic, as in the competitive case, at least in the relevant range).[3] Traditional theory thus proceeded by assuming some rule under which each firm played the game of maximizing its profits: the firm assumes the rivals' outputs to be maintained in the face of a change made by the firm (Cournot); the rivals' price is assumed to be constant (Bertrand; this is the competitive solution); and so on with Fellner and Stackelberg.[4]

3. It is often wrongly thought that the "kinked demand" analysis, developed independently by Hall and Hitch in England and by Sweezy in the U.S.A. in 1939, represented an innovation in oligopoly theory.[5] Actually, it is no more than a variation upon the traditional formulation, designed to explain rigidity in prices. It assumes that, *given* a market price, the firm will argue that a price increase by it will not be followed by its rivals but that a cut will be; hence, the kink. With the demand curve so derived, the firm is assumed to maximize its profits.[6]

4.1. The really fundamental innovation in oligopoly theory came with the realization that oligopoly theory must deal with "potential" competition as

---

[3]This obviously is the well-known Bertrand solution to the oligopoly problem. It is difficult, however, to consider this solution plausible because the firms are going to learn soon that prices will *not* be maintained by their rivals in the face of price cuts!

[4]For an extensive discussion of these various solutions, see Chamberlin, *The Theory of Monopolistic Competition* (4th ed.; Cambridge, Mass.: Harvard University Press, 1942), Chapter III; and W. Fellner, *Competition Among the Few* (New York: A. Knopf, 1949). Edgeworth and Chamberlin were both skeptical about the possibility of a determinate solution of the problem in the general case; cf. Chamberlin, *op. cit.*, Chapter III.

[5]Hall and Hitch, "Price Theory and Business Behaviour," *Oxford Economic Papers*, No. 2 (May, 1939), pp. 12–45; and Sweezy, "Demand Under Conditions of Oligopoly," *Journal of Political Economy*, Vol. XLVII, No. 4 (August, 1939), pp. 568–73; the latter is also reprinted in *Readings in Price Theory*, American Economic Association Series (London: Allen and Unwin Ltd., 1953).

[6]There is thus no radical departure involved in this model and the only advantage of the model consists in providing testable hypotheses relating the variability of prices to the several factors affecting the extent of the kink and hence the magnitude of the discontinuity in the marginal revenue curve. On some elementary tests, see Stigler, "The Kinky Oligopoly Demand Curve and Rigid Prices," *Journal of Political Economy*, Vol. LV, No. 5 (October, 1947), pp. 432–49.

distinct from "actual" competition (with *existing* rivals).[7] In perfect competition (and, indeed, in any "large group" case regardless of product differentiation), the firm does not worry about the reactions of existing rivals; the question of "potential" rivals is hence irrelevant. The distinction between the "short" period and the "long" period, in Marshall, concerns only the question of excess profits in an industry but has nothing to do with each individual firm's economic behavior (which continues to be the same under both periods). This is not so, however, with oligopolistic firms which *do* worry about rivals' reactions. The distinction between the short and long periods becomes of great relevance because the rivals multiply in the long period. More important, except when the firm wants to leave the industry, the firm's decision must *always* be affected by *both* actual competition and the possibility of potential competition.

4.2. This shift of focus makes it necessary to examine afresh the second assumption of traditional oligopoly theory as well. Profit maximization must now be reinterpreted. Firms already in an industry at any point of time will often have the following choice: *either* to maximize profits in the short period (defined, *á la* Marshall, as the period when entry cannot take place)—this being the framework of the traditional oligopoly solutions; or to maximize the value of profits (duly discounted) over the long period, *taking into account the repercussions on entry, and hence on future profitability, of any price policy pursued in the short period*—this being the hallmark of the new approach to oligopoly theory.

4.3. The recent thinking on oligopoly theory, therefore, departs from tradition in two important and related ways: (1) it focuses on the problem of "potential" competition; and (2) it correspondingly distinguishes between short-period and long-period profit maximization and takes the latter to be the objective of firms that maximize profits (excepting, of course, those that are planning to move out of the industry).[8]

---

[7]This is described as a "fundamental innovation" because it represents a radical departure in the theoretical formulation of the problem. Whether this stands up better against the test of empirical verification than the traditional approach is, of course, a separate issue.

[8]Firms may not want to maximize profits. They may desire a stable stream of profits even if the present discounted value thereof may be less than that of an alternative stream that is variable. Alternatively, they may pursue the objective of increasing their share of the market in preference to profit maximization, as W. Baumol has argued in *Business Behavior, Value and Growth* (New York: Macmillan Co., 1959). In either case, however, the impact of the current price-policy on potential competition and thus on the long-period stream of profits and share of the market must still be considered by existing firms.

5. This shift of focus may be primarily associated with the work of P. W. S. Andrews, who has developed this theme in numerous writings on the subject.[9] Several Oxford economists have followed with discussion of the ways in which potential competition affects a firm's price-policy.[10] Much of the analysis, principally of Harrod, Andrews, and Edwards, has assumed that firms, faced with potential competition, will pursue a price-policy designed to prevent the entry of potential competitors—with strong overtones that this is equivalent to long-run profit maximization.[11] However, there is disagreement on the level of the entry-prevention price which reflects, in turn, differences in the postulates made concerning the existing firms' expectations, and hence strategy, with respect to the entrant's evaluation of the possibility of successful entry.

6.1. *The Harrod strategy.* Harrod, explicitly citing Andrews' analysis, has advanced an entry-preventing strategy which is based squarely on the assumption that the potential entrant can be put off if, and only if, the existing firms are making merely normal profits. Hence, the existing firms will equate average cost, inclusive of normal profits, to average revenue instead of maximizing profits in relation to the demand curve derived on the basis of

---

[9]The following are of particular interest: P. W. S. Andrews, *Manufacturing Business* (London: Macmillan and Co., 1949); and P. W. S. Andrews, "Theory of Individual Business," *Oxford Economic Papers*, N.S., Vol. I, No. 1 (January, 1949), pp. 54–89. Mr. Kaldor has drawn my attention to the following paragraph on pp. 69–70 of his paper on "Market Imperfection and Excess Capacity," *Economica* (February, 1935), reprinted in his *Essays on Value and Distribution* (London: Duckworth, 1960):

> Thus a producer, if far-sighted, will take the effect of his own actions not merely on his existing competitors into consideration but also on his *potential competitors.* He will act on the basis of an "imagined demand curve" which shows the amount he can sell at different prices *in the long-run,* under the assumption that his competitors' products, prices and the number of his competitors are all adjusted to his price. If a producer knows that if he charges a high price today a competitor will appear tomorrow whose mere existence will put him in a *permanently worse position,* he will charge a price which will afford him only a low profit, if only he hopes to secure his profit permanently; i.e., he will act in a manner *as if* his own demand curve were very much more elastic than it is.

Indeed, references to the importance of potential competition abound in the literature even prior to Kaldor's paper (including, in the United States, the writings of J. M. Clark). However, nothing like a complete theoretical system appears to have been based on the idea of potential competition until Andrews placed it squarely at the center of his analysis of oligopoly prices and behavior.

[10]The major contributions may be listed here. R. F. Harrod, "Theory of Imperfect Competition Revised," in *Economic Essays* (London: Macmillan and Co., 1952), Chapter VIII; J. R. Hicks, "The Process of Imperfect Competition," *Oxford Economic Papers*, Vol. VI, No. 1 (February, 1954), pp. 41–54; and H. R. Edwards, "Price Formation in Manufacturing Industry and Excess Capacity," *Oxford Economic Papers*, Vol. VII, No. 1 (February, 1955), pp. 94–118.

[11]This equivalence, however, does not necessarily obtain in the case of any of the different strategies discussed in this paper. Hicks, *op. cit.*, however, is explicit on this question.

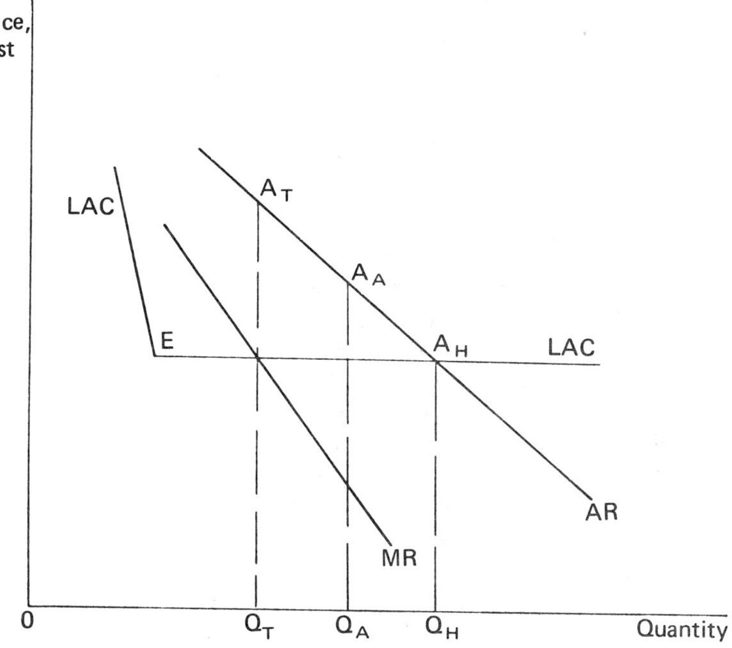

Figure 21-1

competition with existing rivals.[12] Thus, assume that, in view of existing competition, the demand curve facing the (typical) firm is *AR* in Figure 21-1.

[12]Harrod wishes to make this behavior applicable to firms in the "large group" case. This, however, is not persuasive. If firms are unconcerned about the reactions of existing rivals (the definition of the large group), it is impossible to see why they should bother about potential rivals! Harrod's strategy is plausible only in the case of oligopoly. This leads up to a problem which has been treated only cursorily, at best, in the literature on potential competition. How are existing rivals to *agree* on the entry-preventing price? How is such mutual agreement to be obtained? Curiously enough, some of the contributors almost wholly neglect this problem of actual competition in their concern with potential competition: the pendulum has swung to the other end! Hicks, *op. cit.*, skilfully frames his analysis in terms of a single firm which has no current rivals. Harrod does not analyze actual competition either. Edwards, *op. cit.*, in developing Andrews' theory, does have much to offer, however, in this direction. The most efficient firm in the industry, as currently constituted, will usually set the price at the entry-preventing level and other firms will have to follow it as best they can. If they cannot, the efficient firm(s) will expand at their expense and still keep the price at the entry-preventing level. Actual competition, therefore, adjusts itself to the demands of potential competition. Modigliani, *op. cit.*, does not pose the problem in the way it has been formulated here. While concentrating on potential competition, however, he offers several comments, based on Sylos's work, concerning "industrial structure," which closely parallel the arguments of Edwards concerning actual competition. Alternative solutions to the problem raised here would be *either* to have actual collusion *or* to argue, as Schelling has recently done with persuasiveness in *The Strategy of Conflict* (Cambridge, Mass.: Harvard University Press, 1960), that firms will often arrive at similar policies without actual collusion if attractive mutual gains follow from this event.

LAC, the long-run average cost curve of the firm, shows constant costs beyond *E*. Under traditional doctrine, the equilibrium output is Q_T and price A_T. Under Harrod's strategy, however, the output is Q_H and price A_H.[13]

6.2. However, even if this strategy were successful in preventing entry, one must ask why firms should wish to eliminate entry at the cost of all excess profits currently. Why make normal profits throughout (as per Harrod's strategy) instead of making excess profits immediately (ignoring the resulting entry) and normal profits later? Such a curious scale of preference on the part of Harrod's firms may be explained, of course, in terms of the firms seeking, for instance, a "stable" stream of profits or a larger share of the market, at the expense of extra profits. However, a rationale may be found for the Harrod-type behavior even within the framework of profit maximization. The optimum plant may be *different* for the pre-entry and post-entry situations. If the firm decides to invite competition by maximizing profits currently with a plant optimal to this objective, the profits following on entry will become subnormal *until* the plant is adjusted to the post-entry, optimum level. If the time-lag by which an existing plant can be adapted (at worst, through amortization and new purchase) to the post-entry optimal size is greater than the time-lag required for entry (as, one may suspect, may be the case for many plants), then subnormal profits are inevitable initially when entry occurs. If so, Harrod's strategy acquires cogency, from the viewpoint of profit maximization, if the initial losses on entry, duly discounted, exceed the gains that would have accrued from short-period profit maximization.

7.1. *The Andrews strategy.* Much of Andrews' writing suggests, however, that some *premium* in the form of a profit margin in excess of normal profits (as with output Q_A and price A_A) can be secured where entry is not "easy."[14] Entry can be difficult if it is hard to get a "foothold in the market" (i.e., the demand that accrues to the entrant may be insubstantial). A large market may further be needed to reach the "scale of efficient production" (i.e., the minimum size of plant, with least average cost, with which the entrant can come in, may be large).[15] The premium that can be enjoyed by the existing firms will thus reflect both the entrant's requirement of demand (determined by the scale of his plant) and his possibility of securing that demand.

[13]Harrod does allow a firm with advantages "peculiar to itself" to make abnormal profits. But the premium considered here is that which does not rest on such advantages but merely on the fact of being *already* inside the industry. Advantages such as Harrod has in mind are discussed by Bain, *op. cit.*, and are referred to in this paper in paragraph 10.

[14]Thus, Edwards, *op. cit.*, who offers an excellent account and extension of Andrews' theory, shows a premium being charged by an Andrews firm in Figure 2 on p. 110. Edward's analysis seems to be the best formal statement of Andrews' theory, and I shall draw upon it frequently. It is only fair to warn the reader that Andrews does not himself regard this as the correct interpretation of his theory; hence, it is probably best to regard the theory in the text as an "Andrews type" rather than as an Andrews theory.

[15]Edwards, *op. cit.*, pp. 96, 97, 99, among others. Numerous references to Andrews' own statement of the theory can be found in his book, *op. cit.*; for instance, pp. 151–4.

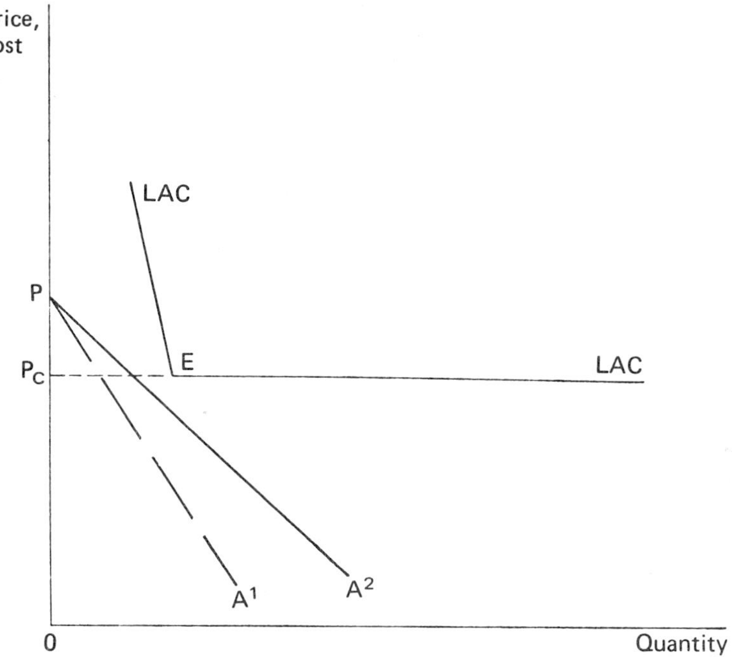

Figure 21-2

7.2. It is assumed that the entrant and the existing firms will expect (1) the existing firms to follow the entrant's price-cuts;[16] and (2) the customers of the existing firms not to switch to the entrant except in pursuit of a price-advantage.[17] Under these assumptions, the demand for the entrant's output is restricted to a share in the *marginal* increment in aggregate (industry) demand when the price falls below the pre-entry level. This increment may be equally divided among the existing firms and the entrant. However, if part of the increment ensues from the buyers attached to the existing sellers, the entrant's share is likely to be lower than that of (at least some of) its rivals. The demand curve so derived for the entrant is PA^1 in Figure 21-2. However, Andrews admits an important qualification to the assumption that buyers do not switch to the entrant except when there is a price-advantage. Buyers *will* be expected to transfer custom (in chagrin) to the entrant if the post-entry

[16] Cf. Edwards, *op. cit.*, pp. 107–9.

[17] With a single exception to be considered shortly, this is one of the central assumptions of Andrews' theory. It is held to be particularly true when the buyers themselves are manufacturing firms. Thus, consider: "The buyers of the product — themselves manufacturers at a higher stage of production — will tend to look first to their customary suppliers because of the confidence gained by previous custom, and it is from these firms that they will normally buy." Edwards, *op. cit.*, pp. 95–6. It should be noticed that this argument contradicts the premise of *random* pairing of buyers and sellers. In the absence of this assumption, the premium that could be charged, consistent with entry-prevention, would be *reduced*.

price reveals the pre-entry price to have been unduly high in relation to cost and hence exploitative.[18] Thus, the demand curve for the entrant will be more elastic — PA^2 in Figure 21-2. If the entrant's demand curve so derived for any given price, say PA^2 for price P in Figure 21-2, is below the average cost of production for the range of outputs at which the minimum average cost obtains,[19] entry will be expected to be unprofitable and hence is barred. The existing firms will then choose the maximum price — P_0 in Figure 21-3 — which is consistent with the prevention of entry.[20]

7.3. The premium charged under Andrews' strategy is then *approximately* given by the formula:

$$P_0 = P_C\left[1 + \frac{\bar{x}}{X_C\{\zeta/(N+1) + \varepsilon\}}\right],$$

where P_0 is the entry-preventing price, P_C the competitive price (equal to the minimum average cost of the potential entrant), $\bar{x}$ the minimum scale of plant (of the entrant) at which the minimum average cost is achieved, X_C the industry demand at price P_C, N the number of existing firms, ζ the price-elasticity of industry demand at price P_C, and ε the elasticity, with respect to change in price, of the current buyers' transfer of custom to the entrant.[21] It follows that the premium obtainable in an industry will vary directly with (1) the minimum size of the scale of most efficient production and (2) the number of existing firms; and inversely with (1) the size of the total market, (2) the price-elasticity of industry demand and (3) the extent to which existing buyers will transfer custom to the entrant consequent upon entry.[22]

[18] "In the event that the price has been maintained high, gratuitously, by otherwise efficient producers, it will very soon be reduced to match the price of the new entrant. But the resentment of the buyer-firms at the high price now revealed to have been not warranted by costs, provides a reservoir of ill-will which, properly exploited, will ensure the new entrant access to the market." (Edwards, *op. cit.*, p. 97.)

[19] Andrews rules out the possibility of a stable equilibrium at levels of production which involve operating at falling costs to the level of the minimum average cost point, the argument being that in this situation firms will feel that they must expand production and drive out existing rivals until at least the efficient scale is achieved. Analogously, the entrant will not enter if he cannot cover his costs at a level of output characterized by *minimum* average costs.

[20] Assuming, of course, that prices and profits are positively correlated. This assumption is shared by Modigliani, *op. cit.*

[21] The sign of ζ is negative and of ε (since custom is lost to the entrant and hence *reduced* when price *falls* with entry) positive. Some of the symbols have been borrowed from Modigliani, *op. cit.* For simplicity, it has been assumed that the increase in demand, as price falls with entry, is shared equally by all firms.

[22] Three observations are in order here. (1) The "Andrews strategy" presented here abstracts, for the purpose of analyzing the problem of price-formation, certain key postulates from, and hence is only a segment of, a full-blooded and rich account of the industrial process contained in Andrews, *op. cit.* (2) On the other hand, the testable hypotheses listed here as deductions from this strategy represent an extension of Andrews' analysis in so far as they are not all to be found (at any rate in the form given here) explicitly in Edwards and Andrews, *op. cit.* (3) It should further be noted that Andrews considers that, with the possibility of entry by multi-product firms into adjacent markets, the relevant minimum size of the entrant's plant will often be sufficiently small to make the premium chargeable negligible.

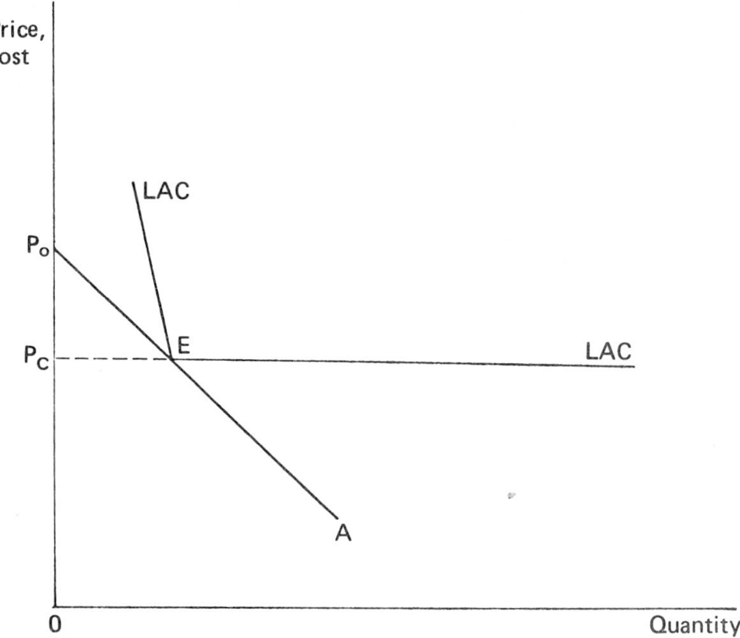

Figure 21-3

8.1. *The attractiveness of entry.* Andrews often appears to argue as though, in addition to making entry easier for the potential entrant, a higher premium also makes entry more "attractive"; however, no cogent discussion of such attractiveness is to be found in his work. It would appear, however, that *the mere enjoyment of lucrative premium by existing firms (no matter how amply justified in terms of difficulty of entry as defined previously) will attract firms into the industry who may want to undergo initial losses with a view to driving some existent firms out, in the hope of surviving and earning the lucrative premiums that are being made in the industry.* If, therefore, it is possible that if the premium charged appears lucrative enough, the entrant will risk coming into the industry in the hope of securing a foothold at the expense of some existing firm(s), the premium that will be charged will be *lower* than otherwise available.

8.2. This argument is illustrated in Figure 21-4. *OE* represents the profits, discounted back to the current period, that will be earned by the existing firms in the industry, *in the absence of entry*, at different premiums.[23] *LP* represents the expected losses and profits, duly discounted again, of an Andrews

[23]It is assumed that the greater the premium charged, the greater the profits made. The schedule could be easily adjusted to incorporate any alternative assumption.

entrant, corresponding to the premiums being charged currently by the existing firms. For premiums up to P_0, the entrant is supposed to take losses; with premiums exceeding P_0, the entrant will expect to make profits.[24] O then represents Harrod's entry-prevention price; and P_0 that of Andrews. If the attractiveness-of-entry argument is considered, however, the entrant will now have a new schedule of profits expected in case of *survival*, corresponding to the range of (lucrative) premiums form O' to P_0. These profits will be expected with uncertainty and are likely to accrue after an initial period of losses; hence, the schedule ought to be left of OE. However, the profits must be computed from the level of losses estimated in deriving LP_0, to permit lateral aggregation with the latter; hence, the schedule *may* be to the right of OE (for some premiums). The resulting schedule is $O'R$ in Figure 21-4. By aggregating LP_0 and $O'R$ for each premium charged, we arrive at the truly relevant curve LR. This curve intersects the Y-axis at P_0^1 which is the entry-prevention price.

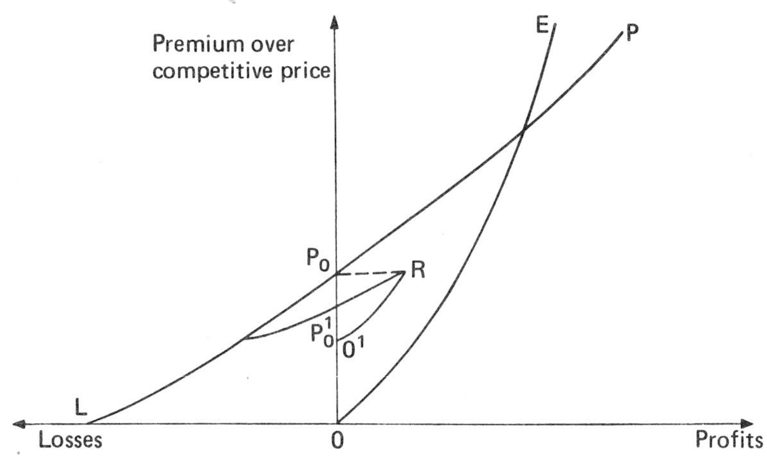

Figure 21-4

9.1. *The SBM strategy.* The Sylos-Bain model, as presented by Modigliani, and referred to hereafter as the SBM model, is startlingly similar to, though not identical with, Andrews' analysis.[25] The SBM firms agree on sharing the following expectations: (1) the potential entrant will not enter if the post-entry price does not cover its average cost of production; and (2)

[24]The expected losses could be estimated presumably at the minimum level of output at which minimum average cost is obtained; and the expected profits in a similar way.

[25]Modigliani, *op. cit.*, in a brief footnote on p. 216, refers to Edwards, *op. cit.*, as having anticipated "many of the conclusions of Sylos and Bain." However, he misses the differences between the two strategies.

the existing firms, assumed to be producing at minimum average cost, maintain their output unchanged when entry occurs. Under these rules, the entrant's demand curve starts from the price-axis at the pre-entry price and is drawn so that the entire increment in aggregate industry demand with each price-reduction accrues to the entrant. In other words, this demand schedule is the industry demand schedule minus the unchanging output of the existing firms. Assuming then that costs fall steeply to the minimum average cost level,[26] the following approximate formula holds for the maximum entry-preventing price (using the notation of paragraph 7.3):

$$P_0 = P_C\left[1 + \frac{\bar{x}}{X_C\,\zeta}\right].$$

9.2. In common with Andrews' results, the following testable hypotheses are obtained: the premium that can be charged, consistent with the prevention of entry, varies directly with the minimum scale of the entrant's plant and inversely with both the size of the total market and the price-elasticity of industry demand. The differences from Andrews, however, are that the premium is not affected by either the number of existing firms or by expectations about the transfer of custom to the entrant by current buyers; further, the premium will now rise if costs do not fall steeply to the minimum average cost level.

9.3. These testable hypotheses relate, however, to *variations* in the profit margins between industries and for an industry at different points of time. It is possible to construe the analysis, however, as also stating something testable about the actual size of the margin: the SBM result,

$$P_0 = P_C\left[1 + \frac{\bar{x}}{X_C\,\zeta}\right],$$

provides such a hypothesis. It is difficult, however, to expect anything except a refutation of this hypothesis. The premium charged according to the SBM strategy is likely to be an over-estimate for a variety of reasons, related to the attractiveness-of-entry factor considered in paragraph 8.1. If lucrative premiums are charged in an attempt to capitalize on the difficulty of entry, the attractiveness of entry becomes great and firms will enter the industry in the hope of survival. The reasons for this type of behavior by the entrant are quite plausible:

(1) When the entrant enters the industry, *every* firm makes losses; it should thus be a matter of chance as to which firm goes out. If the premium is lucrative enough, it could pay the firm to take the chance that it (rather than some existing firm) will survive.

(2) Indeed, if the SBM strategy is pursued, the entrant will be making *smaller* losses than the existing firms, except in a limiting case, under the assumptions made concerning costs; and hence, its chances of survival will be *greater* than those of existing firms,

[26]The SBM model, in contrast to Andrews' model, admits the possibility of equilibrium at ranges of output where the average cost is in excess of the minimum. The formula in the text, however, ignores this complication.

so that the argument about survival is considerably strengthened. In Figure 21-5, designed to illustrate the SBM strategy, AR^1 is the demand curve for an existing firm (symmetry of demand for each firm is assumed for the sake of simplicity; nothing substantive in the following argument hinges on this); P^1 is the entry-preventing price; P^2 is the price *after* entry; OW is the output of the existing firm before entry, which is now maintained, *à la* the Sylos Labini strategy, in the face of entry; OK is the (minimum) plant with which the entrant has entered the industry; and AR^2 is the demand curve for each *existing* firm *after* entry. The pre-entry profits, in excess of normal, are P^1RMN; the post-entry loss for each pre-entry firm is $NMQP^2$; and the post-entry loss for the entrant itself is only $NEHP^2$ ($< NMQP^2$). In the limiting case, when each existing firm produces, prior to entry, at E, each firm (inclusive of the entrant) must make identical losses after entry.

(3) Further, if the question is one of survival, to earn lucrative premiums, it is quite possible that the entrant may have greater financial reserves than some existing firm(s) — an assumption clearly compatible with the assumption of homogeneity of cost curves — and hence, also a greater capacity to survive. Since the entrants are often, and will almost always be assumed to be, multi-product firms, this argument acquires special cogency.

(4) The entrant may quite possibly be willing to take initial losses and to consider them as inevitable "investment in a market," particularly if a market that is already substantially being exploited is being entered.

(5) Finally, multiple-product firms can always set off losses on a new venture against profits from existing activities and hence let the Treasury share the losses, so that the

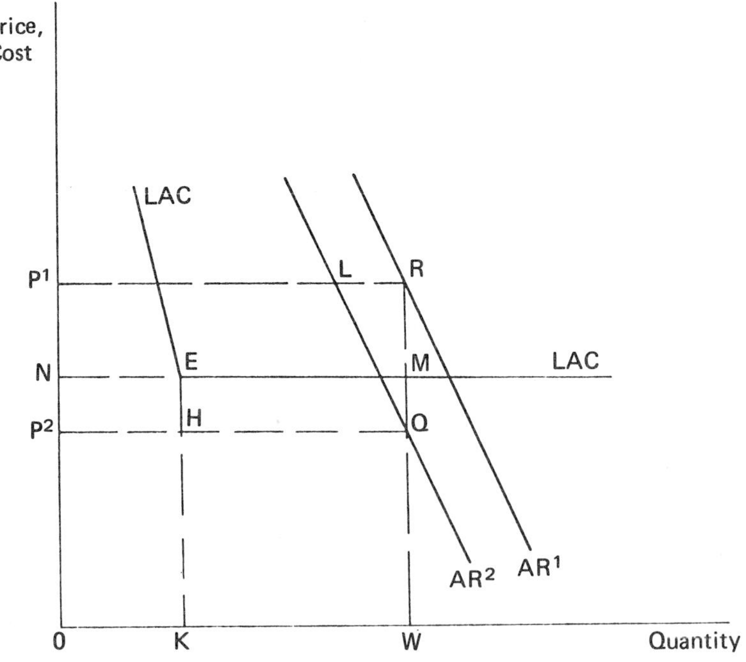

Figure 21-5

prospect of initial losses again is relatively less inhibiting than might otherwise be supposed. For these various reasons, therefore, the premium that will be charged by oligopolistic firms is likely to be overstated by the SBM formulation and is unlikely to be successfully verified empirically.[27]

10. All this is *not* to deny that sometimes existing firms may have absolute cost advantages over entrants, which may persist for long periods. For instance, patents provide an example. Where such advantages obtain and are likely to persist for long periods, the premium charged will be *higher* than that indicated by Andrews', as also Sylos Labini's analysis. Bain provides a careful and valuable analysis of these advantages, and several testable hypotheses about variations in the size of the available premium follow directly from his analysis.[28]

11. Many of the paces through which the entry models are taken involve the assumption of a *given* demand curve for the industry. Sylos Labini and Modigliani argue, for instance, that the implications of a growing demand will be (1) to put a downward pressure on the premium that can be charged (because the aggregate demand is now larger) and hence (2) to cause the existing firms to ration out scarce supplies instead of raising prices if capacity creation has lagged behind the expansion of demand.[29] It is possible, however, to incorporate the effects of growing demand formally into the entry analyses of the variety discussed here; and the results are interesting.

12.1. The formula for the equilibrium price, under the Andrews strategy, should now read:

$$P_0 = P_C\left[1 + \frac{\bar{x} - k\lambda}{X_C\{\zeta/(N+1) + \varepsilon\}}\right]$$

where λ is the growth of aggregate demand subsequent to entry, k the proportion thereof that accrues to the entrant, and X_C now the aggregate demand at the competitive price *after* growth. An Andrews-type version of the share of

---

[27]Of course, under certain assumptions, the issue of survival could be plausibly shown to exercise some *upward* pressure on the premium as well. Thus, for instance, as Mr. Archibald has pointed out to me, if entry is a function of the reserves possessed by existing firms and usable in a "war to the ruin" in case of entry, and reserves in turn depend on the level of profits in the short period, then the best entry-prevention strategy would appear to be to maximize current profits. However, it seems to me that this argument must be balanced against the fact that the worth-whileness of a "war to the ruin" to the entrant is itself a function of the presence of lucrative premiums in the industry. The Archibald-type argument thus merely makes the $O'R$ curve in Figure 21-4 steeper than it would otherwise be, because the expected profits are reduced at higher premiums if the higher premiums improve the existing firms' profits, reserves, and hence fighting strength and thereby dim the entrant's prospect of survival. The result is then to raise the premium that can be obtained by the existing firms.

[28]Modigliani, *op. cit.*

[29]Modigliani draws attention to the fact that these conclusions are found in Edwards, *op. cit.*

the increasing demand accruing to the entrant would probably be: $k\lambda = qm\lambda/(N+1)$, where $(1-m)$ is the proportion of increased demand that accrues through current buyers attached to existing sellers, and $(1-q)$ the fractional scalar by which the entrant's share in the increased demand must be reduced because the existing sellers' "goodwill" gives them a more than equal share of the demand accruing through new buyers. The prospect of increasing demand will thus reduce the premium available; and the reduction will vary directly with q, m, and λ and inversely with the number of current sellers.

12.2 However, there is a further implication which is positively startling. It is no longer possible to argue that entry, even though "free," can be closed by the "very effective and legitimate weapon of a competitive price based on the costs of efficient production."[30] Thus, where $\bar{x} < k\lambda$, the entry-prevention price is lower than P_C. However, the price cannot be set (permanently) below P_C, so that the use of price-policy to prevent entry becomes an ineffective device. From this, there follow two significant conclusions. (1) The entry-prevention approach can now be turned around to provide testable hypotheses concerning the *incidence of entry* itself. Thus, the testable hypothesis provided here is that entry occurs when $\bar{x} < qm\lambda/(N+1)$.[31] Moreover, viewed from the angle of the existing firms, this also becomes a hypothesis about the growth of firms; the share of a firm in increased aggregate demand will fall below its average share of the market when $\bar{x} < qm\lambda/(N+1)$.[32] (2) It is also now evident that the only efficient entry-preventing strategy that the existing firms can pursue, in a situation of increasing demand, is to ensure, in so far as this is feasible, *the maximum appropriation to themselves, rather than to any potential entrant, of the segment of growing demand.* The theoretical problem thus shifts from devising an entry-preventing *price* to a formal analysis of the *non-price* factors which determine the share of the existing firms in the growing market and the ways in which these are within the range of influence of these firms.

---

[30]Edwards, *op. cit.*, p. 96.

[31]Similar hypotheses would be that the incidence of entry would vary directly, for instance, with the rate at which industry demand is growing and inversely with the share thereof that accrues through current buyers.

[32]An SBM-type argument, however, would make the growth of existing firms an independent variable (which determines both entry and price). The SBM formula would now read somewhat like: $P_0 = P_C[1 + \{\bar{x} - (\lambda - \alpha)\}/X_C\,\zeta]$ where α is the creation of new capacity by existing firms in anticipation of growing demand. It in only when this falls short, for reasons such as incorrect anticipation or difficulties of expansion peculiar to some existing firms(s), of the growth in demand that the entry-prevention price could be reduced to the extreme level when entry would become inevitable.

22. PRICE STRATEGY OLIGOPOLY: LIMITING BEHAVIOR WITH PRODUCT DIFFERENTIATION*

Martin Shubik†

In a previous paper Shapley and Shubik [3] set up a model of an oligopolistic market with n firms selling (symmetrically) differentiated products. They solved this model for the noncooperative equilibrium where price is the strategic variable used by each firm. The behavior of the noncooperative equilibrium was examined under the condition that the number of firms in competition became arbitrarily large, and it was shown that under certain circumstances the noncooperative price approached the price that would prevail under pure competition. In that paper, however, the implications of the model concerning the nature of product differentiation and the different ways in which the concept of "the number of firms in a market becomes large" were not discussed. In this paper they are examined.

Limit Processes: Firms, Customers, Capacity and Product Differentiation

"How many is many in a market?" is an old question in the study of the control of industry. With the exception of Cournot [1] and Edgeworth [2] until quite recently this question has been scarcely asked in a precise manner by economic theorists.

A way in which the effect of numbers can be examined precisely in an economic model is to set up a formal mathematical description of the economic activity in which the number of participants appears explicitly, or implicitly in its effect upon certain of the variables or parameters; then investigate the behavior of the model as the number of participants becomes arbitrarily large.

In general there are many different ways in which the model of a market can be constructed and examined for behavior in the limit. The different ways of proceeding to a limit correspond to somewhat different economic phenomena which may not be easy to isolate and distinguish in a verbal or diagrammatic treatment of the subject.

When dealing with oligopolistic competition we make considerable use of symmetry, and in this paper several other simplifications are introduced in order to study a specific model to obtain some simple contrasting results.

The setting-up of the appropriate model of an oligopolistic market involving n single-product firms calls for the specification of the number of

*From *Western Economic Journal*, Vol. VIII, No. 3 (September, 1970), pp. 226–232. Reprinted by permission of the publisher and the author.

†Martin Shubik, Professor of the Economics of Organization, Yale University.

firms, the number of customers, the capacities and costs of the firms and the nature of the differentiation amongst the products. Complete symmetry among the firms is assumed. They are each assumed to manufacture and sell one product to the market, they have identical overheads and production costs and their products are symmetrically differentiated. Another way of stating this is that when all the firms charge the same price, the cross-elasticity between any two firms in the market will be the same as that between any other two firms.

If we assume U-shaped average costs of production, then immediately we are confronted with a problem in comparing markets with different numbers of firms. Intuitively, when the economist talks about the effect of more competitors in the market he usually has in mind a comparison between two markets in which the demand or consumer side has remained constant, but the few competitors have been replaced by more competitors who are in some sense "similar to but smaller than" the previous few competitors. The concepts of "size" and "similarity" are not easy to define precisely when the firms have U-shaped average costs. One way to avoid this difficulty, yet still be able to comment in a useful manner upon the growth in the number of competitors, is by considering a sequence of different markets in which the costs to the individual producer always remain the same; however, the overall size of market demand grows at the same speed as does the supply, due to the presence of new competitors. In other words, although in the sequence of models the market grows larger, if all the firms charge the same price, no matter how many firms there are, each will sell an amount that is independent of the number of competitors. This way of going to the limit leaves the size and cost conditions of the firms the same, but erodes their market share. Hence, this is a useful model to examine the question of how market power is related to market share.

Another way of setting up a limit process would be to hold the overall size of the market fixed, but to chop up the firms. We note that this is difficult to do when we assume U-shaped costs. If however we were to assume that the firms produced under conditions of constant variable costs, c (with no fixed costs) and with a capacity limit k, then it is easy to examine a set of markets where we successively replace few large firms by more firms with the same average costs but with smaller individual capacities.

When fixed average cost and capacities are assumed, then a little reflection will show that the two ways of considering markets with many competitors are equivalent. We can either hold the overall market size fixed and chop up the firms; or we can introduce more firms of the same size and expand the overall size of the market. In the examples in the second section of this paper, fixed average costs and capacities are assumed, and the latter limiting process is used to examine the effect of numbers.

Before any market models are specified and investigated, the role of product differentiation and numbers of firms must be discussed. Consider a duopolistic market and suppose that we had a measure that indicated the degree to which the products of the firms were differentiated substitutes. One such measure might be as follows: consider that one firm sets its price arbitrarily high while the other sets its price equal to cost, the measure is the ratio of the amount sold by the lower-priced firm to the amount that it would have sold, had both firms each set price equal to cost. An example is provided in Figure 22-1. If both firms had charged $p = c$, then the amount sold by the first is indicated by AB and the amount sold by the second by BG, where $BG = AB$ as the firms are selling symmetrically related substitutes. If the second firm raises its price to a level so high that it sells nothing, the first will still not pick up all of the amount BG because the products are differentiated. In Figure 22-1 the final demand for the first firm is indicated by AH, hence the extra demand obtained is BH and the measure that has been suggested is BH/BG. When the firms are selling the identical product the value of this measure is 1, and when they are selling completely isolated products the value of the measure is 0.

Suppose that the overall size of the market were doubled, and that two more firms selling differentiated products were in the market. Once more if all charged $p = c$, each would sell an amount equal to AB in Figure 22-1. If one firm were to change its price slightly with the others remaining fixed, it

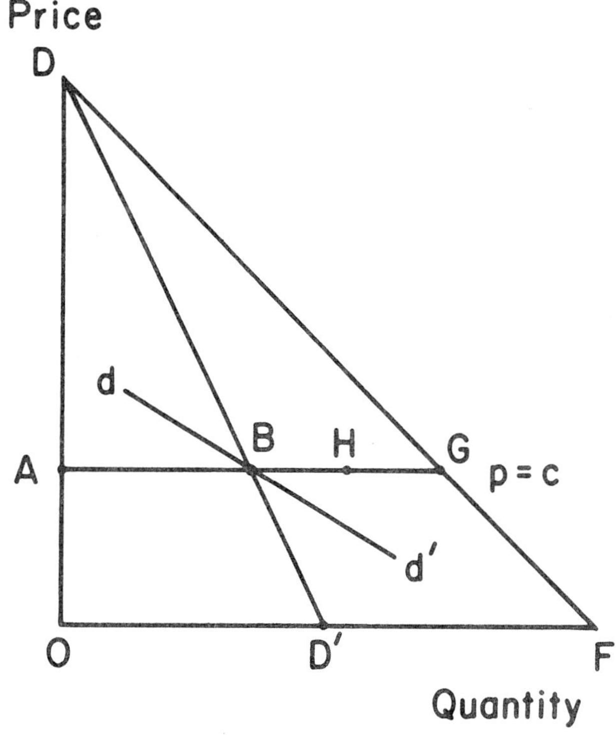

Figure 22-1

would pick up or lose demand along a contingent demand curve indicated by *dd'* in Figure 22-1. Does the slope of this curve remain constant as the number of firms increases or does the slope become flatter? One cannot state which from only a priori considerations. When the market is larger and there are more competing substitutes available, do the substitutes become more competitive or do they stay the same "distance" apart? Are four family cars, in a market twice the size, closer substitutes for each other than two family cars in the original market?

When a market is growing and a few more substitute products appear, it is not unreasonable that the substitutes remain apart. When the number of substitutes becomes large, it is likely that in some sense they become closer substitutes for each other. In the second section of this paper examples of both assumptions are examined. In actual markets there is probably an upper bound of between 5 to 10 perceived different substitutes, beyond which further substitutes pack together.

More powerful mathematical methods than those used here might dispense with the type of replication process used here to compare games of different sizes. This might be achieved by using games with a continuum of players and games with a continuum of commodities. However, staying with the somewhat simpler formulation, there are at least four models that might be considered as are indicated below.

Model	*Number of firms*	*Size of market*	*Capacity*	*Product differentiation*
(1)	n	$O(n)$	k	fixed
(2)	n	$O(n)$	k	$O(1/n)$
(3)	n	fixed	k/n	fixed
(4)	n	fixed	k/n	$O(1/n)$

In the first example the market grows in proportion to the number of firms, but the "distance" of substitutability between the growing number of substitutes remains the same. In the second example the added substitutes are packing closer together as $1/n$. The two other cases are basically the same, however the firms are being cut up and their capacity shrinks while the overall size of the market stays the same.

The Noncooperative Equilibrium and Substitutability

Following the models (1) and (2) suggested above, we consider two aggregate consumer utility functions of the form

$$U(q) = aq - \frac{b}{n}q^2 - \frac{\varepsilon}{n}\left[\Sigma q_i^2 - \frac{q^2}{n}\right] \quad \text{or} \tag{1}$$

(2) $$U(q) = aq - \frac{b}{n}q^2 - \frac{\varepsilon'}{n}\left[\Sigma q_i^2 - \frac{q^2}{n}\right]$$

$$\text{where } q = \sum_{i=1}^{n} q_i \text{ and } \varepsilon' = \varepsilon n.$$

These utility functions are obviously only defined for the appropriate range of the q_i where the marginal utilities are not negative. In the first case the product differentiation comes through the presence of the variance term controlled by ε. The customer likes variety. As the number of commodities increases, they become progressively closer substitutes. In the second case the introduction of the extra term of n in $\varepsilon' = \varepsilon n$ helps to keep the products apart.

It is a relatively straightforward calculation to write down demand in terms of price, to write down the payoff function for each firm in terms of price and to solve for the noncooperative equilibrium with price as the independent variable. This has been done by Shapley and Shubik [3]. Stating only the results we have:

(3) $$q_i = \frac{a - \bar{p}}{2b} - \frac{n}{2\varepsilon}(p_i - \bar{p})$$

(4) $$P = (p_i - c)\, q_i$$

and the noncooperative equilibrium price is given by

(5) $$p_i = \frac{n(n-1)bc + \varepsilon(na + c)}{n(n-1)bc + \varepsilon(n+1)}.$$

As $n \to \infty$, $p_i \to c$. This is the price that would prevail at a competitive equilibrium. Suppose, however, that ε is replaced by $\varepsilon' = \varepsilon n$. The expression for the price prevailing at the noncooperative equilibrium, given in (5) is now modified and becomes

(6) $$p_i = \frac{(n-1)bc + \varepsilon(na + c)}{(n-1)b + \varepsilon(n+1)}.$$

As $n \to \infty$, $p_i \to \dfrac{bc + \varepsilon a}{b + \varepsilon}$.

Even though price will decrease with more competitors, it does *not* approach that of the competitive equilibrium, but a term involving ε remains, indicating that there is always a measure of monopoly power present.

The first model is probably more believable than the second. However, it still involves making the assumptions about substitutability explicit. In a world of monopolies where all products are gross substitutes and where the differentiation among them is continuous, then as numbers grow the noncooperative price approaches that of pure competition. If the substitutes do not pack together, this is not so.

In most markets the truth probably lies in between the two models indicated here. Richard Levitan, in a discussion, has suggested a model in which it is assumed that there is an extra parameter representing the maximum number of different substitutes that a group of customers will consider to be fundamentally different. Beyond this number, if new firms come into the market we may expect that the distinction amongst further substitutes lessens. In such a market the limit is not the competitive equilibrium, but depends upon the extra parameter.

How many competitors constitute "many competitors" in an oligopolistic market? Taking the model of demand based upon (1) we observe that the joint maximum or monopolistic price is given by

$$p_i = \frac{a + c}{2}. \tag{7}$$

We might use as a measure the number of firms for which the noncooperative equilibrium price (given in (5)) comes within 5% of the competitive equilibrium price where the range of 100% is determined by the difference between the monopolistic price and the competitive equilibrium, i.e.,

$$\frac{n(n-1)bc + \varepsilon(na + c)}{n(n-1)b + \varepsilon(n+1)} \leqslant c + .05\left(\frac{a - c}{2}\right) \quad \text{or} \tag{8}$$

$$\frac{\varepsilon n}{n(n-1)b + \varepsilon(n+1)} \leqslant .025. \tag{9}$$

Regarding (9) as an equation, this is a quadratic in n with ε and b as parameters. When $\varepsilon = 0$ the products are identical; when $\varepsilon = b$ the products become completely isolated from each other. A few representative values for ε are:

ε	n
b	40
$b/5$	9
$b/10$	5
$b/20$	3

The first value represents products that are rather distant as substitutes. The others show closer substitutes. It can be seen that the number of firms needed for "many" drops extremely quickly if the initial degree of substitutability is high and the new products crowd together.

Using the model of demand based upon (2), then from (6) we can calculate how close the limiting state with many competitors is to the competitive equilibrium. Calling this distance K, then

$$\frac{bc + \varepsilon a}{b + \varepsilon} = c + K\left[\frac{a - c}{2}\right]. \tag{10}$$

Hence,

$$K = 2\varepsilon/(b + \varepsilon). \tag{11}$$

Thus, unless $\varepsilon < b/40$ in this model oligopolistic price never reaches to within the 5% bandwidth above competitive price.

Although the examples calculated in this paper were specific, the basic model and the results appear to be reasonably general. In particular, when we consider the increase in numbers of competitors in an oligopolistic market with differentiated products, there are many different models that are relevant, each reflecting different conditions on substitutability.

Leaving aside the many other features that characterize an oligopolistic market (indivisibilities, increasing returns to scale, etc.), "many" is determined by the market and cost parameters as well as by the number of firms. With the market structure used here convergence to competition was $O(1/n)$, if substitutes were becoming closer. Otherwise, although price may still decrease with new entrants, it does not approach the competitive price as a limit.

With different market structures we may expect virtually any speed of convergence, although it seems to be reasonable to consider the linear case as a manageable approximation to many markets.

"Many" appears to be a number between 2 and 10 for the most part, unless for special reasons, even with new entrants, the firms find it possible to maintain their distance in product differentiation.

REFERENCES

[1] Cournot, A. A. *Researches into the Mathematical Principles of the Theory of Wealth.* New York: Macmillan, 1897.

[2] Edgeworth, F. Y. *Mathematical Psychics.* London: Keegan Paul, 1881.

[3] Shapley, L., and M. Shubik. "Price Strategy Oligopoly with Product Variation." *Kyklos*, Fasc. 1, Vol. XXII, (1969), pp. 30–44.

23. FURTHER REMARKS ON THE THEORY OF PRODUCT DIFFERENTIATION*

Helmut Schuster†

In a recent article in the *Journal of Political Economy*, W. J. Baumol [2] makes an interesting contribution toward the development of what might be called a theory of product differentiation. His conclusion is, briefly, given a certain number of substitute product characteristics, the optimal strategy of a firm introducing a new product into a market of rival goods would not be to differentiate it as much as possible from any rival product, but, on the contrary, to furnish this product with a combination of characteristics similar to those of some other product already on the market. The explanation given for this apparently paradoxical result that seems to be diametrically opposed to the conclusions of traditional competition theory is essentially a geometrical one. It can perhaps best be translated into verbal terms by saying that the more pronounced the similarity of the new product to one particular already existing rival product, the greater (within certain limits) the demand for that new product, since it will then be regarded as a close substitute for the rival product, and can therefore capture a substantial part of that particular rival product's demand, a gain which is only partly offset by forgoing demand from other more dissimilar rival products.

This contribution undertakes to extend and, at the same time, modify Baumol's findings by relaxing some of the very stringent assumptions he makes. It is basically in these assumptions that the paradox lies. If these assumptions are relaxed then Baumol's theorem can easily be reconciled with and integrated into the traditional theory of competition.

Baumol's main assumptions are (1) absence of any countermoves by other firms against the new product, (2) a constant rate of substitution among the various characteristics of the product for the consumer, and (3) a constant total demand for the entire line of production, that is, for the new product together with its already existing rival products.

Assumption (1) excludes all problems of retaliation. As a general rule, however, it may be expected that retaliation by any one firm will be stronger,

*From *Journal of Political Economy*, Vol. LXXVII, No. 5 (September–October, 1969), pp. 827–833. Reprinted by permission of the University of Chicago Press and the author.

†Helmut Schuster, Professor of Economics, Technische Universitat Berlin. The author is indebted to Professor H. St. Seidenfus for prompting this paper and to Robert A. Mundell for valuable comments on an earlier draft.

the greater the similarity of the new product to its own product. If, on the other hand, the new product's qualities are such that it does not take away a substantial part of any particular rival product's market but rather a small part from several rival products, any such retaliatory action might be avoided altogether or, although involving more firms, its total extent considerably lessened [4, esp. pp. 40–49 and 84–87].

The firm introducing the new product, therefore, has to take at least two counteracting aspects into account. The greater the similarity of its new product to one of the existing products the more substantial, again within certain limits, the immediate gain in demand according to Baumol's theorem; but, at the same time, the greater the probability of extensive retaliation by the one firm mainly affected, leading most likely to costly quality or price warfare. It is then simply a question of whether the addition in demand for the new product whose qualities are similar to those of an existing product is worth the increased risk of a competitive war of this kind.

If the position of the firm introducing the new product is such that it cannot exclude the possibility of being driven out of the market eventually as a result of higher direct costs or inferior capital reserves,[1] then its object must quite clearly be to try to avoid any such conflict, and it will best do so by choosing a combination of product characteristics which affords the highest degree of differentiation from any possibly dangerous retaliator. If, on the other hand, the firm introducing the new product stands a good chance of winning any subsequent price-quality war, then its strategy will essentially be determined by the relative costs of such temporary warfare. The decision will depend mainly on the strength of the opponent in relation to the extra demand gained from the qualitative approximation of the rival product in question. The straight iso-cost lines used by Baumol (figure 1, p. 676), combining points of equal costs for various possible quality combinations but only taking account of costs of production, would therefore have to be modified to include variations in the competitive risks entailed, risks which are dependent on the particular combination of product characteristics chosen. Figure 23-1 helps to illustrate this point. The horizontal axis shows different possible ratios of characteristics, R_1 and R_2 denoting the ratio of two existing rival products. The vertical axis shows demand, costs, and profit. The demand curve for the new product according to Baumol's theorem is represented by *dd*; *kk* represents the shape of the extended cost curve. With equal costs of production for all combinations of product characteristics, total costs (including competitive risks) would reach a peak where the quality of the new product is precisely the same as that of one of the existing products. Total costs decline with a higher degree of differentiation reaching their minimum around the point of equidistance from R_1 and R_2. The optimal point of production for the firm introducing the new product is determined not by the shape of the

[1]In the case of a multiproduct firm, the strategic position of the firm will also be largely dependent on the intensity of competition in the other markets [5, pp. 210–16].

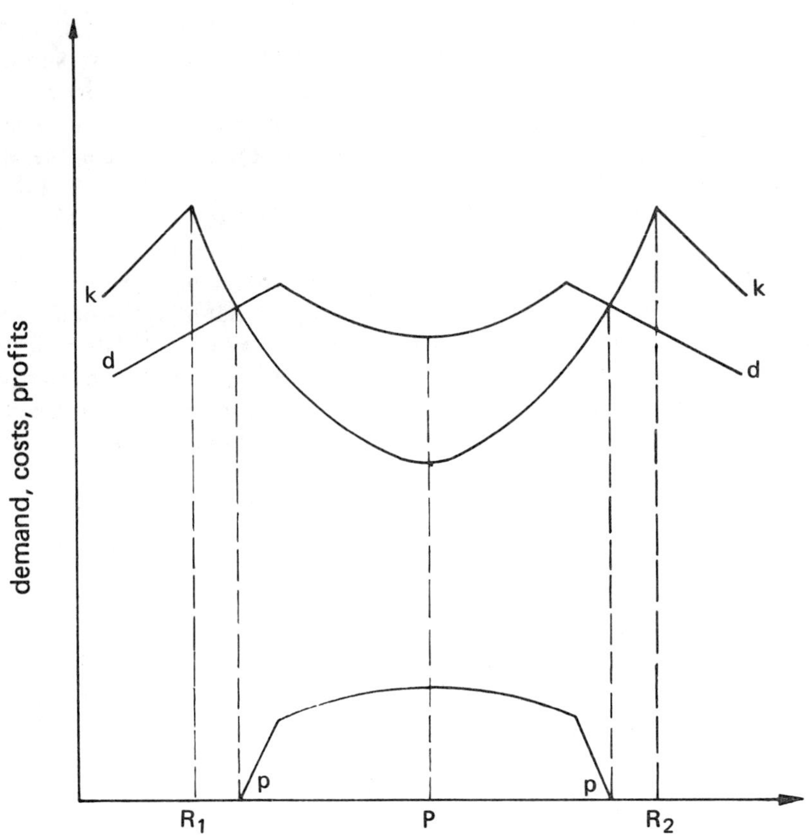

Figure 23-1

demand curve alone, but by the greatest distance between the demand curve, *dd*, and the cost curve, *kk*, resulting in the profit curve, *pp*. In Figure 23-1 the optimal point of production is at *P*. A similar result is always to be expected when the fall in costs toward *P* is more pronounced than the fall in demand. In the reverse situation, however, the peaks of the demand curve are identical with the points of maximum profit.

A second basic assumption, which Baumol makes, is the constant rate of substitution among various characteristics of a product for any one consumer. In the absence of empirical evidence, however, we have no reason to believe that the rate of substitution between two characteristics should not decrease or increase, at least within the relevant part of the model. If the rate of substitution was decreasing, then the tendency on the part of the firm launching the new product to furnish it with a combination of characteristics similar to those of an existing rival product, as Baumol suggests, might in fact be stronger than in the case of a constant rate of substitution.

This stronger tendency will be found if the qualities of the products already on the market are perfectly adapted to consumers' preferences. This is demonstrated in Figure 23-2. The axes show two different product characteristics. The R_1 and R_2 represent two existing products. Together with the "dummy" products R_n and R_m, they make up the supply frontier for the consumer. The existing products can be said to be perfectly adapted to consumers' preferences if their indifference curves, as in Figure 23-2, are tangent to the supply frontier at R_1 or R_2 rather than intersecting it. If this is the case, then at a point A on the iso-outlay curve for the new product, consumer 1

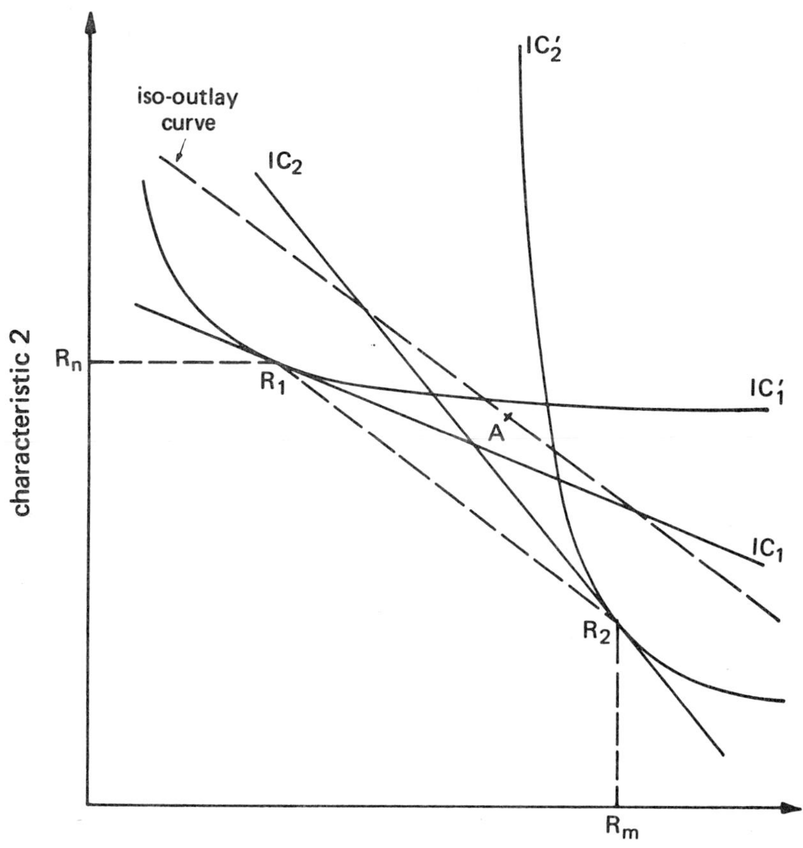

Figure 23-2

with a straight indifference curve, IC_1, would be attracted by the new product. In the case of a bent indifference curve, IC_1', he would remain at R_1, his original point of consumption.

The same holds in the case of consumer 2 originally at R_2 with indifference curves IC_2 and IC_2', respectively. Under these circumstances the convexity of the indifference curves will lead to a smaller demand for a combination of characteristics near the point equidistant from R_1 and R_2 as compared with the case of straight indifference curves and will lead to a greater demand if A moves toward one of these points.

In applying this result to all indifference curves, we first assume that they have the same distribution and each of them the same slope in R_1 or R_2 as described by Baumol. The total demand curve *dd* is determined by the relative position of the points of intersection between the iso-outlay curve and the various indifference curves. The convexity of the indifference curves will lead to a general shift of these points of intersection along the iso-cost curve toward R_1 for all indifference curves going through R_1 and to a general shift toward R_2 for all indifference curves going through R_2. Given the above distribution of indifference curves, the result must be a further concentration of demand for a quality combination in the vicinity of R_1 and R_2.

If the indifference curves are straight lines, then they are tangent either to R_1 or R_2, provided the consumer is behaving rationally. In the case of convex indifference curves this is not necessarily so. The intersection of indifference curves at R_1 or R_2 may reduce or even fully compensate the above concentration of demand near R_1 and R_2. This is demonstrated in Figure 23-3. At A_1 in Figure 23-3, only consumer 1 operating along IC_1 can be led to change from his original position R_1 to the new product, but not consumer 2 operating along IC_2. Similarly at A_2 only consumer 2 can be attracted to the new product, but not consumer 1.

Only combinations of characteristics around A_3 can ensure that both consumer 1 and consumer 2 will change from the existing rival products to the new product. In this case, therefore, the convexity of the indifference curves has the opposite effect, namely, to increase demand around the point of equidistance from R_1 and R_2 and to lessen it in the immediate vicinity of these points.

In reality both cases, shown in Figures 23-2 and 23-3, respectively, can apply to the same product but to different groups of consumers. Whether the overall effect is then an increased demand in the vicinity of R_1 and R_2 together with a decreased demand in the center area between these points, as compared to demand in the case of straight indifference curves or vice versa, is a question of the specific distribution of consumers' preferences in the particular situation observed. As a general rule, however, intersecting indifference curves (as in Figure 23-3) are all the more likely to occur the greater the quality difference between the existing rival products, that is, the greater the distance between R_1 and R_2. Therefore, the greater the quality gap between the

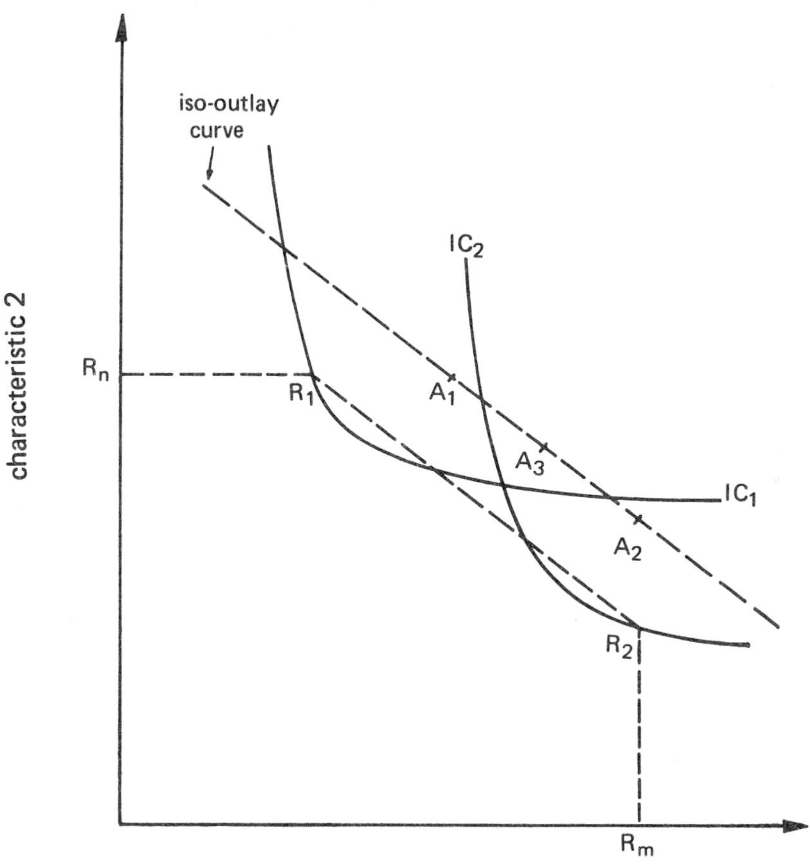

Figure 23-3

existing rival products the less likely Baumol's theorem is to hold and vice versa.

Similar arguments can be developed on the assumption that indifference curves are concave. Again consumers with indifference curves at a tangent would have to be distinguished from consumers with intersecting indifference curves.

The third assumption made by Baumol appears unrealistic insofar as the newly introduced product can be expected to draw its demand not only from its immediate rival products but also from completely different lines of consumption.[2] Generally speaking, one would expect that the greater the differentiation of the new product from its immediate rival products, the greater

[2]The diversity of consumers' wants implies that any additional product variation will result in making that range of products more attractive to consumers, and hence lead to substitution for other lines of consumption [1, pp. 48–51 and 59–65].

the chance of attracting demand from other lines of consumption. This, however, will make a very strong case for differentiating the new product as much as possible from its rivals. For, reverting now to our criticism of assumption (1), demand attracted from outside the industry does not entail the risk of retaliation, or, if so, to a much lesser degree.[3] The firm, in trying to avoid a costly price or quality war, will therefore be well advised to aim at absorbing such outside demand rather than attempting a reshuffle of demand within the industry. For this reason, too, the firm's objective will be a high degree of product differentiation rather than a combination of characteristics similar to that of some existing product.

REFERENCES

[1] Abbot, L. *Quality and Competition.* New York: Columbia University Press, 1955.

[2] Baumol, W. J. "Calculation of Optimal Product and Retailer Characteristics: The Abstract Product Approach." *Journal of Political Economy*, Vol. LXXV (October, 1967), pp. 674–85.

[3] Gaay Fortman, B. de. *Theory of Competition Policy.* Amsterdam: North-Holland, 1966.

[4] Kantzenbach, E. *Die Funktionsfähigkeit des Wettbewerbs.* Göttingen: Vandenhoeck and Ruprecht, 1967.

[5] Seidenfus, H. St. "Mehrproduktunternehmen, preispolitischer Ausgleich und Konzentration." *Kyklos*, Vol. XX (June, 1967), pp. 208–17.

[3]Attracting demand from outside rather than from within the group of rivals also tends to reduce the "tension between the standards and values of the group and the dynamic possibilities of the market" [3, p. 131].

SECTION VI. INCOME DISTRIBUTION THEORY

This section considers the microeconomics of income distribution. The concepts and principles which have been used to explain product pricing are employed to explain the pricing and employment of the factors of production.

After identifying and explaining the pricing and employment of "substitutable," "limitational," and "limitative" factors of production, Finkel and Tarascio focus these concepts on the labor factor and extend their analysis to include the institutional considerations, in addition to the technical and market conditions, of wage determination and employment. Maintaining that bilateral monopoly is largely neglected in the usual textbook coverage of wage theory, Hieser develops a "bargaining power" model of bilateral monopoly in the labor market which is built around an independent measure of bargaining power. Wessel distinguishes between the Ricardian and the Paretian versions of economic rent and examines the relative merits of these two rent concepts in the light of the contributions they make to the theories of distribution and cost. In her review article, Robinson gives particular emphasis to the weaknesses of the neoclassical concept of capital and the shortcomings of the marginal productivity theory of distribution. Bronfenbrenner discusses the major shortcomings of "naive" profit theory and explains his reformulation of this theory. He also examines the question of whether firms seek to maximize total net profit.

The major purpose of Finkel and Tarascio's article is to "develop a theoretical framework to account for institutional, market, and technical aspects of wage determination and employment." The authors maintain that the usual microeconomic theory approach to the pricing and employment of the factors of production has concentrated on "market" and "technical" conditions of production and has not devoted enough attention to "institutional" conditions.

Finkel and Tarascio identify and explain the concepts of "substitutable," "limitational," and "limitative" factors of production. They point out that marginal productivity theory and the conventional theory of the firm utilize the substitutable type of factor. The pricing and employment of these three kinds of factors of production are discussed.

The authors then focus the concepts of substitutable, limitational, and limitative factors of production specifically on the labor factor and extend their analysis to include "institutional considerations" as well as the technical and market conditions of wage determination and employment. Within the general theoretical framework, "union organization and strategies and the impact of labor legislation" are differentiated. In concluding, Finkel and Tarascio briefly consider some of the public policy considerations pertaining to wages and employment within the framework of these concepts.

Hieser states that the usual textbook approach to the treatment of the "theory of wages" is built around the marginal productivity theory of distribution and pays very little, if any, attention to bilateral monopoly. In the real world, however, the "commonest relationship" between employers and employees approximates bilateral monopoly. Maintaining that whenever bilateral monopoly is considered the result is usually a descriptive treatment, Hieser's purpose is to "extend analysis into this area."

He assumes a pure bilateral monopoly, with a pure monopolist seller of a single commodity on one side, and a labor union with unitary control over the labor supply on the other. In his analysis, Hieser emphasizes the importance of the measurable economic factors which motivate the employer and the union. He points out that some of the previous studies of the problem of bilateral monopoly in the labor market argue that the wage outcome is fundamentally indeterminate; others maintain that there is a determinate solution which represents a balance based on the relative bargaining powers of the two parties. Hieser sides with the "bargaining power" thesis, but he maintains that it is "analytically meaningless" without an "independent measure of bargaining power," which he builds into his model.

In developing his static model, Hieser states his assumptions and then delineates the "area of the bargain." He next analyzes the economic factors which determine the relative bargaining power of the two parties. In this context, he discusses the "workers' endurance function" and the "employer's resistance function." From these, Hieser formulates an indifference function for labor and a separate indifference function for the employer which are used in arriving at the static equilibrium solution. Hieser then considers bilateral wage determination as a dynamic process.

Wessel states that, although the concept of economic rent has been widely used by professional economists for many years, "as yet no clear consensus concerning its meaning exists." He points out that at present there are two "very different versions" of the economic rent concept. One of these can be traced back to Ricardo; economic rent is defined by his followers "as the excess amount earned by a factor over the sum necessary to induce it to do its work." The other economic rent concept had its beginnings in the works of Pareto and is defined as "the excess earnings over the amount necessary to keep the factor in its present occupation." For the first concept, the test is "whether the factor is supplied at all or not"; the test of the second is "where it is supplied." Since the concept of economic rent appears most frequently in the theory of distribution and the theory of cost, Wessel tests the merits of these two rent concepts by the contributions they make to the theories of distribution and cost and their applications.

He concludes that the traditional Ricardian approach "passes the distribution test with flying colors." In relation to the theory of cost, the traditional approach has the advantage of distinguishing payments made to overcome "real costs" from "unnecessary bounties." Paretian rent, on the other hand, "has little to contribute to distribution theory" and is a "misfit" from this standpoint. As far as the theory of cost is concerned, Pareto's approach "fares somewhat better." Based on his analysis, Wessel concludes that economic rent is best defined in the traditional manner, "and best defined in this way alone."

In closing, Wessel looks at the argument of whether rents are "price determining" or "price determined." He points out that "rent is neither price determining nor price determined since neither rent nor price is a basic determinant of the system." He maintains that they are "co-determined" as a result of the interaction of the supply of the factors, the technical coefficients, and the preference patterns of consumers. According to Wessel, "rent along with price is a result not a causal factor."

In her review article of Ferguson's *The Neoclassical Theory of Production and Distribution*, Robinson is concerned with neoclassical capital theory. She begins by tracing the history of the "reswitching affair"; part of her discussion in this section is devoted to Samuelson's surrogate production function.

She indicates that the neoclassicals view "capital" as a homogeneous, physical factor of production and she maintains that this concept of capital precludes economic theory from considering such problems as unemployment and imperfect competition.

Robinson discusses the reliance of neoclassical theory on the marginal productivity theory of distribution and points out some of its shortcomings as an explanation of the distribution of the national product between wages and profits. She discusses briefly three types of theories which explain the distribution of the product of industry between wages and profits.

In the final section, entitled "Econometrics," Robinson considers the problem of capital evaluation and the influence of factor prices on investment decisions. She maintains that *ex post* statistical information does not reflect entrepreneurial profit expectations at the time investment decisions were made nor does it indicate what decisions would have been made if "present and expected prices and wage rates" had been different.

Bronfenbrenner states five propositions in which "naive profit theory" is embodied and then covers some of the major arguments made against this theory of profits. These attacks center around Schumpeter, who "reduced both uncertainty and profit to consequences of innovation"; Knight, who maintained that profit "stems from uncertainty or non-insurable risk"; and a set of sociological or institutional profit theories, which have taken several forms, but which generally define profits as accountants' "business net income" and emphasize class distinctions between "profit-receivers" and such other classes as "wage-earners" and "rentiers."

Stating that his article arises from "dissatisfaction" with Schumpeter, with Knight, and with the institutionalists, Bronfenbrenner discusses some of his points of disagreement with their theories. In his reformulation of the naive profit theory, Bronfenbrenner divides economic uncertainties into "those giving rise to profit and those affecting other resource incomes"; he labels this a "specialized" uncertainty theory. He considers profit as compensation for "merely the subset of uncertainties which arises from having no contractual claim to one's income." For purposes of profit theory, he classifies the productive inputs into "contractual" and "entrepreneurial" categories, the distinction being based on whether their remuneration is or is not determined contractually. He points out that this terminology identifies entrepreneurship "exclusively with the precarious nature of its legal claims."

Bronfenbrenner then looks at how his profit theory has affected the five propositions which he earlier indicated embodied the substance of naive profit theory. He examines in greatest detail the proposition that firms seek to maximize total net profit, including in his analysis the views of Baumol and Simon.

24. A THEORETICAL INTEGRATION OF PRODUCTION AND WAGE THEORY*

Sidney R. Finkel and Vincent J. Tarascio†

Although a substantial literature on wage theory exists in the field known as labor economics, this literature has not been incorporated into the main body of microeconomic analysis. The usual approach to the pricing and employment of factors in microeconomic theory has concentrated on what might be called market and technical conditions of production. A state of perfect competition is assumed in the factor markets, and the factors of production are assumed to be technically substitutable, with increased supply forthcoming from increased wages. In general, no provision is made for "institutional" circumstances that affect the degree of competition in the labor market or the conditions of production. In particular, the theory does not account for the existence of union organizations, which may control the supply of labor, influence wages through collective bargaining, and constrain conditions of production.

Wage theorists have, however, recognized the role of labor unions in the wage determination process. This has given rise to the bargaining theories of wages, in which the wage determination process is partially removed from the economic conditions [13], [14]. Studies of the effects of labor unions have also made clear the manner in which unions influence not only conditions of supply, but also conditions of production by preventing factor substitution through featherbedding, work rules, etc. [12].

The major purpose of this study is to develop a theoretical framework to account for institutional, market, and technical aspects of wage determination and employment. Essentially, our approach involves amplifying the relationships in actual production that are part of the technical data. The arguments involve the use of three concepts in production theory: substitutable, limitational, and limitative factors of production. Marginal productivity theory relies on the first type. Since the latter two concepts are less likely to be familiar to most readers, they are discussed in greater detail than substitutable factors. In the second section, wages and employment are considered within the framework of the theoretical analysis.

---

*From *Western Economic Journal*, Vol. VII, No. 4 (December, 1969), pp. 371–378. Reprinted by permission of the publisher and the authors.

†Sidney R. Finkel, Visiting Assistant Professor of Business, Indiana University, and Vincent J. Tarascio, Associate Professor of Economics, University of North Carolina at Chapel Hill.

Pricing and Employment of Substitutable, Limitational, and Limitative Factors of Production

Given a production function of the type

(1) $$Q = F(U, V, W)$$

then for $u_1 > u_2$, $v_1 > v_2$, $w_1 > w_2$, the following types of factors of production can be defined. If, for production function (1)

(2) $$F(u_1, v_1, w_2) > F(u_2, v_2, w_2),\ F(u_2, v_2, w_1) > F(u_2, v_2, w_2)$$

then W is said to be a substitutable factor. If

(3) $$F(u_1,v_1,w_2) = F(u_2,v_2,w_2),\ F(u_2,v_2,w_1) = F(u_2,v_2,w_2)$$

then W is said to be a limitational factor. If

(4) $$F(u_1,v_1,w_2) = F(u_2,v_2,w_2),\ F(u_2,v_2,w_1) > F(u_2,v_2,w_2)$$

then W is said to be a limitative factor.

Marginal productivity theory and the conventional theory of the firm make use of the first type of factor, the substitutable factor. Expression (2) indicates that an increase in w is a sufficient condition for increasing output.[1]

What is important for our purposes is that with respect to marginal productivity theory (and substitutable factors), there are the following conclusions: First, two forces will induce the firm to reduce employment of a factor whose price has risen. It will carry out all economical substitutions increasing its use of the other factors and decreasing its use of the factor whose price has risen. Also, it will reduce output, which will further reduce the amount of the factor employed. Second, in order for a factor to maintain the level of employment it had before the price increase, it is necessary that demand for the product rise so that *more* than the original output is the profit maximizing level of output. Third, the share of the factor whose price has risen will decrease, increase, or remain constant, depending upon whether or not the marginal rate of substitution is greater than one, less than one, or equal to one [6, pp. 117–18]. Consequently, no general conclusion can be made concerning a change in distribution when there is a price increase of a factor.

We turn next to limitational factors.[2] Expression (3) indicates that an increase in W is necessary but not a sufficient condition for increasing output. This condition denotes technical complementarity between W and U, V. An

[1] Under the assumption of perfect competition in the input and output markets, the profit maximizing level of output is that point where marginal cost (MC) is just equal to the price of the output (P_q). Combining this information with the knowledge that the firm will use the least cost of production for every level of output, or maximize output for each level of total cost, yields the fundamental equation of production, $MC = (P_u/f_u) = (p_v/f_v) = (p_w/f_w) = p_q$ where p_u, p_v, and p_w are the prices of the inputs, and f_u, f_v, and f_w are the partial derivatives of (1) or the marginal products of U, V, and W respectively.

[2] The origin of the term "limitational factor" is accorded to Ragnar Frisch by both Georgescu-Roegen [4, p. 42, footnote 6] and Herbert Zassenhaus [5, p. 37]. Frisch

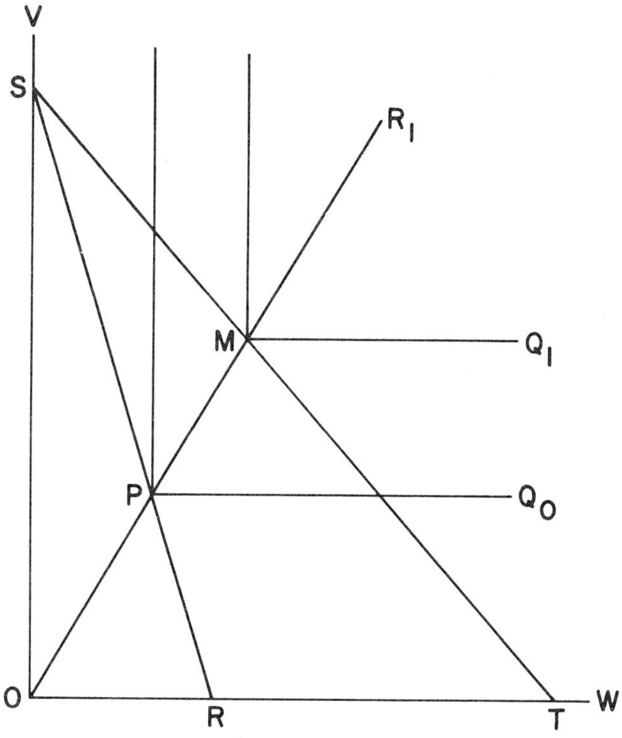

Figure 24-1

increase in the price of a limitational factor cannot be treated using marginal productivity theory discussed above.[3] For a limitational factor, an equation system such as that shown in footnote 1 does not exist; all that is known is that in equilibrium $MC = p_q$, or that the cost of an additional unit of the product is just equal to the price of the additional unit. The isoquant map is similar to Figure 24-1. The isoquants are perpendicular, indicating technical complementarity between *W* and *V*. If *W* is a limitational factor, technical complementarity will exist between *W* and all other factors and all isoquants representing combinations of *W* and any other input will look like Figure 24-1.

first used the term in a discussion of fixed factor coefficients to describe factors for which substitution was not technically possible, as in the case of fixed proportions. Obviously, the limitational factor concept is a short-run consideration. In the long run all factors are substitutable, but there are many examples of short-run limitational factors, such as skilled tradesmen, and specialized capital which cannot be quickly converted to different types of production. For the microeconomic analysis of distribution when limitational factors are present in the production function, see [4] and for production analysis see [3, Chaps. 12-19].

[3]It must be remembered that when we speak of marginal products in a situation where limitational factors exist, the partial derivatives of the production function indicate an increase in production only when sufficient amounts of the other factors are present. When we compute the marginal revenue associated with an increase in a substitutable factor, we must remember that allowance has been made for the revenue that must go to the substitutable factor.

With an initial isocost line of ST, the equilibrium position of the firm is found where the isocost is tangent to the isoquant, or point M in Figure 24-1. An increase in the price of W will shift the isocost to SR, tangent to isoquant Q_0 at point P. The fundamental difference between this case and the case involving marginal productivity is that there is no substitution effect. The only adjustment that the employer can make in response to the increase in the price of W is to reduce output and the amount of W (and V) that is used.

With respect to limitational factors, there are the following conclusions: First, because substitution is not possible, if the price of a limitational factor should rise the factor's share in total receipts will also rise. For limitational factor W, $p_w q_w / pq$ will increase for every level of output. Second, because substitution is not possible, an increase in demand sufficient to bring production back to the original level (before the price increase in the limitational factor) will bring employment of the limitational factor back to its original level. This conclusion is in opposition to the conclusion reached with marginal productivity theory, where it would take an increase in demand sufficient to make production greater than the original level in order to bring employment of the factor whose price has risen back to its original level. Third, since substitution is not possible, attention is turned to the output effect where there is an increase in the price of the limitational factor. The determinant of the output effect is the change in marginal cost brought about by the increase in the price of the factor input. This change may be different among firms, depending upon the degree of intensity with which the limitational factor, whose price has risen, is used in production.[4]

Besides marginal cost changes, another circumstance bearing on the size of the output effect is the slope of the firm's marginal revenue curve. Until now, perfect competition has been assumed in the product market, and the firm's marginal revenue curve has been infinitely elastic. If the firm is operating in a market characterized by imperfect competition, however, the marginal revenue curve has a negative slope that would also influence the output effect. As the firm reduced output, marginal cost would fall, and marginal revenue would rise, so that the two would come into equality sooner than in a situation of perfect competition. Hence, the more inelastic the marginal revenue curve, the less the output effect.

Analysis of a limitative factor is different from the analysis of substitutable and limitational factors because conditions of supply, rather than technical conditions of production, are the primary consideration. Expression (4) indicates that the factor of production, W, is limitative if an increase in its input is both a necessary and sufficient condition for an increase in output. It is possible for both a substitutable and a limitational factor to become a

[4]If 99.99% of total costs consist of the cost of the limitational factor, a doubling of the price of the limitational factor will have a tremendous impact on total and marginal costs, and a large output effect should be experienced. On the other hand, if the limitational factor represents only .01% of total costs, a doubling of its price would have little effect on total and marginal cost, and the output effect would be negligible.

limitative factor if its supply becomes fixed so that the marginal productivity of the other factors is driven down to zero.

Reality prevents us from having a limitative factor in the strictest sense of the term. If a true limitative factor were present, this would mean a zero price for the other factor inputs, which as Georgescu-Roegen points out is a mathematical solution, but not feasible in view of the fact that labor must receive a subsistence wage [5, p. 339]. Also, the cost of production of capital prevents it from having a zero price.[5] Consequently, what is more important is the situation where *starting from some equilibrium point, the supply of a factor is fixed.* In the following analysis, the term "limitative factor" will be used to denote the latter case, and not a limitative factor in the strict sense.

In Figure 24-2, cost minimization exists where isocost JL is tangent to isoquant q_0. Profit maximization is represented in Figure 24-3 where marginal revenue curve MR_1 intersects marginal cost MC_1 at output q_0. If W becomes a limitative factor, as broadly defined above, the only way in which the firm can expand output is by increasing employment of U. Since this method of expansion is not the least-cost-combination path, marginal cost will increase from MC_1 to MC_2. Now suppose there is an increase in demand, so that marginal revenue increases from MR_1 to MR_2. Without the limitative restriction, the firm would like to increase production to q_3, represented by the shift in the isocost from JL to MN, tangent to isoquant q_3, and the intersection of MR_2 with MC_1. Under the assumption of perfect competition, the firm will bid up the price of W in an attempt to attract more W with which to increase production. In Figure 24-2, the isocost MN rotates around M until it is tangent to an isoquant where it also intersects the line of fixed supply, $W_0 W_0$. This is shown in the movement of the isocost from MN to MK, tangent to isoquant q_1 at point R. In Figure 24-3, it is shown by the intersection of MR_2 with the new marginal cost curve, MC_3, at output q_1. Marginal cost has risen, because the price of one of the factor inputs has risen. The result is that there is an increase in the price of the limitative factor, an output effect, but no reduction in employment of the limitative factor. The increase in demand

[5]See Georgescu-Roegen [5, pp. 338–56]. The limitative factor concept has been applied to the analysis of production in countries where overpopulation exists and the supply of capital and land is limited. A result of this type of analysis is that capital and land may become limitative factors, so that if the entire labor force were used in production, the marginal productivity of labor and hence the wage rate would be driven down to zero. Since the price of labor must be above zero to physically sustain the population, production in the underdeveloped countries does not reach the maximum that marginal productivity theory would predict. Consequently, marginal productivity theory as a method of determining distribution does not hold.

The concept of limitativeness has also been used to explain unemployment in developed countries. Keynes was cognizant of the bottlenecks that would prevent the economy from reaching full employment unless there was strong inflationary pressure [8, pp. 300–301]. Kukuoka [9, pp. 23–44] has shown that the application of fixed coefficients in the limitative sense may prevent fiscal and monetary policy from achieving full employment. Kaldor [7, pp. 643–44] has stated that because of fixed supply of some factors in the economy, we should redefine the concept of full employment as full employment of capital or labor, but not both except under extraordinary conditions.

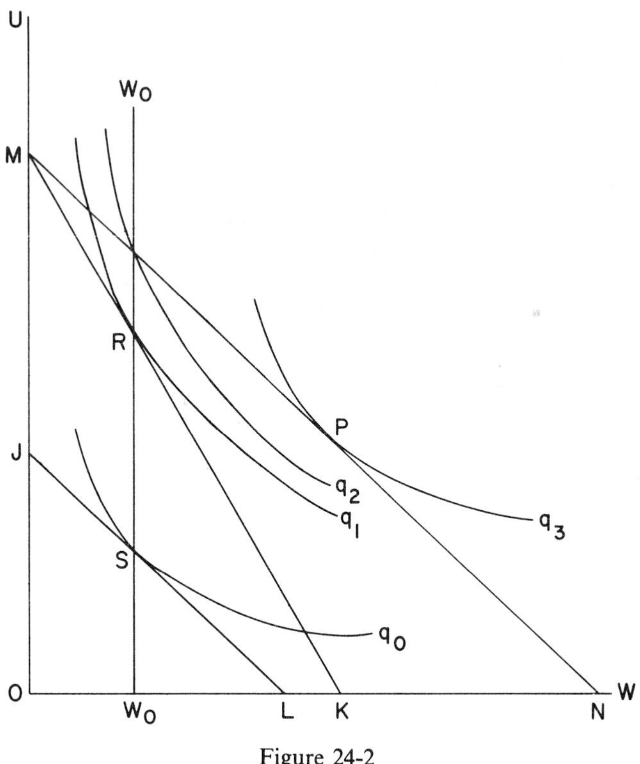

Figure 24-2

necessary to offset the employment has already occurred. In Marshallian terms, the phenomenon of "quasi-rent" has occurred.

If perfect competition is absent in the input market, it may be that the price of the limitative factor will not rise, or if it does rise, it may not rise the full amount that it would have risen had there been perfect competition. A monopsonist (with perfect knowledge of the fixed supply of the limitative factor) would have no reason to bid up the price of W. He would produce q_2 where MR_2 intersects MC_2 in Figure 24-3, or where isocost MN intersects fixed supply line W_0 W_0' in Figure 24-2. The increase in demand is thus accrued as increased profits by the firm. There is no fear of an immediate adjustment in the form of industry expansion, since the fixed supply of W would discourage new firms from entering.

No real economic forces determine the distribution of these excess profits. Both the firm and the factor inputs may claim ownership of the profits that accrue because of the limitative factor. This type of analysis leads to the "bargaining theory of wages" where the wage rate is not determined by economic factors, but by the relative strength of the representatives of management and labor [2]. The bargaining theory, in this case, would maintain that the wage rate under perfect competition and the rate under monopsony would

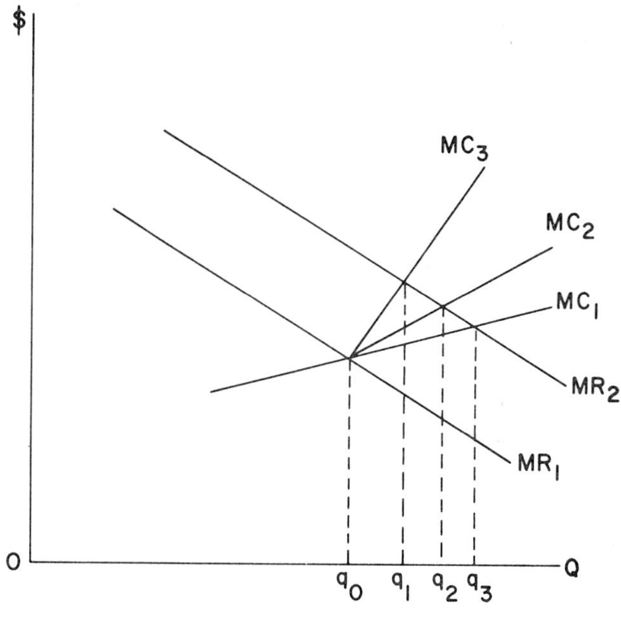

Figure 24-3

be the range for settlement with the exact rate determined by the bargaining ability of the two parties.

Some Extentions of Substitutable, Limitational, and Limitative Concepts to Wage and Employment Theory

The concepts of substitutable, limitational, and limitative factors of production will now be focused upon one type of factor input, labor, and will be extended to include *institutional* considerations in addition to technical and market conditions. Union organization and strategies and the impact of labor legislation will be differentiated within the general theoretical framework. Finally, some wage studies will be related directly to these concepts.

Theoretically the strongest position a labor union can attain in terms of wages and employment is when it represents a factor of production that is *both* limitational and limitative. If a factor is limitational either for technical or *institutional* (work rules, etc.) reasons, it need not fear substitution (employment) effects resulting from wage increases although there will be an output (employment) effect.[6] In so far as the factor is an institutional limitational factor, the union has some control over *demand* for the factor. If a

[6]Since the extent of the output (employment) effect will be influenced by the relation of the wage bill to total costs, the employment effect may be related to capital-labor ratios existing in various employments within or among industries. Such considerations (Contd.)

factor is limitative either because of general market conditions (full employment) or because of *institutional* conditions resulting from the union's control of supply, it need not fear employment effects associated with increased wage rates, for the reasons discussed in the preceding section.

Labor legislation and its effect on the labor movement and the ability of unions to affect employment and wages also fit into this framework. The major impact of the legislation has been to alter the institutional environment in a manner that will either permit or prevent limitationality or limitativeness in organized labor markets. The major impact of early federal legislation has been on permissive limitativeness, i.e., supply conditions. The Norris-La Guardia Act and the Wagner Act made it increasingly difficult for management to draw upon the nonunion labor force when a labor union had been organized by the workers. The election proceedings set up by the Wagner Act, which enabled a union to become certified as sole representatives and bargaining agents of the workers, has been the single most important institution allowing unions to become limitative factors.[7] Later legislation, notably the Taft-Hartley Act, has sought to weaken the power of labor unions by weakening their ability to become limitative and limitational factors. The prohibition of the closed shop was a measure that reduced the ability of the union to become a limitative factor, while the anti-featherbedding section of Taft-Hartley, however weak, was designed to eliminate institutional limitationality.

Nevertheless, some unions have managed to become very strong by becoming institutional limitational and limitative factors, or by taking advantage of natural conditions of limitationality and limitativeness. The construction trades have effected a de facto closed shop through apprentice and licensing requirements, and by taking advantage of their technical limitationality (i.e., plumbers cannot be substituted for electricians).

---

will not be treated here since they further complicate an already difficult discussion.

A factor becomes institutional limitational when a force outside the economic system, such as a labor union or government, is able to secure a type of work rule that prevents substitution. A good example is railroad crew members, where a union work rule requires a specified number for each train. Substitution may be technically possible, but the institutions of the industry prevent it.

[7]In determining a limitative factor, it is the relative and not the absolute amount of excess supply in the labor market that is important. Thus, the auto and steel workers were able to organize during the depression despite a large amount of absolute unemployment. Individual workers in the auto and steel industries were substitutable factors, but collectively in a union they became limitative factors. Even if there were ten or twenty thousand unemployed outside the plant gates, if several hundred thousand workers struck, it was impossible to substitute for them. Once the union membership could convince the members of this, the members were willing to walk out in an organizational strike. In 1968, after an extensive drive, and even though there was a tight labor market and small absolute unemployment, the textile workers were unable to organize the southern mills because of the *relatively* large numbers of unemployed. If workers walk out in an organizational strike, they know that several hundred unskilled workers can be brought in to replace them. The union has no economic power base from which to operate.

The distinction between substitutable and limitational factors also has some bearing on empirical analysis of wage differentials. Reder, for example, uses this approach [11]. During periods of declining demand, skilled (limitational) workers move into unskilled (substitutable) labor markets, increasing the supply of unskilled workers relative to the supply of skilled labor and widening the skilled-unskilled (limitational-substitutable) wage structure.[8] The analysis of labor as "human capital" is also consistent with our analysis, in that limitational factors depict labor in which skills and training represent embodied capital.[9] Oi has proposed that we treat skilled (limitational) labor as more of a fixed factor than a variable factor, by the argument that the firm has significant investment in these workers and that rapid substitution is not available from the labor pool [*10*]. This argument is also used to explain the widening of the skilled-unskilled differential during periods of declining demand. Many similar studies can also be shown to be an application of the concepts of substitutable, limitational and limitative factors.

Finally, our method of analysis points to some public policy considerations pertaining to wages and employment. In areas where labor is limitative and limitational, there will be pressure on wages, and hence prices, to rise independently of monetary and fiscal policy and independently of the state of unemployment in other markets. The limitationality prevents labor in other markets from entering the limitational-limitative markets, and the limitativeness provides continuous upward wage pressure. Thus, economic stability becomes much more difficult in an economy characterized by limitational and limitative factors than in an economy characterized by substitutable factors. The limitational-limitative economy requires more deflationary pressure and higher overall unemployment to reduce inflation. Thus one aspect of union-initiated *institutional* limitativeness and limitationality is to build cost-push pressures into the operation of the economy.[10] Of course, such pressures would also exist in the absence of labor unions because of technical limitationality and market limitative conditions existing in the real world.

[8]The terms "skilled" and "unskilled" are used interchangeably for "limitational" and "substitutable." Although there are exceptions, in most cases a skilled worker will be limitational and an unskilled substitutable with other unskilled workers in other occupations. Also, a technical limitational factor makes for a market limitative factor because the excess supply of labor can exist only if the particular industry is suffering declining demand and unemployment. In normal times, the limitational factor will be close to a limitative factor, and it is demand conditions for that industry and not for the economy as a whole that determine the limitativeness of the technical limitational factor. For the unskilled substitutable factor, it is the general conditions of demand that determine whether or not it becomes limitative, as there must be no excess supply in *any* industry in order for the factor to become a *market* limitative factor. The use of the terms "skilled" and "unskilled" in this manner is an agreement with Behman, [1, pp. 117–42].

[9]See [16] for an analysis of labor as human capital.

[10]This analysis gives a theoretical derivation of the Phillips curve. If there are n labor markets in the economy, with k characterized as limitational-limitative and m as substitutable, then as the economy moves toward full employment, full employment

(Contd.)

REFERENCES

[1] Behman, S. "Wage-Determination Process in U.S. Manufacturing." *Quarterly Journal of Economics*, Vol. LXXXII (February, 1968), pp. 117–42.

[2] Dye, H. "A Bargaining Theory of Residual Income Distribution." *Industrial and Labor Relations Review*, Vol. XXI (October, 1967), pp. 40–54.

[3] Frisch, R. *Theory of Production.* Dordrecht: 1965.

[4] Georgescu-Roegen, N. "Fixed Coefficients of Production and Marginal Productivity Theory." *Review of Economic Studies*, Vol. III (1935), pp. 40–49.

[5] ———. *Analytical Economics: Issues and Problems.* Cambridge, Mass.: Harvard University Press, 1966.

[6] Hicks, J. R. *The Theory of Wages.* London: Macmillan, 1932.

[7] Kaldor, N. "Stability and Full Employment." *Economic Journal*, Vol. XLVIII (December, 1938), pp. 643–44.

[8] Keynes, J. M. *The General Theory of Employment, Interest and Money.* New York: Macmillan, 1936.

[9] Kukuoka, M. "Full Employment and Constant Coefficients of Production." *Quarterly Journal of Economics*, Vol. LXIX (February, 1955), pp. 23–44.

[10] Oi, W. "Labor as a Quasi-Fixed Factor." *Journal of Political Economy*, Vol. LXX (December, 1962), pp. 538–55.

[11] Reder, M. "The Theory of Occupational Wage Differentials." *American Economic Review*, Vol. XLV (December, 1955), pp. 833–52.

[12] Slichter, S. H., J. J. Healy, and E. R. Livernash. *The Impact of Collective Bargaining on Management.* Washington, D. C.: Brookings Institute, 1960.

[13] Stevens, C. M. *Strategy and Collective Bargaining Negotiations.* New York: McGraw-Hill, 1963.

[14] Walton, R. E., and R. B. McKersie. *A Behavioural Theory of Labor Negotiations.* New York: McGraw-Hill, 1965.

[15] Zassenhaus, H. "Dr. Schneider and the Theory of Production." *Review of Economic Studies*, Vol. III (1935), pp. 35–39.

[16] *Journal of Political Economy*, Supplement, Vol. LXX (October, 1962).

---

is most likely reached in the k markets first. Thus while general unemployment continues, mostly in the m markets, there are wage and price pressures, and the economy starts to inflate before general full employment is reached. Adjustments are not possible in the short run because limitationality prevents workers from the m-type markets from coming into the k-type markets.

25. WAGE DETERMINATION WITH BILATERAL MONOPOLY IN THE LABOR MARKET: A THEORETICAL TREATMENT*

Ronald O. Hieser†

INTRODUCTION: INTENTION

The "theory of wages" is dealt with at some length in the textbooks, although the relevance of this theory to the real world is, it must be admitted, purely tangential. Usually we are treated first to a full dress exposition of the marginal productivity theory of distribution erected on the stern assumptions of perfect competition. In due course the analysis is developed to take account of imperfect competition, first in the product market, then in the labor market, and finally taken together: this also at length. Here analysis normally breaks off. The fact that in the real world the commonest relationship between employers and employed approximates to that of bilateral monopoly is reserved for mention, if it is mentioned at all, among the footnotes. Whenever a more ambitious treatment is essayed, we are likely to find analysis soon abandoned in the sands of conglomerate description.[1]

It is the purpose of this paper to extend analysis into this area.[2] For simplicity, we shall assume that there is a situation of pure bilateral monopoly, with a pure monopolist seller of a single commodity on the one side, a trade union with unitary control over the labor supply on the other.

Our aim will not be a "realistic" model in the sense of describing the factors which motivate or underwrite (in defense) employer or union, and certainly not what they say motivates them. Clearly much on the surface and in the overt attitudes of the two parties will be purely rhetorical.[3] Rather, what we have to attempt is to distil from their confrontation situation the essence of

*From the *Economic Record*, Vol. XLVI, No. 113 (March, 1970), pp. 55–72. Reprinted by permission of the publisher and the author.

†Ronald O. Hieser, Professor of Economics, Australian National University.

[1]"I fear when the economic theorist turns to the general problem of wage determination and labor economics, his voice becomes muted and his speech halting." P. A. Samuelson, "Economic Theory and Wages," in *Collected Scientific Papers of Paul A. Samuelson*, Vol. II (Cambridge, Mass.: M. I. T. Press, 1966), p. 1557.

[2]If we need any justification for the abstract, theoretical content of this paper, we may again appeal to Samuelson: "In my view disappointingly little has yet come from theorists in this field." *Ibid.*, p. 1569.

[3]"The practical man of labor affairs has always acted by instinct, and to justify his behavior he has shopped around to choose the most suitable economic rationalizations." *Ibid.*, p. 1557.

the *economic* factors which underlies their respective postures. Once these are determined, much in the parties' actions and attitudes may be explained. In short, we seek an *explanation* of their behavior, not merely a description of it.

Perhaps we should also add at this early juncture that, so far as Australian experience is concerned, we shall be making a further, specific abstraction from reality. Wage determination in Australia is heavily overlain by the legalism and precedent of a compulsory arbitration system. This we ignore as a special case. Rather, we are concerned with the elements of free bargaining between employer and union; and therefore our analysis is to be seen as more relevant to unconstrained collective bargaining situations such as obtain in North America. This is not to say, however, that underlying economic realities do not have a significant effect on arbitration outcomes.

It would, of course, be untrue to say that analytical studies of the problem of bilateral monopoly in the labor market have not been undertaken before. Nevertheless, the literature of the subject is notoriously sparse, and even less convincing. Broadly speaking, there appear to be two main consensi.

In the first place, there are those who argue that the situation is fundamentally indeterminate, with the implication of ever-present possibility of deadlock. At least in the Anglo-Saxon tradition, Edgeworth appears to be the progenitor of this position. He concluded that: "Contract without competition is indeterminate."[4] According to Shackle this answer "absolved economists from trying to explain how in bilateral monopoly a price is ever fixed."[5] Certainly, Edgeworth was followed by Marshall and Pigou.[6]

Generally speaking, those who argue indeterminacy must hold that other than a purely economic calculus is required to define an "equilibrium." Appeal must be had to extra-economic considerations such as psychological propensities, custom, and perhaps Christian togetherness to provide the inertia requisite to stability.[7] This may well be the stuff for Moral Rearmament, but it hardly constitutes a foundation for economic analysis.[8]

---

[4]F. Y. Edgeworth, *Mathematical Psychics* (London: Kegan Paul, 1881), p. 20.

[5]G. L. S. Shackle, "The Nature of the Bargaining Process," in *The Theory of Wage Determination*, edited by J. T. Dunlop (London: Macmillan, 1957), p. 298.

[6]Cf. Pigou: "Where, however, wage rates are settled, not by the action of free competition, but by bargaining between a workmen's association on one side and an employers' association on the other, the rate of wage is no longer determinate at a single point. There is, on the contrary, a *range of indeterminateness*" (Pigou's italics). *The Economics of Welfare* (4th ed.; London: Macmillan, 1938), p. 452.

[7]Jevons has it: "Such a transaction [viz. in bilateral monopoly] must be settled upon other than strictly economic grounds." *The Theory of Political Economy*, quoted by Edgeworth, *op. cit.*, p. 30.

[8]In this connection, Joan Robinson has, as so often, gone to the heart of the matter:

> . . . It is this assumption [of maximization] that makes the analysis of value possible. If individuals act in an erratic way only statistical methods will serve to discover the laws of economics, and if individuals act in a predictable way, but from a large number of complicated motives, the economist must resign his task to the psychologist. It is the assumption that

One of the chief difficulties of the basic-indeterminacy school is that in the real world the general experience is, in fact, achievement of comparatively stable, determinate positions; and it is hard to believe that these positions are underpinned only by incidental, nonmaximizing factors or, worse, derive from pure hit and miss. Deadlock, except in the very shortest term, is infrequent, so much so that when it occurs it is news—strike or lockout news.

Again, it seems to me that this first school of thought is too much influenced by the theory and practice of bilateral monopoly as it is seen to function in the commodity market. The labor market differs from the commodity market in two important respects.

First, in the exchange of commodities, buyer and seller stand in a direct antithetical relationship. Their interests are equal and opposite; the seller's gain is the buyer's loss, and vice versa. But in the labor market this is not altogether so. Indeed, there is a significant area within which a monopoly buyer of labor and the seller of labor have a common interest, namely in extracting the largest divisible surplus from the consumer.

Secondly, commodities are generally mobile in space and, to lesser degree, in time. Deadlock in one market may be countered by transfer to a different market. However, this alternative is not normally applicable in the labor market. Also, it is clear that labor cannot be held over as stocks. Nor is it possible for an employer who has a large fixed capital commitment to a particular place and time to liquidate his position readily. In the not very long run, deadlock will not be acceptable to either side.

The fact is that deadlock involves both sides in *costs* of an order quite different from a commodity market. (Unused labor is lost completely; unsold commodities lose only their carrying costs.) In this matter, as in the exploitation of consumers, labor and capital have a *joint* interest, and these two common factors, it is suggested, lend a greater degree of determinateness and stability to the wage settlement than one might expect from a look at analogous situations in commodity markets.

The second school of thought, which includes the Marxists incidentally, would assert a (determinate) wage outcome representing a balance struck by the relative bargaining powers of the two parties.

The "bargaining power" thesis has a commonsense appeal, and it clearly reflects something significant about the real world. The difficulty with this theory is that, until we are offered an independent measure of bargaining power, the thesis is analytically meaningless. Indeed, it often seems that bargaining power is taken as something given in the situation, substantially exogenous, and therefore largely of non-economic content. Bargaining power

---

any individual, in his economic life, will never undertake an action that adds more to his losses than to his gains, and will always undertake an action which adds more to his gains than to his losses, which makes the analysis of value possible.

The Economics of Imperfect Competition (London: Macmillan, 1933), p. 6.

is made to depend on such factors as the common loyalty of workers, the quality of union leadership, the enlightenment of management, and such like.

However, unless we do define an independent (economic) measure of bargaining power, the analysis becomes quite circular. "High" wages become the result of "strong" bargaining power on the part of the union, "low" wages the result of "weak" bargaining power. Contrariwise, "strong" bargaining power is indicated by "high" wages, "weak" bargaining power by "low" wages. Clearly, there is no explanation here. A break-out from this vicious circle is the primary purpose of this essay.

We have promised a highly abstract model, with the measurable, maximizing elements as its kernel. This does not imply that extra-economic (non-maximizing) factors — for example, corruption of union officials, security-preference of managements, custom, prejudice, political considerations, even violence — do not, in certain circumstances, play an important role in the real world. However, what we seek is a common denominator, general to all bilateral confrontations between labor and capital: we seek an armature about which particular cases of the real world can be molded.

Before launching into our model, it is first necessary to consider certain special conditions which face a trade union intent on maximization.

TRADE UNIONS AND MAXIMIZATION

Our approach leads us immediately to two, not unrelated, problems associated with maximization from a trade union point of view.

In the first place, maximization for a trade union, unlike maximization for the firm, is not a unique criterion. More accurately, certain difficulties attend the idea. A firm, when it maximizes its profits which are then distributed among partners or shareholders according to some predetermined formula, also automatically maximizes the incomes of its individual members. With a trade union, however, incomes accrue directly to individuals, not to the collective. An increase in wage rates may represent higher incomes for some workers, zero incomes for others.

The problem arises, of course, out of the reciprocal relationship between wage rates and employment. Although the strength of this relationship is commonly exaggerated, we must, and a trade union must, take account of it. There may be a clash, then, between maximizing wage rates and maximizing the wage bill (which is equivalent to maximizing the average wage rate of the [assumed] fixed membership of the union). However, divergence of the two criteria only occurs when the demand for labor becomes elastic, i.e., when a further increase in the wage rate will result in a reduction in total wages received. Up to this point, higher wage rates and higher wage bill move in consonance as far as maximization is concerned. We therefore treat this point as an upper limit to wage demands. This means in effect that, up to this limit, pressure to increase the wage rate also serves to maximize the total wage bill. Within this range, the union's objective is unambiguous.

The second way in which a trade union's position is different from that of the firm resides in the fact that, under ordinary circumstances, a trade union cannot pursue maximization by way of marginal adjustment. An employer may employ a few more men or a few less; a trade union cannot normally withdraw labor, except as a whole. It either accepts an offered rate of pay or it rejects it. If it accepts, it will supply all available labor at that price; if it rejects, it will supply no labor at all. (The idea of a continuous, upward-sloping curve for labor is, in general, quite unrealistic!)

In the last analysis, the final sanction of a trade union lies in its ability to exercise control over the *total* labor supply. Hence, in what follows, we shall consider the ordinary strike (withholding of the total labor supply) as the ultimate element of a trade union's bargaining power. In the last resort, when the chips are down, it will be the union's ability to sustain a total withdrawal of labor which will set the limit on its bargaining power.[9] Of course, it is not necessary that actual strike action be invoked: it will be sufficient that the power be there and calculable.

This is not to say that a union cannot, within this limit, maneuver tactically, marginally, in order to bring pressure on an employer or to underline its ultimate power. For example, it may invoke lightning, disruptive strikes, apply overtime bans, or it may restrict output by work-to-rule methods, and so on. Yet it remains basically true that total withdrawal of labor is the ultimate weapon, and this is the assumption we make.[10]

A final preliminary point. We shall use the term "wage" to embrace the Marshallian notion of "net advantages," that is, to include adjustment for working hours, leave and sickness provisions, pension rights, work intensity, and the like.

STATIC MODEL: BASIC ASSUMPTIONS

In establishing our static model, we make explicit two sets of assumptions. There are first the substantive assumptions which provide a static framework for this part of the analysis. There are also certain expository assumptions which have a negligible effect upon the outcome of the argument but greatly facilitate its presentation.

Substantive Assumptions

(1) The demand curve facing the monopolist is given.
(2) The technical production function is given.

---

[9]Clauswitz (or was it Bismarck?) said that war is merely the continuation of politics by other methods. Strike is war, and may be considered to be the continuation of negotiation by other methods. In this sense, it is the limit.

[10]Cf. Hicks: "The weapon by which Trade Unions endeavour to secure more favourable terms for their members than competition would give is the strike: the concerted withdrawal of considerable bodies of men from employment." *The Theory of Wages* (London: Macmillan, 1932), p. 140.

(3) There is a wage at which qualified "free" labor would offer; this we call the *opportunity wage.* Looking at it the other way round, it is the next best wage which members of our particular work force can command.

(4) The trade union has a closed shop, and the membership of the union is given.

Expository Assumptions

(1) The demand curve is linear over the relevant range; or what amounts to the same thing, we take arc elasticity of demand as an approximation to point elasticity over that range.

(2) The prime cost curve is horizontal over the relevant interval, so that average prime cost and marginal cost coincide over that interval. (This particular assumption is introduced so that a common unit may be selected for both output and employment, thus enabling us to use a single output/employment axis on the one diagram).

(3) Our monopolist is fully integrated, i.e., he produces all his own raw materials, so that variable costs are simply wage costs. (It is always open to us to deduct raw materials from both demand and cost curves, but this particular assumption exempts us from that irksome arithmetic and the dual terminology which would be involved.)

AREA OF THE BARGAIN

Having set down our assumptions, we are now in a position to delineate what we shall call the *area of the bargain.* This will define the area within which the ultimate bargain must lie, whatever the relative bargaining strengths of the two parties.

We have a demand curve for the monopolist, DD'; and from this we may derive a marginal revenue curve, DR. Also, we have an initial cost curve, CC', determined by the opportunity wage, W_0. We choose a unit of output representing the output per man in the selected accounting period—say, 1,000 mousetraps per man per week. Then, units of output and units of employment have a one-for-one correspondence along the X-axis. From Figure 25-1, it is clear that, without union intervention, the monopolist would maximize his position where $DR = CC'$, at E, with an output/employment of Q_0.

At a glance it is obvious that any final bargain between the parties must lie within the triangle DEC. However, we may delimit this further. Draw DF such that $OF = FR$, and raise the perpendicular FGH. At the point H on DR, the elasticity of the marginal revenue curve, η, will be equal to unity. Any advance of the wage rate beyond the point H would diminish the total wage payout, and this would conflict with our maximizing assumptions. Hence, the area within which the wage bargain must fall is reduced to the triangle HEG.

Furthermore, any bargain struck within HEG may be extrapolated to the right to HE, since any such move to the right would benefit *both* parties. Therefore, in the end we have only to consider agreements along the segment HE.

Moreover, it may be shown that $\eta = \frac{1}{2}(\varepsilon - 1)$, where ε is elasticity of demand. Then, when $\eta = 1$, at H, $\varepsilon = 3$. Also, since

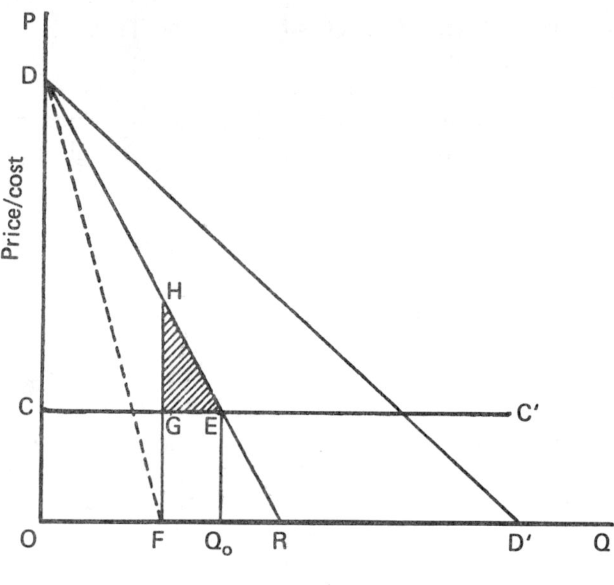

Figure 25-1

$$\frac{W}{P} = \frac{\varepsilon - 1}{\varepsilon} = \frac{2}{3}$$

we may state our first definitive result.

THEOREM I: In a static situation, irrespective of the degree of capitalization or of the comparative bargaining strengths of the two parties, the maximum wage bill cannot exceed two-thirds of value added.[11]

We must now look more closely at the relative bargaining power of the two parties. In substance, this relativity is to be found in the balancing of gains and losses by both sides in the stances of resistance or concession, respectively.[12]

[11]By virtue of our integration assumption, in this context price = value added.
[12]Cf. Hicks:

> When a Trade Union demands an advance in wages, or resists a reduction, it sets before the employer an alternative: either he must pay higher wages than he would have paid on his own initiative (and this generally means a prolonged reduction in profits) or on the other hand he must endure the direct loss which will probably follow from a stoppage of work. . . .one alternative will generally bring him less loss than the other. If resistance appears less costly than concession, he will resist; if concession seems cheaper, he will meet the Union's claims.

(Hicks, *op. cit.*, pp. 140-1). Unfortunately, Hicks scarcely progresses beyond this point.

WORKERS' ENDURANCE FUNCTION

If a union is acting as a simple maximizing unit, it must, if and when it resorts to strike action, balance the cost of such action (to its members) against the possible gains which may flow from that action. We begin with the question of cost.

Cost of Strike Action

We take W as the prevailing wage rate and Q as the obtaining level of employment (= output).

Then, in Figure 25-2 we relate the loss of wages, L, to the duration of a strike, s. In the first instance, we should expect this to be a linear relationship, loss of wages being directly proportional to the length of the strike, as along OA. As a strike continues, however, the position of those involved must progressively worsen. Workers' savings dry up, strike funds tend to exhaustion, credit becomes increasingly difficult. All these factors may be best thought of as increasing the marginal utility of money, as workers' resources become more and more stretched. Hence, we may draw a curve OB describing workers' losses in real terms which we represent by

$$L = sQW + Q.U(s) \tag{1}$$

where sQW is the loss in money terms and $Q.U(s)$ is a supplementary function representing the increasing marginal utility of that money loss as time proceeds. It is appropriate that we should make this function directly proportional with Q, since only those in employment will be affected by a stoppage of work.

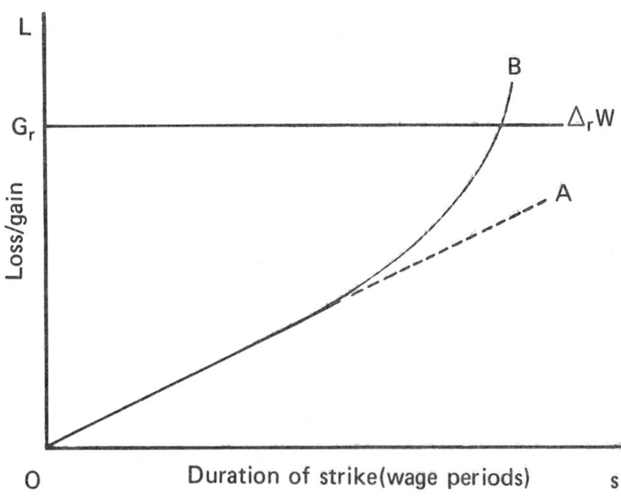

Figure 25-2

Then, $U(s)$ is an average-per-head function relating to those losing wages. After a certain point, one should expect OB to rise fairly sharply.

Now it is clear that there will be a whole family of OB curves, one corresponding to each particular wage, and it is unlikely that $U(s)$ will remain the same for all wage levels. It may increase or decrease as the wage level rises. For example, a higher wage may mean greater worker savings, or it may mean greater overheads such as rent or hire-purchase commitments. At any rate, strictly speaking we should re-write (1) as

$$L = sQW + Q.U(s, W). \tag{2}$$

Finally, it should be observed that $U(s, W)$ may be negative over a greater or lesser range; for instance, (a) when, at a time of full employment, workers can take alternative jobs, or (b) when it may be anticipated that wages lost during a strike will be largely recouped by subsequent overtime.

Gains from Wage Increase

Against these losses we must set off the potential gains. In general, of course, gains will not merely depend on the magnitude of any wage increase achieved. Account must be taken of any corresponding reduction in employment which may be associated with it. If G' represents net gains per wage-period, then[13]

$$\begin{aligned} G' &= Q\Delta W - W\Delta Q \\ &= Q\Delta W - Q\Delta W\left(\frac{W\Delta Q}{Q\Delta W}\right) \\ &= Q\Delta W(1 - \eta) \end{aligned} \tag{3}$$

where η is again the elasticity of the marginal revenue curve (assuming, as we do, that wage moves along the segment HE of Figure 25-1). It will be observed that, when η rises above 1, G' becomes negative, which is our argument of the fourth section of this paper.

A wage increase represents a continuing sequence through time. Future gains must therefore be reduced to the present value if they are to be set off against current losses. The rate of discount applied will depend on a host of factors which will no doubt vary considerably from one situation to another. A similar difficulty arises in relation to the number of periods over which the sum is to be taken. (An analogous problem arises in deciding the number of periods through which profits should be projected when evaluating a business.)

[13]In similar calculations throughout, we ignore quantities of the second order of smallness, in this case $\Delta Q \Delta W$.

All that we can say is that the number of periods will depend on the overall length of time during which conditions are *expected* to remain static. We then write down total gains, G, accruing as the result of a given wage increase as

$$G = Q \Delta W(1 - \eta) V_m(j) \tag{4}$$

where $V_m(j)$ is the sum of unity over m periods, discounted at the rate j.

Labor's Indifference Function

We are now in a position to equate workers' gains and losses, to give us a curve along which they will just break even. In other words, we will have an indifference curve the path of which may be taken as the locus of the union's sticking-points. The equation of this curve will be

$$sQW + Q.U(s, W) = Q \Delta W(1 - \eta) V_m(j)$$

(5) that is,

$$\Delta W = \frac{sW + U(s, W)}{(1 - \eta) V_m(j)}.$$

Geometrically, this result may be reached by superimposing the G_r corresponding to each $\Delta_r W$ on the ordinate of Figure 25-2 and reading off the points of intersection with OB.

Since $V_m(j)$ is a given constant in a particular situation, the curve described in (5) will, for a given W (and hence η) have the same general shape as OB of Figure 25-2. There will of course be a separate indifference curve in respect of

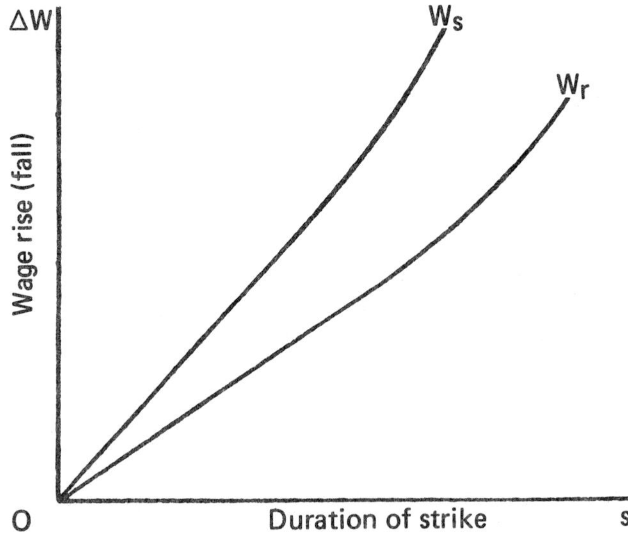

Figure 25-3

each wage. As the wage (and η) increase, the curve moves to the left, with the slope rising (see Figure 25-3).

In view of the fact that $\eta = \frac{1}{2}(\varepsilon - 1)$, we may write (5) alternatively as

$$\Delta W = \frac{sW + U(s, W)}{\frac{1}{2}(3 - \varepsilon)V_m(j)}. \tag{6}$$

EMPLOYER'S RESISTANCE FUNCTION

On his side, the monopolist must match the loss of profits incurred by resistance (i.e., by involvement in a strike) against the extended loss of profits which would result from conceding various wage increases.

Loss of Profits from Strike

At first sight, it might appear that the employer's loss from a strike, L_1, would be simply the profits lost during its currency, namely

$$sQ(P - W).$$

However, there will be some incidental losses to an employer associated with a strike which are likely to increase as the strike is extended. Two of these call for special attention.

First, an interruption of supplies to customers, or failure to meet contract deadlines, may involve the firm in substantial damage. The monopolist could even be faced with a permanent switch to substitutes. Generally we may sum up the whole battery of possible injury of this kind as *loss of goodwill.* Secondly, a protracted strike may involve the firm in financial stringency, or liquidity crisis, as fixed expenditures are met while no revenue flows in.

Loss of goodwill and financial stress will be increasing functions of the duration of the strike. We therefore add the supplementary function $Q.F(s, W)$ to represent these factors. Again, this function could turn out to be negative in the earlier stages of a strike since stocks may hold the line for some time. We have then

$$L_1 = sQ(P - W) + Q.F(s, W) \tag{7}$$

$$= sQW\left(\frac{P}{W} - 1\right) + Q.F(s, W)$$

$$= sQW\left(\frac{\varepsilon}{\varepsilon - 1} - 1\right) + Q.F(s, W)$$

$$= \frac{sQW}{\varepsilon - 1} + Q.F(s, W). \tag{8}$$

Loss of Profits from Wage Increase

The immediate loss of profit, L'_2, consequent on the granting of various wage increases is calculated in the Appendix to this article:

$$L'_2 = Q\Delta W.$$

This loss will of course be a continuing one, and we are again faced with the discounting of a future stream of payments. There is no reason to suppose that the "telescopic faculty" of employers will be the same as that of workers. We therefore introduce $V_n(i)$ to represent the present value of a stream of unit payments over n periods, discounted at the rate i. Then we have

$$L_2 = Q\Delta W.V_n(i). \tag{9}$$

Employer's Indifference Function

Matching L_1 against L_2, we obtain an employer's break-even curve of the form

$$\frac{sQW}{\varepsilon - 1} + Q.F(s, W) = Q\Delta W.V_n(i)$$

(10) that is,

$$\Delta W = \frac{1}{V_n(i)}\left[\frac{sW}{\varepsilon - 1} + F(s, W)\right]$$

"PURE" CASE OF SIMPLE MONETARY GAINS AND LOSSES

To appreciate where we are going, it is worth pausing for a moment to investigate a very special situation. Let us assume that the "telescopic faculties" of both parties are the same, i.e., that $V_m(j) = V_n(i)$; and let us also put aside for the moment the supplementary functions $U(s, W)$ and $F(s, W)$, i.e., assume that $U(s, W) = F(s, W) = 0$. We shall thus be concerned only with gains and losses in simple money terms.

Then, for a given wage (and hence given ε), both (6) and (10) become straight lines whose slopes are given by:

$$\frac{\partial(\Delta W)}{\partial s} = \frac{W}{\frac{1}{2}(3 - \varepsilon)} = \frac{W}{\varepsilon - 1}. \tag{11}$$

These straight lines, OU (union indifference curve) and OE (employer resistence curve), are shown in Figure 25-4. It is clear that $1 < \varepsilon < 3$; and as ε changes,

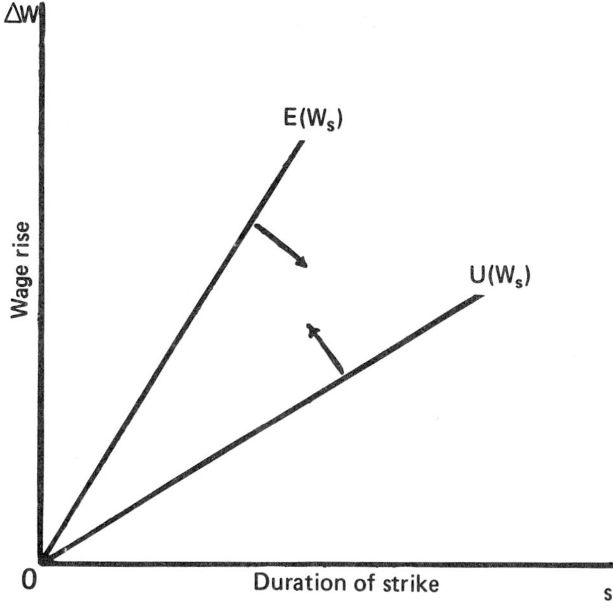

Figure 25-4

OU and OE will change in the following manner: (1) as ε *increases* towards 3, the slope of OU will tend to that of the Y-axis, and the slope of OE will tend to ½ W; and (2) as ε *falls* towards 1, the slope of OE will tend to that of the Y-axis, and the slope of OU will tend to W.

It will be seen then that the slopes of OU and OE move in opposite directions with changes in ε (and hence W). So long as OU lies to the right of OE, the union will always outlast the employer; and vice versa when OE lies to the right of OU. It becomes clear that pressure and counter-pressure from both sides will cease when OU coincides with OE, i.e., when

$$\tfrac{1}{2}(3 - \varepsilon) = \varepsilon - 1,$$

i.e., when

$$\varepsilon = \frac{5}{3}.$$

THEOREM II: If there is no impediment to pursuit of a purely monetary maximum by both sides, and each side discounts the future at the same rate, then the break-even point between the two parties occurs when the elasticity of demand is 5/3.

STATIC EQUILIBRIUM

Our discussion in the previous section gives us the clue to the conditions for equilibrium in the general case, i.e., when *OU* and *OE* may be presumed to be simple monotonic increasing functions but are not straight lines. In addition, it should be recognized explicitly that ε moves in the same direction as W. The slopes of the two functions move in opposite direction, because ε is in the one instance added and in the other subtracted. (Throughout we have followed the usual convention of taking ε itself in the positive sense.) As the wage (and ε) increases, *OU* moves to the left; *OE* moves to the right.

So long as *OU* is anywhere to the right of *OE*, the union can exert pressure for and (on our maximizing assumptions) secure a wage rise. This process will continue to the point where *OU* no longer stands to the right of *OE* at any point, i.e., to the point of tangency between the two curves (Figure 25-5). At this point, union bargaining power in relation to employer's resistance will be exhausted. Of course, the progression to tangency need not be made in one jump but may occur as a succession of steps towards the final equilibrium.

The point of equilibrium occurs when the ordinates of *OU* and *OE* are equal, and their slopes are also equal. If we put $V_m(j)/V_n(i) = v$,[14] our conditions for static equilibrium are:

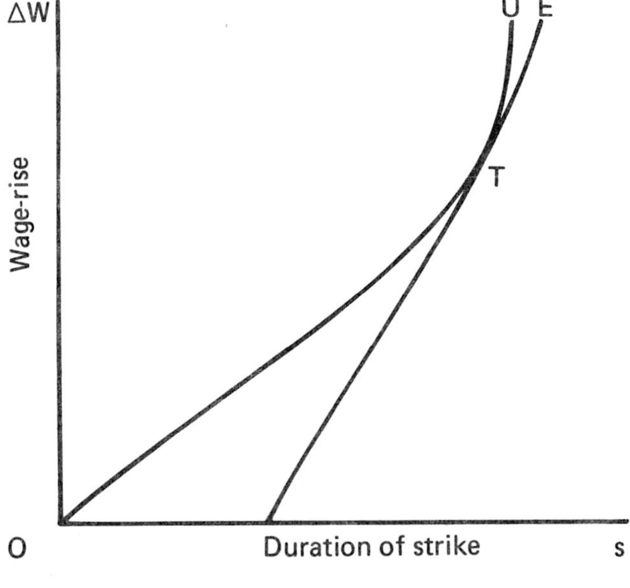

Figure 25-5

[14]One would normally expect the "telescopic faculty" of the firm to range further than that of the workers, in which case we would have $0 < v < 1$.

(12) $$\frac{sW + U(s, W)}{\frac{1}{2}(3 - \varepsilon)v} = \frac{sW}{\varepsilon - 1} + F(s, W)$$

(13) and $$\frac{W + U_s(s, W)}{\frac{1}{2}(3 - \varepsilon)v} = \frac{W}{\varepsilon - 1} + F_s(s, W).$$

It is clear that, once the shapes of U and F are known, we may eliminate s and then solve for W, since v is given in the situation. In summary, we may write

(14) $$W = \phi(\varepsilon, v, U, F)$$

where v, U and F are given parameters of the situation and W varies with ε.

The dependence of W upon ε is complex. In the first place, elasticity of demand will determine the price which the monopolist can charge. Then, by virtue of the relationship $\frac{P - W}{P} = \frac{1}{\varepsilon}$, the proportion of wages as part of total revenue will vary directly with ε. Finally, the value of ε will determine, at one remove, the reciprocity of wage rise and disemployment.

A few further observations on this static solution are in order. First, the reason why an equilibrium may be achieved with OE to the right of OU, but not vice versa, is that the employer is balancing *two losses*, one against the other. He will never want to allow a higher W or an increase in the duration of a strike, since he will incur further losses on either account. He is *pushed* to the point T (Figure 25-5); he will not want to go beyond it of his own accord. On the other hand, the union is balancing a *gain* against a *loss*, and will be in a position to realize some gain so long as OU is anywhere to the right of OE.

Secondly, it will not have passed unnoticed that neither the given membership of the union nor the level of the opportunity wage figures as explicit factors in determining the wage outcome. However, both have an indirect influence. In the first case, although some men may be rendered unemployed and thenceforth cease to enter directly into calculation, the magnitude of this unemployed element must affect the "solidarity" of total union membership and hence influence the shape of U. Likewise, the differential between the attained wage and the opportunity wage will affect (a) the pressure for entry into the industry from outside workers, and (b) the ease with which disemployed members will drop out of the particular industry. However, these two considerations properly belong to the area of dynamics rather than to a static model. What the opportunity wage does do in a static situation is to put a floor under the wage which must be paid by the monopolist; it sets a limit to his monopsonistic power.

Finally, it would be unrealistic to make no mention of a basic factor which we eliminated by virtue of our maximizing assumptions. When we undertook to treat the union as a maximizing entity, we implicitly assumed that it could always act in a cohesive way. This clearly presupposes a high degree of unity between members of the union. The *de facto* degree of unity within a union will obviously have a significant influence on the shape of *OU*.

DYNAMIC FACTORS

When we consider bilateral wage determination as a dynamic process, we must allow ε, v, U and F to vary with time. Formally, the path of the dynamic system will be traced by the simultaneous equations:

$$\frac{sW + U(s, W, t)}{\frac{1}{2}[3 - \varepsilon(t)]v(t)} = \frac{sW}{\varepsilon(t) - 1} + F(s, W, t) \tag{15}$$

$$\frac{W + U_s(s, W, t)}{\frac{1}{2}[3 - \varepsilon(t)]v(t)} = \frac{W}{\varepsilon(t) - 1} + F_s(s, W, t). \tag{16}$$

We shall now need to know how ε, v, U and F behave over time, t.

At one time or another, it has been argued that an increase of demand (say) will increase the elasticity of demand, will decrease it, or will *ceteris paribus* result in an iso-elastic shift of the demand curve. It would require an article in itself to investigate this question. First, the passage of time and increase in demand may result in the development of substitutes which would have the effect of increasing elasticity of demand facing the monopolist. Also, such an increase may pave the way for new entrants (actual or potential) into the field, and this again would tend to increase the value of elasticity of demand. On the other hand, an increase in demand may serve to entrench further the monopolist, when economies of scale are running strongly. Decrease in demand over time would, of course, tend in the opposite direction. Secondly, in so far as an increase in demand is accompanied by a general, all-round increase in *per capita* incomes, this may make buyers less "choosy" and thereby diminish elasticity of demand.

Little can be said, *a priori*, about the behavior of v over time. In general, it is probable that the union has a greater "telescopic range" than its individual members. As unions become better organized and more businesslike, and their members become better informed generally (with time), it is likely that their "telescopic faculty" will increase in range in relation to that of employers. In other words, v might be expected to rise. In so far as increase of demand, growth, and a measure of inflation go hand in hand, this would tend to foreshorten the "telescopic faculty" of both parties, but more especially that of workers who mostly live in the short period. Of course, the wage varies directly with $v = V_m(j)/V_n(i)$, and anything that tends to increase this ratio tends to increase the wage.

How should we expect U and F to behave over time? In the first place, U will depend largely on the general level of prosperity obtaining at a particular time. As we have observed, in times of high employment it is sometimes possible for striking workers to take other (lesser paid) jobs for the duration of the strike. Thus, U may be rendered negative. Also in times of prosperity, workers' reserves are likely to be high; so too are their fixed commitments. In times of recession, these factors should work in the opposite direction. As far as secular change over time is concerned, it is an open question whether higher real incomes increase the staying-power of workers or render them "soft" to hardship such as is involved in strike action.

How then will F behave over the course of time? This will depend to a large extent on the nature of the commodity sold by the monopolist. Goodwill is a very fickle mistress. The maintenance of goodwill will be much more important for some commodities than for others. The more basic or essential the commodity, the less is its continued demand likely to depend on uninterrupted supply; by the same token, the more are the ripples of disruption likely to spread beyond the particular strike-bound industry. The preservation of goodwill by uninterrupted supply is probably most important in service and less essential trades. Also the matter of goodwill probably looms larger in a buyers' market than in a sellers'.

In the long run, a monopolist no doubt builds stature and financial reserves (often hidden) which make him better able to meet a strike, except when engaged in a secularly declining industry. However, if his reserves are invested in outside securities, any loss involved in liquidation of such securities would have to be added to the cost of a strike. Again, during a slump or credit squeeze, with money tight all round, the monopolist might find himself in acute financial stress which would not encourage him to face a protracted strike. On the other hand, there would probably be a build-up of stocks in these circumstances and this would cushion the impact of a strike. All in all, the firm is normally in a stronger position during slump or tight conditions than are the workers. In the long run, the shapes of U and F will largely depend on the progress of each party in organization, efficiency and education; and also in the building of reserves in the case of the union and its members, and in the build-up of stocks and financial reserves in the case of the firm.

Finally we must look at our backroom variables—those ruled out explicitly by our assumptions of a static model. These must be let out of their static boxes. In the first place, demand will change (over time). We have already discussed tentatively how change in the conditions of demand affects elasticity. Increase of demand, as such, and also as part of a general, all-round increase, must be a factor favorable to union pressure. On the one hand, there will be a tendency on the part of the monopolist to hold onto workers, especially skilled workers, beyond the limit of strict profitability against anticipated future expansion. Further, an increase in demand may allow the rate of increase in union membership to be kept lagged behind the rate of increase in the demand for labor. In the final analysis, the union's unity and power will depend on its ability to eliminate or minimize disemployment of its members as it presses for higher wages. To a large extent this ability will reside in the degree of union control over entry of workers into the particular industry.

This control reaches its highest expression in the closed-shop. With control over entry but not over exit, an increasing demand must always work in the union's favor and a decreasing demand against it.

The question of the ratio of labor supply to labor demand pervades all others. For example, technical change will affect the union *directly* in two ways. First, if the innovation is labor-saving, there is the likelihood of unemployment for some union members. The union will attempt to close entry and to allow normal wastage to take up the slack of unemployment so created. Secondly, it may be that the innovation only becomes profitable with an increase in scale, which will necessitate a reduction in price to *expand* the firm's sales. This expansion of demand would usually favor the union since it will probably also expand the demand for labor, always assuming that the union has some control over recruitment into the industry. Lower costs (higher productivity) in themselves do not necessarily benefit the workers.

One facet of technical change is that going on outside the particular industry with which we are concerned. Innovation and increased productivity in the competitive sectors will tend to raise the opportunity wage and thus relieve the pressure on entry into our particular industry. In so far as increased productivity in outside industries manifests itself in lower prices, the real wage of the monopolist's work force will also increase.

On the subject of changes in union membership, we have said nearly all that need be said. However, there is one aspect on which it is worth remarking. To a certain extent the union will have an ambivalent interest. In so far as it attempts to maximize the wage bill with a minimum of unemployment of members, it will want to do its utmost to restrict entry and minimize membership. On the other hand, it is natural for a union—at least from the point of view of union officials—to expand membership, the ordinary and common proclivity for empire-building. In practice this conflict is often plain to see.

CONCLUSION

The foregoing treatment does not purport to be definitive. If some windows have been opened onto an unilluminated subject, the author will be well content.

APPENDIX

Loss of Profit Per Period from Wage Rise ΔW

(1a) Old profit: $Q(P - W)$

(2a) New profit: $[Q - \Delta Q]\,[(P + \Delta P) - (W + \Delta W)]$

Then, the loss of profit per period, L'_2, is given by (1a) minus (2a):

(3a) $$L'_2 = Q\Delta W - Q\Delta P + \Delta Q(P - W)$$

$$= Q\Delta W - Q\Delta P + P\Delta Q\left(\frac{P - W}{P}\right)$$

$$= Q\Delta W - Q\Delta P + \frac{P\Delta Q}{\varepsilon}$$

since $\frac{P - W}{P}$ is the reciprocal of elasticity of demand. Further,

$$L'_2 = Q\Delta W - Q\Delta P + \frac{P\Delta Q}{Q\Delta P} \cdot \frac{Q\Delta P}{\varepsilon}$$

$$= Q\Delta W - Q\Delta P + Q\Delta P$$

(4a) $$= Q\Delta W.$$

This simple result (loss = quantity of employment/output × wage rise conceded) is somewhat surprising, since there are three distinct components entering into its determination: (a) *loss* from increase in wage bill; (b) *loss* from reduction in output; and (c) *gain* from increase in price.

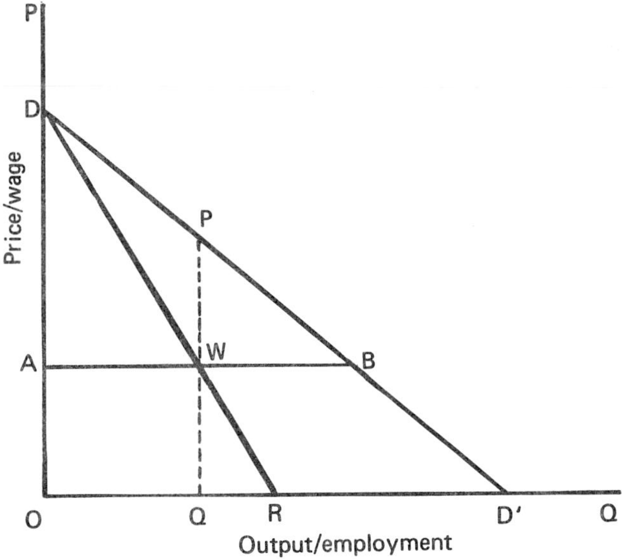

Figure 25-6

As this result is unexpected, it will not be out of order if we demonstrate it geometrically. We have to show that

$$Q\Delta P = \Delta Q(P - W)$$

thereby cancelling these out in (3a), leaving us with the first term only, $Q\Delta W$.

In Figure 25-6, draw the horizontal AB, representing the actual wage, with W assigned to the point where AB intersects the marginal revenue curve, DR.

We have

$$\frac{P - W}{WB} = \frac{\Delta P}{\Delta Q}.$$

But $AW = Q = WB$, since $OR = RD'$;

and therefore
$$\frac{P - W}{Q} = \frac{\Delta P}{\Delta Q}$$

that is,
$$Q\Delta P = \Delta Q(P - W)$$

which was to be shown.

26. A NOTE ON ECONOMIC RENT*

Robert H. Wessel†

Although the concept of economic rent has been widely used by professional economists for many years, as yet no clear consensus concerning its meaning exists. At present two very different versions of the rent idea are usually encountered. The origin of one can be traced through Marshall and Mill back to Ricardo while the other had its beginnings in the works of Pareto. Unfortunately many writers do not recognize the dissimilarity between these concepts and use them interchangeably, while others see the difference but fail to derive any worthwhile advantages from the use of two rent definitions rather than one.[1]

The crux of the definition issue is this. Economic rent is defined by the followers of Ricardo as the excess amount earned by a factor over the sum necessary to induce it to do its work. The Paretian rent concept is the excess earnings over the amount necessary to keep the factor in its present occupation [6, par. 745–55]. Clearly these are very different definitions. In the first the test is whether the factor is supplied at all or not; the second is concerned with where it is supplied. In the latter case it is obvious that opportunity costs created by the competitive uses must be met as a condition of holding the factor in its present use.[2] Only the surplus over these opportunity costs would be rent in this sense.

The first of these definitions had its origin in Ricardo's concept of differential surplus. In essence, it is the same as Taussig's "producer's surplus"

*From *American Economic Review*, Vol. LVII, No. 5 (December, 1967), pp. 1221–1226. Reprinted by permission of the publisher and the author.

†Robert H. Wessel, Professor of Economics and Vice Provost for Graduate Studies, University of Cincinnati.

[1]Even Boulding, in his excellent recent revision of *Economic Analysis*, offers two definitions, one following Ricardo and the other patterned after Pareto without explicitly mentioning that these definitions are different and that they may lend themselves to different uses [1, p. 265 and p. 512]. An examination of the latest editions of most leading intermediate and advanced texts shows this situation to be quite general [7], [3].

[2]At times a distinction is made between the payment needed to hold a factor in its present occupation and the return it could earn in other uses [5]. These could, of course, be different because of nonpecuniary elements involved in different lines of work. This distinction is not employed here because it introduces another, and for our purposes extraneous, variable into the problem. Although we must admit the validity of this contention, it should be ruled out by the simplifying assumption that the net nonpecuniary advantages of the occupations in question are the same.

[8, p. 63] and Marshall's "scarcity rents" [4, pp. 422–30]. It is oriented to the motives and behavior of the supplier of resources and presumably may serve as the basis of moral judgments approving or condemning their rewards.

Pareto's definition is user oriented. Because of the use of the present occupation test, it differentiates payments generated by the industry or firm employing productive resources from those imposed in the market by the competition of other firms or industries. As a result multiple rent concepts appear. First is rent from the point of view of the economy, which coincides with the Ricardian type of definition. Next, however, is rent from the point of view of the industry, which is any payment made by the industry to a factor in excess of the opportunity costs created by other industries. These extra payments are made necessary by the industries' contribution to the total demand for the factor. Finally, rents from the standpoint of the firm are payments by the firm in excess of what other firms in the same industry would offer the agent for its services.

The existence of two significantly different but widely used approaches to the concept of economic rent is obviously unfortunate. It is appropriate, therefore, to examine critically the relative merits of the two types of definitions in order to determine whether significant simplification is possible and desirable.

The concept of economic rent is encountered most frequently in two important areas of economics, the theory of distribution and the theory of cost. Consequently, the merits of the two types of rent concepts can appropriately be tested by the contributions they make to these theories and their applications.

The traditional approach which views rent as the excess payment received by a factor over the minimum required to induce it to do its work passes the distribution theory test with flying colors. This is not unexpected since the concept had its origin in early formulations of distribution theory and was an integral part thereof. In its early as well as its present form it was designed to explain the income received by factors of production. It was first used in connection with the return paid to natural resources where no elasticity of supply was believed to exist. Since the compensation of such a factor generated no increase in productive effort, it was viewed as a surplus payment. Even when this line of reasoning was later extended to other types of agents, the term rent continued to be used to explain all or part of the income shares they received. Here the rent or surplus designation was applied to that part of the compensation of the factor in excess of the payment necessary to bring forth its services. This was true both of the excess over the minimum necessary to get the factor to work at all and the excess over the payment needed to induce each additional increment of performance by the factor. In modern terms, of course, this concept views "economic rent" as the part of the compensation of the factor graphically depicted by the area between the supply curve to all uses of the factor and the horizontal line representing the rate pay received by the factor.

In addition to being a clear-cut distribution concept, the traditional view of rent has the great conceptual merit of being closely related to the basic causes of scarcity. Rent in this sense exists because the supplies of the factors are less than perfectly elastic. This in turn is occasioned by those fundamental forces which cause the services of factors to be available in limited quantities only. When applied to factors other than land, this approach forces us to focus on the behavior of factor suppliers. As a result the study of scarcity must be related to and draw upon the findings of other behavioral sciences.

The traditional rent concept also enables us to divide, conceptually at least, factor compensation into two parts, payments which induce factors to work and surplus which only confers a greater reward for work which would have been done anyway. In classical terms it distinguishes payments made to overcome "real costs," labor pain, abstinence, etc., from unnecessary bounties. Although we no longer subscribe closely to a "real cost" doctrine, it is still worthwhile to have a conceptual separation of those payments which are a necessary condition of production and those which are not. This is particularly important in applied economics where moral judgments are passed and policies suggested.

Pareto's approach has little to contribute to distribution theory. At best the set of concepts which ascribe individual rents to each of the industries or firms using an agent might enable us quantitatively to identify where the components of the total factor rent came from. If available and valid this information might be interesting, but it would contribute nothing that a thorough demand analysis would not provide. However, this type of compilation would be conceptually incorrect. Paretian rent from the point of view of any individual user of a factor is determined by how his demand influences the price of a factor assuming the demands of all other users to be *present in the market*. It is clear that the sum of these influences is not necessarily the same as the sum of the consequences when all of the individual demands are added to or subtracted from the market at the same time. Hence, the total individual user rents would in all probability differ greatly from the total rent received by the factor. This difference would be especially large where supply is highly inelastic. In addition we must remember that, when any user adds his demand to the factor market, the price rise he produces generates "rents" not only for himself but also necessitates additional payments by all other users of the agent.

We should also point out that the multiple-rent concepts are of no value whatsoever when the theory of distribution is used in applied economics. Certainly no moral significance or basis of policy formation can be found in firm or industry rents. It should be clear, therefore, that the Pareto approach is a misfit from the standpoint of distribution theory and must justify itself, if at all, on other grounds.

When the theory of cost is considered, Pareto's approach fares somewhat better. The traditional concept draws its lines of division between necessary and unnecessary payment at the social level. What is necessary or unnecessary for the firm or the industry, however, is far different. Opportunity costs are real and must be met even though from the social point of view most of these payments are rent. Nevertheless, this does not justify separate rent concepts for industries or firms. All that is required by the theory of cost at either firm or industry level is that the conditions of supply of the factor to the firm or the industry be known. Here the concepts of supply curves to industries or firms are entirely sufficient. In situations where a firm or industry can control the market sufficiently to influence costs, the theories of monopsony or oligopsony are adequate. As a result rent concepts at the firm and industry levels that identify and name the income generated by firms or industries are totally unnecessary to the theory of cost. They are worse than useless, however, because they confuse elements of cost and distribution theory. The distribution concept of rent is needlessly brought into the theory of cost while the cost-oriented user classification complicates the theory of distribution without enhancing our knowledge of factor income determination.

It should be clear from what has been said that on theoretical grounds the traditional concept is vastly superior. There is also no suggestion that the multiple-rent concepts are of any particular importance for either the businessman or the social planner. That they are lacking in moral significance and provide no meaningful policy guides should be evident as well. Consequently, the foregoing analyses suggest that economic rent is best defined as the surplus over the payment needed to induce a factor to do its work, and best defined in this way alone.[3]

One final argument in favor of the Pareto concept merits separate attention. Economists have long debated the role of rents in price making, some contending that rents are price determining while others argue that they are price determined. The multiple rent concepts of Pareto's followers seemingly permit a neat compromise which allows one to say that rents are from one standpoint price determined yet from another price determining. The argument proceeds somewhat as follows. Although rents in the sense of payments in excess of the minimum amount needed to induce factors to work are a result of the structure of prices and therefore price determined from the standpoint of the economy as a whole, many components of these payments are price determining to particular industries or firms. This is because the competitive bidding of other industries has built the parts of those rents not generated by the specific industry itself into opportunity costs which the industry must meet and which must be covered in the price of the product. Hence, those components of "rents from the standpoint of the economy" which are embodied in opportunity costs are price determining from the standpoint of the industry

[3]The suggestion that rent be defined as the opportunity cost of land (or for that matter of any other factor) and that any payment in excess of this amount be designated "factor profits" [9, pp. 269–75] must also be rejected. Under conditions of pure competition such a distinction is unimportant. On the other hand, when individual firms play a significant role in the market it is at least misleading and often clearly incorrect.

while rents generated by the industry itself are price determined. Similarly, payments which are rents from the standpoint of the industry are often included in the market price of agents purchased by the firm and are price determining at that level.

This somewhat persuasive line of reasoning, however, misses the basic point in the entire price-determined price-determining controversy. In essence, the controversy arises from a misleading statement of the problem. In fact, under properly constructed sets of assumptions, it is easy to prove that rent is either price determined or price determining. For example, consider a factor X, which is used in the manufacture of product A. Let us assume that X is used in the production of other products and the manufacture of A requires other agents. If now the conditions of supply of all the agents are treated as given, as well as the technical coefficients and the preference patterns for all products except A, a change in the preference pattern concerning A will alter the price of A. This in turn will lead to a change in the demand by the producers of A for X and therefore a change in the price of X, of which the part in excess of the minimum supply price is rent. Consequently, the change in the price of A changes or "determines" the rent of X. On the other hand, if every basic determinant of the system is treated as given, except the supply of X, a change in the supply of X will alter its price including its rent and, in consequence, the price of A. Here rent might be said to be price determining.

In reality, of course, economists have long known that rent is neither price determining nor price determined since neither rent nor price is a basic determinant of the system. They are co-determined as the result of the interaction of more fundamental forces. We know from Cassell's simple general equilibrium model that these forces are the condition of supply of the agents, the technical coefficients, and the preference patterns of consumers [2, pp. 134–55]. Their simultaneous interaction determines the prices of all products and factors, as well as the quantities of all goods produced and the allocation of resources. Rent along with price is a result not a causal factor.[4] The validity of this basic viewpoint is not significantly altered when more sophisticated assumptions are introduced to the system.

Consequently, even this last argument fails to justify the confusion now existing with the rent concept.

REFERENCES

[1] Boulding, Kenneth E. *Economic Analysis*, 4th ed., Vol. I. New York: Harper and Row, 1966.

[2] Cassell, Gustav. *The Theory of Social Economy*, Vol. I. London: Harcourt, 1932.

[4]It is true that autonomously determined rents or prices might themselves be basic elements in a more complex model. This, however, is not the point at issue in the classical controversy.

[3] Due, J. F., and R. W. Clower. *Intermediate Economic Analysis*, 5th ed. Homewood, Ill.: Richard D. Irwin, 1966.
[4] Marshall, A. *Principles of Economics*, 8th ed. London: 1938.
[5] Mishan, E. J. "Rent as a Measure of Welfare Change." *American Economic Review*, Vol. XLIX (June, 1959), p. 386.
[6] Pareto, V. *Cours d' économie politique*, Vol. II. Lausanne, 1896.
[7] Robinson, Joan. *The Economics of Imperfect Competition.* London: Macmillan, 1933.
[8] Taussig, Frank W. *Principles of Economics*, 3d ed., Vol. II. New York: Macmillan, 1921.
[9] Worcester, D. A. "A Reconsideration of Rent Theory." *American Economic Review*, Vol. XXXVI (June, 1946).

27. CAPITAL THEORY UP TO DATE*

Joan Robinson†

The lectures which Professor Solow gave in Holland (published in 1963[1]) opened with the remark: Everybody except Joan Robinson agrees about capital theory. He did not say what it was that they agreed, and a few years later the "reswitching" controversy brought some important differences of opinion to light. Now, fortunately, we have a clear exposition of what Professor Solow must have meant. Professor Ferguson, in *The Neoclassical Theory of Production and Distribution*,[2] asserts that belief in neoclassical theory is a matter of faith. "I personally have the faith" he declares, so that we can learn from him what it is that the neo-classicals believe neoclassical theory to be. But first let us trace the history of the "reswitching" affair.

Reswitching

In the course of investigating the meaning of a production function for output as a whole, I set up what Professor Solow later correctly described as a pseudo-production function, showing the possible positions of equilibrium, corresponding to various values of the rate of profit, in an imagined "given state of technical knowledge." The analysis showed that there is no meaning to be given to a "quantity of capital" apart from the rate of profit, so that the contention that the "marginal product of capital" determines the rate of profit is meaningless. (In the present argument "land" as a separate factor of production is not taken into account.) Incidentally, I found that over certain ranges of the pseudo-production function the technique that becomes eligible at a higher rate of profit (with a correspondingly lower real-wage rate) may be less labor-intensive (that is, may have a higher output per man employed) than that chosen at a higher wage rate, contrary to the rule of a "well-behaved production function" in which a lower wage rate is always associated with a more labor-intensive technique. (I attributed this discovery to Ruth Cohen—a private joke.)

*From *Canadian Journal of Economics*, Vol. III, No. 2 (May, 1970), pp. 309-317. Reprinted by permission of the publisher and the author.

†Joan Robinson, Professor of Economics, Cambridge University, Cambridge, England.

[1]Robert M. Solow, *Capital Theory and the Rate of Return* (Amsterdam: North Holland Publishing Co., 1963).

[2]C. E. Ferguson, *The Neoclassical Theory of Production and Distribution* (London and New York: Cambridge University Press, 1969).

I had picked up the clue from Piero Sraffa's Preface to Ricardo's *Principles* and my analysis (errors and omissions excepted) was a preview of his. When his own treatment of the subject was finally published in *Production of Commodities by Means of Commodities* (in 1960), the "Ruth Cohen case" (which I had treated as a *curiosus*) was seen to have great prominence; the striking proposition was established that it is perfectly normal (within the accepted assumptions) for the same technique to be eligible at several discrete rates of profit. It was from this that the soubriquet "reswitching of techniques" was derived. (The difference between my treatment and Sraffa's was accidental. I put the main emphasis on differences in the amounts of "labor embodied" in the equipment appropriate to different techniques while Sraffa illustrates his point with a case in which two commodities require the same labor applied in different time-patterns. The backward switch, from a lower to a higher output per head with lower wages, is connected with the inter-relations of the time-patterns of the techniques; his examples gave more scope for it than mine.)

The neo-neoclassicals took no notice; they went on as usual drawing production functions in terms of "capital" and labor and disseminating the marginal productivity theory of distribution. In 1961 I encountered Professor Samuelson on his home ground; in the course of an argument I happened to ask him: When you define the marginal product of labor, what do you keep constant? He seemed disconcerted, as though none of his pupils had ever asked that question, but next day he gave a clear answer. Either the physical inputs other than labor are kept constant, or the rate of profit on capital is kept constant.

I found this satisfactory, for it destroys the doctrine that wages are regulated by marginal productivity. In a short-period case, where equipment is given, at full-capacity operation the marginal physical product of labor is indeterminate. When nine men with nine spades are digging a hole, to add a tenth man could increase output only to the extent that nine dig better if they have a rest from time to time.[3] On the other hand, to subtract the ninth man would reduce output by more or less the average amount. The wage must lie somewhere between the average value of output per head and zero, so that marginal product is much greater or much less than the wage according as equipment is being worked below or above its designed capacity.

In conditions of imperfect competition, under-capacity operation of plant is normal (except in an acute seller's market) and, in industry as a whole, it seems that, on average, wages are usually about half of value added. The marginal product of labor, in the short-period sense, is therefore generally about twice the wage.[4]

In long-period equilibrium, with a constant rate of profit, the stock of equipment and the amount of employment have been adjusted to each other. When

[3]See D. H. Robertson, "Wage Grumbles," (1930), republished in *Economic Fragments*.

[4]Cf. A.M. Okun, *Potential GNP. Its Measurement and Significance* (Cowles Foundation Paper), p. 189.

competition prevails in the long-period sense of free entry to all markets, so that a uniform rate of profit tends to be established throughout the economy, the wage is equivalent to what Marshall called the marginal *net* product of labor — that is the value of average output per head *minus* a gross profit sufficient to pay for replacement and net profit at the going rate on the value of capital per man employed, when all inputs are reckoned at the prices appropriate to the given rate of profit. The wage is determined by technical conditions and the rate of profit, as at a particular point on a pseudo-production function. The question then comes up, what determines the rate of profit?

But this was going too far. Professor Samuelson retreated behind what he called a surrogate production function.[5] It was a special case (as Piero Garegnani promptly pointed out[6]) of a pseudo-production function with labor-value prices. When, for any one technique, the capital-labor ratio and the time pattern of inputs are uniform throughout all the processes of production, prices are proportional to labor-time. The value of capital in terms of product, for that technique, is then independent of the rate of profit. When each technique in the "given state of knowledge" has this character and the time-patterns are all alike, the order of techniques in terms of output per head is the same as the order in terms of value of capital per man for each technique at the rate of profit that makes that technique eligible; a higher output per man is associated with a higher wage and lower rate of profit. When a pseudo-production function of this type is set out as a relationship between "capital" and output it looks just like a well-behaved production function.

Professor Samuelson believed that in this he had provided for the "neoclassical parables" of J. B. Clark "which pretend there is a single thing called 'capital' that can be put into a single production function and along with labor will produce total output."[7]

At first the neo-neoclassicals were happy to accept his parable. (This was the period of Professor Solow's lectures and of the first draft of Professor Ferguson's book in which, he tells us, he relied upon the surrogate production function to protect him from what he calls Cambridge Criticism.) For some years they remained cooped up in this position, repelling all attacks with blank misunderstanding. Then, growing bold, they descended to the plains and tried to prove Sraffa wrong.

This rash enterprise was not successful; Professor Samuelson very handsomely admitted that he had been mistaken.[8] But he mistook his mistake. The trouble was not merely that he had ignored Garegnani's warning and treated labor-value prices as the general case. The real mistake was to suppose that a pseudo-production function, which relates the rate of profit to the value of

---

[5]Paul A. Samuelson, "Parable and Realism in Capital Theory: The Surrogate Production Function," *Review of Economic Studies*, Vol. XXIX (June, 1962), pp. 193–206.

[6]*Ibid.*, footnote on p. 202.

[7]*Ibid.*, p. 194.

[8]Paul A. Samuelson, "A Summing Up" in "Paradoxes of Capital Theory: A Symposium," *Quarterly Journal of Economics*, Vol. LXXX (November, 1966), pp. 568–83.

capital at the prices corresponding to that rate of profit, provides the "neoclassical parable." Neoclassical "capital" is a physical quantity which is independent of prices.

Capital

The neo-neoclassicals' concept of capital is derived from Walras, but they have transformed it into something quite different. In a Walrasian market, when dealing begins, there are particular supplies of factors already in existence each measured in physical terms — man-hours, acres, tons, pints, and yards. In the neo-neoclassical concept of capital all the man-made factors are boiled into one, which we may call *leets* in honor of Professor Meade's *steel.*[9] But leets, though all made of one physical substance, is endowed with the capacity to embody various techniques of production — different ratios of leets to labor — and a change of technique can be made simply by squeezing up or spreading out leets, instantaneously and without cost. A higher output per man requires a larger amount of leets per man employed. In Walrasian competitive equilibrium there can never be increasing returns from one factor applied to a given quantity of another. This rule is observed by leets. There is a well-behaved production function in leets and labor for each kind of output, including leets. Moreover, leets can absorb technical progress, without losing its physical identity, again instantaneously and without cost. Then to simplify still further, output is also taken to be made of leets; the whole Walrasian system is reduced to a "one-commodity world."

This is the conception in which Professon Ferguson has re-affirmed his faith.

Many economists, nowadays, who are interested in practical questions are impatient of doctrinal disputes. What does it matter, they are inclined to say, let him have his leets, what harm does it do? But the harm that the neo-neoclassicals have done is, precisely, to block off economic theory from any discussion of practical questions.

When equipment is made of leets, there is no distinction between long and short-period problems. The answer to Dennis Robertson's question is simply fudged. Nine spades are a lump of leets; when the tenth man turns up it is squeezed out to provide him with a share of equipment nine-tenths of what each man had before.

There is no such thing as a degree of utilization of given equipment rising or falling with the level of effective demand. (Professor Solow pretends that his production functions are drawn in terms of concrete capital goods, but the fact that the short-period utilization function is identical with the long-period pseudo-production function gives him away.)

---

[9]J. E. Meade, *A Neoclassical Theory of Economic Growth* (London: Oxford University Press, 1961).

There is no room for imperfect competition. There is no possibility of disappointed expectations — indeed, there is no difference between the past and the future, for the past can always be undone and readjusted to a change in the present situation.

There is no problem of unemployment. The wage bargain is made in terms of product and there is perfect competition both between workers for jobs and between employers for hands. Unemployed workers would bid down wages and the pre-existing quantity of leets would be spread out to accommodate them. The neo-neoclassicals have reconstructed the vague doctrines of the neoclassicals from which was derived the dogma which Keynes had to attack in the great slump of the 'thirties, that unemployment can be caused only by wages being too high.

In long-period analysis, the neo-neoclassics are prone to confuse a comparison of positions of equilibrium (as in a pseudo-production function) with a "Wicksell process" of accumulation without technical progress. "A given state of technical knowledge" consists simply of a production function in terms of leets and labor. Accumulation consists of adding some leets to the pre-existing stock and squeezing it into a new quantity per man employed. This entails raising the wage rate and reducing the return per ton of leets. Thus a process of raising the capital-labor ratio means creeping along the production function, moving step by step from lower to higher ratios of leets to labor. (It is notable that when Professor Samuelson conceded defeat in the "reswitching" controversy, he did so in this form. He seemed to suppose that if the process of accumulation hit a backward switch, where a lower rate of profit is associated with a lower value of capital per man, the economy would suddenly find itself able to consume part of its capital without reducing its productive capacity.)

This brings into play the other aspect of pre-Keynesian theory. Saving consists in a decision not to consume a part of the current output and this causes investment to make a corresponding addition to the stock of "capital." The neo-neoclassicals have succeeded in tying themselves up again in habits of thought from which Keynes had had "a long struggle to escape." However, when it comes to offering advice on questions of national policy many of them propounded quite simple-minded Keynesian views.[10])

Wages and Profits

The main function of the concept of leets is to provide a theory of the distribution of the product of industry between wages and profits.

At any moment, with a given quantity in existence of leets regarded as capital equipment, the wage in terms of leets regarded as product is at the level compatible with full employment of the available labor force. Then, with a

[10]Cf. R. M. Solow, *The Nature and Sources of Unemployment in the United States* (Wicksell Lectures, 1964).

few extra assumptions, such as that there is no charge for interest on the part of working capital which represents the wage fund, it is shown that the wage is equal to the marginal product of the available labor force, that is, the amount of product per week that would be lost if one less man were employed and the stock of leets squeezed up appropriately. If the wage were less than this, competition for hands would drive it up. If it was greater, less men would be employed and competition for jobs would drive it down. The wage being equal to the marginal product of labor, it is shown by Euler's theorem that the product minus the wage is the marginal product of a ton of leets multiplied by the quantity of leets in existence.

Now, capital in the world we live in has two aspects. It consists of the stocks of equipment and materials which (with education and training) permit workers to produce marketable goods and it consists of the command over finance which permits employers to organize the production of goods which they can sell at a profit. In the "one-commodity world" the price of a ton of leets-capital in terms of leets-output is unity. The two aspects of capital are fused. A ton of leets is both a piece of equipment and a sum of purchasing power. Then the return to a unit of leets, leets over leets, is the rate of profit on capital. Thus, labor and capital each receive a "reward" equal to their marginal productivity. As J. B. Clark himself put it: "What a social class gets is, under natural law, what it contributes to the general output of industry."[11]

Here, indeed, we find the origin of the concept of leets. First came the dogma that the rate of profit that the owners of capital enjoy is equal to the productivity of capital equipment, and that saving continues to cause capital to accumulate so long as its marginal product exceeds the rate of interest which represents the "discount of the future" in the minds of its owners. Then the question is asked, what is this "capital" that has a marginal product? Leets had to be invented to give an answer to that question.

Of course, all this is not intended to be taken literally. Even Professor Ferguson admits that capital equipment actually consists of a variety of hard objects that cannot be squeezed up or pressed out, without cost, to accommodate less or more workers. Leets is only a parable, as Professor Samuelson claimed. But as soon as they give it up, their argument comes unstuck.

Professor Ferguson, for instance, incorporates a "vintage model" in his system. The vintage model is taken over from Harrod's conception of an economy realizing the "natural" rate of growth given by technical progress.

Gross investment, in each period, is embodied in equipment for the latest, most superior technique. The conditions for equilibrium growth are that technical progress should be raising output per head at a steady rate and that it should be neutral in Harrod's sense, so that a constant rate of profit on capital is compatible with a constant capital-output ratio and constant relative shares

[11] J. B. Clark, "Distribution as Determined by a Law of Rent," *Quarterly Journal of Economics*, Vol. V (April, 1891), p. 313.

of wages and profits in net output. A constant share of gross investment in total output then produces growth of output per head at a steady rate.

On any one equilibrium path, the rate of profit on capital is constant through time, but there may be different paths (with the same sequence of technical innovations) with different rates of profit. Thus there is a kind of pseudo-production function relating the rate of profit to the value of capital in terms of product and the share of gross investment in output.

The level of wages in terms of product rises in step with output per head (this follows from the condition that the rate of profit and the share of wages in output are constant) and the equipment for each technique is scrapped when the wage absorbs its whole output so that its quasi-rent is reduced to zero. A higher share of profit entails a wider gap between the wage rate and output per head with the latest, best, technique. Thus, it entails a longer service life of equipment, therefore a higher proportion of older, more inferior, techniques in use at any moment, and lower average output per head. There is then a presumption that the pseudo-production function relating the rate of profit to the capital-output ratio will be well-behaved (a lower output per man being associated with a lower value of capital per man) though there still might be some "Cambridge" tricks in it. But what determines the rate of profit?

Professor Ferguson follows Professor Solow's argument that a very small *extra* investment over and above that required by the equilibrium path yields a return equal to the rate of profit. That is true, whatever the rate of profit may be. And he shows that the marginal product of labor in the short-period sense is equal to the wage; the "last man" is employed in the equipment that is just about to be scrapped. This is true because, for a given pseudo-production function, both the wage relative to output per head with the latest technique and the age of the least productive equipment are determined together by the rate of profit. Evidently they are so used to thinking in terms of leets (for whatever he may say, Professor Solow's capital is made of leets) that they forget that,when capital is embodied in specific equipment, the short-period marginal physical product of labor is not the same thing as the value of the net product allowing for profit at a particular rate. They describe the competitive equilibrium position corresponding to a given rate of profit without offering any explanation of what the rate of profit is.

There have been three types of theory of the distribution of the product of industry between wages and profits. In classical theory (of which von Neumann provides the most systematic account) the real wage per man is a technical datum; the rate of profit on capital emerges as a residual. In Marx, the rate of exploitation (the ratio of net profit to wages) is the result of the balance of forces in the class struggle. For Marshall, there is a normal rate of profit and the real wage emerges as a residual; an extension of Keynes' General Theory into the long period finds a clue to the level of profits in the rate of accumulation and the excess of consumption out of profits over saving out of wages.

When the neo-neoclassicals reconstituted orthodoxy after the Keynesian revolution, they eschewed all these and went to Walras, who does not have a theory of profits at all.

Econometrics

The strangest part of the whole affair is that many neo-neoclassicals seek to identify leets-capital with the dollar value of capital as it appears in statistics. Professor Ferguson concludes his account of "reswitching" thus: "The question that confronts us is not whether the Cambridge Criticism is theoretically valid. It is. Rather the question is an empirical or econometric one: is there sufficient substitutability within the system to establish neo-classical results?"[12] And he states in the Preface: "Until the econometricians have the answer for us, placing reliance upon neoclassical economic theory is a matter of faith." Statisticians, though with a very coarse mesh, can catch evidence of the capital-output ratio in terms of dollar values, and the shares of wages and profits in value added, over a particular period in a particular economy, and so they can offer an estimate of the ex-post, over-all rate of profit being realized. They cannot say what expectations of profit were in the minds of the managers of firms, or whether alternative schemes were on the drawing boards of engineers, when the investment decisions were taken that brought a particular stock of capital equipment into existence. Still less can they say what decisions would have been taken if present and expected prices and wage rates had been different from what they were. Professor Ferguson expects too much.

Consider a run of figures for a prosperous period of development in a modern industrial economy which conform more or less (as they often seem to do) to what Kaldor calls the "stylised facts." The capital-output ratio and the wage and profit shares are fairly constant over time, while the dollar value of output per man employed and the dollar value of capital per man have a strong upward trend. This would lend itself to interpretation as an approximation to the story of accumulation on a Harrod path, as in the vintage model, with neutral technical progress and a fairly steady over-all average rate of profit (fluctuations in effective demand being smoothed out).

This will not do for the neo-neoclassicals. They want to separate out increases in the quantity of "capital" from the effects of technical progress. To find this distinction, they puzzle themselves with their leets. Leets can absorb technical progress without any investment being required. An "invention" raises the output per head of a set of workers equipped with a given quantity of leets. But output also consists of leets, so that if the share of saving in income is constant, leets per man employed begins to rise as a result of the invention. Is this to be attributed to accumulation or to the invention? To attribute the

[12] C. E. Ferguson, *op. cit.*, p. 266.

growth of leets per man to saving, it would be necessary to define as saving, refraining from consuming so much of additional leets as to keep leets per man constant.[13]

In any case, the statistics are in dollars, not in tons of leets. Whether technical progress is embodied in new types of equipment or affected by a rearrangement of existing equipment or comes from "learning by doing" by workers without any change in equipment at all, the figures would be the same. The difference would appear only in the amount of gross investment required to keep the economy going.

Output of capital equipment must be reckoned not in tons of any metal or in lists of items (a bus is a bus and a lathe is a lathe) but in terms of productive capacity. Over-all, wages in terms of product are rising in step with output per head, and the rate of profit is constant. The capital-output ratio, over all, does not change much, either way. For embodied technical progress, therefore, the cost per unit of productive capacity is rising at the same rate as output per head.

Equally, the value of equipment absorbing disembodied progress (if there is such a thing) would rise at the same rate. Profit per man employed rises with output per head (since the real wage rises at the same rate) and no depreciation is required. Capitalize the profits at a rate of interest equal to the over-all rate of profit and the value of the equipment rises at the same rate as output per head.

Professor Jorgenson uses just this procedure to account for the rise in the value of capital shown in his statistics but then he attributes its growth entirely to accumulation and maintains that no technical progress has occurred in U.S. industry since 1945.[14] More often a set of statistics is used to draw up a production function in terms of "capital" and labor and to separate the growth of the value of output per head into the part due to the increase in the quantity of "capital" and the "residual" due to technical progress. This requires the statisticians to find out from the record of what actually happened, what the growth of output *would have been* if the value of capital had grown as much as it did without any technical progress having taken place. (It must have needed an even tougher hide to survive Phelps Brown's article on "The Meaning of the Fitted Cobb-Douglas Function"[15] than to ward off Cambridge Criticism of the marginal productivity theory of distribution.)

No doubt Professor Ferguson's restatement of "capital" theory will be used to train new generations of students to erect elegant-seeming arguments in terms which they cannot define and will confirm econometricians in the search for answers to unaskable questions. Criticism can have no effect. As he himself says, it is a matter of faith.

[13]Cf. T. K. Rymes, "Professor Read and the Measurement of Total Factor Productivity," *Canadian Journal of Economics*, Vol. I, No. 1 (May, 1968).

[14]D. W. Jorgenson and Z. Griliches, "The Explanation of Productivity Change," *Review of Economic Studies*, Vol. XXXIV (July, 1967), pp. 249–83.

[15]E. H. Phelps Brown, "The Meaning of the Fitted Cobb-Douglas Function," *Quarterly Journal of Economics*, Vol. LXXI (November, 1957), pp. 546–60.

28. A REFORMULATION OF NAIVE PROFIT THEORY*

Martin Bronfenbrenner†

"Gain is gain, however small."
Robert Browning, *Paracelsus*

Naive Profit Theory and Its Eclipse

This essay is a salvage operation in the economics of distribution under purely competitive conditions. It is concerned with profit—"pure" profit as distinguished from implicit wages and interest, "normal" profit as distinguished from windfall and imperfectly-competitive components. It is therefore little more than a footnote to the economics of profit in the large—as seen by business men or by their critics.

The naive profit theory which we think worth reconsideration enjoyed its heyday in elementary textbooks during roughly the first third of this century.[1] It survives as underpinning for policy pronouncements of a "capitalist-apologist" variety—a fate some consider worse than death. It is embodied

*From *Southern Economic Journal*, Vol. XXVI, No. 4 (April, 1960), pp. 300–309. Reprinted by permission of the publisher and the author.

†Martin Bronfenbrenner, Professor of Economics and Head of the Department of Economics, Carnegie-Mellon University.

[1]In the late forties a survey of 32 English-language elementary economics texts showed 20 presenting some version of this naive theory. (J. Fred Weston, "Profit as the Payment for the Function of Uncertainty-Bearing," *Journal of Business*, Vol. XXII [1949], p. 106.) The percentage would have been higher had Weston's survey been made a generation earlier.

What makes Weston's result remarkable is that neither Alfred Marshall nor J. B. Clark, from whom the theoretical sections of these texts are predominantly derived, adopted the naive theory of profit. Marshall's position is that profit vanishes in the long-run, as per this passage from *Principles of Economics* (8th ed.; London: Macmillan, 1920), p. 605 f.:

> That share of the normal expenses of production of any commodity which is commonly classed as profits, is so controlled on every side by the action of the principle of substitution, that it cannot long diverge from the normal supply price of the capital needed, added to the normal supply price of the ability and energy required for managing the business, and lastly the normal supply price of that organization by which the appropriate business ability and the requisite capital are brought together.

Clark's *Distribution of Wealth* (New York: Macmillan, 1899), p. 70, is even more clear-cut; profit results from dynamic change. As far as static conditions are concerned, he says:

in a set of propositions which we shall restate.[2]

(1) One of the distributive shares in a competitive economy is normal (pure, net, or necessary) profit.

(2) This is usually a positive quantity in the long-run, over and above implicit returns to any services or resources supplied by entrepreneurs to their own enterprises. (It may be zero or negative in the short-run.)

(3) Profit is a return to the related entrepreneurial functions of ultimate decision-making and ultimate uncertainty-bearing. The maker of ultimate decisions (bearer of ultimate uncertainties) is "the entrepreneur" who receives all profit in the long-run.

(4) The quantity which a firm seeks to maximize in its economic operations is the absolute size of the profit component.

(5) In marginal-productivity terms, uncertainty-bearing or decision-making may be looked upon as a separate "factor of production" on the same footing as land, labor, or capital.

The first four of these propositions are the naive ones. They have substantial intuitive appeal, particularly in a world dominated by proprietorships and partnerships. (We shall, however, end by modifying all but the first.) The fifth proposition, more sophisticated and usually omitted from elementary expositions, attempts to fit profit into the Procrustean bed of marginal distribution theory. (We shall abandon it.)

For all its intuitive plausibility, this edifice has fallen into disrepair and disrepute. We may assemble certain of the principal considerations brought against naive profit theory, and outline certain of the rival positions.

(1) In point of time, the initial crack in the structure was implicit in the "adding-up theorem" of distribution theory. This theorem applied the mathematics of the Euler theorem on homogeneous functions to show that there was nothing left over for profit if the production function were linear and homogeneous (with constant returns to scale).

> The prices that conform to the cost of production are, of course, those which give no clear profit to the entrepreneur. A business man whose goods sell at such rates will get wages for whatever amount of labor he may perform, and interest for any capital that he may furnish; but he will have nothing more to show in the way of gain.

Over and beyond business "common sense," the source for the naive theories of the textbooks may be the half-forgotten contributions of a half-forgotton American profit theorist of the century's opening decade, F. B. Hawley. On Hawley, see Frank H. Knight, *Risk, Uncertainty and Profit* (Boston: Houghton Mifflin, 1921), pp. 41–45.

[2]We owe to Weston our most detailed classification of the principal strains of recent profit theory. ("The Profit Concept and Theory: A Restatement," *Journal of Political Economy*, Vol. LXII [1954], p. 152.) In this classification, what we call the naive theory is class "R"—"profits are rewards for bearing uncertainty and risk." (To this position Weston is himself opposed.)

Alternative classifications of profit theories may be found in Knight, *op. cit.*, Chapter 2, and in R. A. Gordon, "Enterprise, Profits, and the Modern Corporation" (originally published 1936) in B. F. Haley and William Fellner (eds.), *Readings in the Theory of Income Distribution* (Philadelphia: Blakiston, 1946), pp. 560–565.

A later extension demonstrated the same theorem under conditions of long-run competitive equilibrium regardless of the form of the production function.[3]

(2) The adding-up theorem seemed to require elevation of decision-making or uncertainty-bearing to separate factors of production. The most ambitious effort in this direction was Pigou's, in *Economics of Welfare*.[4] Pigou's artificial construction was highly tentative, and does not seem to have been followed up.

(3) As these formal difficulties became apparent, two attacks on naive profit theory developed "within the family" of neo-classical economics, centering about the names of Joseph Schumpeter and Frank H. Knight. The earlier of the two, the Schumpeterian attack, reduced both uncertainty and profit to consequences of innovation, and defined entrepreneurship as the introduction and development of innovation.[5] The normal or necessary profits of the naive theory were replaced by the windfalls of the innovator. Monopoly and similar profits, when not traceable to innovation, are defined out of the picture as rents or surpluses.

Knight's position, as stated in *Risk, Uncertainty and Profit*, provides the basis for the more sophisticated versions of contemporary orthodoxy in profit theory.[6] If we may paraphrase Knight and his disciples (of whom Weston has spelled out his own position in greatest detail),[7] profit stems from uncertainty or noninsurable risk. It pervades the entire society, being borne not only by a special entrepreneurial class but by everyone in the economy. It results in positive or negative increments to all incomes from whatever source derived;[8] it is these which Knight calls profit. These elements of profit are not only unplanned but unanticipated. Knight therefore regards them as differences between incomes in disequilibrium and at equilibrium, or between incomes *ex post* and *ex ante*, rather than as compensations for uncertainty-bearing. There is in any

---

[3]The statement and proof of the Euler theorem most available to economists is by R. G. D. Allen, *Mathematical Analysis for Economists* (London: Macmillan, 1938), pp. 317–320. For a history of its application to distribution theory the standard source is George J. Stigler, *Production and Distribution Theories* (New York: Macmillan, 1941), Chapter xii. See also J. R. Hicks, *Theory of Wages* (London: Macmillan, 1932), pp. 233–236, and Joan Robinson, "Euler's Theorem and the Problem of Distribution," (originally published 1934), in *Collected Economic Papers* (New York: Kelley, 1951), pp. 1–18.

The later extension is due primarily to Hicks (*op. cit.*, p. 237 f.), although the basic insights had been suggested earlier by Walras and Wicksell. Compare also Paul A. Samuelson, *Foundations of Economic Analysis* (Cambridge, Mass.: Harvard University Press, 1947), pp. 81–89.

[4]A. C. Pigou, *op. cit.*, (4th ed.; London: Macmillan, 1932), pp. 161–164, and pp. 771–781.

[5]Joseph A. Schumpeter, *The Theory of Economic Development*, originally published 1912 (Cambridge, Mass.: Harvard University Press, 1934), *passim*. In the Weston Classification (Note 2) this theory is placed in category E — "profits are payments for the exercise of managerial or entrepreneurial functions." Knight has pointed out in *Risk, Uncertainty and Profit*, pp. 32–41, and again in an article, "Profit," in *Encyclopaedia of the Social Sciences*, reprinted in Haley and Fellner, *op. cit.*, p. 540, that Schumpeter's profit theory was to some extent anticipated in Clark, *Distribution of Wealth*, Chapter vi, xxv f.

[6]In the Weston classification, Knight and his followers are placed in category U — "profits are deviations arising from uncertainty" between earnings *ex poste* and *ex ante*.

[7]Weston, "Profit as the Payment for the Function of Uncertainty-Bearing" and "Enterprise and Profit," *Journal of Business*, Vol. XXII (1949), "A Generalized Uncertainty Theory of Profit," *American Economic Review*, Vol. XL (1940), "The Profit Concept and Theory," *Journal of Political Economy*, Vol. LXII (1954).

[8]However, "in the case of the owner of the business the difference is the entire income, since under perfect equilibrium the owner as such would have no functions and receive no income." Knight, "Profit," *op. cit.*, p. 537.

event no profit component in distribution, only profit elements in all types of income. As a corollary, the attempt to locate within a corporate body any "entrepreneur" with paramount claim to profit is to look in a dark room for a black cat which is not there. As another corollary, it is meaningless in Knightian language to speak of a firm "maximizing profit" except as a shorthand for maximizing "enterprise net income" to all implicit (non-purchased) productive services lumped together.

(4) The naive theory of profit includes no unequivocal notion of entrepreneurship. Some treat it as primarily a matter of risk- or uncertainty-bearing, others as primarily a matter of decision-making, others as primarily a matter of organization of the factors of production, and yet others as necessary combinations of a number of these activities.[9] None of these concepts proved equal to the task of identifying the entrepreneur in a corporate regime. In a corporate system, ultimate decision-making and organization came to rest mainly on salaried managers with little ownership interest, and ultimate uncertainty-bearing upon absentee stockholders. The distribution of the corporate usufruct, moreover, was difficult to rationalize by any combination of "uncertainty-bearing," "decision-making," or "factor-organization" principles. To use a catch phrase, ownership had become separated from control. The theory of profit and entrepreneurship which assumed the two to be united, now appeared both anachronistic and apologetic, a textbook embalming of the "folklore of capitalism."[10] Nor was a substitute theory helpful, which allocated the entrepreneurial functions to an artificial personage, the firm itself.[11] This theory gives no clue to the allocation or distribution of profit among the natural persons of the firm's ownership and control groups, and leaves this whole issue to the indeterminacy of corporate infighting.

(5) Largely as a result of the diffusion of entrepreneurship, there has arisen a set of sociological or institutional profit theories. These have developed in several forms,[12] although no institutionalist Schumpeter or sociological Knight has yet created a school.[13] Writers of these persuasions agree in defining as profits accountants' "business net income,"[14] including all returns to implicit productive services, all corporate

[9]Once again we turn to Weston for detailed bibliography. Weston, "Enterprise and Profit," *op. cit.*, p. 158 f.

[10]The inapplicability of traditional profit theory to the corporate regime is the basic argument of, *inter alia*, Gordon's attack upon it. (Gordon, *op. cit.*, pp. 558–570.)

[11]James H. Stauss, "The Entrepreneur: The Firm," *Journal of Political Economy*, Vol. LII (1944), pp. 112–127; Richard M. Davis, "The Current State of Profit Theory," *American Economic Review*, Vol. XLI (1951), p. 251 f. In the Weston classification, this strain of thought is related to the category Q—"profits are unimputable quasi-rents." See Weston, "Profit Concept and Theory," *op. cit.*, pp. 152, 166–168.

[12]What are called here sociological or institutional theories include not only Weston's category A—"profits are the difference between accounting revenues and costs," but also categories MC, MN, and W—"profits are gains from 'contrived' monopolistic and predatory activities," "profits are surpluses or rents resulting from uncertainty, indivisibilities, and other 'natural' barriers to entry," and "profits are payments derived from the ownership of productive assets." Weston, "The Profit Concept and Theory," *op. cit.*, p. 152.

[13]See however Paul Streeten, "The Theory of Profit," *Manchester School*, Vol. XVII (1949); R. G. Hawtrey, "The Nature of Profit," *Economic Journal*, Vol. LXI (1951); Jean Marchal, "Essai de construction d'une théorie nouvelle du profit," *Bulletin des Transports* (1952), of which an English translation appeared in the *American Economic Review* the preceding year (1951); Peter L. Bernstein, "Profit Theory—Where Do We Go From Here?" *Quarterly Journal of Economics*, Vol. LXVII (1953); Anatol Murad, "Questions for Profit Theory," *American Journal of Economics and Sociology*, Vol. XIII (1953). These writers' positions do not coincide, as may be seen by Bernstein's criticism of Marchal (*op. cit.*, p. 409 f.) and Murad's attempts to found an aggregative profit theory on Keynes' *Treatise on Money* (Murad, *op. cit.*, pp. 8–10).

[14]The contemporary Western accountant shuns the controversial term "profit" in favor of more colorless concepts like "earnings" or "income." (Cf. Weston, "Profit

(Contd.)

income and profits taxes, and all retained earnings. They usually stress, also, the class distinctions between "profit-receivers" in this sense and such other classes as "wage-earners" and "rentiers."[15] From these class considerations arises, in their view, the principal justification for lumping profit-receivers' diverse income types together under the single head of profit. For some writers, too, such notions as entrepreneurship and pure competition smack of apologetics rather than science. Their views of profit accordingly involve exploitation theorizing in a Socialist tradition.[16]

A Reformulation of the Naive Theory

This essay arises from dissatisfaction with Schumpeter, with Knight, and with the institutionalists. Payments most conveniently regarded as profits apparently persist without justification in Schumpeterian innovation. Business men and promoters continue to estimate profits *ex ante* in defiance of Knightian usage, and the public continues to think of profit as largely the special income of a special class of society. Knight's theory can also be criticized as particularly heavily insulated from both empirical testing and empirical relevance. At the same time the accounting category of "net income" combines elements so numerous and weighted so differently as between firms as to cast doubt on the analytical usefulness of the institutional theories. In this predicament, when both sophistication and iconoclasm seem to fail us, let us explore what can be done by naivete and simplemindedness.

We consider a static society with constant population, tastes, natural resources, social institutions (of a capitalist sort), and an unchanging range of technical alternatives available for use. The society is purely competitive, with complete divisibility of all inputs and outputs, mobility sufficient to assure a single price for most goods and services on each market at any point in time, and full knowledge of all existing prices. The society is not however stationary. Capital may be accumulating or decumulating. The perfection of knowledge does not extend beyond present prices either to cost and production relationships or to the future, although we assume all elasticities of expectations[17] unitary or fractional for the sake of stability. We have in short uncertainty without innovation.

Concept and Theory," *op. cit.*, p. 165.) At the same time, Soviet accountants and economists use the term freely and theorize regarding its role in their own society.

[15]This particular point is made by Knight as clearly as by any of the institutionalist writers: "Under the enterprise system, a special social class, the business men, direct economic activity; they are in the strict sense, the producers, while the great mass of the population merely furnish them with productive services, placing their persons and their property at the disposal of this class." (Knight, *Risk, Uncertainty and Profit*, *op. cit.*, p. 271.)

[16]Marchal and Murad are examples here.

[17]See J. R. Hicks, *Value and Capital* (Oxford: Oxford University Press, 1939), pp. 205–207.

What is this uncertainty about? Fundamentally, about two matters just mentioned: (1) The amount, nature, and consequences of capital accumulation (even with no change in the spectrum of available techniques)[18] and (2) the forms and coefficients of cost and production functions. (There is no need to forget about the vagaries of weather, the breakdown of machinery, the occurrence of illness and accident, or the consequences of variations in morale.) There is assumed to exist no economically efficient method of transforming any significant part of this uncertainty into insurable or otherwise transferable risk.

We follow tradition in considering only a competitive state of things, and only the long run. Imperfect competition and short-run windfalls are admittedly at the heart of concrete problems, but we have no contribution to their unsatisfactory treatment in economic theory. We further eschew the classical commingling of profit with interest, the Marxian commingling of profit with property income generally, and the accountants' commingling of profit with implicit returns to productive services generally.

Starting from this compromising sort of framework, we can outline a compromising sort of profit theory. We divide economic uncertainties into those giving rise to profit and those affecting other resource incomes. This differentiation seems to permit re-establishment of normal profit, positive or negative, as a separate income share. This is a "specialized" uncertainty theory as distinguished from Weston's "generalized" one. It is derived primarily from the confrontation of the naive theories of the textbooks with the sophisticated theories of Knight and his followers in particular. Given this specialized uncertainty theory, it is possible to make peace with marginal analysis and its adding-up theorem, and to consider *en passant* such problems as the meaningfulness of "profit maximizing" and the identification of "the entrepreneur" in a corporate setting.

Of the thousand natural shocks (and uncertainties) that flesh is heir to, those compensated by profit are neither the most pervasive nor the most significant. Considerations of uncertainty alter (in both directions) the supply and demand conditions for all goods and services. The net effect of uncertainty on prices and incomes is itself uncertain. We propose to consider profit as compensation for merely the subset of uncertainties which arises from having no contractual claim to one's income either per hour of labor, per "piece" of product, or per unit of land or capital. We concentrate therefore upon the incomes of those who accept as residual claimants part or all of what

[18]We cannot accept a Knightian dictum: "Many changes, such as the steady growth of population and capital, are fairly predictable, and to a corresponding extent do not occasion imperfect competition or profit." (Knight, "Profit," *op. cit.*, p. 541; see also Knight, *Risk, Uncertainty and Profit*, *op. cit.*, pp. 35–38.) This is more true for the statistician dealing with the economy as a whole than for the business man in any particular branch of trade.

is left after contractual claims are honored and contractual claimants paid.[19] This is not to imply, at one extreme, that contractual claims are always honored or enforced. Varying degrees of uncertainty, called premia rather than profit, attend the fact that particular contracts may be neither honored nor enforceable. Neither is it accurate, at the other extreme, to confine the profit-receiver's risk to the tautological one of not making his profit. He bears in addition the risk of a possible loss on income account, meaning a smaller income than his services or profit would have brought contractually. Further, if property has been contributed non-contractually, the uncertainty-bearer may also lose on capital account by the writing down or wiping out of the value of his assets when a debt investment would have protected him.

For the special purposes of profit theory let us classify productive inputs not into the usual "factors of production" but into "contractual" and "entrepreneurial" categories, according as their remuneration is or is not determined contractually.[20] This terminology identifies entrepreneurship not with managerial, organizational, or innovational responsibilities, but exclusively with the precarious nature of its legal claims. In a partnership entrepreneurship is divided between all partners, silent as well as active. In a corporation it is allocated to common stockholders, coupon-clippers included. (We recall the concept of "drone entrepreneurship," devised in a different setting.[21]) Managers and directors are not in this terminology entrepreneurs except as they

[19]This view is not original. Knight presents it as a "compromise position" between the "theoretical" view of profit (his own uncertainty theory) and the "practical" one which identifies economic profit with the accountant's "business net income." (Knight, "Profit," *op. cit.*, p. 537 f.) Weston likewise considers this view briefly (Weston, "Profit Concept and Theory," *op. cit.*, p. 167 f.)

A word regarding these writers' objections to our position is in order. Knight points out that profit (as he defines it) may be concealed in inflated contractual incomes of "insiders." Weston raises the objection that *all* incomes would be gross profit if institutional arrangements should eliminate the possibility of contractual claims to income. Knight's objection seems valid mainly if not exclusively under conditions of imperfect competition, while Weston's non-contractual world seems inconsistent quite generally with the institutions of an enterprise economy.

[20]This classification is no more water-tight than are most others. We may consider certain intermediate cases:

a. The *preferred stockholder* has a contractual claim, albeit a contingent one. In this he is in a position analogous to that of a salesman on commission.

b. The *convertible bondholder* has a contractual claim, with the privilege of exchanging it on stated terms for an entrepreneurial claim at some future time.

c. The *salaried partner* provides entrepreneurial resources so long as the partnership is in existence, since his claim is not enforceable generally until after the partnership is dissolved. If the partnership goes out of business with his salary in arrears, the salaried partner may then shift to a contractual position.

d. The *executive on the bonus list* is in a hybrid position. He has a contractual claim to his salary. His claim to his bonus is entrepreneurial until it has been voted, and contractual thereafter.

e. The *participating preferred stockholder* is also in a hybrid position. As a preferred stockholder he has a contractual claim; his participation involves an entrepreneurial one.

[21]Clarence Danhof, "Observations on Entrepreneurship in Agriculture," cited by Yale Brozen, "Entrepreneurship and Technological Change," in Harold F. Williamson

are also stockholders. Still less is the entrepreneur "the firm" or any corporate entity abstracted from the people connected with it.

An entrepreneurial service has in pure competition a highly imperfect market, on which several different prices may prevail simultaneously. This is not only because these services are unstandardized, but for special reasons peculiar to the entrepreneurial position. Many of the transactions are implicit, with a resource owner dealing with himself in his other capacity of business manager; demand and supply are identical and neutral equilibrium prevails. In addition, the "price" or "rate of return" of the entrepreneurial service cannot be a contracted, set, or recorded market price or rate of return. It is merely a consensus as to the expected price or rate of return. The expectations and the prices are imprecise; when the buyer and seller deal at arm's length, they may not hold the same expectations. To put the matter geometrically, any "equilibrium position" involves a range, a zone, or a set of points, and not a single point. We shall however use the single-point approximation since, to quote Marshall:[22]

> The adjustment of supply to demand in the case of business ability is somewhat hindered by the difficulty of ascertaining exactly what is the price that is being paid for it in any trade. . . . But though it may be difficult to read the lessons of an individual trader's experience, those of a whole trade can never be completely hidden, and cannot be hidden at all for very long. . . . There is a general agreement among business men that the average rate of profits in a trade cannot rise or fall much without general attention being attracted to the change before long. And though it may sometimes be a more difficult task for a business man than for a skilled labourer to find out whether he could improve his prospects by changing his trade, yet the business man has great opportunities for discovering what can be found out about the present and future of other trades; and if he should wish to change his trade, he will generally be able to do so more easily than the skilled workman could.

We consider in turn each panel of Figure 28-1. The left-hand panel (Figure 28-1-a) relates the *internal* supply and demand for an entrepreneurial service or input to its anticipated gross return. The supply and demand functions are identical, since each entrepreneur as demander is buying entrepreneurial services from himself as supplier. The combined supply and demand function is represented by a single curve *DS*. This curve slopes upward in accordance with the general observation that high rates of gross profit result in increased business population, increased internal investment, and similar signs of increased use of productive services under noncontractual conditions.

The center panel (Figure 28-1-b) represents the *external* supply and demand for the same entrepreneurial service. The demand and supply functions

---

and John A. Buttrick (eds.), *Economic Development: Principles and Patterns* (New York: Prentice-Hall, 1954), p. 205.

[22]Marshall, *op. cit.*, p. 607 f.

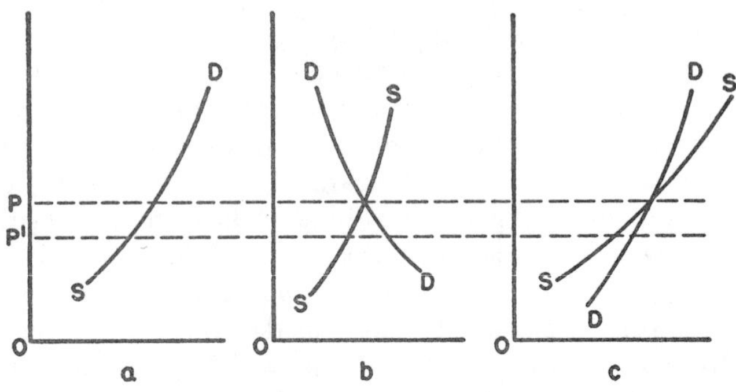

Figure 28-1

are drawn in conventional shapes. The vertical ordinate P of their intersection indicates an equilibrium gross profit.

The right-hand panel (Figure 28-1-c) is the horizontal sum of the other two. It is drawn with the internal supply and demand dominant, so that both the aggregate supply and the aggregate demand function for the entrepreneurial service slope upward. The demand function slopes more steeply as a Hicksian stability condition. This is a common state of affairs in unincorporated business and closed corporations. For corporations whose securities are traded publicly, the external supply and demand are usually dominant. A company's demand function for equity capital is normally inverse to its rate of return.

The supply and demand functions cross at a point with ordinate P (an average value in a zone of equilibrium). This makes OP a gross profit or gross return to the entrepreneurial service. Let OP' (on Figure 28-1) be the price of the physically identical service in its contractual uses.[23] OP' then represents the implicit contractual return to the entrepreneurial service, and PP' represents the net or normal profit which we seek to explain.

These diagrams have drawn P above P', making the normal profit PP' a positive quantity. It may actually be positive, negative, or zero. Its sign depends on many things. What is the relative strength of the "insurance" motive for avoiding uncertainty as against the "gambling" motive for seeking it out?[24] Assuming the former motive to be the stronger at the margin for entrepreneurs as well as for college professors, what are its offsets?

A postitive long-run net profit in a competitive industry may mean that the supply of entrepreneurial resources is *not* associated with such putative advantages as empire-building, tax-avoidance, or being one's own boss. (For

[23]We treat OP' as a constant, unchanging with the amount of the service used entrepreneurially. Dropping this assumption would require the drawing of the horizontal through P' as downward sloping, to allow for the effects of diminishing productivity.

[24]Compare in a different connection Milton Friedman and L. J. Savage, "The Utility Analysis of Choices Involving Risk" (originally published 1948) in George J. Stigler and Kenneth E. Boulding (eds.), *Readings in Price Theory* (Homewood, Ill.: Irwin, 1952), pp. 57–96.

the ordinary small-scale common stockholder, there is no such association.) If these attractions of "the entrepreneurial way of life" exist, their strength is insufficient to outweigh the dislike for uncertainty-bearing by the suppliers of services on non-contractual terms. The industry may also be believed to be facing deflation, obsolescence, or some other prospect which makes a contractual position attractive as compared to an entrepreneurial one.

On the other hand, nothing in our analysis prevents P falling below P' (PP' becoming a negative quantity) either for another entrepreneurial service in the same industry, for the same entrepreneurial service in another industry, or for all entrepreneurial services in all competitive industries. This may mean that the supply of entrepreneurial services is associated strongly with some or all of the attractions mentioned in the last paragraph.[25] It may mean that entrepreneurs see uncertainty-bearing as a positive pleasure. Or it may mean that the industry (or the economy) is facing some prospect such as price inflation, which renders entrepreneurial positions abnormally attractive by comparison with contractual ones.

The preceding analysis shows how physically uniform productive services, types of labor or property, can command even under competition different remunerations when supplied entrepreneurially than their contractual market prices. These differentials cumulate to net, normal, or necessary profit. It can also be shown, using simple indifference analysis, how a firm's budget for a given productive service may be allocated between contractual and entrepreneurial sources of supply.

Both axes of Figure 28-2 measure quantities of a single productive service, available in unlimited amounts to the individual firm on either contractual or entrepreneurial terms.[26] Suppose that we are dealing with money capital, the Keynesian "finance." Funds supplied contractually (debt finance) are measured along the horizontal axis. Funds supplied entrepreneurially (equity finance) are measured along the vertical axis. The straight lines (price lines), drawn with a slope of less than 45 degrees to the horizontal, imply a higher price per dollar of equity than of debt finance. The family of indifference curves (I_0, I_1, . . .) reflect no differences in the liquidity achieved in holding funds raised by the two methods, nor differences in the productivity of goods purchased with funds raised by the two methods. No such differences exist. The indifference curves reflect a variety of considerations in the minds of the management, outgrowths of the pervasiveness of uncertainty. There is a fear of excessive overhead charges for debt service in bad times if too much debt finance is used ("trading on the equity"). There is fear of dilution of both control and profit if too much reliance is put on equity finance. A firm may

[25]At least one profit theorist can cite personal experience (in commercial banking) to support the familiar proposition that many small business men and farmers accept deliberately, and with full knowledge of alternatives, situations in which normal profit is negative. Bernstein, *op. cit.*, pp. 409–411.

[26]No allowance is made here for such practical limitations as lack of access to equity capital markets, rationing of debt finance, or the Kalecki "principle of increasing risk."

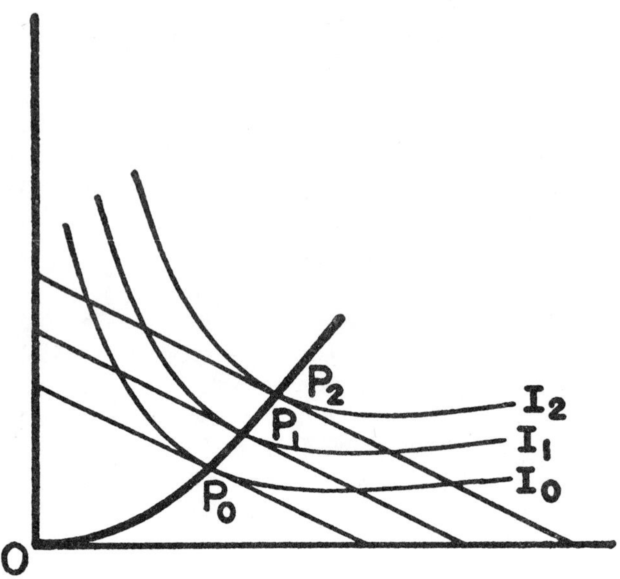

Figure 28-2

prefer a smaller volume of capital in the "right" proportions of debt to equity over a larger volume in the "wrong" proportions. A conventional form of indifference curves, with downward slope and upward concavity, accordingly appears plausible and is adopted on Figure 28-2. The points of tangency (P_0, P_1, . . .) between price lines and indifference curves represent optimal divisions of different outlays budgeted for finance between contractual and entrepreneurial supplies. The expansion path connecting these points of tangency shows how this optimum varies with the size of the budget. For any budget, a weighted average price can be computed for finance as a whole. This weighted average price will be different from the market contractual interest rate. In our example, it will be higher.

We have yet to ask the question — how can normal profit be paid at all? We deal with long-run competitive equilibrium, and with production at minimum average cost. If all productive services receive the value of their marginal products, the entire product is distributed. Yet we have postulated differentials for profit positive or negative. Where do they come from, if they are positive? Where do they go, if they are negative?

Here our weighted averages of contractual and entrepreneurial prices for identical services come to our assistance. The competitive entrepreneur should be looked upon as adjusting the use of productive services so as to equate the values of the marginal products not to their contractual market prices but to weighted averages of contractual and entrepreneurial prices where these diverge and where entrepreneurial inputs are used. This simple device avoids conflict between the persistence of normal profit and the "adding-up theorem." It is consistent with an aspect of the capital market which has aroused comment over the years—the refusal of firms to borrow out to the margin set by contractual interest rates, when their equities earn substantially higher returns. It is equally consistent with the tendency of marginal firms to concentrate on entrepreneurial and avoid contractual inputs whenever possible. This is conventionally criticized as inefficient, but may result from negative normal profit in these enterprises. It may be good marginalism for such firms to consider entrepreneurial services as costing considerably less than the contractual market prices for the same services would suggest.

A welfare complication does however arise from our suggested change in received doctrine. When the competitive firm expands or contracts its output, the proportions normally change in which contractual and entrepreneurial units of identical resources are combined. (The points P_1 on Figure 28-2 need not lie on a single radius vector.) If so, the weighted average price of some productive services to the firm will change with the firm's output, rising or falling as the case may be. Even under pure competition, then, the welfare analysis of the firm's expansion and contraction should involve the considerations now limited to the industry and to imperfect competition—restrictions and over-expansions of output inspired by price changes rather than by "efficiency." The same is true for technological adjustments by which contractual, entrepreneurial, and "mixed" inputs are substituted for each other. Here again firm and industry analysis, pure and imperfectly competitive analysis, move closer to each other in a way which threatens to some extent the conventional welfare economist's preference for pure competition under static conditions.

To present these complications in a form closer to the concrete, suppose that entrepreneurial services for a certain firm cost more than corresponding contractual ones. Suppose also that expansion requires a proportional shift of the firm's input mix in the entrepreneurial direction. This firm's expansion causes its weighted average input prices to rise against it, and vice versa for contraction. The firm will expand less or contract more than is required for optimum resource allocation, always operating below its theoretical optimum scale. Suppose next that the same firm is considering a substitution of machinery for labor at approximately the same level of output, machinery being a mixed and labor a purely contractual input. This substitution would raise the weighted average cost of capital against the firm, which would therefore tend to make it mechanize more slowly and less completely than efficiency would require.

On Optimizing Profit

We have listed five propositions which appear to embody the substance of naive profit theory. Proposition 1 we have accepted: "One of the distributive shares in a competitive economy is normal profit." Likewise Proposition 2: "This is usually a positive quantity in the long run, over and above implicit returns to any services or resources supplied by entrepreneurs to their own enterprises," with some doubts as to the positive sign. Proposition 3 defined profit as "a return to the related entrepreneurial functions of ultimate decision-making and ultimate uncertainty-bearing," which might have been combined as ultimate organizing. Our reformulation has modified this proposition considerably. Gone are decision-making and organizing as bases for profit.[27] Limited is uncertainty-bearing, in its relation to profit, to the assumption of non-contractual positions in the supply of services. As to entrepreneurship, it is scattered among suppliers of various productive services on entrepreneurial terms.[28] Proposition 5 suggests that decision-making or uncertainty-bearing be regarded as a distinct "factor of production," and we have been able to dispense with this proposition entirely. We have as yet said nothing about Proposition 4, that firms seek to maximize total net profit.[29] In this section we shall consider that proposition in the light of our restatement of naive profit theory.

We may state three views baldly. The naive view we have seen already—the rational entrepreneur maximizing his net profit. Sophisticated (Knightian) profit theory has the firm maximizing its net receipts[30]—in our terms, the total return to its entrepreneurial inputs, gross of their contractual input prices.

---

[27]Weston puts the case more strongly, (Weston, "A Generalized Uncertainty Theory of Profit," *op. cit.*, p. 48): "The ultimate decision-makers in a firm need not be compensated as residual income receivers. . . . Judgment is an economic service. The principles explaining the compensation for this service are similar to the principles explaining the compensation for other services. . . . The exercise of judgment may be sold on a fixed-price basis or on a variable-price basis."

[28]Here we part company with Weston, who argues (Weston, "A Generalized Uncertainty Theory of Profit," *op. cit.*, p. 47): "Non-contractual income receivers [may be] identified as entrepreneurs. The application of this term with its varied traditional connotations to a use in which functional activities perform no role, is likely to result in confusion. . . . It would be better if [entrepreneurship] were not used to describe various functional types of factors of production whose common attribute is the non-contractual nature of their returns."

[29]Literature on the realism and relevance of "profit maximization" and "maximizing behavior" generally has burgeoned since the late 1930's. Perhaps the earliest in a series of path-breaking articles was R. L. Hall and C. J. Hitch, "Price Theory and Business Behaviour," (originally published 1938), in T. Wilson and P. W. S. Andrews (eds.), *Oxford Studies in the Price Mechanism* (Oxford: Oxford University Press, 1951), Chapter 3. A good bibliography of the ensuing controversy may be found in A. G. Papandreou, "Some Basic Problems in the Theory of the Firm," in B. F. Haley (ed.), *Survey of Contemporary Economics*, Vol. II (Homewood, Ill.: Irwin, 1952), pp. 205–213.

This writer has profited in this section from the technical contributions of William J. Baumol, Herbert A. Simon, and Tibor Scitovsky, the institutional contributions of Alfred R. Oxenfeldt and Melvin W. Reder, and the "rebuttals" of Armen A. Alchian, James S. Earley, Milton Friedman, and Fritz Machlup. The nature of some of these debts will be clarified later.

[30]Thus Friedman, "The Methodology of Positive Economics," in *Essays In Positive Economics* (Chicago: University of Chicago Press, 1953), p. 21: "Under a wide range of circumstances individual firms behave *as if* they were seeking rationally to maximize their expected returns (generally if misleadingly called 'profits') and had full knowledge of the data needed to succeed in this attempt." And in a footnote to the

(Some such reformulation follows from the definition of profit as a differential between income *ex post* and *ex ante*, or between disequilibrium and equilibrium situations.)[31] "Organization theory" has the firm trying to maximize no quantifiable variable whatever, but instead to survive comfortably and securely as a good-sized organization.[32]

These three alternatives (which by no means exhaust their field) may lead to quite different results under given conditions, as is shown for example by Figure 28-3.[33] The horizontal axis of this diagram measures productive services supplied entrepreneurially; the vertical axis measures their income, gross in some cases and net in others. The alternatives open to the supplier of the entrepreneurial services are plotted as though single-valued on three curves *OX*, *OY*, and *OZ*. The curve *OX* is a path of gross profit; it is drawn with a maximum value *OR* when *OA* units are supplied. The ray *OY* measures the total return to the same service supplied contractually to outside firms under

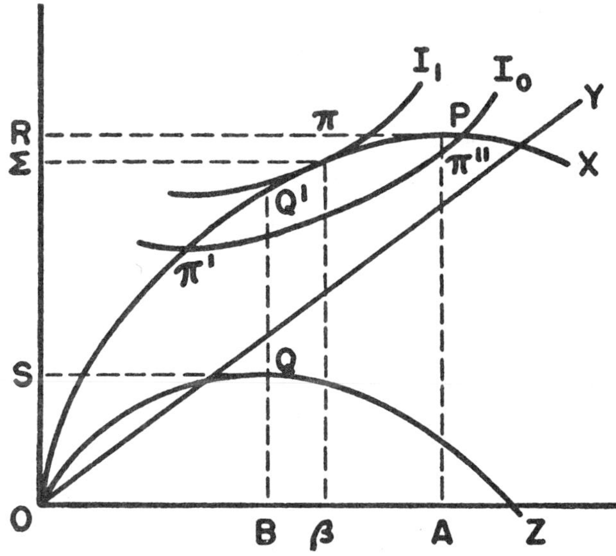

Figure 28-3

above passage: " 'Profits' are a result of uncertainty and . . . cannot be deliberately maximized in advance."

[31]Weston puts this point in italics (Weston, "A Generalized Uncertainty Theory of Profit," *op. cit.*, p. 54): "*To attribute a central role to profit maximization in static equilibrium analysis must lead to confusion because static analysis abstracts from the very conditions which give rise to profit*" (in Knightian terms).

[32]Compare Simon, *Administrative Behavior* (New York: Macmillan, 1947), Chapter 4, and *Models of Man* (New York: Wiley, 1957), Chapter 10. A compromise position is presented for oligopoly cases in Baumol, *Business Behavior, Value and Growth* (New York: Macmillan, 1959), Chapter 4, 6–8.

[33]This diagram is based on Scitovsky, "A Note on Profit Maximization and Its Implications," (originally published in 1943) in Stigler and Boulding, *op. cit.*, Figure 2, p. 354.

competitive conditions; it is a straight line without extreme values. The curve OZ is the vertical difference between OX and OY. In economic terms, it represents normal profit. It too has a maximum value OS (below OR) where OB units (less than OA) are supplied.[34]

According to the naive theory, the firm will aim at point Q, with co-ordinates (OB, OS) at which net profit is maximized. According to the sophisticated theory, more entrepreneurial services will be used and the firm will aim at point P, with co-ordinates (OA, OR) at which net revenue or gross profit is maximized. The two theories give the same result when the quantity of entrepreneurial services is fixed. This case may be the one which Knight and his followers have in mind.

Introduce now a set of indifference curves (I_0, I_1, . . .) expressing reluctance to supply services entrepreneurially, at least beyond a certain point, and expressing also a preference for higher income from any quantity of services so supplied. Geometrically, the indifference curves slope upward with upward concavity. In economic terms, this construction may represent not only aversion to uncertainty-bearing, but tax considerations, devotion to the Hicksian "quiet life," smallness of scale as an end in itself, *rentier* irresponsibility, etc.

In any event, there is generally an "optimizing" tangency point π, with co-ordinates ($O\beta$, $O\Sigma$). This is the point which we maintain that the firm will set as its goal. This point is clearly to the southwest of, and involves smaller supplies of entrepreneurial services than, the point P which the sophisticated theory sets up as the firm's target. We cannot generalize about its relationship to point Q' (the projection of Q on OX) which the naive theory sets up as the firm's target. On the diagram point π lies between points P and Q'.

An interpretation of Simon's organization-theory position may also be presented on Figure 28-3. Suppose that the firm expects to survive with reasonable comfort and security as an organization at any combination of entrepreneurial services and income on or above the indifference curve I_0 (which must cross or touch OX). Suppose further that I_0 crosses OX at two points π' and π'', to the left and right of π. Then according to organization theory any point along OX between the limits π' and π'' is analytically as likely as any other, choice between them being a matter of historical accident. The professional bias of the economist tends to hope for something which will narrow the range of "satisficing" behavior; Baumol's "revenue maximization hypothesis"[35]

[34]It may be useful to present a generalization of this proposition, which is elementary but has many applications:

Let $u = f(x)$ be a function with negative second derivatives over the relevant range, and let $v = g(x)$ be a monotone increasing function. Let u have a maximum at x_1 such that $f'(x_1) = 0$, and let $(u - v)$ have a maximum at x_2 such that $f'(x_2) - g'(x_2) = 0$. Then $x_1 > x_2$, from the negative sign of $f''(x)$.

[35]Baumol, *op. cit.*, Chapter 6.

may be interpreted to suggest that the neighborhood immediately to the left of π'' is more likely than that immediately to the right of π'.

But these are matters for possible empirical testing. At the abstract level of the present discussion, our introductory Proposition 4 (the naive theory of profit maximization) seems to require modification less from sophisticated theories of profit than from notions of "optimizing" rather than "maximizing" profit however defined and isolated.

SECTION VII. GENERAL EQUILIBRIUM AND WELFARE

In this Section, the input-output approach to general equilibrium analysis is examined. There is an extension and modification of the "Arrow-Debreu theory" of value covering markets under conditions of uncertainty. A theory of consumer welfare under conditions of product differentiation is developed, and the welfare effects of externalities under several different market structures are analyzed.

Using the basic, static input-output model developed by Leontief as a base, Dorfman describes input-output, considers its limitations (as well as several dynamic extensions which have been developed to overcome some of these limitations), and discusses its significance. Radner reviews the "Arrow-Debreu theory," extends it to cases in which different economic agents have different information, and argues for the consideration of a model with "a sequence of markets at successive dates." Maintaining that analyses of consumer welfare in product-differentiated markets must be concerned not only with the prices and quantities of goods but also with the number of goods offered, their quality and attributes, and the introduction of new products, Goddard develops a formal, general-equilibrium treatment of consumer welfare in markets with product differentiation. Worcester differentiates between technological and pecuniary externalities and analyzes the welfare effects of these two types of externalities under conditions of competition, simple and discriminating monopsony, and simple and discriminating monopoly. In his analysis, he discusses alternative ways of achieving optimal resource allocation.

Dorfman uses *The Structure of American Economy 1919–1939*, by Leontief, and *Studies in the Structure of the American Economy*, by Leontief and collaborators, as the basis for "surveying the accomplishments of input-output and the direction which its development is taking."

As stated by Leontief in his pioneering work, his objective was "an empirical study of interrelations among the different parts of a national economy." Dorfman indicates that Leontief's procedure was one of simplifying "Walras' general equilibrium schema radically to the point where the equations involved in it could be estimated statistically" and that the result is a general equilibrium system of "impressive simplicity." Dorfman distinguishes between an input-output table or matrix and input-output analysis.

Dorfman then discusses in detail Leontief's basic model, which is concerned with the conditions of static equilibrium. In his analysis, he examines the assumptions (particularly the production assumptions), the conclusions, and the limitations of the basic model. Dorfman also considers three dynamic extensions which have been developed to overcome some of the limitations of the static model. Further, he reviews the results of several tests made by Leontief to gauge the accuracy of the predictions yielded by his static model.

In his concluding section, Dorfman appraises the significance of input-output. He points out that even though it has considerable limitations as a tool for analyzing the operation of a free economy, the model works very well as an instrument of overall industrial planning. Further, it provides a "much-needed framework" for collecting and understanding data about our industrial economy.

Radner states that "the rigorous elaboration of the Walras-Pareto theory of value; that is, the theory of the existence and optimality of competitive equilibrium" is "one of the notable intellectual achievements of economic theory during the past twenty years." Radner refers to this development as the "Arrow-Debreu theory" because of the significant contributions made to it by these two economists. He points out that the Arrow-Debreu theory was not originally put forward for the case of uncertainty but that the work of these two enabled the theory to be reinterpreted to cover the case of uncertainty about the availability of resources and about consumption and production possibilities.

In this paper, Radner uses the Arrow-Debreu theory as a starting point and discusses "certain extensions, limitations, and possible new departures." He initially gives a brief review of the Arrow-Debreu approach to incorporating uncertainty about the environment into a Walrasian model of competitive equilibrium.

Radner next extends the model to account for the case in which different economic agents have different information and for the "production" of information. He then discusses some criticisms of the "extended Arrow-Debreu economy," emphasizing particularly its failure to take account of money, the stock market, and active markets at every date. He further shows how certain improvements can be made in the theory to give some relief from these criticisms.

Radner argues the merits of a model with "a sequence of markets at successive dates" and discusses and evaluates several concepts of equilibrium which might be consistent with such a theory. He concludes by discussing some "unsolved problems" which he considers "promising for further research."

Goddard maintains that an investigation of consumer welfare in markets characterized by product differentiation must be concerned not only with the prices and quantities of goods but also with the number of goods offered, their quality and attributes, and the introduction of new products; he states that formal welfare analysis generally takes the latter as given. Goddard uses Kelvin Lancaster's new theory of consumer behavior as a base for developing a "formal general-equilibrium treatment of consumer welfare in product-differentiated markets."

After summarizing Lancaster's model (which is covered in the seventh article in this book), Goddard distinguishes between a change in the quality of a good and a change in the attributes of a good. He then states the conditions for an unambiguous increase in consumer welfare following any change in the price, quality, or attributes of a good.

With regard to the introduction of new products, Goddard initially examines the possible short-run effects on consumer welfare. He then describes the long-run equilibrium under conditions of relatively free entry and product differentiation, giving the conditions for an ideal range of choice or variety of goods.

He shows that under the conditions of long-run equilibrium in a monopolistically competitive market the equivalence of relative prices and relative marginal costs, which is a necessary but not sufficient condition for a welfare *maximizing* optimum in the Pareto model, is not a necessary condition for an *ideal* allocation of resources in product-differentiated markets.

Worcester distinguishes between technological and pecuniary externalities and uses a linear homogeneous production function to analyze these two types of externalities under conditions of competition, simple and discriminating monopsony, and simple and discriminating monopoly. He demonstrates that the size of the welfare loss associated with economies and diseconomies is "very much affected by the particular type of externality present and the structure of the industry in question."

Worcester indicates that all technological externalities can be converted by appropriate input pricing into pecuniary economies or diseconomies viewed either in terms of specific firms or among industries. He further indicates that different industry structures result in optimal allocation for either technological or pecuniary externalities if the externalities are internal to an industry and if the firms in the industry utilize the same factor proportions. However, when these conditions are not present, "only competitive structures and pecuniary externalities suffice to produce an optimum in the absence of very complicated combinations of taxes and subsidies which require a wealth of accurate detailed data utilized with consummate insight and speed."

In his analysis, Worcester examines the merits and shortcomings of some of the alternative ways of "harmonizing" private and social costs. He also lists and gives examples of eight types of externalities.

29. THE NATURE AND SIGNIFICANCE OF INPUT-OUTPUT *

Robert Dorfman†

There can hardly be an economist who has not watched with amazement that nova of economics, input-output. Into a science characterized by individual research, piddling grants, and hand-me-down data it brought large, well-financed research teams and fresh resources of statistical material. It prodded a government which has practically never encouraged any but descriptive research to sponsor the development of a radical departure in economic analysis. It reversed a trend from aggregative to disaggregative analysis, leavened the thinking of the profession as the Keynesian hypothesis did two decades ago, and taught us all that "matrix" does not necessarily mean "social milieu." It has been discussed in the general press (for example, *Fortune* and *Dun's Review*) and, latterly, like the Keynesian doctrine, its social implications have become a subject of political controversy.

Two authoritative works on input-output have recently appeared: *The Structure of American Economy 1919–1939* by W. W. Leontief [16][1] and *Studies in the Structure of the American Economy* by Leontief and members of the staff of the Harvard Economic Research Project [17]. They provide a good opportunity for surveying the accomplishments of input-output and the direction which its development is taking.

The Structure of American Economy 1919–1939 is an enlarged edition of the monograph of 1941 in which Leontief first presented his system in detail. It consists of two main sections. The first is a reprint of the material of the original edition. The second consists of four essays which reflect the development and application of the method since 1941.

Studies in the Structure is, essentially, a progress report on the work of the Harvard Economic Research Project. It consists of twelve papers, four by Leontief and the rest by other members of the staff. These essays cover the main directions in which research is now progressing: the development of dynamic models, investigation of models for interregional analysis, empirical study of the capital requirements of production and of the determinants of investment in real capital, the detailed study of engineering production functions,

*From *Review of Economics and Statistics*, Vol. XXXVI, No. 2 (May, 1954), pp. 121–133. Reprinted by permission of the publisher and the author.

†Robert Dorfman, Professor of Economics, Harvard University.

[1]Citations to numbered references will be found in the Appendix.

continued study of the determinants of household consumption. Thus, *Structure of American Economy* presents the basic conceptual and empirical framework of input-output analysis, while *Studies in the Structure* deals largely with supplementary material reexamining the technological assumptions of the theory and paving the way for its extension and amplification.

Input-output belongs in the hard-headed, as distinct from the high-flown, category of economic theories. Leontief's objective, announced at the very outset of *Structure of American Economy*, was "an empirical study of interrelations among the different parts of a national economy" [16, p. 3]. He wished to avoid both abstract theoretical schemes supported by casual observation and statistical studies based on rudimentary, unexpressed theoretical underpinnings. He attempts to overcome "the persistent cleavage between a preponderantly deductive type of analysis, on the one side, and radical empiricism, on the other" [17, p. 5]. His method was to erect a sturdy theoretical scaffolding which called for obtainable statistical data, and then to obtain the data.

More specifically, Leontief's procedure was to simplify Walras' general equilibrium schema radically to the point where the equations involved in it could be estimated statistically. There were two essential steps in this simplification. First, he aggregated the countless individual commodities which entered Walras' schema into a comparatively few outputs, one for each industrial sector of the economy. Second, he dropped the supply equations for unproduced raw materials (chiefly various kinds of labor) and the demand equations for final consumption, and adopted the production equations in their simplest, linear form.

The result is a general equilibrium system of impressive simplicity. To set forth the bare bones, conceive of an economy as being divided into some number of sectors, say n. Suppose that the level of output of each sector depends on the levels of some or all of the other sectors, and on nothing else. Then the formulas relating the output of each sector to the outputs of the other sectors will form a set of n equations in n variables. If, further, these formulas are linear, the equations can be solved by straightforward algebra. The result will be a set of sector outputs which are mutually compatible in the sense that each sector produces the quantity called for by the functional relationships assumed at the outset. What we have just sketched is simply a mathematical formalism; Leontief's task was to develop a set of economic concepts which would lead to this kind of mathematical structure and would invest it with meaning. This is just what input-output achieves. An input-output table or matrix is a set of linear formulas connecting the levels of activity in the various segments of an economy. Input-output analysis is the economic justification and interpretation of these formulas and their consequences.

We have already noted that the erection of a well-articulated theory was not Leontief's objective but, rather, only a starting point. Other investigators, for example Walras, might be satisfied with a theory expressed by general functional relationships and connecting constants indicated by letters. Leontief is not satisfied until the functions have been specified and the letters replaced by reliable numerical estimates. The fundamentals of the theory were established some seventeen years ago [15], but the investigations of Leontief and a growing number of followers continue unabated. The major efforts in recent years have taken three main directions. First are applications of the theory to a variety of economic problems with the objectives both of illuminating the problems and appraising the usefulness of the theory. Second are attempts to estimate the empirical data required by the theory. Third are theoretical investigations designed to overcome and explain short-comings revealed by the first two lines of study and to extend the theory's field of application.

The study and development of input-output is now proceeding vigorously. The extent of the effort can be suggested by a simple listing of the organizations which have undertaken major projects: the Bureau of the Budget, the Bureau of Labor Statistics, the Bureau of Mines, the Department of the Air Force, the Department of Commerce, the Cowles Commission, the Harvard Economic Project, Carnegie Institute of Technology, and perhaps others.

It may be well to summarize the general impression given by the revised *Structure* volume and the *Studies* before going into details. It appears that, after seventeen years, the going is still very rough. That same ingenious and severe simplification which made input-output possible contained the seeds of serious difficulties. Economic relationships are not simple and have stubbornly refused to conform to the model. The reams of careful empirical work have revealed the extent of the approximateness of the model, and attempts to refine the model lead to discouraging complexity. These are the facts; Leontief himself is in the forefront of those bringing them out. Whether, in view of these facts, input-output is a brave failure is a question that we must consider carefully.

The Basic Model

A number of excellent concise summaries of Leontief's basic framework have already been published.[2] To restate it very briefly, the model depends on the technological interrelationships of the productive sectors of the economy, these connections being regarded as the most stable and reliable structural characteristics of the economy. The economy is divided into a number of sectors on the basis of the nature of the product produced. In different versions the number of sectors has varied from about a dozen to about four hundred. Whatever the number of sectors, each sector is considered to buy its inputs from other sectors and to sell its output to other sectors and, perhaps,

[2]See [16, pp. 139–46] and [5, pp. 99–102].

to an "autonomous sector" which has no output. The autonomous sector, if there is one, represents final demand and is unexplained within the model.

The model depends on two kinds of relationship: First, the bookkeeping identity that the aggregate sales of any sector must equal the total purchases from the sector by the other sectors, including the autonomous one. Second, the technological relationship that the purchases of any sector (except the autonomous one) from any other sector depend, via a production function, on the level of output of the purchasing sector.

Combining these two relationships we find that the sales of each sector equal autonomous consumption of its output plus a sum each term of which depends only on the output (or sales) of some other sector. For example, the total sales of the coal-mining sector is the sum of its sales to the automobile-producing sector, to the iron and steel products sector, . . . , and finally, to final consumption. Now the coal consumption of the automobile industry depends on the number of automobiles produced, and similarly for all other sectors. Thus, total production (or sales) of coal equals a sum one term of which depends on automobile production, one term on steel production, . . ., plus, finally, autonomous demand for coal. The upshot of this analysis is a system of equations connecting the outputs of all the sectors and the autonomous demand for the products of each sector. Furthermore, there is one equation for each sector. Then the number of equations is just equal to the number of sector output levels, or sales levels, and, if the autonomous demands be regarded as given, this system of equations may determine the level of output of each sector.

This is the heart of the argument, and, before pushing on, let us consider the significance of the assumptions and conclusions thus far. The bookkeeping relationship is unobjectionable, but it should be kept in mind that the bookkeeping balance relates to sales and purchases and not directly to quantities of production and productive consumption. The difference between the sales of any sector and its output is the change in its inventories of finished goods, and the difference between the purchases of any sector and its productive consumption is the change in its inventories of raw materials. Sales can be identified with output and purchases with input only if inventories do not change. We have come to the first of several reasons for emphasizing that the equations connecting industry outputs are not purely technological and are valid only in static equilibrium.

Several objections can be and have been raised to the technological postulate of the model. First, there is the problem of time. The technological relationships express the common sense fact that the quantities of raw materials used by an industry depend on its level of activity. Since the raw materials are the outputs of supplying industries, there is, at first glance, a direct connection between the level of activity in any industry and the levels in its supplying industries. At second glance, though, the connection is not quite so direct (even apart from the inventory problem), for, purely as a matter of technology, inputs (except for services) must be produced before they can be used. Consequently, the technological relationships (except for service inputs) connect the current level of each industry with previous levels of its supply industries and subsequent levels of its customer industries. Since the usual input-output model abstracts from the time sequence of production and exchange, it applies only to a stationary equilibrium, where time is of no consequence.

Second, there is an aggregation problem. This would not arise if each industry consisted of a number of identical single-product firms. But it does arise as soon as we permit an industry to include firms whose technical methods are not identical or to produce products whose technical requirements are not identical. In an industry which includes some variety of products and technical conditions, we can assert that output determines inputs uniquely only if we assume that when the output of one of its products changes, the outputs of all its other products change in the same proportion (in the jargon, we assume that "product-mix" is constant) and also that all technically different segments of the industry (e.g., firms using modern techniques and those using older techniques) expand and contract in the same proportion.[3] The advantage of using a large number of sectors lies, of course, precisely here. The larger the number of sectors in a model, the less need be the diversity within the sectors and the less important is the error incurred by assuming away that diversity. Even with four hundred sectors, however, a considerable amount of variety remains within many sectors.

Third, there is a substitution problem. The model, it will be recalled, assumes that the conditions of production are such that once the level of output of each sector is given the quantity of each of its inputs is uniquely determined. Ordinary production theory, on the contrary, teaches that the amount of each input used in producing a given output will respond to changes in relative input prices. Leontief argues that such responses, that is, factor substitutions, are unimportant, at least in the short run. Samuelson and others[4] have argued that in an economy where labor is the only factor of production not produced within the system, the price structure will lead to the efficient utilization of labor and, since all productive factors will consist in either direct or embodied labor, there will be no scope for changes in relative factor prices, or, therefore, for factor substitutions. Neither of these justifications really disposes of the problem. Leontief's justification applies to time-horizons which are short enough so that the response to changes in final demand does not include changes in technique or in the supply of capital equipment. Such short-run adjustments are inherently transitory and contradict the full static equilibrium assumptions of the model. Samuelson's justification, which assumes that the

[3]These assumptions could be weakened by assuming that the proportions were determinate rather than all the same. But the stricter assumption seems as plausible as the weaker and paves the way for later developments.

[4]See Samuelson [19], Georgescu-Roegen [6], and Chipman [3].

supplies of all factors except labor can be increased at will, is clearly inapplicable except in the very long run and perhaps there also.

Klein also [12] has endeavored to get factor substitutions back into the Leontief model. He assumed a production function of the Cobb-Douglas type which, therefore, permitted factor substitution. Then he showed, just as Cobb and Douglas had done before him, that if producers adopt that combination of factors which minimizes average costs the result will be that in each sector the ratio between the value of purchases from each other sector and the value of the output of the purchasing sector will be the same whatever may be the structure of relative factor prices. On this basis Klein concluded that a Leontief model need not deny the possibility of factor substitution, for the constancy of input-output coefficients is consistent with at least one form of production function which permits substitution. Unfortunately the input-output coefficients whose constancy Klein established are not the ones which appear in a Leontief model. In a Leontief model the coefficients in question are ratios of physical quantities, and Klein's demonstration that ratios of values will not change when prices do is also a demonstration that ratios of physical quantities will change.[5]

The neglect of substitution is the most striking divergence of the Leontief model from conventional economic assumptions. The issue, Leontief maintains, is basically factual, and he suggests that the importance of substitution be decided by empirical studies. We shall consider some statistical results presently, but let us note now that there are not likely to be many empirical data bearing on equilibrium conditions.

Fourth, there is an investment problem. All purchases made by a productive sector may be classified into purchases for purposes of current production and purchases for purposes of investment, that is, increase and replacement of capital plant and equipment. It may be difficult to apply this classification in practice (advertising and maintenance expenditures present problems), but we can consider it in principle. The assumption of a unique relationship between the output of an industry and its purchases from other industries is plausible only with respect to purchases on current account. There are several ways for dealing with capital expenditures. In the first place there is no net investment and therefore no problem in stationary equilibrium, the state in which the model applies best from other points of view, also.[6] Second, capital expenditures may be separated out from other transactions and treated as part of final demand. To the extent that this expedient is used, of course, the model loses explanatory value. On the other hand this expedient is a

[5]The conclusion which Klein came to in his paper was somewhat different from the conclusion imputed to him above, but the bearing on the question of factor substitutions is the same.

[6]Even in stationary equilibrium there would be replacement purchases of durable producers' goods, and these would not necessarily be proportional to output. This complication can be allowed for fairly easily, however.

recognition of the fact that the model is best adapted to describing the level of current production induced by a given level of final demand, an important problem even though not all inclusive. Third, induced capital expenditures may be considered separately as a component of induced activity. This is the approach used in Leontief's dynamic model, discussed below. Finally, and most crudely, the assumption can be made that net investment in any industry is uniquely related to the level of output of that industry. In any event, investment presents a complication which is not handled very conveniently within the basic framework.

Fifth, there is a limitation inherent in the very notion of a production function. Technologically grounded production functions apply very well to a large part of the economy including manufacturing, mining, and utilities. But there are other areas, such as agriculture (with its large stochastic element), trade, foreign trade, government, finance, and services where the concept is not so compelling. Yet these sectors, too, must be included in the model in order to account for the full output of the sectors with stable production functions. This difficulty can be appreciated best by considering an example taken from the 1939 Inter-Industry Transactions Table [16, p. 167]. According to this table the construction industry made purchases valued at $636 million from the trade sector in the course of producing an output valued at $10,089 million. This $636 million is not the value of the materials purchased by the construction sector in that year, but only the aggregate of the trade margins on those materials. Can trade margins be regarded as stable technological inputs? An affirmative answer seems to imply an argument along the lines of full-cost pricing which, whether or not acceptable, is not a technological argument.

These considerations add up to the conclusion that the Leontief model does not follow directly from such simple and necessary productive relationships as the argument for it implies. (Cf. Leontief, [16, pp. 143–45]). They indicate that it is not easy to determine the parameters of the model or to verify its adequacy simply by gathering statistical data on intersector transactions. They limit the model to a specification of equilibrium conditions, which qualifies its significance as a predictive tool and compounds the difficulties of empirical verification. And they indicate the necessity for complicating refinements which endanger the practical manageability of the model.

Production Assumptions

Our description of the model thus far stands as follows. The essential variables are the outputs of the sectors into which the economy is divided. The output of any sector is determined by finding the amount of its product which each other sector consumes, and adding. The amount of each product which each sector (except the autonomous one, if there is one) consumes depends only on the output of the consuming sector. The economy is in equilibrium when the output of each sector equals the total of purchases from that sector, this total being determined by the outputs of the other sectors. It should be noted that in this model considerations of profit maximization, consumer utility maximization, optimal utilization of resources, and motivation occur in the background if at all. The foreground is occupied entirely by the dictates of productive necessity: each output requires its inputs and that is all there is to it.

In order to implement the model practically, it is necessary to specify the production functions involved. This Leontief has done by following the assumption of invariance of technique to its logical conclusion, arriving at the function which Walras originally used. According to this assumption, the quantity of each input consumed by a sector is directly proportional to the quantity of output produced by that sector. The factors of proportionality are Walras' "productive coefficients" and Leontief's "input coefficients."

No one recognizes better than Leontief that constant factors of proportionality are only a crude approximation to actual productive relationships. Where new equipment is involved, geometry herself rebels against the assumption. The capacity of a pipe, for example, increases rather faster than the square of the diameter, but the amount of material required increases only about in proportion to the diameter. Hence, piping in large plants requires a smaller weight of material per unit of output than piping in small ones. Similar dimensional laws apply to warehouses, ships, boilers, electric wires, and almost every other kind of equipment. When old equipment is involved, maintenance and many other direct expenses do not increase in proportion to output. Warehouses and toll roads are extreme examples of the preponderance of inputs which do not respond to output, but the case is similar with railroads and public utilities generally and with much manufacturing.

The most searching critique of the assumption of input coefficients which are the same over a wide range of outputs comes from Leontief's Harvard Economic Research Project and is reported in *Studies in the Structure* [17] in chapters by Chenery, Holzman, Grosse, and Ferguson. In these chapters engineering data were used to study the technical production relationships in natural gas transmission (H.B. Chenery), metal machining (M. Holzman), cotton textile manufacture (A.P. Grosse), and air transport (A.R. Ferguson). Only in the case of cotton textile manufacture was proportionality found to exist between inputs and outputs, and there only by assuming an unchanging product-mix and neglecting maintenance and other indirect inputs.

A theoretical defense of the assumption is, of course, conceivable. It would run along the lines of abstract economic theory and allege that an industry in equilibrium is composed of a number of identical economic units, each of optimum size, and that expansion and contraction of output are attained by changing the number of economic units. Leontief declines to retreat to this level of idealization which, in any event, runs counter to his concept of aggregating firms into broad economic classes. His defense is frankly that only this simple assumption will lead to a manageable theory of general equilibrium. Leontief writes,

> . . .the question is not whether these ratios are constant or not — they certainly cannot be expected to be constant in the strict sense of the word. The real questions are: How does the actual range of their variations affect the empirical validity of the analytical computations based on the assumption of fixed coefficients. . .? [16, p. 214].

In practical application the Leontief system has been freed partially from the assumption of constant input coefficients by using a simple device. To illustrate this device, assume that some industry requires 1 unit of labor per unit of product up to an output of 50 units and that thereafter 1½ units of labor are required per unit of product. Then if we are sure that at least 50 units of product will be required when the equilibrium levels of output are calculated, we can write the equation:

$$\begin{aligned}&\text{Labor units required by this industry}\\&\quad = 50 + 1\tfrac{1}{2} \times (\text{Output} - 50)\\&\quad = -25 + 1\tfrac{1}{2} \times \text{Output}.\end{aligned}$$

That is, we can arrive at the correct result by using the higher, or marginal, input ratio as if it were a constant coefficient and balancing the resulting overstatement by deducting 25 units from the final demand for labor. Rising marginal inputs can thus be incorporated in the model, perhaps to a considerable extent, as Evans and Hoffenberg [5, p. 100] have pointed out.

It is possible that future Leontief models will make extensive use of this and similar devices. The studies of engineering production functions, which permit the calculation of marginal input requirements at different levels of output [17, Chapters 8–11], look in this direction. At the same time those studies indicate that there are serious difficulties involved in developing engineering production functions for broad industrial sectors rather than for well-specified products, and the statistical problems of compiling such functions for all the sectors in the economy are impressive. The assumption of constant input coefficients is therefore of practical importance, even though not theoretically mandatory, and we shall consider it below in the light of empirical testing.

Models: Closed, Open, and Ajar

We have alluded from time to time to the autonomous sector which is present in some versions of the model and absent in others. This sector is of key importance in the interpretation of a Leontief model. The mathematics is always essentially the same, but the economic interpretation changes in response to the treatment of the autonomous sector and final demand.

In the original version, presented in the first edition of *Structure of American Economy* [16], there was no autonomous sector. Consumers were regarded as a "household industry" which consumed the outputs of the other sectors in direct proportion to its output, which consisted chiefly of labor services. The government and foreign trade were treated similarly. Thus, there was no final demand. All consumption was consumption for further production and was explained within the model in the course of determining the levels of output of the household, government, and other sectors which form part of a mutually consistent pattern of sector output levels. This kind of model, since it attempts to account for all consumption, is called "closed." It is the most ambitious version, since it attempts to explain more than any other, but also it requires the most unpalatable assumptions and is the most restrictive since it provides no room for autonomous investment, exogenous changes in government demand, or the like. For these reasons the general tendency has been away from closed models toward "open" models which include a final demand for products of the various sectors which is unexplained within the model. In order to account for this final demand in the input-output framework, an autonomous sector is introduced which consumes but does not produce. There is clearly a wide choice regarding which sources of demand are to be included in the autonomous sector and which are to be explained within the model. The choice depends particularly on the disposition to be made of government demand, household consumption, net exports, and investment.

The most important models for governmental purposes are those in which the autonomous sector comprises final consumption by households, government demand, and net exports. Household consumption cannot be determined within a Leontief model unless the dubious concept of a household production function is invoked. On the other hand, since household consumption does not depend on the details of the outputs of the various sectors, it is frequently placed in the autonomous sector and estimated independently from a general estimate of the level of national income, via some sort of consumption function. Net exports also can best be estimated independently of the internal model by taking account, nowadays, of the government's foreign aid program. Finally, government demand, both civil and military, is almost entirely unrelated to the levels of activity in the private productive sectors. After autonomous demand has been determined by adding these three components, the Leontief equations can be used to estimate private sector outputs consistent with that demand.

No mention has been made thus far of investment in either plant and equipment or inventories, and we have already seen that such investment cannot be derived from the basic Leontief equations. If we regard the model as describing the equilibrium levels of the various sectors in response to a continuing given level of final demand, there would be no need for accumulation of inventories or changes in the stock of capital equipment. The open model, then, does not yield the levels of economic activity consequent upon any government program or assumptions about final demand but, rather, only equilibrium levels in the sense that each sector produces just enough to meet its demands without either drawing down or adding to inventories or capital equipment. In order to have a more complete explanation of the levels of economic activity, investment would have to be allowed for. This may be done by estimating investment independently and including it in the autonomous sector, by the crude assumption that investment is proportional to output, or by making the model dynamic. We shall discuss this last alternative later.

Placing household consumption in the autonomous category is, of course, a serious limitation, all the more so since the modern theory of the consumption function is tending to explain consumption endogenously in terms of the level of economic activity. Leontief early abandoned his first crude approximation in which the consumption of each final product was regarded as proportional to the level of employment. But he has not abandoned the hope of reintroducing the level of consumption as one of the variables explained within the system, using a more realistic consumption function.

Ordinary consumption functions, with household expenditure as a dependent variable and disposable income and the like as independent variables, do not quite fill the needs of Leontief models, because what is required is a formula for predicting the consumption of major categories of goods item by item rather than total consumption expenditure. But individual item consumption predictors should involve prices along with measures of over-all income and activity, and the treatment of prices is one of the weak points of the input-output model. Besides, even with respect to aggregate consumption, attempts at prediction have not been notably successful to date.

Duesenberry and Kistin have been studying this range of problems [17, ch. 12]. Their standpoint is that economic variables like income and prices influence consumption of various goods within a framework set by quasi-economic variables like established consumption habits and the distribution of population among socio-economic strata. Thus, the effects of economic variables have to be studied under circumstances where changes in quasi-economic variables can be avoided or allowed for. This leads Duesenberry and Kistin to use area budget studies, which show the consumption patterns of individual socio-economic groups, in preference to nationwide time-series data. Their method for making over-all consumption estimates, however, does not allow for the effects of changes in the sizes of socio-economic strata, with the consequence that their estimates are no more successful than the results of cruder and more convenient methods of calculation. Their procedure, though, has the very considerable virtue of identifying some of the hitherto anonymous "autonomous variables" which influence consumption, and of paving the way for incorporating those variables in economic analysis. Nevertheless, we are still a long way from being able to estimate consumption with tolerable accuracy within the framework of an input-output model.

The upshot seems to be that the open models omit the two driving forces of economic activity: consumption and investment. What open models amount to then is a device for calculating the level and pattern of gross economic activity (gross in the sense that intermediate goods are counted along with final ones whenever they pass from one sector to another) consistent with any specification of net final output. In normal circumstances this may be a very limited objective for such a formidable apparatus. But in time of war or economic mobilization, when consumption and investment cease being the prime movers of economic activity, this objective is extremely important.

Much of the interest in open models stems from their application to problems of mobilization.

Dynamic Models

The basic Leontief model is concerned with the conditions of a static equilibrium. We have already discussed some of the limitations thereby imposed. The model loses significance as an empirical predictor, it cannot be used to trace the time-paths of readjustment to changed conditions, time-lags in technological relationships have to be neglected, investment cannot be explained within the model. At least three dynamic extensions of the basic model have been proposed to overcome these limitations.

Hawkins [9] and Leontief [17, chapter 3] have developed models based on a generalization of the accelerator principle. The essential idea is that net investment in any sector is proportional to the rate of change of output of that sector. Leontief's accelerator model is, moreover, irreversible, that is, it assumes that the factor of proportionality takes different values according to whether or not there is excess capacity in the sector. The formal mathematics of this model is a natural extension of the basic scheme, the major difference being that total demand for the product of each sector is now the sum of three terms:

(1) the quantity used as inputs by other sectors, which is proportional to the outputs of those sectors;
(2) the quantity required for net investment, which is proportional to the rate of change of output of other sectors; and
(3) the quantity required for final demand exclusive of net investment.

Unfortunately, the irreversibility feature, which seems logically unavoidable in an accelerator model, leads to mathematical complications, because use of the excess-capacity proportionality factor for a sector may imply a level of output inconsistent with the excess capacity while the use of the full-capacity-utilization factor for the same sector implies a level of output inconsistent with full-capacity utilization. This paradox requires further research but need not detain us.

Aside from this ambiguity, the theory of the acceleration Leontief model is neat, and extensive work has been undertaken by the Harvard Economic Research Project to implement it. Two reports on this work are contained in *Studies in the Structure of the American Economy*, Chapter 6, by R. N. Grosse, on the estimation of capital input coefficients, and Chapter 7, by P. G. Clark, on a test of the acceleration theory of investment in the telephone industry.

The estimation of capital input coefficients, that is, the number of units of output of each sector required per unit of new capacity of each sector, presents difficulties beyond those encountered in estimating the ordinary input coefficients. For one thing, the statistical data are less adequate. For another, statistical averaging is less appropriate, since the characteristics of new equipment are not, in general, reflected in the older installed equipment accessible to statistical compilation. Thirdly, the assumption that the value of new investment is directly proportional to the volume of output it will support is particularly questionable. With respect to the inventory investment, Whitin[7] has shown that the optimal level of inventories increases significantly less than in proportion to the level of output. With respect to plant and equipment, the usual theories of long-run economies of scale and the scale laws of geometry and physics to which we have already alluded indicate that capacity is likely to increase faster than the physical volume of equipment inputs.

Leontief, A. P. Grosse, and collaborators are well aware of all these *a priori* difficulties, and others as well, but are not deterred by them. Their policy is to produce estimates on the most practicable assumptions they can find and then submit the results to empirical test. When, however, the same coefficient was computed by two different plausible methods, the results were frequently at variance. It is impossible to say as yet whether the discrepancies are due to the theoretical problems mentioned or to the inadequacy of statistical records. Whatever may be the cause of the difficulties, this type of dynamic model must be regarded as still in the process of construction.

The underlying assumption of the accelerator model is, of course, the acceleration principle. A case study of the reasonableness of this assumption was made by P. G. Clark [17, Chapter 7], who investigated the determinants of investment in the telephone industry. Clark's work, along with that of Chenery, A. P. Grosse, and Duesenberry,[8] seems to be moving toward a new theory of investment which may turn out to be one of the major contributions of the Harvard Economic Research Project. In Clark's hands the acceleration theory is modified almost beyond recognition into a "capital-requirements theory" composed of three hypotheses: "(1) The firm's demand estimates depend via a fixed expectations coefficient upon the recent trend of its output; (2) The firm's net investment depends via a fixed capital coefficient and a fixed spare-capacity coefficient upon these demand estimates; (3) The firm's retirement (plan) depends via a fixed retirement coefficient upon its present stock of capital equipment." [17, p. 249.] Clark has tested each of these hypotheses against data taken from the telephone industry but, I think, tended to be overgenerous in finding conformity between theory and fact. For example, the first hypothesis implies that a firm would expect its demand to grow exponentially, but data given on page 270 indicate that the telephone company expected the volume of messages to grow linearly or a little less. The "confirmations" found for the other hypotheses consist in success in finding *ad hoc*

[7]See T. M. Whitin, *The Theory of Inventory Management* (Princeton: Princeton University Press, 1953), p. 147 ff.

[8]See Hollis B. Chenery, "Overcapacity and the Acceleration Principle," *Econometrica*, Vol. XX (January, 1952), pp. 1–28; A. P. Grosse, "Innovation and Diffusion" (mimeographed); A. P. Grosse and J. S. Duesenberry, "Technological Change and Dynamic Models" (mimeographed).

explanations for discrepancies between hypotheses and fact rather than in finding gratifying degrees of conformity. Nonetheless, this is not a crucial test of the capital-requirements theory of investment and the theory itself is both plausible and empirically usable. If it works out it will free economic models from the mechanistic confines of the acceleration principle.

A second type of model is based on an extension of the multiplier principle. Such models have been developed by Solow [20] and, as by-products to other work, by Goodwin [8] and Chipman [2]. The underlying idea is that of lead-times; the output of a sector in any period is related to the output of other sectors in previous periods. Various justifications of such relationships are possible. Goodwin and Chipman use expenditure considerations; increases in the output of any sectors generate income flows which show up as increases in the demand for other sectors in later periods. Solow relies on an equilibrium argument: because most commodities must be outputs before they are inputs, supplies will not equal demands unless the various sectors expand and contract in an equilibrium sequence. This point of view, also, is appropriate to mobilization planning. It does not, of course, explain investment but, in compensation, it does not require capital coefficients. Theoretical equilibrium conditions have been derived from these models [see especially 9], but little or no empirical work has been done and so they stand aside from the main stream of input-output analysis, which is, above all, empirical.

The third major type of dynamic model rests on the two assumptions that installed capacity must at all times be at least equal to productive requirements and that no capacity should be installed before its product is required (i.e., neither capacity nor product should be stored against future requirements). This type of model was worked out by an Air Force group headed by J. Holley [11] and is the only type whose full operation has been tested. The test consisted in applying flow and capital input coefficients derived for the year 1944 to final consumption data for the years of rapid expansion, 1940–44, and comparing the levels of sector outputs and capital formation resulting from the model with *post hoc* estimates. The only reason for being interested in this model is that it has been tested, because the economic assumption that capacity should be adequate to meet peak loads without drawing on inventories cannot be defended either as a descriptive or as a normative postulate. One would hope that an economic model based on this assumption would lead to substantial overestimates of capital formation and of total output, and that is just what occurred. To this extent the model "makes sense." Its positive contributions are two: (1) it is an ultra-conversative procedure for testing whether a proposed program of outputs can be produced, (2) it established by actual example that a fairly elaborate dynamic model can be worked out numerically.

The present status of dynamic models is one of work still in process. The work bids fair to advance our understanding of the determinants of investment and to produce techniques which will contribute to the planning of economic mobilization. It may lead to formulations useful for more general normative or descriptive economic analyses. As to that, it is a little too early to say.

Empirical Validation

As Leontief sees it, the crucial test of his system, constant input coefficients and all, is the accuracy of the predictions it yields. In this spirit he has applied three separate tests to his static model. First, he has used technical data based on the 1939 Census of Manufactures to calculate a set of sector levels corresponding to the final demand existing in 1929, and compared those levels with the ones actually experienced [16, pp. 152–158]. Second, he has used 1939 technical data to estimate sector outputs corresponding to the final demand patterns of 1919 and 1929 and compared the errors resulting from this method of estimation with the errors found in two simple regression procedures [16, pp. 216–218]. Third, and most elaborate, he has made a study of the pattern of variation in input coefficients over the two decades 1919–39 and made a number of calculations of the effects of the observed changes on the output levels corresponding to observed levels of final demand [17, Chapter 2].

The results of these tests are inconclusive at best. The data available for the testing are known to be subject to appreciable statistical error. The tests are all based on a model in which the economy was divided into about a dozen sectors, involving therefore a violent amount of aggregation. And, in a sense, they are tangential to the main point since they test secular stability over fairly long periods rather than constancy in respect to changes in the scale of output. Because of these considerations, the results of the tests cannot be given decisive weight, and this is just as well because the results are not very encouraging. In the first test, four out of the nine sectors tested showed errors greater than 10 percent. The third test had many aspects. The most significant findings were that over the two decades studied the input coefficients fell at an average rate of about 1 percent per annum (with considerable dispersion, of course), the labor input coefficients fell at better than 3 percent per annum during 1919–29 and at about 1½ percent per annum during 1929–39, and, as a result, if the manpower requirements of the 1939 final demand had been estimated by using 1929 technical data an error of about 23 percent would have been made. Leontief's second test hardly shows more than that two estimating methods can be found which are inferior to input-output, but another investigator has proposed another method which in one test proved superior to input-output.[9]

In sum, the direct statistical testing performed thus far leaves the crucial issue in doubt. There is still another way, though, to test the model. After all, the model is not designed primarily to assist in predictions over a period of a decade or so. Its purpose is to permit the estimation of the impact on an economy of various changes in surrounding circumstances. How successful has the model been in performing this task?

---

[9] H. J. Barnett, "Specific Industry Output Projections," a paper prepared for the Rand Corporation, 1951. Barnett's test involves a number of statistical complications which prevent it from being conclusive either.

Leontief has given his system a number of trial applications. The most interesting are:

(1) Calculation of multipliers which show the effects on the sales of the various sectors and on total employment of a million dollar change in the final demand for products of the various sectors [16, pp. 139–162];

(2) Estimation of the effects on industrial levels and on employment of changes in the level of exports [16, pp. 163–186];

(3) Estimation of effects on the price structure of changes in wage and profit rates [16, pp. 188–202];

(4) Calculation of effects on economic activity in separate geographic regions of changes in the level and pattern of national demand [17, Chapter 5].

The fruitfulness of each of these applications depends on the appropriateness of the assumptions of the basic model to the problem in hand and on the plausibility of the additional assumptions required by the specific problem. The first application flows directly from the basic model without requiring additional assumptions. The most serious restriction on the meaning of the results is the fact that they refer to a static equilibrium. The Leontief model tells how much the equilibrium levels of sector outputs and employment will shift in response to exogenous changes in final demand, and only in this restricted sense does it predict the effects of changes in demand. The second application runs afoul of a difficulty we have noted previously, the ubiquitous application of technical input coefficients. Exports are treated as an industrial sector which purchases from the other sectors in technically fixed proportions and the calculations rest on this convention (it can hardly even be called an assumption). The third application depends on the accounting identity that the total value of output of any sector equals the value of purchases from other sectors plus value added. This plus a little algebra permits the calculation of the effect on the price structure of a change in wage rates in any sector if two additional assumptions be made: (1) that profits, depreciation charges, and taxes per unit of output do not change; and (2) that the change in the price structure does not induce substitutions. These assumptions imply that increases in cost are passed along in full. It seems difficult to grant the additional assumptions. The reverberations which are assumed away are, to be sure, secondary effects, but the whole input-output method depends on the calculation of indirect demand which is also a secondary effect, and who is to say that the secondary effects which are neglected by assumption are not more important than those which are included by calculation? Students of taxation have long ago reached a degree of sophistication about the shifting, incidence, and absorption of cost changes which should not be forgotten when applying the methods of interindustry analysis.

The application to problems of regional economics also requires difficult special assumptions. In effect it requires us to regard each industry in each economic region as a separate economic sector and to regard as constant not only the technological linkages among industries but also the regional distribution of purchases and sales of each industry.

This review of applications of the model is necessarily cursory. It indicates, though, that assumptions and complexities accumulate as soon as the model is pushed beyond the most straightforward technological applications.

Conclusion

It is not surprising that in this appraisal we have found more deficiencies than triumphs. Economic life is just not simple enough to be comprehended within a system of linear equations, and when we impose this format on it we must be content with a pretty liberal degree of approximation. We must be content also to note that the approximate model may be accurate enough for some purposes and still be inapplicable where the changes to be studied are no larger than the errors inherent in the model.

The situation in which these limitations are not crippling or even serious is clear. This is the case of economic mobilization, where large programs are envisaged, technical requirements are the predominant consideration, and consumption and investment are not allowed to interfere with the plan. Leontief's model comprehends the important relationships involved in such a problem, and the errors in the model can be tolerated. The model works better as an instrument of planning than as a tool for analyzing the operation of a free economy.

In using an input-output model for mobilization planning, the major components of final demand — household consumption, government requirements, and net exports — are all regarded as part of the plan and therefore subject to government control. It is true that the government can place an upper limit on these components of demand and, in the circumstances envisaged, it is reasonable to assume that actual final demand will achieve this upper limit. Thus the most difficult problems of economic forecasting are tractable to a mobilization planner.

The input-output model then determines the level of activity of each sector and the total requirement for each original factor as implied by the assumed levels of final demand, on the assumption that the observed input-output ratios will be maintained. If the required quantities of original factors do not exceed the quantities available, the plan can be carried out and this, after all, is the primary question involved in such work. On the other hand, if the factor requirements of the plan exceed the available supplies then either the plan is infeasible or the input-output ratios must be altered by the use of *ersatz* materials or other expedients. In either event the use of the model will lead to a set of final demands and activity levels which are internally consistent though not necessarily optimal.

In focusing our attention on the objectives of input-output and the extent to which they have been achieved, we have done scant justice to one of its most valuable products, the vast amount of organized empirical knowledge concerning the interrelations of industrial sectors which has been obtained. A storehouse of data now exists telling us where the products of various industries go and where their raw materials come from. We are beginning to learn more about the capital requirements of production and even about that well-tilled field, empirical production functions, than was ever before available. In short, input-output analysis provides a much-needed framework for gathering and understanding data about our industrial economy. Much of this information is contained in *Studies in the Structure of the American Economy* [17]; much more will be forthcoming as the work progresses.

It appears now that input-output is not likely to supplant traditional methods for studying industrial or price problems, or even to replace the Walrasian conceptual framework for thinking in terms of general equilibrium. Even so, we are not yet in a position to say what input-output analysis cannot do. The shift from the original closed models to the open models now in use increases the applicability of the technique many fold, though at the cost of theoretical completeness and explanatory content. The study of dynamic and regional models is only beginning at present; they may be susceptible of similar improvement. The Leontief group, and especially Duesenberry and Kistin, are laboring to close the model again in a more sophisticated manner.[10] Not a small part of Leontief's achievement was to open up a vast and hopeful field for exploration, and the work is not yet far advanced.

Whatever is to come of all this work, the improved models will rest on Leontief's original insight. Even in its present unperfected form interindustry analysis is a promising approach to analysis of our complicated industrial structure, and the most feasible technique yet developed for overall industrial planning.

APPENDIX

SELECTED REFERENCES ON INPUT-OUTPUT

[1] Arrow, Kenneth J. "Alternative Proof of the Substitution Theorem for Leontief Models in the General Case." *Activity Analysis of Production and Allocation*, edited by T. C. Koopmans. New York: Wiley, 1951, pp. 155–164.

[2] Chipman, John S. "The Multi-Sector Multiplier." *Econometrica*, Vol. XVIII (October, 1950), pp. 355–374.

[3] ———. "Linear Programming." *Review of Economics and Statistics*, Vol. XXXV (May, 1953), pp. 101–117.

[4] Cornfield, J., W. D. Evans, and M. Hoffenberg. "Full Employment Patterns, 1950." *Monthly Labor Review*, Vol. LXIV (February and March, 1947), pp. 163–190 and 420–432.

[5] Evans, W. D., and M. Hoffenberg. "The Interindustry Relations Study for 1947." *Review of Economics and Statistics*, Vol. XXXIV (May, 1952), pp. 97–142.

[10] See [17, Chapter 12].

[6] Georgescu-Roegen, Nicholas. "Leontief's System in the Light of Recent Results." *Review of Economics and Statistics*, Vol. XXXII (August, 1950), pp. 214–222.

[7] ———. "Some Properties of a Generalized Leontief Model." *Activity Analysis of Production and Allocation*, edited by T. C. Koopmans. New York: Wiley, 1951, pp. 165–173.

[8] Goodwin, R. M. "The Multiplier as Matrix." *Economic Journal*, Vol. LIX (December, 1949), pp. 537–555.

[9] Hawkins, David. "Some Conditions of Macroeconomic Stability." *Econometrica*, Vol. XVI (October, 1948), pp. 309–322.

[10] ———, and H. Simon. "Some Conditions of Macroeconomic Stability." *Econometrica*, Vol. XVII (July–October, 1949), pp. 245–248.

[11] Holley, Julian L. "A Dynamic Model." Part I, *Econometrica*, Vol. XX (October, 1952), pp. 616–642; Part II, *Econometrica*, Vol. XXI (April, 1953), pp. 298–324.

[12] Klein, L. R. "On the Interpretation of Professor Leontief's System." *Review of Economic Studies*, Vol. XX, No. 2 (1952–1953), pp. 131–136.

[13] Koopmans, T. C. (ed.). *Activity Analysis of Production and Allocation*. New York: Wiley, 1951.

[14] ———. "Alternative Proof of the Substitution Theorem for Leontief Models in the Case of Three Industries." *Activity Analysis of Production and Allocation*, edited by T. C. Koopmans. New York: Wiley, 1951, pp. 147–154.

[15] Leontief, Wassily W. "Quantitative Input and Output Relations in the Economic System of the United States." *Review of Economics and Statistics*, Vol. XVIII (August, 1936), pp. 105–125.

[16] ———. *The Structure of American Economy 1919–1939*, 1st ed. Cambridge, Mass.: Harvard University Press, 1941; 2d ed., enlarged. New York: Oxford University Press, 1951.

[17] ———, *et al. Studies in the Structure of the American Economy*. New York: Oxford University Press, 1953.

[18] Samuelson, Paul A. "Abstract of a Theorem Concerning Substitutability in Open Leontief Models." *Activity Analysis of Production and Allocation*, edited by T. C. Koopmans. New York: Wiley, 1951, pp. 142–146.

[19] Solow, Robert. "On the Structure of Linear Models." *Econometrica*, Vol. XX (January, 1952), pp. 29–46.

[20] Von Neumann, J. "A Model of General Economic Equilibrium." *Review of Economic Studies*, Vol. XIII, No. 1 (1945–1946), pp. 1–9.

[21] Wald, Abraham. "On Some Systems of Equations of Mathematical Economics." *Econometrica*, Vol. XIX (October, 1951), pp. 368–403.

[22] Walras, Leon. *Eléments d'économie politique pure ou théorie de la richesse sociale*, 2d ed. Lausanne: 1899.

30. PROBLEMS IN THE THEORY OF MARKETS UNDER UNCERTAINTY*

Roy Radner†

Introduction

One of the notable intellectual achievements of economic theory during the past twenty years has been the rigorous elaboration of the Walras-Pareto theory of value; that is, the theory of the existence and optimality of competitive equilibrium. Although many economists and mathematicians contributed to this development, the resulting edifice owes so much to the pioneering and influential work of Arrow and Debreu that in this paper I shall refer to it as the "Arrow-Debreu theory." (For a comprehensive treatment, together with references to previous work, see [6].)

The Arrow-Debreu theory was not originally put forward for the case of uncertainty, but an ingenious device introduced by Arrow [1], and further elaborated by Debreu [5], enabled the theory to be reinterpreted to cover the case of uncertainty about the availability of resources and about consumption and production possibilities. (See [6, Chap. 7] for a unified treatment of time and uncertainty.)

In the present paper I take the Arrow-Debreu theory as a starting point and discuss certain extensions, limitations, and possible new departures. In particular, I:

(1) show how the theory can be extended to account explicitly for differences in information available to different economic agents, and for the "production" of information;

(2) present a critique of the (extended) theory, especially its failure to explain or take account of money, stock markets, and the presence in the real world of active markets at every date;

(3) argue for the consideration of a theory of a sequence of markets and suggest several concepts of equilibrium that might be appropriate to such a theory; and

(4) present some results on the existence of an equilibrium of plans, prices, and price expectations in a sequence of markets.

The main features of the Arrow-Debreu theory have been available in the literature for more than a decade and were even discussed at a meeting of this

*From the *American Economic Review*, Vol. LX, No. 2 (May, 1970), pp. 454–460. Reprinted by permission of the publisher and the author.

†Roy Radner, Professor of Economics and of Statistics, University of California, Berkeley. This paper is based on research supported in part by the National Science Foundation.

Association six years ago [12]. Nevertheless, it seemed to me wise to begin the paper with a brief review of the elements of the theory, although I fear that the review may be too brief to be intelligible to those who are not already familiar with the material!

The consideration of a sequence of markets under conditions of uncertainty is not new in economics but does not seem to have received much attention from value theorists since the publication of Hick's *Value and Capital* [11]. I would therefore have felt more comfortable presenting this paper in a session entitled, "Old Ideas in Pure Theory," but as far as I know, no such session has been organized for the current meetings.

Review of the Arrow-Debreu Model of a Complete Market for Present and Future Contingent Delivery

In this section I review the approach of Arrow [1] and Debreu [6] to incorporating uncertainty about the environment into a Walrasian model of competitive equilibrium. The basic idea is that commodities are to be distinguished, not only by their physical characteristics and by the location and dates of their availability and/or use, but also by the environmental event in which they are made available and/or used. For example, ice cream made available (at a particular location on a particular date) if the weather is hot may be considered to be a different commodity from the same kind of ice cream made available (at the same location and date) if the weather is cold. We are, thus, led to consider a list of "commodities" that is greatly expanded by comparison with the corresponding case of certainty about the environment. The standard arguments of the theory of competitive equilibrium, applied to an economy with this expanded list of commodities, then require that we envisage a "price" for each commodity in the list, or, more precisely, a set of price ratios specifying the rate of exchange between each pair of commodities.

Just what institutions could, or do, effect such exchanges is a matter of interpretation that is, strictly speaking, outside the model. I shall present one straightforward interpretation, and then comment briefly on an alternative interpretation.

First, however, it will be useful to give a more precise account of the concepts of environment and event that I shall be employing. The description of the "physical world" is decomposed into three sets of variables:

(1) decision variables, which are controlled (chosen) by economic agents;
(2) environmental variables, which are not controlled by any economic agent; and
(3) all other variables, which are completely determined (possibly jointly) by decisions and environmental variables.

A state of the environment is a complete specification (history) of the environmental variables from the beginning to the end of the economic system in question. An event is a set of states; for example, the event "the weather is hot in New York on July 1, 1970" is the set of all possible histories of the environment in which the temperature in New York during the day of July

1, 1970, reaches a high of at least (say) 75° F. Granting that we cannot know the future with certainty, at any given date, there will be a family of elementary observable (knowable) events, which can be represented by a partition of the set of all possible states (histories) into a family of mutually exclusive subsets. It is natural to assume that the partitions corresponding to successive dates are successively finer, which represents the accumulation of information about the environment.

We shall imagine that a "market" is organized before the beginning of the physical history of the economic system. An elementary contract in this market will consist of the purchase (or sale) of some specified number of units of a specified commodity to be delivered at a specified location and date, if and only if a specified elementary event occurs. Payment for this purchase is to be made now (at the beginning), in "units of account," at a specified price quoted for that commodity-location-date-event combination. Delivery of the commodity in more than one elementary event is obtained by combining a suitable set of elementary contracts. For example, if delivery of one quart of ice cream (at a specified location and date) in hot weather costs \$1.50 (now) and delivery of one quart in non-hot weather costs \$1.10, then sure delivery of one quart (i.e., whatever be the weather) costs \$1.50 + \$1.10 = \$2.60.

There are two groups of economic agents in the economy: producers and consumers. A producer chooses a production plan, which determines his input and/or output of each commodity at each date in each elementary event. (I shall henceforth suppress explicit reference to location, it being understood that the location is specified in the term commodity.) For a given set of prices, the present value of a production plan is the sum of the values of the inputs minus the sum of the values of the outputs. Each producer is characterized by a set of production plans that are (physically) feasible for him: his production possibility set.

A consumer chooses a consumption plan, which specifies his consumption of each commodity at each date in each elementary event. Each consumer is characterized by:

(1) a set of consumption plans that are (physically, psychologically, etc.) feasible for him, his consumption possibility set;

(2) preferences among the alternative plans that are feasible for him;

(3) his endowment of physical resources, i.e., a specification of the quantity of each commodity, e. g., labor, at each date in each event with which he is exogenously endowed; and

(4) his shares in producers' profits, i.e., a specification for each producer, of the fraction of the present value of that producer's production plan that will be credited to the consumer's account. (For any one producer, the sum of the consumers' shares is unity.) For given prices and given production plans of all the producers, the present net worth of a consumer is the total value of his resources plus the total value of his shares of the present values of producers' production plans.

An equilibrium of the economy is a set of prices, a set of production plans (one for each producer), and a set of consumption plans (one for each consumer), such that (*a*) each producer's plan has maximum present value in his production possibility set; (*b*) each consumer's plan maximizes his preferences within his consumption possibility set, subject to the additional (budget) constraint that the present cost of his consumption plan not exceed his present net worth; (*c*) for each commodity at each date in each elementary event, the total demand equals the total supply; i.e., the total planned consumption equals the sum of the total resource endowments and the total planned net output (where inputs are counted as negative outputs).

Notice that

(1) producers and consumers are "price takers";

(2) for given prices there is no uncertainty about the present value of a production plan or of given resource endowments, nor about the present cost of a consumption plan;

(3) therefore, for given prices and given producers' plans, there is no uncertainty about a given consumer's present net worth;

(4) since a consumption plan may specify that, for a given commodity at a given date, the quantity consumed is to vary according to the event that actually occurs, a consumer's preferences among plans will reflect not only his "tastes" but also his subjective beliefs about the likelihoods of different events and his attitude towards risk [16].

It follows that beliefs and attitudes towards risk play no role in the assumed behavior of producers. On the other hand, beliefs and attitudes towards risk do play a role in the assumed behavior of consumers, although for given prices and production plans each consumer knows his (single) budget constraint with certainty.

I shall call the model just described an "Arrow-Debreu" economy. One can demonstrate, under "standard conditions":

(1) the existence of an equilibrium,

(2) the Pareto optimality of an equilibrium, and

(3) that, roughly speaking, every Pareto optimal choice of production and consumption plans is an equilibrium relative to some price system for some distribution of resource endowments and shares [6, Chaps. 5 and 6], [7].

In the above interpretation of the Arrow-Debreu economy, all accounts are settled before the history of the economy begins, and there is no incentive to revise plans, reopen the market or trade in shares. There is an alternative interpretation, which will be of interest in connection with the rest of this paper but which corresponds to exactly the same formal model. In this second interpretation, there is a single commodity at each date—let us call it "gold"—that is taken as a numeraire at that date. A "price system" has two parts:

(1) For each date and each elementary event at that date, there is a price, to be paid in gold at date 1, for one unit of gold to be delivered at the specified date and event;

(2) For each commodity, date, and event at that date, there is a price, to be paid in gold at that date and event, for one unit of the commodity to be delivered at that same date and event.

The first part of the price system can be interpreted as "insurance premiums" and the second part as "spot prices" at the given date and event. The insurance interpretation is to be made with some reservation, however, since there is no real object being insured and no limit to the amount of insurance that an individual may take out against the occurence of a given event. For this reason, the first part of the price system might be better interpreted as reflecting a combination of betting odds and interest rates.

Although the second part of the price system might be interpreted as spot prices, it would be a mistake to think of the determination of the equilibrium values of these prices as being deferred in real time to the dates to which they refer. The definition of equilibrium requires that the agents have the access to the complete system of prices when choosing their plans. In effect, this requires that at the beginning of time all agents have available a (common) forecast of the equilibrium spot prices that will prevail at every future date and event.

Extension of the Arrow-Debreu Model to the Case in Which Different Agents Have Different Information

In an Arrow-Debreu economy, at any one date each agent will have incomplete information about the state of the environment, but all the agents will have the same information. This last assumption is not tenable if we are to take good account of the effects of uncertainty in an economy. I shall now sketch how, by a simple reinterpretation of the concepts of production possibility set and consumption possibility set, we can extend the theory of the Arrow-Debreu economy to allow for differences in information among the economic agents.[1]

For each date, the information that will be available to a given agent at that date may be characterized by a partition of the set of states of the environment. To be consistent with our previous terminology, we should assume that each such information partition must be at least as coarse as the partition that describes the elementary events at that date; i.e., each set in the information partition must contain a set in the elementary event partition for the same date.

For example, each set in the event partition at a given date might specify the high temperature at that date, whereas each set in a given agent's information partition might specify only whether this temperature was higher than 75° F. or not. Or the event partition at a given date might specify the temperature at each date during the past month, whereas the information partition might specify only the mean temperature over the past month.

An agent's information restricts his set of feasible plans in the following manner. Suppose that at a given date the agent knows only that the state of the environment lies in a specified set A (one of the sets in his information partition at that date), and suppose (as would be typical) that the set A contains several of the elementary events that are in principle observable at that date. Then any action that the agent takes at that date must necessarily be the same for all elementary events in the set A. In particular, if the agent is a

[1]This section is based upon [14, Sections 2–6].

consumer, then his consumption of any specified commodity at that date must be the same in all elementary events contained in the information set A; if the agent is a producer, then his input or output of any specified commodity must be the same for all events in A. (I am assuming that consumers know what they consume and producers what they produce at any given date.)

Let us call the sequence of information partitions for a given agent his information structure and let us say that this structure is fixed if it is given independent of the actions of himself or any other agent. Furthermore, in the case of a fixed information structure, let us say that a given plan (consumption or production) is compatible with that structure if it satisfies the conditions described in the previous paragraph, at each date.

Suppose that the consumption and production possibility sets of the Arrow-Debreu economy are interpreted as characterizing, for each agent, those plans that would be feasible if he had "full information" (i.e., if his information partition at each date coincided with the elementary event partition at that date). The set of feasible plans for any agent with a fixed information structure can then be obtained by restricting him to those plans in the full information possibility set that are also compatible with his given information structure.

From this point on, all of the machinery of the Arrow-Debreu economy (with some minor technical modifications) can be brought to bear on the present model. In particular, we get a theory of existence and optimality of competitive equilibrium relative to fixed structures of information for the economic agents. I shall call this the "extended Arrow-Debreu economy."[2]

Choice of Information

There is no difficulty in principle in incorporating the choice of information structure into the model of the extended Arrow-Debreu economy. I doubt, however, that it is reasonable to assume that the technological conditions for the acquisition and use of information generally satisfy the hypotheses of the standard theorems on the existence and optimality of competitive equilibrium.

The acquisition and use of information about the environment typically require the expenditure of goods and services; i.e., of commodities.

If one production plan requires more information for its implementation than another (i.e., requires a finer information partition at one or more dates), then the list of (commodity) inputs should reflect the increased inputs for information. In this manner a set of feasible production plans can reflect the possibility of choice among alternative information structures.

Unfortunately the acquisition of information often involves a "set-up cost"; i.e., the resources needed to obtain the information may be independent of the scale of the production process in which the information is used. This

[2]This terminology is not in any way meant to imply that either Arrow or Debreu approve of this way of incorporating information into their model!

set-up cost will introduce a nonconvexity in the production possibility set, and thus, one of the standard conditions in the theory of the Arrow-Debreu economy will not be satisfied [14, Sec. 9].

There is another interesting class of cases in which an agent's information structure is not fixed, namely, cases in which the agent's information at one date may depend upon production or consumption decisions taken at previous dates, but all actions can be scaled down to any desired size. Unfortunately space limitations prevent me from discussing this class in the present paper.

Critique of the Extended Arrow-Debreu Economy

If the Arrow-Debreu model is given a literal interpretation, then it clearly requires that the economic agents possess capabilities of imagination and calculation that exceed reality by many orders of magnitude. Related to this is the observation that the theory requires in principle a complete system of insurance and futures markets, which appears to be too complex, detailed, and refined to have practical significance. A further obstacle to the achievement of a complete insurance market is the phenomenon of "moral hazard" [2].

A second line of criticism is that the theory does not take account of at least three important institutional features of modern capitalist economies: money, the stock market, and active markets at every date.

These two lines of criticism have an important connection, which suggests how the Arrow-Debreu theory might be improved. If, as in the Arrow-Debreu model, each production plan has a sure unambiguous present value at the beginning of time, then consumers have no interest in trading in shares, and there is no point in a stock market. If all accounts can be settled at the beginning of time, then, there is no need for money during the subsequent life of the economy; in any case, the standard motives for holding money do not apply.

On the other hand, once we recognize explicitly that there is a sequence of markets, one for each date, and no one of them complete (in the Arrow-Debreu sense), then certain phenomena and institutions not accounted for in the Arrow-Debreu model become reasonable. First, there is uncertainty about the prices that will hold in future markets, as well as uncertainty about the environment.

Second, producers do not have a clear-cut natural way of comparing net revenues at different dates and states. Stockholders have an incentive to establish a stock exchange, since it enables them to change the way their future revenues depend on the states of the environment. As an alternative to selling his shares in a particular enterprise, a stockholder may try to influence the management of the enterprise in order to make the production plan conform better to his own subjective probabilities and attitude towards risk.

Third, consumers will typically not be able to discount all of their "wealth" at the beginning of time, because (*a*) their shares of producers' future (uncertain) net revenues cannot be so discounted and (*b*) they cannot discount all of their future resource endowments. Consumers will be subject to a sequence of budget constraints, one for each date (rather than to a single budget constraint relating present cost of his consumption plan to present net worth, as in the Arrow-Debreu economy).

Fourth, economic agents may have an incentive to speculate on the prices in future markets, by storing goods, hedging, etc. Instead of storing goods, an agent may be interested in saving part of one date's income, in units of account, for use on a subsequent date, if there is an institution that makes this possible. There will thus be a demand for "money" in the form of demand deposits.

Fifth, agents will be interested in forecasting the prices in markets at future dates. These prices will be functions of both the state of the environment and the decisions of (in principle, all) economic agents up to the date in question.

Equilibrium of Plans, Prices, and Price Expectations in a Sequence of Markets

Consider now a sequence of markets at successive dates. Suppose that no market at any one date is complete in the Arrow-Debreu sense; i.e., at every date and for every commodity there will be some future dates and some events at those future dates for which it will not be possible to make current contracts for future delivery contingent on those events. In such a model, several types of "equilibrium" concept suggest themselves. First, we may think of a sequence of "momentary" equilibria in which the current market is cleared at each date. The prices at which the current market is cleared at any one date will depend upon (among other things) the expectations that the agents hold concerning prices in future markets (to be distinguished from future prices on the current market!). We can represent a given agent's expectations in a precise manner as a function (schedule) that indicates what the prices will be at a given future date in each elementary event at that date. This includes, in particular, the representation of future prices as random variables, if we admit that the uncertainty of the agent about future events can be scaled in terms of subjective probabilities [16].

In the evolution of a sequence of momentary equilibria, each agent's expectations will be successively revised in the light of new information about the environment and about current prices. Therefore, the evolution of the economy will depend upon the rules or processes of expectation formation and revision used by the agents. In particular, there might be interesting conditions under which such a sequence of momentary equilibria would converge, in some sense, to a (stochastic) steady state. This steady state, e.g., stationary probability distribution of prices, would constitute a second concept of equilibrium.

I am not aware of any systematic general theory of markets under uncertainty, incorporating one or both of these two concepts of equilibrium, that has appeared since Hicks's *Value and Capital,* and I don't think that we can rest satisfied with Hicks's treatment in terms of "certainty equivalents" and "elasticities of expectation." The desirability of having a better theory and the importance of the role of expectations are well recognized, of course [3]. In the further development of such a theory, we shall no doubt have to face some of the difficult problems that have appeared in recent work on sequences of momentary equilibria under conditions of certainty [10], [17], [18].

A third concept of equilibrium emerges if we investigate the possibility of consistency among the expectations and plans of the various agents. I shall say that the agents have common expectations if they associate the same (future) prices to the same events. (Note that this does not necessarily imply that they agree on the joint probability distribution of future prices, since different agents might well assign different subjective probabilities to the same event.) I shall say that the plans of the agents are consistent if for each commodity, each date, and each event at that date the planned supply of that commodity at that date in that event equals the planned demand and if a corresponding condition holds for the stock markets. An equilibrium of plans, prices, and price expectations is a set of prices on the current market, a set of common expectations for the future, and a consistent set of individual plans, one for each agent, such that, given the current prices and price expectations, each individual agent's plan is optimal for him, subject to an appropriate sequence of budget constraints.

Of the three concepts of optimality, the last is perhaps the closest in spirit to the Arrow-Debreu theory. How far do the conclusions of the Arrow-Debreu theory (existence and optimality of equilibrium) extend to this new situation? Concerning existence, for particular definitions of "individual optimality" and specifications of the agents' "budget constraints," one can prove the following theorem. Before stating the existence theorem I must define what I shall call a pseudo-equilibrium.

The definition of pseudo-equilibrium is obtained from the definition of equilibrium by replacing the requirement of consistency of plans by the condition that at each date and each event the difference between total saving and total investment (by consumers) is smaller at the pseudo-equilibrium prices than at any other prices.[3]

One can prove [15] that under assumptions about technology and consumer preferences similar to those used in the Arrow-Debreu theory:

(1) there exists a pseudo-equilibrium;

(2) if in a pseudo-equilibrium the current and future prices on the stock market are all strictly positive, then the pseudo-equilibrium is an equilibrium;

(3) in the case of a pure exchange economy, there exists an equilibrium.

---

[3]This second condition will be automatically satisfied at an equilibrium. It should be noted that at each date the set of current prices is normalized; e.g., by taking the sum to be unity.

The crucial difference between this theorem and the corresponding one in the Arrow-Debreu theory seems to be due to the form taken by Walras' law, which in this model can be paraphrased by saying that saving must be at least equal to investment at each date in each event. This form derives from the replacement of a single budget constaint (in terms of present value) by a sequence of budget constraints, one for each date.

With regard to optimality, there is little that can be said at this time. The main difficulty in investigating this question seems to be in characterizing the set of states of the economy that are attainable, given the restrictions on the set of allowable contracts at each date.

Unsolved Problems

I can only list here a few unsolved problems that I personally find interesting and promising for further research.

I have already mentioned the question of the optimality properties (if any) of an equilibrium of plans, prices, and price expectations. One possible approach is to consider more explicitly the information that the observation of prices provides for agents in the economy. One might hope to show that an equilibrium is an optimum relative to the set of states of the economy that could be attained with just the same information that is provided by the equilibrium prices (in addition, of course, to the information structures originally available to the individual agents). Notice that since the equilibrium price expectations are self-fulfilling, the observation of the prices in any current market provides information about the true state of the environment (i.e., the specification of the values of particular prices defines an "event" in the set of possible states of the environment). An approach of this kind was tried in a two-period model [13], which was further complicated, however, by allowing agents to make contracts for future delivery contingent on the values taken on by future prices. (An example of such a contract would be a wage contract with a cost-of-living escalation clause.) It was shown that in this model, if the introduction of such contracts enabled all the agents to discount future receipts and costs back to the initial date (i.e., if all uncertainty about the environment could be reflected in some corresponding uncertainty about future prices), then an equilibrium would be an optimum in the above sense. Unfortunately the existence of an equilibrium in such a model was not demonstrated, and indeed, there might be important economic phenomena that would rule out the existence of equilibrium in such a model [13].

I have also already mentioned the unsatisfactory state of the theory of the evolution of momentary equilibria in a sequence of markets and the question of possible convergence of momentary equilibria to a (stochastic) steady state.

In all of these (potential) theories of a sequence of markets we shall need a more detailed theory of the firm than that used in the Arrow-Debreu model. Simple profit maximization is not well defined if future profits are uncertain and cannot fully be discounted back to the present. The model of the "Equilibrium of Plans, Prices, and Price Expectations in a Sequence of Markets" section of this paper essentially begged this question by assuming that each producer maximizes a utility function whose arguments are his future net revenues in different events. Such an assumption fails to relate the behavior of the firm to the preferences of the stockholders or potential stockholders. (It is rather an expression of the "divorce of ownership from management"!) An alternative candidate that has been discussed is the assumption that at each date a producer maximizes the current stock market value of his firm. (Note that in the Arrow-Debreu model, profit maximization is equivalent to maximization of the value of the stock.) However, except in the context of a special example considered by Diamond [8], I have not seen a formulation of this hypothesis that enables the producer to act as a price-taker; i.e., that does not imply that the producer is able to calculate the effect of his actions on the equilibrium prices.

We shall also want to incorporate into our theories the process of entry and exit of firms. In particular, the results described in the "Equilibrium of Plans, Prices, and Price Expectations in a Sequence of Markets" section of this paper on the relationship between equilibrium and pseudo-equilibrium suggest that the possibility of exit may be important in assuring the existence of such an equilibrium.

Finally, I mention the old problem of incorporating a theory of money and credit in a Walrasian model of general equilibrium [9]. In a sense, the model of the "Equilibrium of Plans, Prices, and Price Expectations in a Sequence of Markets" section of this paper allows "secured" loans that are backed either by physical collateral or by contracts for future delivery of commodities. The theory also provides a framework for explaining the holding of "commodity money." The model does not, however, describe any institutions for carrying over "units of account" from one date to the next; the introduction of such institutions seems a natural next step and one for which the model seems to me to be well suited.

REFERENCES

[1] Arrow, K. J. "Le Rôle de Valeurs Boursières pour la Répartition la Meilleure des Risques." *Econométrie*. Paris: Centre National de la Recherche Scientifique, 1953, pp. 41–48; or see the translation, Arrow, K. J. "The Role of Securities in the Optimal Allocation of Risk Bearing." *Review of Economic Studies* (1964), pp. 91–96.

[2] ———. *Aspects of the Theory of Risk-Bearing*. Helsinki: Yrjo Jahnsson Lecture Series, 1965.

[3] Bowman, M. J. (ed.). *Expectations, Uncertainty, and Business Behavior*. New York: Social Science Research Council, 1958.

[4] Cass, D., and J. E. Stiglitz. "The Implication of Alternative Saving and Expectations Hypotheses for Choices of Technique and Patterns of Growth." *Journal of Political Economy* (July-August, 1969), pp. 586–627.

[5] Debreu, G. "Une Economie de l'Incertain." Paris: Electricité de France, 1953, (mimeographed).

[6] ———. *Theory of Value.* New York: Wiley, 1959.

[7] ———. "New Concepts and Techniques for Equilibrium Analysis." *International Economic Review* (1962), pp. 257–273.

[8] Diamond, P. "The Role of a Stock Market in a General Equilibrium Model with Technological Uncertainty." *American Economic Review* (September, 1967), pp. 759–776.

[9] Hahn, F. H. "On Some Problems of Proving the Existence of an Equilibrium in a Monetary Economy." *The Theory of Interest Rates,* edited by Hahn and Brechling. London: Macmillan, 1965.

[10] ———. "Equilibrium Dynamics with Heterogeneous Capital Goods." *Quarterly Journal of Economics* (November, 1966).

[11] Hicks, J. R. *Value and Capital.* London: Clarendon Press, 1939.

[12] Hirshleifer, J. "Efficient Allocation of Capital in an Uncertain World." *American Economic Review* (May, 1964), pp. 77–85.

[13] Radner, R. "Equilibre des Marchés à Terme et au Comptant en Cas d'Incertitude." *Cashiers d'Econométrie.* Paris: Centre National de la Recherche Scientifique, 1967.

[14] ———. "Competitive Equilibrium under Uncertainty." *Econometrica* (January, 1968), pp. 31–58.

[15] ———. "Equilibrium of Plans, Prices, and Price-Expectations in a Sequence of Markets." Unpublished (1969).

[16] Savage, L. J. *The Foundations of Statistics.* New York: Wiley, 1954.

[17] Shell, K., and J. E. Stiglitz. "The Allocation of Investment in a Dynamic Economy." *Quarterly Journal of Economics* (November, 1967), pp. 592–609.

[18] Uzawa, H. "Market Allocation and Optimum Growth." *Australian Economic Papers* (June, 1968), pp. 17–27.

31. CONSUMER WELFARE AND PRODUCT DIFFERENTIATION*

Frederick Goddard†

Present welfare economics sets forth sufficient conditions for Paretian efficiency in the allocation of resources, given the number of goods and their quality attributes.[1] However, an investigation of consumer welfare and product differentiation must concern itself not only with prices and quantities but also with quality variations and the introduction of new products. In order for an optimal price and output to exist in a meaningful sense, there must also exit an optimal variety of goods embodied in the number of goods offered and their quality and attributes. Economists have intuitively recognized this condition but generally have not formally included it in models of consumer welfare. The problem has been only indirectly approached in analysis of the equilibrium of the firm under monopolistic competition, with the emphasis upon the firm and not upon the consumer.[2]

The failure of traditional welfare economics to meet the challenge of differentiated products is largely due to the inability of the traditional theory of consumer behavior to cope with the introduction of new products and changes in the quality and attributes of old ones. In two recent articles, Kelvin Lancaster has introduced a "New Theory of Consumer Behavior."[3] Although Lancaster is not concerned with an investigation of consumer welfare in general equilibrium, his model provides a convenient framework for a formal, general-equilibrium treatment of consumer welfare in product-differentiated markets. This article in an attempt to develop such a treatment.

---

*From *Quarterly Review of Economics and Business*, Vol. X, No. 2 (Summer, 1970), pp. 27–35. Reprinted by permission of the publisher and the author.

†Frederick Goddard, Assistant Professor of Economics, University of Florida. The author is indebted to the University of Florida Institute of Social Sciences for research support and to Milton Z. Kafoglis for helpful comments and criticisms on an earlier draft.

[1]See, for example, Francis M. Bator, "The Simple Analytics of Welfare Maximization," *American Economic Review*, Vol. XLVII (March, 1957), pp. 22–59, and "The Anatomy of Market Failure," *Quarterly Journal of Economics*, Vol. LXXII (August, 1958), pp. 351–379.

[2]For example, Lawrence Abbott, *Quality and Competition* (New York: Columbia University Press, 1955); Edward Chamberlin, *The Theory of Monopolistic Competition* (6th ed.; Cambridge, Mass.: Harvard University Press, 1948); and Harold Demsetz, "The Welfare and Empirical Implications of Monopolistic Competition," *Economic Journal*, Vol. LXXII (September, 1964), pp. 623–641. Abbott's book contains what is perhaps the best treatment of the problem of consumer welfare with product differentiation.

[3]Kelvin J. Lancaster, "Change and Innovation in the Technology of Consumption," *American Economic Review*, Vol. LVI (May, 1966), pp. 14–23; and "A New Approach

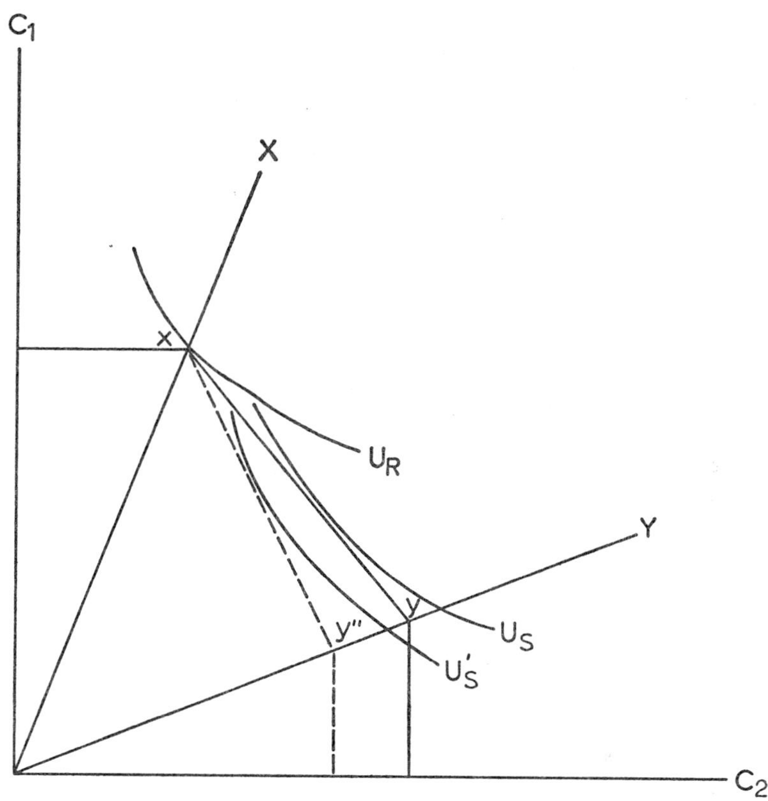

Figure 31-1

A Summary of Lancaster's New Approach

In Lancaster's new approach the utility map of the consumer is considered in what he calls "characteristics space" rather than goods space. Goods themselves are not the direct object of utility or satisfaction, but, instead,

> . . . it is the properties or characteristics of the goods from which utility is derived.
>
> We assume that consumption is an activity in which goods, singly or in combination, are inputs and in which the output is a collection of characteristics. Utility or preference orderings are assumed to rank collections of goods indirectly through the characteristics that they possess. . . .[4]

Lancaster views consumption as a production activity with goods as joint inputs and characteristics as joint outputs. Utility functions rank collections

---

to Consumer Theory," *Journal of Political Economy*, Vol LXXIV (April, 1966), pp. 132–157.

[4]Lancaster, "A New Approach to Consumer Theory," *op. cit.*, p. 133.

of these objective characteristics rather than collections of goods. The consumer, then, is faced with a set of objective efficiency judgments and a set of subjective value judgments in deciding upon his purchases in the marketplace. This new approach promises to be most fruitful in precisely those areas of analysis where the traditional approach has been weakest. The introduction of new products or the modification of existing products becomes a matter of adjusting the characteristic vectors of the products within a given characteristics space and does not involve a change in the utility map or consumers' tastes.

Consider two consumption characteristics, C_1 and C_2. These two characteristics are measured along the axes of Figure 31-1. The vectors X and Y are associated with two goods X and Y, and show the proportions of characteristics C_1 and C_2 that are derived from the consumption of these goods.[5] These vectors are determined objectively by the technical properties of the goods, and the two goods shown are differentiated in that they yield different characteristic vectors. It is assumed that the relationship between goods and obtainable characteristics is both linear and objective, and that the amount of each characteristic obtained in a consumption activity is determined by these characteristic vectors and the amount of the good utilized.[6] Thus, for a given size of budget and set of goods prices, a "consumption-possibilities frontier" can be drawn in characteristics space. The point of intersection of this frontier with a given vector will move out along that vector as the price of the associated good is lowered, and the entire frontier will shift outward or inward as the budget is increased or decreased. The analysis of consumer decision-making resembles the traditional indifference curve analysis, with each consumer maximizing his utility by seeking the highest possible indifference curve obtainable within his consumption-possibilities frontier.[7] As in traditional analysis, an increase in the price of one good will result in a shift in consumption away from that good and toward competitive goods.

Indifference curves for two utility-maximizing individuals with identical budgets but differing tastes are shown in Figure 31-1. Individual R is consuming only good X, whereas individual S is consuming a combination of goods X and Y. An increase in the price of good Y would shift the consumption-possibilities frontier in from xy to xy'' and would result in an increase in S's

[5]It would be more correct to call these "collections of goods" or "goods packages," recognizing the possibility of joint inputs of several complementary goods to produce the combination of characteristics found in a given vector. Throughout this article, however, the less cumbersome term "good" will be used. The reader is warned not to lose sight of this complementary feature of good inputs.

[6]The relationship is assumed to be objective in the sense that the characteristics embodied in a particular consumption activity are identical for all consumers and independent of any individual consumer's tastes.

[7]Since the relationship between goods and obtainable characteristics is assumed to be linear and objective, the consumption-possibilities frontiers of different consumers are geometrically similar and differ only by a change in scale proportional to a change in budget size. Thus, a consumption-possibilities frontier derived from any arbitrarily chosen budget can be analytically representative of all consumers' situations.

consumption of good *X* and a reduction of his consumption of good *Y*. Since *R* was maximizing his satisfaction with a corner solution, there would be no change in his consumption pattern. (If the price of good *Y* were sufficiently reduced, however, *R* would maximize satisfaction with a tangency solution and become a consumer of both goods.) The level of satisfaction of *S* is reduced but the level of satisfaction of *R* is unchanged by the price increase.

Introduction of New Goods

A change in the *quality* of a good is defined as a change that results in a shift of the consumption-possibilities frontier along the existing characteristics vector of that good, whereas a change in the *attributes* of a good is defined as a change that results in a pivoting of the characteristics vector of the good (that is, a change in the relative proportions of the characteristics made available by a unit of the good).[8] A consumer is then indifferent between a 10 percent reduction in price and a 10 percent increase in quality of a good, provided that the attributes of that good remain the same. Given wide variations in consumers' tastes, any change in the price, quality, or attributes of a good that shifts some portion of the consumption-possibilities frontier outward will result in an increase in welfare for some consumers. An unambiguous increase in consumer welfare, therefore, follows only if some portion of the consumption-possibilities frontier is shifted outward and no portion of the frontier is shifted inward.

Now consider the introduction of a new good *Z* that offers yet another characteristic vector to the consumer. As shown in Figure 31-2, good *Z* will be successful provided that it is offered with a price low enough that its introduction results in shifting the consumption-possibility frontier outward from *xy*. The new frontier *xzy* is a definite improvement over the old one for consumers who formerly found themselves consuming combinations of *X* and *Y*. In addition, some consumers that had been specializing in *X* or *Y* will now consume a combination of *X* and *Z* or *Y* and *Z*.

The introduction of this new good has not left the producers of goods *X* and *Y* unaffected. Their demand curves have shifted to the left as a result of *Z*'s successful capture of some of their customers. Their demand curves have also flattened as a result of the increased substitutability of products (lessened

[8]A simple example of these changes can be found in the case of fertilizer. Standard fertilizers are described by three numbers such as 6-6-6 indicating the percentage contents by weight of the three active elements. A quality change might be an increase in all three elements to say 8-8-8. For many purposes a consumer would be indifferent between this change and a 25 percent reduction in the price of 6-6-6. A change to 6-4-10 would represent a change in attributes.

A change in attributes could alternatively be thought of as the replacement of one good by another, but for small changes it is more convenient to retain the continuity of a single good, especially when there is no change of firms. This definition of a change in attributes corresponds to what Abbott terms a "horizontal" change in quality (Abbott, *op. cit.*, pp. 125–131). His "vertical" change corresponds roughly to what is here defined as a quality change.

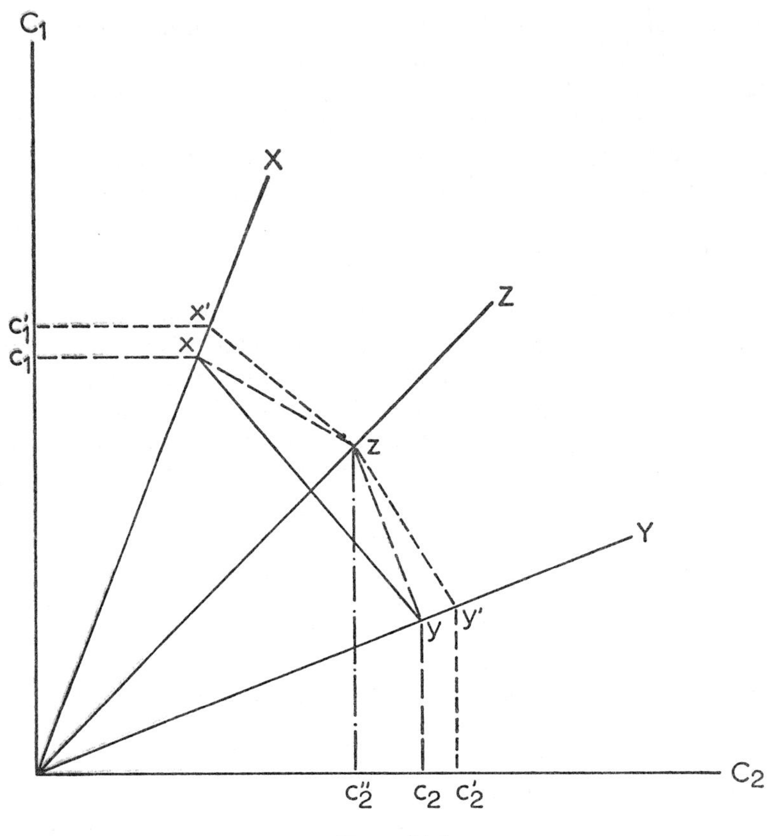

Figure 31-2

product differentiation as exhibited by the closeness of the characteristic vectors). Under these circumstances firms producing *X* and *Y* will find it profitable (or less unprofitable) to lower prices and / or to increase the quality of their products.[9] Thus, consumers will finally be offered the consumption-possibilities frontier *x'zy'*.

The introduction of new goods might also cause existing firms to change not only price and quality but the attributes of their products. Such a case is illustrated in Figure 31-3. Assuming that consumers are evenly distributed in the characteristics space C_1C_2, the introduction of new product *W* makes it profitable for Firm *Z* to change the attributes of its product to correspond to

[9]For an analysis of firms reacting to changes in demand by changing the quality of their product as well as price and output, see Chamberlin, *op. cit.*, pp. 94–104; Abbott, *op. cit.*, pp. 139–170; Lawrence Abbott, "Vertical Equilibrium Under Pure Quality Competition," *American Economic Review*, Vol. XLIII (December, 1953), pp. 826–845; and Robert Dorfman and P. O. Steiner, "Optimal Advertising and Optimal Quality," *American Economic Review*, Vol. XLIV (December, 1954), pp. 826–836.

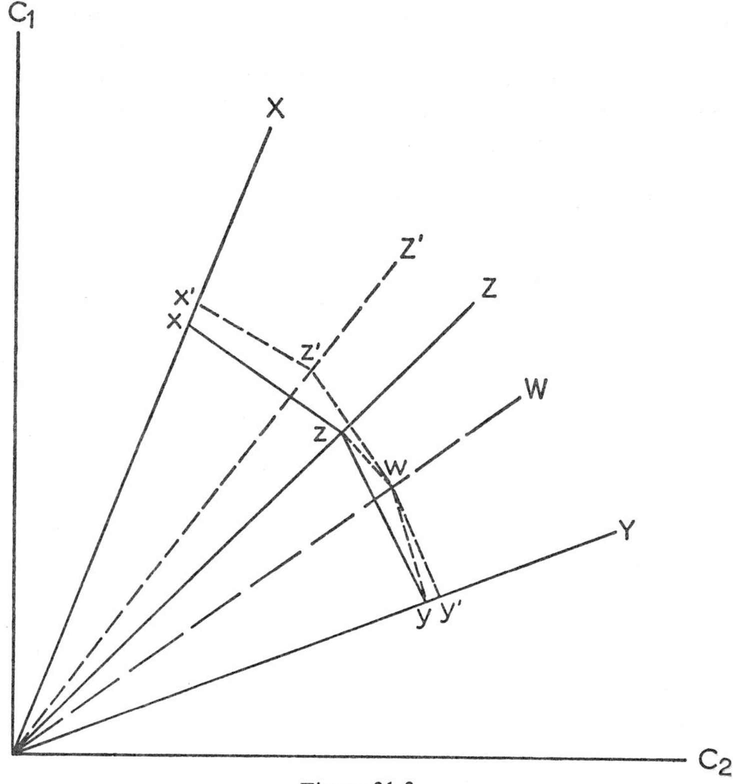

Figure 31-3

the characteristic vector Z'. Initially Firms Y and Z lose customers to the new Firm W as the consumption-possibilities frontier shifts out from *xzy* to *xzwy*. Firm Y will reduce price and increase quality in reaction to the entrance of W, and Firm Z will change its price, quality, and attributes in order to gain some of X's customers as well as recapture some of the consumers lost to W. Firm X will react to the changes of Firm Z by reducing price and/or increasing quality. As in the previous example, the introduction of a new good results in a general outward shifting of the consumption-possibilities frontier, in part because of the change in technologies offered by the new goods and in part because of the changes in price, quality, and attributes of old goods in response to the new entry.

This general outward shift of the consumption-possibilities frontier—and the corresponding increase in consumer welfare—can be expected to result with the introduction of new goods provided that the introduction of the new good does not reduce the demand for an old good to such an extent that the firm involved finds itself with too few customers to sustain profitable operations and quits the market. If this condition is not met, and if some good is withdrawn from the market, then some consumers might find that the consumption-possibilities frontier has shifted in toward the origin in the area concerning them. For example, in Figure 31-2, if Firm *Y* had been driven from the market, the final consumption-possibilities frontier would be $c_1'x'zc_2''$ rather than $c_1'x'zy'c_2'$, and consumers with a strong bias in taste toward C_2 would experience a welfare loss.

Consumer Welfare, Range of Choice, and Price Structure

If entry into the market remains relatively free, that is, if there is quasi-free entry,[10] the introduction of new goods can be expected to proceed so long as normal profits can be made by the firm introducing the new good. The process will resemble that described by Lawrence Abbott and Arthur Smithies[11] in the problem of spatial competition, with firms "locating" their products in characteristics space (that is, determining the characteristic vectors or attributes of their products) according to the distribution of consumers within that space. According to Abbott, Smithies, and Harold Hotelling,[12] there will be a tendency for firms to bunch up too close to the center of a given distribution of consumers, rather than to position their products in the optimal locations within the space under consideration. But their criterion for determining the "optimal" locations of firms or their products is not specifically a welfare-maximizing one. All of these authors consider their models first in terms of locations in a geographic space, and define the "optimal" locations so as to minimize total transportation costs. For Abbott and Smithies, this would also maximize total sales at given prices. There can be no a priori presumption, however, that a set of locations that minimizes total transportation costs and/or maximizes total sales also maximizes community welfare.

A system can be said to be operating *ideally* when it is operating in such a manner that no individual member of the community can be made better off

[10]Quasi-free entry can be defined as the existence of freedom for new firms to produce sufficiently close substitutes to allow them to compete away the economic profits of the existing firms. This concept recognizes that completely free entry would allow firms to duplicate exactly the quality and attributes of competitors (that is, to occupy the same characteristic vector as their competitor). It is consistent with the concept of entry developed by Chamberlin, *op. cit.*, pp. 199–201, and Robert Triffin in *Monopolistic Competition and General Equilibrium Theory* (Cambridge: Harvard University Press, 1940), pp. 85–88, for the theory of monopolitically competitive markets. A less cumbersome term "open competition" has been defined by P. W. S. Andrews in *On Competition in Economic Theory* (New York: St. Martin's, 1964), pp. 15–16, to cover markets ". . . *open to the entry of new competition*," and could be used to describe markets characterized by quasi-free entry.

[11]Abbott, *Quality and Competition*, *op. cit.*, pp. 143–149; and Arthur Smithies, "Optimum Location in Spatial Competition," *Journal of Political Economy*, Vol. XLIX (June, 1941), pp. 423–439; reprinted in *American Economic Association, Readings in Price Theory* (Homewood: Irwin, 1952), pp. 485–501.

[12]Harold Hotelling, "Stability in Competition," *Economic Journal*, Vol. XXXIX (March, 1929), pp. 41–57; reprinted in *American Economic Association, Readings in Price Theory*, *op. cit.*, pp. 467–484.

without some other member being made worse off.[13] This definition does not involve interpersonal utility comparisons and it allows for a multiplicity of ideal solutions. Since the problem of product location involves a large number of consumers with differing tastes, any change in the location of firms or products (for example, changes in the characteristic vector of a good), given prices, must result in a loss of welfare for some consumers and a gain for others. Without interpersonal utility comparisons, no unique welfare-optimal locations can be defined.

Long-run equilibrium will result in the "sort of ideal" described by Edward Chamberlin.[14] The typical firm in the market will be producing under conditions of zero profits at an output corresponding to a tangency of its subjective demand curve with its average-cost curve. The range of choice (that is, the number of characteristic vectors) offered to the consumer can be considered to be an ideal (for a given technology) in the sense that any introduction of a new good can only result in the elimination of an old good, and any reduction in the number of goods will lead only to a shift toward the origin of segments of the consumption-possibilities frontier due to the elimination of some characteristic vectors and the price increase following the reduced competition.

Nor could governmental regulation provide for a smaller range of choice (that is, fewer vectors) and lower prices without a welfare loss for some consumers. The lowest possible price that could be sustained by firms would be that corresponding to production at the minimum average-cost level of production. In order for some firms to produce at this output without a loss of welfare for some consumers, it is necessary that they be able to obtain customers for their output solely through price changes and not through the exit of rival firms. If they cannot, this means that some customers prefer another differentiated product even at a higher price and would suffer a welfare loss if they were denied this choice. But such firms could obtain sufficient customers only if their demand curve passed through or to the right of the minimum point of the average-cost curve, and this is inconsistent with conditions in long-run equilibrium in a monopolistically competitive market.[15]

Under the conditions of long-run equilibrium in a monopolistically competitive market, price will exceed marginal cost, and there is no reason to believe that relative prices will equal relative marginal costs. There can be no assurance, however, that a change in price and output that results in a reduction of the gap between relative prices and relative marginal costs will increase welfare. As indicated previously, any change in price and output

[13]See William J. Baumol, *Welfare Economics and the Theory of the State* (Cambridge: Harvard University Press, 1965), pp. 54–57 and pp. 161–172, for a discussion of alternative welfare criteria.

[14]Chamberlin, *op. cit.*, p. 94.

[15]The conclusions of this paragraph were first arrived at by Chamberlin, *op. cit.*, p. 94.

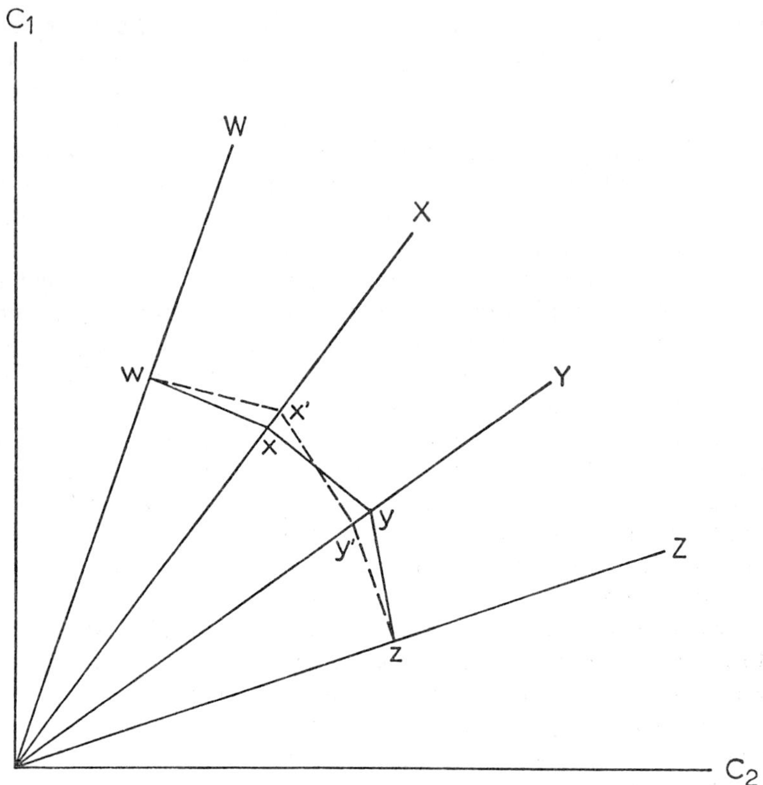

Figure 31-4

that leads to a change in the range of choice may cause a welfare loss for some consumers. Further, if the range of choice is reduced, there is no assurance that the gainers will receive enough improvement to be able to compensate the losers. Marginal cost pricing might be achieved in some markets through the use of declining rate price schedules without affecting the range of choice. But since no individual in a product-differentiated market is a consumer of every good, net losses may be inflicted on some individuals by adjustments in relative prices. In Figure 31-4, the frontier *wxyz* represents a situation in which

$$Px/MCx > Pw/MCw = Pz/MCz \\ > Py/MCy.$$

The frontier *wx'y'z* is obtained after a readjustment of the prices and outputs of *X* and *Y* such as to equate the *P/MC* ratio for all goods. (In a full employment context, any reduction of relative price and increase in output for one good must be accompanied by an increase in relative price and reduction of output for some other goods.) Although some consumers may be better off as a result of this readjustment, it is obvious from Figure 31-4 that any individual with tastes which lead him to specialize in Y or to consume a combination of Y and Z will be made worse off. Hence, the price structure in a product-differentiated market under conditions of long-run equilibrium with quasi-free entry is such that, in the absence of income redistribution, no alternative set of prices can be shown to be a clear improvement for some without losses for others.

Summary

(1) An examination of consumer welfare with product-differentiated markets must include a consideration not only of the relative output of each good, but also the number of goods offered and their quality and attributes.

(2) Under short-run conditions with positive economic profits, the introduction of new goods can be expected to lead to an increase in the welfare of some consumers without a welfare loss for other consumers (but with a loss for some entrepreneurs), provided that no existing good is eliminated. If an existing good is eliminated from the marketplace by a new introduction or a new price structure, it is possible, though not necessary, that the new introduction or price structure could increase consumption opportunities sufficiently to leave all consumers at least as well off as before.

(3) In the long run, with quasi-free entry, the variety of goods offered will reflect the distribution of consumers' tastes, profits will tend toward zero, and prices will be as low as possible given the costs of factors of production, the technical constraints on production, and the range of choice.

(4) In long-run equilibrium, the range of choice or variety of goods offered can be considered ideal in the sense that any change in this range of choice or variety, for a given technology and full employment, must result in a loss of welfare for some individuals.

(5) In long-run equilibrium relative prices will not equal relative marginal costs. The equivalence of relative prices and relative marginal costs is a necessary but not sufficient condition for a welfare *maximizing* optimum in the usual Pareto model. This equivalence, however, is not a necessary condition for an *ideal* allocation of resources in product-differentiated markets. A change reducing the difference between relative prices and relative marginal costs may cause a real loss for some consumers. Such a change is unambiguously an improvement only if compensation is made to the losers.

32. PECUNIARY AND TECHNOLOGICAL EXTERNALITY, FACTOR RENTS, AND SOCIAL COSTS*

Dean A. Worcester, Jr.†

Analysis of external effects in production has turned during the last 15 years from analysis of pecuniary and technological economies and diseconomies of well defined industries (and a belief that the effects are minor),[1] to analysis of interdependence among very few, often only two, individual utility or production functions (and the belief that the effects may be important).[2] This shift seems to have been inspired by Ronald Coase [4]. He is the first to have shown that firms in competitive industries which have interdependent production functions will find negotiations that properly adjust for the externality to be profitable. He also shows that merger of the two firms will result in optimal resource allocation.

No one has argued recently that all of the externalities in even a small enterprise economy can be overcome by negotiation, merger of the interdependent firms, or by wholesale merger of all firms into an administratively planned economy. On the contrary, recent work has emphasized the difficulties that make even conceptual solutions appear virtually impossible for a wide range of cases.

Neoclassical analysis, which rests on the relationships between firms and industries, is utilized in this paper for five reasons.

---

*From the *American Economic Review*, Vol. LIX, No. 5 (December, 1969), pp. 873–885. Reprinted by permission of the publisher and the author.

†Dean A. Worcester, Jr., Professor of Economics, University of Washington. The author wishes to thank José Encarnacion and J. Timothy Peterson for their helpful comments on an earlier draft and the anonymous reader for many helpful suggestions and especially for skillful excisions which sharpened this paper and provided much grist for additional work.

[1]The traditional literature came of age with Pigou's [15] *Economics of Welfare*, which extended Marshall's treatment [11] and Young's [23] constructive review of Pigou's earlier *Wealth and Welfare* before the first World War. It reached its first plateau in the 1920's with the controversy among Clapham [5], Robertson [17], and Pigou [14] over "Those Empty Economic Boxes" and Knight's article [9]. Viner [21] systematized the literature in the early 1930's. Ellis and Fellner [8] and Lerner [10] made contributions during the 1940's. The first satisfactory statement distinguishing between technological and pecuniary economies, Samuelson notwithstanding [18, p. 209], seems to have been made by Baumol [1], although he does not claim originality.

[2]The recent analysis seems to have begun with Meade [12] and has been continued by Scitovsky [19], Buchanan and Stubblebine [3], Davis and Whinston [6], Turvey [20], and Wellisz [22]. It is well summarized up to 1965 by Mishan [13], but continues, in the work of Plott [16], Buchanan [2], Dolbear [7], and others.

(1) It is adequate to reveal the basic source of externalities.

(2) It provides a logical progression of steps for the extension of the analysis.

(3) It is more readily applicable to feasible social controls that can, in many cases, reduce the considerable distortions due to the presence of externalities.

(4) It lends itself to an analysis of the welfare effects of alternative market structures in the presence of externalities.

(5) It is appropriate for both separable and nonseparable cost functions as defined by Otto Davis and Andrew Whinston [6, p. 245].

The principal points to be made here are:

(1) Technological economies and diseconomies occur when the firms comprising the industry are not able to equalize the ratios of marginal products to factor price ratios which reflect alternative costs, because one or more of the factor costs to the firm do not equal opportunity cost to the industry (or to society). This is often the case, arising when the technical production function of an industry is not accommodated properly by the prevailing system of ownership, legal rights and the like. Technological diseconomies exist when, in addition to discrepancies between the ratios of marginal products to opportunity costs, the firms' average and marginal cost curves shift upwards as the total demand for some resource rises thus generating a rising industry supply price.[3] Technological economies exist when the firms' curves fall under these circumstances. Pecuniary economies (diseconomies) exist when the industry average cost is falling (rising) but the marginal equalities between factor prices which reflect alternative social costs and their marginal products prevail.

(2) The size of the welfare loss associated with economies and diseconomies (henceforth referred to simply as economies unless otherwise specified) is very much affected by the particular type of externality present and the structure of the industry in question. The types of externalities considered are pecuniary or technological and the types of industry structures are competition, simple and first degree discriminating monopoly, and simple and first degree discriminating monopsony.

(3) It is useful to distinguish economies that are internal to an industry from those that are external to it because some industry structures offset technological externalities when they are internal to a specific industry, but cannot when they are external.

The plan for this paper is as follows:

(1) A linear homogeneous production function is described which will provide the basis for theoretical analysis.

(2) The analysis relevant to a competitive industry experiencing technological diseconomies is examined in detail so as to provide a solid basis for the treatment of other industry structures and for economies.

(3) The advantages and disadvantages of a few of the alternative ways of harmonizing private and social costs are examined. Analysis of specific cases, however, is left to another occasion.

---

[3] "Industry supply curve" refers to the locus of minimum average cost for a group of one or more firms producing a homogeneous product where the quantity of all factors (which are assumed to be homogeneous) and the numbers of firms are freely variable as industry output expands except that the total supply of some input or inputs may be fixed to the industry. It may be defined alternatively as the summed output of all firms in the industry at each price where the long-run and the short-run marginal cost are both equal to each alternative price. This is often referred to as the long-run supply price (*LRSP*) curve. "Industry marginal cost" (MC_I) is similarly construed, and is marginal to the industry average cost. Under competitive conditions, MC_I is a decision variable for no firm although it denotes marginal social cost (*MSC*) when a technological externality is present.

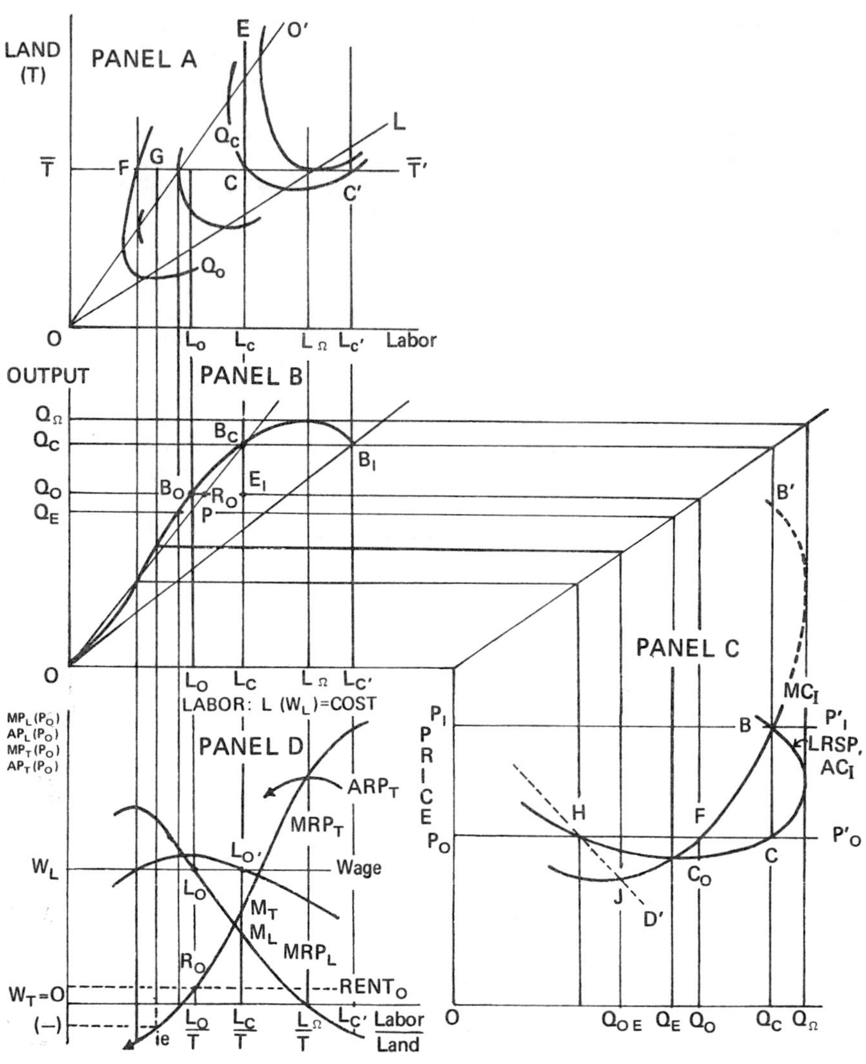

Figure 32-1

Production Function, Cost and Revenue and Related Functions for an Industry

THE PRODUCTION FUNCTION

The following analysis is illustrated by examples based upon a production function homogeneous of degree one, which displays ridge lines in the positive quadrant and which is considered to be relevant to a whole industry whether organized competitively or otherwise. This simple, comparatively well known function is chosen to emphasize the fact that neither technological nor pecuniary economies or diseconomies rest fundamentally upon the nature of the returns to the industry, but rather rest upon violation of the equality of the ratios of marginal products to their factor prices at equilibrium positions.[4]

Figure 32-1 consists of four panels which describe the production function, the costs and revenues, and the demand for factors of production by an industry that will alternately be considered to represent each of five industry structures. Panel A illustrates a production function of the postulated type with two inputs, labor (L), and land (T). Since proportionate increases in inputs yield proportionate increases in output, all outputs are readily determined if the output index is taken as 1.0 where isoquant Q_0 crosses ridge line OL. Land represents some input whose supply is fixed and which is useful only in the industry under consideration. Fixity of supply is not essential to the argument but is a useful simplifying assumption relevant to a number of important industries. Usefulness to but one industry, while not essential to the principal conclusion, is not only relevant to important industries but involves significant theoretical and practical distinctions. Removal of this restriction generates pecuniary externalities, which I wish to ignore. Panel B shows the relationship between output and total cost. It also provides a money scale that permits one to show alternative total revenue functions which correspond to alternative prices. The usual geometric relationships are used to find the industry marginal and average money cost curves shown in Panel C. They are drawn on the assumption that the price of land, W_T, is zero, and the price of labor, W_L, is positive at the level illustrated in Panel D. Rising factor costs to the industry are considered later when pecuniary economies are analyzed.

The lines on Panel D reveal the marginal products of both labor and land, calculated in principle for land as a shadow marginal product implied by the marginal rates of substitution at the intersections of the various isoproduct curves with the expansion path $\bar{T}\bar{T}_1$. The input axis of Panel D shows the proportion between the variable factor (labor) and the fixed factor (land) associated with each level of output. If price is a constant at P_0 (see Panel C), these curves also depict the value of the various marginal and average products, and provide a scale upon which money wages and rents can be shown.

No panel shows the position of an individual firm when the industry is viewed as being competitive. The average cost for the industry (AC_I) is identical to the conventional long-run supply curve (referred to henceforth as $LRSP$) traced out

[4]This point seems to have been made first by Abba P. Lerner in 1943 [10, Ch. 15, 16, 17] but, so far as I know, has not become part of the literature. Lerner did not thus distinguish between technological and pecuniary (dis)economies because his "Rule" is carefully designed to price indivisible and fixed factors according to what might now be termed their shadow marginal products. The present analysis attempts to show that this procedure converts technological into pecuniary diseconomies and thereby supports Lerner's conclusion that misallocation under these circumstances is nothing more than a failure to adhere to the equality of the ratios of factor prices to their respective marginal products. Lerner's handling of technological economies is just as advanced (virtually the 1968 level), if not so satisfactory. Acceptance of Lerner's procedure may have suffered because it directs attention to his proposed social control devices rather than his analysis, but fundamentally it seems simply to have been too neat.

by the loci of the average cost associated with the intersections of the long-run marginal cost and short-run marginal cost as the number of firms fluctuates in response to changed industry demand.[5] Whatever the industry structure, this curve is considered to represent minimum cost of production for each output when factor prices are fixed at W_L and W_T (Panel D).

The *LRSP* of a competitive industry as shown by the *LRSP* in Panel C may be said to reflect technological economies from zero output up to Q_E, and technological diseconomies beyond that point, because with constant factor prices the U-shape depends solely upon the production function for the industry. A corresponding function with the same shape reflects pecuniary economies where an optimal rent is charged. The size of the rent must vary as the industry price and optimal output varies. It will be a charge sufficient to make the private factor cost equal to its social cost.

COMPETITIVE EQUILIBRIUM FOR A SUB-INDUSTRY

To facilitate a clear distinction between rents and profits, consider first a sub-industry, catching a particular kind of fish from a particular fishing ground. It is assumed to comprise so small a part of the market for that species that its price is affected overwhelmingly by the demand for fish in general and only imperceptibly by its own output. Two of these narrowly defined industry demand curves are shown in Panel C, namely P_0P_0', and P_1P_1', and in Panel B by the corresponding total revenue curves, OB_c and OB_1. Such a sub-industry will expand output until profits fall to a level just sufficient to hold the firms in the industry, their summed outputs equalling the quantity demanded. The equilibrium output is in this case the same for both of these demand functions as is shown by Q_c (Panels B and C) and points *c* and *c′* on isoquant Q_c in Panel A. Where labor inputs exceed L_Ω (Panels A, B, and D), this competitive industry exhibits a true backward bending supply curve. Such have been observed in certain fisheries and oil fields with multiple owners, and probably exist for other common property resources and publicly supplied goods.[6] This happens because in the absence of a charge for land, the average value product of labor for each firm is equal to the wage rate at equilibrium, although the marginal factor cost to the industry is much higher. In this instance, all costs are labor

[5]Point *B* is marginal to *LRSP* at point *C*. The marginal cost to *LRSP* at point *B* is far higher and is shown inexactly as *B′*.

[6]An example of publicly supplied goods is streets, especially freeways that are so overloaded at peak hours as to suffer a reduction of traffic flow. If possible, rents should be charged during these periods without further impeding traffic flow. Such a system apparently is technically feasible. I have been told that the Netherland's traffic police use electronic devices which photograph speeding cars on certain freeways. Fines are charged against their owners, the photographed license plate providing the needed information for sending the bill. If such a system exists, it could be expanded to photograph all cars at rush periods; those choosing to use the freeway at that time would be billed for the rent.

costs, and the industry expands or contracts until abnormal profits are eliminated. This occurs where price $=$ *LRSP* in the product market (point *C* in Panel C), although marginal cost to the industry is at point *B*.

At the higher price, P_1, valuable resources with positive opportunity costs are employed, specifically additional labor in the amount of L_cL_c' (Panels A and B), with no net addition to total production, the marginal product of labor being positive at first but negative beyond L_Ω. Lesser, but still substantial waste occurs if price is P_0, output Q_c, and inputs L_c/T. Attention is henceforth confined to the analysis of this lesser amount of waste.

It is immediately evident from Panel D that, where inputs are L_c/T, the marginal product of labor to the industry point M_L is a bit less than 50 percent of the wage rate, and that the marginal product of land, M_T, is far above the (zero) price at which it enters the firms' cost functions. This relationship is also shown in Panel A by the negative slope of the industry isoquant at point *C* where isoquant Q_c is not tangential to the isocost line L_cCE. The latter is vertical because the price of land is zero. The inevitable conclusion follows (however paradoxical it might have seemed to Ricardo or Marx). Although labor gets the whole return, social output is much reduced because labor is being wasted for want of price on land. Labor is being wasted because its alternative marginal contribution to other industries exceeds its marginal value product here. Output should, of course, be contracted until labor's marginal productivity to the industry (rather than its average productivity) equals its wage. This occurs at point L_0/T in Panel D and corresponds to an optimal output of Q_0 in Panels B and C. At that point, a positive rent exists since the marginal product of land is R_0 (Panel D). This is equivalent to the difference between the average and marginal products of labor (Panel D), the gap between total revenue and total cost, B_0R_0, shown in Panel B, and the difference between *LRSP* and price times the output, $C_0F(P_0F)$ in Panel C.

Ownership of the land will tend strongly to produce an optimal level of production. In this case, where output of the sub-industry does not affect the output price, it does not matter whether ownership of land is concentrated or dispersed.

This treatment seems one-sided since the classical remedy via taxation is ignored. In the case under discussion, taxation, either of inputs or outputs is, in principle, an effective means for optimizing output. An optimal license type tax on inputs is equivalent to rents. A tax on the output sufficient to reduce the net price to suppliers to C_0 (Panel C) would also result in optimal output. Taxation is widely regarded as superior to rents because the tax revenues supposedly have more desirable income effects than do rents. There are disadvantages in administration, however, for it is also true that the tax rate, whether levied against inputs or outputs, must be optimally adjusted for every change of product price, factor costs, and technology that affects factor proportions. One can believe that the adjustment process via changing rents will be more finely tuned than via tax adjustment.

WELFARE LOSS DUE TO FAILURE TO CHARGE RENTS

The welfare loss resulting from a failure to charge the optimum rent in the case illustrated by Figure 32-1 can be shown by either of two areas in Panel C, or by a comparison of cost and revenue in Panel B. If price is P_0 and if no rents are charged, equilibrium output is Q_c and both total revenue and total cost for the industry are Q_cB_c (Panel B), or Q_cCP_0O in Panel C.[7] Yet marginal social cost, which is equal to MC_I in Panel C, is Q_cB, about 60 percent higher than P_0. If maximum rents are charged, output drops to Q_0 and unit costs to Q_0C_0 (Panel C) where the social optimum is indicated by the intersection of MC_I with P_0 at point F. Total costs (excluding rents) and revenues are equal to Q_0B_0 and Q_0R_0 respectively on Panel B.

Comparison with the competitive equilibrium shows that consumers lose satisfaction for which they would have paid R_0E_1 (Panel B), while resources valued at B_0E_1 are saved and presumably used to produce an equivalent value of goods and services in other industries. The net gain, which is the largest attainable, is B_0R_0: precisely equal to the maximum rent.

The same result is illustrated, perhaps more persuasively, in Panel C where the rent and the welfare gain appear as different areas. The maximum rent is shown by the rectangle with sides P_0F and FC_0. The welfare gain resulting from the imposition of the rent is shown by the approximately triangular area FCB. The fact that these two areas must be equal appears obvious from Panel B, but it holds only when price is equal to marginal revenue for the industry. Otherwise the rectangular area includes a combined maximum of rent and profit, which occurs when output is restricted below the optimum level and the demand curve is sloping. The profit plus rent rectangle is augmented, but the welfare gain is reduced. This situation is analyzed below.

"TECHNOLOGICAL" DISECONOMIES

Competition, Normal Industry Demand

Now that the flat sub-industry demand curve has enabled us to define the marginal social cost function and to relate it to rents, it is time to admit that even sub-industries typically confront demand curves that slope downward and toward the right as illustrated in Figure 32-2, which is otherwise the equivalent of Panel C. The relationships among physical inputs and outputs, and the prices of the factors remain the same as in Figure 32-1, and the now sloping demand curve is drawn to leave the no rent competitive price P_0 and output Q_c unchanged. The money demand for factors as a whole would (if shown) be rotated clockwise around their former equilibrium positions.

[7]It should be kept in mind that each firm is in zero pure profit equilibrium with $MC=AC=P$ when the industry operates at Q_c, or indeed at any other output where $LRSP = P$.

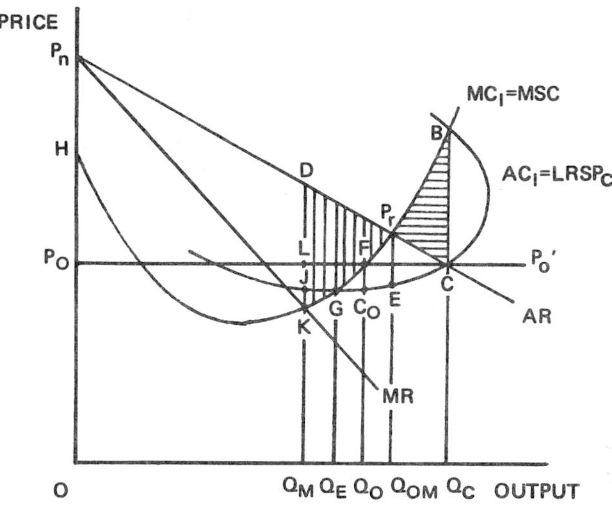

Figure 32-2
Optima: Technological Diseconomies

The principal modification of the analysis is the reduction in the size of the welfare gain incident to the imposition of an optimal rent to the shaded area CBP_r, and an increase of optimal rent to P_rE per unit of output. In this case, optimal rents are approximately doubled while the potential welfare gain is lessened. Each of these modifications follows from the fact that a smaller adjustment of output below the competitive level suffices to achieve the optimal result, since price rises as output is reduced so that optimum output and price occur at Q_{OM} and P_r.

Simple and Discriminating Monopsony

The same situation illustrated by Figure 32-2 can also be viewed as a monopsony. Suppose that the freely competing fishermen must sell to a single cannery (perhaps a local government monopoly). The cannery may be completely devoid of monopoly power, selling its products in distant markets in competition with hundreds of rivals. In this case the appropriate demand curve for the fish is the horizontal line, P_0P_0'. A maximizing simple monopsonist will buy quantity Q_0 at price C_0 which it resells at price OP_0 plus its value added per unit. His profit is equal to FC_0 per unit of output, exactly the maximum rent under competition. Output is induced to the optimal level because his profits are maximized where MC_I (the marginal social cost in this case) equals price. The price paid to the fishermen, C_0, is on the *LRSP* for the industry, so only the correct number of firms and levels of output are induced. If the demand curve is P_nC, the competitive optimum (with rents) is attained at output Q_{OM}, and fishermen's price E.

A discriminating monopsonist, on the other hand, will overproduce. This is illustrated by the extreme case of the perfectly discriminating monopsonist who drives all or nothing bargains with each fisherman, or pays a minimum price for each unit purchased thus making the discriminating monopsonist's marginal cost curve equal to his average cost curve which is the *LRSP* for the industry as shown in Figures 32-1 and 32-2. A discriminating monopolist maximizes profit when output is carried to the competitive no rent level, Q_c. Welfare loss (*FCB*) is the same as under competition; profits exceed optimal rent slightly more than FC_0 C.[8]

Simple Monopoly[9]

Consider again the effect of the sloping industry demand curve $P_n C$. Should the firms in this industry form a perfectly efficient cartel such that the control over output becomes absolute and the industry cost function is not raised above that for competition, the cartel would, if a simple monopolist, maximize its profit at Q_M. Price is then $Q_M D$. Because it has control over entry, it will not overuse the resource (which we have assumed thus far to be useful only in this industry), and it will consider the effect of its output on price. Thus, marginal revenue will be made equal to marginal social cost.

All of the factors (the price of which we continue to hold constant) including the natural resources are underused by monopolists. Compared to the competitive result when an optimal rent is paid, value of output to the consumers is reduced by the area under DP_r while costs are reduced only by the area under KP_r.

---

[8]The appropriate profit calculation is somewhat troublesome because external economies are shown up to Q_E and external diseconomies thereafter. In a later section, we find the direction of adjustments reversed for external economies. In the present instance, it seems most reasonable to assume that the discriminating monopsonist will use his power to hold purchase prices to the minimum average cost, *G*, for supplies up to quantity Q_E. The addition to profit (in addition to the rent equivalent) resulting from perfect discrimination is that shown by $FC_0 C$, plus the difference between buying prices *G* and C_0 for every unit up to Q_E plus a diminishing sliver of profit between Q_E and Q_0.

[9]The nature of costs under monopoly and monopsony are often insufficiently defined. If long-run monopoly and competitive equilibria are to be contrasted on the assumption of long-lived barriers to entry, then full adjustment to alternative output levels must be permitted. This includes alteration of number of establishments, centralized and decentralized control systems, and the like. When this is done, the average cost curve of the monopolist comes from the same family as the *LRSP* of the competitive industry. The U-shapes which are universally drawn for monopolists are questionable generalizations.

It seems much more likely that they are like the *LRSP* under competition plus an additional cost per unit to cover the additional costs of coordination and preservation of the barriers to entry. Yet, some economies may also be forthcoming. Here the *LRSP* under competition and the *LAC* under monopoly are treated as identical, and analysis is confined to the effect of structure on the conditions for equilibrium and their effect on optimal resource allocation. A U-shaped *LRSP* is used only for illustrative purposes and to reduce the number of figures, since that shape contains all three types of returns.

There is a welfare loss of the shaded area $DP_r K$ to be set against the welfare gain of $P_r BC$, the other shaded area, as compared to competitive equilibrium when no rent is paid. Simple monopoly may be either better or worse than competition if no rents are charged depending upon the relative elasticities of the industry demand and of the long-run average cost curve of the monopolist, assuming the latter to be identical to the long-run supply price for the industry when organized competitively.

In this example, rent per unit of output falls to JL, but profit per unit of output is LD. In either case, the gains, if any, to the consumer are small compared to the gains in profits plus rents to the cartelizers, when both are measured in money. One must imagine brutish consumers and epicurean businessmen to be willing to urge the merits of increased efficiency by monopolization even in those cases where there is a clear welfare gain. A government monopoly might find approbation if the industry is thought to be essential and if the profits plus rents were utilized to accelerate economic growth, but it is not a welfare optimum.

A sophisticated combination of subsidies that effect marginal costs and induce larger output and a license type tax to capture pure profits or rents can, in principle, produce an optimum result under simple monopoly. The relevant curves must be accurately known, and prompt adjustments made when they shift if an optimum is to be attained.

Perfectly Discriminating Monopoly

A perfectly discriminating monopolist, whose long-run average cost is identical to the competitive long-run supply curve, would carry output to the socially optimal level (Q_{OM} in Figure 32-2) provided that variable inputs' wages are determined independently of industry output and that fixed inputs are specific to the industry, as is the case here.

Implicit rent is restored to the maximum level (EP_r per unit of output) and profit plus rent is maximized ($P_n P_r KH$). The reason for the good allocation result is that all social costs are internalized by the decision-making unit when such an industry is monopolized, and the demand curve is also the industry marginal revenue curve. This is true with perfect discrimination since the firm need not cut the price on any unit of sales in order to extend its sales further by means of lower prices to otherwise excluded buyers. The transfer to the monopolist is enormous and may be more objectionable to many social critics than the misallocation that is overcome, but this is a different problem.

PECUNIARY DISECONOMIES

Virtually all of the conclusions which relate differing industry structure to optimal allocation in the presence of technological diseconomies must be reversed when pecuniary diseconomies cause cost changes as an industry expands or contracts. Optimal allocation of resources occurs under competition and perfectly discriminating monopsony; restricted production and welfare loss is a consequence of simple monopoly, perfectly discriminating monopoly, and of simple monopsony.

The textbook distinction between technological and pecuniary diseconomies is that the latter is accounted for by rising factor costs per unit of output, not the nature of the production function. The preceding analysis has shown this distinction to be but a special case of a more fundamental difference. Technological diseconomies occur when the cost of output is rising and the cost of some input to the firms is less than its opportunity costs to its industry without reference to the shape of the factor supply curves. Hence, any rise in output cost is pecuniary if the marginal equalities are maintained between the prices of factors which reflect opportunity costs and their respective marginal products. Whenever this is true, the $LRSP$ is the curve of marginal social costs (MSC), and optimal output is found where $LRSP = P$. This is true because any increase in the marginal cost of output per unit reflects either (1) a rise in the opportunity cost of the factors due to expansion of this industry which thereby raises their opportunity costs in each of their uses, or (2) because of lower marginal productivity, or both.

This may be illustrated with Figures 32-1 and 32-2 when optimum rents are charged. The $LRSP$ for a competitive industry becomes identical to the MSC (which, it will be recalled, coincides with the former MC_I). These are shown in Figure 32-3 as $LRSP_{pec}$ and MC_{tech}. The MSC curve, of course, does not shift.

A new marginal cost to the industry arises which is marginal to the new $LRSP$. It is denoted MC_{pec} in Figure 32-3, and is relevant to pecuniary externalities.

The welfare effects relevant to the five alternative market structures are readily compared using the standard definitions of equilibrium. Optimal output occurs at Q_0 where MSC = Demand. This is also the competitive equilibrium because $LRSP_{pec} \equiv MSC$. Simple monopoly operates at Q_M where $MR = MC_{pec}$ and produces a welfare loss of $P_M P_0 N$. Unlike the situation where the diseconomies are technological and monopolistic restriction tends to offset competitive overexpansion, this is an unmitigated, even a multiplied, loss because the firm's marginal cost lies above marginal social cost and its marginal revenue lies below the demand curve in the relevant ranges. A perfectly discriminating monopolist maximizes where MC_{pec} = Price. A welfare loss of $P_s P_0 S$ results since MC_{pec} lies above MSC.

Viewed as a simple monopsony, the supply curve to a single buyer in this competitive market is $LRSP_{pec} = MSC$. The buyer's marginal cost is, therefore, MC_{pec} which he will set equal to his demand curve, and buy Q_{msy} at price S.[10]

[10]The reader may note an anomaly here. $LRSP_{pec}$ is taken as the supply price even to the left of point G where the optimum rent is zero. This implies an optimum negative rent where $LRSP_{pec} < LRSP_{tech}$. This is indeed the correct implication. In this range, technological economies exist which involve negative shadow marginal products for the unpriced fixed factor. This case is discussed in the next section.

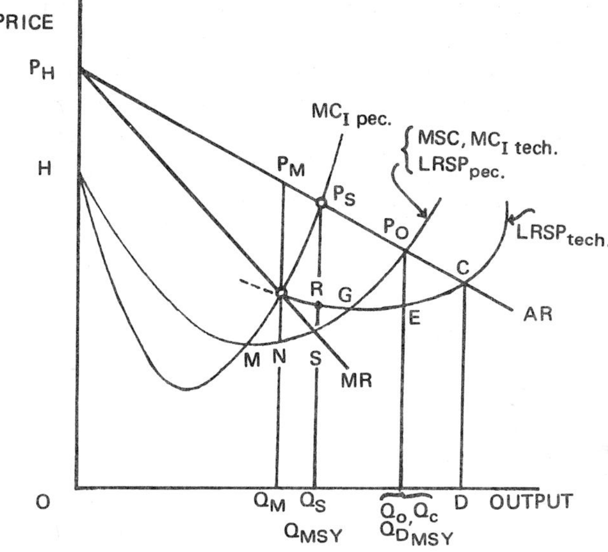

Figure 32-3

Optima: Technological and Pecuniary Diseconomies

Again the welfare loss is $P_s P_O S$. A perfectly discriminating monopsonist will find his marginal factor cost to be equal to the $LRSP_{pec}$. Profit maximization occurs at Q_O which is the same as the competitive output and is a welfare optimum according to the usual definitions. Profits, however, are not normal, being equal to $P_H P_O MH$.

All of the noncompetitive structures garner profits, but the relationship between the size of the profits and the size of the welfare loss is highly irregular.

EXTERNAL ECONOMIES

Figure 32-1 illustrates too the welfare results of alternative structures for external technological and pecuniary economies. The dashed line in Panel C is interpreted as the industry demand curve. The cost curves of Panel C up to Q_E, and the corresponding portions of the associated curves in the other panels in Figure 32-1, relate the alternative equilibria to the basic technological and factor price constraints where external economies accompany the expansion of the industry. Market demand is such that with the most efficient organization of production, competitive equilibrium must occur at point H (with zero price of land) at which point $LRSP$ is still falling. Tracing this equilibrium back to Panel A, we find point F which is outside of the economic sector because the slope of the isoquant denotes a negative marginal product for land. Tracing this combination to Panel D, we discover not only that the marginal product of land is well below its (zero) price to the firms in the industry, but that the marginal product of labor is correspondingly far above its wage rate. Labor is being wasted by insufficiently intensive use. Yet profits are only normal.

Point *J* (Panel C) represents optimal allocation where demand = *MSC*. If its associated output, Q_{0e}, is traced back to Panel A, we find a smaller but still negative marginal product of land implied by the interpolated slope of the isoquant at point *G*. The corresponding points in Panel D seem to suggest a continued failure to bring the marginal cost of labor into equality with its wage rate, but this is an illusion. The price of the product is about one-fourth lower at *J*, as compared to *H*, so that the value of the marginal product in Panel D should be altered proportionately. This produces the desired equality.

The value of the marginal product of land requires a similar adjustment, but it must remain negative at the optimal output and combination of inputs. Thus, the optimal marginal product of land must be negative, and a competitive industry can produce at the optimal rate only if a negative rent (a subsidy) of optimal size be paid for the use of the unpriced resource.

The need for a subsidy to competitive industries to induce optimal levels of operation in the presence of technological economies has long been known. The very similar argument favoring subsidization of regulated monopolies when economies of scale are internal to the firm is based on the same analytical conclusion, that profitable operation is impossible at the socially optimal rate of output.

The equilibrium positions for other industry structures where external technological or pecuniary economies exist are illustrated in Figure 32-4 which reproduces Panel C and also includes the cost curves relevant to pecuniary economies. Subscripts $_t$ and $_p$ are used to designate points relevant, respectively, to technological and pecuniary externalities. The analysis of all four conditions, technological and pecuniary diseconomies and economies, is summarized in Table 32-1.

It is evident that a given structure yields the same general welfare effect whether such external effects are diseconomies or economies, and that a structure that optimizes when economies are pecuniary will fail to do so when they are technological and vice versa.

EXTERNALITIES EXTERNAL TO THE INDUSTRY

One important limitation has been retained thus far, the industry concept and the implication that externalities exist only among firms producing a homogeneous product. When this limitation is removed, choice among means for correcting for externalities is reduced in principle and virtually eliminated as a practical matter. One can argue persuasively that optimization by simple

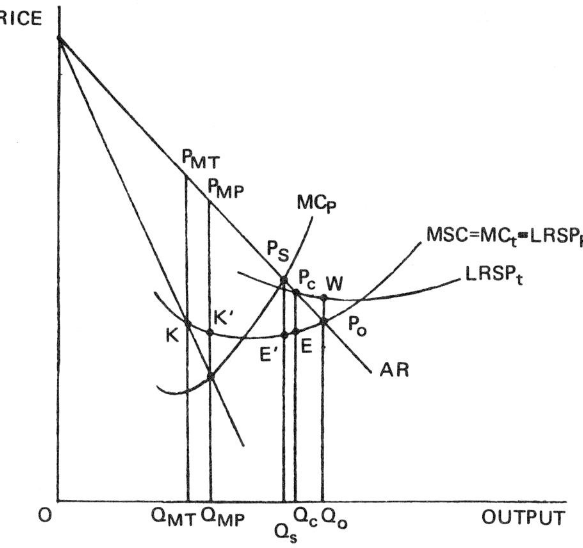

Figure 32-4

Optima: Technological and Pecuniary Economies

monopsony or by organizing perfect monopolistic discrimination is entirely impractical in any case even if income effects should be ignored. If the economies or diseconomies are external not only to the firms in an industry, but also to any given industry, i.e., among firms that are not producing homogeneous products, the structural options are lost even in principle. An optimizing policy must attempt to achieve competitive equilibrium with inputs priced according to their alternative costs. This is true because it is virtually certain that the factor proportions of different users will differ so that the improperly priced factor will not be properly allocated by discrimination or regulation among competing users. The foregoing analysis assumes that the improperly priced factor has but one use and will be given an optimal implied value by a monopolist who treats it as a residual. This implied price is the rent. If the improperly priced factor is used in two or more industries, its allocation among them needs to be such that its implicit marginal value to each industry is the same.[11]

ARE ANY BOXES EMPTY?

It is now possible to list the various types of external economies. They fall conveniently into eight categories. Each is listed below with an illustrative example. This classification should not obscure the more basic fact

[11]This point is also valid within an industry when the various firms utilize different processes and have different implied values for the input fixed to the industry.

that any technological economy or diseconomy can be converted into a pecuniary one by appropriate pricing of inputs. The listing reflects the author's judgment of the typical pricing practices in the United States. These should be examined more carefully after alternative methods of adjusting for technological economies and diseconomies have been surveyed and refined.

Table 32-1

Equilibrium Conditions and Welfare Loss Due to External Diseconomies and Economies, by Type of Industry Structure

Structure	Equilibrium Condition (all cases)	Diseconomies (See Figure 32-3)		Economies (See Figure 32-4)	
		Price Quantity	Welfare Loss	Price Quantity	Welfare Loss
Competition					
Technological	$LRSP_t = P$	C, D	$P_0 CE$	P_c, Q_c	$P_c P_0 E$
Pecuniary	$LRSP_p = P$	P_0, Q_0	optimum	P_0, Q_0	optimum
Simple Monopoly					
Technological	$MC_t = MR$	P_s, Q_s	$P_s P_0 S$	P_{MT}, Q_{MT}	$P_{MT} P_0 K$
Pecuniary	$MC_p = MR$	P_m, Q_m	$P_M P_0 N$	P_{MP}, Q_{MP}	$P_{MP} P_0 K'$
Discriminating Monopoly					
Technological	$MC_t = P$	P_0, Q_0	optimum	P_0, Q_0	optimum
Pecuniary	$MC_p = P$	P_s, Q_s	$P_s P_0 S^*$	P_s, Q_s	$P_s P_0 E'$
Simple Monopsony (where demand is seen as marginal value product and *LRSP* as the supply function)					
Technological†	$MC_t = MFC = P$	E, Q_0	optimum	W, Q_0	optimum
Pecuniary	$MC_p = MFC = P$	S, Q_s	$P_s P_0 S^*$	E', Q_s	$P_s P_0 E'$
Discriminating Monopsony					
Technological	$LRSP_t = P$	C, D	$P_0 CE$	same as simple monopsony**	
Pecuniary	$LRSP_p = P$	P_0, Q_0	optimum		

†Note that the wage lies on the supply curve *LRSP* even when the supply curve lies above the demand curve.

*This is equal to the loss for a simple monopolist under technological economies only by coincidence.

**Discriminating monopsony yields lower profits than simple monopsony when the supply curve is downward sloping because discrimination raises the average price of the factor. Hence a firm with power to discriminate will not utilize it.

A. Externalities which are internal to a specific industry:

(1) Technological diseconomy: common property resources; fisheries, and oil formations used by competing firms.

(2) Technological economy: public utilities; especially electric power, water supply, sewage disposal where a single price covers all costs.

(3) Pecuniary diseconomy: the most common case, where expansion encounters rising factor prices and/or declining marginal productivity.

(4) Pecuniary economy: increased specialization via purchased inputs or subcontracting with expansion of industry output; clothing, aircraft.

B. Externalities which are external to a particular industry:

(5) Technological diseconomy: most public services which are supplied without a charge to the user according to use; city streets, air.

(6) Technological economy: basic research, exploration, law and order, provision of information service.

(7) Pecuniary diseconomy: there are many of these; high cost of living, and wages in the larger cities as city size increases.

(8) Pecuniary economies: general specialization.

The same industry will often appear in both type A and type B. Thus, the internal technological economy for electric power production (#2) can also be cited for external pecuniary economy (#8).

SUMMARY

All external effects are found in principle to be reducible by correct input pricing to economies or diseconomies. This holds for separable and non-separable externalities in production and for externalities viewed either in terms of specific firms or among industries. Different industry structures produce optimal allocation either for technological or for pecuniary externalities if the externalities are internal to an industry and the firms therein use the same factor proportions. When these conditions do not hold, only competitive structures and pecuniary externalities suffice to produce an optimum in the absence of very complicated combinations of taxes and subsidies which require a wealth of accurate detailed data utilized with consummate insight and speed.

REFERENCES

[1] Baumol, W. J. *Welfare Economics and the Theory of the State.* Cambridge, Mass.: Harvard University Press, 1952.

[2] Buchanan, J. M. "Joint Supply, Externality and Optimality." *Economica*, Vol. XXXIII (November, 1966), pp. 404–415.

[3] ———, and W. C. Stubblebine. "Externality." *Economica*, Vol. XXIX (November, 1962), pp. 371–384.

[4] Coase, R. "The Problem of Social Cost." *The Journal of Law and Economics*, Vol. III (October, 1960), pp. 1–44.

[5] Clapham, J. H. "Of Empty Economic Boxes." *Economic Journal*, Vol. XXXII (September, 1922), pp. 305–314. In K. E. Boulding and G. J. Stigler. *AEA Readings in Economic Theory*, Vol. VI. Homewood, Ill.: R. D. Irwin, 1952; and Clapham. "Rejoinder." *Economic Journal*, Vol. XXXII (December, 1922), pp. 560–563.
[6] Davis, O. A., and A. Whinston. "Externalities, Welfare and the Theory of Games." *Journal of Political Economy*, Vol. LXX (June, 1962), pp. 241–262.
[7] Dolbear, F. T., Jr. "On the Theory of Optimal Externality." *American Economic Review*, Vol. LVII (March, 1967), pp. 90–103.
[8] Ellis, H., and W. Fellner. "External Economies and Diseconomies." *American Economic Review*, Vol. XXXIII (September, 1943), pp. 493–511; reprinted in *Readings* [5].
[9] Knight, F. H. "Fallacies in the Interpretation of Social Cost." *Quarterly Journal of Economics*, Vol. XXXVIII (August, 1924), pp. 582–606; reprinted in *Readings* [5].
[10] Lerner, A. P. *The Economics of Control.* New York: Macmillan, 1943.
[11] Marshall, A. *Principles of Economics*, 8th ed. London: Macmillan, 1920.
[12] Meade, J. E. "External Economies and Diseconomies in a Competitive Situation." *Economic Journal*, Vol. LXVII (March, 1952), pp. 54–67.
[13] Mishan, E. J. "Reflections on Recent Developments in the Concept of External Effects." *Canadian Journal of Economics and Political Science*, Vol. XXXI (February, 1965), pp. 1–34.
[14] Pigou, A. C. "Empty Economic Boxes: A Reply." *Economic Journal*, Vol. XXXII (December, 1922), pp. 458–465; reprinted in *Readings* [5].
[15] ———. *The Economics of Welfare*, 4th ed. London: Macmillan, 1952.
[16] Plott, C. R. "Externalities and Corrective Taxes." *Economica*, Vol. XXXIII (February, 1966), pp. 84–87.
[17] Robertson, D. H. "Those Empty Boxes." *Economic Journal*, Vol. XXIV (March, 1924), pp. 16–30; reprinted in *Readings* [5].
[18] Samuelson, P. A. *Foundations of Economic Analysis*, Atheneum edition. New York: 1965.
[19] Scitovsky, T. "Two Concepts of External Economies." *Journal of Political Economy*, Vol. LVII (April, 1954), pp. 143–151.
[20] Turvey, Ralph. "On Divergencies Between Social Cost and Private Cost." *Economica*, Vol. XXX (August, 1963), pp. 309–313.
[21] Viner, J. "Cost Curves and Supply Curves." *Z. Nationalφkon.*, Vol. III (1931), pp. 23–46; reprinted in *Readings* [5].
[22] Wellisz, S. "On External Diseconomies and the Government Assisted Invisible Hand." *Economica*, Vol. XXXI (November, 1964), pp. 345–362.
[23] Young, A. "Pigou's Wealth and Welfare Review." *Quarterly Journal of Economics*, Vol. XXVII (August, 1913), pp. 672–686.

SECTION VIII. SOME APPLICATIONS OF PRICE THEORY

In this Section, some applications of price theory are made to the problems of pricing pioneering products, gasoline price wars, and the adoption of trading stamps by retailers.

In his analysis of the pricing of pioneering products, Dean considers such factors as monopoly pricing, the role of cost, and pricing strategy. Schendel and Balestra suggest an economic motivation for gasoline price cutting and construct a model which considers the reaction of competitors and demonstrates the conditions under which a strategy of price cutting would be profitable. In looking at whether retailers should adopt trading stamps, Sherman considers several possible payoff patterns and some of the problems involved in reaching an equilibrium number of stores giving stamps.

Dean states that pricing pioneer products, which he defines as products which incorporate "a major innovation," is "one of the most important and puzzling of marketing problems." In this article, Dean is concerned with the level of price of the new product and not with its price structure.

Dean maintains that new product pricing, if the product is "truly novel," in essence is monopoly pricing. The controlling consideration is the worth of the new product to the buyer, not the cost of it to the seller. However, he points out several factors which modify this monopoly power. He also indicates the great importance of considering the effect of the price of a new product on its sales volume.

Dean maintains that the buyers' viewpoint should be controlling in the pricing of new products and points out that the producer of a new product may determine its relative attractiveness to potential buyers by comparing it with existing products. An important aspect of this type of comparison is one of determining the price premium over benchmark products which the new product's superiority will most profitably warrant, which Dean calls "the most intricate and challenging problem of new product pricing."

In looking at the use of costs in new product pricing, Dean indicates that three questions of theory must be answered. He discusses these questions, which relate to: (1) Whose cost? (2) Which cost? and (3) What role?

Dean points out that a major strategy decision in pricing a new product involves the choice between "skimming pricing" and "penetration pricing." He distinguishes between these two alternatives and discusses the conditions under which each is most appropriate. He also considers appropriate pricing policies for a new product which is in the later stages of the cycle of market and competitive maturity.

Dean concludes by stating some "pricing precepts" which have been suggested by his analysis.

Schendel and Balestra point out that although gasoline price wars are widespread and frequent, they are not well understood; in particular, it is often claimed that price cutting is not rational in the sense of short-run profit maximization. The purpose of this article is to suggest an "economic, rational motivation for a price cutting strategy intended to yield profits in the short run" and to develop a "reaction model which recognizes the institutional characteristics and legal constraints of retail gasoline marketing."

Schendel and Balestra suggest that the goal of profit maximization can lead to price cutting when cost reductions (particularly a lowered tank wagon price) take place for some competitors. Further, they indicate that the minor brand dealer is the one most likely to obtain lowered tank wagon prices and initiate price cuts from which he can expect some retaliation from his competitor, most frequently a major brand dealer. The authors then examine the two basic types of margin support agreements which are utilized by major brand suppliers to help their dealers to react and compete profitably with a retail price cut. They also consider the effects of the employment of these margin support agreements on the stability of gasoline prices.

Schendel and Balestra construct a reaction model in which they take into consideration the reaction of competitors. This model "suggests the conditions that must be met for profits to be realized and, along with estimates of competitive reaction times, it will permit computation of expected losses or expected gains for an individual firm from a price war." The authors then consider some of the possible pricing policy implications of the reaction model.

Sherman raises the question: "Should a retailer offer trading stamps?" He points out that there is no "ready basis" for answering this question in spite of the widespread use of stamps. Since the retailer's decision is either to offer stamps or not to offer them, a two-strategy, n-person, non-zero-sum game is used by the author to illustrate the effects of the retailer's choices.

One outcome which Sherman examines is that of a prisoner's (retailer's) dilemma. A second pattern of payoffs (no dilemma) is one in which all firms make more profit when all of them give trading stamps. Of these two situations, Sherman states that the former more accurately reflects the conditions facing the retailer who is considering the adoption of trading stamps.

The retailer must consider the possibility that all consumers do not desire trading stamps and that some would prefer to have, as examples, lower prices and/or more service instead of stamps. A third payoff pattern, which is a modification of the prisoner's dilemma, is used by Sherman to illustrate the case in which there are different degrees of consumer interest in stamp premium goods.

Sherman concludes that when a new promotional device, such as trading stamps, is introduced, retailers probably face a prisoner's dilemma type of choice as to whether or not to offer it. He points out that, in the final analysis, whether it is profitable for a firm to adopt trading stamps "depends on the collective choices of consumers; it depends on a voting process." He also relates the consumer choice process to the question of whether there can exist an equilibrium number of stores giving stamps.

33. PRICING PIONEERING PRODUCTS*

Joel Dean†

INTRODUCTION

Pricing pioneer products is one of the most important and puzzling of marketing problems. The high proportion of new products which fail in the market place proclaims the difficulty of pricing them correctly.

A pioneer product is here defined as one which incorporates a major innovation. Its market is therefore, at the outset, ill-defined, since potential applications cannot be foreseen with precision. Pricing decisions usually have to be made recognizing wide margins of error in the forecasts of demand, cost, and competitors' capabilities.

The difficulty of pricing new products is enhanced by the dynamic deterioration of the competitive status of most new products, which decay is speeded by today's high rate of innovation. This makes the life cycle of a new product's economic status a strategic consideration in practical pricing.

This paper is concerned with the level of price of the new product, not its price structure. For example, the average price per pound of a new plastic, not the structure of price differentials depending on quality-spreads, order-size, distribution-channel, geographical location, etc.

DYNAMIC COMPETITIVE SETTING

A product which is new to the world, as opposed to being merely new to the company, passes through distinctive competitive stages in its life cycle. The appropriate pricing policy is likely to be different for each stage.

New products have a protected distinctiveness which is doomed to progressive degeneration from competitive inroads. As new competitor products enter the field, and as their innovations narrow the gap of distinctiveness between your new product and its substitutes, your zone of pricing discretion narrows. Your distinctive "specialty" fades into a pedestrian "commodity" which is so little differentiated from other products that the seller has limited independence in pricing, even if rivals are few.

Throughout the cycle, continual changes occur in promotional and price elasticity and in costs of production and of distribution. These changes may call for adjustments in price policy.

*From *Journal of Industrial Economics*, Vol. XVII, No. 3 (July, 1969), pp. 165–179. Reprinted by permission of the publisher and the author.

†Joel Dean, Joel Dean Associates, Hastings-on-Hudson, New York.

Appropriate pricing over this "competitiveness cycle" depends on three different aspects of maturity, which usually move in approximately parallel time paths:

(1) Technical-maturity, indicated by declining rate of product development, increasing standardization among brands, and increasing stability of manufacturing processes and knowledge about them.

(2) Market-maturity, indicated by consumer acceptance of the basic service idea, by widespread belief that the products of most manufacturers will perform satisfactorily, and by enough familiarity and sophistication to permit consumers to compare brands competently.

(3) Rivalry-maturity, indicated by increasing stability of market shares and price structures.

MONOPOLY PRICING

New product pricing, if the product is truly novel, is in essence monopoly pricing. Stark monopoly pricing, which is the core of new product pricing, considers only what the traffic will bear — the price which will maximize profits taking into account the price-sensitivity of demand and the incremental promotional and production cost of the seller. What the product is worth to the buyer, not what it costs the seller is the controlling consideration.

The competitive setting of the new product has, however, peculiar features that modify monopoly pricing. The monopoly power of the new product is

(1) restricted (i.e., buyers have alternatives in the form of products that compete indirectly),

(2) ephemeral (i.e., subject to inevitable erosion by imitation and obsolescence) and

(3) controllable (i.e., capable of some degree of expansion and prolongation by actions of the seller).

For example, Quanta Welding's new diffusion bonding system, based on a millisecond shaped power pulse is a patented monopoly. But its pricing power is restricted by alternatives. For supersonic aircraft, these are resistance-welding, or rivetting, which are candidate pricing benchmarks. The market-power of Quanta's superior metals-joining process will be eventually eroded. Solid state devices may make obsolete the mercury vapor tube that supplies the controllable massive pulses of electrical energy on which the process depends. Penetration pricing might discourage this competitive entry.

The peculiarities of the new product monopoly introduce dynamism and uncertainty which call for modifications of monopoly pricing:

(1) Substitute ways to get the service set limits on the market power of a new product and hence serve as benchmark for pricing it.

(2) The perishability of the new product's wanted distinctiveness makes the timing of price, promotion and capacity competition crucial (e.g., choice between skimming and penetration pricing).

(3) The ability to influence the amount and the durability of the new product's market power in some degree by your own pricing and promotion actions gives added weight to the effect of today's pricing upon tomorrow's demand.

DEMAND: SENSITIVITY OF VOLUME TO PRICE

Maximum profit monopoly pricing of a new product, even with these dynamic competitive modifications, requires estimates of how price will affect sales. This relationship can be explored in two steps:

(1) find what range of price will make the product economically attractive to buyers;
(2) estimate what sales volumes can be expected at various points in this price range.

Price Range

The price range is determined by the indirect competition of substitutes, which set limits to the monopoly power of the new product. No product serves needs that are totally new; the most novel product merely plugs an abnormally large gap in the chain of substitutes. This gap marks out the potential range of its price.

For industrial products, quick and cheap ways to find this range usually feed on the wisdom of people experienced in looking at comparative product performance in terms of buyers' costs and requirements, for example, distributors, prime contractors, and consulting engineers, as well as purchasing analysts and engineers of prospect companies.

For consumers' goods, different methods are needed. In guessing the price range of a radically novel product of small unit value, the concept of barter equivalent can be useful. For example, a manufacturer of paper specialties tested a dramatic new product this way: a wide variety of consumer products totally unlike the new product were purchased and spread on a big table. Consumers selected the products they would swap for the new product.

Price — Volume Relationship

The effect of the price of the new product upon its volume of sales is the most important and most difficult estimate in pricing. We know in general that the lower the price, the greater the volume of sales and the faster its rate of growth. The air freight growth rate is about 18 percent; priced higher, it will grow slower. But to know the precise position and shape of the price-quantity demand schedule or how much faster sales will grow if the price is 20 percent lower is not possible. But estimate it some way we must.

The best way to predict the effect of price on sales volume for a new product is by controlled experiments: offering it at several different prices in comparable test markets under realistic sales conditions. For example, frozen orange juice was thus tested at three prices. When test marketing is not feasible, another method is to broaden the study of the cost of buyers' alternatives and include forecasts of the sales volume of substitutes (and other indications of the volume of customers of different categories). This approach is most promising for industrial customers because performance comparisons are more explicit and measurable and economics more completely controls purchases. When buyers' alternatives differ widely in service value, the difficulty of translating this disparity into superiority-premiums adds to the imprecision of this method of estimating price-volume relationships.

PRICING BENCHMARKS: BUYERS' ALTERNATIVES

The buyers' viewpoint should be controlling in pricing. For every new product there are alternatives. Buyers' best alternatives are usually products already tested in the marketplace. The new product will, presumably, supply a superior solution to the problem of some categories of buyers. The superiority differential over existing products differs widely among new products. The judgment of degree of superiority over substitutes usually also differs widely among buyers.

Benchmark Alternatives

The prospective buyer of any new product does have alternatives. These indirectly competitive products are the benchmark for the buyers' appraisal of the price-performance package of your new product. This comparison with existing products determines its relative attractiveness to potential buyers. This kind of analysis [of demand] can be make in the following steps:

(1) Determine the major uses for your new product. For each application, determine your product's performance characteristics.

(2) For each important usage area, specify the products that are the buyer's best alternative to your new product. Determine the performance characteristics and requirements which buyers view as crucial for their product selection.

(3) For each major use, determine how well your product's performance characteristics meet the requirements of customers compared with the performance of these buyers' alternative products.

(4) Forecast the prices of alternative products in terms of transaction prices, adjusted for the impact of your new product and translated into units of use. Estimate from the prices of these benchmark substitutes the alternative costs of the buyer per unit of the new product. Real transaction prices (after all discounts) rather than list prices, should be the benchmark, in order to reflect marketplace realities. Prices should be predicted, after the introduction of the new product, so as to reflect probable competitive adaptation to the new product. Where eventual displacement of existing substitutes appears likely, short-run incremental costs supplies a Jeremiah forecast of defender's pricing retaliation.

(5) Estimate your superiority premium, i.e., price the performance differential in terms of what the superior solution supplied by the new product is worth to buyers of various categories.

(6) Figure a "parity price" for your product relative to the buyers' best alternative product in each use, for major categories of customers. Parity is a price which encompasses the premium a customer would be willing to pay for your comparative superiority in performance characteristics.

Pricing the Superiority Differential

Determining this price premium over benchmark products which the new product's superiority will most profitably warrant, is the most intricate and challenging problem of new product pricing.

The value to the customer of the innovational superiority of the new product is surrounded by uncertainties: whether the product will work, whether it will attain its designed superiorities, what its reliability and durability performance will be, and how soon it in turn will become obsolete. These uncertainties influence the price a customer would pay and promotional outlay to persuade him to buy. Thus, customers' uncertainties will cost the seller, either in price or promotion.

In essence, the superiority premium requires translation of differential performance characteristics into dollars, based on value analysis from the buyer's viewpoint. The premium will differ among uses, among alternative products and among categories of customers. For some, it will be negative. Unless it proves practical to segment the market by application and to have widely discriminatory prices, the new product is likely to be priced out of some applications.

A simplistic, single-point premium reflecting "what the product can command in the marketplace" will not do. The customer response-pattern that is needed is the relationship between (1) a series of prospective superiority premiums and (2) the corresponding potential volumes.

What matters is superiority as buyers value it, not superiority as calibrated by technicians' measurements or by the sellers' costs. This means that more and better promotion can raise the premium-volume schedule and make a lower superiority premium achieve the same sales volume or rate of sales growth as would a higher premium without the promotion. This premium-volume schedule will be kicked about by retaliatory pricing of displaceable substitutes as well as by the imitative and innovative new-product-competition of rivals.

The optimizing premium, i.e., the price that would maximize profits in any specified time period will depend upon your future costs as well as upon the hazy and dynamic demand schedule. It will be hard to find. Uncertainty about the future thus makes the appropriate pricing strategy for the long run a matter of sophisticated judgment.

RATE-OF-RETURN PRICING

Application of these principles of economic pricing is illustrated by rate-of-return pricing of new capital equipment. Investment goods are sold to businessmen in their capacity as profit makers. The technique is different for a producer's good (e.g., a truck) than for pricing a consumer's good (e.g., a sports car).

The difference results because the essential service purchased if your product is a producer's good is added profits. Your product represents an investment by your businessman customer. The test of whether or not this investment is a desirable one should be its profitability to the customer. The pricing guide that this suggests is rate-of-return on the capital your customer ties up by his investment in your product.

Rate-of-Return on Customer's Investment

Rate-of-return pricing looks at your price through the investment eyes of the customer. It recognizes that your upper limit is the price which will produce the minimum acceptable rate-of-return on the customer's investment. The added profits obtainable from the use of your equipment differ among customers and among applications from the same customer. Cutoff criteria of required return also differ, so prospective customers differ in the rate-of-return which will induce them to invest in your product. Thus, the rate-of-return approach opens up a new kind of demand analysis for industrial goods. This analysis consists of inquiry into:

(a) the costs of buyers from displaceable alternative ways to do the job;
(b) the cost-saving and profit-producing capability of your equipment in different applications and for different prospects; and
(c) the capital budgeting policies of your customers, with particular emphasis on their cost-of-capital and their minimum rate-of-return requirements.

The rate-of-return analysis just outlined is particularly useful in the pioneering stages of new products, when you compete only with obsolescent ways of doing the job. At more mature stages in the life cycle of a new product, competitive imitation improves your prospective customers' alternatives. These rival investment alternatives must then be taken explicitly into your analysis.

One way is to use your competitor's product as the benchmark in measuring the rate-of-return which your product will produce for specified categories of your prospects. The profitability from your product is measured in terms of its superiority over the best alternative new equipment offered by rivals, rather than by its superiority over the customer's old equipment. Rate-of-return pricing translates your competitive superiority into dollars of added profit for your customer, and relates this added profit to the added investment. In effect, you would say: "To be sure, buying my competitor's product will give you a 25 percent rate-of-return and that is better than keeping your old equipment; but buying my product will give you a 30 percent rate-of-return." For each customer category, rate-of-return analysis reveals a price for your product that makes it an irresistably good investment to your customer in view of his alternatives, but a price which at the same time extracts from your customer all that you can safely demand.

Investigation of (1) the productivity of the buyers' capital investments that you sell in your new product and (2) the required rate-of-return of prospective customers has proven a practical way to predict the demand for some industrial goods. It must be coupled with forecasts of your costs to find the most profitable price, immediately and with considerations of competitive strategy, for the longer run.

ROLE OF COST

To get maximum practical use from costs in new product pricing, three questions of theory must be answered: (1) whose cost? (2) which cost? and (3) what role? As to whose cost, three are important:

(1) the costs of prospective buyers,
(2) the costs of existent and potential competitors, and
(3) the costs of the producer of the new product.

Cost should play a different role for each of the three and the pertinent concept of cost will differ accordingly.

Buyer's Cost

How should costs of prospective customers be used in setting the price of a new product? By applying value analysis to prices and performance of alternative products to find the superiority-premium that will make the new product attractive from an economic standpoint to buyers of specified categories. Rate-of-return pricing of capital goods illustrates this buyer's-cost approach, which is applicable in principle to all new products.

Competitors' Costs

Competitors' costs is usually the crucial estimate in appraisal of their capabilities.

Costs of two kinds of competitive products can be helpful. The first is products already in the marketplace. The purposes are to estimate (1) their staying power and (2) the floor of retaliation pricing. For the first purpose, the pertinent cost concept is the competitor's long-run incremental cost; for the second, short-run incremental cost.

The second kind is the unborn competing product that could blight your new product's future or eventually displace it. Forecasts of competitors' costs for such products are not necessarily wild and can help assess the effectiveness of a strategy of pricing the new product so as to discourage entry. For this purpose, the cost behavior to forecast is the relationship between unit production cost and plant size as you and your rivals move from pilot plant to small scale test production plant to large scale mass production. The cost forecasts should take into account technological progress and should be spotted on a time scale that reflects the potential headstart cost advantages that you could attain under a policy of penetration pricing and under a policy of skimming pricing. Estimates of cost of unborn competitive products are necessarily rough but evaluation of major differences between competitors' costs and your costs can nevertheless be useful. Thus, cost estimates can help formulate a defending product's retaliation-pricing and an invading product's conquest-pricing.

Producer's Cost

The cost of the producer plays several roles in pricing a new product. The first is birth control. A new product must be pre-priced provisionally early in the research and development stage and periodically as it progresses toward market. Forecasts of production and promotional costs at matching stages should play the role of forecasting its economic feasibility in determining whether to continue product development and to ultimately commercialize. The concept of cost relevant for this birth-control role is a prediction of full cost at a series of prospective volumes and corresponding technologies. It should encompass imputed cost of capital on intangible as well as tangible investment.

A second role is to establish a price floor which is also the threshold for selecting from candidate prices that which will maximize return on a new product investment over the long run. For both jobs, the relevant concept is future costs, forecasted over a range of volume, production technologies, and promotional outlays in the marketing plan.

Two categories of cost require separate forecasts and have quite different impact on new product pricing:

(a) Production costs (including physical distribution).
(b) Persuasion costs, which are discretionary and rivalrous with price.

The production costs that matter are the future costs over the long run that will be added by making this product on the predicted scale (or scales) vs not making it. You should estimate the added investment necessary to manufacture and distribute the new product. Investment should include intangibles like R & D, promotion and launching outlays as well as increased working capital. Then you should estimate the added costs of manufacturing and selling the product at various possible sales volumes. Calculate total costs (rather than unit costs) with and without the new product. The difference can then be assigned to the new product. Ignore present overhead that will be the same whether you go ahead with the addition to your product line or not. Future additions to overhead caused by the new product are alone relevant in pricing it. Build up two sets of cost and investment figures—one showing the situation without the new product, and the other showing the situation with the new product added to your line and at several possible volumes. High costs of pilot plant production and of early small scale production plants should be viewed as intangible capital investment rather than viewed as the current operating costs. The losses of a break-in period are part of the investment on which a satisfactory return should be made.

Long-run future incremental costs, including costs of equity capital, (i.e., satisfactory return on the added investment) supply the baseline above which contribution profits of a new product should be maximized—not an impenetrable floor, but a calculation benchmark for optimization.

STRATEGY CHOICES

A major strategy decision in pricing a new product is the choice between:

(1) skimming pricing and
(2) penetration pricing.

There are intermediate positions but the issues are made clearer by comparing the two extremes.

Skimming Pricing

Some products represent a drastic improvement upon accepted ways of performing a service or filling a demand. For these products a strategy of high prices with large promotional expenditure in the early stages of market development (and lower prices at later stages), has frequently proven successful. This I call a skimming price policy. There are four main reasons for its success:

(1) Your sales of the product are likely to be less sensitive to price in the early stages than when the product is "full-grown" and competitive imitations have appeared. In the early stages, the product usually has so few close rivals that cross-elasticity of demand is low. Promotional sensitivity is, on the other hand, quite high, particularly for products with high unit prices, since it is difficult for the customer to value the service of the product.

(2) Launching a new product with a high price is an efficient device for breaking the market up into segments that differ in price elasticity of demand. The initial high price serves to skim the cream of the market that is relatively insensitive to price. Subsequent price reductions tap successively more elastic sectors of the market. This pricing strategy is exemplified by the systematic succession of editions of a book, sometimes starting with a $50 limited personal edition and ending up with a 25-cent pocket book.

(3) A skimming policy is safer, or at least appears so. Facing an unknown elasticity of demand, a high initial price serves as a "refusal" price during the stage of exploration. How much costs can be reduced as the market expands and as the design of the product is improved by increasing production efficiency with new techniques is difficult to predict.

(4) High prices frequently produce a greater dollar volume of sales in the early stages of market development than are produced by low initial prices. When this is the case, skimming pricing will provide you with funds to finance expansion into the larger volume sectors of your market.

Penetration Pricing

Despite its many advantages, a skimming-price policy isn't always the answer to your new product problems. Although high initial prices may maximize profits during the early stages of product introduction, they may also prevent sales to many of the buyers upon whom you must rely for a mass market. The alternative is to use low prices as an entering wedge to get into mass markets early. This I call penetration pricing. This approach is likely to be desirable under these conditions:

(1) When sales volume of the product is very sensitive to price, even in the early stages of introduction.

(2) When you can achieve substantial economies in unit cost of manufacturing and distributing the product by operating at large volume.

(3) When your product faces threats of strong potential competition, very soon after introduction.

(4) When there is no "elite" market—that is, no class of buyers willing to pay a higher price to obtain the newest and the best.

While a penetration pricing policy can be adopted at any stage in the product's life cycle, you should always examine this pricing strategy before your new product is marketed at all. This possibility should be explored again as soon as your product has established an elite market. Sometimes a product can be rescued from premature death by adoption of a penetration price after the cream of the market has been skimmed.

One important consideration in your choice between skimming and penetration pricing at the time you introduce your new product is the ease and speed with which competitors can bring out substitute products. For products whose market potential looks big, a policy of low initial prices makes sense because the big multiple-product manufacturers are attracted to mass markets. If you set your initial price low enough, your large competitor may not feel it worthwhile to make a big investment for slim profit margins.

The speed with which your product loses its uniqueness and sinks from its sheltered status to the level of just another competitive product depends on several factors:

(a) Its total sales potential: A big potential market entices competitive imitation.

(b) The investment required for rivals to manufacture and distribute the product: A big investment barrier deters invasion.

(c) The strength of patent and know-how protection.

(d) The alertness and power of competitors.

Although competitive imitation is almost inevitable, the company that introduces a new product can use price to discourage or delay the introduction of competitive products.

Pricing in Maturity

To determine what pricing policies are appropriate for later stages in the cycle of market and competitive maturity, the manufacturer must be able to tell when a product is approaching maturity. Some of the symptoms of degeneration of competitive status toward the commodity level are:

(1) Weakening in brand preference — this may be evidenced by a higher cross-elasticity of demand among leading products, the leading brand not being able to continue demanding as much price premium as initially without losing position;

(2) Narrowing physical variation among products as the best designs are developed and standardized — this has been dramatically demonstrated in automobiles and is still in process in television receivers;

(3) The entry in force of private-label competitors — this is exemplified by the mail-order houses' sale of own-label refrigerators and paint sprayers;

(4) Market saturation — the ratio of replacement sales to new equipment sales serves as an indicator of the competitive degeneration of durable goods, but in general it must be kept in mind that both market size and degree of saturation are hard to define (e.g., saturation of the radio market, which was initially thought to be one radio per home and later had to be expanded to one radio per room);

(5) The stabilization of production methods — indicated by slow rate of technological advance, high average age of equipment and great uniformity among competitors introduction technology.

PROMOTION AND DISTRIBUTION

Promotion

Initial promotion outlays are an investment in the product that cannot be recovered until some kind of market has been established. As the innovator, you shoulder the burden of educating consumers to the existence and uses of the product. Later imitators will never have to do this job; so, if you, the innovator, do not want to be simply a benefactor to your future competitors, you must make pricing plans to earn a return on all your initial outlays before your pricing discretion evaporates.

Your basic strategic problem is to find the right mixture of price and promotion to maximize your long-run profits. You can choose a relatively high price in pioneering stages, together with large advertising and dealer discounts, and plan to get your promotion investment back early; or you can use low prices and lean margins from the very outset, in order to discourage potential competition when the barriers of patents, and investment in production capacity, distribution channels, or production techniques become inadequate.

Channels of Distribution

Choice of channels of distribution should be consistent with your strategy for initial pricing and for promotional outlays. Penetration pricing and explosive promotion calls for distribution channels that promptly make the product broadly available. Otherwise you waste advertising or stymie mass-market pricing. Distribution policy also concerns the role you wish the dealer to play in pushing your product, the margins you must pay him to induce this action and the amount of protection of territory and of inventory required to do so.

Estimation of the costs of moving the new product through the channels of distribution to the final consumer must enter into the pricing procedure, since these costs govern the factory price that will result in a specified final price. Distributive margins are partly pure promotional costs and partly physical distribution costs. Margins must at least cover the distributors' costs of warehousing, handling, and order taking. These costs are similar to factory production costs in being related to physical capacity and its utilization, i.e., fluctuations in production or sales volume. Hence, these set a floor to trade-channel discounts. But distributors usually also contribute promotional effort — in point-of-sale pushing, local advertising, and display — when it is made worth their while. These pure promotional costs are more optional.

Distributors' margins are best determined by study of distributors' alternatives. This does not mean that your distributor gross margin must be the same as rival products. It should instead produce a better rate of return on the distributors' investment (in inventory, shelf space and sales capacity).

SOME PRICING PRECEPTS

Pricing new products is an art. The important determinants in economic pricing of pioneering innovations are complex and interrelated and hard to forecast. Experienced judgment is required in pricing and repricing the product to fit its changing competitive environment. This judgment may possibly be improved by some pricing precepts suggested by the preceding analysis:

(1) Be clear about corporate goals. Pricing a new product is an occasion for re-thinking them. In this article I have assumed the overriding corporate goal is long-run profit maximization, e.g., making the stock worth most.

(2) Pricing a new product should begin long before its birth. Prospective prices, coupled with forecasted costs, should play the decisive role in product birth control.

(3) Pricing a new product should be a continuing process of bracketing the truth by successive approximations. Rough estimates of the relevant concepts are preferable to precise knowledge of historical irrelevancies.

(4) Costs can supply useful guidance in new product pricing, but not by the conventional wisdom, i.e., cost-plus pricing. Costs to three persons are pertinent: the

buyer, the seller, and his rivals. The role of cost differs among the three, as does the concept of cost that is pertinent to that role: different costs for different purposes.

(5) The role of your cost is to set a reference base for picking the most profitable price. For this job the only costs that are pertinent to pricing a new product on the verge of commercialization (i.e., already developed and tested) are your incremental costs: the added costs of going ahead, at different plant sales. Costs of R & D and of market testing are now sunk and hence irrelevant.

(6) Recognize the pricing implications of the changing economic status and competitive environment of your product as it passes through its life cycle from birth to obsolescence. This cycle, and the plans you make to influence it, are of paramount importance for your pricing policy.

(7) Look at your product through the eyes of your customer and price it just low enough to make it an irresistable investment, in view of his alternatives as he sees them. To estimate successfully how much your product is worth to your prospect is never easy; but it is usually rewarding.

(8) Customers' rate of return should be the main consideration in pricing novel capital goods. Buyers' cost savings (and other earnings) expressed as a return on his investment in your new product is the key to predicting the price-sensitivity of demand and to pricing profitably.

(9) The strategic choice between skimming and penetration pricing should be based on economics. The skimming policy, i.e., relatively high prices in the pioneering stage, cascading downward thereafter, is particularly appropriate for products whose sales initially are comparatively unresponsive to price but quite responsive to education. A policy of penetration pricing, i.e., relatively low prices in the pioneering stage in anticipation of the cost savings resulting from an expanding market, is best when scale-economies are big, demand is price-sensitive, and invasion is threatened. Low starting prices sacrifice short-run profits for long-run profits and discourage potential competitors.

34. RATIONAL BEHAVIOR AND GASOLINE PRICE WARS*

Dan E. Schendel and Pietro Balestra†

INTRODUCTION

Gasoline price wars are a widespread, frequently observed phenomena. For example, from mid-1961 until 1966, over twelve important price wars occurred in the metropolitan Los Angeles region. These price wars ranged in duration from approximately two to greater than twelve weeks, during which periods the average retail price fell as much as eight to ten cents below the so-called normal price. Similar histories characterize other markets (Cassady, [3], [4], [5], and Clover, [9]).

While widespread and frequent, price wars are not well understood and opinion is divided about them. Industry members claim price wars are not rational since only losses are incurred. Critics point out that price wars and the short-term losses they imply are used to assure long-term profits for the large, integrated firms through injury or elimination of weaker competitors. They claim such actions support the need for regulation, divestiture, and other corrections of concentrated economic power, for example, see Federal Trade Commission [11]. Implicit in their argument is that short-term, price cutting behavior is not rational in the sense of short-run profit maximization.

Members and many sympathetic observers of the petroleum industry fail to see where price cutting is rational, i.e., profitable, over any time period, long or short. To them price cutting is not a means to increase profits. Industry sponsored studies purporting to show that price cutting is unprofitable have been made and publicized to the industry (Moir, [16]). Yet price wars persist, suggesting that despite claims to the contrary, price wars may yield profits, at least to some participants.

A short-term profit motivation would offer an alternative explanation for price wars more appealing than the one based on anticompetitive, injurious trade practices such as suggested in the recent Federal Trade Commission [11] report. Such a motivation would offer a less devious and torturous deductive path to profit realization and would not depend upon explaining why any competitor would seek future profits through monopoly control and short-term

*From *Applied Economics*, Vol. I, No. 2 (May, 1969), pp. 89–101. Reprinted by permission of the publisher and the authors.

†Dan E. Schendel, Associate Professor of Industrial Management, Purdue University, and Pietro Balestra, Professor, Universite de Fribourg.

losses. To achieve monopoly control, the would-be monopolist must overcome short-term losses necessary to achieve it,[1] avoid the legal constraints that could be imposed, and prevent entry into refining and marketing of gasoline. All of these represent formidable barriers and are difficult to explain away.

It is the purpose of this paper to suggest an economic, rational motivation for a price cutting strategy intended to yield profits in the short run, and further, to develop a reaction model which recognizes the institutional characteristics and legal constraints of retail gasoline marketing. The reaction model developed suggests the conditions that must be met for profits to be realized and, along with estimates of competitive reaction times, it will permit computation of expected losses or expected gains for an individual firm from a price war.

In the next section, the basic motivation for retail price cutting is developed. In the sections that follow, circumstances that can be readily observed in the market place will be pointed out and used to indicate how price cutting can spread and lead to price wars. Finally, the reaction model will be developed and some of its major implications explored.

THE BASIC MOTIVATION FOR PRICE CUTTING

To have a price war, some competitor first must be led to cut his price. If the price cutting dealer's primary goal is profit maximization, then rational, goal directed behavior suggests the price cut is motivated by an expected gain in profits. Can price cutting be a profitable strategy for the dealer? This is the question we seek to answer.

At the industry level, it has been well documented that gasoline demand is inelastic (Bain, [2]; Cassady, [3]; Cassady and Jones, [6]; and McAllister, [14]). At the brand level, however, many good substitutes exist and the demand curve facing an individual dealer is generally quite elastic (Bain, [2]; Cassady, [3]; Cassady and Jones, [6]; and Clark, *et al.*, [7]). It is the difference in demand elasticity between the industry and brand level that is fundamental to profitable price cutting.

Given that his demand is elastic, a dealer can expect to increase his *total revenue* by cutting price. An increase in total revenue, however, does not mean that *total gross margin* is increased. The relative sizes of the retail price and typical gross margin require that demand elasticity be considerably in excess of unity before a price cut will increase total gross margin (profits).

Gross margin per unit is, of course, the difference between the unit selling price and the cost of a unit sold. For the gasoline dealer, gross margin, M, is:

$$M = p - w \tag{1}$$

[1] The high cost of capital of most integrated petroleum firms and the magnitude of the losses they incur are such that the future return must be relatively large and relatively certain to overcome short-term losses.

where p is the pump price per gallon and w is the so-called dealer tank wagon or wholesale price. Let the demand curve facing the isolated dealer be:

$$q = f(p),\ f'(p) < 0. \tag{2}$$

The total revenue (TR) and total gross margin (TM) may be expressed as:

$$TR = pq = pf(p), \tag{3}$$

$$TM = Mq = (p - w)\,q = (p - w)f(p). \tag{4}$$

If a price cut is to lead to increased total gross margin, the derivative of (4) with respect to quantity must be greater than zero. It is easily shown that this occurs when the elasticity of demand, e, (in absolute terms) is greater than the ratio of the selling price to the margin.[2]

$$|e| > \frac{p}{m} = \frac{p}{p - w}. \tag{5}$$

Expression (5) is the condition sought. It says that total gross margin is increased by cutting price, if the ratio of the percentage increase in volume to the percentage decrease in price (the price elasticity) is greater than the ratio of price to margin.

This result is a direct application of conventional marginal rules, which state that, in equilibrium, the optimal pricing policy for a given dealer would be to equate the ratio of offer price to gross margin with the price elasticity characteristic of his location and its competitive environment. Since our basic interest here is disequilibrium, we prefer to indicate conditions favoring a price cut rather than simply state the equilibrium condition. Accordingly, expression (5) may be thought of as a measure of the intensity of the incentive to cut prices.

DIFFERENTIAL COSTS AND MARGINS

To gain further insight into price cutting and price wars, it is useful to consider the forces, particularly cost differentials, that lead to changing margins and disequilibrium in the sense of expression (5). In restoration of equilibrium,

[2]For a discrete price change, condition (5) becomes:

$$\frac{\Delta q}{\Delta p} \cdot \frac{p^*}{q^*} > \frac{p^*}{p^* - w}$$

where p^* and q^* must be appropriately defined for (5) to hold. Two such definitions are:

(1) $p^* = p_2;\ q^* = q_1$

(2) $p^* = \dfrac{p_1 + p_2}{2};\ q^* = \dfrac{q_1 + q_2}{2}$

where p_1, q_1 and p_2, q_2 are, respectively, the price and quantities before and after the price change.

price cuts occur, which in turn can prompt competitive reactions and cause a price war.

In (5), total *gross* rather than total *net* margin was used. It is not unrealistic to assume that total net margin is maximized when total gross margin is maximized. In any case (5) could be formulated using total net margin. Use of gross margin keeps the analysis simple and focuses on the tank wagon price, the major element of cost and the one most likely to vary over time.[3]

To say that the wholesale price, w, changes frequently and shows greater movement than other costs without any further qualification would overlook a very significant characteristic of gasoline retailing. Wholesale prices may change frequently for minor brand or private-brand operators. They do not change for major brand dealers, or at least, do not change with anything approaching the frequency with which tank wagon prices can change for minor brand dealers.

The reason why the minor brand dealer has a more frequently changing and lower cost basis than the major brand dealer lies in the contractual arrangements between supplier and dealers. The major brand dealer is typically tied through long-term contracts to a supplier—to the integrated oil firm who owns and controls the major brand. These contracts result in a fairly inflexible wholesale price to the major brand dealer. For example, during the two and one-half year period from 1963 to mid-1965, eight different West Coast major brands each changed their tank wagon prices three times. On two of these occasions, tax increases prompted the changes. Yet during this period eight different price wars occurred in Los Angeles and the three changes did not occur at the same time the price wars occurred.

As consideration for this commitment from the supplier, the major brand dealer has use of a well-known brand, credit, training services, financial assistance, and other benefits of value. On the other hand, the minor brand dealer owns his brand and typically has greater independence of operation than does his major brand counterpart. He, of course, receives no help with credit cards and other services.[4]

Of greatest significance here is that the minor brand dealer has much greater freedom in selecting sources of supply. Many minors will "shop around" for their supply, which is typically available at a lower price, sometimes much lower,[5] than to the major dealer who is not free to shift his custom to take advantage of lower cost supplies.

If it is true that minor brand dealers have more frequently changing tank wagon prices and if profit maximization is a basic goal, then we should expect from a consideration of (5) that minor brand dealers in their search for increased

---

[3]In addition to the wholesale price, other costs are incurred in the sale of gasoline. The two most important of these are labor and rental costs. These two costs do not vary markedly in the short run for a given dealer.

[4]Some minor brand suppliers do undertake long-term supply contracts.

[5]Gasoline refining is a joint production process which implies incomplete supply control. At times, for some, if not all refiners, excess gasoline supplies do occur.

profits would be frequent initiators of price cuts that lead to price wars. Moreover, legal precedent and restrictions of the Robinson-Patman Act also are powerful deterrents to initiating price cuts on the part of major brands, at least in market areas where minor brand dealers are competing. Empirical evidence does show that minor brands do lead prices downward during price wars. Of the twelve price wars in Los Angeles mentioned earlier, in every case the minor brand average price led the major brand average downward.[6]

Obviously, there must be some lag or expected lag in competitive reaction time before the minor brand dealer would cut his price. If competitive reaction was expected to be instantaneous, he would have little or no incentive to alter his price. We take up the matter of reaction times below. For now, we can assume reaction is likely to come, but probably not immediately.

What incentive does the major brand dealer have (or minor brand dealer who has no lowered tank wagon price) to match a price reduction made by a competitor? Without some adjustment in tank wagon price (or other cost), he clearly cannot benefit from a lower price-margin ratio. However, the level and elasticity of his demand are likely to shift and if he does not match competitive price cuts, he can lose market share, perhaps permanently.

To permit the major brand dealer to counter price reductions and the possible loss of market share, major brand suppliers have used various means of supporting their dealers during such times without making available on a wide basis a lowered or changed tank wagon price.[7] The support is rendered through what we shall call margin support agreements. They will be discussed in the next section and it will be shown that margin support plans can be in themselves motivation for price cuts and can serve to prolong and spread price wars.

MARGIN SUPPORT AGREEMENTS

Thus far we have suggested: (1) that a lowered tank wagon price, w, can be an incentive to cut a price, and (2) that the minor brand dealer is most likely to receive a lowered tank wagon price and may be expected to be the initiator of price cuts. In this section we take up a mechanism, margin support agreements, commonly employed by major brand suppliers to help dealers selling their brand to react and profitably compete with a retail price cut.

The purpose of these margin support agreements is to maintain the competitive position of the major brand dealer by reducing the disadvantage that these dealers may have in terms of tank wagon prices as compared to minor brand dealers. In maintaining the competitive position of its dealers, the

[6]See also Livingston and Levitt [13]. Very little empirical data have been published on this point. Actual prices as opposed to posted prices show the behavior characteristic of Los Angeles.

[7]Such a solution helps avoid difficulties under the Robinson-Patman Act. It also explains why posted tank wagon prices are inflexible.

supplier is also maintaining his own competitive position and market share. There are two basic types of margin support agreements: (1) the consignment plan, and (2) the margin sharing agreement. The latter is the most interesting since it has the widest use currently.

The Consignment Plan

Under a consignment agreement, the major oil supplier replaces the individual dealer as the price maker. Gasoline is consigned to the dealer who in effect becomes the supplier's agent in selling gasoline.[8] For his services the dealer receives a fee, which is fixed, and may be equal to the normal margin, i.e., the margin received by the dealer during non-price war conditions.

Does this lead to a more stable or a less stable retail price? Given that the major supplier has a much wider horizon than an individual dealer in terms of the retail outlets of interest, it probably means that greater uniformity in price is to be expected in any given market area. Prices may be unstable even though uniform, since under the consignment plan only a handful of companies are price makers. Prices can move and be matched very rapidly for this reason. Prices are more likely to be stable, however, although not necessarily at normal levels. Given the more complete knowledge possessed by the handful of majors and their sensitivity to retaliation by other majors, there may be stickiness in price movements, and lags in adjustment to changed supply conditions.

It is difficult to make any general comments about stability or instability as we move from many competitors to few competitors involved in price making, which is of course what happens under the consignment plan. In some cases, probably most, greater price stability and price uniformity, whatever the price level, is to be expected under consignment.

The Sharing Agreement

The essential feature of this type of dealer support is that the tank wagon price is tied to the retail price. If the dealer decides to lower the price at the pump by one cent, then the tank wagon price that the dealer has to pay is reduced by a fraction of one cent.[9] Let λ be the proportion of the price reduction that is absorbed by the supplier.

Implicit in this agreement is the recognition of a "normal" (or desirable) price and a "normal" margin. The relationship between the tank wagon price

[8]In practice, when a consignment agreement is consummated, the supplier repurchases any dealer inventories. The financial burden of these is thus shifted to the supplier and possible inventory losses to the dealer are eliminated. See Clark, *et al.* [7] for a discussion of the impact of the consignment system in British Columbia, Canada.

[9]The dealer ordinarily does not have complete freedom to lower his price *and* have margin support. Some form of approval must be given by the major supplier, which gives rise to possible delays in price response.

and the retail price is best understood in graphical form (see Figure 34-1). In Figure 34-1, $\bar{p}$ is the "normal" retail price (e.g., 32.9 cents), w the dealer tank wagon price, and C a constant.[10] The shaded area represents the gross margin for the dealer. From Figure 34-1, the following relationship obtains:

$$w = C + \lambda p, \quad 0 < p < \bar{p}$$

(6) $$= C + \lambda \bar{p} = \text{const}, \quad p > \bar{p},$$

where λ is the slope of the line (i.e., the proportion absorbed by the supplier).

In the price range $p > \bar{p}$ for retail prices at or above normal, we are back to the case of constant w. More often, however, because the normal price is usually the highest price attainable in the market, the dealer will operate in the lower range where the tank wagon price declines. It is this lower range which applies during gasoline price wars and is therefore the one we analyze here.

Under the sharing agreement postulated, the margin M, and total margin, TM, of the dealer are defined as follows:

(7) $$M = p - [C + \lambda p] = (1 - \lambda)p - C$$

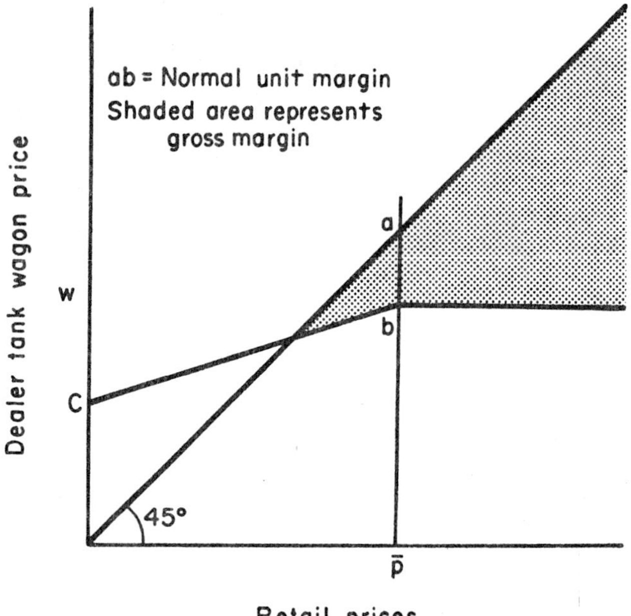

Figure 34-1

[10] This constant includes the sales tax.

(8) $$TM = Mf(p) = [(1 - \lambda)p - C]f(p)$$

the derivative of (8) with respect to q is:

$$\frac{dTM}{dq} = (1 - \lambda)p - C + (1 - \lambda)\frac{f(p)}{f'(p)}$$

(9) $$= M + (1 - \lambda)\frac{p}{e}.$$

Now, for a price cut to be profitable, the expression in equation (9) must be greater than zero, or equivalently, the marginal profit must be positive. This occurs when:

(10) $$|e| > (1 - \lambda)\frac{p}{M}.$$

The significant difference in the above result compared to the one obtained earlier in the case of constant tank wagon prices [see expression (5)], is that a price cut is now desirable whenever the elasticity of demand is greater than the ratio p/M *multiplied* by the factor $(1 - \lambda)$. Since $(1 - \lambda)$ is less than unity, it takes a lower elasticity than before to gain from a price cut. In other words, a smaller increase in volume is sufficient for a dealer to benefit from a price cut than under conditions of constant tank wagon prices.

Consider an example. Suppose that under "normal" conditions the margin is about one-sixth of the retail price (so that the price ratio p/M is equal to six). Without a support program, the elasticity of demand must be greater than six before a price cut becomes attractive. With a sharing agreement of 50–50 ($\lambda = 0.5$), the elasticity need only be three, and in the case of 70 per cent absorption by the supplier, only 1.8. In this last case, a one-cent reduction in the pump price (3 per cent reduction) will increase profits provided that the volume is increased by more than 5.4 per cent (instead of 18 per cent in the case of no support).

To emphasize the destabilizing nature of the sharing agreement, the argument can be pushed to an extreme. For a sufficiently high value of λ, a price cut is profitable *provided only that total revenue is increased.* This result is obtained by letting $\lambda = w/p$ which, in the above example, implies a value of $\lambda = 5/6$ (roughly 83 per cent). It is also clear that with total absorption by the supplier ($\lambda = 1$), profits are increased as long as the elasticity of demand is greater than zero.

Given that many sharing plans have a λ of two-thirds to three-quarters and the dealer tank wagon price is rarely less than 5–6 cents below the prevailing market price, p, (excluding taxes), the margin sharing plan can be a powerful price destabilizing influence. Unless suitable geographic price surveys are made by the companies to identify the source of price cutting, several dealers could agree to a decision to lower their respective prices and thereby receive benefit from their margin sharing plans.

That these margin support agreements do in fact contribute to price wars, at least to their duration, if not to their start, is implied in two articles on two different dates appearing in *The Wall Street Journal* [17], [18]. Several companies were reported as withdrawing their margin supports in order to end price wars in certain of their marketing territories.

These same articles suggest that one company generally ". . . assumes 80 per cent ($\lambda = 0.8$) of the 'loss' in price wars." Another company, American Oil Co. [1] reports that it absorbs ". . . three-quarters ($\lambda = 3/4$) of a cent for each 1 cent reduction in retail price levels. However, at the point where the dealer margin falls to 4½–4 cents per gallon, (this company) generally absorbs the entire amount of the reduction ($\lambda = 1.0$)."[11] Such high support levels suggest that to some dealers, increased revenues are synonymous with increased profits.

Without providing any support for their conclusion, the Federal Trade Commission, on the basis of its recent hearings on gasoline marketing, broadly asserted that ". . . the depth and duration of any particular price war are largely determined by the actions of suppliers in granting price reductions to their dealers. Without their actions in granting price reductions to their dealer customers, price wars would be narrow in scope and limited in duration." (Federal Trade Commission, [11, p. 14]). The model developed here suggests why the FTC conclusion may be warranted, although it is not entirely obvious or necessarily true that price wars would be "narrow in scope and limited in duration" without margin support agreements.

A REACTION MODEL

In the previous two sections we have examined the basic economic or rational motivation for price cutting in the retail gasoline market. Any realistic explanation of price wars must take into consideration the reaction of competitors. We will now generalize the analysis to include the effects of competitive price retaliation. This generalization does not preclude the rational explanation of gasoline price wars we are seeking.

There is probably no other area of economic theory in which the lack of consensus among economists is as vivid as in the field of reaction models. Yet, there are instances in which the institutional characteristics and legal restrictions prevailing in the market permit the formulation of a meaningful and realistic reaction model. The gasoline retail market is a case in point. Without pretending to provide a universal solution to the problem of mutual dependency, it will be shown that, from the point of view of a dealer initiating a price cut, the outcome of a price war is not necessarily indeterminate and can and may actually be predicted. This fact may contradict the view that because of the excessive cost of cutthroat competition a collusive type of solution is to be expected.

The following model presents some dynamic features, inasmuch as the time element plays an essential role. The following assumptions are made:

---

[11]See p. 88 of Learned and Ellsworth [12].

Assumption 1: The minor starts the move. As pointed out earlier, he is typically the dynamic element in gasoline retailing. Hence, we compute the outcome of the price cut from the minor's point of view.

Assumption 2: The major does not undercut the minor, but eventually matches his cut (up to the normal differential of 1 or 2 cents). This is an institutional characteristic of gasoline retailing.

Assumption 3: When the major matches the minor's move, the respective initial volumes or quantities of gasoline sold are restored, but at a lower price. This means that when the major matches the price cut, the gain in gallonage is lost for the minor, but as long as the price war is in effect, the price is depressed. (The implications of relaxing this assumption are discussed later.)

Let T be the *total time* or duration of a price war. Decompose T into two segments: (1) a segment of length t_1 which represents the *lead time* in favor of the minor (when the major does not match), and (2) a segment of length t_2 which represents the matching time (from the moment of the major's match to the end of the price war). Obviously, $T = t_1 + t_2$. From our assumptions it follows that during period t_1 the minor can expect an increase in gallonage.

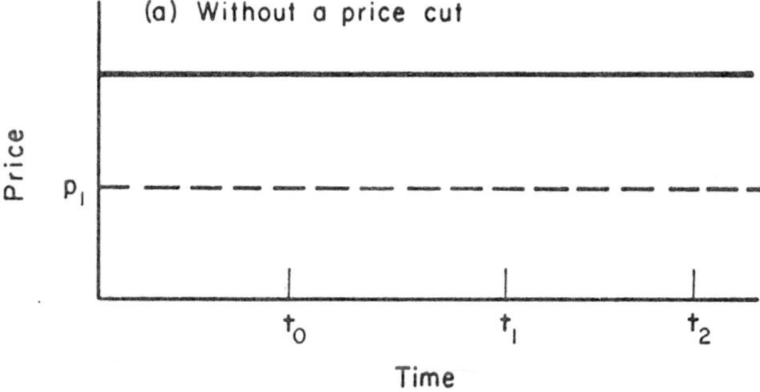

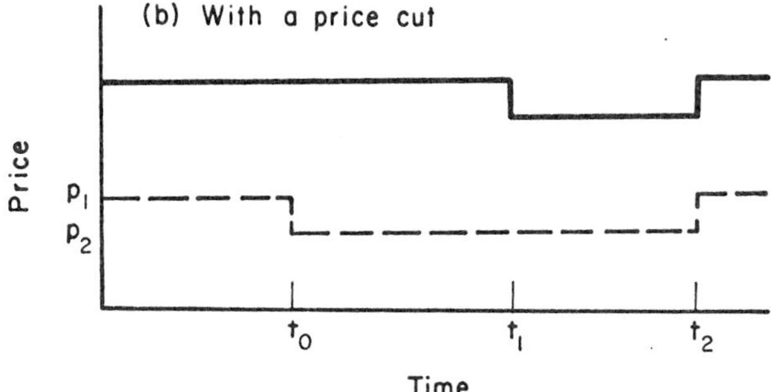

Figure 34-2

The amount of the increase depends on the elasticity of demand. During period t_2, by assumption, the increase in gallonage is lost, but the price stays at the lower level.

Schematically, the price reaction model is represented in Figure 34-2 , where p_1 is the minor brand selling price without a price cut and p_2 the minor price after a cut.

The quantities associated with the price levels shown in Figure 34–2 are:

(a) without a price cut:

$$p_1 \text{———} q_1, \quad \text{for } 0 < t < t_1$$

$$p_1 \text{———} q_1, \quad \text{for } t_1 < t < t_1 + t_2$$

(b) with a price cut:

$$p_2 \text{———} q_2, \quad \text{for } 0 < t < t_1$$

$$p_2 \text{———} q_1, \quad \text{for } t_1 < t < t_1 + t_2$$

where q_1 represents quantities prior to the price cut and q_2 the quantities after the cut, but before retaliation. The point to be stressed is that in period t_2 the quantities do *not* change with respect to the original situation, regardless of the price move. In period t_2, then, the quantities must be understood as constant. (Here, we define quantities as quantities per unit time; hence, for example, the total cumulative quantities in period t_1—with no price cut—are $q_1 t_1$. It is also clear that since we are using cumulated quantities over time, we are bound to use the same lapse of time when comparing the situation with a price cut to that without a price cut.)

To facilitate the understanding of the model, consider the discrete price movement, from p_1 to p_2, if prices are cut. We first compute the total revenue (*TR*), and the total gross margin (*TM*) in the case of no price cut.

(11) $$TR = p_1 q_1 t_1 + p_1 q_1 t_2$$

(12) $$TM = q_1(p_1 - w)\, t_1 + q_1(p_1 - w)\, t_2.$$

If the *price is cut* to the level p_2, the total revenue TR^* and total margin TM^* are:

(13) $$TR^* = p_2 q_2 t_1 + p_2 q_1 t_2$$

(14) $$TM^* = q_2(p_2 - w)\, t_1 + q_1(p_2 - w)\, t_2.$$

For a price cut to be profitable, the case must be that $TM^* > TM$. It can easily be shown that this implies:

(15) $$\frac{q_2 - q_1}{p_1 - p_2} \cdot \frac{p_2}{q_1} > \frac{p_2}{p_2 - w} \cdot \frac{t_1 - t_2}{t_2}$$

or equivalently:[12]

[12]See footnote 2, p. 536 for the proper definition of price elasticity. Equation (16) may be obtained directly by noting that the derivative of

(16) $$|e| > \frac{p}{M} \cdot \frac{t_1 + t_2}{t_1}.$$

This result may now be compared to the one obtained for the isolated dealer [see expression (5)]. The difference between (5) and (16) is that the price/margin ratio is now divided by the factor $t_1/(t_1 + t_2)$, which represents the proportion of lead time enjoyed by the minor with respect to the overall duration of a price war. If $t_2 = 0$, i.e., there is no reaction, the two results are identical. If $t_1 = t_2$, the elasticity must be twice as large as in the case of the isolated dealer in order for the price cut to be profitable.[13] Knowledge of the relative length of t_1 and t_2 and the possibility of controlling them are now instrumental in deriving optimal pricing strategies.

IMPLICATIONS OF RESULTS

The basic economic motivation for price cutting was summarized in expression (5) as:

$$|e| > \frac{p}{M} = \frac{p}{p - w}.$$

This was modified to take account of competitive reaction times. The modification was to multiply (5) by $(t_1 + t_2)/t_1$. Note that $(t_1 + t_2)/t_1 \geqslant 1$. From the viewpoint of the initiator of a price cut, expectations as to the relative lengths of t_1 and t_2 are important in determining whether the expected change in profits is positive or negative. These two time periods, t_1, entirely, and t_2, partly, are in control of the competitor(s) who must react to the price cut. In this section we will explore the results we have obtained from the viewpoint of both the initiator of the price cut and from the competitor's (retaliator's) viewpoint.

The dealer, who makes the price cut, likely to be a minor brand dealer for reasons stated earlier, is under pressure to reduce his price whenever and for whatever reason his cost and therefore his margin basis changes. If he is profit

---

$$TM = q(p - w)\,t_1 + q(p - w)\,t_2$$

with respect to p must be negative. Note, however, that by Assumptions 2 and 3, $dq/dp = O$ during period t_2. This may be made more explicit in the following way. Let q be a function of the minor price, p_m, and the major price, p_M, and let q_m and q_M be the two partial derivatives. The total differential is:

$$dq = q_m dp_m + q_M dp_M.$$

However, by Assumption 3, $q_M = -q_m$ (since q is actually a function only of the difference between the two prices). Hence, we have

$$dq = q_m(dp_m - dp_M).$$

During t_1, $dp_M = O$, since p_M is a constant. Hence, the derivative of q with respect to p_m is simply q_m. During t_2, on the other hand, p_m cannot be supposed constant. Actually by Assumption 2, $dp_M = dp_m$. It follows that $dq = O$, no matter what the price cut.

[13]Note that the concept of elasticity refers to the elasticity during the period in which there is no reaction from the major (the elasticity is zero by assumption in the second period).

oriented, he will only do this if he can *expect* an increase in profits. Whether this occurs is a function of the elasticity he faces and the length of t_1 relative to t_2.

The price cutter can expect t_1 to be of some positive length. For example, it is not uncommon for a minor brand dealer to cut a price on Friday afternoon at 5 o'clock and restore it at 8 o'clock Monday morning. The major brand dealers, unless they wish to incur losses, are unlikely to retaliate because they are unable to get in touch with their suppliers to invoke margin support plans. In this example the minor will benefit from the price cut with $t_2 = 0$.

In all cases, delays are encountered on the part of majors in detecting, reporting, and acting upon price cuts. It does take some finite time for retaliation to occur. Once it occurs, and assuming the initiator does not change his price in either direction, the period t_2 is entered. The longer the initiator expects t_2 to be, the less incentive he has to make the initial cut.

The initiator can take two actions once a reaction to his initial cut is made. First, he can restore his price to the original level. In practice this is not typically done, i.e., the major brands usually lead prices upward. Second, the initiator can cut his price again and enter a new period t_1. By so doing the initiator can control t_2 and make t_1 longer. This might suggest that the initiator should not cut his price by the entire amount immediately, but should do it in a stepwise fashion and in so doing make t_1 longer.

Despite competitive history, although it may be a good predictor, the minor really never knows what the relative lengths of t_1 and t_2 will be. The results shown in (16) tell him how long the relative lengths can be and still permit him to make a profit, but not what they will be. This is a matter of expectation and prediction on his part and errors can be expected which lead to losses, even though the original motivation was increased profits.[14]

Recall that we earlier argued that the competitor who typically responds to a price cut is a major brand. Legal constraints restrain the major brand dealer (supplier) from undercutting a minor brand dealer and in fact they typically only cut their price to maintain the normal 1–2 cents spread between major and minor brands.[15]

From the major's viewpoint there are two possible pricing policy implications from the results developed. First, they should monitor the competitive market price to insure t_1 is as short as possible. Second, they could always make t_2 of sufficient length to restore the minor's total margin, *TM*, to what it would have been had normal prices held during *T*. By reacting consistently to price

[14]Estimates of t_1 and t_2, obtained from past records, may give some notion of the probability distribution of these events. On this basis, the model could be cast in stochastic terms.

[15]The differential or spread between minor and major could be interpreted as a situation where t_1 is of indefinite length and $t_2 = 0$. On the West Coast, the spread prior to 1960 was 2 cents (Cassady, [4]) and a major price war resulted when several majors decided the 2 cent spread was hurting their market share position and that a 1 cent spread balanced the major and minor brand offers.

cuts, and in a manner to restore normal total margin, the minor brand operators will have no short-term profit motivation to cut price.[16] This policy, however effective in preventing the recurrence of price wars, entails a cost to the major supplier which might be greater than the cost of price wars of normal duration because an increase in t_2 can be achieved only at the expense of a further reduction in revenue to the major.

The retaliation strategy just suggested leads to the conclusion that the major *always* loses in total margin during a price war. Perhaps this fact explains why price wars are such an enigma to major brand oil firms.

Thus far we have considered a single market with individual dealers competing. The results apply to "competing" markets too. Consider a given market's price elasticity, along with properly defined, weighted price and margins for all dealers within the market, relative to competing markets. Such more aggregative reasoning may help to explain the geographic spread characteristic of gasoline price wars, since shifts in demand from one market to another may increase the profitability of a price war, at least for the minor. As long as a price war is confined to a given market (in which the minor operates), it can be expected that the total quantities sold even after retaliation are greater than those sold prior to the start of the price war. This is so because there is an incentive to motorists to buy gasoline in the depressed area. This fact (a relaxation of Assumption 3) may have a non-negligible impact on the minor's pricing strategy. On the other hand, a major supplier well represented in all markets may not derive such an advantage.

FURTHER EMPIRICAL WORK

The model developed here, as the discussion of its implications suggests, gives rise to a number of hypotheses about price war behavior. These hypotheses and others are now being empirically tested. The major data base being used is an extensive time series (over 4 years) of retail prices for the Los Angeles metropolitan area. Supplemental price-volume data covering shorter, more frequent time intervals is also being studied. The preliminary results available lend general support to the model developed here.

Specific empirical work intended to examine who in fact cuts price and who acts as catalysts in starting price wars is now underway and will be reported shortly. Also under detailed examination is the matter of reaction times and pricing responses, both interesting aspects of price wars as the reaction model developed here suggests. A report on the detailed anatomy of price wars also is to be made. Such a micro-examination will provide empirical evidence not previously available and will help eliminate some of the folklore surrounding micro-price behavior in retailing.

[16]The minor still may wish to cut price at times he has a cost advantage if he felt permanent market share gains were to be made. Of course, this violates our third assumption above.

CONCLUSION

The purpose of this paper was to examine the economic motivation for gasoline price wars. We conclude that profit goals can lead to price cutting where cost reductions occur for some competitors and that increased profits can be an expected outcome. The initiator of the price cut is typically a minor who can expect some retaliation from his competitor, most frequently a major brand dealer. The outcome of the price war is a function of the time it takes the major to retaliate and for the minor and major to jointly restore price to their original, normal levels.

While not all price wars are explained by the model developed here, it may be that the start, duration, and end of many gasoline price wars is governed by rational, profit seeking behavior and is not the irrational phenomena many observers believe it to be.

REFERENCES

[1] American Oil Co. A Study of Competition in the Refining and Marketing of Petroleum Products. Material for Testimony of B. J. Yarrington and S. Morris Livingston. Submitted before the Federal Trade Commission.

[2] Bain, Joe S. *The Economics of the Pacific Coast Petroleum Industry*, Parts I, II, and III. Berkeley: University of California Press, 1944.

[3] Cassady, Ralph, Jr. *Price Making and Price Behavior in the Petroleum Industry*. New Haven: Yale University Press, 1954.

[4] ———. "Price Warfare — A Form of Business Rivalry." In R. Cox, W. Alderson, and S. Shapiro (eds.). *Theory In Marketing*. Homewood, Ill.: Richard D. Irwin, 1964, pp. 355–379.

[5] ———. *Price Warfare in Business Competition: A Study of Abnormal Competitive Behavior*, Occasional Paper No. 11. Michigan State University: Bureau of Business and Economic Research, 1963.

[6] ———, and Wylie L. Jones. *The Nature of Competition in Gasoline Distribution at the Retail Level.* Los Angeles: University of California Press, 1951.

[7] Clark, S. H., L. Preston, D. E. Schendel, and P. Balestra. *An Analysis of Competition and Price Behavior in the British Columbia Petroleum Industry*. Menlo Park, California: Stanford Research Institute, 1964.

[8] Claycamp, Henry J. "Dynamic Effects of Short Duration Price Differentials on Retail Gasoline Sales." *Journal of Marketing Research* (1966), pp. 175–178.

[9] Clover, Vernon T. "Price Influence in Unbranded Gasoline." *Journal of Marketing*, Vol. XVII, No. 4 (1953), pp. 388–393.

[10] Dixon, Donald F. *Suppliers Pricing Policies and Gasoline Price Wars in Pennsylvania*. Occasional Papers, Temple University, 1966.

[11] Federal Trade Commission. *The Federal Trade Commission's Report on Anticompetitive Practices in the Marketing of Gasoline.* Mimeographed.

[12] Learned, Edmund P., and Catherine C. Ellsworth. *Gasoline Pricing in Ohio.* Boston: Graduate School of Business Administration, Harvard University, 1959.

[13] Livingston, S. Morris, and Theodore Levitt. "Competition and Retail Gasoline Prices." *Review of Economics and Statistics*, Vol. XLI (1959), pp. 119–132.

[14] McAllister, Harry E. *The Elasticity of Demand for Gasoline in the State of Washington*, Bulletin 29. Bureau of Economic and Business Research, State College of Washington, 1956.

[15] McLean, John G., and Robert W. Haigh. *The Growth of Integrated Oil Companies.* Boston: Graduate School of Business Administration, Harvard University, 1954.

[16] Moir, Harry. *Prices or Profits, in Petroleum Marketing: Practices and Problems*, edited by W. H. Day. Tulsa, Oklahoma: Commercial Publishers, 1966.

[17] "Oil Firms Halt Gasoline-Price Allowances in Some Areas Where Price Wars Exist." *The Wall Street Journal* (January 25, 1966), p. 2.

[18] "Price War Allowances to Gasoline Dealers Withdrawn by Phillips, American Petrofina." *The Wall Street Journal* (March 18, 1965), p. 6.

35. A NOTE ON TRADING STAMP STRATEGY*

Roger Sherman†

Should a retailer offer trading stamps? No ready basis for answering that question is yet at hand, despite remarkable growth in the use of stamps and promotional games over the past ten years. These strategic choices differ from price or advertising decisions because they are yes or no choices. Retailers can adjust marginally their prices for their advertising expenditures, but must either offer trading stamps or not offer them.[1] Such bifurcation makes a two-strategy, n-person, non-zero-sum game an especially appropriate model for characterizing these retailer choices, and we shall use it here to illustrate their effects.

The n-person prisoner's dilemma has been elaborated by Weil [11]. Profit outcomes from trading stamp decisions by one firm, which we shall call Firm *A*, are illustrated for a five-firm example in Table 35-1. Firm *A* has a choice either to offer trading stamps or not. Observe the way in which we assume actions by other firms affect Firm *A*'s profit. If Firm *A* does not offer stamps, and no other firm offers them, Firm *A* will enjoy a profit of 100 units. If Firm *A* does offer stamps, but no other firm does, its profit will increase to 120. If two other firms also offer trading stamps, Firm *A's* advantage will be offset; it will make the same profit as before stamps were introduced. And if all five firms offer stamps, Firm *A* will make a lower profit than without stamps in the market at all, only 80 units. But notice that for every combination of actions by the other firms it is always better for Firm *A* to offer stamps rather than not offer them; the "stamps" strategy is therefore a dominant strategy. Because the action that is dominant for each firm, if pursued by all, leads to a result which

Table 35-1

		Profits of Firm *A* No. of Others Offering Stamps				
		4	3	2	1	0
Firm *A*	No Stamps	60	70	80	90	100
	Stamps	80	90	100	110	120

*From *Applied Economics*, Vol. I, No. 3 (August, 1969), pp. 225–228. Reprinted by permission of the publisher and the author.

†Roger Sherman, Professor of Economics, University of Virginia.

[1]Continuous marginal adjustment may also make decisions seem less difficult. See Udell [10]. For an analysis of the effects of trading stamps, see Davis [4].

all would rather avoid, the situation represented in Table 35-1 may be regarded as a prisoner's dilemma.[2]

Is it possible that all firms are better-off (make more profit) rather than worse-off when all give trading stamps? Then if each firm pursues its own independent best interests, all will gain. With such coincidence in motives, we would no longer have a prisoner's dilemma at all, but would have instead a pattern of payoffs as illustrated for the firm in Table 35-2. Even if all four other firms offer trading stamps, each firm's profit will be higher (at 110) than if the market continues without any trading stamps (100).

Table 35-2

		Profits of Firm *A* No. of Others Offering Stamps				
		4	3	2	1	0
Firm *A*	No Stamps	60	70	80	90	100
	Stamps	110	120	130	140	150

A crude test whether there exists a "retailer's dilemma" as in Table 35-1, or no dilemma as in Table 35-2, can be obtained from an examination of monopolies. If all firms benefit when all offer stamps, as in Table 35-2, a monopolist also could benefit and would offer them. But if there exists a dilemma the monopolist, who enjoys a collective market perspective, would have no reason to offer stamps. According to the Trading Stamp Institute of America, monopolists are not important users of trading stamps.[3] This would indicate that of the two situations the n-person prisoner's dilemma illustrated in Table 35-1 best reflects the decision typically faced by retailers concerning the adoption of trading stamps.

But this conclusion holds only in our two-case (Table 35-1 vs. Table 35-2) world, where consumers are implicitly assumed to be identical. If some consumers do not desire stamp premium goods,[4] a store can appeal to them by having a lower price instead of offering stamps. Alternatively, other service

[2]An action is dominant for one person if it offers a greater payoff (profit) than alternative actions, for *any* action by another (or other) person(s). The notion of dominance is presented, together with the prisoner's dilemma, in Luce and Raiffa [6]. That this result might occur is evidenced in "Trading Stamps Become Sticky National Question" [9], where anti-stamp campaigning by retailers is described.

[3]The executive secretary of the Trading Stamp Institute, Hyman Heimowitz, reported in private correspondence that he could think of no instance where a monopoly offered trading stamps save some gas companies that had offered them in an effort to get customers to change from oil to gas.

[4]Although sympathetic to trading stamps, Professor Beem acknowledged that indifference toward them by some consumers would limit their use. See Beem [1], [2] and Strotz [7], [8].

and promotion strategies might be adjusted to attract non-stamp-saving consumers if they have common characteristics that make such service or promotion strategies attractive to them.[5] For example, non-stamp-saving customers might also prefer more service and be willing to pay for it.

Suppose that there are several firms, located close together and all at the same price level, and suppose that the consumers differ in the degree to which they are attracted by stamp premium goods. When only one firm offers stamps, it can increase its price level relative to other stores and still attract those consumers who desire premium goods. If a second firm also offers stamps, the two firms will want to have more consumers save stamps. They can accomplish this either by lowering their prices relative to firms that do not give stamps, or by giving more premiums. Alternatively, the firms that do not give stamps can raise their prices with the same effect, since the difference in price between firms that give stamps and those that do not determines how many consumers will shop where stamps are given and how many will shop elsewhere.

Thus, different degrees of consumer interest in stamp premium goods can lead to a modification of the prisoner's dilemma suggested by Table 35-1, to a payoff pattern for a firm such as that shown in Table 35-3. Once three other firms offer stamps in Table 35-3, no motive remains for Firm *A* to offer them, but when fewer than three firms offer stamps, a prisoner's dilemma holds. If it does not offer stamps, Firm *A*'s profit will eventually begin to improve as more other firms offer stamps, because Firm *A* can maintain a price level closer to that of the stamp offering firms and still win customers who do not desire stamp premium goods. In the Table 35-3 example, this occurs after a third other firm offers stamps.

Table 35-3

		Profits of Firm *A* No. of Others Offering Stamps				
		4	3	2	1	0
Firm *A*	No Stamps	100	90	80	90	100
	Stamps	80	90	100	110	120

We suggested above that total profits to all firms would be lower when all firms offered stamps because monopolists do not offer them. That inference no longer follows if we assume monopolists have only two choices which correspond to all firms or no firms giving stamps. Monopolists might not use stamps then simply because they cannot reach an equilibrium at which only

[5]It has been argued in Klass [5] that stamps have a psychological appeal. But even so, the appeal could be offset by alternative strategies. And some disenchantment with premium programs might arise from considerations emphasized by Bell [3].

some of several competing firms would give stamps, even if that point did offer greater industry profits. Nevertheless, retailers can be trapped into offering stamps in much the same way that a competitor is forced to meet another competitor's price cut. Up to a point of equilibrium, each competitor alone is motivated to offer stamps, so without collusion all or several might offer them, even though they would be less well-off when they did. Whether to offer stamps then becomes an even more difficult question, for beyond that equilibrium point offering stamps will bring a firm less profit, a result that would not hold in the Table 35-1 prisoner's dilemma.

There may thus be a problem in reaching such an equilibrium. Due in part to the discrete nature of the choice, a retailer cannot be expected to have experience that would help him estimate the pay-off matrix he faces. It is difficult to experiment because there are no small steps; trading stamps must either be offered or not.[6] Stores in one community may choose to adopt trading stamp plans almost simultaneously, so none could learn of the opportunity that would have been available had it not offered trading stamps. For example, all firms in Table 35-3 could adopt trading stamps at about the same time, and because abandoning the plan is a risky and abrupt step they might continue the stamp programs without knowing that each could increase its profit by abandoning stamps alone. Such an outcome would have undesirable consequences for consumers as well as firms, inasmuch as some consumers who did not value stamps would have no opportunity to escape them. In any case, firms must make an extra effort to learn consumer preferences regarding stamp plans and similar promotions, in order for profit opportunities to be exploited.

When a new promotional device such as trading stamps is introduced, retailers probably face a prisoners' dilemma choice whether to offer it or not. Stores are individually motivated to offer stamps, but as more stores offer them, the price (or other strategy variable) difference that they can enjoy over non-stamp stores diminishes. Several (not necessarily all) of the firms are to some extent forced into offering stamps if another firm does. This force is modified when some consumers are not attracted by the premium goods for which stamps may be exchanged, for they may prefer lower prices or a different service and promotion mix, which a non-stamp store can achieve. Then the choice is especially difficult, for the individual firm is limited in its opportunity to learn whether it can increase its profit by offering stamps or by not offering them.

Whether it is profitable, in the end, for a firm to add trading stamps depends on the collective choices of consumers; it depends on a voting process. Each consumer chooses whether to shop at a set of stores that give stamps or a set of stores that do not, and to the extent that consumers make such choices, there can exist an equilibrium number of stores giving stamps. But the lack of a marginal adjustment opportunity complicates the retailer's choice, and may prevent achievement of the equilibrium.

[6]Chains can try stamp plans in some stores and not in others, but differences from one market area to another make it difficult to draw general conclusions from such experiments.

REFERENCES

[1] Beem, E. R. "Who Profits from Trading Stamps?" *Harvard Business Review*, Vol. XXXV (November-December, 1957), pp. 123–136.

[2] ———. "On Being Fooled by Statisticians: The Case of Professor Strotz." *Journal of Business*, Vol. XXXII (July, 1959), pp. 279–282.

[3] Bell, Carolyn. "Liberty, Property, and No Stamps." *Journal of Business*, Vol. XL (April, 1967), pp. 194–202.

[4] Davis, O. A. "The Economics of Trading Stamps." *Journal of Business*, Vol. XXXII (April, 1959), pp. 141–150.

[5] Klass, D. *Motivation and the Retail Food Business.* San Francisco: California Grocers Association, 1956.

[6] Luce, R. D., and H. Raiffa. *Games and Decisions.* New York: John Wiley, 1957.

[7] Strotz, R. H. "On Being Fooled by Figures: The Case of Trading Stamps." *Journal of Business*, Vol. XXXI (October, 1958), pp. 304–310.

[8] ———. "Trading Comments on Trading Stamps." *Journal of Business*, Vol. XXXII (July, 1959), pp. 283–286.

[9] "Trading Stamps Become Sticky National Question." *Life* (March 4, 1957).

[10] Udell, Jon G. "The Perceived Importance of the Elements of Strategy." *Journal of Marketing*, Vol. XXXII (January, 1968), pp. 34–40.

[11] Weil, R. L., Jr. "The *N*-Person Prisoner's Dilemma." *Behavioral Science*, Vol. XI (May, 1966), pp. 227–234.